The Irony of Democracy

An Uncommon Introduction to American Politics

Third Edition

The Irony

# of Democracy

An Uncommon Introduction to American Politics

Third Edition

THOMAS R. DYE *Florida State University*

L. HARMON ZEIGLER *University of Oregon*

DUXBURY PRESS *North Scituate, Massachusetts*

Duxbury Press
A DIVISION OF WADSWORTH PUBLISHING COMPANY, INC.

*The Irony of Democracy: An Uncommon Introduction to American Politics,
Third Edition* was edited and prepared for composition by Beatrice Gorm-
ley. The interior and cover designs were provided by Designworks, Inc.

L.C. Cat. Card No.: 74-84838
ISBN: 0-87872-083-9

PRINTED IN THE UNITED STATES OF AMERICA

3 4 5 6 7 8 9 10 — 79 78 77 76 75

Contents

We live in unusual times.

In January 1972 *The Irony of Democracy*, second edition, was published. Since then, this nation has been badly shaken. The Watergate affair and the consequent resignation of President Nixon, a continuing energy crisis, rising inflation and rising unemployment are but a few of the problems that have beset us. A general malaise—marked especially by disillusionment with politics and our political system—has resulted.

The urgency and significance of our message in *The Irony of Democracy* seems ever more clear. Unusual times demanded an unusually thorough revision, and we have made the following major changes in the third edition:

An extended treatment of the presidency, including the issues of presidential war-making powers, impoundment, executive privilege, and impeachment, with special attention to the decline and fall of Richard Nixon.

Additional discussion of elite threats to democracy, again drawing from the revelations of the Watergate affair.

A considerably more detailed treatment of corporate elites, including the military-industrial complex, political contributors, and elite recruitment.

Expanded analysis of elite competition ("Cowboys" versus "Yankees") and consensus (the "liberal establishment").

An elaboration on the role of ideology in electoral choice, with a focus on the 1972 elections.

New material on the decay of the two-party system, with discussions of attempts at party reform and the growing disillusionment with government.

A section on the role of the oil industry in the energy crisis.

Separate chapters on Congress and the courts, with an emphasis on such recent developments in intragovernmental relations as the unstable balance of power between Congress and the president.

An extended discussion of the outcome of the black protest movement—riot, revolution, or repression?—and of the busing issue.

A discussion of the "spillover" effects of black protest, with a focus on the women's movement.

Although this is a long list of revisions, the fundamental thesis of the book remains intact. We maintain our dissent from the prevailing ideology of contemporary political science—pluralism.

Pluralism portrays the American political process as competition, bargaining, and compromise among a multitude of interest groups vying for the rewards distributed by the political system. The multiplicity of such groups and the fact that their memberships overlap are believed to ensure the nation against the eventuality that any one group should emerge as a dominant elite. This pluralist ideology characterizes virtually all of the American government textbooks currently in print.

While the underlying value of individual dignity remains at the core of contemporary pluralist thought, the modern pluralist accepts giant concentrations of power as inevitable in a modern, industrial, urban society. The pluralist realizes that the unorganized individual is no match for giant corporate bureaucracy, but he hopes that "countervailing" centers of power will balance each other and thereby protect the individual from abuse. Groups become the means by which individuals gain access to the political system. The government is held responsible not by individuals but by organized groups and coalition of groups (parties). The essential value becomes participation in, and competition among, organized groups. Pluralism asserts that the dispersed pattern of power among many groups safeguards both individuals and groups against arbitrary and capricious actions of a dominant group. Pluralism contends that the Amercan system is open and accessible to the extent that any interest held by a significant portion of the populace can find expression through one or more groups.

The pluralist ideology went unchallenged for a number of years, not only in American government texts, but also in the general literature of political science. Recently, however, several scholars have challenged the pluralists' claims to empirical validity and, therefore, undermined their claim to normative prescription as well. These scholars, sometimes referred to as "neo-elitists," accept the existence of a multiplicity of groups; however, they look beyond the structural proliferation of interest groups and examine their functional interaction.

Elitist theory contends that all organizations tend to be governed by a small minority of their membership and that the characteristics of the leaders across all groups tend to be similar. The backgrounds and values of these leaders are so similar, in fact, that they constitute an American sociopolitical elite. The members of this elite articulate the values of society and exercise control of society's resources. They are bound as much—if not more—by their elite identities as they are by their specific group attachments. Thus, instead of constituting a balance of power systems within American society, organized interest groups are seen as platforms of power from which a relatively homogeneous group—an elite—effectively governs the nation. These leaders are more accommodating toward each other than they are competitive. They share a basic consensus about preserving the system essentially as it is. They are not really held accountable by the members of their groups. Members have little or nothing to say about policy decisions. In fact, leaders influence followers far more than followers influence leaders.

A generation or more of Amercan have been educated in the pluralist tradition. We do not claim that they have been educated poorly (if for no other reason than that we are among them). Nor do we argue that pluralism is either "wrong" or "dead," for clearly it contains much of value and commands many perceptive adherents. In short, this book was not undertaken to "attack the pluralists." Our primary concern is to make available to students and teachers of political science an introductory analysis of American politics that is *not* based on the pluralist ideology.

The Irony of Democracy is an explanation of American political life based on an elitist theory of democracy. It attempts to organize historical and social science evidence from the American political system. We have deliberately sacrificed some breadth of coverage to present a coherent exposition of the theory of elitist democracy. Those who seek an encyclopedic presentation of the "facts" of American government are advised to look elsewhere. Now have we sought to present a "balanced," or theoretically eclectic, view of American politics. The student can find democratic-pluralist interpretations of American politics everywhere.

The Irony of Democracy is not necessarily "anti-establishment." This book challenges the prevailing, pluralistic view of democracy in America, but it neither condemns nor endorses American political life. To say that America is governed by a small, homogeneous elite may be interpreted either as praise or as criticism of this nation, depending on one's personal values. That is, elitism may be thought of as either "good" or "bad," depending on one's preference for elite or mass governance.

Actually, the authors themselves disagree about whether the elitism they perceive in American politics is "good" or "bad." One author values radical reform as a means of establishing a truly democratic political system in America—a system in which individuals participate in all decisions that shape their lives, a system in which individual dignity is preserved and in which equality is realized in the social, economic, and political life of the nation. He believes that, through radical resocialization and a restructuring of educational, economic, and governmental institutions, the anti-democratic sentiments of the masses can be changed. In contrast, the other author values an enlightened leadership system capable of acting decisively to preserve individual freedom, human dignity, and the values of life, liberty, and property. He believes that a well-ordered society governed by educated and resourceful elites is preferable to the instability of mass society.

In summary, *The Irony of Democracy* challenges the prevailing pluralistic ideology and interprets American politics from the perspective of elite theory. The reader is free to decide for himself whether the political system described in these pages ought to be preserved, reformed, or restructured.

We would like to express our sincere thanks to those many instructors who have used the first and second editions, and who have volunteered their reactions and comments and relayed those of their students. We found such comments unusually helpful, and have incorporated many of their suggestions into the third edition.

We are especially indebted to Harry Scoble (University of Illinois, Chicago Circle), Robert Crew (University of Minnesota), John Sproat (Department of History, University of South Carolina), Bernard Hennessy (California State University, Hayward), Robert Lineberry (Northwestern University), Lyman Kellstedt (University of Illinois, Chicago Circle), John Olson (Portland Community College), Conrad Joyner (University of Arizona), Daniel Vaughn (University of South Carolina), Murray B. Levin (Boston University), David H. Tabb (University of California, Berkeley), Robert G. Striplin and Thomas H. Rhorer (American River College), and Harlan Strauss (University of Oregon) for their extensive and valuable assessments of earlier editions. We also wish to thank Joseph Olexa, Dallas Hardison, and William Eubank (all of the University of Oregon), John Pickering (Memphis State University), and Robert Leonard (University of Evansville) for their assistance in the preparation of the third edition.

CHAPTER 1

THE IRONY OF DEMOCRACY

Elites, not masses, govern America. In an industrial, scientific, and nuclear age, life in a democracy, just as in a totalitarian society, is shaped by a handful of men. In spite of differences in their approach to the study of power in America, scholars—political scientists and sociologists alike—agree that "the key political, economic, and social decisions are made by 'tiny minorities.'"[1]

An *elite* is the few who have power; the *masses* are the many who do not. Power is deciding who gets what, when, and how; it is participation in the decisions that allocate values for a society. Elites are the few who participate in the decisions that shape our lives; the masses are the many whose lives are shaped by institutions, events, and leaders over which they have little direct control. Harold Lasswell writes, "the division of society into elite and mass is universal," and even in a democracy "a few exercise a relatively great weight of power, and the many exercise comparatively little."[2]

Elites are not necessarily conspiracies to oppress or exploit the masses. On the contrary, elites may be very "public-regarding" and deeply concerned with the welfare of the masses. Membership in an elite may be relatively open to ambitious and talented individuals from the masses, or it may be closed to all except top corporate, financial, mili-

1

tary, civic, and governmental leaders. Elites may be competitive or consensual; they may agree or disagree over the direction of foreign and domestic policy. Elites may form a pyramid, with a top group exercising power in many sectors of the society; or plural elites may divide power, with separate groups making key decisions in different issue areas. Elites may be responsive to the demands of the masses and influenced by the outcome of elections, or they may be unresponsive to mass movements and unaffected by elections. But whether elites are public-minded or self-seeking, open or closed, competitive or consensual, pyramidal or pluralistic, responsive or unresponsive, it is elites and not the masses who govern the modern nation.

Democracy is government "by the people," but the responsibility for the survival of democracy rests on the shoulders of elites. This is the irony of democracy: Elites must govern wisely if government "by the people" is to survive. If the survival of the American system depended upon an active, informed, and enlightened citizenry, then democracy in America would have disappeared long ago; for the masses of America are apathetic and ill-informed about politics and public policy, and they have a surprisingly weak commitment to democratic values—individual dignity, equality of opportunity, the right to dissent, freedom of speech and press, religious toleration, due process of law. But fortunately for these values and for American democracy, the American masses do not lead, they follow. They respond to the attitudes, proposals, and behavior of elites. V. O. Key wrote:

The critical element for the health of the democratic order consists of the beliefs, standards, and competence of those who constitute the influentials, the political activists, in the order. That group, as has been made plain, refuses to define itself with great clarity in the American system; yet analysis after analysis points to its existence. If democracy tends toward indecision, decay, and disaster, the responsibility rests here, not with the mass of people.[3]

Although the symbols of American politics are drawn from democratic political thought, the reality of American politics can often be better understood from the viewpoint of elite theory. The questions posed by elite theory are the vital questions of politics: Who governs America? What are the roles of elites and masses in American politics? How do people acquire power? What is the relationship between economic and political power? How open and accessible are American elites? How do American elites change over time? How widely is power shared in America? How much real competition takes place among elites? What is the basis of elite consensus? How do elites and masses differ? How responsive are elites to mass sentiments? How much influence do masses have over policies decided by elites? How do elites accommodate themselves to mass movements?

This book, *The Irony of Democracy*, is an attempt to explain American political life on the basis of elite theory. It attempts systematically to organize the evidence of American history and contemporary social science in order to come to grips with the central questions posed by elite theory. But before we turn to this examination of American political life, it is important that we understand the meaning of *elitism*, *democracy*, and *pluralism*.

The Meaning of Elitism

The central proposition of elitism is that all societies are divided into two classes—the few who govern and the many who are governed. The Italian political scientist Gaetano Mosca expressed this basic concept as follows:

In all societies—from societies that are very underdeveloped and have largely attained the dawnings of civilization, down to the most advanced and powerful societies—two classes of people appear—a class that rules and a class that is ruled. The first class, always the less numerous, performs all of the political functions, monopolizes power, and enjoys the advantages that power brings, whereas the second, the more numerous class, is directed and controlled by the first, in a manner that is now more or less legal, now more or less arbitrary and violent.[4]

For Mosca it was inevitable that elites and not masses would govern all societies, because elites possess organization and unity of purpose.

An organized minority, obeying a single impulse, is irresistible against an unorganized majority in which each individual stands alone before the totality of the organized minority. A hundred men acting uniformly in concert, with a common understanding, will triumph over a thousand men who are not in accord and can be dealt with one by one.[5]

Contemporary writers generally attribute elitism to the impact of urbanization, industrialization, technological development, and the growth of the social, economic, and political organizations in modern societies. Robert Dahl writes, "The key political, economic, and social decisions . . . are made by tiny minorities. . . . It is difficult—nay impossible—to see how it could be otherwise in large political systems."[6] Sociologist Suzanne Keller writes, "The democratic ethos notwithstanding, men must become accustomed to bigger, more extensive and more specialized elites in their midst as long as industrial societies keep growing and becoming more specialized."[7] And according to Harold Lasswell, "The discovery that in all large-scale societies the decisions at any given time are typically in the hands of a small number of people" confirms a basic fact: "Government is always government by the few, whether in the name of the few, the one, or the many."[8]

Elitism also asserts that the few who govern are not typical of the masses who are governed. Elites possess more control over resources—power, wealth, education, prestige, status, skills of leadership, information, knowledge of political processes, ability to communicate, and organization—and elites (in America) are drawn disproportionately from among wealthy, educated, prestigiously employed, socially prominent, white, Anglo-Saxon, and Protestant groups in society. In short, elites are drawn from a society's upper classes, which are made up of those persons in a society who own or control a disproportionate share of the societal institutions—industry, commerce, finance, education, the military, communications, civic affairs, and law.

On the other hand, elite theory admits of some social mobility that enables non-elites to become elites; elitism does not necessarily mean that individuals from the lower classes cannot rise to the top. In fact, a certain amount of "circulation of elites" (upward mobility) is essential for the stability of the elite system. Openness in the elite system siphons off potentially revolutionary leadership from the lower classes, and an elite system is strengthened when talented and ambitious individuals from the masses are permitted to enter governing circles. However, it is important that the movement of individuals from non-elite to elite positions be a slow and continuous assimilation rather than a rapid or revolutionary change. Moreover, only those non-elites who have demonstrated their commitment to the elite system itself and to the system's political and economic values can be admitted to the ruling class.

Elites share in a *consensus* about fundamental norms underlying the social system. They agree on the basic "rules of the game," as well as on the continuation of the social system itself. The stability of the system, and even its survival, depends upon this consensus. According to David Truman, "Being more influential, they (the elites) are privileged; and being privileged, they have, with few exceptions, a special stake in the continuation of the system in which their privileges rest."[9] Elite consensus does not mean that elite members never disagree or never compete with each other for preeminence; it is unlikely that there ever was a society in which there was no competition among elites. But elitism implies that competition takes place within a very narrow range of issues and that elites agree on more matters than they disagree on. Disagreement usually occurs over *means*, rather than *ends*.

In America, the bases of elite consensus are the sanctity of private property, limited government, and individual liberty. Richard Hofstadter writes about American elite struggles:

The fierceness of political struggles has often been misleading; for the range of vision embodied by the primary contestants in the major parties has always been bounded by the horizons of property and enterprise. However much at odds on specific issues, the major political traditions have shared a belief in the rights of property, the philosophy of economic individualism, the value of competition; they have accepted the economic virtues of capitalist culture as necessary qualities of man.[10]

Hofstadter's analysis of consensus among leaders in American history echoes a central principle of elitism.

Elitism implies that public policy does not reflect demands of "the people" so much as it reflects the interests and values of elites. Changes and innovations in public policy come about as a result of redefinitions by elites of their own values. However, the general conservatism of elites—that is, their interest in preserving the system—means that changes in public policy will be incremental rather than revolutionary. Public policies are frequently modified but seldom replaced.

Basic changes in the nature of the political system occur when events threaten the system. Elites, acting on the basis of enlightened self-interest, institute reforms to preserve the system and their place in it. Their motives are not necessarily self-serving; the values of elites may be very "public-regarding," and the welfare of the masses may be an important element in elite decision making. Elitism does not mean that public policy will ignore or be against the welfare of the masses but only that the responsibility for the mass welfare rests upon the shoulders of elites, not upon the masses.

Finally, elitism assumes that the masses are largely passive, apathetic, and ill-informed. Mass sentiments are manipulated by elites more often than elite values are influenced by the sentiments of the masses. For the most part, communication between elites and masses flows downward. Policy questions of government are seldom decided by the masses through elections or through the presentation of policy alternatives by political parties. For the most part, these "democratic" institutions—elections and parties—are important only for their symbolic value. They help tie the masses to the political system by giving them a role to play on election day and a political party with which they can identify. Elitism contends that the masses have at best only an indirect influence over the decision-making behavior of elites.

Naturally, elitism is frequently misunderstood in America, because the prevailing myths and symbols of the American system are drawn from democratic theory rather than elite theory. Therefore, it is important here to emphasize what elitism is *not*, as well as to briefly restate what it *is*.

Elitism does not mean that those who have power are continually locked in conflict with the masses or that powerholders always achieve their goals at the expense of the public interest. Elitism is not a conspiracy to oppress the masses. Elitism does not imply that powerholders constitute a single impenetrable monolithic body or that powerholders in society always agree on public issues. Elitism does not pretend that power in society does not shift over time or that new elites cannot emerge to compete with old elites. Elites may be more or less monolithic and cohesive or more or less pluralistic and competitive. Power need not rest exclusively on the control of economic resources but may rest instead upon other leadership resources—organization, communication, or information. Elitism does not imply that the masses *never* have any impact on the attitudes of elites but only that elites influence masses more than masses influence elites.

Elitism can be summarized as follows:

1. Society is divided into the few who have power and the many who do not. Only a small number of persons allocate values for society; the masses do not decide public policy.

2. The few who govern are not typical of the masses who are governed. Elites are drawn disproportionately from the upper socioeconomic strata of society.

3. The movement of non-elites to elite positions must be slow and continuous to maintain stability and avoid revolution. Only non-elites who have accepted the basic elite consensus can be admitted to governing circles.

4. Elites share a consensus on the basic values of the social system and the preservation of the system. Disagreement is confined to a narrow range of issues.

5. Public policy does not reflect demands of masses but rather the prevailing values of the elite. Changes in public policy will be incremental rather than revolutionary.

6. Active elites are subject to relatively little direct influence from apathetic masses. Elites influence masses more than masses influence elites.

The Meaning of Democracy

Ideally, democracy means individual participation in the decisions that affect one's life. John Dewey wrote, "The keynote of democracy as a way of life may be expressed as the necessity for the participation of every mature human being in formation of the values that regulate the living of men together."[11] In other words, democracy means popular participation in the allocation of values in a society.

In traditional democratic theory, popular participation has been valued as an opportunity for individual self-development: Responsibility for the governing of one's own conduct develops one's character, self-reliance, intelligence, and moral judgment—in short, one's dignity. Even if a benevolent despot could govern in the public interest, he would be rejected by the classic democrat. The English political philosopher J. S. Mill asks, "What sort of human beings can be formed under such a regime? What development can either their thinking or active faculties attain under it?" The argument for citizen participation in public affairs is based not upon the policy outcomes it would produce but on the belief that such involvement is essential to the full development of human capacities. Mill argues that man can know truth only by discovering it for himself.[12]

Procedurally, popular participation was to be achieved through majority rule and respect for the rights of minorities. Self-development means self-government, and self-government can be accomplished only by encouraging each individual to contribute to the development of public policy and by resolving conflicts over public policy through majority rule. Minorities who have had the opportunity to influence policy but whose views have not succeeded in winning majority support would accept the decisions of majorities. In return, majorities would permit minorities to openly attempt to win majority support for their views. Freedom of speech and press, freedom to dissent, and freedom to form opposition parties and organizations are essential to insure meaningful individual participation. This freedom of expression is also necessary for ascertaining what the majority views really are.

The procedural requirements and the underlying ethics of democracy are linked. Carl Becker writes about democracy:

Its fundamental assumption is the worth and dignity and creative capacity of the individual, so that the chief aim of government is the maximum of individual self-direction, the chief means to that end, the minimum of compulsion by the state. . . . Means and ends are conjoined in the concept of freedom: freedom of thought so that the truth may prevail; freedom of occupation, so that careers may be open to talent; freedom of self-government, so that none may be compelled against his will.[13]

The underlying value of democracy is, as we have noted, individual dignity. Man, by virtue of his existence, is entitled to life, liberty, and property. A "natural law," or moral tenet, guarantees to every man both liberty and the right to property; and this natural law is morally superior to man-made law. John Locke, the English political philosopher whose writings most influenced America's founding elites, argues that even in a "state of nature"—that is, a world in which there were no governments—-an individual possesses inalienable rights to life, liberty, and property. Locke meant that these rights were antecedent to government, that these rights are not given to the individual by governments, and that no governments may legitimately take them away.[14]

Locke believed that the very purpose of government was to protect individual liberty. Men form a "social contract" with each other in establishing a government to help protect their rights; they tacitly agree to accept governmental activity in order to better protect life, liberty, and property. Implicit in the social contract and the democratic notion of freedom is the belief that governmental activity and social control over the individual be kept to a minimum. This involves the removal of as many external restrictions, controls, and regulations on the individual as is consistent with the freedom of his fellow citizens.

Moreover, since government is formed by the consent of the governed to protect individual liberty, it logically follows that government cannot violate the rights it was established to protect. Its authority is limited. Locke's ultimate weapon to protect individual dignity against abuse by government was the right of revolution. According to Locke, whenever governments violate the natural rights of the governed, they forfeit the authority placed in them under the social contract.

Another vital aspect of classic democracy is a belief in the equality of all men. The Declaration of Independence expresses the conviction that "all men are created equal." Even the Founding Fathers believed in equality for all men *before the law*, notwithstanding the circumstances of the accused. A man was not to be judged by social position, economic class, creed, or race. Many early democrats also believed in *political equality*—equal access of individuals to political influence, that is, equal opportunity to influence public policy. Political equality is expressed in the concept of "one man, one vote."

Over time, the notion of equality has also come to include *equality of opportunity* in all aspects of American life—social, educational, and economic, as well as political. Roland Pennock writes:

The objective of equality is not merely the recognition of a certain dignity of the human being as such, but it is also to provide him with the opportunity—equal to that guaranteed to others—for protecting and advancing his interests and developing his powers and personality.[15]

Thus, the notion of equality of opportunity has been extended beyond political life to encompass equality of opportunity in education, employment, housing, recreation, and public accommodations. Each person has an equal opportunity to develop his individual capacities to their natural limits.

It is important to remember, however, that the traditional democratic creed has always stressed *equality of opportunity* to education, wealth, and status and not *absolute equality*. Thomas Jefferson recognized a "natural aristocracy" of talent, ambition, and industry, and liberal democrats since Jefferson have always accepted inequalities that are a product of individual merit and hard work. Absolute equality, or "leveling," is not a part of liberal democratic theory.

In summary, democratic thinking involves the following ideas:

1. popular participation in the decisions that shape the lives of individuals in a society;

2. government by majority rule, with recognition of the rights of minorities to try to become majorities. These rights include the freedoms of speech, press, assembly, and petition and the freedom to dissent, to form opposition parties, and to run for public office;

3. a commitment to individual dignity and the preservation of the liberal values of life, liberty, and property;

4. a commitment to equal opportunity for all men to develop their individual capacities.

The Meaning of Pluralism

Despite political rhetoric in America concerning citizen participation in decision making, majority rule, our protection of minorities, individual rights, and equality of opportunity, no scholar or commentator, however optimistic about life in this country, would contend that these conditions have been fully realized in the American political system. No one contends that citizens participate in *all* the decisions which shape their lives, or that majority preferences *always* prevail. Nor do they argue that the rights of minorities are *always* protected, or that the values of life, liberty, and property are *never* sacrificed, or that *every* American has an equal opportunity to influence public policy.

However, modern *pluralism* seeks to reaffirm the democratic character of American society by asserting that:

1. Although citizens do not directly participate in decision making, their many leaders do make decisions through a process of bargaining, accommodation, and compromise.

2. There is competition among leadership groups which helps to protect the interests of individuals. Countervailing centers of power—for example, competition between business leaders, labor leaders, and governmental leaders—can check each other and keep each interest from abusing its power and oppressing the individual.

3. Individuals can influence public policy by choosing between competing elites in elections. Elections and parties allow individuals to hold leaders accountable for their action.

4. While individuals do not participate directly in decision making, they can join organized groups and make their influence felt through their participation in these organizations.

5. Leadership groups are not closed; new groups can be formed and gain access to the political system.

6. Although political influence in society is unequal, power is widely dispersed. Frequently, access to decision making is based on the level of interest people have in a particular decision, and because leadership is fluid and mobile, power depends upon one's interest in public affairs, skills in leadership, information about issues, knowledge of democratic processes, and skill in organization and public relations.

7. There are multiple leadership groups within society. Those who exercise power in one kind of decision do not necessarily exercise power in others. No single elite dominates decision making in all issue areas.

8. Public policy is not necessarily majority preference, but it is an equilibrium of interest interaction. Such equilibrium is the approximate balance of competing interest group influences and is therefore a reasonable approximation of society's preferences.

Pluralism, then, is the belief that democratic values can be preserved in a system of multiple, competing elites who determine public policy through a process of bargaining and compromise, in which voters exercise meaningful choices in elections and new elites can gain access to power.

But pluralism, even if it accurately describes American society, is *not* the equivalent of democracy. Let us explain why. First of all, the pluralist notion of decision making by elite interaction is not the same as the democratic ideal of direct *individual* participation in decision making. Pluralists recognize that mass participation in decision making is not possible in a complex, urban, industrial society and that decision making must be accomplished through elite interaction, rather than individual participation. But a central value of classical democratic politics is *individual* participation in decision making. In modern pluralism, however, individual participation has given way to interaction—bargaining, accommodation, and compromise—between leaders of institutions and organizations in society. Individuals are represented in the political system only insofar as they are members of institutions or organizations whose leaders participate in policy making. Government is held responsible not by individual citizens but by leaders of institutions, organized interest groups, and political parties. The principal actors are leaders of corporations and financial institutions, elected and appointed government officials, the top ranks of military and governmental bureaucracies, and leaders of large organizations in labor, agriculture, and the professions.

Yet, decision making by elite interaction, whether it succeeds in protecting the individual or not, fails to contribute to individual growth and development. In this regard, modern pluralism diverges sharply from classic democracy, which emphasizes as a primary value the personal development that would result from the individual's actively participating in decisions that affect his life.

Pluralism stresses the fragmentation of power in society and the influence of public opinion and elections on the behavior of elites. But this fragmentation of power is not identical with the democratic ideal of political equality. Who rules, in the pluralist view of America? According to political scientist Aaron Wildavsky, "different small groups of interested and active citizens in different issue areas with some overlap, if any, by public officials, and occasional intervention by a larger number of people at the polls."[16] This is not government by the people. While citizen influence can be felt through leaders who anticipate the reaction of citizens, decision making is still in the hands of the leaders—the elites. According to the pluralists, multiple elites decide public policy in America, each in their own area of interest.

Traditional democratic theory envisions public policy as a rational choice of individuals with equal influence, who evaluate their needs and reach a decision with due regard for the rights of others. This traditional theory does not view public policy as a product of elite interaction or interest group pressures. In fact, interest groups and even political parties were viewed by classical democratic theorists as intruders into an individualistic brand of citizenship and politics.

There are several other problems in accepting pluralism as the legitimate heir to classical democratic theory. First of all, can pluralism assure that membership in organizations and institutions is really an effective form of individual participation in policy making? Robert Presthus argues that the organizations and institutions on which pluralists rely "become oligarchic and restrictive insofar as they monopolize access to government power and limit individual participation."[17] Henry Kariel writes, "The voluntary organizations or associations which the early theorists of pluralism relied upon to sustain the individual against a unified omnipotent government, have themselves become oligarchically governed hierarchies."[18] The individual may provide the numerical base for organizations, but what influence does he have upon the leadership? Rarely do corporations, unions, armies, churches, government bureaucracies, or professional associations have any *internal* mechanisms of democracy. They are usually run by a small elite of officers and activists. Leaders of corporations, banks, labor unions, churches, universities, medical associations, and bar associations remain in control year after year. Only a small number of people attend meetings, vote in organizational elections, or make their influence felt within their organization. The pluralists offer no evidence that the giant organizations and institutions in American life really represent the views or interests of their individual members.

Also, can pluralism really assume that the dignity of the individual is being protected by elite competition? Since pluralism contends that different groups of leaders make decisions in *different* issue areas, why should we assume that these leaders compete with each other? It seems more likely that each group of leaders would consent to allow other groups of leaders to govern their own spheres of influence without interference. Accommodation, rather than competition, may be the prevailing style of elite interaction.

Pluralism answers with the hope that the power of diverse institutions and organizations in society will roughly balance out and that the emergence of power monopoly is unlikely. Pluralism (like its distant cousin, the economics of Adam Smith) assures us that no interests can ever emerge the complete victor in political competition. Yet inequality of power among institutions and organizations is commonplace. Examples of narrow, organized interests achieving their goals at the expense of the broader but unorganized public are quite common. Furthermore, it is usually producer interests, bound together by economic ties, which turn out to dominate less organized consumer groups and groups based upon non-economic interests. The pluralists offer no evidence that political competition can prevent monopoly or oligopoly in political power, any more than economic competition could prevent monopoly or oligopoly in economic power.

Finally, pluralism must contend with the problem of how private non-governmental elites can be held accountable to the people. Even if the people can hold governmental elites accountable through elections, how can corporation elites, union leaders, and other kinds of private leadership be held accountable? Pluralism usually dodges this important question by focusing primary attention on *public* decision making involving governmental elites and by largely ignoring *private* decision making involving non-governmental elites. Pluralists focus on rules and orders which are enforced by *governments*, but certainly men's lives are vitally affected by decisions made by private institutions and organizations—corporations, banks, universities, medical associations, newspapers, and so on. In an ideal democracy, individuals would participate in *all* decisions which significantly affect their lives; but pluralism largely excludes individuals from participation in many vital decisions by claiming that these decisions are "private" in nature and not subject to public accountability.

In summary, the pluralism diverges from classical democratic theory in the following respects:

1. Decisions are made by elite interaction—bargaining, accommodation, compromise—rather than by direct individual participation.

2. Key political actors are leaders of institutions and organizations rather than individual citizens.

3. Power is fragmented, but inequality of political influence among powerholders is common.

4. Power is distributed among governmental and non-governmental institutions and organizations, but these institutions and organizations are generally governed by oligarchies, rather than by their members in democratic fashion.

5. Institutions and organizations divide power and presumably compete among themselves, but there is no certainty that this competition guarantees political equality or protects individual dignity.

6. *Governmental* elites are presumed to be accountable to the masses through elections, but many important decisions affecting the lives of individuals are made by *private* elites, who are not directly accountable to the masses.

Frequently confusion arises in distinguishing *pluralism* from *elitism*. Pluralists *say* that the system they describe is a reaffirmation of democratic theory in a modern, urban, industrial society. They offer pluralism as "a practical solution" to the problem of achieving democratic ideals in a large complex social system where direct individual participation and decision making is simply not possible. But many critics of pluralism assert that it is a covert form of elitism—that pluralists are closer to the elitist position than to the democratic tradition they revere. Thus Peter Bachrach describes pluralism as "democratic elitism":

Until quite recently democratic and elite theories were regarded as distinct and conflicting. While in their pure form they are still regarded as contradictory, there is, I believe, a strong if not dominant trend in contemporary political thought incorporating major elitist principles within democratic theory. As a result there is a new theory which I have called democratic elitism.[19]

Mass Threats to Democracy

Democratic theory assumes that liberal values—individual dignity, equality of opportunity, the right of dissent, freedom of speech and press, religious toleration, and due process of law—are best protected by the expansion and growth of mass political participation. Historically, the masses and not elites were considered the guardians of liberty. For example, in the eighteenth and nineteenth centuries, the threat of tyranny arose from corrupt monarchies and decadent churches. But in the twentieth century, it has been the masses who have been most susceptible to the appeals of totalitarianism.

It is the irony of democracy in America that elites, not masses, are most committed to democratic values. Despite a superficial commitment to the symbols of democracy, the American people have a surprisingly weak commitment to individual liberty, toleration of diversity, or freedom of expression for those who would challenge the existing order. Social science research reveals that the common man is not attached to the causes of liberty, fraternity, or equality. On the contrary, support for free speech and press, for freedom of dissent, and for equality of opportunity for all is associated with high educational levels, prestigious occupations, and high social status. Authoritarianism is stronger among the working classes in America than among the middle and upper classes. Democracy would not survive if it depended upon support for democratic values among the masses in America.

Democratic values have survived because elites, not masses, govern. Elites in America—leaders in government, industry, education, and civic affairs; the well-educated, prestigiously employed, and politically active—give greater support to basic democratic values and "rules of the game" than do the masses. And it is because masses in America respond to the ideas and actions of democratically minded elites that liberal values are preserved. In summarizing the findings of social science research regarding mass behavior in American democracy, political scientist Peter Bachrach writes:

A widespread public commitment to the fundamental norms underlying the democratic process was regarded by classical democratic theorists as essential to the survival of democracy . . . today social scientists tend to reject this position. They do so not only because of their limited confidence in the commitment of non-elites to freedom, but also because of the growing awareness that non-elites are, in large part, politically activated by elites. The empirical finding that mass behavior is generally in response to the attitudes, proposals and modes of action of political elites gives added support to the position that responsibility for maintaining "the rules of the game" rests not on the shoulders of the people but on those of the elites. [20]

In short, it is the common man, not the elite, who is most likely to be swayed by anti-democratic ideology; and it is the elite, not the common man, who is the chief guardian of democratic values.

Elites must be insulated from the anti-democratic tendencies of the masses if they are to fulfill their role as guardians of liberty and property. Too much mass influence over elites threatens democratic values. Mass behavior is highly unstable. Usually, established elites can depend upon mass apathy; but, occasionally, mass activism will replace apathy, and this activism will be extremist, unstable, and unpredictable. Mass activism is usually an expression of resentment against the established order, and it usually occurs in times of crisis, when a counter-elite, or demagogue, emerges from the masses to mobilize them against the established elites.

Democracies, where elites are dangerously accessible to mass influence, can survive only if the masses are absorbed in the problems of everyday life and are involved in primary and secondary groups which distract their attention from mass politics. In other words, the masses are stable when they are absorbed in their work, family, neighborhood, trade union, hobby, church, recreational group, and so on. It is when they become alienated from their home, work, and community—when existing ties to social organizations and institutions become weakened—that mass behavior becomes unstable and dangerous. It is then that the attention and activity of the masses can be captured and directed by the demagogue, or counter-elite. The demagogue can easily mobilize for revolution those elements of the masses who have few ties to the existing social and political order.

These ties to the existing order tend to be weakest during crisis periods, when major social changes are taking place. According to social psychologist William Kornhauser:

> . . . communism and fascism have gained strength in social systems undergoing sudden and extensive changes in the structure of authority and community. Sharp tears in the social fabric caused by widespread unemployment or by major military defeat are highly favorable to mass politics.[21]

Counter-elites are mass-oriented leaders who express hostility toward the established order and appeal to mass sentiments—extremism, intolerance, racial identity, anti-intellectualism, equalitarianism, and violence. Counter-elites can easily be distinguished from elites: Elites, whether liberal or conservative, support the fundamental values of the system—individual liberty, majority rule, due process of law, limited government, and private property; counter-elites, whether "left" or "right," are anti-democratic, extremist, impatient with due process, contemptuous of law and authority, and violence-prone. The only significant difference between "left" and "right" counter-elites is their attitude toward change: "right" counter-elites express mass reaction against change—political, social, economic, technological—while "left" counter-elites demand radical and revolutionary change.

All counter-elites claim to speak for "the people." Both "left" and "right" counter-elites assert *the supremacy of "the people"* over laws, institutions, procedures, or individual rights. Right-wing counter-elites, including fascists, justify their policies as "the will of the people," while left-wing radicals cry "all power to the people" and praise the virtues of "people's democracies." In describing this populism, sociologist Edward Shils writes:

the will of the people as such is supreme over every other standard, over the standards of traditional institutions, over the autonomy of institutions, and over the will of other strata. Populism identifies the will of the people with justice and morality.[22]

Extremism is another characteristic of mass politics—the view compromise and coalition-building is immoral. Indeed "politics" and "politicians" are viewed with hostility, because they imply the possibility of compromising mass demands.[23] Occasionally counter-elites will make cynical use of politics, but only as a short-term tactical means to other goals. A commentator on radical student activists observes that they are

indistinguishable from the far right. . . . They share a contempt for rational political discussion and constitutional legal solutions. Both want to be pure. They know nothing about the virtue of compromise. They know nothing about the horror of sainthood or the wickedness of saints.[24]

Counter-elites frequently charge that a *conspiracy* exists among established elites to deliberately perpetuate evil upon the people. The "left" counter-elite charges that the established order knowingly exploits and oppresses the people for its own benefit and amusement; the "right" counter-elite charges that the established order is falling prey to an international communist conspiracy whose goal is to deprive the people of their liberty and property and to enslave them. Richard Hofstadter refers to this phenomena as "the paranoid style of politics."[25] A related weapon in the arsenal of the counter-elite is *scapegoatism*—the designation of particular minority groups in society as responsible for the evils suffered by the people. Throughout American history various scapegoats have been designated—Catholics, immigrants, Jews, blacks, communists, intellectuals, "Wall Street Bankers," munitions manufacturers, etc.

The masses define politics in *simplistic* terms. The masses want simple answers to all of society's problems, regardless of how complex these problems may be. Thus, black counter-elites charge that "white racism" is responsible for the complex problems of under-education, poverty, unemployment, crime, delinquency, ill-health, and poor housing of ghetto dwellers. In a similiar fashion the white counter-elites dismiss ghetto disturbances as a product of "communist agitation." These simplistic answers are designed to relieve both black and white masses of any difficult thinking about social issues and to place their problems in simple, emotion-laden terms. Anti-intellectualism and anti-rationalism are an important part of mass politics.

Counter-elites often reflect mass *propensities toward violence*. Rap Brown inspired black masses in Cambridge, Maryland, in 1967 with:

"Don't be trying to love that honky to death. Shoot him to death. Shoot him to death, brother, cause that's what he's out to do to you. Like I said in the beginning, if this town don't come around, this town should be burned down, it should be burned down, brother."[26]

Early in his political career, George C. Wallace's references to violence were only slightly more subtle:

Of course, if I did what I'd like to do I'd pick up something and smash one of these federal judges in the head and then burn the courthouse down. But I'm too genteel. What we need in this country is some Governors that used to work up here at Birmingham in the steel mills with about a tenth-grade education. A Governor like that wouldn't be so genteel. He'd put out his orders and he'd say, "The first man who throws a brick is a dead man. The first man who loots something what doesn't belong to him is a dead man. My orders are to shoot to kill."[27]

The similarity between the appeals of black and white counter-elites is obvious.

In summary, elite theory views the critical division in American politics as the division between elites and masses. "Left" and "right" counter-elites are similar. Both appeal to mass sentiments; assert the supremacy of "the people" over laws, institutions, and individual rights; reject compromise in favor of extremism; charge that established elites are a conspiracy; designate scapegoat groups; define social problems in simple emotional terms and reject rational thinking; express equalitarian sentiments and hostility toward men who have achieved success within the system; and express approval of mass violence.

Elite Threats to Democracy

While elites are relatively more committed to democratic values than masses, elites themselves frequently abandon these values in crisis periods and become repressive. Anti-democratic mass activism has its counterpart in elite repression. Both endanger democratic values.

Mass activism and elite repression frequently interact to create multiple threats to democracy. Mass activism—riots, demonstrations, extremism, violence—generate fear and insecurity among elites, who respond by curtailing freedom and strengthening "security." Dissent is no longer tolerated, the news media is censored, free speech curtailed, potential counter-elites jailed, and police and security forces strengthened —usually in the name of "national security" or "law and order." Elites convince themselves that these steps are necessary to preserve liberal democratic values. The irony is, of course, that the elites make society less democratic in trying to preserve democracy.

In short, neither elites nor masses in America are totally and ir-revocably committed to democratic values. Elites are generally more committed to democratic procedures than the masses. This is true for several reasons. In the first place, persons who are successful at the game of democratic politics are more amenable to abiding by the rules of the game than those who are not. Moreover, many elite members have internalized democratic values learned in childhood. Finally, the achievement of high position may bring a sense of responsibility for, and an awareness of, societal values. However, elites can and do become repressive when they perceive threats to the political system and their position in it.

The Watergate Affair: Mass Unrest And Elite Repression

The Watergate affair provides an excellent illustration of elite reaction to mass unrest, and the tendency of elites to resort to repression when threatened.

Mass Unrest To understand Watergate, one must first understand the climate of mass unrest in the 1960s which threatened the security of governing elites. A decade of disorder began with the assassination of President John F. Kennedy in 1963 followed by the assassinations of Martin Luther King and Robert F. Kennedy in 1968, and the attempted assassination of George C. Wallace in 1972. Mass demonstrations and civil disobedience were developed and refined as political tactics in the

civil rights movement. Black and white masses did not always understand the distinction between nonviolent demonstrations directed
against injustice, and rioting and violence directed against society itself.
The ghetto riots, which began in Watts in 1965, climaxed in the summer
of 1967 in Newark and Detroit, and flowered anew in many cities after
the death of Martin Luther King in 1968 invited a repressive "law and
order" movement. The decade was also marked by white mass
counter-violence—murders, beatings, and bombings of black and white
civil rights workers. The concern of elites over the increasing legitima-
tion of violence among the masses was reflected in the establishment of
two separate presidential commissions—the National Advisory Commission on Civil Disorders and the National Commission on the Causes
and Prevention of Violence.

But racial unrest and social change were not the only forces contributing to mass unrest. Humiliation and defeat in a prolonged and
fruitless military effort in Vietnam was also undermining the legitimacy
of the government. The Democratic National Convention in Chicago in
1968 featured violent antiwar protest outside of the convention hall; the
police responded with counter-violence of their own. Fears of violence
were heightened in 1969 when "Weathermen" sponsored their "days of
rage" in Chicago, during which they destroyed property and fought with
police. Soon bomb scares became commonplace and bombings increasingly frequent. Three antiwar "Weathermen" were killed when a bomb
they were making accidentally exploded in New York City in 1970.
College protest activity, which had remained nonviolent for most of the
decade, became increasingly violent-prone in 1970. Violence flared on
such diverse campuses as San Francisco State, University of Wisconsin
(Madison), Columbia, and Chicago. After a bombing at the University of
Wisconsin killed a post-doctoral student, underground newspapers glee-
fully reported that another blow had been struck against the "pig-
nation." Increasingly radical elements argued that the use of violence
was justified.

Mass anxieties increased to the point where harsh and repressive
measures by elites were welcomed. Many Americans openly applauded
police violence against students, arguing that students had only themselves to blame if they were killed by police during disruptive or violent
protests. In May 1970, National Guardsmen were sent to Kent State University after the ROTC building had been set afire. When students defied
an order to disperse, some guardsmen fired their weapons; four students
were killed and nine were wounded. Ten days later at Jackson State
College, a black school at Jackson, Mississippi, students set a truck

ablaze and threw bricks and bottles at passing white motorists. In response some policemen fired into a girl's dormitory, killing two black students and wounding twelve. In May of 1970, campus protest activity closed down many of the nation's leading universities. On May 9, 1970, more than sixty thousand people, most of them students, assembled in Washington for an antiwar demonstration. While most demonstrators were nonviolent, a radical minority pledged to "close down the government" and attempted to incite violence. In the inevitable reaction, Washington authorities conducted mass arrests in violation of established procedures.

At the same time, there was a serious split among elites about the handling of the war. While everyone agreed that the war should be terminated, the President's critics did not believe that he was moving fast enough toward that goal. In 1971, the *New York Times* and the *Washington Post* published the so-called "Pentagon Papers," which had been stolen from the files of the Department of Defense by a former Defense Department advisor, Daniel Ellsberg. The President and his senior advisors were convinced that this important segment of the nation's elite—the influential newsmakers—had acted outside of the established "rules of the game" in their effort to end the war quickly.

Thus, by the early 1970s, all of the conditions for elite repression existed: 1) racial unrest and violence; 2) the approval and encouragement of violence as a form of mass protest; 3) defeat and humiliation in war; 4) mass anxieties about crime, street violence, and personal safety; 5) counter-elite violence, including bombings and arson; 6) attacks from segments of the elite which went beyond the established "rules of the game."

Elite Reaction   The Watergate hearings—the hearings before the Senate Select Committee on Campaign Practices chaired by Senator Samuel J. Ervin, Jr. (D-N.C.)—provide a revealing insight into elite behavior. The testimony of top White House advisors, and the statements provided the committee by the President himself, are amazingly candid in their explanation of activities undertaken on behalf of "national security." The testimony of H. R. Haldeman, former White House Chief of Staff, John D. Erlichman, former presidential Domestic Affairs Advisor, and reports by the President himself, all make it clear that the White House "horrors" revealed in the Watergate investigation were reactions of a governing elite to perceived threats to the political system. There is no evidence that the Watergate activities were undertaken for the personal financial gain of any individual or group. Rather, they were undertaken out of a genuine belief that the political system was threatened and that extraordinary measures were required to preserve it. It might be argued that President Nixon and his top White House aides were more paranoid in their assessment of threats to the political system than other elites would have been. But their actions were *typical* of elite behavior in the face of mass threats to the established order.

Let us turn first to the testimony of H. R. "Bob" Haldeman, former White House Chief of Staff, to understand the origins of Watergate in elite fears about mass disruption:

It has been alleged that there was an atmosphere of fear at the White House regarding security matters. I can state categorically that there was no climate of fear at all. There was, however, a healthy and valid concern for a number of matters in the general area of national security and for a number of other matters in the general area of domestic security . . .

With regard to leaks of information, especially in the area of national security, it became evident in 1969 that leaks of secret information were taking place that seriously jeopardized a number of highly sensitive foreign policy initiatives. . . . In order to deal with these leaks, a program of wiretaps was instituted in 1969 and continued into early 1971.

In 1970, the domestic security problem reached critical proportions as a wave of bombings and explosions, rioting and violence, demonstrations, arson, gun battles, and other disruptive activities took place across the country—on college campuses primarily, but also in other areas.

In order to deal with this problem, the President set up an inter-agency committee consisting of the directors of the FBI, the CIA, the Defense Intelligence Agency, and the National Security Agency. This committee was instructed to prepare recommendations for the President . . . for expanded intelligence operations.[28]

This group submitted a forty-three-page report calling for 1) intensified electronic surveillance of both domestic security threats and foreign diplomats; 2) monitoring of American citizens using international communications facilities; 3) increased legal and illegal opening and reading of mail; 4) more informants on college campuses; 5) the lifting of restrictions on "surreptitious entry" (burglary); 6) the establishment of an inter-agency group on domestic intelligence. The President approved the report, but later FBI Director J. Edgar Hoover objected to it—not because he opposed such measures, but because the FBI was not given exclusive control of the program. Hoover's opposition resulted in the formal withdrawal of the plan, but the plan itself clearly reflected elite thinking about the appropriate means of dealing with threats to the political system.

The Plumbers Defended Despite withdrawal of the plan, the White House still believed that the political system was endangered by disruptive and subversive elements, and that "extraordinary" measures were required to protect it. As Mr. Haldeman explains:

In mid-1971, the New York Times started publication of the so-called Pentagon Papers, which had been stolen from the sensitive files of the Department of State and Defense and the CIA and which covered military and diplomatic moves in a war that was still going on. The implications of this security leak were enormous and it posed a threat so grave as to require, in the judgment of the President and his senior advisors, extraordinary action. As a result, the President approved creation of the Special Investigation's Unit within the White House which later became known as the "plumbers."[29]

The Special Investigations Unit within the White House—"the plumbers"—was placed under the supervision of John Ehrlichman and his assistant Egil Krogh. The "plumber's unit" soon included ex-CIA agent and author of spy novels, E. Howard Hunt, Jr., and former FBI agent G. Gordon Liddy. The "plumber's unit" worked independently of the FBI and the CIA (although it received occasional assistance from the CIA) and reported directly to John Erlichman. It undertook a variety of repressive activities—later referred to as White House "horrors"—including: the investigation of Daniel Ellsberg and the burglary of his psychiatrist's office to learn more about his motives in the theft of the Pentagon Papers; investigation of (and later the forgery of) the record of the events surrounding the assassination of South Vietnam's President Diem during the administration of John F. Kennedy; investigation of national security leaks which affected the U.S. negotiating position in the SALT talks; and other undisclosed domestic and foreign intelligence activities. There is additional evidence that the "plumber's unit" also undertook investigations of other White House domestic "enemies," including antiwar protesters; critical reporters and television commentators; assorted liberals and radicals; and even an investigation of the Chappaquiddick scandal and Edward M. Kennedy.

John D. Erlichman strongly defended the activities of the "plumber's unit" before the Ervin Committee. His argument is typical of the justifications which elites make on behalf of repressive actions designed to preserve the political system:

Today the Presidency is the only place in the nation where all of the conflicting considerations of domestic and international politics, economics and society, merge; it is there that street violence and civil rights and relations with Russia and their affect on China and the Cambodian military situation and a thousand *other factors and events are brought together on the surface of one desk and must be resolved.*

Some of these events in 1969 and 1970 included hundreds of bombings of public buildings, a highly organized attempt to shut down the federal government, intensive harrassment of political candidates, and violent street demonstrations which endangered life and property.

Taken as isolated incidents, these events were serious. Taken as a part of an apparent campaign to force upon the President a foreign policy favorable to the North Vietnamese and their allies, these demonstrations were more than a garden variety exercise of the first amendment.[30]

The Watergate Embarrassment The Watergate break-in itself—the burglarizing and wiretapping of the Democratic National Headquarters in the Watergate apartment building in Washington, D.C.—was an outgrowth of earlier elite fears and repressive measures. The work of the "plumber's unit" tapered off at the end of 1971, and Hunt and Liddy found new jobs with the President's re-election campaign organization, the Committee to Re-elect the President, headed by former Attorney General John M. Mitchell. The security co-ordinator for the Committee to Re-elect the President (CRP) was James W. McCord, Jr. who had served 7 years as an FBI agent and 19 years as a CIA agent. It was easy for Hunt and Liddy and McCord to confuse threats to national security with threats to the re-election of the incumbent president, and to employ well-known "national security" tactics, including bugging and burglary, against the president's opponents. On the night of June 17, 1972, five men were arrested in the offices of the Democratic National Committee with burglary and wire-tapping tools, including James W. McCord and Bernard L. Barker.

Later a grand jury charged these five men, together with Hunt and Liddy, with burglary and wire-tapping; at a trial in January 1973, all seven were convicted. U.S. District Court Judge John J. Sirica realized that the defendants were covering up who had ordered and paid for the bugging and break-in. The *Washington Post* also reported that the defendants were under pressure to plead guilty, that they were still being paid by an unnamed source, and that they had been promised a cash settlement and executive clemency if they pleaded guilty and went to jail and remained silent. When Judge Sirica threatened the defendants with heavy sentences, McCord soon broke and told of secret payments and a cover-up.

The White House cover-up of the Watergate affair stemmed in part from the same motives which lead to the original repressive measures —elite concern with mass disorders and threats to national security.

It was probably not so much political embarrassment or fear of prose-cution that led the White House to attempt a cover-up, so much as concern over exposure of the whole series of repressive acts undertaken earlier. The great blunder of the Watergate operation was that certain individuals who were caught in the petty political burglary of the Democratic National Committee—Liddy, Hunt, and McCord—had pre-viously served with the Special Investigations Unit of the White House and with the CIA. The Watergate burglary mixed partisan politics with national security affairs. The President and his top White House aids were prepared to defend repressive tactics employed in defense of "na-tional security"—that is to say, repressive tactics used against radicals, subversives, and antiwar zealots who were leaking national defense sec-rets to the press. Indeed, it is likely that the President would find wide-spread support among both elites and masses for the use of repressive tactics against such opponents. But the use of these same tactics against the Democratic Party clearly violated the established rules of the game in American politics.

The President's major concern was to separate the partisan politi-cal act of the break-in of the Democratic National Committee Headquar-ters from the more important national security activities. Not only was the Watergate affair a political embarrassment, but it also threatened to expose the whole series of repressive measures undertaken by the White House over several years.

A Rationale for Repression   The President's official statements on the Watergate affair clearly indicate his desire to *deplore* the partisan politi-cal act while at the same time *defend* the earlier national security measures. In the words of the President:

The purpose of this statement is . . . to draw the distinction between national security operations and the Watergate case . . . .

In citing these national security matters, it is not my intention to place a national security "cover" on Watergate, but rather to separate them out from Watergate—and at the same time to explain the context in which certain actions took place that were later misconstrued or misused.

Long before the Watergate break-in, three important national security opera-tions took place which have subsequently become entangled in the Watergate case.

The first operation begun in 1969 was a program of wire-taps. All were legal, under the authorities then existing. They were undertaken to find and stop serious national security leaks.

The second operation was a reassessment, which I ordered in 1970, of the adequacy of internal security measures. This resulted in the plan in a directive

© Jules Feiffer

to strengthen our intelligence operations. They were protested by Mr. Hoover, and as a result of his protest, they were not put into effect.

The third operation was the establishment, in 1971, of a special investigation unit in the White House. Its primary mission was to plug leaks of vital security information . . . .[31]

In explaining the cover-up, then, the President contended:

The burglary and bugging of the Democratic National Committee Headquarters came as a complete surprise to me . . . I wanted justice done with regard to Water-

gate; but in the scale of national priorities with which I had to deal. I also had to be deeply concerned with insuring that neither the covert operations of the CIA or the operations of the special investigations unit should be compromised.[32]

It is not necessary that we discuss here the extent of President Nixon's complicity in the cover-up, or whether his real motives were more narrowly self-serving than he admitted. His public defense of his actions is itself a very candid insight into the attitudes of elites who feel themselves threatened. In the words of the President:

In summary, then:
1) *I had no prior knowledge of the Watergate bugging and operations, or of any illegal surveillance activities for political purposes.*
2) *Long prior to the 1972 campaign I did set in motion certain internal security measures, including legal wire taps, which I felt were necessary from a national security standpoint and, in the climate then prevailing, also necessary from a domestic security standpoint.*
3) *People who had been involved in the national security operation later, without my knowledge or approval, undertook illegal activities in the political campaign of 1972.*
4) *Elements of the early post-Watergate reports led me to suspect, incorrectly, that the CIA had been in some way involved. They also led me to surmise, correctly, that since persons originally recruited for covert national security activities had participated in Watergate, an unrestricted investigation of Watergate might lead to and expose those covert national security operations.*
5) *I sought to prevent the exposure of these covert national security activities, while encouraging those conducting the investigation to pursue their inquiry into the Watergate itself.*[33]

Summary

The Watergate affair is important because it illustrates elite behavior in the face of perceived threats to the political system. We believe repressive behavior is typical of elites in crisis situations. We believe there are many other historical examples of such repression—the Alien and Sedition Acts in the administration of John Adams; the suspension of due process rights by Abraham Lincoln during the Civil War; the "red scare" roundup of suspected Bolsheviks in the administration of Woodrow Wilson; the mass incarceration of thousands of Japanese-American families by the Roosevelt Administration; the persecution of suspected communists and "fellow-travelers" during the Truman and Eisenhower Administrations. Most of the practices revealed in the Watergate hearings—extensive wire-tapping, monitoring of mail, paid informants, surveillance of suspected subversives, infiltration of radical organizations, "surreptitious entry," and so forth—have been long-standing practices of federal security agencies. The mass media, the Democratic opposition, and the academic community may contend that the Nixon Administration was especially blameworthy; we do not dispute this contention. But assertions that Watergate is unique or unprecedented are either partisan or naive. Elite repression is a continuing threat to democratic values. And this threat will always be greater in periods of mass unrest, when elites convince themselves that their repressive acts are necessary to preserve the political system.

References

[1]Robert A. Dahl, "Power, Pluralism, and Democracy: A Modest Proposal," paper delivered at 1964 annual meeting of the American Political Science Association, p. 3. See also Peter Bachrach, *The Theory of Democratic Elitism* (Boston: Little, Brown and Co., 1967).

[2]Harold Lasswell and Abraham Kaplan, *Power and Society* (New Haven, Conn.: Yale University Press, 1950), p. 219.

[3]V. O. Key, Jr., *Public Opinion and American Democracy* (New York: Alfred A. Knopf, 1961), p. 558.

[4]Gaetano Mosca, *The Ruling Class* (New York: McGraw-Hill Book Co., 1939), p. 50.

[5]Mosca, p. 51.

[6]Dahl, "Power, Pluralism and Democracy," p. 3.

[7]Suzanne Keller, *Beyond the Ruling Class* (New York: Random House, 1963), p. 71.

[8]Harold Lasswell and Daniel Lerner, *The Comparative Study of Elites* (Stanford, Calif.:

[9]David Truman, "The American System in Crisis," *Political Science Quarterly* (December 1959), 489.

[10]Richard Hofstadter, *The American Political Tradition* (New York: Alfred A. Knopf, 1948), p. viii.

[11]John Dewey, "Democracy and Educational Administration," *School and Society* (April 3, 1937).

[12]John Stuart Mill, *Representative Government* (New York: E. P. Dutton, Everyman's Library), p. 203.

[13]Carl Becker, *Modern Democracy* (New Haven, Conn.: Yale University Press, 1941), pp. 26–27.

[14]For a discussion of John Locke and the political philosophy underlying democracy, see George Sabine, *A History of Political Theory* (New York: Holt, Rinehart and Winston, 1950), pp. 517–541.

[15]Roland Pennock, "Democracy and Leadership," in William Chambers and Robert Salisbury (eds.), *Democracy Today* (New York: Dodd, Mead & Co., 1962), pp. 126–127.

[16]Aaron Wildavsky, *Leadership in a Small Town* (Totawa, N.J.: Bedminster Press, 1964), p. 20.

[17]Robert Presthus, *Men at the Top* (New York: Oxford University Press, 1964), p. 20.

[18]Henry Kariel, *The Decline of American Pluralism* (Stanford, Calif.: Stanford University Press, 1961), p. 74.

[19]Peter Bachrach. *The Theory of Democratic Elitism* (Boston: Little, Brown and Co., 1967), p. xi.

[20]Bachrach, pp. 47–48.

[21]William Kornhauser, *The Politics of Mass Society* (New York: Free Press, 1959), p. 99.

[22]Edward A. Shils, *The Torment of Secrecy* (New York: Free Press, 1956), p. 98.

[23]See John H. Bunzel, *Anti-Politics in America* (New York: Knopf, 1967).

[24]Quotation from Nan Robertson, "The Student Scene: Angry Militants" *New York Times,* November 20, 1967, p. 30.

[25]Richard Hofstadter, *The Paranoid Style of American Politics* (New York: Knopf, 1965).

[26]U.S. Congress, Senate, Committee on the Judiciary, Hearings on H.R. 421, "Anti-riot Bill," 90th Congress, 1st Session, 2 August 1967, p. 32.

[27]Quoted in Seymour Martin Lipset and Earl Raab, *The Politics of Unreason* (New York: Harper and Row, 1970), p. 356.

[28]Testimony of H. R. Haldeman, former White House Chief of Staff, before the U.S. Senate Select Committee on Campaign Practices, July 30, 1973, reprinted in *Congressional Quarterly Weekly Report* August 4, 1973, pp. 2125–2134.

[29]*Ibid.*

[30]Testimony of John D. Ehrlichman, former Advisor to the President on Domestic Affairs, before the U.S. Senate Select Committee on Campaign Practices, July 24, 1973, reprinted in *Congressional Quarterly Weekly Report,* July 28, 1973, pp. 2044–2046.

[31]Statement of President Richard M. Nixon, May 22, 1973, reprinted in *Congressional Quarterly Weekly Report,* May 26, 1973, p. 1265–1269.

[32]*Ibid.*

[33]*Ibid.*

Selected Additional Readings

The Origins of Elite Theory
Michels, Robert. *Political Parties.* Glencoe, Ill.: Free Press, 1915. This book was first published in 1911 in German. Michels was a disciple of Mosca. Like Mosca, he sees elitism as an outcome of social organization. Michels argues that the very fact of organization in society leads inevitably to an elite. His often quoted thesis is "Who says organization, says oligarchy." (p. 418, 1958 Free Press reprint). Political scientists have called this "the iron law of oligarchy."

Mosca, Gaetano. *The Ruling Class,* ed. A. Livingston. New York: McGraw-Hill, 1939. This book was first published in 1896 in Italy. Mosca added to it later in a 1923 edition which reflects the impact of World War I on his ideas. Along with the work of Vilfredo Pareto, Mosca's *Ruling Class* forms the basis of what has been called "classical elitism."

Pareto, Vilfredo. *The Mind and Society: Treatise of General Sociology.* New York: Harcourt Brace, 1935. Originally published in 1915–1916 in four volumes. Pareto begins with a much broader definition of elite. He suggests that in any human activity, those who are the top practitioners are the elite in that activity. Elites can then be grouped into two classes—the governing elite and the non-governing elite—depending on whether the activity of which they are a top practitioner is important to government or not. Pareto also introduces psychological notions into his work. He speaks of "residues" which are human instincts, sentiments, or states of mind. These remain constant over time and from state to state.

Parry, Geraint. *Political Elites*. New York: Praeger Publishers, 1969. An excellent discussion of classical elitism. Includes an extensive treatment of Mosca, Pareto, Michels, Max Weber, James Burnham, C. Wright Mills, and other elite writers.

Current Literature—Books: Elitism, Pluralism, and Democracy
Bachrach, Peter. *The Theory of Democratic Elitism: A Critique*. Boston: Little, Brown, 1967. In addition to a good review of classical elitist literature, Bachrach discusses the distinction between democracy, pluralism, and elitism. He observes that the pluralists' claim that their model is the practical adaptation of democratic theory to the modern, technological state. He concludes that pluralism makes so many alterations in democratic theory as to render it unrecognizable. In fact, Bachrach coins a new term for the model produced by the combination of democratic theory with group theory—he calls it "democratic elitism." We call it "plural elitism."

Bell, Roderick, David V. Edwards, and R. Harrison Wagner. *Political Power: A Reader in Theory and Research*. New York: Free Press, 1969. This collection of important articles on power and elites includes works by Dahl, Polsby, Kornhauser, Simon, Banfield, and Bachrach and Baratz.

Dahl, Robert A. *Pluralist Democracy in the United States, Conflict and Consensus*. Chicago: Rand McNally, 1967. This is one of the few recent theoretical extensions of pluralism on the national level. Most of Dahl's important theoretical work has been at the community level. This book fills an important gap in pluralist literature.

Dye, Thomas R. and Harmon Zeigler, eds. *The Few and the Many*. North Scituate, Mass.: Duxbury Press, 1972. A series of important readings on elite theory and American politics describing the few who have power and the many who do not.

Kornhauser, William. *The Politics of Mass Society*. New York: Free Press, 1959. The argument in this book is that a "mass society" occurs when elites are obvious to masses and masses are accessible to elites. This situation produces a threat of tyranny. To prevent this situation from occurring, Kornhauser argues that intermediate groups are necessary to distract the attention of the masses from elite activities, to give the masses a sense of security and belonging at the local level, and to prevent demogogic manipulation of the masses by the elite.

Lipset, Seymour Martin and Earl Raab. *The Politics of Unreason: Right-Wing Extremism in America, 1790–1970*. New York: Harper and Row, 1970. This is a highly revealing historical account of extremist political movements in the United States.

Ricci, David M. *Community Power and Democratic Theory: The Logic of Political Analysis*. New York: Random House, 1971. This is an excellent review of both past and current philosophical, ideological, and methodological differences between elitists and pluralists of each theory, including the contributions of Joseph Schumpeter ("process" theory of democracy), David Truman ("group" theory of democracy), Floyd Hunter ("reputational" theory of elitism), C. Wright Mills ("positional" theory of elitism), and Robert Dahl ("pluralist" theory of democracy). Also included in the text are an excellent discussion of "the present scholarly impasse" existing between advocates of each point of view and an annotated bibliography of relevant literature.

Current Literature—Journal Articles: Elitism, Pluralism, and Democracy
Bachrach, Peter and Morton Baratz, "Two Faces of Power." *American Political Science Review,* 56 (1962), 947–952. This article argues that power is tied to decision making, but power is also exercised when a decision can be prevented (called a "nondecision"). Thus, power has "two faces."

Dahl, Robert A. "A Critique of the Ruling Elite Model." *American Political Science Review,* 58 (1958), 369–463. This has become a classic critique of elitism from a pluralist point of view.

Walker, Jack L. "A Critique of the Elitist Theory of Democracy." *American Political Science Review,* 60 (1966), 285–295. This critique of both elitism and pluralism treats them as if they were two variations of the same theory. Walker argues that both make too many changes in classical democratic theory to allow it to serve as a meaningful model for government.

CHAPTER 2

THE FOUNDING FATHERS:

THE NATION'S FIRST ELITE

The Founding Fathers—those 55 men who wrote the Constitution of the United States and founded a new nation—were a truly exceptional elite, not only "rich and well-born" but also educated, talented, and resourceful. When Thomas Jefferson, then serving as the nation's minister in Paris, first saw the list of delegates to the Constitutional Convention of 1787, he wrote to John Adams, who was the minister to London: "It is really an assembly of demigods."[1] The men at the Convention were drawn from the nation's intellectual and economic elites—possessors of landed estates, large merchants and importers, financiers and money-lenders, real estate and land speculators, and owners of public bonds and securities. Jefferson and Adams were among the very few of the nation's "notables" who were *not* at the Convention.

Needless to say, the Founding Fathers were not representative of the four million Americans in the new nation, most of whom were small farmers, debtors, tradesmen, frontiersmen, servants, or slaves. However, to say that these men were not representative of the American people, or that the Constitution was not a very democratic document, does not

31

discredit the Constitution or the Founding Fathers. To the aristocratic society of eighteenth-century Europe, the Founding Fathers were dangerous revolutionaries, who were establishing a government in which men with the talent of acquiring property could rise to political power, regardless of birth or nobility. And the Constitution has survived the test of time, providing the basic framework for an ever-changing society.

Elites and Masses in the New American Nation

Visitors from the old aristocratic countries of Europe frequently remarked about the absence of a nobility in America and about the spirit of republicanism that prevailed. Certainly the yeoman farmer or frontiersman in America gave much less open deference to his "betters" than did the peasant of Europe; yet there were class lines in America. At the top of the social structure there was a tiny elite, most of whom were well-born, although there were some who were self-made. This elite group dominated the social, cultural, economic, and political life of the new nation. The French chargé d'affaires of that time reported that although there were "no nobles" in America, there were "gentlemen" who enjoyed a kind of "preeminence" because of "their wealth, their talents, their education, their families, or the offices they hold."[2] Some of these prominent "gentlemen" were Tories and had been forced to flee America after the Revolution; but there were still the Pinckneys and Rutledges in Charleston; the Adamses, Lowells, and Gerrys in Boston; the Schuylers, Clintons, and Jays of New York; the Morrises, Mifflins, and Ingersolls of Philadelphia; the Jenifers and Carrolls of Maryland; and the Blairs and Randolphs of Virginia.

Below this thin layer of educated and talented merchants, planters, lawyers, and bankers was a substantial body of successful farmers, shopkeepers, and independent artisans—of the "middling" sort, as they were known in Revolutionary America. This early middle class was by no means a majority in the new nation; it stood considerably above the masses of debt-ridden farmers and frontiersmen who made up the majority of the population. This small middle class had some political power, even at the time of the Constitutional Convention. This middle group was entitled to vote, and its views were represented in governing circles, even if they did not prevail at the Constitutional Convention. The middle class was especially well represented in state legislatures and was championed by several men of prominence in the Revolutionary period—Patrick Henry, Luther Martin, and Thomas Jefferson.

The great mass of white Americans in the Revolutionary period were "freeholders," farmers who worked their own land, scratching out a minimum existence for themselves and their families. They had little interest in or knowledge about public affairs. Usually the freeholders who were not barred from voting by property-owning or tax-paying qualifications were too preoccupied with debt and subsistence, or too isolated in the wilderness, to vote anyhow. Nearly eight out of ten Americans made a marginal living in the dirt; one in ten worked in fishing or lumbering; one in ten was engaged in commerce in some way, from the dockhand and sailor to the lawyer and merchant.

At the bottom of the white social structure in the new republic were the indentured servants and tenant farmers; this class comprised perhaps 20 percent of the population at this time. There is no evidence that this group exercised any political power at all. Finally, Negro slaves stood below the bottom of the white class structure. While they also comprised almost 20 percent of the population and were an important component of the American economy, they were considered property, even in a country that proclaimed the natural rights and equality of "all men."

Elite Dissatisfaction with the Confederation: The Stimulus to Reform

In July 1775, Benjamin Franklin had proposed to the Continental Congress a plan for a "perpetual union"; and, following the Declaration of Independence in 1776, the Congress appointed a committee to consider the Franklin proposals. The committee, headed by John Dickinson, made its report in the form of Articles of Confederation, which were debated for more than a year before finally being adopted by the Congress on November 15, 1777. It was stipulated that the Articles of Confederation would not go into effect until every state had approved; Delaware withheld its consent until 1779, Maryland until 1781.

The Articles of Confederation, effective from 1781 to 1789, established a "firm league of friendship" among the states "for their common defense, the security of their liberties, and their mutual and general welfare." Each state was reassured of "its sovereignty, freedom, and independence, and every power, jurisdiction, and right, which is not by this confederation expressly delegated to the United States, in Congress assembled." The expressly delegated powers included power to declare war, to send and receive ambassadors, to make treaties, to fix standards of weights and measures, to regulate the value of coins, to manage Indian affairs, to establish post offices, to borrow money, to build and equip an army and navy, and to make requisitions upon the several states for money and manpower. The powers not delegated to Congress remained with the states, and these included two of the most important powers of government—the power to regulate commerce and the power to levy taxes. Congress had to requisition the states for its revenue, but Congress had no authority to compel the states to honor these requisitions. Moreover, since Congress could not regulate commerce, the states were free to protect local trade and commerce even at the expense of destroying the emerging national economy.

Thus, the United States under the Articles of Confederation was comparable to an international organization of thirteen separate and independent governments. The national government was thought of as an alliance of separate *states*, not a government "of the people"; and the powers of the national government were dependent upon state governments.

The Articles of Confederation established Congress as the single branch of the national government. Delegates to Congress were chosen by the legislature of each state, and every state enjoyed one vote in Congress regardless of its population or resources. Executive and judicial functions were performed by committees of Congress, and officials of the United States were appointed and directed by Congress. The Articles guaranteed travel among the states and entitled the citizens of each state to the "privileges and immunities" of citizens of each of the other states, including privileges of trade and commerce. Each state was required to give "full faith and credit" to the records, acts, and judicial proceedings of every other state, and fugitives could be extradited from one state to another. No state could enter into diplomatic relations with foreign governments or engage in war unless it was actually invaded; no state could maintain a navy, but every state was expected to keep a militia force.

Our Founding Fathers were very critical of the first government of the United States under the Articles of Confederation, but the government was not a failure. In the years between 1774 and 1789, the American Confederacy declared its independence from the world's most powerful colonial nation, fought a successful war, established a viable peace, won powerful allies in the international community, created a successful army and navy, established a postal system, created a national bureaucracy, and laid the foundations for national unity.

But despite the successes of the Confederation in war and diplomatic relations, the political arrangements under the Articles were found unsatisfactory, even threatening, by the American elites. Generally, the "weaknesses" of the Articles that were most lamented by the Founding Fathers were the political arrangements that threatened the interests of merchants, investors, planters, real estate developers, and owners of public bonds and securities. Some of these "weaknesses," and the threats that they posed to America's elite, are described below.

The inability of Congress to levy taxes under the Articles of Confederation was a serious threat to those patriots who had given financial backing to the new nation during the Revolutionary War. The war had been financed with money borrowed by the Continental Congress and the states through the issuance of bonds and securities. The United States government owed about $10 million to foreign investors and over $40 million to American investors; in addition, individual states owed over $20 million as a result of their efforts in support of the war.*

Congress was unable to tax the people in order to obtain money to pay off these debts; and although Congress continually requisitioned states for money, the states became less and less inclined, as time passed, to meet their obligations to the central government. Only one tenth of the sums requisitioned by Congress under the Articles was ever paid by the states; and during the last years of the Articles, the United States was unable even to pay interest on its foreign and domestic debt. The result was that the bonds and notes of the United States government lost most of their value, sometimes selling on the open market for only one tenth of their original value. Investors who had backed the American war effort were left holding the bag.

Without the power to tax, and with the credit of the United States ruined, the prospects of the central government for future financial support—and for survival—looked dim. Naturally, the rich planters, merchants, and investors who held public securities had a direct financial interest in helping the central government acquire the power to tax and to pay off its debts.

The inability of Congress under the Articles to regulate commerce between the states and with foreign nations and the practice of the states of laying tariffs on the goods of other states as well as on those of foreign nations were creating havoc among commercial and shipping interests. "In every point of view," Madison wrote in 1785, "the trade of this country is in a deplorable condition."[3] The American Revolution had

---

*A debt of $70 million is very small by today's standards, but the total taxable land value in all of the thirteen states in 1787 was only about $400 million. Thus, the public debt was about 20 percent of the total value of all of the lands in the thirteen states.

been fought, in part, for the purpose of defending American commercial and business interests from oppressive regulations by the British government. Now the states themselves were interfering with the development of a national economy. Merchants and shippers with a view toward a national market and a high level of commerce were vitally concerned that the central government acquire the power to regulate interstate commerce and that the states be prevented from imposing crippling tariffs and restrictions on interstate trade.

State governments under the Articles posed a serious threat to investors and creditors through the issuance of cheap paper money and the passage of laws impairing the obligations of contract. Paper money issued by the states permitted debtors to pay off their creditors with money that had less value than the money originally loaned. Even the most successful farmers were usually heavily in debt, and many of these farmers were gaining strength in state legislatures. They threatened to pass laws delaying the collection of debts and even abolishing the prevailing practice of imprisonment for unpaid debts. Obviously, creditors had a direct financial interest in the establishment of a strong central government that could prevent the states from issuing public paper or otherwise interfering with debts.

The political success of debtors in Rhode Island particularly alerted men of property to the need for action that would offset the potential power of the agrarian classes. In Rhode Island, the paper-money faction secured a majority in the legislature and issued so much state currency that Rhode Island money was almost valueless. When merchants and creditors refused to accept Rhode Island paper money as "legal tender," the Rhode Island legislature passed a law making such refusal a punishable offense. In one of the first exercises of judicial review in history, the Rhode Island Supreme Court, still safe in the hands of propertied men, declared the law to be a violation of the Rhode Island Constitution. But the lesson to America's elite was clear: Too much democracy could threaten the rights of property, and only a strong central government with limited popular participation could safeguard property from the attacks of the masses.

A strong central government would help to protect creditors against social upheavals by the large debtor class in America. In several states, debtors had already engaged in open rebellion against tax collectors and sheriffs attempting to repossess farms on behalf of creditors. The most serious rebellion broke out in the summer of 1786 in Massachusetts, when bands of insurgents—composed of farmers, artisans, and laborers—captured the courthouses in several western districts and momentarily held the city of Springfield. Led by Daniel Shays, a veteran of Bunker Hill, the insurgent army posed a direct military threat to the governing elite of Massachusetts. Shays' Rebellion, as it was called, was put down by a small mercenary army, paid for by well-to-do citizens who feared that a wholesale attack on property rights was imminent.

The growing radicalism in the states was intimidating the propertied classes, who began to suggest that a strong central government was needed to "insure domestic tranquility," guarantee "a republican form of government," and protect property "against domestic violence." The American Revolution had a disturbing effect on the tradition among the masses of deferring to those in authority. Extremists, like Thomas Paine, who had reasoned that it was right and proper to revolt against England because of political tyranny, might also call for revolt against creditors because of economic tyranny. If debts owed to British merchants could be legislated out of existence, why not also the debts owed to American merchants? Acts of violence, boycotts, tea parties, and attacks on tax collectors frightened all propertied men in America.

A strong central government with military power sufficient to oust the British in the Northwest and to protect Western settlers against Indian attacks could open the way for the development of the American West. In addition, the protection and settlement of Western land would skyrocket land values and make rich men of land speculators.

Speculation in Western land was a very active pastime for men of property in early America. George Washington, Benjamin Franklin, Robert Morris, and even the popular hero Patrick Henry were involved in land speculation. During the Revolutionary War, the Congress had often paid the Continental soldiers with land certificates. After the war, most of the ex-soldiers sold these certificates to land speculators at very low prices. The Confederation's lack of proper military forces for America's frontiers had kept the value of Western lands at low prices, for ravaging Indians discouraged immigration to the lands west of the Alleghenies, and the British threatened to cut off westward expansion by continuing to occupy (in defiance of the peace treaty) seven important fur-trading forts in the Northwest. The British forts were also becoming centers of anti-American influence among the Indians.

The development of a strong American navy was also important to American commercial interests; for the states seem to have been ineffective in preventing smuggling, and piracy was a very real danger at the time and a vital concern of American shippers.

Manufacturing was still in its infant stages during the Revolutionary era in America, but farsighted investors were anxious to provide protection for infant American industries against the importation of British goods. While it is true that all thirteen states erected tariff barriers against foreign goods, state tariffs were unlikely to provide the same degree of protection for industry as a strong central government with a uniform tariff policy, because foreign goods could be brought into low-tariff states and then circulated throughout the country.

Finally, a strong sense of nationalism appeared to motivate America's elites. While the masses directed their attention to local affairs, the educated and cosmopolitan-minded leaders in America were concerned with the weakness of America in the international community of nations. Thirteen separate states failed to manifest a sense of national purpose and identity. The United States were held in contempt not only by Britain, as evidenced by the violations of the Treaty of Paris, but even by the lowly Barbary states. Hamilton expressed the indignation of America's leadership over its inability to swing weight in the world community:

There is something . . . diminutive and contemptible in the prospect of a number of petty states, with the appearance only of union, jarring, jealous, and perverse, without any determined direction, fluctuating and unhappy at home, weak and insignificant by their dissentions in the eyes of other nations.[4]

In short, America's elite wanted to assume a respectable role in the international community and exercise power in world affairs.

The Formation of a National Elite

In the spring of 1785, delegates from Virginia and Maryland met at Alexandria, Virginia, to resolve certain difficulties that had arisen between the two states over the regulation of commerce and navigation on the Potomac River and Chesapeake Bay. It was fortunate, indeed, for the new nation that the most prominent man in America, George Washington, took a personal interest in this meeting. As a rich planter and land speculator who owned over 30,000 acres of Western lands upstream on the Potomac, Washington was keenly aware of commercial problems under the Articles. He lent great prestige to the Alexandria meeting by inviting participants to his home at Mount Vernon. Out of this conference came the idea for a general economic conference for all of the states. The Virginia legislature issued a call for such a convention to meet at Annapolis in September 1786.

In terms of its publicly announced purpose—that of securing interstate agreement on matters of commerce and navigation—the Annapolis

Convention was a failure; only twelve delegates appeared to represent five commercial states: New York, New Jersey, Pennsylvania, Delaware, and Virginia. But these twelve men saw the opportunity to use the Annapolis meeting to achieve greater political successes. Alexander Hamilton, with masterful political foresight, persuaded Egbert Benson, John Dickinson, George Reed, Edmund Randolph, James Madison, and others in attendance to strike out for a full constitutional solution to all of the ills of America. The Annapolis Convention adopted a report, written by Alexander Hamilton, which outlined the defects in the Articles of Confederation and called upon the states to send delegates to a new convention to suggest remedies for these defects. The new convention was to meet in May 1787 in Philadelphia. It was rumored at the time that Hamilton, with the behind-the-scenes support of James Madison in the Virginia legislature, never intended that the Annapolis Convention should be successful in its stated purposes and had planned all along to make Annapolis a stepping stone toward larger political objectives.

Shays' Rebellion could not have occurred at a more opportune time for men like Hamilton and Madison, who sought to galvanize America's elite into action. Occurring in the fall of 1786, after the Annapolis call for a new convention, the rebellion convinced men of property in Congress and state legislatures that there was cause for alarm. Even George Washington, who did not frighten easily, expressed his concern: "I feel . . . infinitely more than I can express . . . for the disorders which have arisen. . . . Good God! Who besides a Tory could have foreseen, or a Briton have predicted them!"

On February 21, 1787, Congress confirmed the call for a convention to meet in Philadelphia "for the sole and express purpose of revising the Articles of Confederation and reporting to Congress and the several legislatures such alterations and provisions therein as shall, when agreed to in Congress and confirmed by the states, render the federal Constitution adequate to the exigencies of government and the preservation of the union." Delegates to the convention were appointed by the state legislatures of every state except Rhode Island, the only state in which the debtor classes had won political control.

Men of Principle and Property   The 55 men who met in the summer of 1787 to establish a new national government were the most prestigious, wealthy, educated, and skillful group of "notables" ever to be assembled in America for a political meeting. The Founding Fathers were truly the elite of elites—an elite both willing and able to act with creative boldness in establishing a government for an entire nation.

The Founding Fathers quickly chose George Washington, their most prestigious member—indeed, the most prestigious man on the continent—to preside over the assembly. Just as quickly, the Convention decided that its sessions would be held behind closed doors and that all proceedings would be a carefully guarded secret. This decision was closely adhered to, and neither close friends nor relatives were informed of the nature of the discussions underway. Apparently the Founding Fathers were aware that elites are most effective in negotiation, compromise, and decision making when operating in secrecy.

The Convention was also quick to discard its congressional mandate to "revise the Articles of Confederation"; and without much hesitation, it proceeded to write an entirely new constitution. Only men self-confident of their own powers and abilities, men of principle and property, would be capable of proceeding in this bold fashion. Let us examine the characteristics of the nation's first elite more closely.

The Founding Fathers were, first of all, men of *prestige and reputation*. Washington and Franklin were men of world-wide fame; and Johnson, Livingston, Robert Morris, Dickinson, and Rutledge were also well known in Europe. Gorham, Gerry, Sherman, Ellsworth, Hamilton, Mifflin, Wilson, Madison, Wythe, Williamson, Whitney, and Mason were men of continental reputations; and the others were major figures in their respective states.

It is hardly possible to overestimate the prestige of George Washington at this time in his life. As the commander-in-chief of the successful Revolutionary army and founder of the new nation, he had overwhelming charismatic appeal among both elites and masses. In addition to his preeminence as soldier, statesman, and founder of the nation, George Washington was one of the richest men in the United States at this time. Despite all the years that he had spent in the Revolutionary cause, he had refused any remuneration for his services. He often paid his soldiers from his own fortune. In addition to his large estate on the Potomac, he possessed many thousands of acres of undeveloped land in western Virginia, Maryland, Pennsylvania, Kentucky, and the Northwest Territory. He owned major shares in the Potomac Company, the James River Company, the Bank of Columbia, and the Bank of Alexandria. Finally, he held large amounts in United States bonds and securities. In short, Washington stood at the apex of America's elite structure.

As men of great reputations, the Founding Fathers knew one another and had *frequent communications and interaction*. The Convention was said to be a happy reunion of old friends and comrades. They had shared many activities in their elite experiences. As Clinton Rossiter points out:

Washington could look around the room and see a half a dozen men who had voted him into command far back into 1775, a dozen who had been with him at Trenton, Monmouth, or Yorktown, and another dozen who had won his friendship by supporting him in Congress or fishing with him in the Potomac. . . . Yates had studied law with Livingston, Livingston had been a patron of Hamilton, Hamilton had brightened the life of Madison, Madison had swapped books with Williamson, Williamson had done experiments with Franklin, Franklin had been amused by Sherman, Sherman had sold books to Baldwin, Baldwin had talked of the ancients with Johnson, Johnson was an old friend of Morris' of Morrisania, and Gouverneur Morris had worked closely with Yates in New York's dark days of 1776–1777. Bedford and Madison were classmates from Princeton; so too were Ellsworth and Luther Martin. Robert Morris knew at least ten men intimately from the early days in Congress; ten others had been his associates in schemes for bolstering the credit of the United States or improving the fortunes of Robert Morris.[5]

The Founding Fathers had extensive experience in governing, and a glance at their previous governing responsibilities reveals that these same men had made all the key decisions in American history from the Stamp Act Congress to the Declaration of Independence to the Articles of Confederation. They controlled the Congress of the United States and had conducted the Revolutionary War. Dickinson, Rutledge, and Johnson had been instrumental in the Stamp Act Congress at the very beginning of revolutionary activity. Eight delegates—Sherman, Robert Morris, Franklin, Clymer, Wilson, Gerry, Reed, and Wythe—had signed the Declaration of Independence. Langdon, Livingston, Mifflin, Rutledge, Hamilton, Dayton, McHenry, Mercer, A. Martin, Davie, and Pierce had all served as officers in Washington's army. Forty-two of the 55 Founding Fathers had already served in the Congress of the United States, and Gorham and Mifflin had served as president of the Congress. Even at the moment of the Convention, more than forty delegates held high offices in state governments; Franklin, Livingston, and Randolph were governors. The Founding Fathers were unexcelled in political skill and experience.

In an age when no more than a handful of men on the continent had ever gone to college, the Founding Fathers were conspicuous for their great educational attainment. Over half the delegates had been educated at Princeton, Yale, Harvard, Columbia, Pennsylvania, William and Mary, or in England. The tradition of legal training for political decision makers, which has continued in America to the present day, was already evident in Philadelphia. About a dozen delegates were still active members of the bar in 1787, and about three dozen had been trained in law. Aristotle, Plutarch, Cicero, Locke, and Montesquieu were familiar names in debate. The Founding Fathers continually made historical and comparative references to Athenian democracy, the Roman republic, the Belgian and Dutch confederacies, the German empire, the English constitution, and even the Swiss cantons. The Convention was as rich in learning as it was in property and experience.

The 55 men at Philadelphia formed a major part of the nation's economic elite. The *personal wealth* represented at the meeting was enormous. Even Luther Martin, who showed more sympathy for the debtors of the nation than anyone else in attendance, was a Princeton graduate, successful attorney, planter, slaveowner, and bondholder, although his fortune was modest compared to his fellow delegates. It is difficult to determine accurately who were the richest men in America at this time, because the finances of the period were chaotic and because wealth assumed a variety of forms—land, ships, credit, slaves, business inventories, bonds, and paper money of uncertain worth (even George Washington had difficulty at times in converting his wealth in land into hard cash). But at least forty of the 55 delegates were known to be holders of public securities; 14 were known to be land speculators; 24 were moneylenders and investors; 11 were engaged in commerce or manufacturing; and 15 owned large plantations.[6] (See Table 2–1.)

Robert Morris was perhaps the foremost business and financial leader in the nation in 1787. This Philadelphia merchant owned scores of ships that traded throughout the world; he engaged in iron manufacturing, speculated in land in all parts of the country, and controlled the Bank of North America in Philadelphia, probably the nation's largest financial institution at the time. In business and financial dealings, he associated with many other eminent leaders, including Hamilton, Fitzsimons, G. Morris, Langdon, Clymer, and John Marshall. He earned his title "the patriot financier" by underwriting a large share of the debts of the United States during and after the Revolutionary War. George Washington was later to ask Morris, described as Washington's most intimate friend and closest companion, to become his first Secretary of the Treasury, but Morris declined in order to pursue his personal business interests. Later in his life, his financial empire collapsed, probably because of overspeculation, and he died in debt. But at the time of the Convention, he stood at the apex of the financial structure of America.

Perhaps what set off the men of Philadelphia from the masses more than anything else was their *cosmopolitanism*. They approached political, economic, and military issues from a "continental" point of view. Unlike the allegiances of the masses, the loyalties of the elites extended beyond their states; they experienced the sentiment of nationalism half a century before this sentiment would begin to seep down to the masses.

Table 2-1 / Founding Fathers Classified by Known Membership in Elite Groups

Public Security Interests		Real Estate and Land Speculation	Lending and Investments	Mercantile, Manufacturing, and Shipping	Planters and Slaveholders
Major	Minor				
Baldwin	Bassett	Blount	Bassett	Broom	Butler
Blair	Blount	Dayton	Broom	Clymer	Davie
Clymer	Brearley	Few	Butler	Ellsworth	Jenifer
Dayton	Broom	Fitzsimons	Carroll	Fitzsimons	A. Martin
Ellsworth	Butler	Franklin	Clymer	Gerry	L. Martin
Fitzsimons	Carroll	Gerry	Davie	King	Mason
Gerry	Few	Gilman	Dickinson	Langdon	Mercer
Gilman	Hamilton	Gorham	Ellsworth	McHenry	C. C. Pinckney
Gorham	L. Martin	Hamilton	Few	Mifflin	C. Pinckney
Jenifer	Mason	Mason	Fitzsimons	G. Morris	Randolph
Johnson	Mercer	R. Morris	Franklin	R. Morris	Read
King	Mifflin	Washington	Gilman		Rutledge
Langdon	Read	Williamson	Ingersoll		Spaight
Lansing	Spaight	Wilson	Johnson		Washington
Livingston	Wilson		King		Wythe
McClurg	Wythe		Langdon		
R. Morris			Mason		
C. C. Pinckney			McHenry		
C. Pinckney			C. C. Pinckney		
Randolph			C. Pinckney		
Sherman			Randolph		
Strong			Read		
Washington			Washington		
Williamson			Williamson		

Professor John P. Roche summarizes the characteristics and strengths of this national elite:

A small group of political leaders with the continental vision and essentially a consciousness of the United States' international impotence, provided the matrix of the movement. To their standard other leaders rallied with their own parallel ambitions. Their great assets were (1) the presence in their caucus of one authentic "father figure," George Washington, whose prestige was enormous; (2) the energy and talent of their leadership (in which one must include the towering intellectuals of the time, John Adams and Thomas Jefferson, despite their absence abroad) and their communications "network," which was far superior to anything on the opposition side; (3) the preemptive skill which made "Their Issue" "The Issue" and kept the locally oriented opposition permanently on the defensive; (4) the subjective consideration that these men were spokesmen of a new and compelling credo: American nationalism, that illdefined but none the less potent sense of collective purpose that emerged from the American Revolution.[7]

Elite Consensus   By focusing upon the debates *within* the Convention, many historical scholars tend to overemphasize the differences of opinion among the Founding Fathers. While it is true that many conflicting views had to be reconciled in Philadelphia and that innumerable compromises had to be made, the more striking fact is that the delegates were in almost complete accord on the essential questions of politics. They agreed that the fundamental end of government was the *protection of liberty and property*. They accepted without debate many of the precedents set by the English constitution and by the constitutions of the new states.

Reflecting the rationalism of their times, the Founding Fathers were much less devoutly religious than most Americans today. Yet they believed in a law of nature with rules of abstract justice to which the laws of men should conform. They believed that this law of nature endowed man with certain inalienable rights that were essential to a meaningful existence for a man. Man had the right to life, liberty, and property; and these rights should be recognized and protected by law. They believed that all men were equal, in that they were entitled to have their natural rights respected regardless of their station in life. Most of the Founding Fathers were even aware that this belief ran contrary to the practice of slavery and were embarrassed by this inconsistency in American life.

But "equality" did *not* mean to the Founding Fathers that men were equal in birth, wealth, intelligence, talent, or virtue. Inequalities in society were accepted as a natural product of diversity among men. It was definitely not the function of government to reduce these inequalities; in fact, "dangerous leveling" was a serious violation of man's right to property, his right to use and dispose of the fruits of his industry. On the contrary, it was the very function of government to protect property and to prevent "leveling" influences from reducing the natural inequalities of wealth and power.

The Founding Fathers agreed that *the origin of government is an implied contract among men.* They believed that men pledged allegiance and obedience to government in return for protection of their natural rights, the maintenance of peace, and protection from foreign invasion. The ultimate legitimacy of government—that is, sovereignty—rested with the people themselves, and not with gods or kings; and the basis of government was the consent of the governed.

The Founding Fathers believed in republican government. They were opposed to hereditary monarchies, the prevailing form of government in the world at the time. While they believed that men of principle and property should govern, they were opposed to an aristocracy or a governing nobility. By "republican government" they meant a representative, responsible, and non-hereditary government. But by "republican government" they certainly did not mean mass democracy, with direct participation by the people in decision making. They expected the masses to consent to government by men of principle and property out of recognition for their abilities, talents, education, and stake in the preservation of liberty and order. The Founding Fathers believed that the masses should only have a limited part in the selection of government leaders. There was some bickering over how much direct participation should take place in the selection of decision makers, and some bickering over the qualifications of public office. But there was general agreement that the masses should have only a limited and indirect role in the selection of decision makers, and that decision makers themselves should be men of wealth, education, and proven leadership ability.

The Founding Fathers believed in *limited government*. Government should be designed so that it would not become a threat to liberty or property. Since the Founding Fathers believed that power was a corrupting influence and that the concentration of power was dangerous, they believed in dividing governmental power into separate bodies capable of checking each other, in the event that any one branch should pose a threat to liberty or property. Differences of opinion among honest men, particularly differences between elites located in separate states, could best be resolved by balancing representation of these several elites in the national government and by a system of decentralization that permitted local elites to govern their states as they saw fit, with limited interference from the national government.

It should be noted that the laissez-faire principles of Adam Smith were *not* a part of elite consensus in 1787. Quite the contrary, the men who wrote the Constitution believed that government had the obligation not only to protect private property but also to nourish it. They expected government to foster trade and commerce, protect manufacturing, assist in land development, and provide other positive economic assistance. And, to protect the rights of property, they expected government to enforce contracts, maintain a stable money supply, punish thievery, assist in the collection of debts, record the ownership of property in the form of deeds, punish counterfeiting and piracy, protect copyrights and patents, regulate the value of money, establish courts, and regulate banking and commerce.

Finally, and perhaps most importantly, the Founding Fathers believed that only *a strong national government*, with power to exercise its will directly on the people, would be able to "establish justice, insure domestic tranquility, provide for the common defense, promote the general welfare, and secure the blessings of liberty."

The compromises that took place in the Convention were relatively unimportant in comparison to this consensus among the Founding Fathers on fundamentals. It was the existence of a national elite and its agreement on the fundamentals of politics that enabled the American government to be founded. If there had been any substantial cleavage among elites in 1787, any substantial competition or conflict, or any divergent centers of influence, a new government would never have emerged from the Philadelphia convention. Elite consensus in 1787 was profoundly conservative, in that it wished to preserve the status quo in the distribution of power and property in America. Yet, at the same time, this elite consensus was radical in comparison with the beliefs of other elites in the world at this time. Nearly every other government of the time adhered to the principle of hereditary monarchy and privileged nobility, while American elites were committed to republicanism. Other elites asserted the divine right of kings, while American elites talked about government by the consent of the governed. American elites believed in the equality of man with respect to his inalienable rights, while the elites in Europe rationalized and defended a rigid caste system.

An Elite in Operation—Conciliation and Compromise

On May 25, 1787, sessions of the Constitutional Convention opened in Independence Hall, Philadelphia. After the selection of Washington as president of the Convention and the decision that the proceedings of the Convention should be kept secret, Governor Edmund Randolph, speaking for the Virginia delegation, presented a draft of a new constitution.

Under the Virginia Plan, little recognition was given to the states in the composition of the national government. The plan proposed a two-house legislature, the lower house to be chosen by the people of the several states with representation accorded by population. The second house was to be chosen by the first house. This Congress would be empowered to "legislate in all cases in which the separate states are incompetent, or in which the harmony of the United States may be interrupted by the exercise of individual legislation." Moreover, Congress would have the authority to nullify state laws that it felt violated the Constitution, thus insuring national supremacy. The Virginia Plan also proposed a parliamentary form of government, with members of the executive and judiciary branches chosen by the Congress.

It is interesting that the most important line of cleavage at the Convention was between elites of large states and elites of small states over the representation scheme in the Virginia Plan. This was not a great question of economic interest or ideology, since delegates from large and small states did not divide along economic or ideological lines. But the Virginia Plan did not provide certainty that elites from small states would secure membership in the upper house of the legislature.

After several weeks of debate over the Virginia Plan, delegates from the small states presented a counterproposal, in a report by William Patterson of New Jersey. The New Jersey Plan may have been merely a tactic by the small state elites to force the Convention to compromise on representation, for it was debated only a week before it was set aside, and despite this defeat the small state delegates did not leave the Convention nor did they seem particularly upset with their defeat. The New Jersey Plan proposed to retain the representation scheme in Congress under the Articles, where each state was accorded a single vote. But separate executive and judiciary branches were to be established, and the powers of Congress were to be greatly expanded to include the right to levy taxes and regulate commerce.

The New Jersey Plan was *not* an attempt to retain the Confederation. Indeed, the plan included words that were later to appear in the Constitution itself as the famous "national supremacy clause":

This constitution, and the laws of the United States which shall be made in pursuance thereof, and all treaties made, or which shall be made, under the authority of the United States shall be the Supreme Law of the land; the judges in every state shall be bound thereby, anything in the Constitution or laws of any state to the contrary notwithstanding.

Thus, even the small states did not envision a confederation. Both the Virginia and New Jersey plans were designed to strengthen the national government; they differed only in the degree to which it would be strengthened and in its system of representation.

On June 29, William Samuel Johnson of Connecticut proposed the obvious compromise; namely, *that representation in the lower house of Congress be based upon population whereas representation in the upper house would be equal* — two senators from each state. The Connecticut Compromise also provided that equal representation of states in the Senate could not be abridged, even by constitutional amendment.

The next question to be compromised, that of slavery and the role of slaves in the system of representation, was more closely related to economic differences among America's elite. It was essentially the same question that was to divide America's elite and result in the nation's bloodiest war 75 years later. Planters and slaveholders generally believed that wealth, particularly wealth in slaves, should be counted in apportioning representation. Non-slaveholders felt that "the people" should only include free inhabitants. The decision to apportion direct taxes among the states in proportion to population opened the way to compromise, since the attitude of slaveholders and non-slaveholders was just the reverse as to which person should be counted for the purposes of apportioning taxes. The result was the famous Three-Fifths Compromise, in which *three fifths of the slaves of each state would be counted for the purposes of representation, and three fifths would also be counted in apportioning direct taxes.*

Agreement between Southern planters and Northern merchants was still relatively easy to achieve at this early date in American history. But latent conflict could be observed on issues other than slavery. While all the elite groups agreed that the national government should regulate interstate and foreign commerce, Southern planters had some fear that the unrestricted power of Congress over commerce might lead to the imposition of export taxes. Export taxes would bear most heavily on the Southern states, which were dependent upon foreign markets for the sale of indigo, rice, tobacco, and cotton. However, planters and merchants were able to reach another compromise in resolving this issue: *No tax or duty should be levied on articles exported from any state.*

Finally, a compromise had to be reached on the question of trading in slaves. On this issue, the men of Maryland and Virginia, states that were already well supplied with slaves, were able to indulge in the luxury of conscience and support proposals for banning the further importation of slaves. But the less developed Southern states, particularly South Carolina and Georgia, could not afford to be so moral, since they still needed additional slave labor. Inasmuch as the Southern planters were themselves divided, the ultimate compromise permitted Congress to prohibit *the slave trade—but not before the year 1808.* This twenty-year delay would allow the undeveloped Southern states to acquire all the slaves they needed before the slave trade was cut off.

Another important compromise, one which occupied much of the time of the Convention although it has received little recognition by subsequent writers, concerned qualifications for voting and holding office in the new government. While no property qualifications for voters or officeholders appear in the text of the Constitution, the debates revealed that members of the Convention generally favored property qualifications for voting and almost unanimously favored property qualifications for officeholding. The delegates showed little enthusiasm for mass participation in democracy. Elbridge Gerry of Massachusetts declared that "the evils we experience flow from the excess of democracy." Roger Sherman protested that "the people immediately should have as little to do as may be about the government." Edmund Randolph continually deplored the turbulence and follies of democracy, and George Clymer's notion of republican government was that "a representative of the people is appointed to think for and not with his constituents." John Dickinson considered property qualifications a "necessary defense against the dangerous influence of those multitudes without property and without principle, with which our country like all others, will in time abound." Gouverneur Morris also insisted upon property qualifications: "Give the votes to the people who have no property and they will sell them to the rich who will be able to buy them." Charles Pinckney later wrote to Madison, "are you not . . . abundantly depressed at the theoretical nonsense of an election of Congress by the people; in the first instance, it's clearly and practically wrong, and it will in the end be the means of bringing our councils into contempt." Many more such statements could be cited from the records of the Convention.[8]

There was even stronger agreement that property qualifications should be imposed for senators and for the president. The Senate, according to C. C. Pinckney, "was meant to represent the wealth of the country. It ought to be composed of persons of wealth." He also proposed that no pay be given presidents or senators, because "if no allowance was made, the wealthy alone would undertake the service." Alexander Hamilton ably expressed elitist feeling on the representation of property:

All communities divide themselves into the few and the many. The first are the rich and well-born, the other the masses of people. The voice of the people has been said to be the voice of God; and however generally this maxim has been quoted and believed, it is not true in fact. The people are turbulent and changing; they seldom judge or determine right. Give therefore to the first class a distinct, permanent share in the government. They will check the unsteadiness of the second, and as they cannot receive any advantage by change, they therefore will ever maintain good government. Can a democratic assembly who annually revolves in the mass of the people, be supposed steadily to pursue the public good? Nothing but a permanent body can check the imprudence of democracy.[9]

In the light of these views, how then do we explain the absence of property qualifications in the Constitution? Actually, a motion was carried in the Convention instructing a committee to fix property qualifications for officeholding, but the committee could not agree upon the nature of the qualifications to be imposed. Various propositions to establish property qualifications were defeated on the floor, not because they were believed to be inherently wrong but, interestingly enough, because of differences in the *kind* of property represented by elites at the Convention. Madison pointed this out in the debate in July, when he noted that a requirement of land ownership would exclude from Congress the mercantile and manufacturing classes, who would hardly be willing to turn their money into large quantities of landed property just to make them eligible for a seat in Congress. Madison rightly observed that "landed possessions were no certain evidence of real wealth. Many enjoyed them to a great extent who were more in debt than they were worth." The objections by merchants and investors led to a defeat of the "landed" qualification for Congressmen. Also, a motion to disqualify persons from public office who had "unsettled accounts" with the United States (an early-day version of conflict-of-interests law) was also struck down by an overwhelming vote of the delegates.

Thus, the Constitution was approved *without any property qualifications on voters, except those which the states themselves might see fit to impose.* Failing to come to a decision on this issue of suffrage, the delegates merely returned the question to state legislatures by providing that "the electors in each state should have the qualifications requisite for electors of the most numerous branch of the state legislatures." At the time, it did not seem that this expedient course of action would result in mass democracy. Only one branch of the new government, the House of Representatives, was to be elected by popular vote anyhow. The other three controlling bodies—the President, the Senate, and the Supreme Court—were removed from direct voter participations. Finally, the delegates were reassured by the fact that nearly all of the state constitutions then in force included property qualifications for voters.*

The Constitution as an Elitist Document

The text of the Constitution, together with interpretive materials in *The Federalist* papers written by Hamilton, Madison, and Jay, provide ample

---

*Historians disagree about the number of people who were disenfranchised by property qualifications in 1787. All states had property-owning or tax-paying qualifications for voting and even higher qualifications for officeholding. But we do not really know how many people met these qualifications. For example, Massachusetts conferred the suffrage on all males owning an estate with an annual income of three pounds or a total value of sixty pounds. And a Massachusetts senator was required to be "seized in his own right of a freehold within this Commonwealth of the value of 300 pounds at least, or possessed of a personal estate of the value of 600 pounds at least, or both to the amount of the same sum." It is difficult to estimate what percentage of Massachusetts males owned an estate with an annual income of three pounds. But whether or not many citizens were *legally* disenfranchised, very few voted.

evidence that elites in America benefited both politically and economically from the adoption of the Constitution. While both elites and non-elites—indeed, all Americans—may have benefited by the adoption of the Constitution, elites benefited more directly and immediately than non-elites. And it is reasonable to infer that the advantages contained in the document for America's elite provided the direct, impelling motive for their activities on behalf of the new Constitution. Indeed, if elites had not stood to gain substantially from the Constitution, it is doubtful that this document would have been written or that the new government would have been established. We can discover the elitist consensus by examining the underlying philosophy of government contained in the Constitution.

According to Madison in *The Federalist, controlling factions* was "the principal task of modern legislation."[10] A "faction" is a number of citizens united by a common interest that is adverse to the interest of other citizens or of the community as a whole. The causes of factions are found in human diversity: "A zeal for different opinions concerning religion, concerning government, and many other points, as well of speculation as of practice; an attachment to different leaders ambitiously contending for preeminence and power; or to persons of other descriptions whose fortunes have been interesting to human passions." But at the heart of the problem of faction is inequality in the control of economic resources:

But the most common and durable source of factions has been the various and unequal distribution of property. Those who hold and those who are without property have ever formed distinct interests in society. Those who are creditors and those who are debtors fall under like discrimination. A landed interest, a manufacturing interest, a merchantile interest, a monied interest, with many lesser interests, grow up of necessity in civilized nations, and divide them into different classes, actuated by different sentiments and views. [Federalist No. 10]

In Madison's view, the most important protection against mass movements that might threaten property was the establishment of the national government. By creating a national government encompassing a large number of citizens and a great expanse of territory "you take in a greater variety of parties and interests; you make it less probable that a majority of the whole will have a common motive to invade the rights of other citizens; or if such a common motive exists it will be more difficult for all who feel it to discover their own strength, and to act in unison with each other."

The structure of the new national government was supposed to insure that "factious" issues would be suppressed. And Madison does not hedge on naming the factious issues that must be avoided: "A rage for paper money, for an abolition of debts, for an equal division of property, or any other improper or wicked project. . . ." Note that all of Madison's factious issues are challenges to the dominant economic elites. Madison's defense of the new Constitution was that its republican and federal features would help to keep certain threats to property from ever becoming public issues. In short, the new American government was deliberately designed by the Founding Fathers to make it difficult for any mass political movement to challenge property rights.

Now let us turn to an examination of the text of the Constitution itself and its impact upon American elites. There are seventeen specific grants of power to Congress in Article I, Section 8, followed by a general grant of power to make "all laws which shall be necessary and proper for carrying into execution the foregoing powers." The first and perhaps the most important enumerated power is the "power to lay and collect taxes, duties, imposts, and excises." The *taxing power* is, of course, the basis of all other powers, and it enabled the national government to end its dependence upon states. The taxing power was essential to the holders of public securities, particularly when it was combined with the provision in Article VI that "All the debts contracted and engagements entered into before the adoption of this Constitution shall be valid against the United States under this Constitution as under the Confederation." This meant that the national government would be obliged to pay off all those investors who held bonds of the United States, and the taxing power would give the national government the ability to do this on its own.

The text of the Constitution suggests that the Founding Fathers intended Congress to place most of the tax burden on consumers in the form of custom duties and excise taxes, rather than direct taxes on individual income or property. Article I, Section 2, required that direct taxes could be levied only on the basis of population; it follows that such taxes could not be levied in proportion to wealth. This provision prevented the national government from levying progressive income taxes, and it was not until the Sixteenth Amendment was passed in 1913 that this protection for wealth was removed from the Constitution.

Southern planters, who depended for their livelihood on the export of indigo, rice, tobacco, and cotton, strenuously opposed giving the national government the power to tax exports. Protection for their interests was provided in Article I, Section 9: "no tax or duty shall be laid on goods exported from any state." However, Congress was given the power to tax imports so Northern manufacturers could erect a tariff wall to protect American industries against foreign goods.

Congress was also given the power to "regulate commerce with foreign nations and among the several states." The *interstate commerce clause,* together with the provision in Article I, Section 9, prohibiting the states from taxing either imports or exports, created a free trade area over the thirteen states. In *The Federalist* No. 11, Hamilton describes the advantages of this arrangement for American merchants: "The speculative trader will at once perceive the force of these observations and will acknowledge that the aggregate balance of the commerce of the United States would bid fair to be much more favorable than that of the thirteen states without union or with partial unions."

Following the power to tax and spend, to borrow money, and to regulate commerce in Article I, there is a series of *specific powers designed to enable Congress to protect money and property.* Congress is given the power to make bankruptcy laws, to coin money and regulate its value, to fix standards of weights and measures, to punish counterfeiting, to establish post offices and post roads, to pass copyright and patent laws to protect authors and inventors, and to punish piracies and felonies committed on the high seas. Each of these powers is a specific asset to bankers, investors, merchants, authors, inventors, and shippers. Obviously, the Founding Fathers felt that giving Congress control over currency and credit in America would result in better protection for financial interests than would leaving this essential responsibility to the states. Likewise, control over communication and transportation ("post offices and post roads") was believed to be too essential to trade and commerce to be left to the states.

All of the other powers in Article I deal with military affairs—raising and supporting armies, organizing, training, and calling up the state militia, declaring war, suppressing insurrections, and repelling invasions. These powers in Article I, together with the provisions in Article II making the president the commander-in-chief of the army and navy and of the state militia when called into the federal service, and the power of the president to make treaties with the advice and consent of the Senate and to send and receive ambassadors, all combined to centralize diplomatic and military affairs at the national level. This centralization of diplomatic-military power is confirmed in Article I, Section 10, where the states are specifically prohibited from entering into treaties with foreign nations, maintaining ships of war, or engaging in war unless actually invaded.

It is clear that the Founding Fathers had little confidence in the state militia, particularly when it was under state control; General Washington's painful experiences with state militia during the Revolutionary War were still fresh in his memory. The militia had proven adequate when defending their own states against invasion; but when employed outside their own states, they were often a disaster. Moreover, if Western settlers were to be protected from the Indians, and if the British were to be persuaded to give up their forts in Ohio and open the way to American westward expansion, the national government could not rely upon state militia but must instead have an army of its own. Similarly, a strong navy was essential to the protection of American commerce on the seas (the first significant naval action under the new government was against the piracy of the Barbary states). Thus, a national army and navy were not so much protection against invasion (for many years the national government would continue to rely primarily upon state militia for this purpose), but rather for the protection and promotion of its commercial and territorial ambitions. In addition, a national army and navy, as well as an organized and trained militia that could be called into national service, also provided *protection against class wars* and rebellion by debtors. In an obvious reference to Shays' Rebellion, Hamilton warns in *The Federalist* No. 21:

The tempestuous situation from which Massachusetts has scarcely emerged evinces that dangers of this kind are not merely speculative. Who could determine what might have been the issue of her late convulsions if the malcontents had been headed by a Caesar or a Cromwell? A strong military force in the hands of the national government is a protection against revolutionary action.

Further evidence of the Founding Fathers' intention to protect the governing classes from revolution is found in Article IV, Section 4, where the national government guarantees to every state "a republican form of government" as well as protection against "domestic violence." Thus, in addition to protecting Western land and commerce on the seas, a strong army and navy would enable the national government to back up its pledge to protect governing elites in the states from violence and revolution.

Protection against domestic insurrection also appealed to the Southern slaveholders' deep-seated fear of a slave revolt. Madison drives this point home in *The Federalist* No. 23:

I take no little notice of an unhappy species of population abounding in some of the states who, during the calm of regular government were sunk below the level of men; but who, in the tempestuous seeds of civil violence, may emerge into human character and give a superiority of strength to any party with which they may associate themselves.

As we have already noted, the Constitution permitted Congress to outlaw the *importation of slaves* after the year 1808. But most of the

Southern planters were more interested in protecting their existing property and slaves than they were in extending the slave trade, and the Constitution provided an explicit advantage to slaveholders in Article IV, Section 2:

No person held to service or labor in one state, under the laws thereof, escaping into another, shall, in consequence of any law or regulation thereof, be discharged from such service or labor, but shall be delivered upon claim of the party to whom such service or labor may be due.

This was an extremely valuable protection for one of the most important forms of property in America at the time. The slave trade lapsed in America after twenty years, but slavery as a domestic institution was better safeguarded under the new Constitution than under the Articles.

The restrictions placed upon state legislatures by the Constitution also provided protection to economic elites in the new nation. States were prevented from coining money, issuing paper money, or passing legal tender laws that would make any money other than gold or silver coin tender in the payment of debts. This restriction would prevent the states from issuing cheap paper money, which could be used by debtors to pay off their creditors with less valuable currency. The authors of *The Federalist* pointed to this prohibition on paper money in their appeal to economic elites to support ratification of the Constitution:

The loss which America has sustained since the peace from the pestilential effects of paper money on the necessary confidence between man and man, on the necessary confidence in the public councils, on the industry and the morals of the people, and on the character of republican government constitutes an enormous debt against the states chargeable to this unadvised measure, which must long remain unsatisfied, or rather an accumulation of guilt, which can be expiated no otherwise than by a voluntary sacrifice on the altar of justice which has been the instrument of it. [Federalist No. 44]

In other words, the states had frequently issued paper money to relieve debtors; they were now to be punished for their "unadvised" behavior by removing their power to issue money. Moreover, the states were denied the power to pass legal tender laws obliging creditors to accept paper money in payment of debts.

The Constitution also prevents states from passing any law "impairing the obligation of contracts." The structure of business relations in a free enterprise economy depends upon government enforcement of private contracts, and it is essential to economic elites that the government be prevented from relieving persons from their obligations to contracts. If state legislatures could relieve debtors of their contractual obligations, or relieve indentured servants from their obligations to their masters, or prevent creditors from foreclosing on mortgages, or declare moratoriums on debt, or otherwise interfere with business obligations, the interests of investors, merchants, and creditors would be seriously damaged.

The heart of the Constitution is the *supremacy clause of Article VI:*

This Constitution, and the laws of the United States which shall be made in pursuance thereof, and all treaties made, or which shall be made under the authority of the United States, shall be the Supreme Law of the Land and the judges in every state shall be bound thereby, anything in the Constitution or laws of any state to the contrary notwithstanding.

This sentence made it abundantly clear that laws of Congress would supersede laws of the states and it made certain that Congress would control interstate commerce, bankruptcy, monetary affairs, weights and measures, currency and credit, communication, and transportation, as well as foreign and military affairs. Thus, the supremacy clause insures that the decisions of the national elite will prevail over the decisions of the local elites in all of those vital areas allocated to the national government.

The structure of the national government—its republicanism and its system of separated powers and checks and balances—was also designed to provide for protection of liberty and property. To the Founding Fathers, a *republican government* meant the delegation of powers by the people to a small number of citizens "whose wisdom may best discern the true interest of their country, and whose patriotism and love of justice will be least likely to sacrifice it to temporary or partial considerations."[11] Madison goes on to explain, in classic elite fashion, "that the public voice, pronounced by representatives of the people, will be more consonant to the public good than if pronounced by the people themselves." It is clear that the Founding Fathers believed that representatives of the people were more likely to be enlightened men of principle and property than the voters who chose them, and thus more trustworthy and dependable.

Moreover, voters had a very limited voice in the selection of decision makers. *Four major decision-making bodies were established in the Constitution*—the House of Representatives, the Senate, the Presidency, and the Supreme Court—but only *one* of these bodies was to be elected by the people themselves. The other bodies were to be at least twice removed from popular control. In the Constitution of 1787, only United States representatives were directly elected by the people, and they were elected for short terms of two years. In contrast, United States senators were to be elected by state legislatures, not by the people, for six-year terms. The president was not elected by the people, but by "electors," who themselves were to be selected as state legislatures saw fit. The states could hold elections for presidential "electors," or could appoint the electors through the state legislatures. The Founding Fathers hoped that presidential "electors" would be prominent men of wealth and reputation in their respective states. Finally, federal judges were to be appointed by the president for life, thus removing these decision makers as far from popular control as possible. Of course, it would be unfair to brand the Founding Fathers as "conservative" because of these republican arrangements. In 1787, the idea of republicanism itself was radical, since few governments provided for *any* popular participation in government, even a limited role in the selection of representatives. While the Founding Fathers believed that government ultimately rested upon the will of the people, they hoped that republicanism could reduce the influence of the masses and help insure government by elites.

The system of separated powers in the national government —separate legislative, executive, and judicial branches—was also intended by the Founding Fathers as a bulwark against majoritarianism and an additional safeguard for liberty and property. The doctrine derives from the French writer, Montesquieu, whose *Spirit of Laws* was a political textbook for these eighteenth-century statesmen. *The Federalist* No. 51 expresses the logic of the checks and balances system:

Ambition must be made to counteract ambition. . . . It may be a reflection on human nature, that such devices should be necessary to control the abuses of government. But what is government itself, but the greatest of all reflections on human nature? If men were angels, no government would be necessary. If angels were to govern men, neither external nor internal controls on government would be necessary. In framing a government which is to be administered by men over men, the great difficulty lies in this: you must first enable the government to control the governed; and in the next place oblige it to control itself.

The separation of powers concept is expressed in the opening sentences of the first three articles of the Constitution: "All legislative powers herein granted shall be invested in the Congress of the United States. . . . The Executive power shall be vested in a President of the United States. . . . The Judicial power shall be vested in one Supreme Court and such inferior courts as Congress may from time to time ordain and establish." If this system divides responsibility and makes it difficult for the masses to hold government accountable for public policy, then it is achieving one of the purposes intended by the Founding Fathers. Each of the four major decision-making bodies of the national government is chosen by different constituencies—the House by the voters in the several states, the Senate by the state legislatures, the president by electors chosen by the states, and the judiciary by the president and the Senate. A sharp differentiation is made in the terms of these decision-making bodies, so that a complete renewal of government by popular vote at one stroke is impossible. The House is chosen for two years; the Senate is chosen for six, but not in one election, for one third go out every two years. The president is chosen every four years, but judges of the Supreme Court hold office for life. Thus the people are restrained from working immediate havoc through direct elections; they must wait years in order to make their will felt in all of the decision-making bodies of the national government.

Moreover, each of these decision-making bodies has an important check on the decisions of the others. No bill can become law without the approval of both the House and the Senate. The president shares in legislative power through his veto and his responsibility to "give to the Congress information of the state of the union, and recommend to their consideration such measures as he shall judge necessary and expedient." He can also convene sessions of Congress. But the appointing power of the president is shared by the Senate; so is his treaty-making power. Also, Congress can override executive vetoes. The president must execute the laws, but in order to do so he must rely upon executive departments, and these must be created by Congress. Moreover, the executive branch cannot spend money that has not been appropriated by Congress. Thus, the concept of "separation of powers" is really misnamed, for what we are really talking about is a sharing, not a separating, of power; each branch participates in the activities of every other branch.

Even the Supreme Court, which was created by the Constitution, must be appointed by the president with the consent of the Senate, and Congress may prescribe the number of judges. More importantly, Congress must create lower and intermediate courts, establish the number of judges, fix the jurisdiction of lower federal courts, and make "exceptions" to the appellate jurisdiction of the Supreme Court.

All of these checks and counterchecks were defended in The Federalist as a means of restraining popular majorities, particularly those which might arise in the House of Representatives. Perhaps the keystone of the system of checks and balances is the idea of judicial review, an original contribution by the Founding Fathers to the science of government. In the case of Marbury v. Madison in 1803,[12] Chief Justice John Marshall argued convincingly that the Founding Fathers intended the Supreme Court to have the power of invalidating not only state laws and constitutions but also any laws of Congress that came in conflict with the Constitution of the United States. Marshall reasoned (1) that the "judicial power" was given to the Supreme Court, (2) that historically the judicial power included the power to interpret the meaning of the law, (3) that the Supremacy Clause made the Constitution the "Supreme Law of the Land," (4) that laws of the United States should be made "in pursuance thereof," (5) that judges are sworn to uphold the Constitution, and (6) that judges must therefore declare void any legislative act that they feel conflicts with the Constitution.

The text of the Constitution nowhere specifically authorizes federal judges to invalidate acts of Congress; at most, the Constitution implies this power. But Hamilton apparently thought that the Constitution contained this power, since he was careful to explain it in *The Federalist* No. 78 prior to the ratification of the Constitution:

The complete independence of the courts of justice is peculiarly essential in a limited constitution. By a limited constitution, I understand one which contains certain specified exceptions to the legislative authority; such, for instance, as that it shall pass no bills of attainder, no ex post facto laws, and the like. Limitations of this kind can be preserved in practice no other way than through the medium of courts of justice, whose duty it must be to declare all acts contrary to the manifest tenor of the constitution void. Without this, all the reservations of particular rights or privileges would amount to nothing. . . . The interpretation of the laws is the proper and peculiar province of the courts. A constitution is, in fact, and must be regarded by the judges as a fundamental law. It therefore belongs to them to ascertain its meaning, as well as the meaning of any particular act proceeding from the legislative body. If there should happen to be an irreconcilable variance between the two, that which has the superior obligation and validity ought, of course, to be preferred; or, in other words, the constitution ought to be preferred to the statute, the intention of the people to the intention of their agents.

 Thus, the Supreme Court stands as the final defender of the fundamental principles agreed upon by the Founding Fathers against the encroachments of popularly elected legislatures.

Ratification—an Exercise in Elite Political Skills

When the work of the Constitutional Convention ended on September 17, 1787, the document was sent to New York City, where Congress was then in session. The Convention suggested that the Constitution "should afterwards be submitted to a convention of delegates chosen in each state by the people thereof, under the recommendation of its legislature for their assent and ratification." The Philadelphia Convention further proposed that when *nine* states had ratified the new constitution, it should go into effect. On September 28, Congress sent the Constitution to the states without making any recommendations of its own.

The ratification procedure suggested by the Founding Fathers was a skillful political maneuver. The Convention itself had been held in secret, so there was little advance word that the delegates had not merely amended the Articles of Confederation, as they had been instructed, but instead had created a whole new scheme of government. Their ratification procedure was a complete departure from what was then the law of the land, the Articles of Confederation. The Articles provided that all amendments should be made by Congress only with the approval of *all* of the states. But since Rhode Island was firmly in the hands of small farmers, the unanimity required by the Articles was obviously out of the question; and the Founding Fathers felt obliged to act outside of the existing law. Hence the proclamation that only nine states need ratify the new Constitution.

It is important to note that the Founding Fathers also called for special ratifying conventions in the states, rather than risk submitting the Constitution to the state legislatures. This extraordinary procedure gave clear advantage to supporters of the Constitution. Nathaniel Gorham argued effectively at Philadelphia that submitting the plan to state legislatures would weaken its chances for success:

Men chosen by the people for the particular purpose will discuss the subject more candidly than the members of the legislature who are about to lose the power which is to be given up to the general movement. Some of the legislatures are composed of several branches. It will consequently be more difficult in these cases to get the plan through the legislatures than through a convention. In the states, many of the ablest men are excluded from the legislatures but may be elected to a convention . . . the legislatures will be interrupted by a variety of little business . . . if the last Article of the Confederation is to be pursued the unanimous concurrence of the states will be necessary.[13]

In other words, it was politically expedient to by-pass the state legislatures and to ignore the requirement of the Articles for unanimity among the states. Thus, the struggle for ratification began under ground rules designed by the national elite to give them the advantage over any potential opponents.

In the most important and controversial study of the Constitution to date, Charles A. Beard compiled a great deal of evidence in support of the hypothesis "that substantially all of the merchants, money lenders, security holders, manufacturers, shippers, capitalists and financiers, and their professional associates are to be found on one side in support of the

Constitution, and that substantially all of the major portion of the opposition came from the non-slaveholding farmers and debtors."[14] While historians disagree over the solidarity of class divisions in the struggle for ratification, most concede that only about 160,000 persons voted in elections for delegates to state ratifying conventions and that not more than 100,000 of these voters favored the adoption of the Constitution. This figure represents about one in six of the adult males in the country, and not more than five percent of the population in general. Thus, whether or not Beard is correct about class divisions in the struggle for ratification, one thing is clear: The total number of persons who participated in any fashion in the ratification of the Constitution was an extremely small minority of the population.

Some men of property and education did champion the views of the common people. Men like Patrick Henry and Richard Henry Lee of Virginia vigorously attacked the Constitution as a "counterrevolutionary" document that could undo much of the progress made since 1776 toward freedom, liberty, and equality. According to the opponents of the Constitution, the new government would be "aristocratic," all-powerful, and a threat to the "spirit of republicanism" and the "genius of democracy." They charged that the new Constitution created an aristocratic upper house and an almost monarchial presidency. The powers of the national government could trample the states and deny the people of the states the opportunity to handle their own political and economic affairs. The Antifederalists repeatedly asserted that the Constitution removed powers from the people and concentrated them in the hands of a few national officials who were largely immune from popular control; moreover, they attacked the undemocratic features of the Constitution and argued that state governments were much more representative of the people. The secrecy of the Philadelphia Convention and the actions of the Founding Fathers, which were contrary to both the law and the spirit of the Articles of Confederation, also came under attack.

While the Antifederalists deplored the undemocratic features of the new Constitution, their most effective criticism centered on the absence of any Bill of Rights. The omission of a Bill of Rights is particularly glaring, since the idea of a Bill of Rights was very popular at the time and most of the new state constitutions contained them. It is an interesting comment on the psychology of the Founding Fathers that the idea of a Bill of Rights was never even mentioned in the Philadelphia Convention until the final week of deliberations; even then it was given little consideration. The Founding Fathers certainly believed in the idea of limited government. A few liberties were written into the body of the Constitution—protection against bills of attainder and ex post facto laws, a guarantee of the writ of *habeas corpus*, a limited definition of treason, a guarantee of jury trial—but there was no Bill of Rights labelled as such. Perhaps the Founding Fathers were so confident that men of principle and property would control the new government that they believed limitations on this government were unnecessary.

When criticism about the absence of a Bill of Rights began to mount in the states, supporters of the Constitution presented an interesting argument to explain this deficiency: (1) the national government was one of enumerated powers and could not exercise any powers not expressly delegated to it in the Constitution; (2) the power to interfere with free speech or press or otherwise to restrain liberty was not among the enumerated powers in the Constitution; (3) it was therefore unnecessary to specifically deny the new government this power. But this logic was unconvincing; the absence of a Bill of Rights seemed to confirm the suspicion that the Founding Fathers were more concerned with protecting property than with protecting the personal liberties of the people. Many elites and non-elites alike were uncomfortable with the thought that personal liberty depended upon a thin thread of inference from enumerated powers. Supporters of the Constitution were forced to retreat from their demand for unconditional ratification; the New York, Massachusetts, and Virginia conventions agreed to the new Constitution only after receiving the solemn promise of the Federalists that a Bill of Rights would be added as amendments. Thus the fundamental guarantees of liberty in the Bill of Rights were political concessions by the nation's elite. While the Founding Fathers deserved great credit for the document that they produced at Philadelphia, nonetheless, the first Congress to meet under that Constitution was obliged to submit twelve amendments to the states, ten of which were ratified by 1791.

Historians disagree as to whether or not class lines were as clearly drawn in the struggle for ratification as Beard contends. But Beard's summary of the strengths and weaknesses of the Federalist and Antifederalist in the struggle over ratification is a classic statement of the political advantages of an elite over a numerically superior mass:

At all events, the disenfranchisement of the masses through property qualifications and ignorance and apathy contributed largely to the facility with which the . . . [Federalists] carried the day. The latter were alert everywhere, for they knew, not as a matter of theory, but as a practical matter of dollars and cents, the value of the new Constitution. They were well informed. They were conscious of the identity of their interests. They were well organized. They knew for weeks in advance, even before the Constitution was sent to the states for ratification, what the real nature of the contest was. They resided for the most part in the towns or in the more thickly populated areas and they could marshal their forces *quickly and effectively. . . . Talent, wealth, and professional abilities were, generally speaking, on the side of the Constitutionalists. The money to be spent in the campaign of education was on their side also; and it was spent in considerable sums for pamphleteering, organizing parades and demonstrations, and engaging the interests of the press. A small percentage of the enormous gain to come through the appreciation of securities, a loan would have financed no mean campaign for those days.*[15]

In contrast, Beard describes the plight of the Antifederalists in this struggle:

The opposition, on the other hand, suffered from the difficulties connected with getting a backwoods vote out to the town and country elections. This involved sometimes long journeys and bad weather, for it will be remembered that elections were held in late fall and winter. There were no such immediate personal gains to be made through the defeat of the Constitution, as were to be made by the security holders on the other side. It was true that the debtors knew that they would probably have to settle their accounts in full, and the small farmers were aware that taxes would have to be paid to discharge the national debt if the Constitution was adopted; and the debtors everywhere waged war against the Constitution—of this there is plenty of evidence. But they had no money to carry on their campaign; they were poor and uninfluential—the strongest battalions were not on their side. The wonder is that they came so near defeating the Constitution at the polls.[16]

Summary

Elite theory provides us with an interpretation of the Constitution of the United States and the basic structure of American government. The following propositions can be derived from our analysis of Constitutional politics:

1. The Constitution of the United States was not "ordained and established" by the "the people." Instead, it was written by a small, educated, talented, wealthy elite in America, representative of powerful economic interests—bondholders, investors, merchants, real estate owners, and planters.

2. The Constitution and the national government that it established had its origins in elite dissatisfaction with the inability of the central government to pay off its bondholders, the interference of state governments with the development of a national economy, the threat to investors and creditors with state issuance of cheap paper money and laws relieving debtors of contractual obligations, the threat to propertied classes arising from post-Revolutionary War radicalism, the inability of the central government to provide an army capable of protecting Western development or a navy capable of protecting American commercial interests on the high seas, and the inability of America's elite to exercise power in world affairs.

3. Ratification of the Constitution was achieved through the political skills of

the elite. The masses of people in America did not participate in the writing of the Constitution nor in its adoption by the states, and they probably would have opposed the Constitution had they the information and resources to do so.

4. Founding Fathers shared a consensus that the fundamental role of government was the protection of liberty and property. They believed in a republican government by men of principle and property. They opposed an aristocracy or a governing nobility, but they also opposed mass democracy with direct participation by the people in decision making. They were fearful of mass movements that would seek to reduce inequalities of wealth, intelligence, talent, or virtue. "Dangerous leveling" was a serious violation of men's rights to property.

5. The structure of American government was designed to suppress "factious" issues, that is, threats to dominant economic elites. Republicanism, the division of power between state and national governments, and the complex system of checks and balances and divided power were all designed as protections against mass movements threatening liberty and property.

6. The text of the Constitution itself contains many direct and immediate benefits to America's governing elite. Although all Americans, both elite and mass, may have benefited by the adoption of the Constitution, the advantages and benefits in that document for America's elite provided the impelling motive for their activities on behalf of the new Constitution.

References

[1]Lester Cappon (ed.), *The Adams-Jefferson Letters*, Vol. I (Chapel Hill: University of North Carolina Press, 1959), p. 196.

[2]Max Farrand (ed.), *The Records of the Federal Convention of 1787*, Vol. 3 (New Haven, Conn.: Yale University Press, 1937), p. 15.

[3]Farrand, *Records of the Federal Convention of 1787*, Vol. 3, p. 32.

[4]See Clinton Rossiter, *1787, The Grand Convention* (New York: Macmillan Co., 1966), p. 45.

[5]Rossiter, pp. 152–153. Rossiter's discussion of the events leading to the Convention of 1787 and of the Convention itself is excellent.

[6]Charles Beard, *An Economic Interpretation of the Constitution of the United States* (New York: Macmillan Co., 1913), pp. 73–151.

[7]John P. Roche, "The Founding Fathers: A Reform Caucus in Action," *American Political Science Review*, 55 (December 1961), 799.

[8]See especially Beard, *Economic Interpretation of the Constitution*.

[9]Farrand, *Records of the Federal Convention of 1787*, Vol. 1, pp. 299–300.

[10]James Madison, Alexander Hamilton, John Jay, *The Federalist* No. 10 (New York: The Modern Library, 1937).

[11]Madison, Hamilton, and Jay, *The Federalist* No. 10.

[12]*Marbury v. Madison*, 1 Cranch 137 (1803).

[13]Beard, *Economic Interpretation of the Constitution*, pp. 217–238.

[14]Beard, pp. 16–7. Beard's "economic" interpretation differs from an elitist interpretation in that Beard believed the economic elites supported the Constitution and the masses opposed it. Our elitist interpretation asserts only that the masses did not participate in the writing or adoption of the Constitution, and that elites benefited directly from its provi-

sions. Our interpretation does not depend upon showing that the masses opposed the Constitution, but merely upon showing that they did not participate in its establishment. Beard's thesis about class conflict over adoption is a controversial one among historians. Attacks on Beard are found in Forrest McDonald, *We the People: The Economic Origins of the Constitution* (Chicago: University of Chicago, 1963); and Robert E. Brown, *Charles Beard and the Constitution* (Princeton, N.J.: Princeton University Press, 1956). A balanced view is presented in Lee Benson, *Turner and Beard: American Historical Writing Reconsidered* (New York: Free Press, 1960).

[15]Beard, pp. 251–252.

[16]Beard, p. 252.

Selected Additional Readings

Beard, Charles A. *An Economic Interpretation of the Constitution of the United States.* New York: Macmillan, 1913. A Free Press paperback edition was issued in 1965. Much of the second chapter of *Irony* is grounded in the data presented by Beard in this classic work. Beard traces the events leading up to the writing of the Constitution and the events surrounding ratification from an economic point of view. He discovers that economic considerations played a major, if not central, role in the shaping of the Constitution.

For several critiques of Beard see:

a. Benson, Lee. *Turner and Beard: American Historical Writing Reconsidered.* New York: Free Press, 1960.

b. Beale, Howard K., ed. *Charles A. Beard: An Appraisal.* Lexington: University of Kentucky Press, 1954.

c. McDonald, Forrest. *We The People: The Economic Origins of the Constitution.* Chicago 1958.

Corwin, Edward S. and J. W. Peltason. *Understanding the Constitution,* 6th ed. New York: Holt, Rinehart, and Winston, 1973. There are many books on the market which deal with explanations of parts of the Constitution. This paperback is one of the best in this area. It contains explanations of The Declaration of Independence, the Articles of Confederation, and the Constitution in a section-by-section manner. The book is clearly written and is well suited for undergraduate as well as graduate and faculty use.

Lipset, Seymour Martin. *The First New Nation.* Garden City, N.Y.: Doubleday—Anchor Books edition, 1963. This book is a comparative treatment of the factors necessary for the development of a new nation. Lipset argues that any new nation must develop legitimacy of government, national identity, national unity, opposition rights, and citizen payoffs. The book is important because the United States is examined as the first "new nation" in light of these five factors and is then compared to other developing nations.

Madison, James, Alexander Hamilton, and John Jay. *The Federalist.* New York: Modern Library Edition, 1937. This is a collection of the articles published in support of ratification of the Constitution. They are perhaps the most important contemporary comments available on the Constitution.

Rossiter, Clinton L. *1787, The Grand Convention.* New York: Macmillan Co., 1966. This readable and entertaining account of the men and events of 1787 contains many insights into the difficulties the Founding Fathers had writing the Constitution.

CHAPTER 3

THE EVOLUTION OF AMERICAN ELITES

A stable elite system depends upon the movement of talented and ambitious individuals from the lower strata into the elite. An open elite system providing for "a slow and continuous modification of the ruling classes" is essential for the continuation of the system and the avoidance of revolution. Of course, only those non-elites who accept the basic consensus of the system can be admitted into the ruling class. Although popular elections, party competition, and other democratic institutions in America have not enabled the masses to govern, these institutions have been helpful in keeping the elite system an open one. They have assisted in the circulation of elites, even if they have never been a means of challenging the dominant elite consensus.

This chapter presents an historical analysis of the evolution of American elites. In this analysis, we shall show that American elite membership has evolved slowly, without any serious break in the ideas or values underlying the American political and economic system. America has never experienced a true revolution, in which governing elites were forcefully replaced with non-elites. Instead, American elite membership has been open to those individuals who have acquired wealth and property and who have accepted the national consensus about private enterprise, limited government, and individualism. Thus, industrialization, technological change, and new sources of wealth in the expanding economy have produced new elite members, and America's elite system has permitted the absorption of the new elites without upsetting the system itself.

It is our contention that America's political leadership over the years has been essentially conservative, in that it has accepted the basic consensus underlying the American political and economic system. Whatever the popular political label has been—"Federalist," "Democrat," "Whig," "Republican," "Progressive," "Conservative," or "Liberal" —American leadership has remained committed to the same values and ideas that motivated the Founding Fathers. No drastic revisions of the American system have ever been contemplated by the American elites.

While it is true that basic changes in public policy and major innovations in the structure of American government have taken place over the decades, we shall argue in this chapter that these changes and innovations have been *incremental* rather than revolutionary. Public policies have been frequently modified but seldom replaced. Structural adaptations have been made in the constitutional system designed by the Founding Fathers, but the original framework of American constitutionalism remains substantially intact.

Finally, we shall contend that policy changes in America have not come about as a result of demands by "the people." Instead, changes and innovations in public policy have occurred when events have threatened the system and when elites, acting in enlightened self-interest, have instituted reforms in order to preserve the system and their place in it. Reforms have been designed to strengthen the existing social and economic fabric of society with a minimum of dislocation for governing elites. Political conflict in America has continually centered on a very narrow range of issues; only once, in the Civil War, have American elites been deeply divided over the nature of American society. The Civil War reflected a deep cleavage between Southern elites—dependent upon a plantation economy, slave labor, and free trade—and Northern industrial and commercial elites, who prospered under free labor and protective tariffs.

Hamilton and the Nation's First Public Policies

The most influential figure in George Washington's administration was Alexander Hamilton, Secretary of the Treasury. More than anyone else, Hamilton was aware that the new nation, to survive and prosper, must win the lasting confidence of business and financial elites. Only if the United States were established on a sound financial basis would it be able to attract investors both at home and abroad and to expand its industry and commerce. Great Britain remained the largest source of investment capital for the new nation, and Hamilton was decidedly pro-British. Also, he favored a strong central government as a means of protecting property and stimulating the growth of commerce and industry.

Hamilton's first move was to refund the national debt at face value. Most of the original bonds were no longer in the hands of the original owners but had fallen to speculators who had purchased them for only a fraction of their face value. Since these securities were worth only about 25 cents on the dollar, the Hamilton program for refunding the national debt meant a 300 percent profit for the speculators. But Hamilton's program did not end with refunding the debts owed by the United States; he also undertook to pay the debts incurred by the states themselves during the Revolutionary War. The object was to place the creditor class under a deep obligation to the central government.

Hamilton also acted to establish a Bank of the United States, which would receive government funds, issue a national currency, facilitate the sale of national bonds, and tie the national government even more closely to the banking community. The Constitution did not specifically grant to Congress the power to create a national bank, but Hamilton was willing to interpret the "necessary and proper" clause broadly enough to include the creation of a bank to help carry out the taxing, borrowing, and currency powers enumerated in the Constitution. Obviously, Hamilton's broad construction of the "necessary and proper" clause looked in the direction of a powerful central government that would exercise powers not specifically enumerated in the Constitution. Thomas Jefferson, who was Secretary of State in the same Cabinet with Hamilton, expressed growing concern over Hamilton's tendency toward centralization at the national level. Jefferson argued that Congress could not establish the bank because the bank was not, strictly speaking, "necessary" to carry out delegated functions. But Hamilton won out, with the support of President Washington; and Congress voted to charter a Bank of the United States. For twenty years the bank was very successful, especially in stabilizing the currency of the new nation.

It was not until 1819 that the constitutionality of the Bank of the United States was decided by the Supreme Court. In the famous case of *McCulloch* v. *Maryland*, the Supreme Court upheld the broad definition of national power suggested by Hamilton under the "necessary and proper" clause. At the same time, the Court established the principle that when a state law interferes with a national activity the state law will be declared unconstitutional.[1] "Let the end be legitimate," Chief Justice John Marshall wrote, "let it be within the scope of the Constitution, and all means which are appropriate, which are plainly adopted to that end, which are not prohibited, but consistent with the letter and spirit of the Constitution, are constitutional." The McCulloch case firmly established the principle that Congress has the right to choose any appropriate means for carrying out the delegated powers of the national government. The "necessary and proper" clause is now sometimes referred to as the "implied powers" clause or the "elastic" clause, because it gives to Congress many powers that are not explicitly given in the Constitution. Of course, Congress must still trace all of its activities to some formal grant of power, but this is usually not a difficult task.

By 1793, the centralizing effect of Hamilton's program and its orientation toward merchants, manufacturers, and ship builders had aroused serious opposition in governing circles. Southern planters and large landowners benefited very little from Hamilton's policies, and they were joined in their opposition by many small farmers and frontiersmen. These agrarian interests, both large and small, resented especially Hamilton's pro-British policy and gave little support to debt refunding, national banking, or other projects designed to strengthen commerce and manufacturing.

The Rise of the Jeffersonians

The opposition to the Hamiltonian or "Federalistic" programs was a coalition of those who had opposed the adoption of the Constitution in the first place—men who feared strong central government as a threat to freedom and the sovereignty of the states; landed interests who sought to export foodstuffs and opposed high tariffs; anti-British elements in the population who denounced the Anglophilia of Federalists; and those small farmers, tradesmen, and frontiersmen who opposed Hamilton's financial program of support for commerce and industry and resented the aristocratic trends in the new government. These groups were first called "Antifederalists," and later "Republicans" and "Democratic Republicans" when these terms became popular after the French Revolution. When Thomas Jefferson resigned from Washington's Cabinet in protest of Hamilton's program, opposition to the Federalists began to gather around Jefferson.

Jefferson is portrayed in history as a great democrat and champion of the common man. And it is true that in writing the Declaration of

Independence, the Virginia Statute for Religious Freedom, and the famous *Notes on Virginia*, Jefferson expressed concern for the rights of all men and a willingness to trust in the wisdom of "the people." But when Jefferson spoke warmly of the merits of "the people," he meant those who owned and managed their own farms and estates. He firmly believed that only those who owned their own land could make good citizens. Jefferson disliked aristocracy, but he also held urban masses in contempt. He wanted to see the United States become a nation of free, educated, informed, incorruptible, landowning farmers. Democracy, he believed, could only be founded on a propertied class in a propertied nation.

Jefferson's political views differed very little from those of the Founding Fathers. In 1788 he wrote to James Madison praising *The Federalist* as "the best commentary on the principles of government which was ever written." He shared the concern of the Founding Fathers about unrestrained rule by the masses. While Jefferson expressed more confidence in the judgment of small landowning farmers than most of his contemporaries, he also believed in republican government with its checks and balances and safeguards against popular majorities. Jefferson was willing to base republican government on large and small landowners, but he distrusted merchants, manufacturers, laborers, and urban dwellers. In 1787 he wrote:

I think our governments will remain virtuous for many centuries; as long as they remain chiefly agricultural; and this will be as long as there shall be vacant lands in any part of America. When they get piled upon one another in large cities, as in Europe, they will become corrupt as in Europe.

Later on he exclaimed: "Those who labor in the earth are the chosen people of God, if ever he had a chosen people." His belief that land ownership was essential to virtuous government explains in part his Louisiana Purchase, which he hoped would provide the American people with land "to the hundredth and thousandth generation."[2]

The dispute between Federalists and Antifederalists in early America was not between aristocrats and democrats, nor was it a dispute between elites and masses. As Richard Hofstadter explains:

. . . although democratically minded Americans did stand with Jefferson, the line of division was essentially between two kinds of property, not two kinds of philosophy. The Federalists during Hamilton's service as Secretary of the Treasury had given the government a foundation of unashamed devotion to the mercantile and investing classes . . . the landed interests, however, were in a majority, and it was only a matter of time before they could marshal themselves in a strong party of their own. Jefferson's party was formed to defend specific prop-

erty interests rather than the abstract premises of democracy, and its policies were conceived and executed in the sober, moderate spirit that Jefferson's generation expected of propertied citizens when they entered the political arena.[3]

The Antifederalists, or "Republicans," did not elect their first president, Thomas Jefferson, until 1800. John Adams, a Federalist, was chosen to succeed Washington in the election of 1796. Yet the election of 1796 was an important milestone in the development of the American political system. For the first time, two candidates, Adams and Jefferson, did not campaign as individuals but as members of political parties. For the first time, the candidates for the electoral college announced themselves before the election as either "Adams' men" or "Jefferson's men." More importantly, for the first time, the American political leaders saw the importance of molding mass opinion in organizing the masses for political action. It was the Republican party that first saw the importance of working among the masses to rally popular support. The Federalist leaders made the mistake of assuming that they could maintain the unquestioning support of the less-educated and less-wealthy without bothering to mold their opinions.

Rather than follow the Republicans in attempts to manipulate public opinion, the Federalists tried to outlaw public criticism of government officials by means of the Alien and Sedition Acts of 1798. Among other things, these acts made it a crime to conspire to oppose the legal measures of the government or to interfere with their execution, or to publish any false or malicious writing directed against the president or Congress, or to "stir up hatred" against them. These acts directly challenged the newly adopted First Amendment guarantee of freedom of speech and press. But the Supreme Court had not yet asserted itself in declaring laws of Congress unconstitutional, as it would in *Marbury* v. *Madison*[4] a few years later.

In response to the Alien and Sedition Acts, Jefferson and Madison put forward their famous Kentucky and Virginia Resolutions. These measures proposed that the states should assume the right to decide whether Congress has acted unconstitutionally and, furthermore, that the states might properly "interpose" their authority against "palpable and alarming infractions of the Constitution." The Virginia and Kentucky legislatures passed these resolutions and declared the Alien and Sedition Acts were "void and of no force" in these states.

Republicans in Power—The Stability of Public Policy

In the election of 1800, the Federalists finally went down to defeat; Thomas Jefferson and Aaron Burr were elected over John Adams and C.

C. Pinckney. Only New England, New Jersey, and Delaware, where commercial and manufacturing interests were strongest, voted Federalist. The vast majority of American people won their living from the soil, and landed elites were able to mobilize these masses behind their bid for control of the government. The Federalists had failed to recognize the importance of agrarianism in the economic and political life of the nation. Another half century would pass and America's industrial revolution would be in full swing before manufacturing and commercial elites would reestablish their dominance.

But the real importance of the election of 1800 is not that landed interests gained power in relation to commercial and industrial interests. The importance of 1800 is that for the first time in America's history control of the government passed peacefully from the hands of one faction to an opposition faction. This may seem commonplace, but there are few nations in the world today where government office changes hands in orderly or peaceful fashion. The fact that an "out" party peacefully replaced an "in" party is further testimony to the strength of the consensus among the elite of the new nation. Despite bitter campaign rhetoric, Federalists and Republicans agreed to abide by the basic "rules of the game," to view an opposition faction as legitimate, and to accept the outcome of an election. The Federalists relinquished control of the government without fear that the fundamental values of the American society would be destroyed by a new governing faction. There was clearly more agreement among American leaders than there was disagreement.*

The "Virginia Dynasty"—Thomas Jefferson, James Madison, and finally James Monroe—was to govern the country for a total of six presidential terms, nearly a quarter of a century. It is interesting to note that, once in office, the Republicans made few changes in Federalist and

---

*The original text of the Constitution did not envision an opposition faction. Presidential electors were permitted to cast two votes for president, with the understanding that the candidate with the second highest vote total would be vice-president. A total of 73 Republican electors pledged to Jefferson were sent to the electoral college, and 65 Federalists pledged to Adams. Somewhat thoughtlessly, all of the Republicans cast one vote for Jefferson and one vote for Aaron Burr, his running mate, with the result that, when the votes were tallied, each man was equally eligible for the Presidency. Because of the tie vote, the decision went to the Federalist-controlled House of Representatives, where a movement was begun to elect Burr, rather than Jefferson, in order to embarrass the Republicans. But Alexander Hamilton used his influence in Congress to swing the election to his old political foe Jefferson, suggesting again that their differences were not so deep that either would deliberately undermine the presidency to strike at the other. Once in power, the Republicans passed the Twelfth Amendment to the Constitution, providing that each presidential elector should thereafter vote separately for president and vice-president. This reform was promptly agreed to by both Federalists and Republicans in the states and was ratified in time for the election of 1804.

Hamiltonian policy.† No attack was made on commercial or industrial enterprise; in fact, commerce and industry prospered under Republican rule as never before. No attempt was made to recover money paid out by Hamilton in the refunding of national or state debts. Speculations in public lands continued. Instead of crushing the banks, Republicans were soon flirting with the financial interests they were sworn to oppose. Jefferson's Secretary of the Treasury, Albert Gallatin, wrote:

I am decidedly in favor of making all of the banks Republican by sharing deposits among them in proportion to the disposition they show. . . . It is material to the safety of Republicanism to detach the mercantile interest from its enemies and incorporate them into the body of its friends. A merchant is naturally a Republican and can be otherwise only from a vitiated state of things. [5]

When the Bank of the United States expired in 1811, problems of cheap currency and unreliable state banks began to plague Republican men of property; and by 1816, the Republicans themselves chartered a Second Bank of the United States. Soon Republican newspapers were reprinting Alexander Hamilton's arguments in favor of the constitutionality of the First Bank of the United States! Jefferson was an ardent expansionist; to add to America's wealth in land, he purchased the vast Louisiana Territory. Later a stronger army and a system of internal roads were required to assist in the development of Western land. Jefferson's successor, James Madison, built a strong navy and engaged in another war with England, the War of 1812, to protect American commerce on the high seas. The Napoleonic Wars and the War of 1812, by depressing trade with Britain, stimulated American manufacturing. In 1816 Republicans passed a high tariff in order to protect domestic industry and manufacturing from foreign goods. As for Republican tax policies, Jefferson wrote in 1816:

To take from one, because it is thought his own industry and that of his fathers has acquired too much, in order to spare to others, who, or whose fathers have not, exercised equal industry and skill, is to violate arbitrarily the first principle of association, 'the guarantee to everyone of free exercise of his industry and the fruits acquired by it.' [6]

In short, the Republicans had no intention of redistributing wealth in America. Indeed, before the end of Madison's second term, the Republi-

---

†The only major pieces of legislation to be repealed by the Republicans were the Alien and Sedition Acts. And it seems clear that in these acts the Federalists had violated elite consensus. Even John Marshall, who was elected as a Federalist congressman in 1798, pledged to support repeal of these acts.

cans had taken over the whole complex of Hamiltonian policies—a national bank, high tariffs, protection for manufacturers, internal improvements, Western land development, a strong army and navy, and a broad interpretation of national power. So complete was the elite consensus that by 1820 the Republicans had completely driven the Federalist party out of existence, largely by taking over their programs.

The Rise of the Western Elites

According to Frederick Jackson Turner, "The rise of the New West was the most significant fact in American history."[7] Certainly the American West had a profound impact on the political system of the new nation. People went West because of the vast wealth of fertile lands that awaited them there; nowhere in the world could one acquire wealth so quickly as in the new American West. Because aristocratic families of the Eastern seaboard seldom had reason to migrate westward, the Western settlers were mainly middle- or lower-class immigrants. With hard work and good fortune, a penniless migrant could become a wealthy plantation owner or cattle rancher in a single generation. Thus, the West meant rapid upward social mobility.

New elites arose in the West and had to be assimilated into America's governing circles. This assimilation had a profound effect on the character of America's elites. No one exemplifies the new entrants into America's elite better than Andrew Jackson. Jackson's victory in the presidential election of 1828 was not a victory of the common man against the propertied classes but rather a victory of the new Western elites against established Republican leadership in the East. Jackson's victory forced America's established elites to recognize the growing importance of the West and to open their ranks to the new rich who were settled west of the Alleghenies.

Since Jackson was a favorite of the people, it was easy for him to believe in the wisdom of the common man. But "Jacksonian Democracy" was by no means a philosophy of leveling equalitarianism. The ideal of the frontier society was the self-made man, and wealth and power won by competitive skill was very much admired. It was only wealth and power obtained through special privilege that offended the frontiersmen. They believed in a *natural aristocracy*, rather than an aristocracy by birth, education, or special privilege. Jackson himself best expressed this philosophy in his famous message vetoing the bill to recharter the national bank:

Distinctions in society will always exist under every just government. Equality of talents, of education, or wealth cannot be produced by human institutions. In the full enjoyment of the gifts of heaven and the fruits of superior industry, economy, and virtue, every man is equally entitled to protection by law; but when the laws undertake to add to these natural and just advantages artificial distinctions, to grant titles, gratuities, and exclusive privileges, to make the rich richer and the potent more powerful, the humble members of society—the farmers, mechanics, and laborers,—who have neither the time nor the means for securing like favors to themselves, have a right to complain of the injustice of their government.[8]

Thus it was not absolute equality that Jacksonians demanded but rather a more open elite system—a greater opportunity for the rising middle class to acquire wealth and influence through competition.

In an attempt to win a place for themselves in America's governing circles, the new Western leaders attempted to convince the public that politics and administration should be taken from the hands of social elites and opened to men like themselves, who could boast of natural ability and talent. Jackson himself expressed this philosophy in his first annual message to Congress in December 1829: "The duties of all public offices are, or at least admit of being made, so plain and simple that men of intelligence may readily qualify themselves for their performance, and I cannot but believe that more is lost by the long continuance of men in office than is generally to be gained by experience." Rotation in office became a leading principle of Jacksonian Democracy.

In their struggle to open America's elite system, the Jacksonians appealed to mass sentiment. Jackson's humble beginnings, his image as a self-made man, his military adventures, his frontier experience, and his rough, brawling style served to endear him to the masses. As beneficiaries of popular support, the new elites of the West developed a strong faith in the wisdom and justice of popular decisions. All of the new Western states that entered the Union granted universal white male suffrage, and gradually the older states fell into step. Rising elites, themselves often less than a generation away from the masses, saw in a widened electorate a chance for personal advancement that they could never have achieved under the old regime. Therefore, the Jacksonians became noisy and effective advocates of the principle that all men should have the right to vote and that no restrictions should be placed upon officeholding. They also launched a successful attack upon the Congressional caucus system of nominating presidential candidates. Having been defeated in Congress in 1824, Jackson wished to sever Congress from the nominating process. In 1832, when the Democrats held their first national convention, Andrew Jackson was renominated by acclamation.

Jacksonian Democracy also brought changes in the method of selecting presidential electors. The Constitution left to the various state legislatures the right to decide how presidential electors should be chosen, and in most cases the legislatures themselves chose the electors. But after 1832 all states selected their presidential electors by popular vote. In most of these states the people voted for electors who were listed under the name of their party and their candidate.

The Jacksonian drive to open America's elite system did not stop with electoral reforms. The Western elites also tried to curtail the privileges of the established Eastern elites. As a Westerner, Jackson despised the Bank of the United States, which was controlled by conservative Eastern bankers, and supported the free lending policies of the state banks. State bank men were prominent in Jackson's first administration; Roger Taney, for instance, was a lawyer for and stockholder of the Union Bank of Maryland before Jackson appointed him Chief Justice of the United States Supreme Court. Thus when, prior to the election of 1832, Easterners Daniel Webster and Nicholas Biddle pushed through Congress a new charter for the Bank of the United States to replace the charter that was to expire in 1836, Jackson vetoed the new charter with a ringing message that cemented his popularity with the masses. He denounced the banks as a "granted monopoly and exclusive privilege." Again, Jackson emerged as the apparent champion of the common man.

Following his re-election in 1832, Jackson decided to make war upon the Bank and its president, Nicholas Biddle. Jackson withdrew all deposits of the United States government from the bank and placed them in selected state banks—"pet banks," as they were called—which were prepared to extend credit to the new empire builders and land speculators of the Western states. The result was that money began to move from east to west in America and the way was paved for the rise of new Western capitalism. Jacksonian Democracy broke the exclusive monopoly of the Eastern elites over money and political power in America.

Yet the evidence is clear that the changes in the character of elites, from the administration of John Adams through Thomas Jefferson to Andrew Jackson, were very minor. Historical research by sociologist Sidney H. Aronson reveals that, contrary to the general assumption, Jackson's administration was clearly upper class in origin, college educated, prestigiously employed, professionally trained, and probably wealthy. (See Table 3–1.) In fact, Jackson's administration is not much different in class character from that of Thomas Jefferson or even that of the Federalist, John Adams! Over half of Jackson's top appointees were

Table 3-1 / Social Class Characteristics of Presidential Appointments of Adams, Jefferson, and Jackson

Characteristics	Adams (*N* = 96)	Jefferson (*N* = 100)	Jackson (*N* = 127)
Father held political office	52%	43%	44%
Father attended college	17	13	12
Class I[1] family social position	62	58	51
High-ranking occupation	92	93	90
Political office prior to appointment	91	83	88
Class I[1] social position	86	74	74
Family in America in seventeenth century	55	48	48
Attended college	63	52	52
Professional training	69	74	81
Relative an appointive elite	40	34	34

[1] "Class I" is the highest of four classes described as follows:
  Class I: "national and international aristocracy";
  Class II: "prosperous and respectable";
  Class III: "respectable";
  Class IV: "subsistence or impoverished."
Breakdowns by each class are as follows:
  Adams: I: 62%, II: 19%, III: 5%, IV: 1%, unknown: 13%.
  Jefferson: I: 58%, II: 15%, III: 6%, IV: 1%, unknown: 20%.
  Jackson: I: 51%, II: 25%, III: 11%, IV: 2%, unknown: 11%.
Source: Sidney H. Aronson, *Status and Kinship in the Higher Civil Service* (Cambridge: Harvard University Press, 1964), p. 195.

born into America's distinguished upper-class families, and three-quarters enjoyed high class standing, prior to their appointment, either through birth or achievement.

Elite Cleavage — The Civil War

America's elites were in substantial agreement about the character and direction of the new nation during its first 60 years. Conflicts over the Bank, the tariff, internal improvements (roads, harbors, etc.), and even the controversial war with Mexico in 1846 did not threaten the basic underlying consensus in support of the American political system. In the 1850s, however, the role of the Negro in American society—the most divisive issue in the history of American politics—became an urgent question that drove a wedge among America's elites and ultimately led to the nation's bloodiest war. The American political system was unequal to the task of negotiating a peaceful settlement to the problem of slavery because America's elites were themselves deeply divided over the question.

In 1787, the Southern elites—cotton planters, land owners, exporters, and slave traders—had been prepared to envision an end to slavery; but after 1820, the demand for cotton became insatiable, and cotton could not be profitably produced without slave labor. Over half the value of all American goods shipped abroad before the Civil War was in cotton; and a broad belt of Southern land, ranging in width from about 500 miles in the Carolinas and Georgia to 600 or 700 miles in the Mississippi Valley, was devoted primarily to cotton culture. While Virginia did not depend upon cotton, it sold great numbers of slaves to the cotton states, and "slave raising" itself became immensely profitable. The price of a good slave for the fields increased from $300 in 1820 to over $1,000 in 1860, in spite of the fact that the slave population grew from about a million and a half to nearly four million during this period.

It was the white *elites* and not the white *masses* of the South who had an interest in the slave and cotton culture. On the eve of the Civil War, probably not more than 400,000 Southern families—approximately one in four—held slaves. And many of these families held only one or two slaves each. The number of great planters—men who owned fifty or more slaves and large holdings of land—was probably not more than 7,000. Yet the views of these men dominated Southern politics.

The Northern elites were merchants and manufacturers who depended upon free labor. However, Northern elites had no direct interest in the abolition of slavery in the South. Some Northern manufacturers were making good profits from Southern trade; and with higher tariffs, they stood a chance to make even better profits. Abolitionist activities imperiled trade relations between North and South and were often looked upon with irritation even in Northern social circles. But both Northern and Southern elites realized that control of the West was the key to future dominance of the nation. Northern elites wanted a West composed of small farmers who produced food and raw materials for the industrial and commercial East and provided a market for Eastern goods. Southern planters feared the voting power of a West composed of small farmers and wanted Western lands for the expansion of the cotton and slave culture. Cotton ate up the land and, because it required continuous cultivation and monotonous rounds of simple tasks, was suited to slave labor. Thus, to protect the cotton economy, it was essential to protect slavery in Western lands. This conflict over Western land eventually precipitated the Civil War.

Yet despite these differences, the underlying consensus of American elites was so great that compromise after compromise was devised to maintain unity. In the Missouri Compromise of 1820, the land in the

Louisiana Purchase exclusive of Missouri was divided between free ter-
ritory and slave territory at 36° 30'; and Maine and Missouri were admitted as free and slave states, respectively. After the war with Mexico, the
elaborate Compromise of 1850 caused one of the greatest debates in
American legislative history, with Senators Henry Clay, Daniel Webster,
John C. Calhoun, Salmon P. Chase, Stephen A. Douglas, Jefferson Davis,
Alexander H. Stevens, Robert Tombs, William H. Seward, and Thaddeus
Stevens all participating. Elite cleavage was apparent, but it was not yet
so divisive as to split the nation. A compromise was achieved, providing
for the admission of California as a free state; for the creation of two new
territories, New Mexico and Utah, out of the Mexican cession; for a
drastic fugitive slave law to satisfy Southern planters; and for the prohibition of slave trade in the District of Columbia. Even the Kansas-
Nebraska Act of 1854 was intended to be a compromise; each new territory was supposed to decide for itself whether it should be slave or free,
with the expectation that Nebraska would vote free and Kansas slave.
But gradually the spirit of compromise gave way to cleavage and conflict.

Beginning in 1856, pro- and anti-slavery forces fought it out in
"bleeding Kansas." Senator Charles Sumner of Massachusetts delivered a
condemnation of slavery in the Senate and was beaten almost to death
on the Senate floor by Preston Brooks, a relative of Senator Andrew P.
Butler of South Carolina. Intemperate language in the Senate became
commonplace, with frequent threats of secession, violence, and civil
war.

In 1857, the Supreme Court decided, in *Dred Scot* v. *Sanford*,[9] that
the Missouri Compromise was unconstitutional because Congress had
no authority to forbid slavery in any territory. Slave property, said Chief
Justice Roger B. Taney, was as much protected by the Constitution as
was any other kind of property.

In 1859, John Brown and his followers raided the United States
arsenal at Harper's Ferry, as a first step to freeing the slaves of Virginia
by force. Brown was captured by Virginia militia under the command of
Colonel Robert E. Lee, tried for treason, found guilty, and executed.
Southerners believed that Northerners had tried to incite the horror of
slave insurrection, while Northerners believed that Brown died a martyr.

The conflict between North and South led to the complete collapse
of the Whig party and the emergence of a new Republican party composed exclusively of Northeners and Westerners. For the first time in the
history of American parties, one of the two major parties did not spread
across both sides of the Mason-Dixon line. Robert Dahl describes the
decline of unity among American elites:

Congress, hitherto the forum of compromise, became in the 1850s a battleground where almost every issue split the membership in the same two camps. In 1858–1859, Congress had lengthy deadlocks on almost every issue: The admission of Kansas, transcontinental railroads, rivers and harbors appropriations, a homestead bill, the tariff. Deadlock and conflict so much dominated the session that the Congress was not even able to agree on the annual appropriation for the post office; at the end of the session the post office department was left without funds.[10]

1860 was the only year in American history that four, rather than two, major parties sought the Presidency. The nation was so divided that no party came close to winning the majority of popular votes. Lincoln, the Republican candidate, and Douglas, the Democratic candidate, won most of their votes from the North and West, while Breckenridge, the Southern Democratic candidate, and Bell, the Constitutional Union candidate, received most of their votes from the South (see Table 3–2).

Table 3-2 / The Election of 1860

	Percent of Total Vote	Percent of Vote from North and West	Percent of Vote from South
Republicans: Lincoln	40	98.6	1.4
Democrats: Douglas	30	88.0	12.0
Southern Democrats: Breckenridge	18	33.0	67.0
Constitutional Union: Bell	12	13.0	87.0

Source: Robert A. Dahl, *Pluralist Democracy in the United States* (Chicago: Rand McNally, 1966), pp. 312–313; data from W. Dean Burnham, *Presidential Ballots, 1836–1892* (Baltimore: Johns Hopkins Press, 1955).

More important, the cleavage had become so deep that many prominent Southern leaders announced that they would not accept the outcome of the presidential election if Lincoln won. Threats of secession were not new, but this time it was no bluff. For the first and only time in American history, prominent elite members were prepared to destroy the American political system rather than compromise their interests and principles. Shortly after the election, on December 20, 1860, the state of South Carolina seceded from the Union. Within six months, ten other Southern states had followed.

Yet even in the midst of this disastrous conflict, one finds extensive evidence of continued devotion to the principles of constitutional government and private property among both Northern and Southern elites. There were many genuine efforts at compromise and conciliation. Abraham Lincoln never attacked slavery in the South; his exclusive concern was to halt the spread of slavery in the Western territories. He wrote in 1845: "I hold it a paramount duty of us in the free states, due to the union of the states, and perhaps to liberty itself (paradox though it may seem), to let the slavery of the other states alone."[11] Throughout his political career he consistently held this position. On the other hand, with regard to the Western territories he said: "The whole nation is interested that the best use shall be made of these territories. We want them for homes and free white people. This they cannot be, to any considerable extent, if slavery shall be planted within them."[12] In short, Lincoln wanted the Western territories to be tied economically and culturally to the Northern system. As for Lincoln's racial views, as late as 1858 he said:

I will say, then, that I am not, nor ever have been, in favor of bringing about in any way the social and political equality of the white and black races; that I am not, nor ever have been, in favor of making voters or jurors of Negroes, nor qualifying them to hold office, nor to intermarry with white people . . . and in as much as they cannot so live while they do remain together, there must be a position of superior and inferior; and I as much as any other man am in favor of having the superior position assigned to the white race.[13]

Lincoln's political posture was essentially conservative: He wished to preserve the long-established order and consensus that had protected American principles and property rights so successfully in the past. He was not an abolitionist, and he did not set as his goal the destruction of the Southern elites or the rearrangement of the South's social fabric. His goal was to bring the South back into the Union, to restore orderly government, and to establish the principle that the states cannot resist national authority with force. At the beginning of the war, Lincoln knew that a great part of conservative Northern opinion was willing to fight for the Union but might refuse to support a war to free Negroes. Lincoln's great political skill was his ability to submerge all of the issues of the Civil War into one single overriding theme—the preservation of the Union. On the other hand, he was bitterly attacked throughout the war by radical Republicans who thought that he had "no anti-slavery instincts."

As the war continued and casualties mounted, opinion in the North became increasingly bitter toward Southern slave owners. Many Republicans joined the abolitionists in calling for emancipation of the slaves simply to punish the "rebels." They knew that the power of the South was based on the labor of slaves. Lincoln also knew that if he proclaimed to the world that the war was being fought to free the slaves, there would be less danger of foreign intervention. Yet even in late summer of 1862, Lincoln wrote:

My paramount object in this struggle is to save the Union. If I could save the Union without freeing any slaves, I would do it; if I could save it by freeing some and leaving others alone, I would also do that. I shall do less whenever I shall believe what I am doing hurts the cause, and I shall do more whenever I believe doing more will help the cause. I shall adopt new views as fast as they shall appear to be true views.[14]

Finally, on September 22, 1862, Lincoln issued his preliminary Emancipation Proclamation. Claiming his right as commander-in-chief of the army and navy, he promised that "on the first day of January 1863, all persons held as slaves within any state or designated part of a state, the people whereof shall then be in rebellion against the United States shall be then, thence forward, and forever free." Thus one of the great steps forward in human freedom in this nation, the Emancipation Proclamation, did not come about as a result of demands by the people, and certainly not a result of demands by the slaves themselves. It was a political and military action by the President for the sake of helping to preserve the Union. It was not a revolutionary action but a conservative one.

The Rise of the New Industrial Elite

The importance of the Civil War for America's elite structure was the commanding position that the new industrial capitalists won during the course of the struggle. Even before 1860, Northern industry had been altering the course of American life; the economic transformation of the United States from an agricultural to an industrial nation reached the crescendo of a revolution in the second half of the nineteenth century. Canals and steam railroads had been opening up new markets for the growing industrial cities of the East. The rise of corporations and of stock markets for the accumulation of capital upset old-fashioned ideas about property. The introduction of machinery in factories revolutionized the conditions of American labor and made the masses dependent upon industrial capitalists for their livelihood. Civil War profits compounded the capital of the industrialists and placed them in a position to dominate the economic life of the nation. Moreover, when the Southern planters were removed from the national scene, the government in Washington became the exclusive domain of the new industrial leaders.

The protective tariff, long opposed by the Southern planters, became the cornerstone of the new business structure of America. The industrial capitalists realized that the Northwest Territory was the natural market for their manufactured goods, and the protective tariff restricted the vast and growing American market to American industry alone. When the passage of the Homestead Act threw the national domain wide open to settlers, Eastern capital hastened to build a system of transcontinental railroads to link expanding Western markets to Eastern industry. Northeast America was rich in the natural resources of coal, iron, and water power; and the large immigrant population streaming in from Europe furnished a dependable source of cheap labor. The Northeast also had superior means of transportation—both water and rail—to facilitate the assembling of raw materials and the marketing of finished products. With the rise of the new industrial capitalism, power in America flowed from the South and West to the Northeast and Jefferson's dream of a nation of free farmers faded.

The new industrial elite found a new philosophy to justify its political and economic dominance. Drawing an analogy from the new Darwinian biology, Herbert Spencer undertook to demonstrate that just as an elite was selected in nature through evolution, so also society would near perfection as it allowed natural social elites to be selected by free competition. In defense of the new capitalists, Herbert Spencer argued: "There cannot be more good done than that of letting social progress go on unhindered; an immensity of mischief may be done in . . . the artificial preservation of those least able to care for themselves."[15] Spencer hailed the accumulation of new industrial wealth as a sign of "the survival of the fittest." The "social Darwinists" found in the law of survival of the fittest an admirable defense for the emergence of a ruthless ruling elite, an elite which defined its own self-interest more narrowly, perhaps, than any other in American history. It was a philosophy that permitted the conditions of the masses to decline to the lowest depths in American history.

Spencer's social Darwinism forbade restrictive "meddling" legislation. If trusts and monopolies proved to be the natural results of competition, worshippers of competition could not logically prohibit them. Yet, ironically, the industrial elites saw no objection to legislation if it furthered their success in business. Unrestricted competition might prove who was the "fittest"; but as an added precaution to insure that industrial capitalists themselves emerged as the "fittest," these new elites also insisted upon government subsidies, patents, tariffs, loans, and massive giveaways of land and other natural resources.

Railroads were at the heart of the early industrial expansion in America. The excitement over the completion of the first transcontinental railroad in 1869 was accentuated by the fact that railroad progress was general throughout the United States. The expansion of the railroads created new members of elites: Leland Stanford of the Union Pacific, Commodore Vanderbilt of New York Central, Jay Gould of the Erie, Henry Villard of the Northern Pacific, and James J. Hill of the Great Northern. So ruthless were these men in exploiting their customers, the Western farmers, that an organization called the Patrons of Husbandry, or the Grange, emerged to battle with the railroads. The Grangers actually succeeded in winning control of some Western state legislatures, including Illinois, and in passing some state legislation regulating railroad practices. But these Granger Laws, the railroad attorneys claimed, were unconstitutional "impairments of contracts" and took private property without "due process of law."

In 1877, the Supreme Court, which still reflected pre-Civil War landed interests, ruled against the railroads in *Munn* v. *Illinois*. The Court asserted the "right of a state to regulate a business that is public in nature though privately owned and managed."[16] However, *Munn* v. *Illinois* was soon relegated to an obscure position in court policy when the makeup of the court finally caught up with the industrial revolution. In the 1880s, Justice Stephen A. Field gave a new interpretation to the Fourteenth Amendment. Business corporations were "persons" under the Fourteenth Amendment, and no "corporate person" could be deprived of property by a state without "due process of law."[17] Since legislative regulation of railroad rates or other business decisions might reduce a corporation's profits, such regulations were unconstitutional under the Fourteenth Amendment, Field held. The Court soon became a bulwark against the occasional attempts by states to challenge industrial dominance. In a dissenting opinion in 1905, Justice Oliver Wendell Holmes said that "the Fourteenth Amendment does not enact Mr. Herbert Spencer's *Social Statics*."[18] But Holmes' observation was a *dissenting* opinion; the majority of the Court helped to sustain the capitalist impulse by using the "due process clause" of the Fourteenth Amendment to halt all challenges of industrial dominance.

After the Civil War, businessmen became more numerous in Congress than at any other time in American history. They had little trouble in voting high tariffs and hard money, both of which heightened profits. Very little effective regulatory legislation was permitted to reach the floor of Congress. After 1881 the Senate came under the spell of Nelson Aldrich, son-in-law of John D. Rockefeller, who controlled Standard Oil. Aldrich served 30 years in the Senate. He believed that geographical representation in the Senate was old-fashioned and openly advocated a Senate manned officially by representatives from the great business "constituencies"—steel, coal, copper, railroads, banks, textiles, and so on.

As business became increasingly national in scope, only the strongest or most unscrupulous of the competitors survived. Great producers tended to become the cheapest producers, and little companies tended to disappear. Industrial production rose rapidly, while the number of industrial concerns steadily diminished. Total capital investment and total output of industry vastly increased, while ownership became concentrated. One result was the emergence of monopolies and near monopolies in each of the major industries of America. Another result was the accumulation of great family fortunes.[19] (See Table 3–3, which was compiled from 1924 tax returns and admittedly fails to record other great personal fortunes, such as Armour and Swift in meat packing, Candler in Coca-Cola, Cannon in textiles, Fleischman in yeast, Pulitzer in publishing, Golet in real estate, Harriman in railroads, Heinz in foods, Manville in asbestos, Cudahy in meat packing, Dorrance in Campbell's Soup, Hartford in A & P, Eastman in film, Firestone in rubber, Sinclair in oil, Chrysler in automobiles, Pabst in beer, and others.)

Typical of the great entrepreneurs of industrial capitalism was John D. Rockefeller. By the end of the Civil War, Rockefeller had accumulated a modest fortune of $50,000 in wholesale grain and meat. In 1865, with extraordinary good judgment, he invested his money in the wholly new petroleum business. He backed one of the first oil refineries in the nation and continually reinvested his profits into his business. In 1867, backed by two new partners—H. M. Flagler and F. W. Harkness—Rockefeller founded the Standard Oil Company of Ohio, which in that year refined 4 percent of the nation's output. By 1872, with monopoly as his goal, he had acquired 20 of the 25 refineries in Cleveland and was laying plans that within a decade would bring him into control of over 90 percent of the oil refineries of the country. Rockefeller bought up pipelines, warehouses, and factories and was able to force railroads to grant him rebates. In 1882, he formed a giant trust, the Standard Oil Company, with a multitude of affiliates. Thereafter, the Standard Oil Company became a prototype of American monopolies. As Rockefeller himself put it: "The day of combination is here to stay. Individualism has gone, never to return."

Perhaps the greatest American success story is that of Andrew Carnegie, a Scottish immigrant boy who came penniless to America. He worked first as a bobbin boy for $1.25 a week in a western Pennsylvania cotton factory, then as a messenger at $2.50 a week in a Pittsburgh telegraph office. Quite soon, he became the private secretary of Thomas

A. Scott of the Pennsylvania Railroad and began to amass railway and oil stocks. Then, on a trip to England, he saw steel being made by the new Bessemer process, and he returned to the United States determined to begin manufacturing steel. In Pittsburgh, in 1873, he opened the J. Edgar Thompson Steel Mill, carefully named after the president of the Pennsylvania Railroad. Carnegie soon monopolized the steel industry in Pittsburgh and much of the nation, and steel replaced railroads as the backbone of the new industrialism. In 1901, Carnegie Steel plus three other steel giants—the Tennessee Coal and Iron Company, the Illinois Steel Company, and the Colorado Fuel and Iron Company—arranged one of the nation's most colossal business mergers, creating the United States Steel Corporation. Unlike his fellow capitalists Carnegie believed that "The amassing of wealth is one of the worst species of idolatry" and he gave away over $350,000,000. Most of his philanthropy went to public libraries in cities throughout the nation.

At the apex of America's new corporate and industrial elite stood J. Pierpont Morgan, master of industrial finance. Morgan knit together the U.S. Steel Corporation, America's first billion dollar corporation, and later established International Harvester Corporation. During World War I, J. P. Morgan and Company was the purchasing agent in America for the Allies at a commission of 1 percent. J. P. Morgan himself was not the wealthiest of America's wealthy men, but the Morgan firm derived its unprecedented power from the combined resources of many families and corporations in which it had an interest. The extent of Morgan power in American industry and finance defies statistical measurement. Direct Morgan *control* of banking and non-banking corporations often shades into Morgan *dominance,* and Morgan dominance often shades into Morgan *influence.* Morgan partners or executives were found in dominant positions on the boards of American Telephone and Telegraph Company, U.S. Steel Corporation, General Electric Company, Consolidated Edison Company, United Gas Improvement Company, American & Foreign Power Company, Electric Bond and Share Company, Niagara Hudson Power Corporation, Montgomery Ward and Company, International Telephone and Telegraph Corporation, American Can Company, Kennecott Copper Corporation, Chesapeake and Ohio Railroad, New York Central Railroad, General Motors Corporation, E. I. du Pont de Nemours and Company, and many others. The Morgan firm exercised dominance over the Guarantee Trust Company of New York, the Banker's Trust Company, the First National Bank of New York, and the New York Trust Company. The combined Morgan commercial banks outweighed all other banking interests in total assets, deposits, and re-

Table 3-3 / The Industrial Fortunes, 1924

Family and Number of Tax Returns	Primary Source of Wealth	Aggregate 1924 Tax	Approximate Net Aggregate Income Taxed	Net Aggregate Fortune Taxed	Gross Adjusted Fortune after Multiplying by 3	Maximum Estimated Fortune
1. 21 Rockefellers	Standard Oil	$7,309,989	$17,955,000	$359,100,000	$1,077,300,000	$2,500,000,000
2. 34 Morgan Inner Group	J. P. Morgan & Co.	4,796,263	12,620,000	276,000,000‡	728,000,000‡	
(Including Morgan partners and families and eight leading Morgan corporation executives)						
3. 2 Fords	Ford Motor Co.	4,766,863	11,000,000	220,000,000	660,000,000	1,000,000,000
4. 5 Harknesses	Standard Oil	2,776,735	7,550,000	150,200,000	450,600,000	800,000,000
5. 3 Mellons	Aluminum Company	3,237,876	7,550,000	150,000,000	450,000,000	1,000,000,000
6. 22 Vanderbilts	N.Y. Central R.R.	2,148,892	6,005,000	120,100,000	360,300,000	800,000,000
7. 4 Whitneys	Standard Oil	2,143,992	5,375,000	107,500,000	322,000,000	750,000,000
8. 28 Standard Oil Group	Standard Oil	1,737,857	5,435,000	118,700,000	356,000,000	
(Including Archbolds, Rogerses, Bedfords, Cutlers, Flaglers, Pratts, and Benjamins, but excepting others)						
9. 20 Du Ponts	E. I. du Pont de Nemours	1,294,651	3,925,000	79,500,000	238,500,000	1,000,000,000
10. 8 McCormicks	Int. Harvester and Chi. Tribune	1,332,517	3,500,000	70,400,000	211,200,000	
11. 2 Bakers	1st National Bank	1,575,482	3,500,000	70,000,000	210,000,000	500,000,000
12. 5 Fishers	General Motors	1,424,583	3,225,000	64,500,000	193,500,000	500,000,000
13. 6 Guggenheims	Amer. Smelting & Rfg. Co.	817,836	2,185,000	63,700,000	190,100,000	
14. 6 Fields	Marshall Field & Co.	1,197,605	3,000,000	60,000,000	180,000,000	
15. 5 Curtis-Boks	Curtis Pub. Co.	1,303,228	2,900,000	58,000,000	174,000,000	
16. 3 Dukes	Am. Tobacco Co.	1,045,544	2,600,000	52,000,000	156,000,000	
17. 3 Berwinds	Berwind-White Coal Co.	906,495	2,500,000	50,000,000	150,000,000	
18. 17 Lehmans	Lehman Brothers	672,897	2,150,000	43,000,000	129,000,000‡	
19. 3 Wideners	Am. Tob. & Pub. Utilities	772,720	1,975,000	39,500,000	118,500,000	
20. 7 Reynolds	R. J. Reynolds Tobacco Co.	652,824	1,950,000	39,000,000	117,000,000	
21. 3 Astors	Real Estate	783,002	1,900,000	38,000,000	114,000,000	300,000,000
22. 6 Winthrops	Miscellaneous	651,188	1,735,000	34,700,000	104,100,000	
23. 3 Stillmans	National City Bank	623,614	1,700,000	34,000,000	102,000,000	500,000,000
24. 3 Timkens	Timken Roller Bearing Co.	781,435	1,850,000	37,000,000	111,000,000	
25. 4 Pitcairns	Pittsburgh Plate Glass Co.	752,545	1,660,000	33,200,000	99,600,000	
26. 8 Warburgs	Kuhn, Loeb & Co.	598,246	1,620,000	32,400,000	97,200,000‡	
27. 4 Metcalfs	Rhode Island textile mills	623,817	1,510,000	30,200,000	90,600,000	
28. 3 Clarks	Singer Sewing Mach. Co.	583,087	1,475,000	30,000,000	90,000,000	
29. 16 Phipps	Carnegie Steel Co.	431,969	1,485,000	29,700,000	89,100,000	600,000,000

No.	Name	Business					
30.	4 Kahns	Kuhn, Loeb & Co.	565,608	1,440,000	28,800,000	86,400,000‡	
31.	2 Greens	Stocks and real estate	443,021	1,200,000	24,000,000	72,000,000	
32.	2 Pattersons	Chicago Tribune, Inc.	365,211	1,015,000	20,300,000	60,900,000	
33.	3 Tafts	Real Estate	329,689	900,000	18,000,000	54,000,000	
34.	3 Deerings	International Harvester	315,701	825,000	16,500,000	49,500,000	
35.	3 De Forests	Corp. law practice	202,013	685,000	13,700,000	41,100,000‡	400,000,000
36.	6 Goulds	Railroads	154,563	565,000	11,300,000	33,900,000	150,000,000
37.	5 Hills	Railroads	226,827	360,000	7,000,000	21,600,000	100,000,000
38.	2 Drexels	J. P. Morgan & Co.	131,616	350,000	7,000,000	21,000,000	
39.	Thomas Fortune Ryan*†	Stock market	791,851	1,800,000	36,000,000	108,000,000	
40.	H. Foster (Cleveland)	Auto Parts	569,894	1,700,000	34,000,000	106,000,000	
41.	Eldridge Johnson	Victor Phonograph	542,627	1,250,000	25,000,000	75,000,000	
42.	Arthur Curtiss James	Copper and railroads	521,388	1,200,000	24,000,000	72,000,000	
43.	C. W. Nash	Automobiles	459,776	1,100,000	22,000,000	66,000,000	
44.	Mortimer Schiff	Kuhn, Loeb & Co.	459,410	1,100,000	22,000,000	66,000,000	
45.	James A. Patten	Wheat market	425,348	1,000,000	20,000,000	60,000,000‡	
46.	Charles Hayden*	Stock market	427,979	1,000,000	20,000,000	60,000,000	
47.	Orlando F. Weber	Allied Chemical & Dye Corp.	406,582	900,000	18,000,000	54,000,000	
48.	George Blumenthal	Lazard Frères	415,621	900,000	18,000,000	54,000,000‡	
49.	Ogden L. Mills	Mining	372,827	800,000	16,000,000	48,000,000	
50.	Michael Friedsam*†	Merchandising	292,396	700,000	14,000,000	42,000,000	
51.	Edward B. McLean	Mining	281,125	700,000	14,000,000	42,000,000	
52.	Eugene Higgins	New York real estate	279,265	700,000	14,000,000	42,000,000	
53.	Alexander S. Cochran*†	Textiles	271,542	700,000	14,000,000	42,000,000	
54.	Mrs. L. N. Kirkwood		268,556	625,000	12,500,000	37,500,000	
55.	Helen Tyson		258,086	600,000	12,000,000	36,000,000	
56.	Archer D. Huntington*†	Railroads	226,353	575,000	11,500,000	34,500,000	
57.	James J. Storrow*†	Lee Higginson & Co.	222,571	575,000	11,500,000	34,500,000‡	
58.	Julius Rosenwald*†	Sears, Roebuck & Co.	208,812	500,000	10,000,000	30,000,000	
59.	Bernard M. Baruch	Stock market	268,142	625,000	12,500,000	37,500,000	
60.	S. S. Kresge	Merchandising	188,608	500,000	10,000,000	30,000,000	

*Deceased.

†Fortune left to family.

‡Partly theoretical as income consisted in varying measure of fees.

Source: Ferdinand Lundberg, America's Sixty Families (New York: Citadel Press, 1937).

sources. As late as 1932, it was estimated that the Morgan interests, with their varying degrees of control, dominance, and influence, totaled more than one quarter of all American corporate wealth. The boards of directors of most of these banks and corporations reveal the same names again and again and point up the close interlocking community of interest among America's industrial elite.

The American Telephone and Telegraph Company is an excellent example of the interlocking nature of America's industrial, corporate, and banking elites. This company has a virtual monopoly on telephone and telegraph communications in America. This monopoly was in part a product of government patent laws, which protected Alexander Graham Bell's invention of the telephone in 1876. On the other hand, while the A. T. & T. advertises that no individual owns as much as 1 percent of its stock, actual working control of the corporation resides in a small and elite board of directors. In the mid-1930s, this board was composed as follows:

The Morgan men on the A. T. & T. board are George F. Baker, president of the First National Bank of New York; Samuel A. Walldon, vice-president of the First National Bank of New York; John W. Davis (Democratic presidential candidate in 1924), chief council for J. P. Morgan and Co.; and Myron C. Taylor, chairman of the finance committee of the U.S. Steel Corp. The Rockefellers are represented by Winthrop Aldrich (brother of Senator Nelson Aldrich), chairman of the Chase National Bank. A Boston group, closely identified with J. P. Morgan and Co., is represented by Charles Francis Adams (of the famous Adams family), director of the Union Trust Co. of Boston and numerous corporations and former Secretary of the Navy and father-in-law of Henry Sturgis Morgan, J. P. Morgan's son; W. Cameron Forbes, of J. M. Forbes and Co., a Boston enterprise, and former governor-general of the Philippines; George P. Gardner, director of the Morgan controlled General Electric Co.; Thomas Nelson Perkins, lawyer; Philip Stockton, director of the First National Bank of Boston. Presidents of three railroads dependent upon J. P. Morgan Co. for financing, two insurance company heads, and James F. Bell of General Mills, Inc., fill out the board, along with three A. T. & T. executives, who have little to say outside the technical field. [20]

In the 1930s, the assets of A. T. & T. exceeded the total wealth of 21 states in the United States and were greater than the assets of 8,000 average-sized corporations.

The Political Dominance of the Industrial Elite

The condition of the masses during the age of great industrial expansion was perhaps the lowest in American history. At the turn of the century, American workers earned, on the average, between $400 and $500 a year (or only $1,500 a year by today's standards). Unemployment was frequent, and there were no unemployment benefits. A working day of ten hours, six days a week, was taken for granted. Accidents among industrial employees were numerous and lightly regarded by employers. The presence of women and children in industry tended to hold down wages but was an absolute necessity for many families. Child labor was ruthlessly exploited in the cotton mills of the South, in the sweat shops of the East, and in the packing plants of the West.

By 1900, almost 40 percent of the population lived in urban areas, in which the living conditions for the masses varied from bad to unspeakable. Very few owned their own homes; from 80 percent to 90 percent rented the space in which they lived.

Both the Republican and Democratic parties reflected the dominance of the industrial elites. Richard Hofstadter comments on the influence that the industrial capitalists exercised over the party system in America:

The Republicans were distinguished from the Democrats chiefly by being successful. From the war and Reconstruction onwards, when it sought actively to strengthen its social base by espousing policies of American industrialists, the Republican party existed in an unholy and often mutually hostile conjunction with the capitalistic interests. Capitalists, seeking land grants, tariffs, bounties, favorable currency policies, freedom from regulatory legislation, and economic reform, supplied campaign funds, fees, and bribes, and plied politicans with investment opportunities. Seward had said that "a party is in one sense a joint stock company in which those who contribute the most direct the action and management of the concern."[21]

V. O. Key also describes the Republican Party machine of the 1870s and 1880s:

The inner strength of Republicanism did not rest on sentiment alone. Sentiment clothed the bonds of substance. To the old soldiers—old Union soldiers—went pensions. To manufacturers of the Northeast went tariffs. To the farmers of the Northwest went free land under the Homestead Act. To railroad promoters went land grants for the construction of railroads that tied together the West and the North—and assured that the flow of commerce would bypass the South. The synthesis of self-interest and glory formed a cohesive combination. The G. O. P. represented a wonderfully effective contrivance, not only for preserving the Union but for holding together East and West, for the magnate and factory worker, homesteader and banker, and the great enterprise of continental unification, development, and exploitation.[22]

The Democratic Party under Grover Cleveland was little different from the Republican Party. Perhaps the single exception was that Cleveland called upon businessmen to improve their morals and become trustees of the public interest. Nevertheless, Cleveland used federal troops to break the Pullman strike in 1894 and to help keep down the urban working class. He supported the gold standard and alienated the debt-ridden farmers of the West. He hedged on the tariff question, refusing to adopt the traditional position of landed interests on behalf of low tariffs. He even negotiated a much-publicized gold purchase loan from J. P. Morgan. Hofstadter remarks: "Out of heartfelt conviction he gave to the interests what many a lesser politician might have sold them for a price."[23]

The only serious challenge to the political dominance of Eastern capital came over the issue of "free silver." Leadership of the "free silver" movement came from mine owners in the silver states of the Far West. Their campaigns convinced thousands of Western farmers that free silver was the answer to their economic distress. The Western mine owners did not care about the welfare of small farmers, but the prospect of inflation, debt relief, and expansion of the supply of money and purchasing power won increasing support among the masses in the West and South.

When William Jennings Bryan delivered his famous "Cross of Gold" speech at the Democratic Convention in 1896, he swept the Cleveland "Gold Democrats" out of control of the Democratic Party. Bryan was a Westerner, a talented orator, an anti-intellectual, and a deeply religious man; he was antagonistic to the Eastern industrial interests and totally committed to the cause of free silver. Bryan tried to rally the nation's have-nots to his banner; he tried to convince them they were being exploited by Wall Street finance. Yet it is important to note that he did not severely criticize the capitalist system, nor did he call for increases in the regulatory powers of the federal government. In his acceptance speech he declared, "our campaign has not for its object the reconstruction of society. . . . Property is and will remain the stimulus to endeavor and the compensation for toil."[24] He was uninterested in labor legislation; his only issue was free silver.

The Republican campaign, directed by Marcus Alonzo Hanna of Standard Oil, was aimed at persuading the voters that what was good for business was good for the country. Hanna raised an unprecedented $16,000,000 campaign fund from his wealthy fellow industrialists (an amount that would not be matched in presidential campaigns until the 1960s) and advertised his candidate, William McKinley, as the man who would bring a "full dinner pail" to all. The heavy expenditures of the Republicans suggests that Bryan was considered capable of rallying the masses. Republican machines were mobilized across the nation. As the end of the campaign drew near, threats were cast about freely. Working men were told that the election of McKinley would mean high wages and prosperity, whereas the election of Bryan would bring the loss of their jobs. Some employers bluntly told their employees that if Bryan were elected they could not come back to work. Farmers were told that a Democratic victory might mean their mortgages would not be renewed.

Bryan's attempt to rally the masses was a dismal failure; McKinley won by a landslide. Bryan would run twice again under the Democratic banner, in 1900 and 1908, but he would lose by even greater margins. Although Bryan carried the South and some Western states, he failed to rally the masses of the populous Eastern states or the people of America's growing cities. Republicans carried working-class, middle-class, and upper-class neighborhoods in the urban industrial states. As V. O. Key explains:

While the election of 1896 is often pictured as a lasting fight between the haves and have-nots, that understanding of the contest was evidently restricted to the plains of leadership and oratory. It did not extend to the voting actions of the electorate. . . . In 1896 the industrial cities, in their aggregate vote at least, moved toward the Republicans in about the same degree as did the rural farming communities . . . the Republicans gained in the working class wards, just as they did in the silk stocking wards, over their 1892 vote. . . . Instead of a sharpening of class cleavages within New England, the voting apparently reflected a more sectional antagonism and anxiety, shared by all classes, expressed in opposition to the dangers supposed to be threatening the West.[25]

The Liberal Establishment: Reform as Elite Self-interest

In 1882, William H. Vanderbilt of the New York Central Railroad expressed the ethos of the industrial elite in his famous declaration, "The public be damned." There was little sense of public responsibility among America's first generation of great capitalists. They had built their empires in the competitive pursuit of profit. They believed that their success could be attributed to the immutable laws of natural selection, the survival of the fittest; and they believed that society was best served by allowing these laws to operate freely. In 1910, Woodrow Wilson, forerunner of a new elite ethos, criticized America's elite for its lack of public responsibility. At a widely publicized lecture to a meeting of bankers, with J. P. Morgan sitting at his side, Wilson declared:

The trouble today is that you bankers are too narrow-minded. You don't know the country or what is going on in it and the country doesn't trust you. . . . You take no interest in the small borrower and the small enterprise which affect the future of the country, but you give every attention to the big borrower and the rich enterprise which has already arrived. . . . You bankers see nothing beyond your own interests. . . . You should be broader-minded and see what is best for the country in the long run. [26]

Wilson urged America's elite to reject a narrowly self-interested view of things and to take the welfare of others, especially that of "the community," into account as an aspect of their own long-run welfare. Wilson did not wish to upset the established order; he merely wished to develop a sense of public responsibility within the establishment. He believed that the national government should see that industrial elites operated in the public interest, and his New Freedom program reflected these high-minded aspirations. In the Federal Reserve Act, the nation's banking and credit system was placed under public control. The Clayton Antitrust Act attempted to define specific business abuses, such as charging different prices to different buyers, granting rebates, or making false statements about competitors in order to take business away from them. A Federal Trade Commission was established and authorized to function in the "public interest" to prevent "unfair methods of competition and unfair and deceptive acts in commerce." An eight-hour day was established for railroad workers in interstate commerce; and the Child Labor Act attempted to eliminate the worst abuses of children in industry (this act was declared unconstitutional, however, by a much less public-regarding Supreme Court). Wilson's program aimed to preserve competition, individualism, enterprise, opportunity—all things that were considered vital in the American heritage. But he also believed fervently that elites must function in the public interest and that some government regulation might be required to see that they do so.

Wilson's New Freedom was forgotten during America's participation in World War I, and its gains were largely wiped out by the postwar reaction to reform. During the 1920s, America's elite rejected Wilsonian idealism. The established order clung to the philosophy of rugged individualism and rejected Wilson's appeal to a higher public interest.

Herbert Hoover was the last great advocate of the rugged individualism of the old order. The economic collapse of the Great Depression undermined the faith of both elites and non-elites in the ideals of the old order. Following the stock market crash of October 1929, and in spite of elite assurances that prosperity lay "just around the corner," the American economy virtually stopped. Prices dropped sharply, factories closed, real estate values declined, new construction practically ceased, banks went under, wages were cut drastically, and unemployment figures mounted. By 1932, one of every four persons was unemployed, and one of every five persons was listed on welfare roles. Persons who had never known unemployment before lost their jobs, used up their savings or lost them when banks folded, cashed in their life insurance, gave up their homes and farms because they could not continue the mortgage payments. Economic catastrophe struck far up into the ranks of the middle classes. Once a man lost a job, he could not find another. Tramps abounded, panhandlers plied the streets, transients slept on the steps of public buildings, on park benches, on lawns, or on highways. Mines were no longer worked; steel mills, iron foundries, and every variety of industrial plant put out only a fraction of the goods that they could produce; trains ran with only a handful of passengers; stores lacked customers, and many closed their doors; ships stayed in port; hospitals were empty, not because they were unneeded but because people could not afford them.

The election of Franklin Delano Roosevelt to the Presidency in 1932 ushered in a new era in American elite philosophy. The Great Depression did not bring about a revolution; it did not result in the emergence of new elites; but it did have important impact on the thinking of America's governing elites. The economic disaster that had befallen the nation caused American elites to consider the need for economic reform. The Great Depression also gave force to Wilson's advice that elites acquire a greater public responsibility. The victories of fascism in Germany and communism in the Soviet Union and the growing restlessness of the masses in America combined to convince America's elite that reform and regard for the public welfare were essential to the continued maintenance of the American political system and their dominant place in it. In December 1933, John M. Keynes wrote an open letter to Roosevelt, emphasizing the importance of saving the capitalist system:

You have made yourself the trustee for those in every country who seek to mend the evils of our conditions by reasoned experiment within the framework of the existing social system. If you fail, rational change will be gravely prejudiced throughout the world, leaving orthodoxy and revolution to fight it out.[27]

And Roosevelt himself was aware of the necessity of saving capitalism from itself:

As I see it, the task of government in its relation to business is to assist the development of an economic declaration of rights, an economic constitutional order. . . . Happily, the times indicate that to create such an order not only is the proper policy of government, but it is the only line of safety for our economic structures as well.[28]

Roosevelt sought to elaborate a New Deal philosophy that would permit government to devote much more attention to the public welfare than did the philosophy of Hoover's somewhat discredited "rugged indi-vidualism." The New Deal was not a new or revolutionary system but rather a necessary reform of the existing capitalist system. There was no consistent unifying plan to the New Deal; it was a series of improvisa-tions, many of them adopted very suddenly and some of them even contradictory. Roosevelt believed that more careful economic planning by government was required in order to adapt "existing economic organiza-tions to the service of the people." And he believed that the government must act humanely and compassionately toward those who were suffer-ing hardship. Relief, recovery, and reform, not revolution, were the objec-tives of the New Deal. Roosevelt called for "full, persistent experimenta-tion. If it fails, admit it frankly and try something else. But above all try something. The millions who are in want will not stand by silently forever while the things to satisfy their needs are within easy reach."[29]

For anyone of Roosevelt's background, it would have been surpris-ing indeed if he had tried to do other than preserve the existing social and economic order. Roosevelt was a descendant of two of America's oldest elite families, the Roosevelts and the Delanos, patrician families whose wealth predated the Civil War and the industrial revolution. The Roosevelts were not schooled in social Darwinism or the survival of the fittest or the scrambling competition of the new industrialists. From the beginning Roosevelt expressed a public-regarding philosophy. In Hofstadter's words:

At the beginning of his career he took to the patrician reform thought of the progressive era and accepted a social outlook that can best be summed up in the phrase "noblesse oblige." He had a penchant for public service, personal philan-thropy, and harmless manifestos against dishonesty in government; he displayed a broad easy-going tolerance, a genuine liking for all sorts of people; he loved to exercise his charm in political and social situations.[30]

Roosevelt's personal philosophy was soon to become the prevailing ethos of the new liberal establishment.

In his first administration, Roosevelt concentrated on relief (a Fed-eral Emergency Relief program, a Public Works Administration program, and a Works Project Administration) and on national economic planning through the National Recovery Administration (NRA). The NRA sought unsuccessfully to organize businessmen for the purposes of self-regulation in the public interest. The NRA failed, as did the Agricultural Adjustment Administration, which had tried to compensate farmers in various ways for reducing output. The National Labor Relations Act of 1935 was not a product of demands by the workers for government protection but rather a scheme for alleviating the depression by protecting unions, in the hopes that unions could raise wage rates and hence income levels in the nation. Established leaders of the American Federation of Labor actually opposed the measure at its time of passage. The Social Security Act of 1935 was designed to reduce the burdens of government welfare programs by compelling people to purchase insurance against the possibility of their own poverty. Later, the Housing Act of 1937 and the Fair Labor Standards Act continued the President's efforts to restore the health of capitalism.

In the New Deal, American elites accepted the principle that the entire community, through the agency of the national government, had a responsibility for mass welfare. In Roosevelt's second inaugural address he called attention to "one third of a nation, ill housed, ill clad, ill nourished." Roosevelt succeeded in saving the existing system of private capitalism and avoiding the threats to the established order of fascism, socialism, communism, and other radical movements.

Of course, some capitalists were unwilling to be "saved" by the New Deal. Roosevelt was genuinely hurt by criticisms from American industrialists, whom he felt he had protected with his reforms; he cried out in anger against the "economic royalists" who challenged his policies. He believed that the economic machinery of the nation had broken down and that the political fabric of America was beginning to disintegrate. He believed he had stabilized the economy and turned politics safely back to its normal democratic course. While he had engaged in some novel experiments (including the dangerous concept of public ownership, in TVA), he believed that for the most part he had avoided disturbing vital property interests. He rejected cries to nationalize America's banks during the bank crisis of 1933 and instead merely urged the American people to have greater confidence in their bankers. His basic policies in industry and agriculture had been designed by the large industrial and agricultural interests themselves. He believed that his relief and reform measures were mainly of the kind that any wise and humane conservative would admit to be necessary. He believed he had headed off the demagogues—Huey Long, Father Coughlin, and others—who had attempted to stir up the masses.

Eventually, Roosevelt's philosophy of noblesse oblige—elite responsibility for the welfare of the masses—won widespread acceptance within America's established leadership. The success of Roosevelt's liberal philosophy was in part a product of the economic disaster of the Great Depression and in part a tribute to the effectiveness of Roosevelt himself as a mobilizer of opinion among both elites and masses. But the acceptance of liberal establishment ideas may also be attributed in part to the changes that were occurring in the economic system.

One of these was a decline in the rate of new elite formation. Most of America's great entrepreneurial families had built their empires before World War I. The first-generation industrialists and entrepreneurs were unfriendly toward philosophies of public responsibility and appeals to "the public interest." But among the children and grandchildren of the great empire builders these ideals won increasing acceptance. Those who are born to wealth seem to accept the idea of noblesse oblige to a greater degree than those who had to acquire wealth for themselves, and available evidence indicates that there were more self-made men in 1900 than in 1950. Table 3–4 shows that only 39 percent of the richest men in

Table 3-4 / Social Origins of America's Richest Men, 1900–1950

Social Origin	1900	1925	1950
Upper class	39%	56%	68%
Middle class	20	30	20
Lower class	39	12	9
Not classified	2	2	3

Source: Adapted from C. Wright Wills, *The Power Elite* (New York: Oxford University Press, 1956), pp. 104–105. The percentages are derived from biographies of the 275 people who were and are known to historians, biographers, and journalists as the richest people living in the United States — the 90 richest of 1900, the 95 of 1925, and the 90 of 1950. At the top of the 1900 group is John D. Rockefeller; at the top in 1925 is Henry Ford I; at the top in 1950 is H. L. Hunt.

America in 1900 came from the upper classes, while 68 percent of the nation's richest men in 1950 were born to wealth. Thirty-nine percent of the richest men in 1900 had struggled up from the bottom, whereas only 9 percent of the richest men of 1950 had done so. This suggests that America's elite in the mid-twentieth century was more receptive to the ideas of responsibility for the common good and concern for the welfare of the masses. In other words, while Wilson's appeals for elite responsibility fell on the deaf ears of John D. Rockefeller in 1910, a sense of public responsibility would motivate the careers of John D. Rockefeller's grandsons—Nelson Rockefeller, Governor of New York; Winthrop Rockefeller, Governor of Arkansas; David Rockefeller, President of Chase Manhattan Bank of New York; and John D. Rockefeller III, Chairman of the Board of the Lincoln Center for Performing Arts in New York City.

Summary

According to elite theory, the movement of non-elites into elite positions must be slow and continuous to maintain stability and avoid revolution.

Furthermore, potential elite members must demonstrate their commitment to the basic elite consensus before being admitted to elite positions. Elite theory recognizes competition among elites, but contends that elites share a broad consensus about preserving the system essentially as it is. It views public policy changes as a response to elite redefinition of its own self-interest, rather than as a product of direct mass influence. Finally, elite theory views changes in public policy as incremental rather than revolutionary. All of these propositions can be supported with reference to America's political history:

1. America's elite membership evolved slowly with no serious break in the ideas or values of the American political and economic system. When the leadership of Hamilton and Adams—Federalists—was replaced by that of Jefferson, Monroe, and Madison—Republicans—the policies of American government changed very little, owing to the fundamental consensus among elite members.

2. As new sources of wealth were opened in an expanding economy, America's elite membership was opened to new groups and individuals who acquired wealth and property and who accepted the national consensus about private enterprise, limited government, and individualism. The West produced new elites, which were assimilated into America's governing circle. Public policies were modified, but not replaced. The Jacksonians wanted a more open elite system where men of new wealth could acquire influence, but they were no more in favor of "dangerous leveling" than the Founding Fathers.

3. The Civil War reduced the influence of the Southern planters in America's elite structure and paved the way for the rise of the new industrial capitalists. The Industrial Revolution produced a narrowly self-interested elite of industrial capitalists. Mass movements resulted —Populism and free silver—but they met with failure.

4. Although industrial elites were never ousted from power, they were prevailed upon to assume a more public-regarding attitude toward the welfare of the masses. Economic collapse undermined the faith of elites and non-elites and the rugged individualism of the nineteenth-century industrial elite. But even economic collapse did not bring revolution; it did not result in the emergence of new elites. Instead, the Great Depression, the victories of fascism in Germany and communism in the Soviet Union, and growing restlessness of the American masses combined to convince America's elites that a more public-regarding philosophy was essential to the maintenance of the American political system and their prominent place in it.

5. The new liberal establishment sought to preserve the existing social and economic order, not to overthrow it. Eventually, Franklin D. Roosevelt's philosophy of noblesse oblige—elite responsibility for the welfare of the masses—won widespread acceptance within America's established leadership. The change from isolationism to world-wide involvement of America's foreign policy was a product of this new redefinition of American elite responsibility.

6. Political conflict in America has centered on a narrow range of issues. Consensus rather than conflict has characterized America's elite history. Political rhetoric and campaign slogans should not obscure the fundamental consensus of

America's elites. Whatever the popular political label has been—"Federalist," "Democratic," "Whig," "Republican," "Progressive," "Conservative," or "Liberal"—America's leadership has been essentially conservative.

7. America's elites have been deeply divided on the nature of American society only once. This elite cleavage produced the Civil War—the nation's bloodiest conflict. The Civil War was a conflict between Southern elites—dependent on a plantation economy, slave labor, and free trade—and Northern industrial commercial elites—who prospered under free labor and protective tariffs. But before, during, and after the Civil War, Northern and Southern elites continued to strive for compromise in recognition of shared consensus on behalf of liberty and property.

8. Policy changes, even those seemingly as revolutionary as the New Deal, did not cause any serious break in the ideals and values of the American system. Nor did they result from demands by "the people." Instead policy changes, including the New Deal, occurred when events threatened the system; governing elites—acting on the basis of enlightened self-interest—instituted reforms to preserve the system. Even the reforms and welfare policies of the New Deal were designed to strengthen the existing social and economic fabric of society with a minimum of dislocation for elites.

References

[1]*McCulloch v. Maryland*, 4 Wheaton 316 (1819).

[2]See Richard Hofstadter, *The American Political Tradition* (New York: Alfred A. Knopf, 1948), pp. 18–44.

[3]Hofstadter, pp. 32–33.

[4]*Marbury v. Madison*, 1 Cranch 137 (1803).

[5]Hofstadter, *American Political Tradition*, pp. 36–37.

[6]Hofstadter, p. 38.

[7]Frederick Jackson Turner, "The West and American Ideals," in *The Frontier in American History* (New York: Holt, 1921).

[8]See Hofstadter, *American Political Tradition*, pp. 45–67.

[9]*Dred Scott v. Sanford*, 19 Howard 393 (1857).

[10]Robert A. Dahl, *Pluralist Democracy in the United States* (Chicago: Rand McNally, 1966).

[11]Hofstadter, *American Political Tradition*, p. 109.

[12]Hofstadter, p. 113.

[13]Hofstadter, p. 116.

[14]Hofstadter, pp. 132–133.

[15]Herbert Spencer, *Social Statics* (1851).

[16]*Munn v. Illinois*, 94 U.S. 113 (1877).

[17]*San Mateo County v. Southern Pacific Railroad Co.*, 116 U.S. 138 (1885).

[18]*Lochner v. New York*, 198 U.S. 45 (1905).

[19]See Gustavus Myers, *A History of the Great American Fortunes*, 3 vols. (Chicago: 1910).

[20]Ferdinand Lundberg, *America's Sixty Families* (New York: Citadel Press, 1937), pp. 43–44.

[21]Hofstadter, *American Political Tradition*, p. 170.

[22]V. O. Key, Jr., *Politics, Parties, and Pressure Groups* (New York: Thomas Y. Crowell Co., 1942), pp. 185–186.

[23]Hofstadter, *American Political Tradition*, p. 185.

[24]Hofstadter, p. 190.

[25]Key, *Politics, Parties, and Pressure Groups*, pp. 189–191.

[26]Hofstadter, *American Political Tradition*, p. 251.

[27]Hofstadter, p. 332 (emphasis added).

[28]Hofstadter, p. 330.

[29]Hofstadter, p. 316.

[30]Hofstadter, pp. 323–324.

Selected Additional Readings

Hofstadter, Richard. *The American Political Tradition*. New York: Random House—Vintage Books edition, 1948. This book is an important political history from an elite perspective. Hofstadter deals with the development of American political elites and their philosophies from Jefferson and the Founding Fathers through Jackson, Bryan, Wilson, and Franklin Roosevelt. He emphasizes the fact that at every stage of American history, elites have been in considerable agreement over major issues (with the possible exception of the Civil War). Finally, Hofstadter discusses the elite practice of incrementalism—i.e., that elite leaders have always moved to preserve the established order with as little change in the system as possible.

Lundberg, Ferdinand. *America's Sixty Families*. New York: Citadel Press, 1937. This is a classic work on elites which systematically traces the development of the entrepreneurial elite of the late nineteenth and early twentieth centuries.

CHAPTER 4

MEN AT THE TOP:

POSITIONS OF POWER IN AMERICA

Power in America is organized into large institutions—corporate, governmental, educational, military, religious, professional, occupational. Positions at the top of the major institutions in American society are sources of great power. Not all power, it is true, is anchored in and exercised through institutions. And the potential for power lodged in giant institutions is not always exercised by the leadership. But institutional positions provide a continuous and important base of power. Sociologist C. Wright Mills describes the relationship between institutional authority and power as follows:

If we took the one hundred most powerful men in America, the one hundred wealthiest, and the one hundred most celebrated away from the institutional positions they now occupy, away from their resources of men and women and money, away from the media of mass communication that are now focused upon them—then they would be powerless and poor and uncelebrated. For power is not of a man. Wealth does not center in the person of the wealthy. Celebrity is not inherent in any personality. To be celebrated, to be wealthy, to have power, requires access to major institutions, for the institutional positions men occupy determine in large part their chances to have and to hold these valued experiences.[1]

103

In this chapter we shall describe the men who occupy high positions in the major private and governmental institutions of American society. We include high positions in the major *private* institutions—in industry, finance, law, and other "non-governmental institutions"—because we believe that these institutions allocate values for our society and shape the lives of all Americans. Our definition of an elite member is anyone who participates in decisions that allocate values for society, not just those who participate in decision making as part of the government.[2] The decisions of steel companies to raise prices, of defense industries to develop new weapons, of banks to raise or lower interest rates, of electrical companies to market new products, of the mass media to determine what is "news," and of educational institutions to decide what shall be taught—all affect the lives of Americans as much as do governmental decisions. Moreover, these private institutions have the power and resources to enforce their decisions.

The men at the top of institutional structures need not overtly exercise their power. Decisions may reflect the values of the persons in high institutional positions, even if these persons do not directly participate in the decisions, because the subordinates who carry on the day-to-day business of industry, finance, government, and so on, know the values of the top elite and understand the great potential for power that the top elite possesses. These subordinates were selected for their jobs in part because they reflected dominant values in their thinking and actions. Whether consciously or unconsciously, their decisions reflect the values of the men at the top.

It should be noted also that high positions in industry, finance, government, education, and the military, as well as great wealth, do not necessarily *guarantee* great power. Persons who occupy high formal positions in the institutions of society may have great potential for power and yet be restrained in the actual *exercise* of power.

The institutional structure of society exercises power when it limits the scope of public decision making to issues that are relatively harmless to the elite. Institutions facilitate the achievement of some values while they obstruct the achievement of other values. For example, we already know that the American governmental system was deliberately constructed to suppress certain values and issues. James Madison, in *The Federalist* No. 10, defended the structure of the new American government, particularly its republican and federal features, on the grounds that it would suppress "factious issues." And Madison named outright the factious issues which must be avoided: "a rage for paper money, for an abolition of debts, for an equal division of property, or any other improper or wicked project. . . ."[2] It is interesting that all of the issues that Madison wished to avoid involved challenges to the dominant economic interests. To select a non-governmental example: By placing owners of large blocks of company stock on governing boards of directors and by increasingly allocating large blocks of stock to top management personnel, the American business corporation tends to encourage the values of profit and investment security in corporate decision making. The structure of the American corporation deters it from pursuing a policy of public welfare at the expense of profit.

The fact that institutional structures maximize certain values (private enterprise, limited government, the profit system) while obstructing other values (absolute equality or "leveling," government ownership of industry) is an important aspect of American politics, one which was recognized even by our Founding Fathers. It is another reason for examining the major institutions of society and the men who occupy high positions in them.

The Governing Elites

Top governmental executives—Cabinet members, presidential advisors, department officers, special ambassadors—are frequently men who have occupied key posts in private industry, finance, or law, or who have sat in influential positions in education, in the arts and sciences, or in social, civic, and charitable associations. These men move easily in and out of government posts from their positions in the corporate, financial, legal, and educational world. They often assume government jobs at a financial sacrifice, and many do so out of a sense of public service.

Obviously, there is some overlapping of top leadership in America, but it is difficult to measure precisely *how much*. The plural elite model of power (described in Chapter 1) suggests that there is very little overlap, that *different* groups of individuals exercise power in different sectors of American life. In contrast, the single elite model of power envisions extensive overlap, with a single group of men exercising power in many different sectors of American life. In order to understand position overlap among American elites, let us examine the career backgrounds of several key governmental executives in recent presidential administrations.[3]

Neil H. McElroy: *Secretary of Defense, 1957–1959; former president and member of the board of directors of Procter and Gamble Co.; member of the board of directors of General Electric Company, of Chrysler Corporation, and of Equitable Life Insurance Company; member of the board of trustees of Harvard University, of the National Safety Council, and of the National Industrial Conference.*

Charles E. Wilson: Secretary of Defense, 1953–1957; president and member of the board of directors of General Motors Corporation.

Thomas S. Gates: Secretary of Defense, 1959–1960, and Secretary of the Navy, 1957–1959; Chairman of the Board and Chief Executive Officer, Morgan Guaranty Trust Co. (J. P. Morgan, New York); member of the board of directors of General Electric Corp., Bethlehem Steel Corp., Scott Paper Co., Campbell Soup Co., Insurance Co. of North America, Cities Service Co., Smith, Kline and French (pharmaceuticals), and the University of Pennsylvania.

Robert S. McNamara: Secretary of Defense, 1961–1967; president and member of the board of directors of the Ford Motor Company; member of the board of directors of Scott Paper Company; president of the World Bank, 1967 to date.

John Foster Dulles: Secretary of State, 1953–1960; partner of Sullivan and Cromwell (one of twenty largest law firms on Wall Street); member of the board of directors of the Bank of New York, of the Fifth Avenue Bank, of the American Bank Note Company, of the International Nickel Company of Canada, of Babcock and Wilson Corporation, of Gold Dust Corporation, of the Overseas Security Corporation, of Shenandoah Corporation, of United Cigar Stores, of American Cotton Oil Company, of United Railroad of St. Louis, and of European Textile Corporation. He was a trustee of the New York Public Library, of the Union Theological Seminary, of the Rockefeller Foundation, and of the Carnegie Endowment for International Peace; a delegate to the World Council of Churches.

Dean Rusk: Secretary of State, 1961–1968; former president of Rockefeller Foundation.

George M. Humphrey: Secretary of the Treasury, 1953–1957; former chairman of the board of directors of the M. A. Hanna Company; member of the board of directors of the National Steel Corporation, of Consolidated Coal Company, of Canada and Dominion Sugar Company; a trustee of the Massachusetts Institute of Technology.

Robert B. Anderson: Secretary of the Treasury, 1957–1961; Secretary of the Navy, 1953–1954; Deputy Secretary of Defense, 1954–1955; member of the board of directors of the Goodyear Tire and Rubber Company; member of the executive board of the Boy Scouts of America.

Douglas Dillon: Secretary of the Treasury, 1960–1963; chairman of the board of Dillon, Reed, and Company, Inc. (Wall Street investment firm); member of the New York Stock Exchange; director of U.S. and Foreign Securities Corporation and of U.S. International Securities Corporation; member of the board of governors of the New York Hospital and of the Metropolitan Museum.

Clark Clifford: Secretary of Defense, 1967–1969; senior partner of Clifford and Miller (Washington law firm); member of the board of directors of the National Bank of Washington, and of the Sheridan Hotel Corporation; Special Counsel to the President, 1949–1950; member of the board of trustees of Washington University in St. Louis.

David Kennedy: Secretary of the Treasury, 1969–1971; president and chairman of the board of Continental Illinois Bank and Trust Company; a director of International Harvester Company, of Commonwealth Edison, of Pullman Company, of Abbott Laboratories, of Swift and Company, of U.S. Gypsum, and of Communications Satellite Corporation; and a trustee of the University of Chicago, of the Brookings Institution, of the Committee for Economic Development, and of George Washington University.

George Romney: *Secretary of Housing and Urban Development, 1969–1972; former president, American Motors Corporation; Governor of Michigan.*

Melvin Laird: *Secretary of Defense, 1969–1973; former Republican congressman from Wisconsin.*

James R. Schlesinger: *Secretary of Defense, 1973–; former director, Central Intelligence Agency; former chairman, Atomic Energy Commission; former economics professor and research associate, Rand Corporation.*

George P. Shultz: *Secretary of Treasury, 1971–1974; former Secretary of Labor; former Dean of Graduate School of Business, University of Chicago; former director of Borg-Warner Corporation, and General American Transportation.*

Henry Kissinger: *Secretary of State, 1973–; former Special Assistant for National Security Affairs; former Harvard Professor of International Affairs, and project director for Rockefeller Brothers Fund.*

All of the individuals mentioned above held cabinet posts. But of almost equal importance are the men who serve as special assistants to the president or as special ambassadors in periods of international crisis.

Cyrus R. Vance: *U.S. negotiator at Paris Peace Conference on Vietnam; senior partner, Simpson, Thacher and Bartlett (Wall Street law firm); member of the board of directors of Pan American World Airways, Aetna Life Insurance Co., IBM Corporation, Council on Foreign Relations, American Red Cross, University of Chicago, and the Rockefeller Foundation. He was formerly Secretary of the Army and Undersecretary of Defense.*

W. Averell Harriman: *U.S. Ambassador-at-Large and Undersecretary of State for Political Affairs, 1961–1969; United States negotiator at Paris Peace Conference on Vietnam; former Governor of the State of New York, 1955–1958; former chairman of the board of directors of the Union Pacific Railroad and of the Merchant Ship Building Corporation; partner in Brown Brothers, Harriman, and Company (Wall Street investment firm).*

John J. McCloy: *Special Advisor to the President on Disarmament, 1961–1963; chairman of the Coordinating Committee on the Cuban Crisis, 1962; member of the President's commission on the assassination of President Kennedy; U.S. High Commissioner for Germany, 1949–1952; president of the World Bank, 1947–1949; partner in Milbank, Tweed, Hadley, and McCloy (Wall Street law firm); member of the board of directors of Allied Chemical Corporation, of American Telephone and Telegraph Company, of Chase Manhattan Bank, of Metropolitan Life Insurance Company, of Westinghouse Electric Corporation, of E. R. Squibb and Sons; member of the board of trustees of the Ford Foundation, of the Council of Foreign Relations, and of Amherst College.*

Arthur H. Dean: *chairman of the U.S. Delegation on Nuclear Test Ban Treaty; chief U.S. negotiator of the Korean Armistice Agreement; partner, Sullivan and Cromwell (Wall Street law firm); member of the board of directors of American Metal Climax, of American Bank Note Company, of National Union Electric Corporation, of El Paso Natural Gas Company, of Crown Zellerbach Corporation, of Campbell Soup Company, of Northwest Production Corporation, of Lazard Fund, Inc., and of the Bank of New York; a member of the board of trustees of New York Hospital, of Cornell Medical Center, of Cornell Medical College, of Cornell University, of the Carnegie Foundation, and of the Council of Foreign Relations.*

Ellsworth Bunker: *former Ambassador to India, Ambassador to Vietnam; former president and chairman of the board of National Sugar Refining Company;*

member of the board of directors of the Centennial Insurance Company, of the Curtis Publishing Company, of Lambert International Corporation, and of Atlantic Mutual Insurance Company; former president of the American Red Cross; a trustee of the Hampton Institute, of the Asia Foundation, of the Council on World Affairs, and of the Foreign Policy Association.

There was some tendency for the Kennedy Administration to rely more on educational elites in staffing key governmental executive posts, whereas the Eisenhower administration relied more upon business and financial elites. The Kennedy administration brought into government McGeorge Bundy as Special Assistant to the President for National Security Affairs, 1961–1966; Bundy was formerly Dean of the Faculty of Arts and Sciences at Harvard University. Kennedy appointed Gardner Ackley as chairman of the Council of Economic Advisors; Ackley had been an economics professor at the University of Michigan, a director of the Social Science Research Council, and a Fulbright Scholar. Walt Whitman Rostow, who was made Special Assistant to the President for National Security Affairs in 1961 and chairman of the Policy Planning Council of the Department of State, had been a professor of economic history at Massachusetts Institute of Technology and a member of the staff of the Center for International Studies. Walter Heller was made chairman of the Council of Economic Advisors in 1961; he had been a professor of economics at the University of Minnesota.

In contrast, Eisenhower tended to rely upon people like Marion B. Folsom, Under Secretary of the Treasury, 1953–1955, and Secretary of Health, Education, and Welfare, 1955–1958. Folsom had been director of the Eastman Kodak Company, of the Eastman Savings and Loan Association, and of Rochester Savings Bank. He had also served as a trustee of the Committee for Economic Development, of the National Bureau of Economic Research, of the University of Rochester, of the Brookings Institution, and of Harvard College. Eisenhower's Secretary of Commerce was Sinclair Weeks, chairman of the board of the United Car Fastener Corporation, and a director of John Hancock Mutual Life Insurance Company, of West Point Manufacturing Company, of the First National Bank of Boston, of Reed and Barton Corporation, of New Hampshire Insurance Company, and of Lancaster National Bank. Eisenhower's first Secretary of Health, Education, and Welfare was Oveta Culp Hobby, president of the Houston Post Publishing Company, and a member of the board of directors of the Bank of Texas and of the Mutual Insurance Company of New York.

The top personnel in the first Nixon Administration resembled the Eisenhower team in many respects. In fact, several of Nixon's lieutenants served in the Eisenhower Administration—former Secretary of State

William P. Rogers, a partner in the Wall Street law firm of Dwight, Royall, Harris, Koegal, and Caskey, had served as Attorney General, 1957–1961; former Treasury Secretary David Kennedy and former Commerce Secretary Maurice Stans had both served under President Eisenhower. Nixon's selection of Wisconsin Congressman Melvin Laird as Secretary of Defense was somewhat surprising, inasmuch as previous appointees to this influential position had been top corporate elites. But in an apparent attempt to overcome this deficiency, Nixon appointed as Deputy Secretary of Defense David Packard, whose elite credentials are impeccable: the president of Hewlett-Packard Company, a director of Palo Alto Mutual Savings and Loan Association, of Pacific Gas and Electric Company, of Systems Development Corporation, and of National Airlines; a trustee of Stanford University, of the Stanford Research Institute, of the Hoover Institute on War and Revolution, and of the World Affairs Council. Packard was required to put over 300 million dollars in trust in order to accept the $30,000-a-year government job.

Other top Nixon appointments included Secretary of Housing and Urban Development George Romney, who was former president of American Motors Corporation and governor of Michigan; Agricultural Secretary Clifford Hardin, who was former chancellor at the University of Nebraska, a director of Fairmont Foods and of Bankers Life Insurance Company of Nebraska, a trustee of the Rockefeller Foundation, former president of the Association of State Universities and Land Grant Colleges and director of the American Council of Education; and Attorney General John M. Mitchell, who was Nixon's partner in the Wall Street law firm. Just like his predecessors, Nixon sought the advice of Harvard University intellectuals—Henry Kissinger, Special Presidential Assistant for Foreign Affairs, and later Secretary of State, was Professor of Government at Harvard; and Daniel P. Moynihan, Nixon's chief advisor on domestic affairs and later Ambassador to India, was Professor of Education and Urban Politics.

The Corporate Elites

Formal control over the economic life of the nation is concentrated in the hands of a very few men: the presidents, vice-presidents, and boards of directors of the nation's corporate institutions. A major reason for this concentration of control is the increasing consolidation of economic enterprise into a small number of giant corporations. The following statistics can only suggest the scale and concentration of modern corporate enterprise in America.

There are more than 200,000 industrial corporations in the United

States, with total assets of $554 billion; but the 100 corporations listed below control 52 percent ($290 billion) of all industrial assets in the nation. The five largest industrial corporations (Standard Oil, General Motors, Texaco, Ford Motor, and Gulf Oil) control 10 percent of the nation's industrial assets themselves. (See Table 4–1.) Concentration in utilities, transportation, and communications is even greater! Thirty-three corporations, out of 67,000 in these fields, control 50 percent of the nation's assets in transportation, communication, electric, and gas. This sector of the nation is dominated by the American Telephone and Tele-graph Company (AT&T)—the nation's single largest corporation by total assets. (See Table 4–3.)

The financial world is equally concentrated. The fifty largest banks, out of 13,500 banks serving the nation, control 48 percent of all banking assets. Three banks (Bank of America, First National City, and Chase Manhattan) control 14 percent of all banking assets themselves. (See Table 4–2.) In the insurance field, eighteen companies, out of 1,790, control two thirds of all insurance assets. Two companies (Prudential and Metropolitan) control over one quarter of all insurance assets. (See Table 4–4.)

Control of these corporate resources is officially entrusted to the presidents and directors of these corporations. In 1970 there were a total of 3,572 persons listed as presidents or directors of these top corpora-tions. Collectively, these people controlled half of the nation's industrial assets, half of all assets in communications, transportation, and utilities, nearly half of all banking assets, and two thirds of all insurance assets.

A. A. Berle, Jr., a corporation lawyer and corporate director who has written extensively on the modern corporation, explains that corpo-rate power is lodged in the hands of the directors of these corporations plus the holders of large "control blocks" of corporate stock:

The control system in today's corporations, when it does not lie solely in the directors as in the American Telephone and Telegraph Company, lies in a com-bination of the directors of a so-called control block (of stock) plus the directors themselves. For practical purposes, therefore, the control or power element in most large corporations rests in its group of directors, and it is autonomous—or autonomous if taken together with a control block. . . . This is a self-perpetuat-ing oligarchy.[4]

Corporate power does not rest in the hands of the masses of corporate employees or even in the hands of the millions of middle- and upper-middle-class Americans who own corporate stock.

Corporate power is further concentrated by a system of interlock-

Table 4-1 / Top Industrial Corporations

Rank	Name	Rank	Name
1	Standard Oil (N.J.) (Now Exxon)	51	Republic Steel
2	General Motors	52	Caterpillar Tractor
3	Texaco	53	Weyerhaeuser
4	Ford Motor	54	Anaconda
5	Gulf Oil	55	McDonnell Douglas
6	I.B.M.	56	Std. Oil (Ohio)
7	Mobil Oil	57	Kennecott Copper
8	G.T. & E.	58	Georgia-Pacific
9	I.T. & T.	59	Rapid-American
10	Standard Oil (Calif.)	60	Nat'l. Cash Reg.
11	U.S. Steel	61	Singer
12	General Elec.	62	Kaiser Aluminum
13	Std. Oil (Ind.)	63	Celanese
14	Chrysler	64	Allied Chemical
15	Shell Oil	65	W. R. Grace
16	Atlantic Richfield	66	National Steel
17	Tenneco	67	United Aircraft
18	Western Elec.	68	Continental Cars
19	E. I. duPont	69	N. American Rockwell
20	Union Carbide	70	Lykes-Youngstown
21	Westinghouse Elec.	71	Deere
22	Bethlehem Steel	72	Minn. Mining & Mfg.
23	Phillips Petroleum	73	American Can
24	Eastman Kodak	74	Burroughs
25	Continental Oil	75	Sperry Rand
26	Goodyear	76	Burlington Industries
27	R.C.A.	77	Inland Steel
28	Dow Chemical	78	General Foods
29	Sun Oil	79	Marathon Oil
30	Alcoa	80	Signal Companies
31	Boeing	81	Avco
32	Ling-Temcs-Vought	82	Owens-Illinois
33	Occidental	83	Uniroyal
34	Union Oil of Cal.	84	B. F. Goodrich
35	Boise Cascade	85	Control Data
36	International Harv.	86	PPG Industries
37	Cities Service	87	Ill. Central Ind.
38	Gulf & West. Ind.	88	International Util.
39	Monsanto	89	American Std.
40	Firestone	90	Philip Morris
41	International Paper	91	Greyhound
42	Honeywell	92	Borden
43	American Brands	93	U.S. Plywood-Papers
44	Armco Steel	94	City Investing
45	Getty Oil	95	Amerada Hess
46	Litton Industries	96	Olin
47	R. J. Reynolds	97	General Dynamics
48	Xerox	98	United Brands
49	Proctor & Gamble	99	TRW
50	Reynolds Metals	100	American Metal Climax

Source: Fortune Magazine (May 1971).

Table 4-2 / Top Commercial Banks

Rank	Name	Rank	Name
1	Bank America	26	Rep. Nat'l. Bk. of Dallas
2	First Nat'l City Corp	27	PNB (Philadelphia)
3	Chase Manhattan	28	Seattle-1st Nat'l Bk.
4	Mfgrs. Hanover	29	Girard Co. (Phila.)
5	J. P. Morgan	30	Wachovia (Win. Sal.)
6	Western Bancorp.	31	Detroit Bank & Tr.
7	Chemical N.Y. Corp.	32	First Wisconsin
8	Bankers Trust	33	Nat'l Bk. of N. Amer.
9	Conill Corp	34	Mfgrs. Nat'l. Bk.
10	Security Pacific	35	Nortrust (Chicago)
11	First Chicago Corp.	36	First Nat'l., Dallas
12	Marine Midland	37	Harris Trust
13	Charter New York	38	Pittsburgh Nat'l.
14	Wells Fargo	39	Lincoln First
15	Crocker Nat'l.	40	Bank of Calif. (S.F.)
16	Mellon Nat'l B&T	41	Valley Nat'l.
17	Nat'l Bk. of Detroit	42	Citizens & S. Nat'l. (Atlanta)
18	First Nat'l. Boston	43	U.S. Bancorp (Port.)
19	First Bank (Minn.)	44	BancOhio
20	N. W. Bancorp.	45	Shawmut (Bos.)
21	Franklin N.Y.	46	NCNB (Charlotte)
22	First Pennsylvania	47	Fidelity Penn (Phil)
23	Bank of New York	48	Nat'l. City (Cleve.)
24	Unionamerica	49	Marine BkCorp (Seattle)
25	Cleveland Trust	50	Commonwealth (Det.)

Source: Fortune Magazine (May 1971).

Table 4-3 / Top Communication, Transportation, and Utility Corporations

Rank	Name	Rank	Name
1	Am. Tel. & Tel.	18	Philadelphia Electric
2	Penn. Central*	19	Columbia Gas System
3	Consolidated Edison	20	Consumers Power
4	Pacific Gas & Elec.	21	Detroit Edison
5	Commonwealth Edison	22	El Paso Natural Gas
6	American Elec.	23	Pan Am World Airway
7	Southern Cal. Edison	24	Virginia Elec. & Pow.
8	Southern Co.	25	Duke Power
9	Southern Pacific	26	Texas Eastern Trans.
10	Burlington Northern	27	Middle South Utilities
11	Norfolk & W. Ry.	28	Pennzoil United
12	Union Pacific	29	Texas Utilities
13	Chesapeake & Ohio Ry.	30	American Natural Gas
14	Publ. Ser. El. & Gas	31	Niagara Mohawk Power
15	Santa Fe Industries	32	Southern Ry.
16	United Air Lines	33	American Airlines
17	Gen. Public Utilities		

*Bankruptcy; control by court-appointed directors.

Source: Fortune Magazine (May 1971).

Table 4-4 / Top Insurance Corporations

Rank	Name	Rank	Name
1	Prudential Ins. Co.	10	Mass. Mutual Life
2	Metropolitan Life	11	Mutual Life of N.Y.
3	Equitable Life	12	New England Mut. Life
4	New York Life	13	Connecticut Mutual
5	John Hancock	14	Mutual Benefit Life
6	Aetna Life	15	Penn. Mutual Life
7	Northwestern Mut.	16	Tchrs. Ins. & Ann.
8	Connecticut Gen. Life	17	Lincoln Nat'l. Life
9	Travelers Ins. Co.	18	Bankers Life

Source: Fortune Magazine (May 1971).

ing directorates and by a corporate ownership system in which control blocks of stock are owned by financial institutions rather than by private individuals. Interlocking directorates, in which a director of one corporation also sits on the board of other corporations, enable key corporate elites to wield influence over a large number of corporations. It is not uncommon for top elites to hold six, eight, or ten directorships. Let us illustrate the concept of interlocking directorates by examining the positions held by a few top corporate elite members. We shall also note the key positions that these top corporate elites hold outside the corporate system—in government, in the arts and sciences, and in charities, education, and civic affairs.

Richard King Mellon: *chairman of the board of Mellon National Bank and Trust Company; president, Mellon and Sons; member of the board of directors of Aluminum Company of America, of General Motors Corporation, of Gulf Oil Corporation, of the Koppers Company, of the Pennsylvania Company, and of the Pennsylvania Railroad. Fortune magazine lists Mellon's personal wealth in excess of one-half billion dollars. He is a lieutenant general in the Reserves, a member of the board of trustees of the Carnegie Institute of Technology, of the Mellon Institute, and of the University of Pittsburgh.*

David Rockefeller: *chairman of the board of directors of the Chase Manhattan Bank; member of the board of directors of the B. F. Goodrich Company, of the Rockefeller Brothers, Inc., and of the Equitable Life Insurance Society; a trustee of the Rockefeller Institute for Medical Research, of the Council on Foreign Relations, of the Museum of Modern Art, of Rockefeller Center, and of the Board of Overseers of Harvard College.*

Paul C. Cabot: *partner, State Street Research and Management Company (investment firm); member of the board of directors of J. P. Morgan and Company, of the Continental Can Company, of the Ford Motor Company, of the National Dairy Products Corporation, of the B. F. Goodrich Company, and of the M. A. Hanna Company; former treasurer of Harvard University, and a trustee of the Eastern Gas and Fuel Association.*

Crawford H. Greenewalt: *chairman of the board of directors of E. I. du Pont de Nemours; member of the board of the Equitable Trust Company, of the Christiana Securities Company, and of the Morgan Guaranty Trust Company; a trustee of Massachusetts Institute of Technology, of Wilmington General Hospital, of the Philadelphia Academy of Natural Sciences, of the Philadelphia Orchestra Association, of the American Museum of Natural History, of the Carnegie Institute of Technology, and of the Smithsonian Institute.*

Arthur A. Houghton: *president and chairman of the board of directors of Corning Glass Works; member of the board of directors of the Steuben Glass Company, of the Erie-Lackawanna Railroad Company, of the New York Life Insurance Company, and of the United States Steel Corporation; trustee of the Corning Museum of Glass, of the J. Pierpont Morgan Library, of the Philharmonic Symphony Society of New York, of the Fund for the Advancement of Education, of the Lincoln Center of Performing Arts, of the Cooper Union, of the Metropolitan Museum of Art, of the New York Public Library, of the Rockefeller Foundation, and of the Institute for Contemporary Art of Boston.*

H. L. Romnes: *chairman of the board and chief executive officer, American Telephone and Telegraph Company.* He is a director of United States Steel Corporation, Chemical Bank of New York, Colgate-Palmolive Co., Cities Service Co., Mutual Life Insurance and Co. He is also active at the national level in the United Negro College Fund, the Urban League, and the Salvation Army. He is a trustee of M.I.T., the National Safety Council, and the Committee on Economic Development.

Henry Ford, II: *chairman and chief executive officer, Ford Motor Company.* He is a director of General Foods Corporation and a trustee of the Ford Foundation. His brother, Benson Ford, is also a director of Ford Motor Company and the Ford Foundation, as well as a director of the American Safety Council and United Community Funds of America. Another brother, William Clay Ford, is president of the Detroit Lions Professional Football Club and a director of the Girl Scouts of America, Thomas A. Edison Foundation, and the Henry Ford Hospital. These Fords are centi-millionaires and heavy political contributors.

Ellmore C. Patterson: *president, J. P. Morgan & Co.* He is a director of Atlantic Richfield Co., Canadian Life Assurance Co., International Nickel, Atcheson, Topeka and Santa Fe Railroad, Warner Patterson Co. He is a trustee of the Alfred P. Sloan Foundation, the Carnegie Endowment for International Peace, and the University of Chicago.

Albert L. Williams: *chairman of the board of directors of the International Business Machines Corp. (IBM).* He is a director of General Motors Corporation, Mobil Oil Corporation, First National City Bank of New York, General Foods Corporation. He is a trustee of the Alfred P. Sloan Foundation.

Leslie B. Worthington: *former president, United States Steel Corporation, and a current director.* He is also a director of Mellon National Bank and Trust Co., TRW Inc., American Standard, Greyhound Corporation, Westinghouse Air Brake Co., and the Pittsburgh Pirates. He is a trustee of the University of Illinois and the University of Pittsburgh.

James Stillman Rockefeller: *chairman and director of First National City Bank of New York; member of the board of directors of the International Banking Corporation, of the National City Foundation, of the First New York Corporation, of the First National City Trust Company, of the Mercantile Bank of Canada, of the National City Realty Corporation, of Kimberly-Clark Corporation, of the Northern Pacific Railway Company, of the National Cash Register Company, of Pan American World Air Lines, and of Monsanto Company.*

Some of these top corporate elite members, such as Rockefeller, Ford, Mellon, Cabot, and Houghton, inherited their position and power. Others, such as Greenewalt, Romnes, Patterson, and Williams came to power through the ranks of corporate management. But almost all members of the American business elite, according to recent studies, share similar social backgrounds. Suzanne Keller, in a study of more than 1,000 business leaders, reports that 57 percent of the business leaders had fathers who were businessmen (owners or managers).[5] Only one fourth of the businessmen studied originated in lower-class homes —laborers, farmers, clerks, or salesmen. Over 60 percent of the business leaders were college graduates, and almost one half had post-graduate training in either law (15 percent), engineering (15 percent), or other professions (15 percent).

Concentration of power among corporate elites occurs not only through interlocking directorates but also through the system of ownership in which one corporation or financial institution owns controlling blocks of the common stock of other corporations or financial institutions. It is very difficult to trace the ownership of a corporation. For example, because the Federal Power Commission requires that the ten largest stock holders of electric utilities companies be reported, one might assume that it would be easy to identify the owners of these companies. However, this is not the case, because these utilities are owned by other corporations rather than by individuals. The list of the ten top stockholders of Pacific Gas and Electric, the fourth largest utility in the country, was reported as follows:[6]

1. Merrill Lynch
2. Equitable Life
3. New York Life
4. Savings Fund and Plan
5. Prudential Life
6. King and Company
7. Raymond and Company
8. Sigler and Company
9. Mack and Company
10. Cudd and Company

Some of these companies are identifiable; but others are "street names," or aliases, of leading banks and investment firms, which hold the stock in trust for unnamed individuals. Mack and Company, for example, translates into Mellon National Bank, which represents the Mellon family interest, headed by Richard King Mellon.

Economist Gabriel Kolko summarizes what we know about corporate power in America:

The concentration of economic power in a very small elite is an indisputable fact. . . . A social theory assuming a democratized economic system—or even a trend in this direction—is quite obviously not in accord with social reality. Whether the men who control industry are socially responsive or trustees of the social welfare is quite another matter: it is one thing to speculate about their motivations, another to generalize about economic facts. And even if we assume that these men act benevolently toward their workers and the larger community, their actions still would not be the result of social control through a formal democratic structure and group participation, which are the essentials for democracy; they would be an arbitrary noblesse oblige by the economic elite. When discussing the existing corporate system, it would be more realistic to drop all references to democracy.[7]

Wealth in America

Corporate ownership in America is highly concentrated. Despite the publicity given the idea of "people's capitalism"—the official concept of the New York Stock Exchange, which urges American families to buy stock—fewer than 10 percent of the American people own any stock at all. And, as might be expected, stock ownership is very inequitably distributed among income classes. In 1959, only 6 percent of the persons with an income of $5,000 or less owned stock, while 55 percent of the persons with an income of $15,000 or more owned stock.

Moreover, many individual owners of stock own very small numbers of shares. A Brookings Institution study of stock ownership in nearly 3,000 major corporations discovered that the top 2 percent of the shareholders owned nearly 58 percent of the common stock of these corporations[8] The next 31 percent of the shareholders owned 32 percent of the shares. But fully two thirds of all common stock shareholders owned only one tenth of the shares. (See Figure 4–1.)

Income inequality is and has always been a significant component of American social structure.[9] The top fifth of income recipients in America receives over 40 percent of all income in the nation, while the bottom fifth receives only about 5 percent (see Table 4–5). However, the income share of the top fifth has declined since the pre-World War II years. The income share of the top 5 percent of families has declined dramatically from 30.0 to 14.4 percent. But the bottom fifth of the population still receives a very small share of the national income. The only significant rise in income distributions has occurred among the middle classes, in the second, third, and fourth income fifths. It is widely believed that the progressive income tax substantially levels incomes, but this is not really the case. The best available evidence suggests that taxation has not altered the unequal distribution of income.

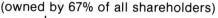

(owned by 67% of all shareholders)

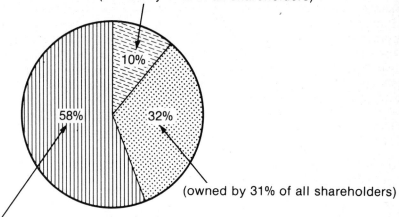

(owned by 31% of all shareholders)

(owned by 2% of all shareholders)

Figure 4-1. The distribution of common stock in publicly owned corporations. (From Lewis H. Kimmel, *Share Ownership in the United States*, Washington, D.C.: Brookings Institution, 1952, pp. 43, 46.)

Millionaires in America are no longer considered among the *really* rich of the nation. *Fortune* magazine estimates that there are at least 153 Americans who are "centi-millionaires"—worth more than $100,000,000 each—and the numbers of these great fortunes are growing.

The editors of *Fortune* report that in 1957, 45 persons in the United States had fortunes over $100,000,000. In the following ten years, the "centi-millionaire" population tripled; those with $150,000,000 or more grew to 66. *Fortune* also states that half of the people with $150,000,000 or more inherited most of it and that the Du Ponts, the

Table 4-5 / The Distribution of Family Income in America

	By Quintiles and Top 5 Percent						
Quintiles	1929	1936	1944	1950	1956	1962	1972
Lowest	3.5	4.1	4.9	4.8	4.8	4.6	5.5
Second	9.0	9.2	10.9	10.9	11.3	10.9	12.0
Third	13.8	14.1	16.2	16.1	16.3	16.3	17.4
Fourth	19.3	20.9	22.2	22.1	22.3	22.7	23.5
Highest	54.4	51.7	45.8	46.1	45.3	45.5	41.6
Total	100.0	100.0	100.0	100.0	100.0	100.0	100.0
Top 5 Percent	30.0	24.0	20.7	21.4	20.2	19.6	14.4

Source: U.S. Bureau of the Census, Current Population Reports Series P-60 No. 80; Data for early years from Edward C. Budd, *Inequality and Poverty* (New York: W. W. Norton and Co., 1967).

Fords, the Mellons, and the Rockefellers *are* among America's wealthiest citizens.[9]

Economist Gabriel Kolko observes:

Insofar as economic power in the United States derives from savings and income, it is dominated by a small class, comprising not more than one tenth of the population, whose interests and style of life mark them off from the rest of American society. And within this class, a very small elite controls the corporate structure, the major sector of our economy, and through it makes basic price and investment decisions that directly affect the entire nation.[10]

America's Centi-Millionaires*

1. J. Paul Getty (oil)
2. Howard Hughes (Hughes Tool Co., real estate)
3. H. L. Hunt (oil)
4. Edwin H. Land (Polaroid)
5. Daniel K. Ludwig (shipping)
6. Alisa Mellon Bruce (Mellon)
7. Paul Mellon (Mellon)
8. Richard King Mellon (Mellon)
9. N. Bunker Hunt (oil, son of H. L. Hunt)
10. John D. MacArthur (Bankers Life and Casualty)
11. William L. McKnight (Minnesota Mining and Manufacturing)
12. Charles S. Mott (General Motors)
13. R. E. (Bob) Smith (oil)
14. Howard F. Ahmanson (Home Savings & Loan Association)
15. Charles Allen, Jr. (investment banking)
16. Mrs. W. Van Alan Clark, Sr. (Avon Products)
17. John T. Dorrance, Jr. (Campbell Soup)
18. Mrs. Alfred I. Du Pont (Du Pont)
19. Charles W. Engelhard, Jr. (mining and metal fabricating)
20. Sherman M. Fairchild (Fairchild Camera, I.B.M.)
21. Leon Hess (Hess Oil & Chemical)
22. William R. Hewlett (Hewlett-Packard)
23. David Packard (Hewlett-Packard)
24. Amory Houghton (Corning Glass)
25. Joseph P. Kennedy (banking, real estate, investments; father of John F. Kennedy)
26. Eli Lilly (Eli Lilly & Co.)
27. Forrest E. Mars (Mars candy)
28. Samuel I. Newhouse (newspapers)
29. Marjorie Merriweather Post (General Foods)
30. Mrs. Jean Mauze (Abby Rockefeller)
31. David Rockefeller
32. John D. Rockefeller III
33. Laurance Rockefeller
34. Nelson Rockefeller
35. Winthrop Rockefeller
36. Cordelia Scaife May (Mellon)
37. Richard Mellon Scaife (Mellon)
38. DeWitt Wallace (*Reader's Digest*)
39. Mrs. Charles Payson (Joan Whitney)
40. John Hay Whitney
41. James S. Abercrombie (oil, iron)
42. William Benton (*Encyclopaedia Britannica*)
43. Jacob Blaustein (Standard Oil of Indiana)
44. Chester Carlson (inventor of xerography)

*In descending order of approximate wealth, from $1.5 billion to $150 million. These assessments include holdings of spouses and minors, of trusts, and of foundations established by the individuals or their spouses.

45. Edward J. Daly (World Airways)
46. Clarence Dillon (investment banking)
47. Doris Duke (tobacco)
48. Lammot Du Pont Copeland (Du Pont)
49. Henry B. Du Pont (Du Pont)
50. Benson Ford (Ford Motor)
51. Mrs. W. Buhl Ford II (Ford Motor)
52. William C. Ford (Ford Motor)
53. Helen Clay Frick (steel)
54. William T. Grant (variety stores)
55. Bob Hope (entertainment)
56. Arthur A. Houghton, Jr. (Corning Glass)
57. J. Seward Johnson (Johnson & Johnson)
58. Peter Kiewit (construction)
59. Allan P. Kirby (Woolworth heir, Alleghany Corp.)
60. J. S. McDonnell, Jr. (McDonnell Douglas, aircraft)
61. Mrs. Lester J. Norris
62. E. Claiborne Robins (A. H. Robins, drugs)
63. W. Clement Stone (insurance)
64. Mrs. Arthur Hays Sulzberger (New York *Times*)
65. S. Mark Taper (First Charter Financial Corp.)
66. Robert W. Woodruff (Coca-Cola)

Source: Fortune, May 1968.

"This is one injustice we're just going to have to live with."

Szep, reprinted by permission

The Managerial Elites

We have defined management (presidents and directors) and controlling stockholders as the corporate elites. But A. A. Berle, Jr., has suggested that the managers, rather than the major stockholders, have come to exercise dominant influence in American corporations. Berle describes power in corporation as follows:

Management control is a phrase meaning merely that no large concentrated stock holding exists which maintains a close working relationship with the management or is capable of challenging it, so that the board of directors may regularly expect a majority, composed of small and scattered holdings, to follow their lead. Thus, they need not consult with anyone when making up their slate of directors, and may simply request their stock holders to sign and send in a ceremonial proxy. They select their own successors. . . . Nominal power still resides in the stockholders; actual power in the board of directors.[11]

In contrast to Berle's thesis, other scholars continue to assert the importance of large stockholders operating through holding companies, "street names," and family trusts.[12] It is generally conceded that a 5 percent ownership stake in a large corporation is sufficient in most cases to give corporate control. The Rockefellers, Fords, Du Ponts, Mellons, and others are still said to exercise prevailing influence over the large corporations. One example is the Mellon interest group which controls, among others, Mellon National Bank, Gulf Oil, Westinghouse Electric, Aluminum Company of America, and Koppers. *Forbes* magazine reports:

When Gulf executives speak reverently of "The Board," they are normally referring to a single man, diffident Richard King Mellon, senior member of one of the world's richest families. The only Mellon on Gulf's board, Dick Mellon looks after his family's two billion, 32 percent interest in Gulf—though he rarely is concerned with the day-to-day operation.[13]

But it does not matter a great deal whether the managers or the owners of the controlling blocks of stock really control America's largest corporations; the end result appears to be the same. Management is just as interested in profits as stockholders. Moreover, managers themselves generally own sizeable blocks of stock in their own corporations. For example, Charles E. Wilson of General Motors had accumulated $2.5 million in stock in that company before he became Secretary of Defense; and Robert McNamara had accumulated $1.5 million worth of stock in the Ford Motor Company before he became Secretary of Defense. It is doubtful that the values of management and of large stockholders differ a great deal.

Today the requirements of technology and planning have greatly increased the need in industry for specialized talent and skill in organization. Capital is something that a corporation can now supply to itself. Thus there is a shift in power in the American economy from capital to organized intelligence, and we can reasonably expect that this shift will be reflected in the deployment of power in society at large.

Individual capitalists are no longer essential to the accumulation of capital for investment. Approximately three fifths of industrial capital now comes from retained earnings of corporations, rather than from the investments of individual capitalists. Another one fifth of industrial capital is borrowed, chiefly from banks. Even though the remaining one fifth of the capital funds of industry come from "outside" investments, the bulk of these funds are from large insurance companies, mutual funds, and pension trusts, rather than from individual investors. Thus, the individual capitalist investor is no longer in a position of dominance in American capital formation.

American capital is primarily administered and expended by managers of large corporations and financial institutions. Stockholders are supposed to have ultimate power over management, but individual stockholders seldom have any control over the activities of the corporations they own. Usually "management slates" for the board of directors are selected by management and automatically approved by stockholders. Occasionally banks and financial institutions and pension trust or mutual fund managers will get together to replace a management-selected board of directors. But more often than not, banks and trust funds will sell their stock in corporations whose management they distrust, rather than used the voting power of their stock to replace management. Generally, banks and trust funds vote their stock for the management slate. The policy of non-action by institutional investors means that the directors and managements of corporations whose stock they hold become increasingly self-appointed and unchallengeable; and this policy freezes absolute power in the corporate managements.

Most of the capital in America is owned not by individuals but by corporations, banks, insurance companies, mutual funds, investment companies, and pension trusts. A. A. Berle writes:

Of the capital flowing into non-agricultural industry, 60 percent is internally generated through profits and depreciation funds (within corporations). Another 10 or 15 percent is handled through the investment staffs of insurance companies and pension trusts. Another 20 percent is borrowed from banks. Perhaps 5 percent represents individuals who have saved and chosen the application of their savings. This is the system. . . . The capital system is not in many aspects an open market system. It is an administered system.[14]

Of course, the profit motive is still important to corporate managers, since profits are the basis of capital formation within the corporation. Increased capital at the disposal of corporate managers means increased power; losses mean a decrease in the capital available to the managers, a decrease in their power, and perhaps eventual extinction for the organization.

There is some evidence that management today has more concern for the interest of the public than did the individual industrial capitalists of a few decades ago. The management class is more sympathetic to the philosophy of the liberal establishment, to which they belong; they are concerned with the public interest and express a devotion to the "corporate conscience." As Adolph Berle explains:

This is the existence of a set of ideas, widely held by the community and often by the organization itself and the men who direct it, that certain uses of power are "wrong," that is, contrary to the established interest and value system of the community. Indulgence of these ideas as a limitation on economic power, and regard for them by the managers of great corporations, is sometimes called—and ridiculed as—the "corporate conscience." The ridicule is pragmatically unjustified. The first sanction enforcing limitations imposed by the public consensus is a lively appreciation of that consensus by corporate managements. This is the reality of the "corporate conscience."[15]

Management fears loss of prestige and popular esteem. While the public has no direct economic control over management, and government control is more symbolic than real, the deprivation of prestige is one of the oldest methods by which any society enforces its values upon individuals and groups. Moreover, most of the values of the prevailing liberal consensus have been internalized by corporated managers themselves; that is, they have come to believe in a public-regarding philosophy.

Galbraith summarizes the changes in America's economic elite:

Seventy years ago the corporation was the instrument of its owners and a projection of their personalities. The names of these principals—Carnegie, Rockefeller, Harriman, Mellon, Guggenheim, Ford—were well known across the land. They are still known, but for the art galleries and philanthropic foundations they established and their descendents who are in politics. The men who now head the great corporations are unknown. Not for a generation did people outside Detroit in the automobile industry know the name of the current head of General Motors. In the manner of all men, he must produce identification when paying by check. So with Ford, Standard Oil, and General Dynamics. The men who now run the large corporations own no appreciable share of the enterprise. They are selected not by the stockholders but, in the common case, by a board of directors which narcissistically they selected themselves.[16]

Corporate and financial elites have access to government officials which ordinary citizens could never hope to acquire. Several years ago Herbert P. Patterson, president of Chase Manhattan Bank, bemoaned his heavy schedule in Washington and listed a single day's appointments on Capitol Hill:

8:30 A.M.	Arrive National Airport
9:15 A.M.	Sen. Ernest Hollings of South Carolina
9:45 A.M.	Rep. William Widnall of New Jersey
10:30 A.M.	Sen. Warren Magnuson of Washington
11:00 A.M.	Sen. Alan Cranston of California
11:45 A.M.	Rep. Gerald Ford of Michigan, House Minority Leader. (I'm asked to note that if he's delayed at a White House conference the appointment will be rescheduled for 3:45 p.m.)
Noon	Luncheon in House dining room with Rep. Leslie Arends of Illinois, the House Minority Whip, and Rep. Harold Collier of Illinois
1:30 P.M.	Sen. Henry Jackson of Washington
2:00 P.M.	Sen. Wallace Bennett of Utah
2:30 P.M.	Sen. Robert Packwood of Oregon
3:15 P.M.	Rep. Hale Boggs of Louisiana, the House Majority Leader
3:45 P.M.	Rep. Gerald Ford (who was delayed at the White House)

Also on the schedule, if time permitted and they could break free, were Rep. Benjamin Blackburn of Georgia and Sen. William Brock of Tennessee.[17]

Needless to say, it is unlikely that very many Americans would ever be able to schedule meetings with so many congressmen in a lifetime, let alone in a single day. Mr. Patterson goes on to note with approval that:

My banking colleague, A. W. Clausen of the Bank of America, is no stranger to Capitol Hill. Men like Edward Cole of General Motors, John Connor of Allied Chemical and Charles Myers of Burlington Industries, among others, have made a real effort to provide legislators with information, to discuss with them problems of mutual interest, and to give them their best judgment as to how particular issues can be handled in the national interest.[18]

The Military-Industrial Complex

In his farewell address to the nation in 1961, President Dwight D. Eisenhower warned of "an immense military establishment and a large arms industry." He observed:

In the councils of government, we must guard against the acquisition of unwarranted influence, whether sought or unsought, by the military industrial complex. The potential for the disastrous rise of misplaced power exists and will persist. We must never let the weight of this combination endanger our liberties or democratic processes. We should take nothing for granted. Only an alert and knowledgeable citizenry can compel the proper meshing of the huge industrial and military machinery of defense with our peaceful methods and goals, so that security and liberty may prosper together.[19]

These words were prepared by political scientist Malcolm Moos, an Eisenhower advisor who was later to become president of the University of Minnesota. But they accurately reflect Eisenhower's personal feelings about the pressures which had been mounting during his administration from the military and from private defense contractors for increased military spending. The "military-industrial complex" refers to the Armed Forces, the Defense Department, military contractors, and congressmen who represent defense-oriented constituencies.

While some radicals view the military-industrial complex as a conspiracy to promote war and imperialism, it is not really anything like that. Liberal economist John K. Galbraith portrays the military-industrial complex as a far more subtle interplay of forces in American society:

It is an organization or a complex of organizations and not a conspiracy. . . . In the conspiratorial view, the military power is a collation of generals and conniving industrialists. The goal is mutual enrichment; they arrange elaborately to feather each other's nests. The industrialists are the deus ex machina; their agents make their way around Washington arranging the payoff. . . .

There is some enrichment and some graft. Insiders do well. . . . Nonetheless, the notion of a conspiracy to enrich the corrupt is gravely damaging to an understanding of military power. . . . The reality is far less dramatic and far more difficult of solution. The reality is a complex of organizations pursuing their sometimes diverse but generally common goals. The participants in these organizations are mostly honest men. . . . They live on their military pay or their salaries as engineers, scientists, or managers, or their pay and profits as executives, and would not dream of offering or accepting a bribe. . . .

The men who comprise these organizations call each other on the phone, meet at committee hearings, serve together on teams of task forces, work in neighboring offices in Washington or San Diego. . . . The problem is not conspiracy or corruption, but unchecked rule. And being unchecked, this rule reflects not the national need but the bureaucratic need—not what is best for the United States, but what the Air Force, Army, Navy, General Dynamics, North American Rockwell, Gruman Aircraft, State Department representatives, intelligence officers, and Mendel Rivers and Richard Russell believe to be best.[20]

What are real facts about the military-industrial complex? Military spending runs about $80 billion per year—less than one third of the federal budget and about 7 percent of the gross national product. The 100 largest industrial corporations in the United States depend on military contracts for less than 10 percent of their sales. In other words, American industry does not depend upon war or the threat of war for any significant proportion of its income or sales.

Nonetheless, there are a few companies which depend heavily on defense contracts—Lockheed Aircraft, General Dynamics, McDonald Douglass, Boeing Co., Martin-Marietta Co., Grumman Aircraft, and Newport News Shipbuilding. But in the world of corporate giants, these firms are considered only medium-sized. None appears in the list of the top 100 corporations in America. While General Electric and American Telephone and Telegraph, among the real corporate giants, appear near the top of defense contracts, their military sales are only a small proportion of total sales. Yet there is enough military business to make it a real concern of certain companies, the people who work for them, the communities in which they are located, and the congressmen and other public officials who represent these communities.

A frequent criticism of the military-industrial complex is that defense-oriented industries have become dependent on military hardware orders. Any reduction in military spending would result in a severe economic setback for these industries, so they apply great pressure to keep defense spending high. This is particularly true of the industries that are almost totally dependent upon defense contracts. The military, always pleased to receive new weapons, joins with defense industries in recommending to the government that they purchase new weapons. The military identifies and publicizes "gaps" in U.S. weapon strength relative to that of the Soviet Union—the missile gap, the bomber gap, the atomic submarine gap, the surface ship gap—frequently overestimating Soviet military capabilities to obtain new weapons. Finally, congressmen from constituencies with large defense industries and giant military bases can usually be counted on to join with the armed forces and defense industries in support of increased defense spending for new weapons. Of course, heavy military spending by the United States prompts the Soviet Union to try to keep pace, thus accelerating the arms race.

But American business is not interested in promoting war or international instability. The defense industry is considered an unstable enterprise—a feast or famine business for industrial companies. The price earnings ratios for military-oriented companies are substantially lower than for civilian-oriented companies. More importantly, corporate America seeks planned stable growth, secure investments, and guaranteed returns. These conditions are disrupted by war. The stock market, reflecting the aspirations of businessmen, goes up when peace is announced, not down.

A more rational critique of the relationship between government and business centers on the gradual blurring of the distinction between private and public activity in the economy. In his popular book, *The New Industrial State*, John K. Galbraith argues effectively that the military-industrial complex is part of a general merger of corporate and governmental enterprise into a giant "technostructure." Corporate planning and governmental planning are replacing market competition in America. Corporations avoid vigorous price competition, and the government also endeavors to fix over-all prices. Both corporations and governments seek stable relations with large labor unions. Solid prosperous growth is the keynote of the planned economy, without undue, disruptive, old-style competition. Wars, depressions, or over-heated inflations are to be avoided in the interest of stable growth. Big government, big industry, and big labor organizations share in this consensus. Within this consensus, the big quietly grow bigger and more powerful. Government protects this secure stable world of corporate giants, unless they abuse the accepted standards of behavior or openly try to aggrandize their positions.

According to Galbraith:

The industrial system, in fact, is inextricably associated with the state. In notable respects the mature corporation is an arm of the state. And the state, in important matters, is an instrument of the industrial system. This runs strongly counter to the accepted doctrine that assumes and affirms a clear line between government and private business enterprise. . . . In fact, the line between public and private authority in the industrial system is indistinct and in large measure imaginary, and the abhorrent association of public and private organizations is normal. When this is perceived, the central trends in American economic and political life become clear.[21]

The interests of the government and the corporate world come together on behalf of a consensus for stable planned growth:

The state is strongly concerned with the stability of the economy. And with its expansion or growth. And with education. And with technical and scientific advance. And, most notably, with the national defense. These are the national goals; they are sufficiently trite so that one has a reassuring sense of the obvious in articulating them. All have their counterpart in the needs and goals of the technostructure. It requires stability in demand for its planning. Growth brings promotion and prestige. It requires trained manpower. It needs government underwriting of research and development. Military and other technical procurement support its most developed form of planning. At each point the government has goals with which the technostructure can identify itself.[22]

Galbraith is concerned with the dangers in this merger of governmental and corporate power. He believes the industrial system has proven its ability to serve man's material desires, but that it threatens his industrial liberty. He expresses his fear of this "new industrial state" in his concluding section:

Our wants will be managed in accordance with the needs of the industrial system; the policies of the state will be subject to similar influence; education will be adapted to industrial need; the disciplines required by the industrial system will be the conventional morality of the community. All other goals will be made to seem precious, unimportant or antisocial. We will be bound to the ends of the industrial system. The state will add its moral, and perhaps some of its legal, power to their enforcement. What will eventuate, on the whole, will be the benign servitude of the household retainer who is taught to love her mistress and see her interests as her own, and not the compelled servitude of the field hand. But it will not be freedom.[23]

The Big Political Contributors

Political campaign financing provides important linkage between corporate and personal wealth and the political system. Campaigns for public office cost money—a great deal more money than candidates themselves are willing or able to spend. President Richard Nixon spent an estimated $60 million in his 1972 re-election campaign, and his "poorer" opponent, Senator George McGovern, spent an estimated $30 million. Even an unsuccessful presidential *primary* campaign can cost $5 to 10 million. Few candidates can even begin a political career for state or local office without first securing financial support from wealthy "angels." Far-sighted men of wealth may chose to back a promising young congressman or senator early in his career and continue this support over many years. Richard Nixon has been supported by W. Clement Stone since young Nixon's early days as a California congressman, and Stewart Mott has supported the political career of Senator George McGovern. There are few congressmen or senators who do not have wealthy financial sponsors.

Top political contributors are drawn from the corporate and financial world and the nation's wealthiest strata of the population. Lists of political campaign contributors contain many familiar names— Rockefellers, Fords, DuPonts, Mellons, etc.—these names are found on both Republican and Democratic lists. In 1972, Richard Nixon's top financial backers included:

W. Clement Stone. *President and chairman of the board of Combined Insurance Company of America, and a director of Alberto-Culver Co. Publisher of Success Unlimited Magazine, and president of Religious Heritage of America, Inc. A* director of Boys Clubs of America, Chicago Mental Health Assn., National Center for Voluntary Action, and the Richard Nixon Foundation. A centi-millionaire. (Contributed $2 million.)

Richard Mellon Scaife. Director of Mellon Bank and Trust, and Gulf Oil Corporation. An heir of the Mellon fortune, a centi-millionaire, and a trustee of Carnegie-Mellon University. (Contributed $1 million.)

Arthur K. Watson. Former president and chairman of board, IBM Corporation. A director of Pan American World Airways, Continental Insurance, Carnegie Endowment of International Peace, Hotchkiss School, Metropolitan Museum of Art, and Yale University. (Contributed $300,000.)

Cornelius Vanderbilt Whitney. President of Whitney, Inc., Hudson Bay Mining and Smelting, and Whitney Farms. A director of Churchill Down racetrack and New York Philharmonic Symphony. Heir to Vanderbilt and Whitney family fortunes. (Contributed $300,000.)

Other large Nixon contributors included John DuPont (DuPont Corporation), Harvey Firestone (Firestone Tire & Rubber), Henry Ford II (Ford Motors), J. Paul Getty (oil), Howard Hughes, Walter Annenberg (Ambassador to England), J. Willard Marriot (Motels), Elmer Bobst (Warner-Lambert Pharmaceuticals), Henry J. Heinz II (Ketchup), Bob Hope, and Frank Sinatra.

Democrats do not usually receive as much money from the corporate world as Republicans, although about half of Democratic funds come from this source. The Xerox Corporation, for example, has been a major source of support for Democratic candidates. Traditionally, Democrats have turned to big labor for support, notably the Committee on Political Education (COPE) of the AFL-CIO and the larger international unions—United Automobile Workers, United Steel Workers, etc. Democrats have also relied on wealthy Jewish investment interests, including Wall Street investment firms (Lehman Brothers; Goldman, Sachs; and Kuhn, Loeb), and conservative Democratic oil and gas money from the Southwest. Liberal Democrats have been supported by upper-class liberal philanthropists. These "Limousine Liberals" provided much of the financial support for the civil rights movement, the peace movement, the ecology movement, and other liberal causes.

In 1972, Senator George McGovern's "liberalism" was backed by:
Stewart Mott. President, Compo Industries. Heir to General Motors fortune of his father Charles Stewart Mott, who was president and chairman of the board of General Motors and U.S. Sugar Corporation. Stewart Mott is also a director of U.S. Sugar Corp., Michigan National Bank, Rubin Realty, Planned Parenthood, Urban League of New York, United Peace Foundation, Center for the Study of Democratic Institutions. (Contributed $725,000.)

Max Palevsky. Chairman of board of the Xerox Corporation. (Contributed $310,000.)

Nicholas and Daniel Noyes. *Students who are heirs to Eli Lilly Pharmaceutical fortune.* (Contributed $400,000.)

Richard Saloman. *President, Charles of the Ritz, Inc. of New York (fashions, cosmetics). A director of Federation of Jewish Philanthropies and trustee of Brown University.* (Contributed $137,000.)

Elite Recruitment: Getting to the Top

How do people at the top get there? Certainly we cannot provide a complete picture of the recruitment process in all sectors of society. But we can learn whether the top leadership in government is recruited from the corporate world, or whether there are separate and distinct channels of recruitment.

Biographical information on individuals occupying positions of authority in top institutions in each sector of society reveals that there are separate paths to authority. Table 4–6 shows the principle lifetime occupational activity of individuals at the top of each sector of society. This categorizing of individuals by their principle activity in life depended largely on their own designation of principle occupation in *Who's Who.*

Table 4-6 / Recruitment to Top Institutional Positions

	Elites		
	Corporate[a]	Public Interest[b]	Governmental[c]
Primary Sector from Which Top Elites Were Recruited:			
Corporate	89.1	37.2	16.6
Public Interest	8.8	50.8	62.1
Governmental	1.7	7.0	16.7
Other (Labor, Press, Religion, etc.)	0.4	5.0	4.6

[a]Presidents and directors of largest corporations in industry, communication, transportation, utilities, banking, and insurance, (See listings in previous tables.) N = 3,572.

[b]Trustees of prestigious private colleges and universities (see note for Table 4-7); directors of twelve largest private foundations; senior partners of top law firms, directors of trustees of twelve prestigious civic and cultural organizations. N = 1,345.

[c]President and vice president; secretaries and undersecretaries and assistant secretaries of all executive departments; White House presidential advisors; congressional leaders, committee chairmen, and ranking minority members; Supreme Court justices; Federal Reserve Board; Council of Economic Advisors; all four star generals and admirals. N = 286.

It turns out that the corporate sector supplies a majority of the occupants of top positions in only the corporate sector (89.1 percent). The corporate sector supplied only 37 percent of the top elites in the public interest sector, and only 16.6 percent of government elites. Top leaders in government are recruited primarily from the legal profession (56.1 percent); some have based their careers in government itself (16.7 percent) and education (10.6 percent). This finding is important. Government and law apparently provide independent channels of recruitment of high public office. High position in the corporate world is *not* a prerequisite to high public office.

What do we know about the men who occupy authoritative positions in American society? There are a number of excellent social background studies of political decision makers,[24] federal government executives,[25] military officers,[26] and corporate executives.[27] These studies consistently show that top business executives and political decision makers are *atypical* of the American public. They are recruited from the well-educated, prestigiously employed, older, affluent, urban, white, Anglo-Saxon, upper and upper-middle class, male population of the nation. We expected our top institutional leaders to conform to this pattern, and we were not at all disappointed. (See Table 4–7.)

Table 4-7 / Social Characteristics of Corporate, Governmental and Public Interest Elites

	Corporate	Public Interest	Governmental
Average Age	61	64	58
Female Percentage	0.3	7.2	1.4
Schools			
Public	81.8	73.2	90.9
Private	7.0	8.8	3.0
Prestigious[a]	11.2	18.0	6.1
Colleges			
Public	31.8	12.8	43.9
Private	13.3	8.4	12.1
Prestigious[b]	55.0	78.8	43.9
Education			
College Educated	90.1	95.7	100.0
Advanced Degree	49.2	75.7	77.4
Urban Percent	89.0	84.9	69.7

[a]Andover, Buckley, Cate, Catlin, Choate, Cranbrook, Country Day, Deerfield, Exeter, Episcopal, Gilman, Groton, Hill, Hotchkiss, Kingswood, Kent, Lakeside, Lawrenceville, Lincoln, Loomis, Middlesex, Milton, St. Andrew's, St. Christopher's, St. George's, St. Mark's, St. Paul's, Shatluck, Taft, Thatcher, Webb, Westminister, Woodbary Forest.

[b]Harvard, Yale, Chicago, Stanford, Columbia, M.I.T., Cornell, Northwestern, Princeton, Johns Hopkins, Pennsylvania, and Dartmouth.

Age The average age of all of the corporate leaders identified in our study is 61. Leaders in foundations, law, education, and civic and cultural organizations are slightly older—average age 64. Top positions in the governmental sector are filled by slightly younger men.

Sex The feminine half of the population is seriously underrepresented at the top of America's institutional structure. Male dominance in top positions is nearly complete in the corporate world.* The same is true in government; in 1970 only one woman served as Secretary of Undersecretary or Assistant Secretary in any executive department; none served as chairman of any standing committee of either the House or Senate; only two served as ranking minority committee members; none served as a member of the Supreme Court, the Council of Economic Advisors, or Federal Reserve Board. Only in civic and cultural affairs, education, and foundations are women found among the top position-holders.

Race We were able to identify only two blacks in five thousand positions of authority in top-ranked institutions in 1970. Both were in government. One was Thurgood Marshall, associate justice of the Supreme Court, former Solicitor General of the United States and former director of the Legal Defense and Educational Fund of the NAACP. The other was James Farmer, assistant secretary of HEW and former national director of the Congress of Racial Equality. We were unable to identify any blacks in top institutional positions in industry, banking, communications and utilities, insurance, law, etc., although it is possible that some may have escaped identification in our biographical search. Certainly it is justifiable to conclude that very few blacks are in any positions of authority in America.

Education Nearly all our top leaders are college educated, and more than half held advanced degrees. Some 25.8 percent hold law degrees, and 23.8 percent advanced academic or professional degrees. (These are earned degrees only; there were a host of honorary degrees that were not counted.) Governmental leaders are somewhat more likely to hold advanced degrees than corporate leaders.

A glance at the precollegiate education of our top elites reveals that about 18 percent of the corporate leaders and 10 percent of the governmental leaders attended private school. Perhaps the more surprising fact is that 11 percent of corporate leaders and 6 percent of the governmental

---

*Data for this study is from 1970. Recent attention to women's role in society may result in greater female representation on top corporate boards. In 1972 General Motors Corporation appointed its first woman director, *Ms. Catherine B. Cleary*, president of First Wisconsin Trust, and now a director of AT&T, Kraftco, and Northwestern Mutual Life. *Patricia Roberts Harris*, Washington attorney and former Ambassador to Luxemburg, has been named a director of IBM, Chase Manhattan, and Scott Paper. Barnard College President *Martha E. Peterson* has been named to the board of Metropolitan Life, and Chicago attorney *Jewel Stradford Lafontant* to the board of T.W.A. *Time*, October 16, 1972.

leaders attended one of the 30 prestigious prep schools in America. When these men were attending school, only six or seven percent of the school population of the nation attended private school. Needless to say, only an infinitesimal proportion of the population had the benefit of education at a "name" prep school. What is even more impressive is the fact that 55 percent of the corporate leaders and 44 percent of the governmental leaders are alumni of 12 prestigious, heavily endowed private universities—Harvard, Yale, Chicago, Stanford, Columbia, M.I.T., Cornell, Northwestern, Princeton, Johns Hopkins, Pennsylvania, and Dartmouth. Elites in America are notably Ivy-League. (Table 4–7.)

Urban origin Most of our top leaders were urban dwellers. Governmental leaders are somewhat more likely to draw from rural areas than leaders in business and finance and law, but still less than one third of key government posts are filled by individuals from rural areas.

These social background characteristics suggest a slight tendency for corporate elites to be more upper class than governmental elites. There are somewhat lower proportions of prestigious prep school types and Ivy-Leaguers among governmental leaders than among corporate or public interest sector leaders. There is a slight tendency for governmental leaders to have more advanced professional education.

Elite Consensus: The Liberal Establishment

Elites in America share a consensus about the fundamental values of private property, limited government, individual liberty, and due process of law. Moreover, since the Roosevelt era, American elites have generally supported liberal, public-regarding, social welfare programs, including social security, fair labor standards, unemployment compensation, a graduated income tax, a federally aided welfare system, government regulation of public utilities, and counter-cyclical fiscal and monetary policies. Today, elite consensus also includes a commitment to equality of opportunity for black Americans and a desire to end direct, lawful discrimination. Finally, elite-consensus includes a desire to exercise influence in world affairs, to oppose the spread of communism, to maintain a strong national defense, and to protect pro-Western governments from internal subversion and external aggression.

The prevailing philosophy of American's elite is liberal and public-regarding. By this we mean a willingness to take the welfare of others into account as an aspect of one's own sense of well-being, and a willingness to use governmental power to correct perceived wrongs done to others. It is a philosophy of noblesse oblige—elite responsibility for the welfare of the poor and downtrodden, particularly blacks. Today's liberal elite believes that it can change men's lives through the exercise of governmental power: end discrimination, abolish poverty, eliminate slums, insure employment, uplift the poor, eliminate sicknesses, educate the masses, and install dominant culture values in everyone. The prevailing impulse is to do good, to perform public services, and to assist the poorest in society, particularly blacks. This philosophy is *not* widely shared among America's masses.

Leadership for liberal reform has always come from America's upper social classes. This leadership is more likely to come from established "old family" segments of the elite, rather than "new rich," self-made men. Before the Civil War, abolitionist leaders were "descended from old and socially dominant Northeastern families"[28] and were clearly distinguished from the new industrial leaders of that era. Later, when the children and grandchildren of the rugged individualists of the industrial revolution inherited positions of power, they turned away from the Darwinist philosophy of their parents and moved toward the more public-regarding ideas of the New Deal. Liberalism was championed not by the working class but by men like Franklin D. Roosevelt (Groton and Harvard), Adlai Stevenson (Choate School and Princeton), Averell Harriman (Groton and Yale), and John F. Kennedy (Choate School and Harvard).

The liberal, public-regarding character of America's elite defies simplistic Marxian interpretations of American politics; wealth, education, sophistication, and upper-class cultural values do not foster attitudes of exploitation, but rather of public service and do-goodism. Liberal elites are frequently paternalistic toward segments of the masses they define as "underprivileged," "culturally deprived," "disadvantaged," etc., but they are seldom hostile toward them. Indeed, hostility toward blacks is more characteristic of white masses than of white elites. Political divisions in America do not take the form of upper classes versus lower classes, but rather upper class, allied with certain minority segments of the lower classes, notably blacks, in opposition to the white middle-class and working-class masses.

The liberal philosophy of noblesse oblige—elite responsibility for the welfare of the masses—leads inevitably to a sense of national responsibility for the welfare of the world, which in turn involves the United States in war. The missionary spirit of liberalism strives to bring freedom—self-determination, civil liberty, limited government, and private enterprise—to all the peoples of the world. America's major wars of the twentieth century occurred during the administrations of liberal Democratic presidents—Wilson (World War I), Roosevelt (World War II), Truman (Korea), and Johnson (Vietnam). Is it accidental that wars occurred during these administrations? Or is it this element of the liberal philosophy which propels the nation toward international involvement and war?

Both World Wars were fought to "make the world safe for democracy." Following World War II, the United States embarked upon a policy of worldwide involvement in the internal and external affairs of nations in an effort to halt the expansion of communism. The "containment policy," as it came to be known, was a commitment by America's liberal elite to halt revolutionary communist movements and to support non-communist governments attempting to resist revolutionary influences either within or outside their borders.

As a result of this containment policy, the United States acquired a staggering number of international obligations. In addition to numerous specific treaty commitments, the containment policy committed the United States to resist the expansion of communism in every non-communist nation in the world. We were committed to resist not only overt military aggression, but also internal takeovers, economic penetration, and even successful campaigning in free elections. But many peoples of the world were ignorant and ungrateful; they did not wish to "improve" their lives and their society by accepting American social, political, and economic ideals. The "good" that the liberals sought to do throughout the world was neither appreciated nor understood by the elites and masses of many nations. The result was a great deal of bloodshed and violence committed by well-meaning liberal administrations for the finest of motives. An American field commander in Vietnam summed up the liberal dilemma: "It was necessary to destroy the village in order to save it."[29]

The failure of America's political and military leadership to achieve victory in Vietnam seriously undermined the legitimacy of the established elite. The original decision to commit American troops to a land war in Vietnam is widely viewed as a serious mistake—militarily and politically—by both elites and masses. The obvious errors in political and military judgment, the heavy loss of life over a prolonged period, the humiliation of the military establishment in a war with a third-rate power, the revelations of incompetency and brutality, and the moral and philosophical questions posed by American involvement in a distant war, all combined to spawn a rash of criticism of the established leadership.

The Limits of Consensus Among Elites

Elite theory does *not* contend that disagreement never occurs among elites. On the contrary, the multiple bases of power in American society—industry, finance, law, government, mass media, etc.—insure that different segments of America's elite will view public issues from slightly different vantage points. However, elite theory does assert that disagreement occurs *within* a framework of consensus on fundamental values, that the range of disagreement among elites is relatively narrow, and that disagreement is generally confined to means rather than ends.

We have already suggested the broad outlines of elite consensus on behalf of private enterprise, due process of law, liberal and public-regarding social welfare programs, equality of opportunity, and a strong national defense posture. But let us examine more closely the nature and extent of elite disagreement.

Over 500 top elites in business, labor, government, the Democratic and Republican parties, and the mass media were interviewed in 1971–72 by Columbia University's Bureau of Applied Social Research. These interviews defined the limits of agreement and disagreement on specific policy questions among these separate elite segments. Table 4–8 reveals the limits of consensus on selected key economic policy questions. At the left of the table are those questions suggesting "liberal consensus" on which all groups agreed to help the poor and use government power to stabilize the economy. Next are those questions which won agreement by every group of leaders except businessmen. Businessmen dissented on issues involving the environmental problem and its control and the causes and remedy for poverty. At the right of the table are those issues which reveal a "conservative" consensus on behalf of the private enterprise economy, unlimited opportunity to acquire wealth, and confidence in the opportunities provided the working class in the American system. Next are those questions which won disagreement by every group of leaders except labor union officials. Labor is cut off from other elites when it comes to governmental intervention into labor disputes (labor is opposed, while others favor such intervention) and labor's demand for a greater role in management of the plant.

In the middle are those questions which actually divided elites along the lines suggested by pluralist political theory: Republican politicians and business leaders disagreed with Democratic politicians, labor leaders, government officials, and the mass media. It seems safe to say that only in this relatively narrow range of issues—the oil depletion allowances, federal versus state and local government control of social

Table 4-8 / Elite Consensus: Economic Policy Questions (Percent Giving Liberal Answers)

		Business Owners & Executives	Republican Politicians & Officials	Career Civil Servants	Mass Media Execs. & Professionals	Democratic Politicians	Labor Union Leaders	Total Sample
Conservative Consensus	Worker's son doesn't have a chance	8	6	4	11	9	10	7
	Take big corps. out of private ownership	3	3	4	9	7	17	7
	Limit job incomes	4	3	12	30	17	37	16
Bi-partisan Conservatism with Labor Dissenting	DISAGREE: Pricing system competitive	11	15	31	40	33	63	29
	Tax capital gains 50% or more	13	20	68	36	47	54	33
	Larger workers's role in management	12	16	33	48	33	65	33
	DISAGREE: Compulsory arbitration needed	30	26	21	22	44	88	34
	Welfare reform not generous enough	15	11	31	54	43	71	35
Pluralist Division: Business and Repub. Disagree with Labor and Demo.	More effective inheritance tax	21	24	56	46	56	93	45
	Reduce income differences	20	38	56	56	49	70	45
	DISAGREE: Local control of social programs	43	34	53	69	44	80	50
	End oil depletion allowance	32	35	67	80	68	85	57
Bi-partisan Liberalism with Business Dissenting	Increase political power of poor	36	60	60	69	75	82	59
	DISAGREE: Poverty mainly cultural	48	62	64	66	65	77	62
	DISAGREE: Environmental problem exaggerated	41	60	75	84	77	84	66
	Tax polluting industries	45	57	76	84	70	88	68
Liberal Consensus	Wage-price controls are needed	69	62	82	82	82	63	74
	Federal govt. should create jobs	59	70	81	91	83	98	77
	DISAGREE: Govt. spending should be cut in recession	73	78	94	76	83	88	81
	DISAGREE: Too much done for poor	75	84	90	93	82	95	86

(Table reads: 75% of business owners and executives disagree with the statement that too much is done for the poor. 69% of business owners and executives favor wage and price controls, etc.)

programs, inheritance taxes, and the proper range of income differences—are traditional notions of pluralist politics applicable.

Professor Alan Barton, director of the study, summarized his findings in part as follows:

> While there were sharp divisions on some economic policies, there were certain general actions favored by a majority of every one of the groups studied. These include some kind of action to help the poor, deficit spending in times of recession, wage-price controls against inflation, and federal job creation in the public sector for the unemployed. "Keynesian economics" and the welfare state in some form are now orthodoxy among American leaders; so also—since the Republican administration adopted them shortly after our interviewing began—are direct controls on wages and prices in periods of inflation. . . .
>
> Some issues sharply divided the businessmen from the labor and liberal interest-group leaders, with differences of over 50 percentage points on most: the Republicans come close to the business position on all of these issues, while Democrats tend toward the labor position. . . .
>
> Just as there are some things which "everyone" now favors, like Keynesian economics, controls, and the welfare state, there are some things which "everyone" opposes. Three such items rejected by large majorities in every group are: a top limit on incomes, taking big corporations out of private hands, and the belief that a worker's son doesn't have much chance to get ahead in our society. There are very few socialists among American leaders—only one out of every six labor leaders give even qualified support to socializing large corporations, and 90 percent of them subscribe to the Horatio Alger theory.[30]

Elite Competition: Sun-Belt "Cowboys" and Established "Yankees"

There are multiple structures of power in American society—industry, utilities, finance, law, government, education, the news media, personal health, etc.—and some competition among these separate power centers is inevitable. Moreover, in any society, various leaders will compete with each other for power and pre-eminence. Finally, the circulation of elites insures that new elite members are continually being admitted to elite circles and these new elites bring slightly different interests and experiences to their roles than older established elites. Elite theory does not contend that conflict, competition, and factionalism never occur among elites.

A major source of factionalism among America's elite today is the division between the new-rich, Southern and Western *Cowboys* and the established, Eastern, liberal *Yankees*. This factional split transcends partisan squabbling among Democrats and Republicans, or traditional rifts between Congress and the president, or petty strife among organized interest groups. The conflict between Cowboys and Yankees derives from differences in their sources of wealth and the newness of the elite status of the Cowboys.

The Cowboys are new-money people who acquired their wealth in the post-World War II era of erratic growth and expansion. Their wealth and power was generated in 1) independent oil and natural gas exploration and development; 2) real-estate operations in the population boom areas running from Southern California and Arizona, through Texas and from the new South to Florida; 3) aerospace and defense contracting and allied businesses, and in some cases new commercial inventions. In contrast, the Yankees are men whose fortunes are linked to the great corporate and financial institutions established in the nineteenth century. Many of the Yankees are themselves second-generation descendants of the great entrepreneurial families of the Industrial Revolution (the Rockefellers, Fords, Mellons, DuPonts, Kennedys, Harrimans, etc.). Other Yankees have been recruited through established corporate institutions, Wall Street and Washington law firms, Eastern banking and investment firms, prestigious foundations, and Ivy League universities.

The Cowboys do not fully share in the liberal, public-regarding values of the dominant Eastern establishment. However, the Cowboys do not exercise power which is proportional in any way to the overwhelming hegemony of the established Yankees. The Cowboys may have gained in influence in recent years. And much of the petty political fighting reported in today's press has its roots in Cowboy-Yankee factionalism. But the liberal establishment remains dominant. And Cowboys and Yankees agree on the overriding importance of preserving political stability and a healthy free-enterprise economy.

The Cowboys are self-made men who acquired wealth and power in an intense competitive struggle which continues to shape their outlook on life. Their upward mobility, their individualism, and their competitive spirit influence their view of society and the way they perceive their new elite responsibilities. In contrast, Yankees either inherit great wealth or attach themselves to established institutions of great wealth, power, and prestige. The Yankees are socialized, sometimes from earliest childhood, into the responsibilities of wealth and power. They are secure in their upper-class membership, highly principled in their relationships with others, and public regarding in their exercise of elite responsibilities.

The Cowboys are new to their position; they lack old school ties, and they are not particularly concerned with the niceties of ethical conduct. The Yankees frequently regard the Cowboys with disdain—as uncouth and opportunistic gamblers and speculators, shady wheeler-dealers and influence-peddlers, and uncultured and selfish bores.

The Cowboys are newly risen from the masses—many had very humble beginnings. But it is their experience in rising from the masses that shapes their philosophy, rather than their mass origins. The Cowboys are less public regarding and social-welfare oriented than the Yankees. They tend to think of solutions to social problems in individualistic terms—they place primary responsibility for solving life's problems on the individual himself. Cowboys believe that they made it themselves through initiative and hard work, and they believe that anyone who wants more out of life can get it the same way they did. The Cowboys do not feel guilty about poverty or discrimination—neither they nor their ancestors had any responsibility for these conditions. Their wealth and position were not given to them—they earned it themselves and they have no apologies for what they have accomplished in life. They are supportive of the political and economic system which helped them rise to the top; they are very patriotic, sometimes vocally anti-communist, and moderate to conservative on most national policy issues.

An examination of the backgrounds of some of the new-rich, sun belt Cowboys reveals their connections with the oil, defense, and real estate industries.

Clint Murcheson. *Murcheson Brothers Investments, Dallas, Texas. A director of the First National Bank of Dallas, Delhi-Australian Petroleum Co., and the Dallas Cowboys professional football team. He owns substantial interest in Atlantic Life Insurance, Transcontinental Bus, Southeastern Michigan Gas, and Holt, Rinehart, and Winston, publishers. He is a former director of the New York Central Railroad, which he purchased with partner Sid W. Richardson. (Trinity College, Texas.)*

John B. Connally. *Special advisor to President Richard Nixon. Former Secretary of Treasury, Secretary of the Navy, Governor of Texas, and administrative assistant to Lyndon B. Johnson. Wounded in the assassination fire which killed President John F. Kennedy. Attorney for oilman Sid W. Richardson and formerly a director of New York Central Railroad. (University of Texas.)*

Roy Ash. *Director, Office of Management and Budget, under President Richard Nixon. Former president and director of Litton Industries. Director of Bank of America, Global Marine Inc., Pacific Mutual Life Insurance; a trustee of California Institute of Technology, Marymont College, Loyola University. Formerly chief financial officer of Hughes Aircraft. (No undergraduate college.)*

H. L. Hunt. *Hunt Oil Co., Dallas, Texas. Owner of Life Line Inc. (radio broadcasts). Son Lamar Hunt owns Kansas City Chiefs professional football team. A billionaire and heavy contributor to presidential campaign of Barry Goldwater. (Fifth grade education.)*

Howard Hughes. *Owner and president of Hughes Oil Co., Houston, Texas; Hughes Aircraft Co., Silver City, California; extensive real estate holdings, Las Vegas, Nevada; holder of world's land plane speed record, transcontinental speed record, and world flight record in 1930s. A billionaire recluse. (Rice University.)*

Cowboys have risen to the top echelons of government in both the Democratic administration of President Lyndon B. Johnson and the Republican administration of Richard M. Nixon. Johnson and Nixon themselves were self-made men, from the South and West respectively. Both devoted many years of their lives to the task of convincing established Eastern elites of their trustworthiness—Johnson in the U.S. Senate as a leader in civil rights and poverty legislation, and Nixon as vice-president and Wall Street corporation lawyer. Yet many of the attacks on these two presidents arose from their closeness to the new-wealth components of America's elite, and the resulting distrust of them by influential segments of the Eastern liberal establishment.*

The Watergate affair and the subsequent movement to impeach President Nixon also involved Cowboy-Yankee conflict. Early in the affair, the Eastern liberals were content merely to chastise the President; there was little open talk of impeachment. The President appointed a Yankee, Elliot Richardson (Harvard Law, clerkship under Supreme Court Justice Felix Frankfurter, prestigious Boston law firm, prior to government service as Secretary of HEW and Secretary of Defense), as Attorney General to replace Richard Kleindienst (Arizona attorney and former assistant to Senator Barry Goldwater). Richardson appointed, as Special Prosecutor, Yankee Archibald Cox (Harvard Law Professor, U.S. Solicitor General under Kennedy and Johnson) to conduct the Watergate investigation. When President Nixon fired Cox over the use of taped presidential conversations, Richardson resigned and the Eastern establishment turned against the President.

Eastern liberals in both parties charged that President Nixon had surrounded himself with Southern and Western sunbelt "wheeler-dealers" whose opportunism and lack of ethics created the milieu for Watergate. Easterners decried the unwholesome influence of many White House staffers whose careers were tied to Southern and Western interests: H. R. (Bob) Haldeman (California public relations), John Ehrlichman (Seattle lawyer), Ronald Ziegler (California public relations), Herbert Klein (California press executive), Frederick Dent (South Carolina textile millionaire).

The prestigious *New York Times*, voice of the Eastern establishment, published an article blaming Watergate on the Cowboys:

---

*Yankee distrust of Cowboys may have begun with the assassination of President John F. Kennedy in Dallas, Texas, and the rash of conspiracy theories linking the assassination to reactionary Texas oil interests. President Johnson acted decisively to discredit these rumors with the appointment of the prestigious Warren Commission, composed mainly of Eastern liberals, which assured the liberal establishment and the entire nation that Kennedy's death was the act of a lone gunman.

The Nixonian bedfellows, the people whose creed the President expresses and whose interests he guards, are, to generalize, the economic sovereigns of America's Southern rim, the "sun-belt," that runs from Southern California, through Arizona and Texas down to the Florida Keys. . . . They are "self-made" men and women in the sense that they did not generally inherit great riches . . . whether because of the newness of their position, their frontier heritage, or their lack of old school ties, they tend to be without particular concerns about the niceties of business ethics and morals, and therefore to be connected more than earlier money would have thought wise, with shady speculations, political influence-peddling, corrupt unions, and even organized crime. . . .

Other scandals are sure to follow, for it seems obvious that the kind of milieu in which the President has chosen to immerse himself will continue to produce policies self serving at best, shady at average, and downright illegal at worst . . . the new-money wheeler-dealers seem to regard influence-peddling and back scratching as the true stuff of the American dream.[31]

Of course, this charge overlooks the fact that former Attorney General John Mitchell, who as chairman of the Committee to Re-Elect the President was directly responsible for campaign tactics, possesses impeccable Eastern establishment credentials: senior partner, top Wall Street law firm of Mudge, Rose, Guthrie, Alexander, and Mitchell; specialist in tax-free municipal bond investing (a favorite tax shelter for establishment fortunes).

Summary

Elite theory does not limit its definition of elites to those who participate in governmental decision making. On the contrary, an elite member is anyone who participates in decisions that allocate values for society. Power in America is organized into large institutions, private as well as public—corporations, banks and financial institutions, universities, law firms, churches, professional associations, and military and governmental bureaucracies. Several propositions were developed in our analysis of power and the institutional structure of America:

1. Great potential for power is lodged in the giant institutions and bureaucracies of American society. High positions—in industry, finance, government, education, and the military—and great wealth do not necessarily guarantee great power. Those who occupy high positions in the institutions of society may have potential power, yet be restrained in the actual exercise of it.

2. The institutional structure of American society concentrates great authority in a relatively small number of positions. About 3,500 presidents and directors of the nation's largest corporations possess formal authority over half of the nation's industrial assets, half of all assets in communications, transportation, and utilities, nearly half of all banking assets, and two thirds of all insurance assets.

3. Wealth in America is unequally distributed. The top fifth of income recip-

ients receive over 40 percent of all income in the nation, while the bottom fifth receives about 5 percent. Inequality is lessening very slowly over time.

4. Managerial elites are replacing owners and stockholders as the dominant influence in American corporations. Most capital investment comes from the retained earnings of corporations and bank loans, rather than from individual investors.

5. Political campaign finance provides an important linkage between corporate and personal wealth and the political system. Top political contributors for both Democratic and Republican parties are drawn from the corporate and financial world and the nation's wealthiest strata of the population.

6. Despite concentration of institutional power, there is clear evidence of specialization among different elites. Less than 20 percent of top governmental officeholders are recruited from the corporate world. Most are recruited from the legal profession; some have based their careers in government itself and in education. Thus, there are separate channels of recruitment to top elite positions.

7. Elites are recruited disproportionally from the well-educated, prestigiously employed, older, affluent, urban, white, Anglo-Saxon, upper- and upper-middle-class male population of the nation.

8. Elites in America share a consensus about the fundamental values of private enterprise, due process of law, liberal and public-regarding social welfare programs, equality of opportunity, and opposition to the spread of communism. The prevailing impulse of the "liberal establishment" is to Do Good, to perform public services, and to use government power to change men's lives. In world affairs, this missionary spirit has involved the United States in a great deal of bloodshed and violence, presumably in pursuit of high motives: the self-determination of free peoples resisting aggression and suppression.

9. Disagreement among elites occurs within a framework of consensus on fundamental values. The range of disagreement among elites is relatively narrow, and generally confined to ends rather than means.

10. A major source of factionalism among America's elite today is the division between the new-rich, Southern and Western, sun-belt "Cowboys," and the established, Eastern, liberal "Yankees." Their differences in style derive from differences in sources of wealth and the newness of the elite status of the Cowboys. The establishment Yankees remain overwhelmingly dominant in national affairs, but new Southern and Western elites have gained influence in recent years.

References

[1] Wright Mills, The Power Elite (New York: Oxford University Press, 1956), pp. 10–11.

[2] James Madison, Alexander Hamilton, and John Jay, The Federalist No. 10 (New York: Modern Library, 1937).

[3] Biographical data in this chapter compiled from various volumes of Who's Who in America (Chicago: Marquis Who's Who).

[4] A. A. Berle, Jr., Economic Power and the Free Society (New York: Fund for the Republic, 1958), p. 10.

[5] Suzanne Keller, Beyond the Ruling Class (New York: Random House, 1963).

[6]See William Domhoff, *Who Rules America?* (Englewood Cliffs, N.J.: Prentice-Hall, 1967), p. 55.

[7]Gabriel Kolko, *Wealth and Power in America* (New York: Praeger, 1962), pp. 68–69.

[8]Lewis H. Kimmel, *Share Ownership in the United States* (Washington D.C.; Brookings Institution, 1952).

[9]See Kolko, *Wealth and Power in America*; see also Clair Wilcox, *Toward Social Welfare* (Homewood, Ill.: Richard D. Irwin, 1969), pp. 7–24.

[10]Kolko, *Wealth and Power in America*, p. 127.

[11]A. A. Berle, Jr., *Power Without Property* (New York: Harcourt, Brace & World, 1959), p. 73

[12]See Ferdinand Lundberg, *The Rich and the Super Rich* (New York: Lyle Stuart, 1968).

[13]*Forbes*, May 1, 1964, p. 22; also cited by Domhoff, *Who Rules America?*, p. 49.

[14]Berle, *Power Without Property*, p. 45.

[15]Berle, *Power Without Property*, pp. 90–91.

[16]John K. Galbraith, *The New Industrial State* (Boston: Houghton Mifflin, 1967), p. 14.

[17]Herbert P. Patterson in *Nation's Business*, February 1971, p. 61.

[18]*Ibid.*

[19]Excerpt from "Farewell to the Nation" speech by President Dwight D. Eisenhower, delivered over radio and television, January 17, 1961.

[20]John Kenneth Galbraith, *How to Control the Military* (New York: Signet Books, 1969), pp. 23–31.

[21]John Kenneth Galbraith, *The New Industrial State* (New York: Signet Books, 1967), pp.304–305.

[22]*Ibid.*, p. 316.

[23]*Ibid.*, p. 405.

[24]Donald R. Mathews, *The Social Background of Political Decision-makers* (New York: Doubleday, 1954).

[25]David T. Stanley, Dean E. Mann, and Jameson W. Doig, *Men Who Govern* (Washington, D.C., The Brookings Institution, 1967).

[26]Morris Janowitz, *The Professional Soldier: A Social and Political Portrait* (New York: The Free Press, 1960).

[27]Lloyd Warner and James C. Abegglen, *Big Business Leaders in America* (New York: Harper, 1955).

[28]David Donald, *Lincoln Reconsidered* (New York: Knopf, 1956), p. 33.

[29]See David Halberstam, *The Best and the Brightest* (New York: Random House, 1973), for a full account of how U.S. involvement in Vietnam grew out of the "good" motives of "good" men.

[30]Allen H. Barton, "The Limits of Consensus Among American Leaders," Bureau of Applied Social Research, Columbia University, 1972, p. 8–9.

[31]Kirkpatrick Sale, "The World Behind Watergate," *New York Times Review of Books*, 20, May 3, 1973.

Selected Additional Readings

Elite Literature
Amory, Cleveland. *Who Killed Society?* New York: Pocket Books, Inc.—Giant Cardinal edition, 1960. This is a popularly written account of the "decline of

high society" by an "insider." Amory is also the author of *The Proper Bostonians*, of which he is one. In *Who Killed Society?* he discusses the early sources of society in America, the most important families (the "400"), and the supposed decline of society in recent years. Note: Domhoff disagrees with this latter aspect of Amory's work.

Andreano, Ralph L., ed. *Superconcentration/Supercorporation: A Collage of Opinion on the Concentration of Economic Power.* Andover, Mass.: Warner Modular Publications, 1973. The articles in this edited reader present a wide variety of opinions concerning the nature and implications of corporate concentration of economic power in America. Included are articles from such diverse sources as *Ramparts*, the *American Economic Review*, and *Hearings Before Antitrust Subcommittee on the Judiciary, House of Representatives.* As a result, the articles vary widely as to rhetoric, scholarship, factual content, and methodology, but they do present an interesting collage of opinions.

Baltzell, E. Digby. *Philadelphia Gentlemen: The Making of a National Upper Class.* Glencoe, Ill.: The Free Press, 1958. *The Protestant Establishment: Aristocracy and Caste in America.* New York: Random House—Vintage Books edition, 1964. The first of these books is a detailed analysis of how a national and associational upper class replaced the local and communal gentry in America between the close of the Civil War and 1940. The second book considers another question—will the Anglo-Saxon-Protestant caste which evolved into a national upper class remain intact, or will the descendants of newer immigrants gain access to upper-class status? He concludes that this caste is still powerful but that it has lost its position as an authoritative aristocracy. This has left the upper class in an uneasy state with an uncertain future.

Berle, Adolf A. *Power Without Property.* New York: Harcourt, Brace, and World, Inc.—Harvest Book edition, 1959. This work by a corporate lawyer and upper-class "insider" presents some interesting views of the American corporate economy. He argues that control of the corporate economy has passed out of the hands of owners and into the hands of managers. The effect of this change will be a return of the corporation to public accountability. This view has been widely debated. See, for example, the Kolko book cited below.

Domhoff, G. William. *Who Rules America?* Englewood Cliffs, N.J.: Prentice-Hall—Spectrum Books edition, 1967. *The Higher Circles.* New York: Random House—Vintage Books edition, 1970. In these books, Domhoff argues that there is a "governing class" in America. By this he means the part of the national upper class which holds positions of power in the federal government and industry and their upper-middle-class hired executives. He spends a great deal of time in both books developing the notion of social indicators. In *Who Rules America?* he examines elite control of the federal government, while in *The Higher Circles*, he develops in detail the role of private planning organizations in the formation of foreign and domestic policy.

Epstein, Edwin M. *The Corporation in American Politics.* Englewood Cliffs, N.J.: Prentice-Hall, Inc., 1969. A good introduction to the interdependence of government and corporations. It contains a historical overview of corporate political activities, a discussion of the types and general methods of corporate political involvement, and a discussion of pluralism vs. elitism.

Galbraith, John Kenneth. *The New Industrial State.* Boston: Houghton Mifflin—Sentry Books edition, 1969. Galbraith's book presents the notion of an intimate partnership between government officials and corporate specialists. General national goals (which Galbraith observes are "trite") are produced by this partnership. Decisions are made in this atmosphere of interrelationship between government and business. Needs and interests of the industrial system are "made to seem coordinate with the purposes of society." (p. 379)

Halberstam, David. *The Best and the Brightest.* Greenwich, Conn: Fawcett Publications, Inc., 1973. This book deals with the men who advised Presidents Kennedy and Johnson with regard to the conduct of the War in Vietnam. Based on interviews of former *New York Times* Vietnam correspondent, David Halberstam, this book reveals an excellent view of the men and processes responsible for decision making at the highest levels of the federal executive.

Kolko, Gabriel. *Wealth and Power in America.* New York: Praeger Publishers, 1962. Kolko discusses the distribution of wealth and income in America, the inequality of taxation, and the concentration of corporate power. He considers the questions 1) do a small group of very wealthy men have the power to guide industry, and thereby much of the total economy, toward ends that they decide upon as compatible with their own interests? and 2) do they own and control the major corporations? He concludes both questions in the affirmative and then relates these facts to the problem of poverty in America.

Lundberg, Ferdinand. *The Rich and the Super Rich.* New York: Lyle Stuart, 1968. An extensive, well-documented, popularly written but unsystematic book which discusses both the corporate-governmental power partnership and elite life styles. Lundberg is the author of the more systematically written but dated book, *America's Sixty Families.*

Mills, C. Wright. *The Power Elite.* New York: Oxford University Press, 1956. This is one of the classics of elite literature. Mills takes an institutional approach to roles within an "institutional landscape." Three particular institutions—the big corporations, the political executive, and the military—are of greatest importance. The individuals who fill the positions within these institutions form a "power elite." These "higher circles" share social attributes (like similar life styles, prep schools, clubs, etc.) as well as positions of power. Thus, Mills' power elite is relatively unified. It is also practically free from mass accountability, which leads Mills to complain of the "higher immorality" of the power elite.

Pluralist Critique

Keller, Suzanne. *Beyond the Ruling Class.* New York: Random House —paperback, 1963. Keller presents an essentially pluralist group theory argument. She begins by adopting Pareto's notion of a series of elites—one for each type of human activity. The ones which are important to governmental and societal policy making are called "strategic elites." These strategic elites are becoming, according to Keller, more specialized and more isolated from one another. Thus, she disagrees sharply with C. W. Mills, who argues that inter-institutional elite movement is becoming easier and more common.

Rose, Arnold M. *The Power Structure.* New York: Oxford University Press—A Galaxy Book edition, 1967. This book is a more direct and systematic critique of elite literature as well as a restatement of pluralist theory. Rose presents the notion of "multi-influence" groups headed by elites. This notion is similar to Keller's strategic elite hypotheses. He asserts that the "power structure is highly complex and diversified," "that the political elite is ascendant over and not subordinate to the economic elite," and "that the political system is more or less democratic." (p. 492)

CHAPTER 5

ELITES AND MASSES:

THE SHAKY FOUNDATIONS OF DEMOCRACY

One might suppose that the survival of democracy depended upon a substantial and widespread consensus among the American people on the principles of democratic government. Actually, only a small portion of the population is committed to the principles of democracy. While most people voice agreement with abstract expressions of democratic values, they are not willing to translate abstract principles into democratic patterns of behavior. The question is not whether most Americans are in accord with the principles of democracy. The question is how democracy and individual freedom can survive in a country where most people do *not* support these principles in practice.

Mass Attitudes toward Democracy

The readiness of the American public to restrict the civil rights of deviant groups has been known for quite some time. As early as 1937, it was found that the majority of voters were in favor of banning communist literature and denying communists the right to hold public office, or even to hold public meetings.[1] During World War II, when the

United States and the Soviet Union were allies, tolerance of the rights of communists rose somewhat; but even after the Battle of Stalingrad, two out of five Americans would have prohibited any communist party member from speaking on the radio. This proportion rose during the Cold War years; it was 77 percent by 1952 and 81 percent by 1954.[2] Willingness and, occasionally, eagerness to abridge the civil liberties of groups other than communists is also very much in evidence.

The first systematic examination of the intolerant frame of mind was made by sociologist Samuel Stouffer in 1954.[3] Stouffer realized that he was conducting his surveys of attitudes toward communism and other minority ideologies during one of the periodic reactions to communism that characterize our nation. He argued, however, that he was concerned not with transient opinions but with deeper attitudes. For example, he measured popular support for freedom of speech, a fundamental democratic value. Stouffer asked a national sample of Americans whether various minorities should be allowed to "speak in your community." Twenty-one percent would not permit a man to speak if his loyalty had been *questioned* before a congressional committee, even if *he swore he was not a communist.* Nearly a third of Stouffer's sample would not permit a socialist to speak; 60 percent would not permit an atheist to speak; and fully two thirds would not permit a communist to speak.

This important study indicates that the extension of democratic rights to communists, socialists, and other minorities cannot be accepted by the average American. Granted, these minorities are very unpopular groups in the United States, but the important point is that the questions are phrased in terms of *legitimate activities.* The respondents were not asked to approve sabotage or other conspiratorial behavior; they were only asked whether these minorities should be given the right to speak.

Out-groups—disapproved minorities—are not stable. In the 1950s, with the Cold War raging, communists were a clearly perceived threat. In the 1960s, particularly the latter half of the decade, the locus of the threat had shifted. The masses generally opposed the activities —whether merely verbal or more active—by "extremists"; but the nature of extremism shifts. A recent replication of the Stouffer study found substantial increases in the willingness of the masses to tolerate nonconformists, as defined by the original study.[4] The communist conspiracy has clearly receded as a threat.

In place of the communist conspiracy, the student radicals of the 1960s became the dreaded enemy, and "law and order" the phrase used by elites to mobilize support for repression. There was a strong revulsion against street demonstrations, even among those who had sympathy with the stated goals of the protesters. A substantial majority disapproved of civil disobedience *and* lawful protest. Popular approval of active dissent was at its lowest point as the 1960s drew to a close. Although estimates of trends are difficult, it appears that, at the end of the last decade: "Before 1950 a maximum of 49 percent would have allowed an extremist to speak freely. During the 1950s permissiveness toward radicals never climbed above 29 percent. Since 1960 only two in ten would approve free expression to an extreme view."[5] Thus, a CBS poll released in 1970 revealed that a majority (54 percent) did not agree with the notion that everyone has the right to criticize the government, even if the criticism is damaging to our national interests. Seventy-five percent opposed the idea of nonviolent protest by extreme groups.

The early 1970s have—as yet—produced no object of mass intolerance. In 1972, substantial majorities disapproved amnesty for those who refused to participate in the war in Vietnam, and equally strong majorities opposed legalization of marijuana. (The movement to legalize marijuana is perhaps the most visible ideological hangover from the 1960s.)

Whatever the focus of hostility, there is one consistent pattern: elites exhibit a greater support for tolerance than do masses. As an illustration of the more tolerant attitudes of elites, Stouffer's original study compared the willingness of community leaders (mayors, presidents of school boards, political party leaders, etc.) to tolerate nonconformists with the willingness among the general public. A replication of the study in 1973 found virtually identical results. Whereas 55 percent of the general public were classified as "more tolerant," 82 percent of the community leaders were so classified.[6]

Social Class and Democratic Attitudes

The studies cited above suggest the correctness of Senator Fulbright's comment that Americans believe in the right of freedom of speech until someone tries to exercise that right.[7] The evidence seems quite clear that "a large proportion of the electorate has failed to grasp certain of the underlying ideas and principles on which the American political system rests."[8] We are left with the question, why does the system survive?

One possible answer to this question can be found in the distribution of anti-democratic attitudes, for commitment to the norms and procedures of a democratic system is directly related to social class. Seymour Lipset has observed that "extremist and intolerant movements in modern society are more likely to be based on the lower classes than on the middle and upper classes."[9] Analyzing the ideologies of the lower classes, Lipset notes:

The poorer strata everywhere are more liberal or leftist on economic issues; they favor more welfare state measures, higher wages, graduated income taxes, support of trade unions, and so forth. But when liberalism is defined in non-economic terms—as support of civil liberties, internationalism, and so forth—the correlation is reversed. The more well-to-do are more liberal; the poorer are more intolerant.[10]

Intolerance in the Lower Classes The argument is that such intolerance—disproportionately concentrated in the lower classes—is characteristic of an "either-or" approach to political and social life: "Change and opposing belief systems are not the natural outcome of endemic social processes or the working of a democratic society, but rather reflect the triumph, or the existence of, evil." Such a configuration of beliefs is called the "cultural intolerance factor."

As can be seen in Table 5–1, cultural intolerance is heavily concentrated in the poorly educated, economically impoverished portions of the populations whose social class is defined (by them) as low.

Table 5–1 / Correlates of the Cultural Intolerance Factor (Percentage High)

	Percent
Education	
8th Grade	52%
High School	39
Some College	28
College Graduate	12
Income	
Under $5,000	47%
$5,000 to $9,999	35
$10,000 to $14,999	29
$15,000 and over	27
Subjective Class	
Lower	43%
Middle	37
Upper	27

Source: Seymour Martin Lipset and Carl Root, *The Politics of Unreason* (New York: Harper and Row, 1971), p. 447.

Lipset has expanded these ideas into his concept of "working class authoritarianism." He observes, from Stouffer's data, that only 30 percent of those in manual occupations are "tolerant," compared with 66 percent of the professionals. The question that Lipset sought to answer is, what aspects of lower-class life make an authoritarian or anti-democratic personality? He argued that a number of elements, such as low education, low participation in political organizations, little reading, economic insecurity, and rigid family patterns, contribute to the making of the anti-democratic personality.

Taken collectively, many features of the subculture of the working and lower classes support the idea of a class-linked, anti-democratic pattern. There is no doubt, for example, that the childrearing patterns of the lower classes are substantially more authoritarian than those of the middle and upper classes. Also, the work life of the lower classes is depressing. Unskilled workers are substantially less satisfied with their jobs than are skilled workers and, as a partial consequence of their job dissatisfaction, have a more fatalistic attitude toward life. Workers who are conscious of having little control over their own lives show a tendency to view the social and political worlds as unchangeable. Unskilled workers are also more likely to view both big business and big government as cynically manipulative. Most important, the skill level in manual jobs is clearly related to mental health. Anxiety, hostility, negative self-feelings, and social alienation are associated quite consistently with unskilled labor; and people in skilled occupations have higher mental health scores than those whose jobs require a repetitive unskilled operation.[11] In addition to the relationship between mental health and work-life, there is a very strong link between the socioeconomic status of one's parents and the probability of poor mental health. The higher the social class of one's parents, the better one's mental health.

Given this evidence, Claude Bowman has concluded that "the world of the semi-skilled and especially of unskilled workers is an unhealthful environment for them and their families."[12] Lipset provides the following depressing summary of the lower-class individual:

> He is likely to have been exposed to punishment, lack of love, and a general atmosphere of tension and aggression since early childhood—all experiences which tend to produce deep-rooted hostilities expressed by ethnic prejudices, political authoritarianism, and chiliastic transvaluational religion. His educational attainment is less than that of men with higher socioeconomic status, and his association as a child with others of similar background not only fails to stimulate his own intellectual interests but also creates an atmosphere which prevents his educational experience from increasing his general social sophistication and his understanding of different groups and ideas. Leaving school rather early, he is surrounded on the job by others with a similarly restricted cultural, educational, and family background.[13]

Social Class, Education, and Commitment to Democracy The main thrust of the preceding argument is that the circumstances of lower-class life make commitment to democratic ideas virtually impossible. However, the relative contribution of each of these circumstances to the making of the anti-democratic personality is not clear. Is it family life, or work life, or education that produces the authoritarian or anti-democratic personality?

Lipset suggested that lack of education might be more important than any of the other characteristics of lower-class life. By examining the tolerance responses of people of various educational and occupational strata, he found that within each occupational level, higher educational status makes for greater tolerance. He also found that increases in tolerance associated with educational level are greater than those related to occupation. An no matter what the occupation, tolerance and education were strongly related.

Numerous studies found that commitment to free speech was also closely related to educational levels; college graduates were far more tolerant of the speech of unpopular minorities than were persons with only a grade school or high school education. Kornhauser found that *within* a given occupation (auto workers) those with poor education were more authoritarian than were those with more education.[14]

Lewis Lipsitz, by examining a variety of surveys administered in the 1950s, finds that the upper and middle classes are less authoritarian primarily because of the greater frequency in these classes of post-high school education. Very few of the relationships between class and authoritarianism remain strong when education is held constant. Thus, the greater authoritarianism of the working classes is largely a product of low education.[15]

Comparable findings are reported by Trow in his analysis of political tolerance and support for Senator Joseph McCarthy. He finds that, among those with less than four years of high school education, the manual workers are less tolerant than small businessmen; but, among those who have some college training, occupational differences are virtually destroyed. He concludes:

Occupation and economic class, and all the variant discontents that flow from membership in different class and occupational groups, seem to have little bearing on political tolerance, certainly as compared with the bearing of formal education and cultural sophistication. . . . Tolerance of dissidence appears to be almost wholly a function of the degree to which men have learned and internalized the rules of the democratic political game: in the United States this, in turn, is closely related to general political awareness and sophistication, acquired in part through formal education and through exposure to the serious political media which support those norms, rather than through economic or occupational experience.[16]

The problem of separating out the effects of education is best illustrated by the device of examining education and income *simultaneously*—that is, by looking at variation in attitude according to education *within* selected income categories. With regard to one indicator of tolerance—willingness to accept the legitimacy of lawful protest—the results suggest an *independent,* strong effect of education (Table 5–2). Within each income group, tolerance increases significantly with education. It is also true, however, that within each education group, tolerance increases with income, but the increases are far less dramatic.

We conclude, then, that the key factor in understanding variations in tolerance is education. Indeed, education is a more significant variable now than it was in the 1950s, when the original Stouffer study was conducted. In the Stouffer study, the correlation between education and tolerance was .44; in the 1973 replication it increased to .55, suggesting considerably more tolerant attitudes among the highly educated. Lest we be overly optimistic, however, note in Table 5–2 that, with the exception of the wealthy, college-educated population, tolerance is—in the aggregate—very low.

Table 5-2 / Joint Effects of Income and Education of Noneconomic "Liberalism"

	Percent Liberal (of Opinion Holders) on Lawful Protest					
	Education					
Family Income	Non-High School Graduate		High School Graduate		Some College	
Under $6000	27%	(214)	33%	(76)	55%	(61)
$6000–$9,999	29	(113)	41	(143)	48	(103)
$10,000 and over	39	(57)	44	(140)	71	(181)

Source: Robert S. Erikson and Norman R. Luttbeg, *American Public Opinion: Its Origins, Content, and Import* (New York: John Wiley, 1973), p. 176.

Social Class and the Anti-democratic Personality   Another opportunity to examine the relationship between education and commitment to democratic norms is provided by the research of Herbert McClosky, the most thorough inventory available of the psychological underpinnings of a democratic society.[17] McClosky administered a variety of attitude and personality scales to a national cross-section of 1,484 respondents. Most of the scales were also administered by a mail survey to 3,000 Democratic and Republican leaders, ranging from federal officials to local officials and precinct workers.* By dividing the national sample into educational categories, we can compare the responses of both well-educated and poorly educated people with the responses of the sample of national leaders.

McClosky examines the following attributes of elites, of the educated public, and of the uneducated public: (1) psychological flexibility, (2) feelings of marginality or lack of identification with one's class, (3) intellectuality, (4) dichotomous, or black-and-white, thinking, (5) liberalism and conservatism, (6) attitudes toward democracy and politics, (7) political alienation, and (8) extreme beliefs. The analysis measures both personality and attitude (Table 5–3). A good introduction to the characteristics of elites and masses can be gained from determining what proportion of each of the three groups scores high on the rigidity scale. A person who scores high on this scale is likely to view the world in black-and-white terms and is especially given to stereotypic categorizations and overgeneralizations. The world consists of "them" and "us." "They" are unquestionably bad, while "we" are unquestionably good. A division of the world into two opposing camps simplifies problems that would otherwise require thought and makes the world manageable. Notice that rigidity is higher among low-education groups than among either the leaders or the high-education group.

A more explicit measure of dichotomous thinking can be observed in the we-they scales, the chauvinism scale, the ethnocentrism scale, the anti-Semitism scale, and the segregation-integration scale. All of these scales indicate quite clearly that leaders are distinguished from followers by their rejection of dichotomous thinking. Such simplistic views of the world are compatible with those who have a feeling of marginality. The alienation scale (which refers to feelings of personal isolation), the anomie scale (which measures the degree to which individuals feel society is lacking in direction and meaning), and the cruel-world scale (which measures the tendency to regard the world as cold and indifferent) point up some of the problems of the poorly educated individual. Clearly, these individuals feel estranged, bewildered, and overwhelmed by a complex world and seek simple explanations of this world.

A hostile, dangerous, or indifferent world can be explained most easily as the consequence of a conspiracy; and lower-class movements are typically concentrated upon a scapegoat. Scapegoating is linked with intellectuality, since prejudice declines with information about the

---

*One might quarrel with McClosky's definition of leaders; certainly it is not intended to be inclusive. However, political party leaders are at least a part of the elite as we have defined it.

Table 5-3 / Democratic and Anti-democratic Attitudes among Elites and Masses (Percent Scoring High)

	Leaders	General Public	
		High Education	Low Education
	(N = 3,020)	(N = 787)	(N = 697)
Democratic commitment	49%	36%	13%
Elitism-inequalitarianism	23	31	47
Faith in democracy	40	24	13
Faith in direct action	26	32	53
Faith in freedom	63	53	43
Faith in procedural right	58	32	15
Tolerance	61	55	30
Political cynicism	10	23	41
Sense of political futility	4	22	39
Political suspiciousness	9	20	34
Left wing	7	16	41
Right wing	17	22	46
Populism	13	24	50
Totalitarianism	10	22	47
Authoritarianism	15	21	48
Rigidity	28	33	52
Alienation	17	26	43
Anomie	8	21	51
Cruel, indifferent world	10	16	35
Intellectuality	57	47	23
We-they (general)	23	24	44
We-they (specific)	12	24	49
Chauvinism	13	16	47
Ethnocentrism	17	22	39
Anti-Semitism	28	36	54
Segregation-integration	29	28	49
Pro-business attitudes	50	40	42
Classical conservatism	17	23	53
Economic conservatism	42	23	16
Opposition to government welfare	57	41	25
Support for liberal issues	24	23	22

Source: Adopted from Herbert McClosky, "Personality and Attitude Correlates of Foreign Policy Orientation," in James N. Rosenau (ed.), *Domestic Sources of Foreign Policy* (New York: Free Press, 1967), pp. 51–110.

"out-group." The under-educated strata do not read and are poorly informed about public matters. For example, a Gallup poll indicated that whereas 41 percent of the college graduates had read a book in the past month, only 9 percent with a grade-school education had done so. In the past, prior to the development of a permanent Cold War ideology, the scapegoat for lower-class movements seemed to alternate between Catholics and "Wall Street," but in present-day America, the scapegoat for all the evils of the world is communism or "radicalism." Leaders like Spiro Agnew or Richard Nixon can encapsulate all of these scapegoating tendencies and give them direction.

To a considerable degree, the presidency of Richard Nixon provided masses with a much more tangible scapegoat: radical student demonstrators and militant blacks. The testimony of his key aides makes clear that Nixon's—and Agnew's—attacks upon the "counter culture" were based at least partially upon fear. Thus, simultaneously with public attacks on students (for example, references to students as "bums"), Nixon's staff sought intelligence about demonstration leaders which would link them to a foreign power. (Failure to locate such evidence resulted, apparently, in intensification, rather than termination, of this intelligence effort.) At any rate, Nixon's articulation of strong distaste for radical students fits well with the traditional use of scapegoats by elites to gain mass support.

It is a curious attribute of elite-mass exchanges surrounding the development and maintenance of scapegoats that the scapegoated group frequently has little or no influence within the body politic. Evidence indicating a marked decline of radical sentiment on campuses was available, presumably, to Nixon and his staff. But the domestic intelligence operation was actually escalated as the radicals began to lose their base of support.

Social Class, "Liberalism," and Political Alienation

We are accustomed to associating conservatism with the upper classes, but the configuration of attitudes is not that simple. The poorly educated public may be more "liberal" with respect to economic matters; they favor more welfare measures and more government intervention into economic life than do the upper strata of the society. But the upper strata are much less conservative when conservatism is defined as an emphasis on tradition, order, status hierarchy, duty, obligation, obedience, and authority. Commitment to order and authority is much more a characteristic of poorly educated people. (See Table 5–3.)

On the other hand, notice that both leaders and followers have a relatively pro-business attitude. One might assume that the economic liberalism of the poorly educated people would dispose them against the business system; but, actually, there is considerable evidence that the ideology of business is shared by *all* strata of society. The idea of starting a business with one's savings, for instance, is sufficiently alive to prompt literally millions of American workers to establish a business of their own. In the Oakland labor mobility study by Lipset and Bendix, two thirds of the manual workers interviewed had considered going into business for themselves, and about two fifths of them had actually tried to start their own firms. Despite the fact that most of these businesses ultimately fail, self-employment is a career that many Americans regard as desirable. Lipset and Bendix note that "with the exception of the workers at the very bottom of the occupational structure, the majority of Americans are probably related to or know individuals who have become self-employed."[18] It appears, therefore, that the dream of becoming an independent entrepreneur is not restricted to those who have any genuine possibility of achieving this status. However, in spite of the commitment of all sections of the system to a business ideology, this ideology is more characteristic of the elite than of the masses. Notice, however, that a pro-business attitude is not linked as much with classical conservatism as it is with economic conservatism. The elite exhibits more congruence of values (consistency of ideology) than poorly educated segments of society (this point will be discussed in the next chapter).

A footnote might be added to the description of the elite as relatively more liberal than the masses. Janowitz describes the military elite as conservative, although his measure of conservatism is limited to the respondent's self-evaluation. He notes that since military elites are well educated, the emphasis they place upon conservatism is especially noteworthy as an exception to the general rule.[19] Indeed, Janowitz describes the ideology of the military elite in terms that make this particular elite more comparable to the masses. Military ideology is concerned with a respect for authority and is characterized by a lack of respect for the compromises inherent in the political process—the same kind of impatience toward democracy and politics that characterizes the poorly educated population.

The rejection of politics and politicians is a basic feature of the rejection of democracy itself. In the minds of the poorly educated, politics in a democracy is "all talk and no action." Moreover, the poorly educated view the government as a manipulating "they." Feelings of helplessness are, of course, not necessarily all in the minds of the poorly educated; indeed, their feeling of helplessness might be a rational and accurate evaluation of the real situation. The poorly educated have no faith in the system because the system has not rewarded them.

Those who feel helpless are not likely to undertake any sort of political activity. However, given the appropriate provocation, those who reject participation in the official procedures of democratic society may initiate more radical types of activities, such as rioting. The blacks who led the riots in the urban ghettos, for example, were much more inclined than non-rioters to think that the country is not worth fighting for and were substantially less trusting of the city government. Whites of similar social-economic status were reacting similarly to their feelings of help-lessness when they attacked the Alabama freedom riders. The point is that political behavior of the disadvantaged segments of the society is likely to be violent and illegal rather than to be within the normal framework of democratic decision making.

The potential violence of the under-educated strata is shown by their extreme political beliefs. The appeals of both the left wing and the right wing are more attractive to the masses than to the elite. It is not the content of the ideology that attracts the masses but rather the emotional symbolism that both left and right ideologies offer. As McClosky says:

Both are inspired by chauvinism, both conceive themselves as the nation's defenders against its enemies; both are impatient with or suspicious of the political process, and both regard themselves as dispossessed, pushed aside by men of doubtful patriotism and questionable objectives. The supporters of both political objectives are nostalgic for an era no longer possible; they continue to yearn for a return to the simplicity of an earlier period when the nation was invincible and its own master. Xenophobia has characterized both, and their portraits of foreigners and foreign nations have been remarkably alike. Both have been given to jingoism and heroic postures, and both have repudiated the artificial, corrupt, and declining cultures of the Old World. Both are attracted to conspiratorial explanations of human affairs, and both are inclined to attribute American reverses to softness, duplicity, or even treason.[20]

Political Socialization of the Masses

If education is the key to how commitment to a democratic system is developed, then we need to know something about the quality of the educational experience. The evidence presented so far has suggested, tentatively, that there is a fundamental difference between the college educated and non-college educated population.

This distinction is generally blurred and needs to be sharpened. If one examines the association between education and a variety of attitudes normally attributed to the political elite, it can be discovered that commitment to democratic rules of the game becomes apparent only after substantial exposure to higher (as distinguished from secondary) education. At least through high school, learning how to be a good citizen does not necessarily include respect for the rights of minorities.[21]

Making the usual assumption that racial progress and education are highly related in the South, Matthews and Prothro were surprised to learn that there was a substantial *negative* correlation between median school years completed by whites and black voting registration. As the average education of whites in a county increases, black voter registration decreases. Puzzled by this contradiction to one of the "laws" of political behavior, Matthews and Prothro remarked: "These findings . . . are completely contrary to what we would have expected from earlier studies and 'common sense' interpretations."[22]

However, such findings are not surprising if we regard the social function of the public school as one of the insulation of children from controversial ideas in order to attempt to preserve the *status quo*. As Key puts it: "All national educational systems indoctrinate the oncoming generation with the basic outlooks and values of the political order."[23] Illustrations of these ideas are not hard to find. An early study by Pressey indicated that changes in moral and religious values of society were reflected in shifting beliefs of college students but had no impact upon the ideas of high school students.[24] More recently, Campbell and Schuman's analysis of racial attitudes in 15 cities reaches the conclusion that:

The schools appear to have accepted without question the prevailing culture of race relations. Since World War II, those white students who have gone to college have evidently been exposed to influences which have moved their attitudes away from the traditional pattern. . . . In contrast, the high schools . . . seem to have been little more involved in the nation's racial problems than they were during the pre-war period. Or, to be more precise, their involvement has been so peripheral that it has had relatively little influence on the racial attitudes of their graduates.[25]

The point is that there is a fundamental qualitative as well as quantitative distinction to be made about education. The liberating effects of free inquiry are, in large measure, reserved for the potential elite who enter college. For those who terminate their education at the level of high school, the learning process is better characterized as "schooling." As Lane and Sears put it: "The home, and, to some extent, early formal education, encapsulate the past; higher education subjects it to scrutiny in the light of different ideas."[26]

Illustrations of the "encapsulation of the past" can be uncovered by looking at the attitudes of those who discontinued their education at high school, compared to those who go to college. The numerous studies of racial attitudes which have appeared since 1964 have been consistent in indicating that whites view America as a land of equal opportunity. To take one illustration, the Gallup Political Index of July 1968 reported that a substantial majority believe that blacks are treated the same as whites and only a minority agrees with the conclusions of the President's Commission on Civil Disorders that our nation is moving toward two societies. In Table 5–4, we can see that the only appreciable impact of education upon attitudes occurs after high school.

Table 5-4 / Attitudes of Various Educational Groups Toward Racial Problems (Percentages)

	Grade School	High School	College
Believe Negroes are treated the same as whites	71%	75%	71%
Believe Negroes are more to blame for present condition than whites	56	58	42
Believe that businesses discriminate against Negroes in hiring	17	19	30
Believe that labor unions discriminate against Negroes in membership practices	15	13	30
Believe that looters should be shot on sight	54	55	45

Source: Gallup Political Index (July 1968): 15-22.

One cannot, of course, assume that the lack of exposure to critical thinking is a *sufficient* explanation for the unrealistic attitudes of the masses. For instance, Langton reveals that high school students who *intend* to go to college are more tolerant than those who do not.[27] Nevertheless, it is clear that public education does not provide the opportunity for critical thinking required of decision makers.

The main thrust of the literature on the school as an agent of political socialization is that the formal instructional process is generally unrelated to changes in the values of students. This is the case primarily because the instructional efforts in public schools are redundant; they are largely symbolic reinforcements of the "democratic creed"—a liturgy heard by most students so many times that sheer boredom would allow for, at the most, slight increments in loyalty, patriotism, and other virtues presumed to be the goal of civics and social studies courses.

We can get some general notion of what students are told in social studies courses from the texts they use and from the attitudes of those who teach. The chief conclusion of such an examination is that controversy is to be avoided. Massialas conducted an exhaustive survey of texts and found them to be of extraordinarily poor quality. Among the more significant of his conclusions are:

Textbooks generally present an unrealistic picture of American society and government. Many social problems that exist today are not discussed. In statements about democracy and the good life textbooks often do not separate prescriptions from descriptions. Thus the persuasive usage of concepts are not distinguishable from descriptive and explanatory ones. America is presented as the champion of freedom, good will, and rationality, while all other nations are depicted as aggressors or "second raters." . . . Many authors assume naively that the political system functions in accordance with the fundamental laws of the land. . . . Controversial issues are not dealt with in an ethically or intellectually responsible manner. Nowhere do authors outline a defensible model for dealing with social cleavages and value incompatibility.[28]

Some excerpts from texts analyzed by Massialas illustrate his point. Take, for example, this statement about the American economic system:

One needs only to look at the great achievements and the standard of living of the American people to see the advantages of our economic system. . . . We believe that a well-regulated capitalism —a free choice, individual incentives, private enterprise system —is the best guarantee of the better life for all mankind.[29]

There is no discussion of any alternative to this economic system, not even in the "some say—others say" style that characterizes some efforts to consider alternatives. Further, a picture accompanying this discussion shows people waiting in line in the rain to be treated by the English National Health Service!

Race relations are regarded as a "controversial social issue" which is treated with extreme caution. While some texts are more realistic than others, the following quotation is typical.

In 1954, the United States Supreme Court made a decision stating that separate schools for Negro children were unconstitutional. This decision caused much controversy, but there has been general agreement, however, that some system must be developed to provide equal educational opportunity for all children —regardless of race, nationality, religion or whether they live in cities or rural areas.[30]

Of course, this statement is patently false. There is no discussion of the vigor with which Southern states resisted the order. Presumably, students were given no explanation for the fact that race relations remain America's most divisive problem.

Patriotism, which is characteristic of the study of American government in the public schools, may be less jingoistic than it once was. However, texts carefully intersperse discussion of government structure (considered in purely legalistic terms) with appropriate exhortations such as: "No other country has more nearly approached the goals of true democracy as our United States. . . . No doubt many of the early settlers were inspired men. . . ,"[31] and, "because the nations of the world have not yet learned to live permanently at peace, the United States today must maintain large defensive forces."[32]

The treatment of the American political process is generally totally unreal. A single example selected from the abundance of current texts should serve to make the point. One text devotes an entire chapter to the electoral process, but fails to mention the twenty-five years of research conducted on elections. As Massialas observed:

The five main ideas of the chapter on voting are: (1) "Voting is a process that makes possible peaceful change," (2) "Voting promotes citizen participation in govern-

ment," (3) "Voting helps to promote equality," (4) "Voting promotes obedience to government," (5) "Voting promotes the self respect of every individual."[33]

The manner in which texts treat communism is even more astonishing. In both the "Challenge of Communism" courses which have become quite popular recently and the general civics courses, communism is pictured as a total evil. Most state departments of education are primarily concerned with demonstrating the fallacies of communism rather than encouraging objective comparison. An unswerving, ruthless conspiracy dominated by the Soviet Union (texts have an understandable inability to shift their bias with the direction of U.S. foreign policy) is the image that is presented, almost without exception. Texts warn students that they will be "badly fooled" if they "take the Russians at their word"; the "errors" of Marx are listed (no communist sources are cited); and the contrast of good versus evil is made quite explicit. In the event that the students fail to get the message, end-of-chapter assignments, maps, and other visual aids are equally biased. For instance, four projects accompanying one text are: (1) Write a short paper on agreements with other nations broken by the Soviet Union. (2) Draw a chart contrasting the way of life in a democracy and in a totalitarian government. (3) Organize a panel to discuss United States policy toward Cuba (preceded by the statement, "The presence of a Communist dictatorship in Cuba poses a threat to the people of the Western Hemisphere."). (4) Compile a list of Marx's errors.[34]

To provide a sense of geographical continuity, maps frequently are included in social studies texts. One such map divides the world into four camps: The United States, the Communist Bloc, the uncommitted nations, and the Free World—including Spain, Portugal, Formosa, and Haiti (presumably "free" is a synonym for friendliness with the United States, rather than a description of the internal politics of a country). If, given the boredom which might be expected to accompany class discussions of such simplistic notions, the class still has not figured out how to get a good grade, the final assignment should reduce any remaining ambiguities: "List as many criticisms of Communism as you can."[35]

There are, surely, some social studies teachers who can contradict the pap of textbooks and produce an element of realism, but they are rare. Most social studies teachers are not trained to distinguish facts from values and, in any case, probably find the anticommunism and ethnocentrism of texts quite compatible with their own values. Therefore, little contrary information filters into the classroom. Further, since such unreal descriptions are reinforced by other sources of information (such as the family), we should expect little attitude change to occur during formal schooling. What probably occurs is attitude *organization*.

The notion of attitude organization, as developed by Jules Henry, consists of grouping and focusing poorly articulated attitudes.[36] Given the conservative goals of the educational system, its success might better be measured in terms of providing order to attitudes and directing them toward larger social goals, such as the maintenance of positive affect toward national symbols. We suggest, moreover, that the crude indoctrination typical of texts is less effective in achieving attitude organization than the more subtle learning experiences manifested by means of teacher-student interaction and the norms of school organization. Teachers, in keeping with the general ethos of public education, are overly concerned about authority. The style of teaching emphasizing the authority of the teacher, is in contrast to even the symbolic norms of participation presented in texts. The available evidence, such as that in Table 5–5, suggests that teachers are not prepared to engage students in a process of critical exchange of ideas.[37]

Table 5-5 / Attitudes of Teachers toward Authority

Item	Percent Agree	Percent Disagree
Children should be given greater freedom in expressing their natural impulses and desires, even if these impulses are frowned upon by people.	42	58
Schools should return to the practice of administering a good spanking when other methods fail.	59	41
A good teacher never lets students address him or her except as Mr., Miss, or Mrs.	75	25
What youth needs most is strict discipline, rugged determination, and the will to work and fight for family and country.	69	31
The main purpose of social studies courses is to teach students to be good citizens	83	17
Obedience and respect for authority are the most important virtues children should learn.	60	40
Students today don't respect their teachers enough.	57	43

Such attitudes provide a strong propensity for creating a rigid classroom situation. Furthermore, in spite of the shibboleths of texts, to which teachers undoubtedly pay lip service, they appear to be as unclear about the application of democratic ideals to concrete situations as is the general population. A minority believe that police should not have the power to censor books and movies; a majority do not wish to provide First Amendment freedoms to social or political nonconformists.

Given the nature of our public education, the lack of commitment to (and understanding of) democracy on the part of the masses is hardly surprising. Most students who do not pursue education beyond high school have really been taught little more than loyalty to symbols. Symbolic loyalty can be deceptive. Merelman's study of education in the Los Angeles area is suggestive of such a result. Although he found teachers to be more open to controversy than is normally the case, he also found students to be poorly equipped to become responsible citizens. He finds that the educational process sustains support for the most obvious democratic symbols, thus enhancing approval for the existing structure of democracy. However, he is cognizant of the conservative implications of symbolic loyalties and remarks that formal education

> . . . seems unable to convey much tolerance for or comprehension of those minorities who would criticize the democratic system. Educational quality, as it presently operates, therefore supports the status quo rather than those who would change the status quo.[38]

Loyalty, rather than tolerance, is the message of public education. An ingenious study by Pock probes beyond the abstract values of "symbolic democrats" among the high school population. Rather than relying upon attitude scales, Pock presented high school seniors with a series of constitutional cases, each raising a separate constitutional issue. Respondents were asked to agree or disagree with the specific actions or decision involved in the case. He concluded,

> confronted by description of situations in which both explicit and implicit civil rights have been violated, a preponderance of students responded approvingly to use of improperly gathered evidence, secret trials, search without probable cause, setting of excessive bail, and to the use of anonymous witnesses.[39]

We have seen, then, that schools teach loyalty and, to some extent, a belief in the efficacy of individual political participation. However, there is a final irony to the story. Langton and Jennings found that overwhelming majorities of students defined being a "good citizen" in two dimensions: loyalty and participation. However, for blacks, loyalty rather than participation emerges as the dominant factor.[40] For blacks, education means that a good citizen is above all loyal rather than active. Similar results are found by examining the perceptions of citizenship on the part of lower-class whites. Litt examined the civic education programs in three schools, one serving an upper-middle-class community, one serving a lower-middle-class community, and one serving a working-class community. In all three communities, texts heavily emphasized the "democratic creed." However, in the lower-class school, there were few references to norms that encourage voting. Civic education courses in the lower-class community do not encourage participation. It is only in the upper-class school that politics is viewed as a feasible process for the resolution of conflict.[41] Thus, in the case of both blacks and lower-class whites, the results of civic education are to encourage obedience and conformity to the beliefs of elites. Both groups are being told to "keep in their place" and to leave the decision-making authority to elites. The college-bound, future elites, are given a somewhat more realistic appraisal of the use of the political process.

Clearly, then, the public educational process operates not to change beliefs, but to reinforce established values; not to encourage diversity, but to demand conformity. Public education serves established elites quite well. It denies political skills and knowledge to the masses. As Lane and Sears aptly put it: "The Platonic Code (only the 'guardians' to be educated for leadership) here, in fact, had its modern incarnation."[42]

How Does Democracy Survive?

This portrait of the elite and the masses indicates that survival of a democratic system does not depend upon a consensus that penetrates to every level of society. It is apparently not necessary that most people commit themselves to a democracy; all that is necessary is that they fail to commit themselves actively to an anti-democratic system. One might therefore conclude that American democracy is on shaky foundations. However, it is important to keep in mind that although the masses may have anti-democratic attitudes, they are also inclined to avoid political activity. And those with the most dangerous attitudes are the least involved in politics. As sociologist Herbert Hyman notes, "the normal apathy of the public provided some restraint on violent action against possible victims and also made the public less responsive to appeals to intolerance from national figures."[43] The apathy of the masses acts to counterbalance the radically conservative and potentially irrational nature of their values. It takes an unusual leader, such as George Wallace, to raise them from their apathy. Wallace is a "counter-elite," a clear threat to the values of the established elite. His typical appeal plays upon the fears of the masses:

I think there is a backlash in this country against the theoreticians —some of them in some of our colleges and some of our courts and some of our newspaper editors' offices and some of our pulpits —who look down their nose at the steelworker and the paper worker and the communications worker and the beautician and the barber and the policeman and the fireman and the little businessman and the clerk and the farmer and say that you don't have enough intelligence to decide how to get up in the morning and when to go to bed at night, and people are tired of theorists running their country.[44]

The response of the "little people" to Wallace is indicated by his strength in the lower strata of American society.

Conditions for Mass Activism

Occasionally, mass activism replaces mass apathy. This activism reflects the anti-democratic, extremist, hateful, and violence-prone sentiments of the masses, and constitutes a serious threat to democratic values.

Mass activism tends to occur in crisis situations—defeat or humiliation in war, economic depression and unemployment, or threat to public safety. William Kornhauser correctly observes:

There appears to be a close relation between the severity of crises and the extent of mass movements in Western societies. The more severe the depression in industrial societies, the greater the social atomization, and the more widespread are mass movements (for example, there is a high [inverse] association between level of employment and increase in the extremist electorate). The stronger a country's sense of national humiliation and defeat in war, the greater the social atomization, and the greater the mass action (for example, there is a close association between military defeat and the rise of strong mass movements).[45]

Defeat in war, or even failure to achieve any notable victories in a protracted military effort, reduces mass confidence in established leadership and makes the masses vulnerable to the appeals of counter-elites. Both fascism in Germany and communism in Russia followed on the heels of national humiliation and defeat in war. The current anti-establishment culture in America owes a great deal to the mistakes and failures of the nation's leadership in Vietnam.

Mass anxiety and vulnerability to counter-elites are also increased by economic dislocation—depression, unemployment, or technological change—which threatens financial security. It is not so much poverty itself which breeds anxiety, but change or threatened change in the level of affluence. Another source of anxiety among the masses is their perceived level of personal safety. Crime, street violence, and terrorism can produce disproportionately strong anxieties about personal safety. Historically, when they believe their personal safety is threatened, masses in America have turned to vigilantes, the Ku Klux Klan, and "law and order" movements.

The masses are most vulnerable to extremism when they are alienated from group and community life and when they feel their own lives are without direction or purpose. According to William Kornhauser:

People become available for mobilization by [counter] elites when they lack or lose an independent group life. The term masses applies only where we deal with people who . . . cannot be integrated into any organization based on common

interest, into political parties or municipal governments or professional organiza-
tions or trade unions. The lack of autonomous relations generates widespread
social alienation. Alienation heightens responsiveness to the appeal of mass
movements because they provide occasions for expressing resentment against
what is, as well as promises of a vitally different world. In short, people who are
atomized readily become mobilized. Since totalitarianism is a state of total
mobilization, mass society is highly vulnerable to totalitarian movements and
regimes.[46]

Counter-elites: George C. Wallace as Voice of the People

Threats to established elite values occur periodically, from both left and right. The counter-elite pattern is similar, no matter which ideological direction it moves from. Both left and right counter-elite movements base their appeal upon the desire of those who perceive themselves as powerless to overthrow the established elite. Lipset and Raab refer to this appeal as "anti-elitism,"[47] but counter-elitism is a better term.

Though "left" counter-elites in America are just as anti-democratic, extremist, intolerant, and violence-prone as "right" counter-elites, their appeal is currently limited to small numbers of alienated blacks, intellectuals, and college students. "Left" counter-elites have no mass following among workers, farmers, or middle-class Americans. In contrast, "right" counter-elites have been more indigenous to American life, and have mobilized broad mass followings. Many changes in American society have contributed to the popular appeal of "right" counter-elites: shifts in power and prestige from the farms to the cities, from agriculture to industry, from the South to the North; shifts away from individual enterprise toward collective action; shifts away from racial segregation toward special emphasis on opportunities for blacks; shifts from old values to new, from religion to secularism, from work to leisure; shifts in scale from small to large, from personal to impersonal, from individual to bureaucratic; increases in crime, racial disorder, and threats to personal safety. Any genuine "people's" revolution in America would undoubtedly take the form of a right-wing nationalist, patriotic, religious-fundamentalist, anti-black, anti-intellectual, anti-student, "law and order" movement.[48]

Counter-elite movements may seem from their rhetoric to be equalitarian but (like all political activity) are well within the control of the articulate few. Rarely, of course, do counter-elites achieve sufficient resources to put any portion of their values into practice. They can, however, threaten established elites and prod them into providing symbolic satisfaction, in the hope that the anxieties expressed in the counter-elite movement can be reduced. Nixon's "Southern strategy," for instance, is certainly partially generated by his fear of George C. Wallace. Similarly, during the 1930s, Roosevelt's economic policies were partially inspired by a desire to de-fuse the more radically left political movements of the time.

There is perhaps too much significance placed upon the "left" or "right" ideology of counter-elites, and not enough placed upon their deep-seated antagonism toward established elites. For example, granted that Wallace's opposition to integration and his strong support of the Vietnam war are in stark contrast to the professed values of today's radical left, there are some striking similarities in appeal of these two counter-elites. Wallace's economic proposals are appreciably toward the (economically defined) left. For instance, he advocates a federal job-training program, increase in social security, improving Medicare, increases in minimum-wage levels, and other programs quite compatible with the left counter-elite. As one commentator noted:

He is talking about poor people, "ordinary folks," and if you strip him of the southern accent and some of the surrounding rhetoric you might mistake him for a New Left advocate of the poverty program, urging maximum feasible participation of the poor and returning local government to the people, "participatory democracy."[49]

Wallace's early career was typical of many counter-elites in its populism, extremism, anti-elitism, and equalitarianism. But Wallace was particularly important because of his mass base: In the 1968 presidential election, 14 percent of the American electorate completely abandoned the two-party system to support Wallace's independent candidacy. Given the historic, institutional role of the two-party system in America, the strength of traditional party loyalties, family ties, and socialization patterns, the fact that so many people would abandon both parties for an independent candidate is truly astounding.

Both North and South, Wallace appealed to racial sentiments—a mass characteristic of whites which Wallace successfully exploited.* But it is a mistake to dismiss Wallace as merely a racist. He appealed to "little people" throughout the nation by expressing a wide variety of mass sentiments.

---

*Whether Wallace is personally a racist is open to question. In his first run for Governor of Alabama in 1958, Wallace shunned KKK support and ran as a Southern "moderate," against strong segregationist John Patterson. Wallace was badly beaten, and was widely quoted as saying "They out-niggered me that time but they'll never do it again." One Wallace observer says, "I would term the Governor a pseudo-demagogue, because he doesn't really believe what he says about the race question. He uses it only as a technique to get the vote of the nonsophisticated white man." But another observer adds, "He used to be anything but a racist, but with all his chattering he managed to talk himself into it." See Robert Sherrill, *Gothic Politics in the Deep South* (New York: Grossman, 1968), p. 283.

Wallace spoke in *populist* terms about the role of "the people":

The Wallace for President movement is a movement of the people and it doesn't make any difference whether top leading politicians endorse this movement or not. I think that if the politicians get in the way in 1968, a lot of them are gonna get run over by this average man in the steel mill, this barber, this beautician, the policeman on the beat, they're the ones —and the little businessman —I think those are the mass of people that are going to support a change on the domestic scene in this country.[50]

His *anti-intellectualism* and *anti-elitism* held a great deal of mass appeal.

Wallace was *equalitarian* on everything except race. He attacked the "Eastern money interests" and "the over-educated ivory-tower folks with pointed heads looking down their nose at us." He identified communism with wealth: "I don't believe in all this talk about poor folks turning Communist! It's the damn rich who turn Communist. You ever seen a poor Communist?"[51] Republicans were attacked as "bankers and big money people" who exploit "us ordinary folks." Wallace's welfare and public-works programs, when he was Governor of Alabama, were the most liberal in the state's history, and he was regarded as a threat to conservative business interests in that state.

Mass fears about personal safety were just as influential as racial prejudice in stimulating Wallace support. Wallace frequently referred to demonstrators as "the scum of the earth"; he pledged that if a demonstrator ever tried to lie down in front of a Wallace motorcade "it would be the last car he ever lies down in front of." Wallace's simplistic solution to rioting was "to let the police run this country for a year or two and there wouldn't be any riots."

If we were President today, you wouldn't get stabbed or raped in the shadow of the White House, even if we had to call out 30,000 troops and equip them with 2-foot long bayonets and station them every few feet. . . . That's right, we gonna have a police state for folks who burn the cities down. They aren't gonna burn any more cities.[52]

Wallace correctly judged that his mass audience would welcome a police state in order to insure their personal safety. Opinion surveys consistently reported that "crime and violence," "riots," and "law and order" were rated as the most important issues by Wallace's mass following.[53]

Wallace frequently expressed contempt for established institutions and procedures, and an undercurrent of violence is easily detectable in his speeches.

There is one thing more powerful than the Constitution . . . than any constitu-
tion. That's the will of the people. What is a Constitution anyway? They're the
products of the people, the people are the first source of power, and the people
can abolish a Constitution if they want to.[54]

He symbolized popular resistance to court-decreed desegregation by
"standing in the schoolhouse door in person" at the University of
Alabama when he personally interposed his body between federal
marshals and the entrance to the registrar's office. Wallace expressed
very little tolerance of diverse views. Intellectual critics of the Vietnam
War were "long-hairs who ought to be treated as traitors, which they
are." As for courts and constitutional rights of defendants: "Of course if I
did what I'd like to do I'd pick up something and smash one of these
federal judges in the head and then burn the courthouse down. But I'm
too genteel."

The response of conservative intellectuals (e.g., William Buckley)
and conservative politicians (e.g., Barry Goldwater) to Wallace is indicative of their recognition of his status as a counter-elite representative,
rather than as a spokesman of the conservative wing of the established
elite. He was widely condemned by Buckley's *National Review* as a
Populist demagogue. At the same time, he was denounced by the liberal
wing of the established elite as a racist. In the 1968 election, the establishment contenders (with Nixon representing the "moderate" wing of
the conservative portion and Humphrey representing the "moderate"
wing of the liberal portion) were alarmed by Wallace's potential, although each based his fear upon the potential loss of a different constituency. Nixon was afraid of losing the strength in the South established
by Goldwater, while Humphrey feared Wallace's erosion of Democratic
support among the South.

It is not unusual—indeed it is normal—for major parties to absorb,
and de-radicalize, the protest of third-party movements. For they are,
indeed, "movements." Wallace was *initially* concerned more about the
articulation of protest than with immediate electoral success; an upris-
ing against established elites is not likely to propel its leaders into national office. Nevertheless, the fear generated in dominant elites was immediately apparent. Nixon's civil rights policy was a faithful reflection
of his "Southern strategy." He vigorously opposed busing, a major Wallace rallying point, sought to subvert the desegregation guidelines
adopted by the Department of Health, Education and Welfare, and
nominated two Southerners to the Supreme Court. Although Nixon was
unsuccessful in many such efforts, the symbolic gratification to the

South was apparent—in increased support for Nixon in Congress, in Nixon's success in the 1972 election, and in his higher popularity in public opinion polls in the South. Wallace's extraordinarily strong showing in the Democratic primaries of 1972 led both parties to continue their cooptation efforts. Nixon, George Meany, and Edward Kennedy have made overtures to Wallace, and the Democrats have accommodated Wallace's followers within the party. Wallace supporters are represented on the Democratic National Committee and on all other party commissions.

Wallace himself has moved appreciably away from the ideological postures of his early populism. He has built solid strength *within* the party. His image has become more centrist, and his political admirers more astute. In 1972, Wallace knew virtually nothing about the mechanisms of delegate selection. He won preferential primaries without entering delegates, thus depriving himself of votes. He missed filing deadlines in primaries when he could have expected substantial voter support, and he paid scant attention to non-primary states. His organization now has made certain that such errors will not be repeated. The rules of the Democratic party have been revised to maximize the advantages of candidates like Wallace, who demonstrate exceptional strength in primary elections. Rather than "winner-take-all" primaries, in 1976 a proportional-vote system will apply, meaning that delegates will be assigned in proportion to voting strength.

Coming to terms with Wallace is necessary for the Democrats because Wallace's strength has been the traditional Democratic coalition: the South, the young, the undereducated; in short, the working class. With the exception of blacks, Wallace has seized the heart of the Democratic coalition, a coalition which elected Roosevelt, and remained intact until 1968. These voters are personally loyal to Wallace. For the Democrats, then, capturing Wallace's supporters by coopting Wallace is a necessity.

If the Democrats need Wallace, he needs the party. While he probably would have increased his percentage of the vote in the general election from 13 percent in 1968 to 19 percent in 1972, he can expect no appreciable success without the support of the Democratic party. He is clearly the preferred candidate of the right-wing Democrats, but certainly not the left-wing Democrats, nor is he as well received with the center as the traditional centrist candidates. Thus, the move to the center, accompanied by a rejection of the "new politics" by the traditional Democratic elites, heralds the transformation of the Wallace "movement" into the Wallace "organization." The counter-elite has now been admitted to elite circles.

Failure of Elites

Although the masses can usually be counted on to leave politics to the elites, we should not necessarily assume that our freedoms are safe in the hands of the elites. In periods of crisis, support for our civil liberties does not appear to be very great even among those with college educations. For example, a poll taken in Minnesota indicates that the educated citizenry had an unfavorable opinion about those who took part in demonstrations against the war in Vietnam, even though no laws were broken. Only 25 percent of the college-educated population had a favorable impression of people who took part in demonstrations.[55] Further, 50 percent of the college-educated population felt that communists were heavily involved in anti-Vietnam demonstrations. To take another example, the elected leaders of the country, notably President Johnson and Vice-President Humphrey (not to mention Mayor Richard Daley of Chicago), left little doubt that they considered the demonstrations at the 1968 Democratic Convention unpatriotic, and thus provided tacit approval to police attacks on demonstrators.

The failure of the elite to defend the right to demonstrate against the war in Vietnam is not a unique example of the failure of elites to support civil liberties. The career of Senator Joseph McCarthy, and the response of elites to his career, is another example of the failure of elites to respond to a challenge to the system. To be sure, McCarthy's assault upon traditional freedoms was especially popular with those of less education, which is consistent with what we know about the relationship between education and political attitudes. The less-educated were undoubtedly also strongly attracted by McCarthy's anti-intellectual and anti-aristocratic appeals (it is rare that the anti-intellectualism of the masses is provided with articulate leadership). However, for a long period McCarthy's career went virtually unchallenged even by the elites. As David Truman phrases it, "The response in that segment [the elite] during the years 1950–1954 was not reassuring. Though the evidence is not beyond contradiction, it seems clear that among the elites the threat was not generally seen for what it was.[56]

When elites feel threatened, their response is not necessarily more extreme than that of masses; but it is considerably more direct. In its reaction to the New Left, the Nixon Administration was not merely exploiting the tendency of the masses to resort to scapegoating. It perceived a genuine threat—both to its policy and to the "national interest." The Watergate matter was, among other things, a response to the threat of mass unrest. The visible threat to the *status quo*—disruptive demonstrations, flag-burnings, flouting of traditional patterns of sexual behavior, and, in general, a decline of respect for authority, made it apparent to Nixon that the established traditions were under serious attack. Although Wallace's counter-elite movement articulated the majority backlash to sudden change, Wallace himself could serve as nothing more than a symbol of reaction.

Nixon could, and did, do more. Two of Nixon's aides, John Dean and H. R. Haldeman, described the atmosphere in the White House in the early 1970s: "The Watergate Matter was an inevitable growth of a climate of excessive concern over the political impact of demonstrations. . . . Taken as part of an apparent campaign to force upon the President a policy favorable to the North Vietnamese, these demonstrations were more than just a garden variety exercise of the First Amendment."[57]

As a consequence of these fears, domestic intelligence units were organized to cope with the threat. Such units were to deal with demonstrations on a basis independent from the "normal" intelligence apparatus. These domestic intelligence units were responsible for the various abuses now associated with the Watergate affair.

But Watergate was not the first example of elite repression, nor will it be the last. The backlash against social change after World War I led to the establishment of a General Intelligence Division in the Justice Department to investigate domestic radicals. Dossiers were kept on 200,000 suspects, and more than 10,000 were actually arrested. The repression of the 1920s, moreover, was led by the national government, but many state and local governments followed the example of Washington.

Thus, Watergate is one of a series of elite responses to mass unrest; it is not unique, with the possible exception of the fact that the elite response was apparently generated within the office of the President.

If the masses, acting in accordance with their values, would destroy freedom, then we are left with the elites as the defender of this freedom. Though the elites may be "carriers of the creed" in their attitude, their actions in support of liberty have often been less than adequate. Thus, mass apathy, rather than elite activism, seems to be the key to the survival of democracy.

Elite—Mass Communication

Because of the political apathy of the masses, the elite policy makers generally operate with minimal restriction from the masses. However, they are still constrained by their perception of the opinions of the masses. These perceptions can often be incorrect, unless elites are able to undertake sophisticated analyses of public opinion. For instance, if congressmen pay special attention to their mail, they may reach a conclusion about the opinions of their constituency that is actually quite the reverse of the true structure of opinion.

Congressmen affirm that most of their mail is in agreement with the position that they advocate. The congressman therefore has considerable initiative in organizing the nature of the communications that he wishes to receive. By establishing his image in the minds of his constituents, and by establishing relationships with constituency groups whose attitudes are congruent with his own, the congressman can create a world of public opinion that is self-reinforcing: "He makes the world to which he thinks he is responding."[58]

These conclusions suggest that the flow of influence is from the elite to selected sub-elites, rather than the reverse. Elites create pressure to which they respond, if they wish. The phenomenon of elites creating opinions among the masses is sometimes referred to as "the mobilization of bias" or as a "false consensus."[59] Its ramifications for popular democratic theory are great; for elites, by controlling the values and norms of society, can thereby also control the issues upon which governmental decision makers act. Control of this type is subtle and effective. Peter Bachrach and Morton Baratz describe it as follows:

Of course power is exercised when A participates in the making of decisions that affect B. But power is also exercised when A devotes his energies to creating or reinforcing social and political values and institutional practices that limit the scope of the political process to public consideration of only those issues which are comparatively innocuous to A. To the extent that A succeeds in doing this, B is prevented, for all practical purposes, from bringing to the fore any issues that might in their resolution be seriously detrimental to A's set of preferences.[60]

This same effect can be achieved whether elites covertly control social values or overtly control the mechanism through which wants and demands are transmitted to government. In either case, issues do not receive governmental attention without the approval of the elite. Nor is it obvious to the casual observer that such demands exist, for they remain silent and unarticulated. Since such issues never enter the visible political arena, they arouse no perceptible conflict or debate.

Elite Perception of Mass Attitudes   Given the relative freedom of elites from pressure from below, it should be understood that this freedom varies with the type of issue. In the case of the reduction of tariffs, the low level of public visibility (interest in the issue) undoubtedly contributed to elite freedom. Some evidence for the relationship between issue visibility and congruence of attitude between elites and masses can be gleaned from a study of the interrelations between constituency attitude and congressional attitude in three key areas of public policy: social welfare, foreign affairs, and civil rights. The greatest agreement between the representative and his constituents occurred in the area of civil

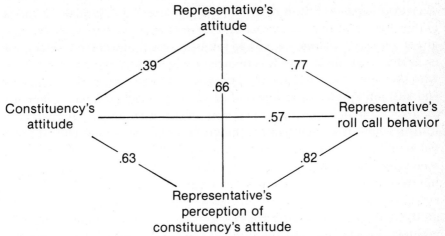

Figure 5-1. Intercorrelations of variables pertaining to civil rights. (From Warren E. Miller and Donald E. Stokes, "Constituency Influence in Congress," *American Political Science Review*, 57:1 (March 1963), pp. 45–56.)

rights, the next closest in the area of welfare, and the smallest correlation in the area of foreign affairs.[61] Civil rights clearly provokes more interest than social welfare or foreign policy and seems to require that the congressman conform more closely to the wishes of his constituents.

We have already noted that communications between elites and masses are tenuous and that perceptions of mass opinions by elites are distorted. The crucial question, then, is to what extent does the actual voting behavior of the representative reflect the attitudes of constituents, rather than the representative's *perception* of these attitudes? As Figure 5–1 shows, there is generally a stronger correlation between constituency attitude and the representative's *perception* of constituency attitude than there is between constituency attitude and the representative's actual attitude. For example, the association between constituency attitude and the representative's attitude on the question of civil rights is only .39, while the correlation between constituency attitude and the representative's *perception* of constituency attitude is .63. Naturally, since congressmen select the groups with which they wish to communicate, their perception of constituency attitudes is distorted. The greatest correlation occurs between the representative's vote and his perception of his constituents' attitudes, while the weakest correlation occurs between the representative's vote and the actual attitude of his constituents. Thus, perceptual distortions are translated into actual voting behavior. Only on the issue of civil rights are legislators acting in reasonable conformity to the attitudes of the people.

Congressmen's Response to Mass Attitudes   There is no evidence to suggest that a congressman will alter his behavior in accordance with his perceptions of constituents' attitudes. Charles Jones groups members of the House of Representatives into three categories: those whose margin of victory from one election to the next was reduced by 5 percent or more, those whose margin was reduced by less than 5 percent, and those who increased their margin of victory. He reasons that if the campaign and election are not issue-oriented events, there should be no difference in changes in voting behavior between these three groups. Alternatively, if the election is issue-oriented, the group of congressmen who suffered the greatest decrease in margin of victory should be expected to change their behavior more radically, since they should perceive from the election results that many constituents disapprove of their voting behavior. He finds that there is no appreciable difference between any of the groups, whether the election is issue-oriented or not. Indeed, the representatives who suffered the greatest decline in support exhibited the least change in voting behavior.[62] Thus, even though representatives perceive the outcome of an election to be related directly to their voting behavior, they do not change their behavior because of the results of an election.

The persistence of voting patterns indicates that congressmen do not necessarily respond uncritically to constituent demands. No evidence of the self-perception of congressmen is available, but the self-images of state legislators support this assertion. Wahlke, Eulau, Buchanan, and Ferguson found that the majority of representatives filled the role of the *trustee*; that is, they believed that the representative is a free agent who should follow the dictates of his conscience.[63] The delegate role, an alternative orientation which holds that the representative should act according to the constituency's wishes, was filled by about 25 percent of the legislators. Miller and Stokes, on the other hand, concluded from their research that no single model of representative behavior can be adequate to explain their data. On the issue of civil rights, the representatives behaved more like delegates; on foreign policy, they behaved more like trustees.[64] Although it is unwise to make inferences from these data beyond the setting in which they were gathered, we can at least conclude that elites do not regard effective communication with constituents as a prerequisite for rational decision making.

Mass Perception of Elite Roles Given the fact that the representative has extremely imperfect information about the preference of his constituency, and given the complementary fact that the constituency is unaware of most of the policy stands of the representative, it seems likely that the delegate role is rarely played by congressmen. The constituency may well believe that this role is appropriate, but they are not able to make it a possibility. For example, one study indicates that only 18 percent of a sample of constituents have a trustee perception of legislators. Twenty-six percent of the respondents supported both delegate and trustee models simultaneously; and by far the largest group, 47 percent, felt that representatives should behave as instructed delegates.[65] In relating these varying perceptions of the proper role of the legislator to certain socioeconomic characteristics of the respondents, the researchers found that the upper socioeconomic groups were more likely to support the trustee perception than were the lower socioeconomic groups. For example, only 3 percent of those with grade school education have trustee orientations, compared to 25 percent of those with college education (Table 5–6). Similarly, professional and

Table 5-6 / Education and the Perception of Legislators by Constituents

Education	Instructed Delegate	Trustee	Ambivalent	Politico
Grade school	50%	3%	47%	
High School	49	17	23	11%
College	43	25	22	10

Source: Carl D. McMurray and Malcolm B. Parsons, "Public Attitudes toward the Representational Roles of Legislators and Judges," *Midwest Journal of Political Science*, 9:2 (May 1965), 167–185.

managerial occupations provide a high proportion of the support for the trustee role. The greatest commitment to the delegate role occurs among the lower strata of society, those who are least likely to take an active role in the political process. Nearly 60 percent of the nonparticipants in politics support the delegate role, as against 35 percent of the high participants. Ironically, the citizens most jealous of their potential for control over elites are those least likely to try to use that control.

TV and the Liberal Establishment Bias

It is chiefly by mass media that elites instruct masses about politics. Network television is far more important in elite-to-mass communication than newspapers; the masses watch television hours each day, but seldom do more than glance through newspapers. Television broadcasting in America is overwhelmingly controlled by three private corporations—the American Broadcasting Company (ABC), National Broadcasting Corporation (NBC), and Columbia Broadcasting System (CBS). They determine almost all that will be seen by the viewing audience; there is little public regulation of network broadcasting. Individual television stations are privately owned and licensed to use public broadcast channels by the Federal Communication Commission. All but a few of the largest and wealthiest of these stations are forced to receive news and programming from the networks because of the high production costs involved in *producing* news or entertainment at the local station level. The top officials of the networks, particularly those in charge of the news, are indeed "a tiny, enclosed fraternity of privileged men."*

The Liberal Bias of TV News   This elite permits far *less* diversity of views on television than is in the press, which presents a wide spectrum of views. Conventionally "liberal" and "conservative" news can be found, respectively, in such publications as *The New York Times* versus *The Chicago Tribune; Time Magazine* versus *U.S. News and World Report; The New York Post* versus *The Wall Street Journal; The New Republic* versus *The National Review; The Village Voice* versus *Barron's Weekly.* One reason for this greater diversity in print than in television is the mass appeal of television versus the specialized appeal of print. The larger the audience, the less the opportunity to satisfy a well-articulated ideological constituency. As the audience for television grows, so does the proportion of people relying upon it primarily for their view of what is happening. Given the general apathy of the masses, the growth of television as an information source was inevitable. Reading about politics is largely the information-gathering device of the educated strata; passively observing the playing out of a political drama is a characteristic of the less educated masses.

Granted that television is truly mass (that is, unspecialized) communication, and granted that it takes very little effort to flip on the set, networks—and politicians—seem to have overestimated the audience for the major networks' nightly news shows. About 20 percent of the adult population are *regular* news viewers and 80 percent irregular or non-news viewers. Indeed, a slight majority of the population watches *no* network news![66]

Most people watch television to be entertained, not informed. For in-depth information, the half-hour news format is unsatisfactory. So, network news resembles entertainment—but without the audience entertainment has. Norman Nie, drawing upon the extensive research of Gary Steiner, concludes: "When citizens have the opportunity to choose between public information and entertainment, they choose entertain-

---

*The phraseology is courtesy of former Vice President Spiro T. Agnew, who also used the more colorful description of the network top brass—"super-sensitive, self-anointed, supercilious electronic barons of opinion." See *Newsweek* (November 9, 1970), p. 22.

ment."[67] These data call into question the popular view of an entire nation waiting breathlessly for the latest *pronunciamentos* from David Brinkley. Once again, elites transfer to masses their own intense interest in politics: Because these elites *believe* that news commentators attract huge audiences, they tend to treat them as a surrogate public. Even so, 20 percent of the adult population is larger than the readership of the mass-circulation weekly news sources or newspapers.

If the audience for TV news is smaller than most people believe, it is still large and still characterized by a preponderance of less educated persons. That TV news programs have taken on a distinctly moderate-liberal, Eastern-establishment point of view is therefore ironic, because it falls upon the ears of those least likely to find it attractive, *if they perceive overt bias.* As Hennessy argues: "The liberalization of the big media has been most noticeable with regard to Vietnam, but apparent too since 1965 on black power, poverty in America, military-industrial complex, environmental pollution, and most of the other quality-of-life issues the new left is seized with."[68]

Such a bias is most likely to appear in the selection of topics to be covered. As David Brinkley explained candidly, "News is what I say it is. It's something worth knowing by my standards."[69] In newspaper reporting, such selection (or "agenda-setting") is possible, but less necessary. On a half-hour news program, *most* of what has happened in the past 24 hours must be excluded. But Brinkley is only part right. The agenda-setting of news broadcasts is partially a function of the entertainment or dramatic potential of the story. There can be very little background analysis; there must be "action." Stories are therefore chosen for their dramatic quality; "people doing something, preferably involving disagreement, conflict, or adventure."[70] Thus, news programs and other media might be significant in telling people *what* they should have opinions about even if they do not sell them an opinion.

The complaint that TV news shows the bad side of America is correct. The bad side is more interesting and intriguing to watch, and TV is in the business of attracting large audiences who will buy the products offered by its sponsors. A particularly intriguing piece of evidence bears upon the presentation of the "worst" about America (e.g., riots, protests, the Vietnamese War). Comparison of CBS Evening News with the Canadian counterpart, CBC National News, indicates that the American news concentrated much more of its time on violence, protest, and war. Even cancelling out the effects of the Vietnam War, CBS news is bloody compared to CBC (CBC, by arrangement, originates about 20 percent of its news from CBS and NBC). Of course, one can hardly conclude that CBS "distorts reality." One can just as easily argue that since America is considerably more violent than Canada,[71] CBS is simply telling it like it is. The author of the study concludes that the heavy dose of violence in American television news might be a function of three factors: (1) passive reporting of a violent society, (2) reflections of popular interest in violence, or (3) an emphasis by TV on the more violent aspects of life in America.[72]

Assuming, then, that through a combination of editorial bias in selection, the necessity to entertain the audience, and the responsibility to report (with inevitable bias) the unpleasant facts about life in America, the TV audience is told what to think about—to what extent does the presentation of news induce any appreciable change in attitude?

Mass Resistance to Indoctrination

By most evidence, mass media do not directly change opinion. For example, media coverage of the 1968 Democratic Convention was biased, according to Efron, for the rioters and against the police.[73] Contrary to the expectations of the newscasters, public opinion samples revealed that the masses remained unsympathetic to antiwar demonstrators, and the networks were flooded with mail protesting the newsmen's interpretation of events. What had happened is quite predictable. People "selectively perceive" reality: What the media present and what people see are often quite different. Selective perception is especially applicable to TV because of the low attention level required to absorb information. The media thought they were presenting a picture of innocent "kids" being brutally assaulted; people saw radical troublemakers getting what they deserved. Previously, when the ghetto riots were in full swing, the Kerner Commission concluded that TV coverage emphasized the control of riots and the activities of police in restoring order rather than actual acts of violence.[74] Yet most of the ghetto dwellers remembered TV as depicting the actual riot, with only a few remembering arrests and crowd control.[75] Finally, there is Vietnam. Presumably, Americans were made more aware of the horrors of death by the uniqueness of the "Living Room War." However, Mueller finds that events reported on TV—the Tet offensive, General Westmoreland's retirement, the emergence of peace candidates, etc.—did not have enought impact to "reduce support for the war below the levels attained by the Korean War, when television was in its infancy, until casualty levels had far surpassed those of the earlier war."[76]

Attitudes—particularly deeply held ones—are not changed easily. The liberal-establishment bias of the mass media runs into strong resistance: the filtering mechanics of the human perceptual system. Perceptions of reality—as distinguished from attitudes—might be more amenable to manipulation. In spite of occasional protests, most people think TV is unbiased. (Those who watch it most, the relatively uneducated, think it is less biased than those who watch it least, the college educated.) Thus, information from a relatively trusted source might gradually change images of reality. For instance, although the majority still supported the government's position in Vietnam, the percentage believing the Americans and South Vietnamese were losing ground rose 15 percent after the 1968 Tet offensive. While attitudes remained firm, the government's assurances that we were winning became suspect as the siege of Saigon unfolded.[77]

It should be kept constantly in mind that—whatever is intended by the media—there is the solid rock of mass apathy against which their persuasive efforts founder. Moreover, as we have just shown, the direction of mass response to the liberal media is not always as intended by the media. As a further illustration of this point, any casual observer of television will have had little trouble in detecting the fact that most correspondents opposed Nixon's election to the presidency. Yet Nixon *was* elected president, certainly in spite of, but perhaps to a limited degree *because* of television. By concentrating upon the "bad" as opposed to the "good" in the 1960s, newscasts presented an image of reality that suggested chaos, disorder, and deterioration of respect for authority. In such an environment, Richard Nixon thrived:

For a long time there were two basic issues in National politics: foreign policies, a traditional advantage to the Republicans, and economics, a plus for the Democrats. Now there is a third: law and order's shorthand for street crime, race, protest tactics, and "revolution." It has been forty years since American politics generated an issue so intense that it could change partisan loyalties for vast numbers of citizens. Law and Order may be such an issue. Where did it come from?

We suggest that the essential midwives in birth of the issue were Messrs. Cronkite, Brinkley, and their brethren—television's newsmen who, we hasten to add, are probably as strongly revolted by the appearance of Law and Order as any group in America.[78]

Robinson's careful analysis of audience response strongly suggests that the unintended consequences of television are paramount.[79] The case under investigation was the program *The Selling of the Pentagon*, produced by CBS. His results suggest that "malaise"—and television viewing are linked. Indeed, television has escalated cynicism and feelings of helplessness in America. Robinson's experimental audience roughly approximated the center of the political spectrum, that is, the "real majority" of Middle Americans. Most had seen or heard nothing about the controversy surrounding the showing of the documentary; the fury within the governmental elite was, of course, quite unjustified. Shown opposite Marcus Welby, *The Selling of the Pentagon* lost four to one. Among those who did watch, while some shift in opinion about the military did occur, very little opinion shift took place concerning the alleged power of the military-industrial complex. Indeed, most viewers had no opinion before or after watching. Robinson did observe, however, that political self-confidence (the feeling that one can influence political events) declined after watching. In fact, those who depend upon television news are generally less self-confident than those who do not (even taking into account the tendency of poorly educated people, who are less self-confident, to depend heavily upon television). Further, heavy reliance upon television tends to increase disinterest and political cynicism. Not surprisingly, those who watch great amounts of television—whether news or entertainment—significantly overestimate the probability of being the victim of a crime.

One of the ironies of the elite-mass communication through television is that the sophistication of the mass media is forced to reduce its message to the simplistic level of good versus evil. Possessed of a shallow, primitive liberalism, the newscasters view politicians as good or bad largely because of their image. For example, Senator Muskie is "Lincolnesque," Nixon is "shifty." In general, news commentators view politics as a game played by politicians to advance themselves personally. Falling upon the ears of the politically unsophisticated, the message of TV news may enter an echo chamber, for the less educated are a good deal less sanguine that most elites about the benevolence of their leaders. Such a combination may contribute to "videomalaise," a general feeling of frustration, and a longing for quick solutions, which is susceptible to the appeals of counter-elites. George Wallace, for example, drew a slightly higher vote among excessive television viewers than did either Nixon or Humphrey.[80] It goes without saying that commentators disapproved of Wallace, but television actually assisted his candidacy, as it had Nixon's, by making him a viable candidate.

Perhaps the best example of the distorted message of television is not George Wallace, nor Richard Nixon, both of whom profited by the description of the country as on the verge of anarchy; but rather Archie Bunker, the bigoted hero of CBS's *All in the Family*. The producer of the show reasoned that, by poking fun at Bunker's bigotry, the absurdity of his views would become apparent. By holding Archie Bunker up to ridicule, he believed, racism would be combated. To achieve this goal, scripts called for Bunker's son-in-law, Mike (a long-haired college student) to "make sense." In contrast, Archie is portrayed as one whose reasoning is "convoluted." However, only 10 percent of a sample of American adolescent viewers named Archie as the person most often ridiculed; 46 percent named Mike! Most viewers simply did not see the program as satire: ". . . highly prejudiced adolescents are more prone than less prejudiced adolescents to watch *All in the Family* in particular . . . [it] seems to be appealing more to the racially and ethnically prejudiced members of society than to the less prejudiced members."[81] Yet the myth of television influence persists. *All in the Family,* a program which attracts a highly prejudiced audience, was given the 1972 Image Award by the Los Angeles Chapter of the NAACP for its contribution to race relations!

We began this section by asserting that elites use media to instruct masses. We can conclude that quite a bit is lost in the translation. Most Americans now believe there is genuine danger of social and political disintegration. The liberal establishment (in this case, television news reporters) believes the causes of disintegration are systemic. The masses, agreeing that "the country is going to hell" do not accept or understand systemic explanations and look for scapegoats.

Summary

Elite theory suggests that elites are distinguished from the masses not only by their socioeconomic background but also by their attitudes and values. Elites give greater support to the principles and beliefs underlying the political system. Our analysis of elite and mass attitudes suggests the following propositions:

1. Elites give greater support to democratic values than masses. Elites are also more consistent than masses in applying general principles of democracy to specific individuals, groups, and events.

2. Extremist and intolerant movements in modern society are more likely to be based in lower classes than in middle and upper classes. The poor may be more liberal on economic issues, but when liberalism is defined in noneconomic terms—as support for civil liberties, for example—then the upper classes are more liberal and the lower classes more conservative. Masses demonstrate antidemocratic attitudes more often than elites. Mass movements exploit the alienation and hostility of lower classes by concentrating upon scapegoats.

3. The masses are less committed to democratic rules of the game than elites and more likely to go outside these rules to engage in violence. Mass activism tends to be undemocratic, unstable, and frequently violent.

4. The survival of democracy depends upon the commitment of elites to democratic ideals rather than upon broad support for democracy by the masses.

5. Political apathy and nonparticipation among the masses contribute to the survival of democracy. Fortunately for democracy, the anti-democratic masses are generally more apathetic than elites. Only an unusual demagogue or counter-elite can arouse the masses from their apathy and create a threat to the established system.

6. Occasionally mass apathy is replaced by mass activism, which is generally extremist, intolerant, anti-democratic, and violence-prone. Conditions which encourage mass activism include defeat or humiliation in war, economic dislocation, or perceived threats to personal safety.

7. Counter-elites appeal to mass sentiments and express hostility toward the established order and its values. Both "left" and "right" counter-elites are anti-democratic, extremist, impatient with due process, contemptuous of law and authority, and violence-prone. Counter-elites express racial prejudices, populism, equalitarianism, anti-intellectualism, and simplistic solutions to social problems.

8. Although "left" counter-elites are just as anti-democratic as "right" counter-elites, their appeal is limited to small numbers of alienated blacks, college students, and intellectuals. In contrast, "right" counter-elites have mobilized mass support among large numbers of farmers, workers, and middle-class Americans. George C. Wallace is a typical mass counter-elite, not only in his appeal to racial sentiments but in his appeal to other mass values.

9. Although elites are relatively more committed to democratic values than masses, elites may abandon these values in crisis periods. When war or revolution threatens the existing order, elites themselves may deviate from democratic values to maintain the system. Dissent is no longer tolerated—the mass media are censored, free speech curtailed, counter-elites jailed, police and security forces strengthened.

10. Elite-mass communication is very difficult. Most of the communication received by decision makers is from other elite members rather than the masses. The decision maker's perceptions of mass attitudes are likely to be affected by his own values; consequently he interprets public opinion to support his own position.

11. Although elites are relatively free of mass influence, this freedom varies with the issue. The masses are ignorant about most political issues and consequently cannot convey any message to decision makers about them. But on issues of race and civil rights mass attitudes are well-formed. Decision makers have a reasonably accurate perception of mass attitudes on civil rights and are more likely to vote their perception of mass attitudes than their own feelings on civil rights questions.

12. The masses believe that elected decision makers should behave as instructed delegates, but very few decision makers consider themselves delegates. Instead decision makers believe they are free agents who should follow the dictates of their own conscience.

13. Efforts by elites to change mass attitudes are not uniformly successful, although elites believe that they are very influential. Television serves as an example.

References

[1]*Fortune* (June 1940).

[2]Herbert H. Hyman and Paul B. Sheatsley, "Trends in Public Opinion on Civil Liberties," *Journal of Social Issues*, 9 (1953), 6–16.

[3]Samuel A. Stouffer, *Communism, Conformity and Civil Liberties* (New York: John Wiley, 1966). Originally published in 1955.

[4]J. Allen Williams, "Communism, Conformity, and Civil Liberty: Highlights of a 1973 Replication of Stouffer's 1954 Study." Paper presented at the Southwestern Sociological Association Convention, Dallas, March 1974.

[5]Hazel Erskine, "The Polls: Freedom of Speech," *Public Opinion Quarterly*, 34 (February 1970), 484.

[6]Williams, "Communism, Conformity, and Civil Liberty," p. 6.

[7]William Fulbright, *The Arrogance of Power* (New York: Vintage, 1966), p. 27.

[8]McClosky, "Consensus and Ideology in American Politics," 365.

[9]Seymour Martin Lipset, *Political Man* (Garden City, N.Y.: Doubleday & Co., 1963), p. 87.

[10]Lipset, p. 92.

[11]Lewis Lipsitz, "Work Life and Political Attitudes: A Study of Manual Workers," *American Political Science Review*, 58:4 (December 1964), 959.

[12]Claude E Bowman, "Mental Health in the Worker's World," in Arthur B. Shostk and William Gomberg (eds.), *Blue Collar World: Studies of the American Worker* (Englewood Cliffs, N.J.: Prentice-Hall, 1964), p. 374.

[13]Lipset, *Political Man*, p. 114.

[14]Lipset, p. 110.

[15]Lewis Lipsitz, "Working-class Authoritarianism: A Reevaluation," *American Sociological Review* 30 (1965), 103–109.

[16]Martin Trow, "Small Businessmen, Political Tolerance, and Support for McCarthy," *American Journal of Sociology*, 64:270 (November 1958), 280.

[17]Herbert McClosky, "Personality and Attitude Correlates of Foreign Policy Orientation," Publication A-48, Survey Research Center, University of California at Berkeley, in J. Rosenau (ed), *Domestic Sources of Foreign Policy* (New York: Free Press, 1967), pp. 51–110.

[18]Seymour Lipset and Reinhard Bendix, *Social Mobility in Industrial Society* (Berkeley: University of California Press, 1960), p. 103.

[19]Morris Janowitz. *The Professional Soldier: A Social and Political Portrait* (New York: Free Press, 1970), p. 238.

[20]McClosky, "Personality and Attitude Correlates of Foreign Policy Orientation," p. 90.

[21]This section draws heavily upon Harmon Zeigler and Wayne Peak, "The Political Functions of the Educational System," *Sociology of Education*, 43 (Spring 1970), 115–142.

[22]Donald R. Matthews and James W. Prothro, *Negroes and the New Southern Politics* (New York: Harcourt, Brace and World, 1966), p. 129.

[23]V. O. Key, Jr., *Public Opinion and American Democracy* (New York: Alfred A. Knopf, 1963), p. 316.

[24]S. Pressey, "Changes From 1923 to 1943 in the Attitudes of Public School and University Students," *Journal of Psychology*, 21 (1946), 173–188.

[25]Angus Campbell and Howard Schuman, "Racial Attitudes in Fifteen American Cities,"

Supplemental Studies for the National Advisory Committee on Civil Disorders (Washington: Government Printing Office, 1968), p. 35.

[26]Robert E. Lane and David O. Sears, *Public Opinion* (Englewood Cliffs, N.J.: Prentice-Hall, Inc., 1964), p. 25.

[27]Kenneth P. Langton, *Political Socialization* (New York: Oxford University Press, 1969), p. 18.

[28]Byron G. Massialas, "American Government: We Are the Greatest!", in C. Benjamin Cox and Byron G. Massialas, *Social Studies in the United States*, (New York: Harcourt, Brace and World, 1967), pp. 191–192.

[29]William A. McClenoghan, *Magruder's American Government* (Boston: Allyn and Bacon, 1966), p. 20. Cited in Massialas, *op. cit.*, p. 179.

[30]Cited in Mark N. Krug, *History and the Social Sciences* (Waltham, Mass.: Blaisdell Publishing Co., 1967), p. 202.

[31]Cole and Montgomery, *op cit.*, pp. 341–342. Cited in Girault, *op. cit.*, p. 227.

[32]Robert P. Ludlum, *et. al.*, *American Government* (Boston: Houghton, Mifflin, 1965), p. 2. Cited in Massialas, *op. cit.*, p. 180.

[33]Massialas, *op. cit.*, p. 182.

[34]Stuart Gary Brown and Charles L. Pelthier, *Government in Our Republic* (New York: Macmillan, 1964), pp. 20–21. Cited in Massialas, *op. cit.*, p. 183.

[35]McClenoghan, *op. cit.*, pp.26–27. Cited in Massialas, *op. cit.*, p. 184.

[36]Jules Henry, "Attitude Organization in Elementary School Classrooms," in W. W. Charters, Jr. and N. L. Gage (eds.), *Readings in the Social Psychology of Education* (Boston: Allyn and Bacon, 1963), pp. 254–263.

[37]Zeigler and Peak, *op. cit.*, p. 133.

[38]Richard M. Merelman, *Political Socialization and Educational Climates* (New York: Holt, Rinehart and Winston, Inc., 1971), p. 129.

[39]John C. Pock, *Attitudes Toward Civil Liberties Among High School Seniors* (Washington: U.S. Department of Health, Education, and Welfare, 1967), p. 134.

[40]Kenneth P. Langton and M. Kent Jennings, "Political Socialization and the High School Civics Curriculum," *American Political Science Review*, 62 (September 1968), 864.

[41]Edgar Litt, "Civic Education, Community Norms, and Political Indoctrination," *American Sociological Review*, 28 (Feb. 1963), 69–75.

[42]Lane and Sears, *op. cit.*, p. 27.

[43]Herbert H. Hyman, "England and America: Climates of Tolerance and Intolerance, 1962," in Daniel Bell (ed.), *The Radical Right* (Garden City, N.Y.: Doubleday & Co., 1963), p. 229. Although England went through the same postwar stress as America, English investigations of suspected subversives were more limited. Hyman concludes that "when millions of individuals . . . are brought under official scrutiny as possible security risks, it validates the belief that everyone ought to be regarded with suspicion. . . . It thus encourages in the public at large a climate of intolerance toward those who may exhibit nonconformist opinions."

[44]*Life* (August 2, 1969), p. 20.

[45]William Kornhauser, *The Politics of Mass Society* (New York: Free Press, 1959), p. 174.

[46]Kornhauser, p. 33.

[47]Seymour Martin Lipset and Earl Raab, *The Politics of Unreason* (New York: Harper and Row, 1970), p. 348.

[48]Lipset and Raab, p. 3.

[49]Ward Just, "Discontent Is the Mood of Wallace Audiences," *Washington Post*, October, 12, 1967, p. B-4, Cited in Lipset and Raab, *op. cit.*, p. 349.

[50]Lipset and Raab, *op. cit.*, p. 349.

[51]Lipset and Raab, *op. cit.*, p. 350.

[52]*Newsweek*, September 16, 1968, p. 27.

[53]Lipset and Raab, *op. cit.*, p. 406.

[54]Marshall Frady, *Wallace* (New York: World, 1968), p. 227.

[55]*Gallup Political Index*, June 1967, Report No. 24.

[56]David B. Truman, "The American System in Crisis," *Political Science Quarterly*, 74 (December 1959), 495.

[57]*The Watergate Hearings* (New York: Bantam Books, 1973) pp. 266, 500.

[58]Bauer, Pool, and Dexter, *American Business and Public Policy*.

[59]E. E. Schattschneider, *The Semisovereign People: A Realist's View of Democracy in America* (New York: Holt, Rinehart, and Winston, 1960), p. 71; and Robert A. Dahl, "A Critique of the Power Elite Model," *American Political Science Review*, 52 (June 1958), 468.

[60]Peter Bachrach and Morton S. Baratz, "Two Faces of Power," in Willis D. Hawley and Frederick M. Wirt (eds.) *The Search for Community Power* (Englewood Cliffs, N.J.: Prentice-Hall, 1968), pp. 241–242. Also see Peter Bachrach, *The Theory of Democratic Elitism: A Critique* (Boston: Little, Brown and Co., 1967). A critical appraisal of this analysis is contained in Richard M. Merelman, "On the Neo-elitist Critique of Community Power," *American Political Science Review*, 62 (June 1968), 451–460.

[61]Warren E. Miller and Donald E. Stokes, "Constituency Influence in Congress," *American Political Science Review*, 57: 1(March 1963), 45–56.

[62]Charles O. Jones, "The Role of the Campaign in Congressional Politics," in Zeigler and Jennings (eds.) *The Electoral Process* (Englewood Cliffs, N.J.: Prentice-Hall, 1966), p. 36.

[63]Wahlke, Eulau, Buchanan, and Ferguson, *The Legislative System: Explorations in Legislative Behavior* (New York: John Wiley, 1962), p. 281.

[64]Miller and Stokes, "Constituency Influence in Congress," pp. 45–56.

[65]Carl D. McMurray and Malcolm B. Parsons, "Public Attitudes toward the Representational Roles of Legislators and Judges," *Midwest Journal of Political Science*, 9:2 (May 1965), 167–185.

[66]John P. Robinson, "The Audience for National TV News Programs," *Public Opinion Quarterly*, 35 (Fall 1971), 403–404.

[67]Norman Nie, "Communication and Citizen Participation," in Harold Sackman and Norman Nie, *The Information Utility and Social Choice* (Montvale, N.J.: AFIPS Press, 1970), p. 239. See also Gary A. Steiner, *The People Look at Television: A Study of Audience Attitudes* (New York: Knopf, 1963), p. 201.

[68]Bernard Hennessy, "Welcome, Spiro Agnew," *The New Republic* (December 13, 1969), 14. Edith Efron, *The News Twisters* (Los Angeles: Nash, 1971), makes much the same point. Unfortunately, the content analyses upon which she bases her conclusions are methodologically faulty.

[69]Efron, *op. cit.*, p. 6.

[70]Herbert J. Gans, "How Well Does TV Present the News", *New York Times Magazine* (January 11, 1970), p. 32.

[71]Ted Robert Gurr, "A Comparative Study of Civil Strife," in Hugh Davis Graham and Ted Robert Gurr, *Violence in America* (New York: Signet 1969), p.550.

[72]Benjamin D. Singer, "Violence, Protest, and War in TV News," *Public Opinion Quarterly*, 34 (Winter 1970–71), 612.

[73]Efron, *op. cit.*, p. 178.

[74]Report of the National Advisory Commission on Civil Disorders (New York: Bantam, 1969), p. 369.

[75]Benjamin D. Singer, "Mass Media and Communication Processes in the Detroit Riot of 1967," *Public Opinion Quarterly,* 34 (Summer 1970), 239.

[76]John E. Mueller, "Trends in Popular Support for the Wars in Korea and Vietnam," *American Political Science Review,* 65 (June 1971), 374.

[77]Richard H. Pride, "Television Network News: Re-thinking the Iceberg Problems," *Western Political Quarterly,* forthcoming.

[78]Byron Shafer and Richard Larson, "Did Television Create the Social Issue?" *Columbia Journalism Review,* (September–October 1972), 10.

[79]Michael Robinson, "Public Affairs Television and the Growth of Political Malaise: The Case of *The Selling of the Pentagon*" (mimeo, 1973).

[80]Michael Robinson, "TV and the Wallace Vote in 1968: Implications for 1976," paper presented to the 1974 Annual Convention of the American Association of Public Opinion Research, Bolton Landing, New York.

[81]Neil Vidmar and Milton Rokeach, "Archie Bunker's Bigotry: A Study in Selective Perception and Exposure," *Journal of Communication,* 24 (Winter 1974), 45.

Selected Additional Readings

Devine, Donald J. *The Political Culture of the United States.* Boston: Little Brown, 1972. Devine has provided an exhaustive analysis of the content of mass ideologies.

Edelman, Murray. *The Symbolic Uses of Politics.* Chicago: University of Illinois Press—Illini Books edition, 1967. Edelman deals with the general uses of symbols in society and then specifically the uses of political phenomena as symbols. He discusses the fact that myth and symbolic reassurance have become key elements in the governmental process. Edelman argues that the masses are generally uninterested in and inattentive to political phenomena as symbols. Only when the masses perceive symbolic or real threats or reassurances do they notice things political. Masses react to stimuli. Therefore, it is political action which "shape men's political wants and 'knowledge,' not the other way around." (172) Edelman also argues that mass demands, when they are articulated, are most often met with "symbolic" rather than "tangible" rewards.

Epstein, Edward Jay. *News from Nowhere.* New York: Random House, 1973. Epstein argues that television news is partially determined by the necessities of commercial television.

Erikson, Robert S. and Norman R. Luttbeg. *American Public Opinion: Its Origins, Content, and Impact.* New York: John Wiley, 1973. In this book, Erikson and Luttbeg have brought together and updated through 1970 several aspects of American public opinion research, including the formulation and content of opinion and the linkage between opinion and public officials. Especially important for the argument made in *Irony* are the chapters on political socialization, the potential of elections for "popular" control, and the impact of voter opinion on the policy choices of governmental officials.

Fromm, Eric. *Escape from Freedom.* New York: Avon Books, 1941. This book examines the notion of authoritarianism as an "escape" from the isolation produced by a large society. It is written primarily from a popular psychoanalytic point of view, interesting comparative reading with the political science and sociological works on authoritarianism.

Kornhauser, William. *The Politics of Mass Society*. New York: Free Press, 1959. (See Chapter 1, page 29.)

Lane, Robert E. *Political Ideology*. New York: Free Press, 1962, and *Political Life*. New York: Macmillan—Free Press edition, 1965. *Political Ideology* is a series of case studies, using in-depth interviews on 15 randomly selected "common men" in "Eastport." Lane attempts to probe the nature and extent of their political ideas. He finds that they do support the democratic ideal but that their political beliefs are held as a subpart of their job orientation and beliefs. *Political Life* was originally published in 1959. It is a diverse book with sections on the historical development of suffrage, conditions for the success of democracy, political behavior of the American people, etc. Perhaps the most interesting sections are those on the sociopsychological factors which affect political behavior. Lane discusses not only the *determinants* of man's political life but also the *effects* of social institutions (mass media, parties, economic organizations, etc.) on his political life.

Lipset, Seymour Martin. *Political Man*. Garden City, N.Y.: Doubleday & Co. (Anchor Books edition), 1963. This interpretation of American politics by an eminent political sociologist covers a myriad of factors that affect or are affected by the dynamics of political activity. Parts I and III—respectively entitled "The Conditions of the Democratic Order" and "Political Behavior in American Society"—are particularly germane to the discussion in this chapter.

Schattschneider, E. E., *The Semisovereign People: A Realistic View of Democracy in America*. New York: Holt, Rinehart and Winston, 1960. This book deals with the nature of conflict and change in America. Schattschneider argues against the pluralist-group theory bias which he perceives as the common view of the political system today. He also recognizes the elite-masses dichotomy which exists in the American social and political system. For example, he develops the notion that elites, by virtue of their organizational strengths, can manage conflict within the political system. They can alter it, exploit it, and/or suppress it. (pp. 15, 17)

Stouffer, Samuel A. *Communism, Conformity, and Civil Liberties*. New York: John Wiley, 1966. This book, originally published in 1955, reports the results of a national survey of 6000 which was designed to "examine in some depth the reactions of Americans to two dangers. One, from the communist conspiracy outside and inside the country. Two, from those who in thwarting the conspiracy would sacrifice some of the very liberties which the enemy would destroy." The study was one of the first systematic attempts to study the *intolerant* frame of mind and indicates that a large portion of America's masses would be willing to severely restrict even *legitimate* activities of unpopular minorities.

CHAPTER 6

ELECTIONS: IMPERFECT INSTRUMENTS

OF ACCOUNTABILITY

Can masses hold elites responsible through elections? Over half a million governmental officials are chosen through the ballot in America, but the extent of popular control of government through elections is undetermined. Although voters help to select the men who occupy prominent positions in government, voters do not order troops to Vietnam, or enact civil rights laws, or write tax legislation; and the effect of elections on these and other actions by governmental elites is unclear. The ballot is widely considered a panacea for social ills, but there is little evidence that voters can directly affect public policy through the exercise of their franchise.

In order for elections to serve as mandates, and for voters to exercise influence over public policy through elections, four conditions would need to be fulfilled: (1) Competing candidates would offer clear policy alternatives; (2) voters would be concerned with policy questions; (3) majority preferences on these questions could be ascertained in election results; (4) elected officials would be bound by the positions they assumed during the campaign.

In this chapter and the next, we shall contend that none of these conditions are fulfilled in American politics and, consequently, that voters cannot exercise direct control over public policy. First of all, the parties do not offer clear policy alternatives. Both parties agree on the major direction of public policy; they disagree only over the *means* of implementing public policy. Therefore, the voters cannot influence public policy by choosing between the parties.

Moreover, voter decisions are not motivated primarily by policy considerations. For a mandate to be valid, the electorate must make informed, *policy-oriented* choices; but traditional party ties and candidate personalities are more influential in most voting decisions than are policy questions. When voters cast their ballot because of traditional party ties, their party loyalty dilutes their influence over policy.

Even if the voters were primarily concerned with policy questions, it would be difficult to ascertain majority preferences on these questions from the election results. Victory for the party of a candidate does not necessarily mean that the voters support that party's programs. For one reason, voters are inconsistent in their policy preferences, and they frequently misinterpret or pay little attention to the policy preferences of a candidate. Generally a candidate's voters include not only advocates of his position but also some who oppose his position, as well as some who vote for him for other reasons. Moreover, a popular majority may really be composed of many policy minorities. How is a candidate to know which of his policy positions resulted in his election? It is unlikely that his election can be interpreted as a mandate for *all* of his policy positions.

Finally, in order for voters to exercise control over public officials through elections, it would be necessary for elected officials to be bound by their campaign pledges. Needless to say, campaign pledges are frequently ignored by elected officials.

The Functions of Elections

If elections do not provide a means for voters to exercise direct control over public policy, what is the purpose of elections? Elections are a symbolic exercise for the masses to help tie them to the established order. Political scientist Murray Edelman agrees that voters have little effect on public policy and contends that elections are primarily "symbolic reassurance." According to Edelman, elections serve to "quiet resentments and doubts about particular political acts, reaffirm belief in the fundamental rationality and democratic character of the system, and thus fix conforming habits of future behavior."[1] Even though electoral participation does not permit the masses to determine public policy, it nonetheless gives them a feeling that they play a role in the political system.

The second function of elections is to give the masses an opportunity to express themselves about the conduct of the public officials who have been in power. Elections do not permit the masses to direct *future* events, but they do permit the masses to render judgment about *past* political conduct. For example, in 1968, voters could not choose a specific policy by voting for Nixon. They had no way of knowing what policies Nixon would follow in Vietnam, because Nixon did not set forth any specific proposals regarding that conflict. But the voters *were* able to express their discontent with Johnson's handling of the war by voting against a continuation of the Democratic administration. As Gerald Pomper explains:

The voters employ their powerful sanction retrospectively. They judge the politician after he has acted, finding personal satisfactions or discontents as the results of these actions. . . . The issue of Viet Nam is illustrative. . . . For their part, critics of the war did not emphasize their own alternative policies, but instead concentrated on retrospective and adverse judgments. . . . Declining public support of the war brought all major candidates to promise its end. The Republican Party, and particularly Richard Nixon, joined in this pledge, but provided no specific programs, instead seeking the support of all voters inclined to criticize past actions.[2]

The voters' retrospective judgment on past administrations may have an impact on the behavior of current and future elected officials. Pomper contends, rather optimistically, that even though the voters have no *power* over government, they nonetheless have an *influence* on government. He accepts Carl Friedrich's definition of influence: "Influence flows into the human relation whenever the influencer's reaction might spell disadvantage and even disaster for the actor, who foresees the effect the action might have and alters more or less in accordance with his foresight."[3] Pomper contends that because "politicians might be affected by the voters in the next election, they regulate their conduct appropriately."[4]

But he fails to say how elected officials are supposed to know the sentiments of voters on policy questions in order to "regulate their conduct appropriately." As we shall see, most voters do not have an opinion that can be communicated to elected officials; and elected officials have no way of interpreting voters' policy preferences from electoral results. By ousting the Democratic administration from power in 1968, were the voters saying they wanted a military victory in Vietnam? Or that they wanted a negotiated peace and compromise with the Viet Cong?

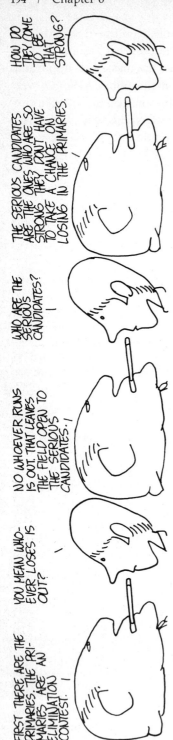

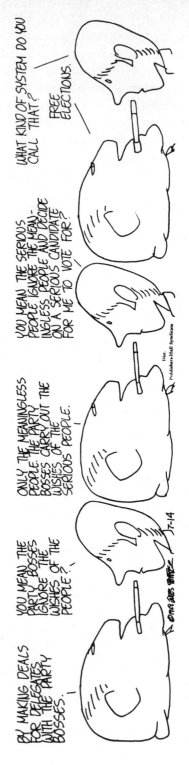

Perhaps all that we can really say is that the retrospective judgment that voters can render in an election helps to make governing elites sensitive to mass welfare. Elections do not permit masses to decide what should be done in their interests, but they do encourage governing elites to consider the welfare of the masses. Knowing that a day of reckoning will come on election day, elected officials strive to make a good impression on the voters in the meantime.

The existence of the vote does not make politicians better as individuals; it simply forces them to give greater consideration to demands of enfranchised and sizeable groups, who hold a weapon of potentially great force. . . . The ability to punish politicians is probably the most important weapon available to citizens. It is direct, authoritative, and free from official control.[5]

It has been argued that elections have a third function—that of protecting individuals and groups from official abuse. John Stuart Mill wrote: "Men, as well as women, do not need political rights in order that they might govern, but in order that they not be misgoverned."[6] He went on:

Rulers in ruling classes are under a necessity of considering the interests of those who have the suffrage; but of those who are excluded, it is in their option whether they will do so or not, and however honestly disposed, they are in general too fully occupied with things they must attend to, to have much room in their thoughts for anything which they can with impunity disregard.[7]

Certainly the long history of efforts to insure black voting rights in the South suggests that many concerned Americans believed that if blacks could secure access to the polls, they could better protect themselves from official discrimination. Some major steps in the struggle for voting rights were the abolishment of the "white primary" in 1944; the Civil Rights Acts of 1957, 1960, 1964, and 1965, all of which contained provisions guaranteeing free access to the polls; and the Twenty-fourth Amendment to the Constitution, which eliminated poll taxes. But the high hopes stirred by the development of new law were often followed by frustration and disillusionment when blacks realized that their problems could not be solved through the electoral process alone. No doubt William R. Keech is correct when he asserts that the vote is a symbol of full citizenship and equal rights, which may contribute to black self-respect.[8] But it is still open to question how much blacks can gain through the exercise of their vote. In the North, blacks have voted freely for decades, but conditions in the urban ghettos have not been measurably improved through political action. In signing the Voting Rights Act of 1965, President Johnson said:

The right to vote is the most basic right, without which all others are meaningless. It gives people—people as individuals—control over their own destinies. . . .

The vote is the most powerful instrument ever devised by man for breaking down injustice and destroying the terrible walls which imprison men because they are different from other men.

But the black experience in both the North and the South suggests that the ballot cannot eliminate discrimination, much less enable men to "control their own destinies." It is probably true that men can *better* protect themselves from government abuse when they possess and exercise their voting rights, but the right to vote is not a guarantee against discrimination.

The Ignorance of the Electorate

If elections are to be a means of popular control over public policy, voters must be reasonably well informed about policy issues and must hold opinions on these issues. Yet available evidence suggests that large numbers of the electorate are politically uninformed and inarticulate.

Some years ago, public-opinion analysts reported what is now a typical finding about the low level of political information among adult Americans (see Table 6–1). Only about one half of the public knew the elementary fact that each state has two United States senators; fewer still knew the length of the terms of congressmen or the number of Supreme Court justices.[9]

Table 6-1 / Proportion of Adult Americans Informed about Various Aspects of the American Political System

	Percentage of Correct Responses
How many senators are there in Washington from your state?	55
When a man is elected to the United States House of Representatives, how many years does he serve in one term of office?	47
Do you happen to know whether all United States Senators come up for re-election this fall?	46
Can you tell me how many justices there are normally on the United States Supreme Court, including the Chief Justice?	40
Do you happen to know whether federal or state governments make the laws about who can vote in a presidential election?	33
What do you know about the Bill of Rights? Do you know anything it says?	23

Source: Fred I. Greenstein, *The American Party System and the American People* (Englewood Cliffs, N.J.: Prentice-Hall, 1963).

Herbert McClosky discovered that 28 percent of the public was unable (or unwilling) to classify itself as either "liberal," "middle-of-the road," or "conservative."[10] In contrast, only a tiny fraction of the elite was unable to do so. Further, the ordinary voters who did classify themselves showed a poor understanding of the components of an ideology. McClosky and his associates devised a scale of conservatism constructed from the writings of conservative political philosophers. In applying this scale to the mass electorate, he found that the way the respondents classified themselves was unrelated, in many cases, to the objective classification of the respondent on the conservatism scale.

Typically, elites wage their battles over political issues, while the unconcerned masses occupy themselves with other matters. Even an issue such as the Vietnam War had difficulty in penetrating to a significant degree. In the 1968 Democratic primaries, Senators Eugene McCarthy and Robert Kennedy waged strenuous campaigns based largely upon their opposition to the Vietnam War; yet about two thirds of the voters were unable to identify the position of these candidates on the war.[11]

A particularly apt example of the ability of the masses to exert an extraordinarily effective screen against information is provided by the saturation of television viewers with the byzantine details of the Watergate affair. Between May 17 and August 7 of 1973, the networks jointly telecast approximately 235 hours of live Watergate hearings, excluding network news programs, for an average of five hours per day. Such coverage—a veritable telethon—was clearly unique in the history of commercial television.

As a consequence, the Watergate affair achieved a remarkably high mass awareness: fully 97 percent of the respondents in a series of national polls indicated that they had heard of Watergate.[12] Since more people had heard of Watergate than could identify the governor of their state, the depth of penetration was remarkable.

But beneath these figures—easily interpretable by elites as indications of mass concern—lurks disquieting evidence of boredom. Daytime television audiences are, of course, biased against employed persons. Nevertheless, the audience for daytime television is enormous. During the Watergate hearings, about three fourths of those with television sets tuned in at least one session of the hearings. But this audience was actually smaller than normal for those hours! About one third of the audience who watched the hearings did so regularly. Thus, Watergate proved less popular than *The Edge of Night*.

One could legitimately argue that the electorate should not be expected to inform itself about complicated political issues. In general, one could expect that the more complicated the issue, the less information will filter down to the masses. But it can be demonstrated that substantial

"Then shut up and impeach him . . . it's almost time for Kojak . . ."

portions of the mass electorate cannot identify even such clearly symbolic terms as "Cold War," "monopoly," "welfare state," "GOP," and "fallout." Accurate information about political issues is confined to those with superior education. For example, Campbell, Converse, Miller, and Stokes found that 59 percent of those who had attended college were familiar with a variety of domestic and foreign policy issues, compared to 31 percent of those who had attended high school and 21 percent of those who had attended school through the eight grade.[13] (See Table 6–2.) Perhaps it is a truism to observe this relationship; for the purpose of education is, of course, to increase knowledge.

Table 6–2 / Education and Familiarity with Policy Issues

Familiarity with Issues	Less Than 8 Years of School	High School	College
High	21%	31%	50%
Medium	37	47	44
Low	42	22	6
Total	100	100	100

Source: A. Campbell, P. Converse, W. Miller, and D. Stokes, *The American Voter* (New York: John Wiley, 1960), p. 175.

Contradictions in the Beliefs of Masses

Closely related to the fact that the masses have less information than the elite is the inability of the masses to sort out and relate information that they do possess. We are all familiar with the vagaries of elections and have come to expect that the public will offer simultaneous approval to candidates with fundamentally different outlooks. Such apparent contradictions can be explained partially by low levels of information and low awareness of candidate position. However, it is equally likely that broad segments of the public hold opinions that are contradictory, as a study by Philip Converse shows. Converse uses the word *constraint* to describe the success we might have in predicting a person's attitude in one area if we know his opinion in another. If, for example, we know that a person believes that the federal government should reduce its aid to education, can we assume that this person also wishes the federal government to reduce its spending in other areas? If a person is opposed to expansion of social security, is he also opposed to progressive income tax? Most elite observations of mass behavior assume that constraints are present within the belief systems of the masses. In fact, they are conspicuously *absent*.[14]

Except for those issues which are unusually salient to large numbers of people (such as civil rights), constraints do not characterize the attitude structure of mass publics toward domestic issues. For example, those who support an enlargement of public services do not necessarily support taxes to pay for these services. In fact, many of those persons who support a tax cut also favor federal expansion of welfare measures.

Persons who hold inconsistent positions are most likely to come from the lower social strata. These people, although they demand an expansion of federal services and a reduction of the federal budget, hold extreme negative attitudes toward the worth of the services they require. Obviously, self-interest makes simultaneous support for tax reduction and expansion of federal welfare activities quite compatible; one might very well wish to have his tax burden reduced while enjoying the benefits of expanded services. However, for the political system as a whole, the combination of opinions described above is irrational. Even if the elite attempts to interpret and do what the masses want, it cannot satisfy both demands.

A possible reason for these inconsistencies is that opinions that the masses are supposed to hold are frequently created by public opinion polls. For a substantial portion of the population the questions asked in opinion polls are meaningless; therefore, so are their answers. Many people have never thought about the question before it is asked and will never think about it again; the very absence of consistency in mass opinions is evidence of lack of interest. As one moves down the socioeconomic ladder from elites to masses, consistent political beliefs fade away rapidly. As constraints decline, objects of beliefs shift from abstract principles to simple and concrete goals. As Converse phrases it, the central focus of belief systems shifts from "ideological principles to the more obviously recognized social groups and chauvinistic leaders."[15]

In order to estimate the ability of the electorate to conceptualize, to think abstractly, the Survey Research Center examined the responses of the electorate to questions concerning the good and bad points of the two major parties.[16] The following categorization was derived. *Ideologues* are those respondents who are either "liberal" or "conservative" and are likely to rely upon abstract principles in their evaluation of candidates and issues. *Near ideologues* are those respondents who mentioned an abstract principle, but clearly did not place as much reliance upon it as did the ideologues. With the near ideologues, ideology was peripheral and used in a fashion that raised doubts about the understanding of the terms employed. The next level of respondents, the *group benefits* class, were those who did not exhibit any overriding ideological dimension in their thinking, but were able to evaluate parties and candidates in terms of expected favorable or unfavorable treatment for social groups. A favored candidate was seen as "for" a group with which the subject was identified. Politics, for the *group benefits* portion of the electorate, was perceived as an arena of group conflict. Unless an issue could be linked to the welfare of their own grouping, these respondents could not understand it well enough to respond appropriately to issues and candidates. A fourth level of conceptualization defines respondents whose judgment is based upon their perception of the *"goodness"* or *"badness" of the times.* They blame or praise parties and candidates because of their association with conditions of war or peace, prosperity or depression. This category of respondents also includes those whose only point of reference to public policy is a single issue with which they feel a unique personal identification. The last level includes those respondents whose evaluations of the political scene hold *no relationship whatever to policy,* even in the broadest and most symbolic use of the term. Some of these people profess a loyalty to one of the two parties but have no idea about the positions advocated by that party.

An examination of the entire electorate in terms of the various levels of conceptualization shows quite clearly that ideological commitments are significant in the political decisions of only a tiny fraction (see Table

Table 6-3 / Relation of Education to Levels of Conceptualization, 1956

	Grade School	High School	College
Ideologue	0%	2%	10%
Near ideologue	5	8	22
Group benefits	40	49	38
Nature of the times	29	25	20
No issue content	26	16	10
Total	100	100	100

Source: Adapted from Angus Campbell, Philip Converse, Warren Miller, and Donald E. Stokes, *The American Voter* (New York: John Wiley, 1960), p. 250.

6–3). Three and one half percent of the total electorate are "ideologues," another 12 percent are "near ideologues," and the remainder display no ideological content in their evaluations.

It is clear, therefore, that the majority of the public does not conceptualize politics in the manner of the highly educated. Indeed, of the tiny fraction of the electorate classified as ideologues, 65 percent are highly educated. The proportion of highly educated respondents at each level of descending conceptualization drops consistently: 42 percent of the near ideologues are highly educated, but the proportion of highly educated respondents drops precipitously to 18 percent among those who perceive the political process in terms of group benefits. Only 17 percent of those who view candidates and issues in terms of the nature of the times, and a mere 11 percent of those who lack any issue content, are college educated. Thus, except for the small educated portion of the electorate, the ideological debate between the elites has very little meaning. Since the masses lack the interest and level of conceptualization of the educated, they cannot be expected to possess an organized ideology.

Converse has examined the levels of constraint among beliefs on a range of domestic and foreign issues in both an elite and a mass range population. The elite population for his study consisted of candidates for the United States Congress in the year 1958; however, Converse expects that the same properties of an elite would have been discovered if the elite had been any other group of politically active people. Table 6–4 provides the average coefficients of correlation between issues for both the elites and the masses. It can be seen that in every case there is a stronger correlation between beliefs on the part of elites than on the part of the masses. As Converse notes, "The strongest constraint within a domain for the mass public is less than that between domestic and foreign domains for the elite sample."[17]

Converse relates the unsophisticated conceptual processes of mass

Table 6-4 / Summary of Differences in Level of Constraint within and between Domains

	Average Coefficients			
	Within Domestic Issues	Between Domestic and Foreign	Within Foreign Issues	Between Issues and Party
Elite	.53	.25	.37	.39
Mass	.23	.11	.23	.11

Source: Adapted from Philip E. Converse, "The Nature of Belief Systems in Mass Publics," in David E. Apter (ed.), *Ideology and Discontent* (New York: Free Press, 1964).

publics with the findings of McClosky, which were discussed in the previous chapter. Those findings showed that there was widespread support for abstract principles of democracy but substantially less support for specific application of these principles. Converse argues that the findings are less a demonstration of cynicism than a demonstration of the inability of the masses to link a specific case to a general principle. That is to say, the inconsistency is simply not recognized.

Another obstacle to mass influence over public policy is the instability of mass opinions. A longitudinal study of the electorate indicated that in responding to a particular controversy only about 13 out of 20 people took the same side that they had taken four years earlier (10 out of 20 would have done so by chance alone). Indeed, an examination of the correlation between opinions over time indicates that, with the exception of party identification, there is a remarkable instability (Table 6–5). This instability suggests once again that issues and ideology are simply not

Table 6-5 / Individual Stability of Different Belief Elements for Individuals, 1958–1960

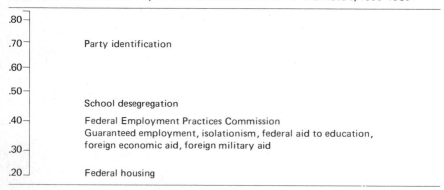

Numbers are rank (tau_b) correlation between individual's positions in 1958 and 1960 on the same items.

Source: Philip Converse, "The Nature of Belief Systems in Mass Publics," in David E. Apter (ed.), *Ideology and Discontent* (New York: Free Press, 1964), p. 240.

relevant to the mass electorate. Furthermore, the most consistent attitudes relate to clearly identifiable groups, such as blacks. Attitudes about school desegregation and federal employment practices commissions are substantially more stable than attitudes toward foreign policy. Evidently, the mass electorate thinks about race relations, but does not think about foreign policy unless someone happens to ask the question. Hence, the answers to questions about foreign policy vary randomly through time. This instability is, of course, also associated with an absence of information.

Looking at the instability of mass attitudes, Converse concludes that "large portions of the electorate do not have meaningful beliefs, even on those issues that have formed the basis for intense political controversy among elites for substantial periods of time."[18] Edelman, reflecting upon the belief systems of masses, concludes that, rather than communicating demands to elites, masses absorb a crude and simplified version of elite attitudes.

The basic thesis is that mass publics respond to currently conspicuous political symbols: not to "facts," and not to moral codes embedded in the character or soul, but to the gestures and speeches that make up the drama of the state. . . . The mass public does not study and analyze detailed data about secondary boycotts, provisions for stock ownership and control in a proposed space communications corporation, or missile installations in Cuba. . . . It ignores these things until political actions and speeches make them symbolically threatening or reassuring and it then responds to the cues furnished by the actions and speeches, not to direct knowledge of the facts. . . . It is therefore political actions that chiefly shape men's political wants and "knowledge," not the other way around. The common assumption that what democratic government does is somehow always a response to the moral codes, desires, and knowledge embedded inside people is as inverted as it is reassuring. This model, avidly taught and ritualistically repeated, cannot explain what happens; but it may persist in our folklore because it so effectively sanctifies prevailing policies and permits us to avoid worrying about them. . . . The public is not in touch with the situation, and it "knows" the situation only through the symbols that engage it.[19]

Are Election Choices Related to Issues?

Given the ignorance of the masses, one might wonder what is actually decided through elections. In congressional elections, the incumbent is usually re-elected. The tendency of the electorate to return incumbents to office, and the voters' lack of awareness of the policies of the challengers to incumbents, is related to the relatively low-keyed nature of congressional elections, especially in off-years. In presidential elections there is greater awareness of the candidates, but this does not necessarily mean that the issues are more completely discussed. It is somewhat disconcerting to examine the campaigns of presidential aspirants when we realize how little of the issue content of the candidates' efforts penetrates into the mass of the electorate.

The ideal model of democracy requires that the two major parties offer policy alternatives to the electorate and compete for votes on the basis of their contrasting programs. This competition helps keep the elite responsible. Therefore, the masses, although not necessarily completely informed about the explicit nature of the programs advocated by the elites, should at least be aware of the broad outline of a program.

In order for this model to work, the voters must perceive alternatives and determine which alternatives most closely match their own ideological positions. However, the preponderance of evidence suggests that voters are not capable of making choices along the lines suggested by the model. For example, in examining the responses of the electorate in the 1952 and 1956 elections, Campbell, Converse, Miller, and Stokes concluded that only about one third had an opinion, were aware of what the government was doing, and perceived a difference between the parties. This one third is the *maximum* pool of issue-oriented people. While it is true that the nature of the election influences to some extent the size of the issue-oriented portion of the electorate, it is probable that two thirds of the electorate make a choice unrelated to the issues raised by the competing candidates.

It is important to recognize that these blurred perceptions may be caused by the behavior of elites as much as by the ignorance of masses. If the parties do not, in fact, provide clear alternatives, then perhaps those who fail to perceive these alternatives are correct rather than uninformed. Party activists are separated by a wide ideological gulf, but party followers are not. For example, the leaders of the Democratic party are "liberal," and the leaders of the Republican party are "conservative" (when conservatism is measured in terms of economic policy). However, the extent to which these differences are translated into clear statements by either party is questionable, and most Democratic and Republican voters hold fairly similar opinions on most issues. Indeed, Republican voters' opinions are closer to the opinions of Democratic leaders than they are to those of Republican leaders. Thus, although the Republican party traditionally argues for reduced federal expenditures, rank-and-file Democrats are more likely to support cutting taxes than are rank-and-file Republicans. The blurring of the linkage between leader opinions and follower opinions probably occurs in this case because low-income, low-education voters are less willing to support a high level of federal expenditures. These same voters are most likely to identify with the Democratic party.

Since most voters are incapable of making a distinction between the parties and, in any case, do not necessarily share the attitudes of party leaders, it seems that American national elections are not high in their ideological or issue content and that successful candidates are therefore not directed by mass opinion. This is not to suggest that voters are fools who are easily manipulated by clever use of the mass media and other instruments of persuasion. The stability of partisan attitudes and the operation of such screening factors as selective perception reduce the manipulative qualities of campaigns considerably.

Party identification is remarkably stable, while opinions are quite unstable. Ironically, the party is substantially more central to the belief system of mass electorates than are the policies it pursues. Short-term forces, such as a candidate's religion, can deflect voters away from the choice indicated by their party identification, but these short-term forces are, in many cases, unrelated to issues.

Our discussion does not preclude the possibility that *some* voters are issue-oriented and informed. Recall that we described about one third of the electorate as having an opinion, being aware of what the government was doing, and perceiving a difference between parties. V. O. Key has chosen to characterize the electorate as "responsible," but his conclusion is based solely upon those who switch from one party to another.[20] depending upon the election, one fifth to one eighth of the electorate does this. Since we have described about one third of the electorate as *potential* switchers, Key's findings and ours are not inconsistent. Indeed, Key's argument indicates that, from the reservoir of potential switchers, relatively few voters actually switch parties. Nevertheless, Key's thesis merits response, because it does tend to portray the electorate in more flattering terms than we have. Key asserts, for instance, that: "From our analyses *the voter* emerges as a person who appraises the actions of the government, who has policy preferences, and who relates his vote to those appraisals and preferences."[21] Granted that in close elections switching voters might be crucial, to describe "the voter" as Key does is to ignore the fact that only a tiny fraction of voters can be properly called "responsible." Even assuming that this fraction has political preferences gives no evidence that they "appraise" the actions of government. A critical problem in Key's work is his failure to explore information levels. As Converse aptly remarked, "opinions, be they ever so fervent, are no proof of information."[22] For instance, on the surface the McCarthy supporters seemed drawn from the ranks of those who opposed

Johnson's policy in Vietnam, yet once the surface is broken we discover that such people voted contrary to their policy preference. As Converse and his colleagues note: ". . . pushing beyond the expression of narrow or superficial attitudes in the mass public to the cognitive nature which underlies the attitudes is a rather disillusioning experience."[23]

We do not wish to suggest that the "responsible electorate" is a complete myth; rather, we suggest that it takes an unusually vigorous assertion of beliefs on the part of a candidate to cause the electorate to link issues with candidates. McCarthy, speaking in his intellectually oriented style, failed. However, George Wallace, whose appeal to his electorate was far less sophisticated, succeeded. The evidence suggests that among Nixon and Humphrey supporters issue positions minimally determined candidate choice. Wallace supporters, by contrast, displayed much stronger issue orientation.[24] Ironically, Key's "responsible electorate" consists largely of the followers of a counter-elite movement using the electoral process to challenge the consensual elite system.

1972: An "Ideological" Election?

The McGovern candidacy in 1972 helped to develop a more discernible ideological difference between the candidates of the two major parties. McGovern appealed to an ideologically committed cadre, leaving the rest of the electorate to Nixon. The resulting landslide was indeed remarkable. In carrying every state save Massachusetts (and Washington, D.C., with its black majority), Nixon gained 61 percent of the vote, roughly equal to the margin by which Johnson defeated Goldwater in 1964. McGovern's 38 percent was the lowest proportion by a major party candidate since 1936, when Alf Landon was engulfed by Franklin Roosevelt's victory. And his proportion was the lowest by a Democratic candidate since 1920, when Cox was defeated by Harding. Not only did Nixon receive 94 percent of the vote among Republicans and 66 percent among Independents, he also captured 42 percent of the vote among Democrats.

What was the voter response? Were issues the crucial variable? Had the electorate, given the stimulus of disparate candidate images, become "ideological"? Yes and no. McGovern was clearly the Goldwater of the 1972 election. The American voters obviously found vast differences between McGovern and Nixon, regarding McGovern as too far from the ideological mainstream. It was not so much the *what* of McGovern, but rather the *how* and *when*. On the eve of the election, a Harris poll reported that, by a margin of two to one, the electorate felt McGovern wanted to "change things too much."

Table 6-6 / Ideological Differences among 1972 Voters

	% More Likely to Vote for Candidate Who Favored:	
	Nixon Supporters	McGovern Supporters
Ending U.S. involvement in Vietnam	74%	93%
Busing School Children to Achieve Racial Balance	10	37
Stricter Control on Firearms	57	74
Greater Equality—More Opportunity for Women	60	79
Checking the Rising Cost of Living	91	95
Removing Wage and Price Controls	28	38
Increasing Aid to Parochial Schools	42	49
Allowing Men Who Left the Country to Avoid Draft to Return Without Punishment	15	39
Decreasing Defense Spending	45	66
Tougher Sentences for Lawbreakers	87	72
Improving Opportunities for Blacks & Other Minority Groups	60	82
Providing National Health Insurance for All Americans	60	82
Lessening Penalties for Marijuana Possession	23	40
Increasing Spending to Control Air & Water Pollution	79	85

Source: Gallup Political Index, September 7, 1972, pp. 5–12.

If the dispute between the two groups was over the *speed* of change, rather than the content of change, we should expect substantial consensus between McGovern and Nixon supporters. As Table 6–6 reveals, of fourteen issues, in only *one* (decreasing defense spending) did a majority of McGovern supporters take a position in opposition to a majority of Nixon supporters. This is not, of course, to deny a difference. What we are asserting is that the differences occur *within a basic consensus.* Speaking of the electorate, Lipset and Raab conclude:

> *What they resist is change that takes place in a non-traditional manner . . . the basic threat perceived by the electorate in the McGovern candidacy was not so much to existing social arrangements as to the social order itself. And especially to due process. That is the "extremism" which the voters finally rejected, not any liberal social or economic policy per se.*[25]

Nevertheless, one should not minimize ideological differences; one should simply remember their relatively *minor* nature. For instance, both sets of voters were strongly committed to getting out of Vietnam. McGovern said, "Now"; Nixon said, "Later." Thus, when asked to place themselves on a scale ranging from "left" to "right," respondents who favored immediate withdrawal were "left," those who wanted gradual withdrawal "right."

Such a self-classification scheme was used by the University of Michigan Survey Research Center's analysis of the election. As one would expect, McGovern supporters were appreciably more "left" (or liberal) than Nixon's supporters. However, on highly skewed issues, those issues which strike at the chords of the counter-culture and consequently produced the greatest left-right disparity, a majority of *both* Nixon and McGovern supporters took a "right" perspective. The majority of McGovern supporters did not want to legalize marijuana or bus children out of neighborhoods. Nevertheless, the major thrust of *half* of McGovern's supporters' ideology was one of social change. In contrast, *half* of Nixon's supporters displayed an opposing control orientation. Such a split is hardly indicative of the widely portrayed "either-or" election (half of McGovern's supporters did *not* display a social change orientation; half of Nixon's did *not* reveal a social control orientation). Actually, the division of opinion *within* the ranks of Democratic identifiers was greater than the differences *between* Democrats and Republicans. By looking at those Democrats (42 percent) who voted for Nixon, in comparison with those who stayed with McGovern, the polarizing effects of McGovern's candidacy *within* the ranks of the party faithful becomes apparent: ". . . with respect to the liberal-conservative measure, the differences between Democrats and Republicans were less than those between the two Democratic factions."[26]

Such massive defections left McGovern, as we noted, with a relatively tight, ideologically constrained, intense following. Issues, as distinguished from partisan identification or candidate perception, clearly had an exceptional impact upon the 1972 vote; it was, in some aspects, the most ideologically potent election in modern history. A portion of the electorate was responding in a relatively sophisticated manner. We refer here again to the notion of constraints, the ability of an individual to organize beliefs and relate beliefs to events.

Given the weeding-out process begun by McGovern's candidacy, it should be expected that Democrats (including those who defected to Nixon) would exhibit higher degrees of ideological sophistication. Such is indeed the case. Democrats (and Independents) responded to the issues of 1972 in a substantially more ideological manner than did Republicans. If the *mood* of the elections was one of the counter-culture versus the establishment, the Democrats—in accepting or rejecting McGovern —found it easier than Republicans to develop a coherent ideology. Roughly one fourth of the population has sympathy with counter-culture goals; the rest of the population is the establishment. The counter-culture vs. the establishment dispute is as much one of style as

Table 6–7 / Correlations Between Liberal-Conservative Scale and Specific Issues

	Vietnam	Amnesty	Busing	Marijuana	Health Insurance	Women's Rights	Minorities	Defense Spending	Total
Non-College	.22	.33	.26	.21	.15	.11	.31	.21	.22
College	.43	.52	.46	.44	.49	.30	.48	.44	.44

Source: Arthur H. Miller, Warren E. Miller, Alden S. Raine, and Thad A. Brown, "A Majority Party in Disarray: Policy Polarization in the 1972 Election." Paper presented at the 1973 Annual Meeting of the American Political Science Association, New Orleans, p. 10.

ideology, but it is a potent mobilizer of an ideological response. Pro-counter-culture individuals (with the exception of blacks) are typically more ideologically sophisticated. They are well-educated, young, and either Democratic or Independent.

Especially noteworthy is the role of the highly educated, for their participation is a crucial element in understanding the role of issues in elections. The college-educated electorate was appreciably more ideologically coherent than those of lesser education. In Table 6–7, correlations between self-placement on the liberal-conservative scale and specific issues indicates the magnitude of the difference. The correlation between ideology and issue position are about twice as high for the college-educated group. For the college-educated voter, "new political events have more meaning, retention of political information is far more adequate, and political behavior increasingly approximates that of sophisticated 'rational' models, which assume relatively full information."[27]

What did such sophistication—normally associated with the educated minority—mean in 1972? Specifically, did the educated minority translate its issue orientation into a *vote*? In Table 6–8, the percent of

Table 6–8 / Variance in Vote Related to Candidate Perception and Ideology

	Candidate Ratings		Liberal-Conservative Ideology
	Nixon	McGovern	
Grade School	45%	15%	1%
High School	37	16	7
College	12	6	45
Total Population	41	14	5

Source: Miller *et al.,* "A Majority Party in Disarray," p. 68.

variance in the vote (the higher the percentage, the greater the contribution of each factor to the vote) is related to candidate perception and ideology for college and non-college groups. As can be readily seen, the role of ideology increases dramatically as one moves up the education ladder. The college-educated group casts an ideological vote, but no other group does.

It may be, therefore, that the "issue voting" of 1972 was a consequence of a *shift* in the electoral participation of the various educational groups. Turnout among the less well educated has declined from 68 percent in 1964 to 58 percent in 1962; turnout among the college-educated group has remained constant (89 percent and 88 percent). Thus, while the college-educated population contributed 25 percent to the electorate in 1964, in 1972 it contributed 37 percent. As interest in politics declines, elections assume more elitist characteristics, and hence resemble typical elite behavior.

In sum, McGovern lost because he was the least popular Democratic candidate in twenty years. Issues were more important than usual, but the most important factor was McGovern himself. Nixon, by contrast, was clearly an extraordinarily popular candidate, receiving positive ratings from voters of all ideological leanings. McGovern was associated with permissivism, the "welfare ethic," marijuana abuse, even sexual excess. His radical image was counterpoised against that of Nixon the reliable, and it was no contest.

What Factors Win Elections?

If most voters are not capable of perceiving the alternative policy positions of political parties, what do campaigns accomplish? Candidates confer extensively with their advisors, planning elaborate political statements and making public appearances to discuss the issues that they perceive as relevant to the election. While they direct themselves almost exclusively to the issues, the *presentation* of their ideologies apparently produces more voter support than do the ideologies themselves. It is the "image" of the candidate and not his policies that affect voter choice.

The "Floating Vote" The evidence indicates that about one fifth to one third of the electorate makes up its mind during the campaign. Most of these late deciders are independents and weak partisans who form the potential "floating vote" (those who change their vote from one election to another). In close elections, of course, those who make up their minds during the campaign can be critical. It is very likely that late deciders, if they do play a critical role, are those least qualified to play such a role;

they are those least likely to keep themselves informed about the issues and the campaign. Concerning the "floating voters," Converse comments that "susceptibility to party shifting seems higher for some types of voters than for others, and in any given shift between two elections . . . the less involved and less informed voters are disproportionately represented."[28] One should draw a distinction between those who switch their votes during a campaign and those who change their partisan identification on a permanent basis. Those who change their party identification permanently appear to be well organized ideologically; they change because of a desire to achieve congruence between their ideological posture and the perceived policy positions of a political party. These long-term realignments can contribute to the party victory or defeat on an ideological basis. However, those who change their party identification constitute only about 10 percent of the electorate. Those who maintain a stable party identification but switch their votes in a particular election are not ideologues. Thus, short-term instability in voting is greatest among those who pay little attention to campaigns, ideologies, and issues, simply responding according to broad-gauged perception of whether times are good or bad.

Even though they are not especially well informed, the "floating voters" do provide some mechanism of control. Unfortunately for those seeking political office, the stimulus to which the "nature of the times" voters respond is usually beyond their control. The information level of the "floating voters" is substantially less than that of those who are consistent partisans but is greater than that of those who are infrequent participants in the electoral process. Since their information level is moderate at best and their commitment to partisan symbols unstable, these voters are susceptible to short-term influences. Any new information that reaches them at all is likely to have more effect than the same information that reaches the stable partisans. Ironically, candidates campaign more or less on the issues, but the change occurs most among those to whom the issues are not especially significant.

Voters' Attitudes Toward Foreign Policy   Generally speaking, unless the country is involved in war, domestic issues (to the extent that voters concern themselves with any issues) are more important than is foreign policy. The public typically gives the president a great degree of latitude in making foreign policy (partly because information on foreign policy is more difficult to acquire) and is less capable of maintaining the stability of their opinions in this area. However, a president's persistent perceived failure can, in conjunction with other grievances, take an electoral toll. For instance, the struggle in Korea was initially widely supported by the

American population, but as the war dragged on, enthusiasm declined appreciably. In the elections of 1952, the failure of the Democratic administration to end the Korean War was a partial contributor to the partisan surge to the Republican party.[29]

The political situation during the Vietnam War is virtually identical with the situation that faced Truman during the Korean War. The initial enthusiasm for the war in Vietnam diminished and was replaced by gradual lack of support. However, the decline in support could be temporarily arrested by any decisive action by President Johnson. If bombing of the North was increased—or if bombing was halted—enthusiasm spurted upward. As Lipset has noted, the president does not follow opinion, he creates it.[30] This is especially the case in foreign policy because the government is the only source of information for the public.

Furthermore, conflicts such as Vietnam blur a distinction between the attitudes of elites and masses as the population unites against the feared and hated communists. In foreign policy, even more than in domestic policy, the information gap between the elite and the masses is enormous. However, when the country is involved in a protracted and controversial conflict, the shape of opinion between elites and masses is not appreciably different. Nevertheless, a leader can adopt any position and find support for it. Given the general instability of opinion on foreign policy, the control that the masses can exercise over governmental elites is minimal.

It is important to note parallels between the Korean War and the Vietnam War in presidential campaign politics. In neither case was there much relationship between campaign statements and policy performance. Warren Miller remarks of Eisenhower's victory:

Mr. Eisenhower's election was made possible because of dissatisfaction with Democratic foreign policy. He immediately rejected the policy preferences of his supporters and by so doing gained the uncritical gratitude of the same supporters, who forthwith accepted the tenets of the opposition and became more like Mr. Stevenson's supporters than Stevenson supporters themselves.[31]

Specifically, Eisenhower adopted Stevenson's policy toward Korea by easing out of the war. Johnson, who ridiculed Goldwater's position on foreign policy in general and the Vietnam War in particular, received enthusiastic support at the beginning of his Vietnam intervention, even though he was taking the same actions advocated by Goldwater, whom the public tended to regard as "trigger happy." Nixon was elected in 1968 in part because of dissatisfaction over the conduct of the Vietnam War, yet Nixon pledged throughout the campaign to continue the policy position of the Johnson administration. The point of these examples is that the impact of the candidates during an election seems to be greater than the impact of issues. Thus, candidates can operate virtually independently of electoral control over policy making. Voters make their choice on the basis of a candidate's personal style, filtered through partisan commitment, and presidential elections do not necessarily offer a policy choice.

The Results of Ideological Campaigning   The impotence of the campaign can well be illustrated by the frustrations of George McGovern. Nixon did virtually no personal campaigning, while McGovern exhausted himself futilely, ending up with virtually the same support that he had at the time of his nomination. The publicity associated with McGovern's nomination did nothing to improve his image. On the contrary, support for *Nixon* increased immediately after the Democratic Convention! (Figure 6–1). A similar phenomenon occurred in 1964, when Goldwater was nominated from the minority wing of the Republican party.

   McGovern, like Goldwater, was a factional leader, contemptuous of the majority sentiment in his party. Goldwater's famous remark, "extremism in defense of liberty is no vice," found its counterpart in the

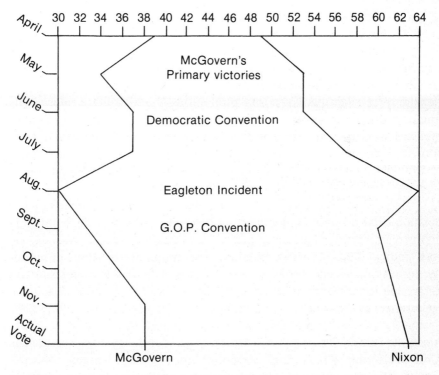

Figure 6–1. Trends in candidate support: percentages indicating voting intention, 1972. (From *Gallup Political Index*, April-November, 1972.)

behavior of the McGovern faction at the Democratic National Convention. Party regulars, leaders of urban machines (such as Daley of Chicago), and labor activists (the old Democratic coalition) were deliberately ignored (or actually expelled from the convention) in favor of the radical activists who had led the fight in the turbulent Democratic primaries. Symbolic of the entire debacle was the spectacle of Senator Eagleton, having been refused his request for a seconding speech by Governor Hearns of Missouri, being seconded by an undergraduate coed!

McGovern eagerly cast his lot with the devotees of the "new politics" at the convention, only to discover that the extremism of the primaries had little place in a general election in which the winning candidate must occupy the center ground. Table 6–9 shows a distribution of McGovern, Nixon, and the public, arrayed on a liberal-conservative continuum.

Table 6–9 / Distribution of Opinions Along an Ideological Continuum

	Nixon's Image	McGovern's Image	Public's Ideology
Conservative	52	11	44
Middle-of-the-road	25	22	30
Liberal	11	44	24

Source: Gallup Political Index, May 1972.

Whether or not McGovern knew the true distribution of preferences, he swiftly began to disengage himself from the left wing of the party. Consider, for example, his position on amnesty and welfare reform. His final position on amnesty was that amnesty would be granted only after the war was over and the prisoners of war returned; excluded from amnesty were deserters. With regard to welfare, he abandoned his scheme of $1,000 to every American in favor of a National Income Insurance Program.

It made no difference. By the time of the election, McGovern's issue position differed only in degree from Nixon's, and was well within the mainstream of the Democratic party. The *image*, however, was set. He was "radical." Additionally, in spite of his frequent assertions of morality, he was regarded—by a margin of five to two—as less credible and believable than Nixon. It was a question of style, and the intricacies of welfare had no impact.

Elections Decide Personnel, Not Policy　Presidential elections are means for the selection of personnel, not policy. As William Flanigan notes, "It is perfectly appropriate to attribute policy significance to an election on the basis of policy preferences of winning candidates, so long as it is not implied that the voters had these policy implications in mind when they voted."[32] That is, an elected official might interpret election results in a manner unintended by the electorate. In general, the electoral system is not a way of imposing policy standards on elected officials.

One might be tempted to believe that elections at the state and local level are more accurate examples of traditional democratic theory, since they are less complex than national elections. Some state elections are concerned almost exclusively with a single issue. For example, Epstein's study of the 1962 gubernatorial election in Wisconsin indicates that tax policy was the issue that dominated the campaign of both candidates. The question was whether to increase the income tax or to extend the sales tax. Each position developed strong partisans; the Republicans, in keeping with their traditional image, advocated a sales tax extension, while the Democrats, the incumbent party, supported an increase in the income tax. Each candidate took a firm position linked to the ideological perspective of his party.

As is typically the case, the turnout for this election was substantially less than the turnout in presidential elections. Low turnout means an overrepresentation of high-status, well informed people. Given this type of an election, information should have penetrated substantially beyond the better educated voters. However, about one third of the voters could not identify the position of the Democrats. The victory of the Democratic candidate, therefore, can hardly be attributed solely to his position on the sales tax. His majority included a large number of people who disagreed with his tax policy, and many who voted for him for reasons unrelated to the tax issue. Therefore, Epstein concludes that the election, although centered on a single policy, cannot be interpreted as a wish by the majority to extend the income tax.[33]

At the local level, participation in the electoral process is substantially less than at the state or national level. Thirty-five to 45 percent of the eligible population abstain from voting in national elections, but 50 to 90 percent frequently do not vote in local elections. These habitual non-voters are drawn disproportionately from the poor and uneducated, who typically have very little interest in politics. It is difficult for them to become enthusiastic about bond issues and tax referenda, for example, when there are no personalities to relate to the issues. Most voters are not issue-oriented, but rather are attracted to parties and candidates; the relative unimportance of either parties or candidates in local politics contributes substantially to the low turnout. Only citizens who are intensely committed to the community are likely to vote in local elections. These are the interested, committed, high-status citizens who make up the "normal" local electorate. They feel they have a stake in community decision making and therefore participate frequently in local affairs. Also, their better education makes it possible for them to comprehend elections even in the absence of parties and candidates.

Occasionally an abnormal election occurs. People who typically do not vote are stimulated into political activity, perhaps for the first and only time. When local elections generate a substantial increase in turnout, one can infer that the election is a symptom of a deeply felt community conflict. The election has become "heated," and has generated interest among the strata of the population normally unconcerned about local affairs. The added voters are usually from the poorly educated classes of the population, who have few organizational and emotional ties to the community. Abstract issues mean little to them, and they respond only to campaigns that appeal to the frustrations of an economically inferior position.[34]

Electoral Participation and Nonparticipation

Another problem with the theory of popular control over public policy through elections is the fact that nearly half of the adult population fails to vote, even in presidential elections.

Since the 1960 presidential race between John F. Kennedy and Richard Nixon, voter turnout has steadily slipped from 64 percent of the eligible voters, to 63 percent in the Johnson-Goldwater race in 1964, to 60 percent in the Nixon-Humphrey-Wallace race in 1968, and to 56 percent in 1972. "Off-year" elections bring out fewer than half of the eligible voters. Yet in these "off-year" contests the nation chooses all of its U.S. representatives, one third of its senators, and about one half of its governors. (See Figure 6–2.)

Lester Milbrath listed six forms of "legitimate" political participation.[35] Individuals may run for public office, become active in party and campaign work, make financial contributions to political candidates or causes, belong to organizations that support or oppose candidates, take stands on political issues, attempt to influence friends while discussing candidates or issues, and vote in elections. Activities at the top of this list require greater expenditure of time, money, and energy than those activities at the bottom, and they involve only a tiny minority of the population. Less than 1 percent of the American adult population ever runs for public office. Only about 5 percent are ever active in parties and campaigns, and only about 10 percent make financial contributions. About one third of the population belong to organizations that could be

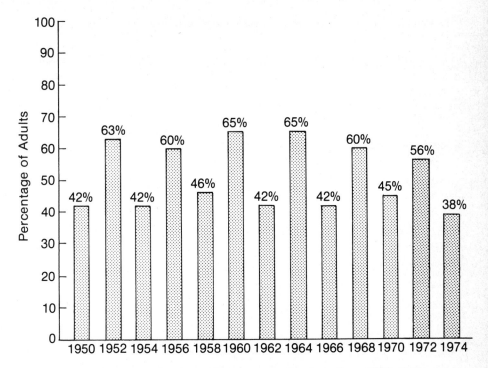

Figure 6-2. Participation in presidential and congressional elections, 1950–1974. (From *Statistical Abstract of the United States*, Washington, D.C.: U.S. Government Printing Office. Composite of data from annual editions.)

classified as political interest groups, and only a few more ever try to convince their friends to vote a certain way. And finally, about 60 to 65 percent of the American people will vote in a hard-fought presidential campaign.

Nonparticipation does not occur uniformly throughout all segments of the population. The Michigan Survey Center recorded the percentages (found in Table 6–10) of non-voting for various groups in the 1960 election. Non-voting is associated with lower education levels, unskilled occupations, rural living, non-membership in organizations, and the especially deprived status of large numbers of blacks. Of course, membership in these categories overlaps. High voter turnout is related to college education; to professional, managerial, or other white collar occupations; to metropolitan residence; and to membership in voluntary associations. On the whole, Catholics and Jews (not shown) vote more frequently than Protestants. While these figures pertain only to voting, other forms of participation follow substantially the same pattern. White, middle-class, college-educated, white-collar, urban Americans participate more in all forms of political activity than non-white, lower-class,

Table 6-10 / Non-voters Classified by Group Characteristics, 1960

Group Characteristic	Percentage Not Voting*
Education	
Grade school	33
High School	19
College	10
Occupation	
Professional and managerial	12
Other white collar	16
Skilled and semi-skilled	22
Unskilled	32
Farm	23
Community	
Metropolitan area	18
Towns and cities	22
Rural areas	23
Race	
White	19
Negro	46
Labor	
Union	23
Non-union	20
Religion	
Protestant	24
Catholic	15

*The exact percentages may change from one election to another, but the general pattern remains very stable.

Source: Fred I. Greenstein, *The American Party System and the American People* (Englewood Cliffs, N.J.: Prentice-Hall, 1963).

grade-school-educated, unskilled, and rural Americans. Marches and demonstrations, which are special tactics of minority groups, are excepted.

Election turnout figures in the United States are lower than those of several other democracies. The turnout in recent elections has been 74 percent in Japan, 77 percent in Great Britain, 83 percent in Israel, 88 percent in West Germany, and 93 percent in Italy. Of course, the lower turnouts in the United States may be explained by our stricter residence and registration requirements and by the fact that we hold elections more frequently. It may also be that Americans are less "political" than citizens of other democracies, less likely to care about the outcome of elections, and less likely to feel that government makes much of an impact on their lives. This disinterest in politics may be a product of an underlying consensus in America that brings opposing parties and candidates so close to each other on major political issues that it does not matter much which party or candidate wins.[36]

Voter participation is highly valued in American political theory. Popular control of government, control of leaders by followers, is supposed to be affected through the electoral process. The majority of Americans do vote, and by so doing they indicate they have some stake in the outcome of elections, but a sizeable group of Americans never vote or participate in politics in any accepted fashion. It is possible to interpret this non-voting as a reflection of "alienation" from the political system. Political "alienation" involves a feeling that voting and other forms of participation are useless, that nothing is really decided by an election, and that the individual cannot personally influence the outcome of political events. The fact that non-voting occurs most frequently among those at the bottom of the income, occupation, education, and status ladder tends to confirm this view; alienation *should* occur more frequently in groups who have not shared in the general affluence of society. However, this interpretation is discouraging for those who wish well for the democratic ideal, because it suggests that not all groups in society place a high value on democratic institutions.

Of increasing significance to those who value popular participation is the *expansion* of the alienated, coupled with a decline in participation. As distrust in government soars, the alienated tend to be more evenly distributed among *all* population groups, rather than concentrating among the traditional have-nots.

The growing disillusionment and distrust of government—and attendant feelings of helplessness and inability to exercise influence —began about 1964 and has continued virtually unabated. About one third of the electorate was classified as cynical in 1964, compared to about half in 1972. About one fourth thought government operated more to the benefit of special interests than to that of the general public in 1964, compared to nearly 60 percent in 1973. Not only are cynicism and alienation becoming less of a class-linked phenomena; they are also reaching across generations. Figure 6–3, tracing the rise of distrust in two separate generations, dramatically indicates how pervasive the feeling of distrust has become. The trend toward increasing dissatisfaction with governmental performance, coupled with a sharp decline in participation in elections, hardly supports the hypothesis that a low turnout indicates a calm and tranquil mass. Although traditional democratic theory argues that a low turnout and a wide majority for an incumbent are indicative of a feeling of well-being on the part of the

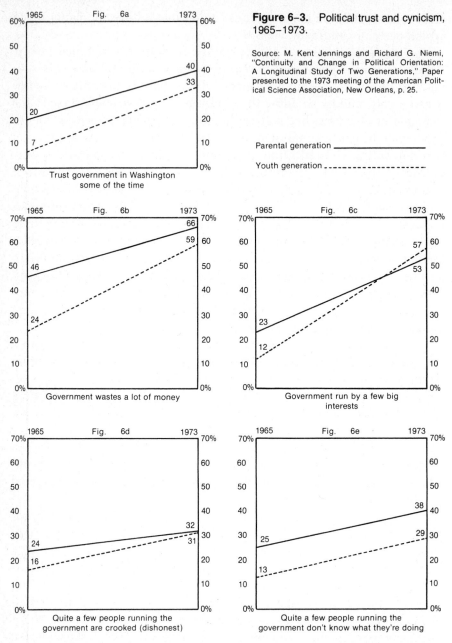

Figure 6-3. Political trust and cynicism, 1965–1973.

Source: M. Kent Jennings and Richard G. Niemi, "Continuity and Change in Political Orientation: A Longitudinal Study of Two Generations," Paper presented to the 1973 meeting of the American Political Science Association, New Orleans, p. 25.

Parental generation ——————————

Youth generation - - - - - - - - - - - - -

masses, the election of 1972 does not fit this theory. Clearly, the masses expressed no such feeling of well-being. On the contrary, dissatisfaction was seething. McGovern did do better among the cynical than among the trusting, but not as well as he *should* have done (assuming a "normal" Democratic vote).

The forces at work in 1972—notably the correlates of cynicism and disinterest—made it impossible for an anti-establishment candidate to capitalize upon widespread malaise. The continuing drift away from participation defused any potential impact of the discontented. McGovern's greatest support came from people who were both cynical and inefficacious. This depressing combination of characteristics is found in the predominant population group in the country (44 percent). However, such people simply did not vote at the level of other population groups. And McGovern simply could not raise the dismal level of motivation among those who felt helpless. Even among the inefficacious cynics who *did* vote, McGovern received only 49 percent of the vote.

Thus the surface appearances of 1972 are deceptive. Beneath the Nixon landslide lurked widespread discontent, waiting for an elite, or counter-elite, to channel it into participation. For the present, "a major segment of the population will go unrepresented at the presidential level. . . . Such a condition of perceived non-responsive government can only lead to further political dissatisfaction, discontent and disaffection."[37]

Violence as an Alternative to Elections

There is a strong relationship between status deprivation and political violence. Perhaps this deprivation explains why many blacks, rather than taking their hostility to the ballot box, have increasingly participated in violence. As Table 6–11 shows, the rioters in recent disorders were better educated than the non-rioters, but were likely to hold menial jobs, and their intense racial pride was strengthened by the discrepancy between their education and their occupation. For these people, conventional political participation lost its meaning, and violence became a device to

Table 6–11 / Education, Occupation, and Participation in Riots

	Newark		Detroit	
	Rioters	**Non-rioters**	**Rioters**	**Non-rioters**
Education				
Grade school	1.9%	14.3%	7.0%	27.9%
Some high school	63.2	46.8	53.5	33.8
High school graduate	29.2	31.0	23.3	26.1
Some college or college graduate	5.7	7.9	16.2	12.2
Occupation				
Unskilled	50.0	39.6		
Semiskilled or better	50.0	60.4		

Source: Report of the National Advisory Commission on Civil Disorders (Washington, D.C., 1968).

Table 6-12 / Racial Hostility and Participation in Riots in Newark

	Rioters	Non-rioters
Who do you think are nicer?		
Negroes	78.1%	57.3%
Whites	21.9	37.3
About the same	0.0	5.4
Sometimes I hate white people.		
Agree	72.4	50.0
Disagree	27.6	50.0
Political information test		
High score	68.9	51.2
Low score	31.1	48.8
How much did anger with politicians have to do with causing riot?		
Great deal	43.2	19.6
Something	31.8	39.1
Nothing	18.2	24.5
Don't know	6.8	6.6
Is the country worth fighting for?		
Yes	33.0	50.8
No	52.8	27.8
Don't know	14.2	21.4

Source: *Report of the National Advisory Commission on Civil Disorders* (Washington, D.C., 1968).

communicate intense dissatisfaction. (See Table 6–12.) The rioters were not vagrants or criminals; they were long-time residents of the city and were, in fact, cited among the more intellectually oriented and politically sophisticated of the black community.[38]

Furthermore, actions of the militant rioters are supported by substantial portions of blacks who did not participate directly in the riots. Post-riot survey information indicated that roughly 20 percent of the blacks in the Watts area participated actively in the riot of 1964, and more than half of the residents supported the activities of the rioters. Interviews found that 58 percent of the Watts residents felt that the long-run effects of the riots would be favorable; 84 percent said that whites were now more aware of black problems; 62 percent said that the riot was a black protest. In summary, the riots are looked upon favorably by a large proportion of the ghetto residents.

Conventional political participation is often deemed hopeless by ghetto dwellers. The election of black mayors in Cleveland, Ohio, and Gary, Indiana, in 1967 does not indicate that blacks elsewhere will find it possible to return to conventional participation as the sole method of influencing political decisions. In Cleveland, more than 90 percent of the white Democrats who voted in the Democratic primary election switched to a Republican candidate in the general election, presumably because the Democratic candidate was a black.[39]

Rioting is an alternative to voting, taken when the results of elections provide no tangible rewards, but rioting and political violence are not considered political participation by political scientists. Perhaps this is because we wish to regard political violence as an atypical and temporary aberration. However, the fact that rioters are otherwise typical black citizens and have a strong commitment to the redress of the grievances of the black community suggests that violence may become a common pattern of political participation. Actually, the American political system is not as stable as we like to assume.[40] Although most whites regard the political system as a legitimate one, a substantial proportion of blacks do not, because they believe that the political system has not provided adequate rewards for their conventional political participation.

Almond and Verba describe Americans as proud of their governmental and political institutions, and further comment that a substantial majority of Americans also expect equal treatment by government officials and police.[41] This description of the American political culture does not apply to blacks; they do not share this opinion of the police. Even though perceptions of unequal treatment by the police are a major precipitating cause of racial violence, whites are unwilling to accept the possibility of brutality and discrimination on the part of police.

In short, middle- and upper-class whites tend to look upon our system of government as extremely satisfactory and find it difficult to understand why a minority group communicates its dissatisfaction violently. In Milbrath's hierarchy of political involvement (discussed on p. 187) violence is excluded, because the hierarchy of participation does not apply to behavior "designed to disrupt the normal operation of democratic political processes."[42] But it is quite likely that a new pattern of political participation—violence as a response to both deprivation and resentment—is emerging. To be sure, this form of protest is a criminal one. And it may be irrational and self-defeating, for the great majority of the casualties of the riots—the dead, the injured, and the arrested—were rioters themselves, and much of the property destroyed belonged to ghetto residents. Moreover, the riots may have changed the attitudes of many whites toward the black community and toward the civil rights movement from sympathy or disinterest to opposition. Nonetheless, violence must be recognized as a form of political participation by the masses.

"Politics as usual" is not an apt description of the mood of the nation with regard to the crisis in civil rights. The shattering of consensus produced by violence and reaction to violence has presented the two major political parties with their most severe crisis since the Civil War.

Summary

Elite theory contends that the masses do not participate in policy making, and that the elites who do are subject to little direct influence from apathetic masses. But many scholars who acknowledge that even "democratic" societies are governed by elites seek to reaffirm democratic values by contending that voters can influence elite behavior by choosing between competing elites in elections. In other words, elitism is sometimes challenged by modern pluralists on the grounds that elections give the masses a voice in policy making by holding governing elites accountable to the people.

Our analysis suggests that elections are imperfect instruments of accountability. But even if the people can hold *governmental* elites accountable through elections, how can corporation elites, financial elites, union leaders, and other private leadership be held accountable? The accountability argument usually dodges the problem of *private* decision making and focuses exclusive attention on *public* decision making by elected elites. But certainly men's lives are vitally affected by the decisions of private institutions and organizations. So the first problem with the accountability thesis is that, at best, it applies only to elected governmental elites. However, our analysis of elections also suggests that it is difficult for the voters to hold even *governmental* elites accountable.

1. Elections are primarily a symbolic exercise that helps tie the masses to the established order. Elections offer the masses an opportunity to participate in the political system, but electoral participation does not enable them to determine public policy.

2. Competing candidates in elections do not usually offer clear policy alternatives; hence it is seldom possible for the voter to affect policy by selecting a particular candidate for public office.

3. Voters are not well-informed about the policy stands of candidates, and relatively few voters are concerned with policy questions. The masses cast their votes in elections on the basis of traditional party ties, personality of the candidates, group affiliations, and a host of other factors having little relation to public policy.

4. Mass opinion on public policy is inconsistent and unstable. Relatively few voters (generally well-educated, upper-class voters from whom elites are drawn) hold reasonably consistent political ideologies. Mass opinion is unguided by principle, unstable, and subject to change.

5. Available evidence suggests that elites influence the opinions of masses more than masses influence the opinion of elites. Mass publics respond to political symbols manipulated by elites, not to facts or political principles.

6. The only reasonably stable aspect of mass politics is party identification. But party identification in the mass electorate is unaccompanied by any wide policy gaps between Democrats and Republicans. Democratic and Republican voters hold fairly similar opinions on most issues.

7. It is difficult to use election results to ascertain majority preferences on policy questions because (a) campaigns generally stress the presentation of political ideologies rather than the *content* of the ideologies; (b) victory for a party or a candidate does not necessarily mean that the voters support any particular policy position of the candidate; (c) voters frequently misinterpret the policy preferences of a candidate; (d) often a candidate's voters include not only advocates of his position, but some who oppose his position and some who vote for him for other reasons; (e) a candidate may take positions on many different issues, so he cannot know which of the policy positions he has taken resulted in his election; (f) for voters to influence policy through elections, winning candidates would be bound to follow their campaign pledges.

8. Elections are means for selecting personnel, not policy. Voters choose on the basis of a candidate's personal style, filtered through partisan commitment. A candidate's election does not imply a policy choice by the electorate.

9. At best, elections provide the masses with an opportunity to express themselves favorably or unfavorably about the conduct of past administrations, but not to direct the course of future events. A vote against the party or candidate in power, however, does not identify the particular policy being censured. And there is no guarantee that an ousted official's replacement will pursue any specific policy alternatives.

10. Few individuals participate in any political activity other than voting. One third of the adult population fails to vote even in presidential elections.

References

[1] Murray Edelman, *The Symbolic Uses of Politics* (Urbana: University of Illinois Press, 1964), p. 17.

[2] Gerald Pomper, *Elections in America: Control and Influence in Democratic Politics* (New York: Dodd, Mead, & Co., 1968), pp. 255–256.

[3] Carl Friedrich, *Man and His Government* (New York: McGraw-Hill Book Co., 1963), pp. 199–201.

[4] Pomper, *Elections in America*, p. 254.

[5] Pomper, pp. 254–255.

[6] John Stuart Mill, *Considerations on Representative Government* (Chicago: Henry Regnery, Gateway edition, 1962), p. 144.

[7] Mill, pp. 130–131.

[8] William R. Keech, *The Impact of Negro Voting: The Role of the Vote in the Quest for Equality* (Chicago: Rand McNally, 1968), p. 3.

[9] Fred I. Greenstein, *The American Party System and the American People* (Englewood Cliffs, N.J.: Prentice-Hall, 1963), p. 12.

[10] Herbert McClosky, "Consensus and Ideology in American Politics," *American Political Science Review*, 58: 2 (June 1964), 372.

[11] Public opinion survey in Oregon by Ray Bardsley (not published).

[12]Michael J. Robinson, "The Import of the Televised Watergate Hearings," *Journal of Communications*, 24 (Spring 1974), 17.

[13]A. Campbell, P. Converse, W. Miller, and D. Stokes, *The American Voter* (New York: John Wiley, 1960), p. 175.

[14]Philip E. Converse, "The Nature of Belief Systems in Mass Publics," in David E. Apter (ed.), *Ideology and Discontent* (New York: Free Press, 1964), p. 210.

[15]Converse, "The Nature of Belief Systems," pp. 213–230.

[16]Campbell *et al.*, The American Voter, p. 227.

[17]Converse, "The Nature of Belief Systems," p. 229.

[18]Converse, "The Nature of Belief Systems," p. 245.

[19]Edelman, *The Symbolic Uses of Politics*, p. 172.

[20]V. O. Key, Jr., *The Responsible Electorate* (Cambridge: Harvard University Press, 1966).

[21]V. O. Key, Jr., pp. 58–59.

[22]Philip E. Converse, review of *The Responsible Electorate*, in *Political Science Quarterly* (December 1966), 631.

[23]Converse, *et al.*, *op. cit.*, 1096.

[24]Converse, pp. 1097–1101.

[25]Seymour Martin Lipset and Earl Raab, "The Election and the National Mood," *Commentary*, 55 (January 1973), p. 44.

[26]Arthur H. Miller, Warren E. Miller, Alden S. Raine, and Thad A. Brown, "A Majority Party in Disarray: Political Polarization in the 1972 Election," paper presented to the 1973 annual meeting of the American Political Science Association, p. 12.

[27]Converse, "The Nature of Belief Systems," p. 227.

[28]Philip E. Converse, "Information Flow and the Stability of Partisan Attitudes," *Public Opinion Quarterly*, 26:4 (Winter 1962), 579.

[29]Angus Campbell, "Voters and Elections: Past and Present," *Journal of Politics*, 26:4 (November 1964), 745–757.

[30]S. M. Lipset, "The President, the Polls, and Vietnam," *Transaction* (September-October 1966), 22.

[31]Warren E. Miller, "Voting and Foreign Policy," in James Rosenau (ed.), *Domestic Sources of Foreign Policy* (New York: Free Press), p.216.

[32]William H. Flanigan, *The Political Behavior of the American Electorate* (Boston: Allyn and Bacon, 1968), p. 115.

[33]Leon D. Epstein, "Electoral Decision and Policy Mandate: An Empirical Example," *Public Opinion Quarterly*, 28:4 (Winter 1964), 572.

[34]James S. Coleman, *Community Conflict* (New York: Free Press, 1957), p. 19.

[35]Lester Milbrath, *Political Participation* (Chicago: Rand McNally, 1965), pp. 23–29.

[36]Robert E. Lane, "The Politics of Consensus in an Age of Affluence," *American Political Science Review*, 61:4 (December 1965), 880.

[37]Miller *et al.*, "A Majority Party in Disarray," p. 90.

[38]*Report of the National Advisory Commission on Civil Disorders* (Washington, D.C., 1968), pp. 111–112; pp. 128–135.

[39]Jeffrey Hadden, Louis H. Masotti, and Victor Thiessen, "The Making of the Negro Mayors, 1967," *Transaction*, 5:3 (January–February 1968), 24.

[40]See Ted Gurr, "Urban Disorder: Perspectives from the Comparative Study of Civil Strife," *American Behavioral Scientist*, 4 (March–April 1968), 50–55; Ivo K. Feierabend and Rosalind L. Feierabend, "Aggressive Behaviors."

[41]Gabriel A. Almond and Sidney Verba, *The Civic Culture: Political Attitudes and Democracy in Five Nations* (Boston: Little Brown and Co., 1965), pp. 69–75.

[42]Milbrath, *Political Participation*, p. 18.

Selected Additional Readings

Burnham, Walter Dean. *Critical Elections and the Mainsprings of American Politics.* New York: W. W. Norton and Co., Inc., 1970. Burnham argues that a realignment of party loyalties is probable.

Campbell, Angus, et al. *The American Voter: An Abridgement.* New York: John Wiley, 1964. This is an abridgement of the classic study of voting behavior in the United States conducted by the Survey Research Center at the University of Michigan.

Congressional Quarterly. *Dollar Politics.* Washington D.C.: Congressional Quarterly Inc., 1971. This short publication provides an excellent review of campaign fund raising, spending, and costs, as well as a chronological summary of federal legislation regulating campaign finances from 1945 through the 1971 Campaign Spending Act.

Flanigan, William H. *The Political Behavior of the American Electorate,* 2nd ed. Boston: Allyn and Bacon, 1972. In this short book, Flanigan draws on a wide range of previous voting studies in explaining American voting behavior. Of particular interest are the discussions in Chapters 3 and 4 of social, economic, and psychological correlates of voting.

Lipset, Seymour Martin. *Political Man.* Garden City, N.Y.: Doubleday & Co. (Anchor Books edition), 1963. (See Chapter 5, page 189.)

Milbrath, Lester. *Political Participation.* Chicago: Rand McNally, 1965. Milbrath presents a propositional survey of the literature on political participation through the early 1960s.

Pomper, Gerald. *Elections in America: Control and Influence in Democratic Politics.* New York: Dodd, Mead, & Co., 1968. This is an outstanding study of the American electoral process. In addition to analyzing voting behavior per se, Pomper focuses on the impact of that behavior on public policy.

CHAPTER 7

THE AMERICAN PARTY SYSTEM:

A SHRINKING CONSENSUS

The Two-Party Consensus

There is a great deal of truth to the "Tweedledum and Tweedledee" image of American political parties. American parties do, in fact, subscribe to the same fundamental political ideology. Both the Democratic and the Republican parties have reflected prevailing elite consensus on basic democratic values—the sanctity of private property, a free enterprise economy, individual liberty, limited government, majority rule, and due process of law. Moreover, since the 1930s both parties have supported the public-oriented, mass-welfare domestic programs of the "liberal establishment"—social security, fair labor standards, unemployment compensation, a graduated income tax, a national highway program, a federally aided welfare system, counter-cyclical fiscal and monetary policies, and government regulation of public utilities. Finally, both parties have supported the basic outlines of American foreign and military policy since World War II—international involvement, anticommunism, the Cold War, European recovery, NATO, military preparedness, selective service, and even the Korean and Vietnam wars. Rather than promoting competition over national goals and programs, the parties reinforce societal consensus and limit the area of legitimate political conflict.[1]

The major parties are not, of course, *identical* in ideology; there are nuances of difference. For instance, Republican leaders are "conservative" on domestic policy, while Democratic leaders are "liberal." Moreover, the social bases of the parties are slightly different. Both parties draw their support from all social groups in America, but the Democrats draw disproportionately from labor, urban workers, Jews, Catholics, and blacks, while the Republicans draw disproportionately from rural, small-town, and suburban Protestants, businessmen, and professionals (see Table 7–1). To the extent that the aspirations of these two broad groups of supporters differ, the thrust of party ideology also differs. However, the magnitude of this difference is not very great. Since there are only two parties and a non-ideological electorate, "consumer" demand (as perceived by leadership) requires that party ideologies be ambiguous and moderate. Therefore, we cannot expect the parties, who wish to alienate the minimum number of voters and attract the maximum number, to take up a cause supported by only a minority of the population.

Since parties are organizations whose basic motive is to capture political office, strong ideology and innovation are virtually out of the question. Firmer and more precise statements of ideologies by the political parties would probably create new lines of cleavage and eventually fragment the parties. The development of a clear "liberal" or "conservative" ideology by either party would cost the party votes unless the electorate, stimulated by elites, became more ideologically oriented. Even so, it is doubtful that the country could divide itself into two warring camps, one consisting of liberals and the other of conservatives.

Both the 1964 and 1972 presidential elections are examples of the fact that a strong ideological stance will not win elections in America. In 1964, the Republicans came as close to offering a clear ideological alternative to the majority party as has occurred in recent American political history. Goldwater, the Republican presidential candidate, made a genuine effort to provide the electorate with a "choice, not an echo." He specifically rejected moderation ("moderation in defense of liberty is no virtue") and defended extremism ("extremism in defense of liberty is no vice"). He rejected the "peace" image of Eisenhower in favor of an aggressive, military-oriented stance on foreign policy.

While most voters did not perceive a *foreign* policy difference between Goldwater and Johnson, they did perceive a *domestic* policy difference. Public opinion data indicate that Johnson's campaign presentation and the general mood of the public were very similar. A Louis

Harris poll taken during the campaign revealed that only 1 percent of the respondents considered themselves "radical," but 45 percent considered Goldwater radical. However, 80 percent of the respondents defined themselves as either conservatives or middle-of-the-roaders, and 67 percent identified Johnson as sharing this ideological orientation.[2] Goldwater received 27 million votes, but a Harris poll of January 11, 1965, indicates that 18 million people voted for Goldwater only out of party loyalty; they had doubts about or disagreements with his position on the issues. Also, Goldwater gained 2 million Southern Democratic votes because of his opposition to the Civil Rights Act of 1964. This leaves a total of about 7 million hardcore "conservative" supporters of Senator Goldwater, and this small cadre of ideologues is probably the basic strength of the highly motivated right wing of American politics (at least in 1964).

This overwhelming defeat of the "pure" conservative position is significant, in that it reveals the fallacy of the argument that the non-ideological two-party system suppresses basic ideological cleavages within the masses. The magnitude of Goldwater's defeat indicates that few ideologues will rally to the call. If there *were* strong divisions of opinion within the electorate, the parties, given their "consumer" orientation, would surely reflect them. Parties reflect the consensual, moderate nature of the American public and will continue to do so as long as the majority of voters share the consensus.

The same can be said with regard to the 1972 election. Table 7–2 presents the population and candidate distributions on political philosophy. The percentage indicate the public's self-image, and their image of the candidates before and after the conventions. McGovern's position was unknown, even in the most general and symbolic terms, to one third and one fourth of the voters. McGovern made the same error in perception as did Goldwater: there are not enough voters who prefer alternatives to the dominant value consensus. McGovern did well among that minority of voters seeking a liberal policy alternative, but could not retain the support of Democratic voters preferring middle-of-the-road or conservative policies.

While Goldwater erred in the direction of the "hidden conservatives," McGovern's error was in seriously overestimating the liberal change-orientation of the electorate, particularly the younger voters. In both cases, the mistake was natural. Communication patterns enhance supportive statements, making it inevitable that a candidate exaggerate his support. Given the wide publicity extended to the youth movement, and the great potential for support in the newly enfranchised eighteen-year-olds, McGovern's expectations appeared justified. Indeed, he

Table 7-1 / Who Votes for Each Party: Differences in Voter Support Given the Democratic and Republican Parties (by Major Social Groups)

	1948		1956		1960		1964		1968		1972	
	D	R	D	R	D	R	D	R	D	R	D	R
Religion												
Protestant	47%	53%	36%	64%	37%	63%	63%	37%	38%	62%	30%	66%
Catholic	66	34	52	48	83	17	79	21	60	40	37	57
Jewish	100	0*	74	26	89	11	89	11	93	7	66	29
Race												
White	53	47	40	60	47	53	64	36	41	59	30	66
Black	65	35	82	18	72	28	100	0*	97	3	84	13
Education												
Grade school	69	31	49	51	55	45	80	20	62	39†	38	57
High school	54	46	43	57	53	47	69	31	48	52	36	63
College	24	76	26	74	36	64	54	40	37	63	36	61
Age												
34 and younger	63	37	45	55	52	48	72	28	48	52	43	54
35 to 44	61	39	45	55	51	49	68	32	52	48	32	63
45 to 54	47	53	42	58	55	45	69	31	43	57	31	63
55 to 64	43	57	35	65	44	56	70	30	41	59	26	69
65 and over	50	50	36	64	38	62	55	45	45	55	29	65
Sex												
Male	57	43	43	57	53	47	65	35	45	55	30	66
Female	53	47	40	60	46	54	69	31	47	53	37	59
Occupation												
Professional and managerial	19	81	32	68	45	55	58	42	38	62	31	65

White collar	50	50	35	65	48	52	65	35	45	55	32	64
Skilled and semi-skilled workers	77	23	52	48	59	41	77	23	52	48	35	60
Unskilled workers	74	26	68	32	59	41	83	17	60	40	55	43
Farm operators	64	36	37	63	33	67	64	36	45	55	31	69
Union membership												
Labor union families	82	18	56	44	64	36	84	16	43	57	41	54
Non-union families	44	56	36	64	44	56	62	38	56	44	32	64
Income‡												
Lower (less than $5000)	65	35	42	58	47	53	74	26	51	49	41	53
Lower middle ($5000–$9999)	69	31	46	54	46	54	71	29	45	55	38	57
Middle ($10,000–$14,999)	38	62	26	74	46	54	56	44	52	48	34	63
Upper middle ($15,000+)	49	51	42	58	55	45	71	29	32	68	30	66
Community Size												
Metropolitan areas	60	40	43	57	58	42	72	28	60	40	38	58
Cities (over 50,000)	—	—	52	48	50	50	64	33	55	45	43	55
Towns (2,500–49,999)	48	52	37	63	40	60	61	39	45	55	33	62
Rural (under 2,500)	67	33	39	61	48	52	69	31	37	63	25	69

*Fewer than 1 percent of respondents favored the Republican candidate in these instances.

†Rounding error.

‡Cut-points for 1972 are slightly different than for previous years.

Source: Survey Research Center, University of Michigan. (Composite from SRC studies.)

Table 7-2 / Population and Candidate Distributions on Political Philosophy

	Conservative		Middle-of the-Road		Liberal		No Opinion	
	April	July	April	July	April	July	April	July
Public's ideology	37%	41%	26%	30%	26%	24%	4%	5%
Nixon's image	51	52	24	25	15	11	10	12
McGovern's image	18	11	15	22	33	44	34	23

Source: Gallup Political Index, April–July, 1972.

counted on a three to one advantage among eighteen-year-olds, particularly among the college students who participated so enthusiastically in the primary elections and convention.

His advantage did not materialize, due to the fact that the "generation gap" was largely (insofar as political behavior is involved) unsupported by empirical information. Not only should one make a distinction between college and non-college youth; one should also note that the college population is far less homogeneous than McGovern assumed. (See Table 7–3.)

The result of such a division of opinion was that McGovern and Nixon split the new voters at roughly 50–50. In contrast, Humphrey in 1968 had actually enjoyed a five to four advantage over Nixon among new voters. Further, if one takes the "under 30" generation as the cut-off point,

Table 7-3 / McGovern Support Among College Students

	% Support for McGovern
Class	
Freshmen	40%
Sophomores	45
Juniors	55
Seniors	52
Graduate Students	68
Place of Residence	
On Campus (dorms, fraternities, sororities)	44
Off Campus (apartments, rooming houses)	56
At Home	44
Type of College	
Public	49
Private	54
Denominational	26
Major	
Humanities & Social Science	55
Physical Science	44
Business & Professionals	42

Source: Gallup Political Index, February 1971.

McGovern fared even worse: in the 18 to 24 age group he received half the vote, while in the 25 to 29 age group he received 43 percent. In truth, the voting behavior of the youth was not very dissimilar to that of the parental generation:

Looking at the reported vote in the presidential election of 1968, the Congressional election of 1970, and the Presidential election of 1972 [indicates that] both generations manifest signs of Nixon's hairline victory of 1968, the traditional "decline" in the off-year election, and the spectacular "surge" represented by Nixon's landslide of 1972.[3]

Assessing the implications of such findings, Kent Jennings and Richard Niemi are struck by the similarity between the younger and older generations, especially in view of "open efforts to pit the young against the middle-aged." They predict a "smoothing out" of intergenerational antagonisms, which would make the lesson of 1964 and 1972 even more apparent.

To repeat the lesson: the strategy is to attract voters from the center of the political spectrum, for here lies the majority and the way to victory. "If young, poor, and black are what most voters aren't, let us consider the electorate for what it largely is: white, median family income of $8,622; median age of about forty-seven. In short, middle aged, middle-class whites. . . . There are no two strategies for victory—they are the same strategy with different rhetoric. This single strategy involves a drive to the center of the electorate . . . this moving attitudinal center involves progressivism on economic issues and toughness on the social issue . . . the winning coalition in America is the one that holds the center group on an attitudinal battleground. . . . For the seventies, the battlefield shows signs of splitting into two battlefields: the old economic one and the new social one that deals with crime, drugs, racial pressure, and disruption. To the extent that this transformation occurs, then the party and the candidate that can best occupy the center ground of the two battlefields will win the election."[4]

Political Parties as Organizations

Unlike European mass-membership parties, American parties are not "organizations" in the sense normally understood by that term. To be a "Democrat" or a "Republican" involves no greater commitment to the organization than supporting, occasionally, the nominees of that party.

There is, of course, a party organization, consisting of the formally chosen leadership, informal power-holders (who do not hold government or party office), and the party activists who contribute their time and money and consequently acquire the right to make decisions in the name of the party. However, neither political party is structurally hierarchical. Both are decentralized to the extent that no chain of command from national through state to local levels can be said to exist. But the structure of power within the activist group in each party is not especially relevant to our concern. Rather, we are interested in interaction *between* this group and the overwhelming majority of Democrats and Republicans, who do not involve themselves in formulation of party objectives or the selection of candidates (except in primaries) but merely accept or reject the product offered to them by the party activists. For all but a tiny portion of the participants in the political system, the major political act is that of a consumer. The association with the party is entirely passive.

It is somewhat of an irony that the parties, as the agents of democratic decision making, are not themselves democratic in their structures. One of the most sweeping indictments of political parties on this count comes from Roberto Michels, whose "iron law of oligarchy" leads him to conclude that "every party . . . becomes divided into a minority of directors and a majority of directed."[5] However, the organizational characteristics of American parties supply few relevant data to either support or refute Michels' assertion. There is, indeed, an active minority, but there is no passive majority because the party in the electorate, the masses, are not really members of the party. The party as an organization is composed of those persons who exercise varied degrees of influence within the activists' cadre. Sorauf describes American parties in this way:

Despite recent trends, the American parties remain largely skeletal, "cadre" party organizations, manned generally by small numbers of activists and involving the great masses of their supporters scarcely at all. . . . By the standards of the parties of much of the rest of the world, American party organization continues to be characterized by its unusual fluidity and evanescence, by its failure to generate activity at non-election times, and by the ease by which a handful of activists and public officeholders dominate it.[6]

The evidence suggests that American parties, within the activists' cadre, are not a perfect fit for Michels' model, for party activists are neither as homogeneous nor as numerically small as his model requires. A more appropriate analytic construct would appear to be one developed by Harold Lasswell and Abraham Kaplan, and most recently employed by Samuel Eldersveld—the "stratarchy."[7] A stratarchy is a hierarchical structure best described as a flat-topped pyramid, in which power resides at the top level (just as it does with conical-shaped hierarchies), but in which there are a number of persons occupying that level. In the case of American party stratarchies, those who are at the top level—the activists—are both numerous and heterogeneous. Power is diffused among them rather than centralized. The exception to this rule is a few large city political machines, such as those found in Chicago, Pittsburgh, and Philadelphia; these political machines are tightly and hierarchically controlled.

In essence, power in American parties tends to rest in the hands of those who have the time and the money to make it a full-time, or nearly full-time, occupation. Party activists—consisting of no more than 3 or 4 percent of the adult population—can decide what product is to be offered to political consumers (the party in the electorate). Beyond this, there is little interaction between the party in the electorate and the party activists. The crucial question is, therefore, who are the party activists? We know, from research cited in previous chapters, that the activists are strongly ideological and committed to the norms of the democratic decision-making process. Since these characteristics describe the upper socioeconomic groups, it is not surprising to discover that party activists are of relatively high socioeconomic status, and come from families with a history of party activity. The highest socioeconomic levels are found in the highest echelons of the party organization. As Sorauf notes, "the parties . . . attract men and women with the time and financial resources to be able to afford politics, with the information and knowledge to understand it, and with the skills to be useful in it."[8]

It is, of course, true that—reflecting the basis of support among the party in the electorate—Democratic activists are of somewhat lower socioeconomic status than their Republican counterparts. The activists of both parties are somewhat representative of their clientele. Nevertheless, the socioeconomic status of both Democratic and Republican activists is above the average for the area they represent. This distinction between elite and mass, then, is especially characteristic of American political parties.

But what does it matter whether or not the parties are democratic in structure? If the competition between parties is similar to the competition between businesses, the structural characteristics of each group of producers are not very important. Each competitor, democratic or not, has the primary function of satisfying his customers. For instance, it is of no concern to the average consumer that he does not have a voice in determining the type of electric toaster manufactured by the General Electric Corporation. If he does not like this toaster, he can always buy one from Sunbeam or Westinghouse or any one of a number of competitors.

Unfortunately, this analogy is not especially apt for American political parties. The political alternatives offered by parties are much more constricted than are the alternatives offered in business. The voter cannot choose from a number of competing products, but is limited to a choice between two. If the voter finds the product of one competitor unsatisfactory, he must either accept the single alternative or decline to become a consumer. Given the consensual nature of American parties, the range of alternatives is quite narrow.[9]

Further, it is difficult for consumers to force the producers to change their product. At first glance, it would seem easy to become an activist in a party and change the agenda-setting personnel. At most levels of political participation, this is superficially quite simple. State legislatures generally require that the party machinery be "open," so anyone can become an activist. Indeed, thousands of party positions are unfilled. However, gaining control of the political party apparatus takes longer than the normally short-term commitment that even more active portions of the citizenry are willing to make. Also, challenges to the dominant group of activists are generally focused around a candidate such as Eugene McCarthy or George McGovern. Thus, a relatively small number of party leaders can control the decisions of a large proportion of the delegates to the national conventions. The choice of a nominating convention will be, therefore, the choice of the party activists who have long-term commitments to the party, rather than the choice of those activists who are occasionally mobilized by a particular candidate. Only on the rare occasions when temporarily mobilized activists encounter the power of the permanent activists are we able to see the extent to which the parties are the property of the small cadre willing to commit themselves to politics as an avocation.

Attempts at Party Reform

The debacle of the 1968 Democratic Convention, with huge television audiences observing total anarchy, led to an effort to reform the delegate selection process. In 1969 the Commission on Party Structure and Delegate Selection (the "McGovern Commission") adopted as its purpose the maximization of rank and file participation, so that the nominee of the Democratic Convention would accurately reflect the views of the Democratic electorate. The commission, chaired by McGovern and dominated by McGovern supporters, proposed a quota system (whereby "blacks, youth and women" would achieve representation in "reasonable relationship" to the group's presence in the population of a state). Further, delegate selection in state conventions and local caucuses was to be opened to participation by non-regulars. The goal here was the reduction, if not the elimination, of the traditional dominance of party activists. Consequently, many local party machines decided to use primary elections for the election of delegates to state conventions (which, in turn, named delegates to the national convention).

The focus upon increased participation by non-regulars coincided well with McGovern's ambitions, since he was not the choice of more than a handful of the county chairmen. However, what impact did the reform have upon the representative characteristics of the preconvention primary elections and the composition of the convention itself? Did McGovern's commission succeed in reducing the elitist nature of parties, or was one elite substituted for another?

Let us first consider the nature of primary elections. Primary elections generate considerably *lower* turnout than do general elections. The average turnout in primary elections is usually 30 percent less than in general elections. What does this lower turnout mean for the representation of presidential primaries, especially in 1972? In low turnout elections, a cohesive minority can generate considerably more support than it can in a general election. The strategies of victory can therefore be quite different, since the "vital center" is not so vital. In Table 7–4, we trace the fortunes of the various Democratic primaries to illustrate the success that non-centrist candidates can enjoy.

As we can see, both McGovern and Wallace did exceptionally well against the mainstream Democratic candidates, with McGovern winning in Wisconsin, Massachusetts, Nebraska, Oregon, Rhode Island, California and New Mexico, while Wallace scored victories in Florida, Tennessee, North Carolina, Maryland and Michigan. Between the two insurgents, twelve out of eighteen primary victories were recorded. In terms of delegate strength, Wallace was a strong second to McGovern until he withdrew after being wounded in Maryland.

While McGovern, after Wallace's injury and withdrawal, pulled away to a strong lead in the primaries (ultimately, 51 percent of the delegates elected in primaries were committed to McGovern), his success in state conventions was considerably more mixed. Granted that the new open rules permitted non-regulars to replace established party leadership, it is nevertheless true that McGovern entered the convention with only a slight edge in support among delegates who had been elected at state conventions.

In any case, McGovern's preconvention showing clearly created the impression that "the people" were replacing "the bosses." Who, then, were "the people?" To what extent did McGovern's display of strength in the primaries reflect an increasing move away from the center by rank and file Democrats? To some degree, opinions did parallel the primary elec-

Table 7-4 / Results of 1972 Democratic Primaries

	Percentage of votes cast		
	McGovern	Wallace	Center Candidates
New Hampshire (March 7)	38		48
Florida (March 14)	6	42	42
Illinois (March 12)			63
Wisconsin (April 4)	30	22	39
Pennsylvania (April 25)	20	21	58
Massachusetts (April 25)	52	7	30
Indiana (May 2)		42	59
Ohio (May 2)	40		61
Tennessee (May 4)	7	68	18
North Carolina (May 6)		50	4
Nebraska (May 6)	41	13	39
West Virginia (May 9)		33	67
Maryland (May 16)	22	39	30
Michigan (May 16)	27	51	16
Oregon (May 23)	50	20	18
Rhode Island (May 23)	41	15	41
California (June 6)	45	5	40
New Mexico (June 6)	33	29	30

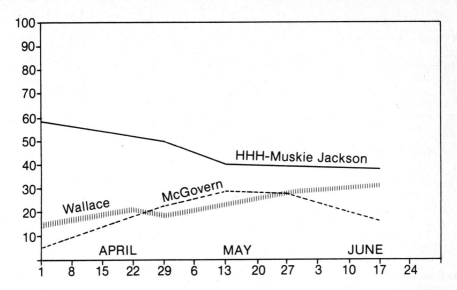

Figure 7-1. Percentage among Democratic rank and file—public opinion polls. (Compiled from delegate data from *National Journal*, April 15-July 1, 1972, and public opinion data from *Gallup Opinion Index*, with the exception of a May 9-10 Harris Poll including Independents as well as Democrats. Gallup question reads as follows: "Which one of the men on this list would you like to see nominated as the Democratic candidate for President in 1972?"

tion (Figure 7-1). As McGovern's campaign proved itself, support for McGovern's nomination grew, and support for the Democratic center declined. But Wallace, too, was gaining in popularity, and in delegate strength. Both non-centrist candidates were gaining, to the point that they were virtually equal in May. Indeed, the insurgency of Wallace appears to have taken support away from the center to a greater extent than did the insurgency of McGovern.

McGovern's first ballot nomination, then, did not necessarily reflect the views of the rank and file. The Democratic party was truly polarized, with no candidate having a clear edge. McGovern's primary voters represented a minority faction. The turnout in primary elections produced a set of voters biased in favor of McGovern. His supporters were, on the basis of their policy preferences, clearly atypical among Democrats, as is demonstrated in Table 7-5.

At the convention, the McGovern reform had an immediate impact upon the nature of the representation. As Table 7-6 shows, the quota system gave blacks, women, and youth a solid block, whereas in 1968 these groups had been virtually excluded.

In addition to these demographic representational changes, delegates in 1972 (as compared with 1968) were substantially less likely to have attended a previous convention, and to have a weak identification

Table 7-5 / Policy Preferences Among Democrats

	McGovern Primary Voters	All Democrats
Vietnam		
Left	79%	52%
Center	17	24
Right	15	24
Amnesty		
Left	52	34
Right	48	66
Marijuana		
Left	41	20
Center	19	8
Right	41	72
Minorities		
Left	49	39
Center	25	22
Right	26	39
Busing		
Left	19	14
Center	10	5
Right	70	81

Source: Arthur H. Miller, Warren E. Miller, Alden S. Raine, and Thad A. Brown, "A Majority Party in Disarray: Policy Polarization in the 1972 Election." Paper presented at the 1973 Annual Meeting of the American Political Science Association, New Orleans, p. 10.

with the Democratic party. Only the delegates supporting the center candidates were strong party identifiers with previous convention experience.

Given the distinctly amateur characteristics of the 1972 convention, and the visible replacement of party regulars, it is not surprising to learn that McGovern and Wallace delegates (as distinguished from mainstream delegates) adopted a "purist" position. That is, they viewed their mission as a crusade, with compromise to be avoided.[10]

Thus it was the purists who successfully challenged the Illinois delegation led by Mayor Richard Daley, on the grounds that the Daley organization had not invited its opponents to participate in the drawing

Table 7-6 / Representation at Democratic Conventions

	1968	1972
Blacks	6%	15%
Youth	2%	21%
Women	14%	40%

Source: Denis G. Sullivan, Jeffrey C. Pressman, Benjamin I. Page, and John J. Lyons, *The Politics of Representation: The Democratic Convention of 1972* (New York: St. Martin's Press, 1974), p. 23.

up of slates. The Daley-led delegation was replaced by one led by Jesse Jackson, who had not voted in the primary, since he was not a registered Democrat (the Jackson-led slate was drawn up at closed meetings from which Daley supporters had been excluded.).

McGovern's supporters asserted that the reform rules, and the expulsion of the "bosses," would make the 1972 convention "the most representative group ever gathered in one spot in one party's history." From the point of view of issue congruence, Democratic elites have always been more liberal than Democratic masses. Therefore, to achieve the desired congruence, either the 1972 convention would have had to have been more conservative, or the masses more liberal, than had been true in previous years. Such was clearly not the case in 1972. The gap between elites and masses was *wider* than usual. Seventy percent of the Democratic rank and file opposed busing, compared with 21 percent of the delegates; 69 percent of the Democratic rank and file opposed amnesty, compared with 18 percent of the delegates; 57 percent of the Democratic masses opposed a guaranteed annual income, compared with 26 percent of the delegates.

The Democratic party platform, which reflected the views of the delegates, was thus in opposition to the views of the masses. It is probable, then, that McGovern's insurgency provided the *least* representative convention in the history of the party. However, the center had not been obliterated. It would reappear in November to bury the Democratic candidate, who represented a new elite—the amateurs—which was extraordinarily unrepresentative.

After the defeat by Nixon, the Democratic party took prompt steps to return control to the traditional party activists. A Commission on Delegate Selection was appointed, with much greater representation given to party regulars, to undo as quickly and quietly as possible the quota system. A new Charter Commission was created to present a new scheme to an extraordinary 1974 convention. Most significantly, McGovern's personal choice as party chairman, Jean Westwood, was replaced by Robert Strauss, Dallas lawyer and Farm Treasurer of the Democratic National Committee. Described by McGovern forces as a symbol of old-guard Democrats, Strauss was supported by organized labor, supporters of the centrist candidates, and a newly formed Coalition for a Democratic Majority (an organization designed to re-construct the old traditional liberal-organized labor alliance).

So it ended, as had Goldwater's insurgency in 1964, with the summary removal of the amateurs and the return of the old guard to positions of influence.

The Development of Party Consensus

Although the beginnings of the welfare-capitalism consensus can be traced to the very origin of the country, the consensus was considerably broadened in the years after the Civil War. Both parties, caught up in the industrial expansion of the era, came under the control of those favoring maximization of private enterprise. Since both parties espoused a virtually identical ideology, neither was able to represent adequately certain disadvantaged segments of the population, especially farmers and urban workers, who were not sharing in the prosperity. These groups became progressively alienated from the established order. The result of this alienation was the mass Populist movement, agrarian rebels who gained control of the Democratic party and nominated William Jennings Bryan in 1896. This rebellion did not develop within elite circles; it was clearly from the "outsiders." But it was a disaster—for the agrarians, for the Democrats, and for participatory democracy in the United States. Probably because an alliance of agrarian farmers and urban workers is unrealistic, the Democratic party was crushed in urban areas of the North, while conservative Democrats completed their hegemony in the South. Consequently, both parties became even more conservative. The triumph of the business system, accomplished by a nonviolent expulsion from the political arena of the disadvantaged segments, was total.

A severe decline in voting participation occurred after the election of 1896, and the decline has not been reversed since then. Many of the masses who had supported Bryan simply dropped out of the electoral system. Turnout decreased from 85 percent in 1896 to 68 percent in the period 1952–1960. The destruction of political competition, with the crushing of the Populist rebellion in 1896, is largely responsible for the marked decline in the active voting population. As Burnham concludes:

This revolutionary contraction in the size and diffusions in the shape of the voting universe was almost certainly the fruit of the heavily sectional party realignment which was inaugurated in 1896. . . . It is difficult to avoid the impression that while all the forms of political democracy were more or less scrupulously preserved, the functional result of the "system of 1896" was a conversion of a fairly democratic regime into a rather broadly based oligarchy.[11]

The party system of 1896 was modified by the Great Depression and the election of 1932, which established a liberal elite and replaced the Republicans as the majority party. As result of this realigning election, the consensus shifted gradually from "rugged individualism" to a more public-oriented philosophy under Franklin D. Roosevelt. The Republican party clung to the philosophy of rugged individualism in the 1936 election with the candidacy of the "Kansas Sunflower," Alf Landon, but the prevailing mood of both elites and masses favored economic reform and social welfare. By 1940, the GOP candidate, Wendell Willkie, president of a giant public utilities empire, was expressing support for social security, fair labor standards, unemployment compensation, public welfare, and most other New Deal programs. The Republican party found itself promising to administer reform programs more efficiently and more effectively than the Democrats! The Republican party, as a part of the shifting consensus, came to accept most of the innovations introduced by the Democrats. The Eisenhower administration was conservative rather than reactionary, and the Eisenhower years illustrated the extent to which the consensus had become solid.

This apparent resolution of the conflicts of the 1930s had led some observers to proclaim an "end to ideology."[12] Some viewed the alleged end to ideology with contentment, others with dissatisfaction. Perhaps the most explicit statement of the consequences of an "end to ideology" comes from Barrington Moore, Jr.:

Once the ideal has been achieved, or is even close to realization, the driving force of discontent disappears, and a society settles down for a time to a stolid acceptance of things as they are. Something of this sort seems to have happened to the United States.[13]

In such a situation, political parties cannot produce genuine alternatives. Evidence of consensus politics is found in patterns of partisanship and attitudes toward political parties. Lane notes that, as increasing proportions of the working class achieve security and adopt middle-class values, they nevertheless remain Democrats.[14] Also, members of the middle class now associate their own well-being with the welfare state. Nominally Republicans, they recognize the stability of economic planning and retain only their symbolic identification with laissez-faire capitalism. Thus values are not necessarily stable or related to party affiliation, which in contrast is extremely stable. Since both classes are generally satisfied, and neither party proposes a serious modification of the status quo, there is a low sense of electoral crisis. Campaigns tend to be moderate and calm. Surveys show that only 3 percent of Americans think that Democrats would endanger their country's welfare; in contrast, 17 percent of the English think that the Labour Party would do so. Two thirds of the American population do not think that they would be personally any better or any worse under either party.[15] The level of tension is low among members of the consensual majority because personal stakes in electoral outcomes are not very great. However, when marginal individuals and groups that are not members of the majority are considered in conjunction with those who embrace middle-class values, tension is very high.

In spite of the bureaucratization of the economy, people are able to maintain symbolic values that buttress the individualistic consensus. For instance, most people believe that personal achievement can produce economic success, and that environmental handicaps are easily overcome. In a recent Gallup survey[16] the question was asked: "In your opinion, what is more to blame if a person is poor: lack of effort on his part, or circumstances beyond his control?" Notice that the largest proportion of respondents in 1967 indicated that a lack of effort rather than circumstances produced poverty (see Table 7–7). Apparently, however,

Table 7-7 / Reasons for Poverty

	1964	1967
Lack of Effort	33%	42%
Circumstances	29	19
Both	32	36
No opinion	6	3

Source: Gallup Opinion Index, Report No. 25 (July 1967), p. 17.

commitment to the individualistic ethic is flexible. The proportion of respondents giving this answer has increased since 1964, perhaps partly as a negative reaction to the increased visibility of poverty, produced by riots and poor people's marches. The strength of the symbolic attachment to the Protestant ethic is shown by the fact that only 36 percent of the population favored a guaranteed annual income of at least $3,200, but 78 percent favored guarantee of enough work so that $3,200 a year could be earned. The lesson that emerges from these data is that it is possible to accept federal intervention in the economy while maintaining an attachment to the symbols of laissez-faire capitalism.

When a candidate or a party seriously threatens the continuation of government intervention in the economy, he is soundly defeated. In general, therefore, candidates of the major parties do not propose radical alternatives to the economic status quo; the party system in the United States strengthens the national consensus. The consensus is also strengthened by other institutions of society, such as public schools and the mass media. Education in this country indoctrinates the youth with the basic values of the political order; teachers' political values are moderate to conservative, and they tend to avoid the introduction of controversy into the classroom. The mass media also avoid serious criticism of the political system. A few minor publications, such as Ramparts, have leveled fundamental criticisms, but mass circulation newspapers and magazines limit themselves to mild scoldings of specific policies. In short, the entire environment of the United States reinforces a commitment to the *status quo*. Most people are, therefore, immersed in an established political system and are totally unaware of radical alternatives.

The abandonment of Goldwater by big business in 1964 had its parallel in the abandonment of McGovern by big labor in 1972. In 1968, with Hubert Humphrey as the Democratic nominee, labor's effort was herculean. The AFL-CIO registered 4.6 million voters, printed and distributed 55 million pamphlets, mobilized 72,000 house-to-house canvassers, and recruited 94,000 election-day volunteers. Since its formation in 1955, the AFL-CIO had consistently backed Democratic candidates. However, in 1972, the AFL-CIO voted to remain neutral, and spent its six million dollars on congressional campaigns. The elite relentlessly hammers away at deviants, whatever the nature of the deviation. After McGovern's defeat, labor's George Meany, moving to head off another public confrontation, began meeting with George Wallace. Meany expected to form a powerful coalition between the populist Wallace, whose support among rank-and-file union members has always been high, and labor's organizational elite.

Strains on Party Consensus

The economic and political assimilation of labor into the middle class has produced the age of consensus that settled the question of the welfare state. However, the benefits of the welfare state have not been evenly distributed in this country. Major pockets of poverty exist, and hard-core poverty groups remain untouched by the general affluence of the society. Although income in this country is undoubtedly more equitably distributed than in many others, the level of poverty remains quite stable. In the 1930s, the lowest fifth of the income scale received 4.1 percent of the total personal income of the country. This percentage has increased only to about 4.7 percent.[17] The fact that the poverty issue is linked to the racial question makes it doubly difficult for the parties to resolve. However, the inability of the parties to assimilate the lowest classes has meant that about 40 percent of Americans are outside of the political, economic, and social system. Consequently, they are not socialized to the consensus.

The level of participation in American politics has never returned to the level of the nineteenth century. This means that socially and economically disadvantaged groups are underrepresented in the active electorate. The 40 percent or so of American adults who are excluded from the political, economic, and social system of the consensual society pose a threat to the existence of the consensus, since they have the potential to be mobilized by counter-elites. A major crisis or an authoritarian movement might pull the outsiders into the political system, with the possible effect of destroying that system.

But this conclusion does not mean that widespread participation is in and of itself bad for democracy. After all, in the nineteenth century America enjoyed participation rates as great as those of the European democracies of today. However, increased, participation must be structured by the parties so that the newly mobilized voters will not be captured by the radicalism of the left or right. The failure of the parties to mobilize these voters leaves the danger of rapid mobilization unchecked. This failure, argues Burnham, is due primarily to the unwillingness of the American political system to accept the legitimacy of non-middle-class values. Thus, we have constructed a political system that has achieved stability by keeping out dissidents, and, within the walls of the political community, the politics of consensus is appropriate. However, by narrowing the political community, we have created a total system that is potentially unstable.

But even as both parties struggle to insure consensus, their efforts appear to be unsuccessful, for larger numbers of people on both the Left and Right in American politics are deserting the Democratic and Republican parties. To be sure, there is substantial evidence that the poor and the blacks were never wholly within the two-party system in the first place. Figures on non-voting indicate that a majority of blacks and a majority of the poor (families earning less than $3,000 per year) do not participate in American party politics. It is true, of course, that the Civil Rights Act of 1964, the most sweeping civil rights act in American history, and the Economic Opportunity Act of 1964, an outgrowth of the "War on Poverty," represented attempts to incorporate the black and the poor communities into the national consensus. But the actual impact of these acts seemed to be one of raising expectation levels without really bringing about any noticeable changes in the lives of most black and poor people. The effect of these efforts seemed to increase alienation from the political systems rather than reduce it, as promises went unfulfilled and expectations unmet. In the words of the Commission on Civil Disorders, "The expectations aroused by the great judicial and legislative victories of the civil rights movement have led to frustration, hostility, and cynicism in the face of the persistent gap between promise and fulfillment."[18]

Several trends support the notion of the decay of the established parties. As we have noted, voter participation had declined to the point in 1972 where only slightly more than half of the eligible voters participated in an election which was supposed to offer the "clearest choice in this century." The percentage of the electorate expressing a personal concern over the outcome of the election was the lowest in twenty years. Due partially to the extreme polarization with the ranks of the Democrats, partisan affiliation was not an especially helpful indication of how a person would vote.

The declining importance of political parties continues a trend in deterioration of partisan loyalty—along with trust—which began before Watergate, probably during the turbulent confrontation politics of the 1960s. In the past two presidential elections, the majority of voters have supported the presidential choice of one party while supporting the congressional candidates of the other. As split-ticket voting increases, party identification decreases. In 1964, 23 percent of the eligible electorate were independents. By 1972 the percentage of independents had increased to 34 percent. Democratic identification declined from 52 percent in 1960 to 41 percent in 1972, while the strength of the Republicans remained stable at 25 percent. As is clear from the above percentages, there is no majority party. Further, the traditional minority party, the Republican, places third.

Such an erosion of traditional party strength tends to minimize the conservative effects of parties. Parties traditionally absorb social protest, making change incremental rather than radical. Protest movements find it difficult to dislodge the loyalty of the voters to major parties. George Wallace, as an example, has suffered at the polls by a fall-off in support among older voters who, while supporting Wallace's policies, find it difficult to vote against the party. Hence Wallace's strong showing in primaries, without the constraint of party, was substantially better than his actual vote in the 1968 general election.

The erosion of parties in 1972 created, at least temporarily, the danger (from the point of view of elites) of political instability. The election was in reality a fierce dispute between the liberal and conservative wings of the Democratic party. The left wing won the nomination, but the right wing won the election. Nixon, totally disassociating himself from his party, added to the decline of parties.

The decay in parties coincided with a period of exceptional political instability. Indeed, partisan decay and political instability seem inextricably intertwined. In the 1960s, as Pomper has lamented:

The loss of stability and moderation is readily apparent, as extremists ranging from Wallace to Weathermen gain significant support and publicity. The methods of political action have extended far beyond the accustomed bargaining and the restrained control of the parties. Assassinations have become a political tactic, looting a political message, and assault an expression of patriotism.[19]

If parties cannot modify, mute, and disguise the passions of the masses, they cannot serve as mechanisms of compromise and orderly change. In such circumstances, masses begin to view direct action, violence, as opposed to traditional political participation, as the only channel of elite influence open to them. Characterized by extreme political alienation, masses either withdraw from participation (as in 1972), or become emotionally committed to charismatic leaders, such as George Wallace. While civil disturbances began declining after 1970, major crime increased by 126 percent in the decade from 1962 to 1972. Further, the Symbionese Liberation Army introduced a new idea in American political warfare: the political kidnapping. Such an act is clearly indicative of the rapidly growing sense of powerlessness, to a deep feeling that those with power seek to abridge, deny, and even strip away the ultimate power of the governed.

It is likely, however, that the parties can re-establish themselves in their traditional roles. The massive decline in Nixon's popularity has shattered his party's electoral chances. Simultaneously, the Democrats appear to be working to achieve an agreement with George Wallace, who is moving steadily toward the center of the Democratic party. Even if the Democrats regain the White House, the Republicans can rebuild the party to provide an effective—centrist—challenge in 1980.

Summary

Elitism asserts that elites share a consensus about the fundamental values of the political system. This elite consensus does not mean that elite members never disagree or never compete with each other for preeminence. But elitism implies that competition centers on a narrow range of issues and that elites agree on more matters than they disagree. The single elite model suggests that parties agree about the direction of public policy and disagree only on minor details. Our analysis of the American party system suggests the following propositions:

1. American parties share consensus both on basic democratic values and on major directions of American policy. They believe in the sanctity of private property, the free enterprise economy, individual liberty, and limited government. Moreover, both parties have supported the same general domestic and foreign policy—including social security, a graduated income tax, counter-cyclical fiscal and monetary policies, anticommunism, the Cold War, and the Korean and Vietnamese wars.

2. The American parties do not present clear ideological alternatives to the American voter. Both American parties are overwhelmingly middle class in organization, values, and goals. Deviation from the shared consensus by either party ("a choice not an echo") is more likely to lose than attract voters.

3. Both parties draw support from all social groups in America, but the Democrats draw disproportionately from labor, workers, Jews, Catholics, and blacks, and the Republicans draw disproportionate support from rural, small-town, and suburban Protestants, businessmen, and professionals.

4. Democratic and Republican party leaders differ over public policy more than Democratic or Republican mass followers. The consensus about welfare economics extends to Democratic leaders, Democratic followers, and Republican followers; only the Republican leadership is outside this consensus, with a more laissez-faire position. However, all party differences observed fall well within the range of elite consensus on the values of individualism, capitalism, and limited government.

5. American parties are dominated by small groups of activists who formulate party objectives and select candidates for public office. The masses play a passive role in party affairs. They are not really "members" of the party; they are "consumers."

6. Among party activists, power is generally diffused, not centralized. Power within parties is not in the hands of a single elite, but rather a "stratarchy" of elites. The exceptions to this rule are the few large city machines, particularly in the Democratic party.

7. Party activists differ from the masses, because they have the time and financial resources to be able to "afford" politics, the information and knowledge to understand it, and the organization and public relations skills to be successful in it.

8. The choice of party nominees is a choice of party activists, not a choice of the masses of party members.

9. With neither party proposing a serious modification of the *status quo*, there is a low sense of electoral crisis. Thus, the stakes in electoral outcomes in any American election are not very great. This contributes to the relative ease with which public offices are transferred between the "in" party and the "out" party.

10. The American party system strengthens the national consensus. Serious political issues strain the American party system; the system appears unable to handle any real issues. Both the black movement of the 1960s and the lower-class (Wallacite) white reaction took place outside the framework of the Democratic and Republican party system. In 1968 a majority of Americans did not vote for either the Republican or Democratic candidates for president.

REFERENCES

[1]See Walter Dean Burnham, "The Changing Shape of the American Political Universe," *American Political Science Review*, 59 (March 1965), 28; and Walter Dean Burnham, "Party Systems and the Political Process," in William Nisbet Chambers and Walter Dean Burnham (eds.), *The American Party Systems: Stages of Political Development* (New York: Oxford University Press, 1967), pp. 305–307.

[2]Charles O. Jones, "The 1964 Presidential Election—Further Adventures in Wonderland," in Donald G. Herzberg (ed.), *1965–1966 American Government Annual* (New York: Holt, Rinehart and Winston, 1965), p. 17.

[3]M. Kent Jennings and Richard G. Niemi, "Continuity and Change in Political Orientations: A Longitudinal Study of Two Generations," paper presented to the 1973 Annual Meeting of the American Political Science Association, New Orleans, p. 15.

[4]Richard M. Scammon and Ben J. Wattenberg, *The Real Majority* (New York: Coward-McCann, 1970), pp. 59, 78, 80.

[5]Roberto Michels, *Political Parties: A Sociological Study of the Oligarchical Tendencies of Modern Democracy* (New York: Dover Publications, 1959; originally published in English in 1915), p. 32.

[6]Frank J. Sorauf, *Party Politics in America* (Boston: Little, Brown and Co., 1968), pp. 79–80.

[7]Harold D. Lasswell and Abraham Kaplan, *Power and Society* (New Haven, Conn.: Yale University Press, 1950), pp. 219–220; and Samuel J. Eldersveld, *Political Parties: A Behavioral Analysis* (Chicago: Rand McNally, 1964), pp. 9, 98–117.

[8]Sorauf, *Party Politics in America*, p. 94.

[9]See the consideration of the party-voter-as-business-firm-customer relationship in Robert A. Dahl, *Pluralist Democracy in the United States: Conflict and Consent* (Chicago: Rand McNally, 1967), pp. 247–252.

[10]Denis G. Sullivan, Jeffrey C. Pressman, Benjamin I. Page, and John J. Lyons, *The Politics of Representation: The Democratic Convention of 1972* (New York: St. Martin's Press, 1974), p. 124.

[11]Walter Dean Burnham, "The Changing Shape of the American Political Universe," p. 23.

[12]Daniel Bell, *The End of Ideology: On the Exhaustion of Political Ideas in the Fifties* (New York: Collier Books, 1961).

[13]Barrington Moore, Jr., *Political Power and Social Theory* (Cambridge, Mass.: Harvard University Press, 1958), p. 183.

[14]Robert E. Lane, "The Politics of Consensus in an Age of Affluence," *American Political Science Review*, 59 (March 1965), 880.

[15]Lane, p. 883.

[16]*Gallup Opinion Index*, Report No. 25 (July 1967), p. 17.

[17]Michael Harrington, *The Other America: Poverty in the United States* (Baltimore: Penguin Books, 1963), p. 179.

[18]*Report of the National Advisory Commission on Civil Disorders* (Washington, D. C., 1968), p. 204.

[19]Gerald M. Pomper, "Party Functions and Party Failures," in Pomper, ed., *The Performance of American Government* (New York: The Free Press, 1972), p. 88.

Selected Additional Readings

Downs, Anthony. *An Economic Theory of Democracy*. New York: Harper and Row, 1959. Downs develops an abstract model of party politics based upon traditional democratic political theory. The relationships among voters, parties, and governmental policy according to the democratic model are clearly presented, and empirical propositions are deduced therefrom.

Key, V. O., Jr. *Politics, Parties, and Pressure Groups*. New York: Thomas Y. Crowell Co., 1967. This work is a classic in the area of American party politics. Key traces the historical development of our present parties and discusses their role in the political system.

Ladd, Everett Caroll, Jr. *American Political Parties*. New York: W. W. Norton and Co., Inc., 1970. The consensual nature of American parties is treated historically.

Michels, Robert. *Political Parties*. Glencoe, Ill.: Free Press, 1915. (See Chapter 1, page 28.)

Pomper, Gerald. *Elections in America: Control and Influence in Democratic Politics*. New York: Dodd, Mead Co., 1968. In focusing on the linkage between electoral behavior and public policy, Pomper discusses at some length the role of political parties, historically and within the contemporary context. Chapters 5, 7, and 8 are most useful in this regard.

Sorauf, Frank J. *Party Politics in America*, 2nd ed. Boston: Little, Brown and Co., 1972. Sorauf employs the organizing concept of the political system in this theoretical work. He focuses on the parties within the American political system—their structure and the functions they perform.

CHAPTER 8

THE ORGANIZED INTERESTS:

DEFENDERS OF THE STATUS QUO

Interest groups, private non-governmental organizations, should be a more effective method of political participation than individual voting. Presumably, a combination of voices is more effective than a single one. The "interests'"with their better organization achieve more tangible benefits than do the unorganized "people" (voters). In fact, serious studies of the policy-making process indicate that cohesion and organization *do* contribute disproportionately to political success. The myth that interest groups are the "real" influence behind policy making contains just enough truth to make the study of them worthwhile.

What are the functions of interest groups? Why are some groups powerful and others not? Why are some issues vulnerable to group influence and others not? Do some political systems contribute to interest-group strength?

The Premises of Interest Group Theory

Some contemporary writers contend that interest groups perform important functions for their members and for the total society. First, the organized group is said to serve as a link between the individual and his government:

Voluntary associations are the prime means by which the function of mediating between the individual and the state is performed. Through them the individual is able to relate himself effectively and meaningfully to the political system.[1]

Actually, the extent to which this particular function is served is open to question, as is the extent of the power of groups. Is the organization, operating as a mediating link between the individual and the government, any more efficient than a direct citizen-government interaction? Why do we need a "middleman"?

It is also said that interest groups contribute to individual well-being. In a mass society, with primary associations (small groups, such as the family) diminishing in importance, secondary associations may help the individual overcome the sense of powerlessness characteristic of mass societies. Groups may integrate the individual with society.

Finally, interest groups are said to help reduce potentially divisive conflicts. At first glance, it might be assumed that interest groups intensify conflict. In America, political parties are deliberately devoid of firm ideologies. Interest groups, so the argument runs, since they represent narrower sets of values, can afford to sharpen conflict. An individual who is a Republican might also be a member of the National Association of Manufacturers. While his party membership does not encourage competition, his NAM membership might. Thus, while parties moderate conflict, groups—in working for a favorable allocation of resources or for some symbolic point—increase conflict.

However, one can also argue that groups can *mute* conflict because of overlapping affiliations. The theory of overlapping memberships suggests that all citizens are members of groups (unorganized and organized).[2] Each person can be summed up as a product of his group affiliations. A person may be, for example, a lawyer, a Southerner, and a Protestant, each of these affiliations imposing contradictory values upon him. A person who was raised in a Southern conservative family might begin a teaching career in a Northern university with a predominately liberal environment. Under these circumstances, neither group affiliation would be able to claim the total loyalty of the individual, and thus full mobilization of group resources is impossible, given divided loyalties. If an organization that attempts to represent a value imposes demands that conflict with the wishes of a substantial proportion of its members, it faces a loss of cohesion and thus a reduction in bargaining position. Hence, group demands are modified and societal conflict reduced. A problem with this theory is that the conflict management function of interest groups is difficult to test, because of the difficulty of measuring affiliation with unorganized groups.

To sum up, interest groups are now considered "good" because they provide for a more effective voice for citizens competing for the allocation of resources. They reduce the anxiety produced by a feeling of powerlessness, and they provide an element of stability for the society. The "old theory" that interest groups are "bad" because they are opposed to the "public interest" has been replaced.

In replacing it, political scientists have performed a subtle but significant transformation on pluralism by making interest-group theory part and parcel of pluralist thinking. Organized group activity is considered to be a means whereby individuals who want something from a government can pool their resources and get it. Indeed, there are thousands of organizations making their demands on Congress, various administrative agencies, state legislatures, city councils, and even school boards. A glance at the list of registered lobbyists in Washington and in the various state capitals gives superficial credence to the argument. Each group, or potential group, is free to organize. Consequently, organization produces counter-organization. In the process of resolving group demands, each interest is given a voice, and public policy is formed in response to these competitive demands. Interest groups, then, serve pluralistic democracy well by insuring that governmental decision makers respond to the claims of the various publics. It is in the *competition* among the varieties of competitive groups that pluralism finds its most frequently stated defense. Pluralistic interest-group theory does not deny the existence of elites, but rather contends that each elite is specialized, representative of a set of mass demands, and counter-balanced by a set of opposing demands. As Arnold Rose puts it:

[the multi-influence hypothesis] conceives of society as consisting of many elites, each relatively small numerically and operating in different spheres of life, and of the bulk of the population classifiable into organized groups and publics as well as masses. Among the elites are several that have their power through economic controls, several others that have power through political controls, and still others that have power through military, associational, and other controls. While it is true that there are inert masses of undifferentiated individuals without access to each other (except in the most trivial respects) and therefore without influence, the bulk of the population consists not of the mass, but of integrated groups and publics, stratified with varying degrees of power.[3]

As described by Rose, a typical exponent, interest-group theory contains a series of assumptions which must be verified if the theory is to be judged correct. The assumptions are: (1) Membership in organizations is widespread and thus broadly representative of *all* the relevant publics. (2) Organized groups efficiently translate membership expectation into political demands. Nothing is lost in the translation, but a great deal is gained by the presentation of demands from a representative association. (3) Although representation by an interest group is not uniformly successful (some groups win and some lose), each group has equal access to the political resources necessary for success, irrespective of the nature of its demands. (4) By their representative functions, organizations contribute to a feeling of political efficacy among their members; they strengthen the social fabric.

We contend that the first three of these assumptions are incorrect; and we will present evidence to refute them. And though we concede that the final assumption has empirical evidence in its behalf, we will argue that *because* of their integrative function, organizations help to guide their members toward an acceptance of the *status quo*. We suggest that interest groups, rather than articulating the demands of masses, serve to protect the values of established elites.

How Widespread is Formal Group Affiliation?

It is popularly assumed that "Americans are joiners." It appears that a majority of the population belong to at least one formal organization. However, membership in voluntary associations is clearly linked to socioeconomic status (see Table 8–1). A variety of evidence has demonstrated that membership is greatest among the professional and managerial classes, among college-trained people, and among people with high incomes. Voluntary association membership is primarily an upper-middle-class to upper-class phenomenon. For instance, 80 percent of the

Table 8–1 / Percentage of Respondents Who Belong to Some Organization by Nation and Education

	Total		Primary or Less		Some Secondary		Some University	
	(%)	(no.)*	(%)	(no.)	(%)	(no.)	(%)	(no.)
United States	57	(970)	46	(339)	55	(443)	80	(188)
Great Britain	47	(963)	41	(593)	55	(322)	92	(24)
Germany	44	(955)	41	(792)	63	(124)	62	(26)
Italy	30	(995)	25	(692)	37	(245)	46	(54)
Mexico	24	(1,007)	21	(877)	39	(103)	68	(24)

*Numbers in parentheses refer to the bases upon which percentages are calculated.

Source: Gabriel A. Almond and Sidney Verba, *The Civic Culture: Political Attitudes and Democracy in Five Nations* (Boston: Little, Brown and Co. 1965) p. 249.

respondents in the Almond-Verba study with "some college" are members of associations, compared to 46 percent of those respondents with a primary education or less.[4]

The upper-class bias of voluntary associations varies, of course, with the nature of the organization. Unions (which frequently are not voluntary) recruit from the lower strata, as do civil rights organizations and the Ku Klux Klan. However even within the civil rights movement, the masses of blacks are uninvolved. Civil rights organizations are lower class in comparison to white organizations, but within the black community, participation and social status are still related. For example, the National Association for the Advancement of Colored People represents the moderate black "establishment", not the blacks in urban ghettos who take direct and violent action. Liberal causes, such as the women's movement and Common Cause, are likely to attract a disproportionate element of the university "liberal establishment," and rarely appeal to the lower classes. At any rate, the social bias in voluntary association membership, whether or not the association is "political," is complemented by the high social origins of lobbyists and the predominance of business organizations in *effective* lobbying.

This bias has obvious implications for the ascribed functions of interest groups. Whatever they do, they do it mostly for the upper-middle and upper classes, not for the total population. As Schattschneider observes, "The notion that the pressure system is automatically representative of the whole community is a myth fostered by the universalizing tendencies of modern group theory."[5] For one thing, even if interest groups are an effective link between the citizen and his government, many citizens do not avail themselves of this benefit. For example, 87 percent of the farm laborers do not belong to an organization, compared to 58 percent of the farm owners. Even if the voluntary association does reduce anxiety or increase feelings of power, it does not serve the very people whose alienation from the society is the greatest and whose need for such services is most extreme.

The point is well made by Verba and Nie, whose exhaustive study of political participation elaborates the notion of the upper-class bias of political groups. Their concern is with the "interaction" of organizational membership and social status. That is, does organizational activity exaggerate, or minimize, the class bias of American politics? They argue that to a greater extent than is true of other countries, political activity is linked to social status. Does organizational membership increase this disparity between the classes? By looking at the organizational membership of a variety of social classes, they find that, while lower-class persons individually do increase their political activity if they belong to organizations, so few of them do so that the net effect is to *increase* the upper-class bias of the political system: "Do voluntary associations increase political equality or diminish it? . . . In fact, organizations increase the political gap, for the simple reason that those who come from advantaged groups are more likely to be organizationally active."[6]

Further, among those who are members of associations, active participation—and the holding of formal organizational office—is directly related to social status. Whereas membership in associations is characteristic of the majority of Americans, *active* participation is characteristic of a minority of members. All organizations are typically controlled by a small elite. Michels' "iron law of oligarchy" describes the fact that even the most democratically inclined organizations gradually evolve into oligarchies. The oligarchs, who help to shape the goals of the organization, are drawn disproportionately from the upper social classes.[7]

Here again, the oligarchy's social status may vary according to the nature of the organization. Cesar Chavez, leader of the Chicano movement, can hardly be thought of as an aristocrat. True, his early life was above average for Chicanos. He is a native-born American citizen whose parents were prosperous farmers until the depression forced his family to live the grim life of the migrant laborer. As leader of the National United Farm Workers, however, Chavez is typically autocratic—indeed, authoritarian. Work assignments are handled by the union; any worker who fails to report to a job assigned by the union gets to the bottom of the list. Chavez has opposed placing farmers under the jurisdiction of the National Labor Relations Board, since they would make this practice illegal.

Within the union, there are no bylaws, and no election of officers. Union dues may be raised or lowered by Chavez without approval from the members. In brief, an organization which is, in Chavez's words, dedicated to the dissolution of "the existing social order" is as dictatorial as any in the country—certainly as autocratic as the Teamsters Union with which Chavez struggles for power.

Participation in organizations is also related to satisfaction with one's life situation. The more satisfied one is with his job, for example, the more likely he is to participate in union affairs. Hence, those who have the least to complain about are most likely to guide the affairs of formal organizations. Naturally, the higher one's social status, the less one has to complain about.

Thus, our first empirical test of contemporary interest-group theory fails to corroborate an important assumption upon which such theory is based. Those who are active in interest groups constitute only a small portion of the populace; moreover, they tend to be from a higher socioeconomic status than those who are not active. In short, it is the elites who are the most active in interest groups in America.

Given the class bias in organizational membership, it is not surprising that business associations are the single largest lobbying group at the state and national levels. In Washington, of the 25 top spenders among lobbying groups, nine are business (see Table 8–2). Further, of the 269

Table 8–2 / Top Spenders for Lobbying, 1972 (of those recorded)

Common Cause	$558,839
AFL-CIO	216,294
Veterans of World War I of the U.S.A. Inc.	213,743
American Postal Workers Union	208,767
United States Savings & Loan League	191,726
National Council of Farmer Cooperatives	184,347
American Farm Bureau Administration	180,678
Disabled American Veterans	159,431
National Association of Letter Carriers (AFL-CIO)	154,188
American Trucking Association Inc.	137,804
Farmers Educational Cooperative Union of America	113,156
United Mine Workers of America	110,045
American Nurses Association Inc.	109,643
National Association of Home Builders of the United States	99,031
American Medical Association	96,146
Brotherhood of Railway, Airline and Steamship Clerks	88,540
Recording Industry Association of America Inc.	88,396
American Insurance Association	82,259
National Federation of Federal Employees	82,080
National Housing Conference Inc.	77,906
International Brotherhood of Teamsters	76,897
National Limestone Institute Inc.	75,777
American Civil Liberties Union	73,131
National Association of Real Estate Boards	70,941
Liberty Lobby Inc.	70,019

Source: Congressional Quarterly Weekly Report, June 9, 1973, p. 1426.

organizations that reported any lobbying expenditures, 143 are business organizations. At the state level, the domination of business associations is equally apparent. In a survey of interest groups represented in the states, it was found that business lobbyists were clearly the most visible and most numerous. No matter what kind of economy a state has, business dominates its lobbying. Even in a state such as South Dakota, which has 30 percent of its population employed in non-industrial occupations, two thirds of the registered lobbyists represent business.[8] As Schattschneider concludes:

The business or upper-class bias of the pressure system shows up everywhere. . . . The data raise a serious question about the validity of the proposition that special interest groups are a universal form of political organization reflecting all interests.[9]

Interest-group conflict, then, reflects merely the most visible disputes between factions within the established elite. Business and labor may contest over the raising of the minimum wage, but both unite to keep demands for radical reform out of the pressure system. The game of pressure-group politics has rules which exclude the masses.

How Well Do Groups Mediate?

The next test of group theory concerns the function of transmitting member demands into political action. Since we have seen in the previous section that membership demands are rarely made, we can hardly expect that organizational leadership is merely a middleman. Still, group leaders *do* lobby and, to the extent that they are successful, protect their membership (even though the membership may not know or care) in most cases.

The size of the group is an important variable in its leadership's effectiveness as a middleman. Access to legislators is enhanced by a large membership, since elected officials are sensitive to numbers. However, large groups find it difficult to commit themselves to an explicit position, since their membership is so heterogeneous. The policy positions of mass membership organizations must be vague and broad, devoid of specific content, and thus harmless. The Chamber of Commerce, for example, seeks to represent "businessmen," without regard for the nature of the business. Since intrabusiness disputes are often as bitter as labor-management disputes, the Chamber cannot take a position on many of the minute legislative and administrative details that involve the economic health of various portions of the business community.

Generally, mass membership groups achieve symbolic success, while smaller, more cohesive groups are able to persist in the pursuit of limited objectives and gradually exhaust their enemy. Edelman makes the point that tangible benefits are rarely redistributed by legislatures, the arena of the large groups. Rather, they are redistributed in the *administration* of legislation, an activity in which small groups have the advantage. Numbers are not as important to administrators, who are only indirectly concerned with election results, as they are to legislators. When administrative action reverses legislative intent, "deprived groups often display little tendency to protest or to assert their awareness of the deprivation. . . . The most intensive dissemination of symbols commonly attends the enactment of legislation, which is most meaningless in its effects upon resource allocation."[10]

Groups seeking symbolic achievement exhibit the following characteristics: (1) shared interest in the improvement of status through protest activity, (2) an unfavorably perceived strategic position with respect to reference groups, (3) stereotyped, inexact information and perception, (4) response to symbols connoting suppression of threats, (5) relative ineffectiveness in achieving tangible rewards as a result of political activity, (6) little organization for purposive action, (7) quiescence (inactivity), and (8) relatively large numbers.

Most of the groups active in the legislative process display many, but not all, of these characteristics. Labor unions, for example, are large and well organized. Still, many of their achievements are symbolic. Much the same can be said of those civil rights organizations that seek to achieve political results through established democratic procedures. In spite of the turmoil since the 1954 decision outlawing segregation in public schools, the economic condition of blacks has changed very little, for the law itself has not been enforced by government sanctions. Indeed, for the first decade after the desegregation decision, many of the demands of black organizations were symbolic. What, for instance, is the significance of forcing Woolworth's to integrate their lunch counter? Clearly, nothing other than the conferring of legitimacy upon the goals of the movement was achieved. Gusfield notes the symbolic value of desegregation efforts:

Desegregation is a status issue par excellence. Its symbolic characteristics lie in the deference which the norm of integration implies. The acceptance of token integration, which is what has occurred in the North, is itself prestige-conferring because it establishes the public character of the norm supporting integration. It indicates what side is publicly legitimate and dominant. Without understanding this symbolic quality of the desegregation issue the fierceness of the struggle would appear absurd. Since so little actual change in concerted behavior ensues, the question would be moot if it were not for this characteristic as an act of deference toward Negroes and of degradation toward whites.[11]

However, it may be that symbolic victories are needed as a prelude to the achievement of tangible ones. The civil rights movement, as leadership is wrested away from the moderate elements, is directing itself more toward equality of economic opportunity.

In contrast to these groups, organizations enjoying tangible benefits are small and highly organized, with rational procedures related to realistic goals. Their members have precise information. The group has an effective interest in a specifically identified, tangible resource. Members have a favorably perceived strategic position with respect to reference groups. Small groups, based upon narrow interests, can achieve cohesion more readily and concentrate their resources upon a limited objective. They can act decisively and persistently. Such organizations are most frequently business or industrial; the business groups employ the majority of lobbyists at the state and national level. Many businessmen are organized into trade associations representing varieties of industrial and commercial activity. Their membership is limited to a specific form of business activity—for example, insurance—so the trade associations are frequently quite small, some with as few as 25 members. Trade associations also provide non-collective benefits, but they can provide tangible, collective benefits that the larger groups cannot offer. They have disproportionate power with regard to the *specific* values they advocate, while the business community *as a whole* fights symbolic battles.

The "businessmen in politics" movement, in which the United States Chamber of Commerce distributed a "practical politics" package to companies to be used in classes for junior executives, exhibits the symbolic nature of the struggles of the larger, undifferentiated business community. A similar, widely distributed package was offered by the Manufacturers Association of Syracuse. Executives were provided with a text. Recordings (by Richard Nixon) and pamphlets (including homework assignments) were included in the package, and training couses, designed to activate businessmen as a force to combat the alleged domination of American politics by organized labor, were conducted. Executives spoke of labor's "domination of Congress," alleging business to be "powerless."[12]

The practical politics seminars were profitable for those who organized and staffed them and were perhaps symbolically meaningful. Tangibly, however, they were valueless. Business is *not* powerless with regard to the allocation of tangible rewards to specific kinds of business, and it is symbolically powerful as a whole. How often does one turn from the business section of a newspaper to a "union section"? The symbol of success in America *is* the businessman. Does the American success story include the image of a union organizer? Do the mass media of communication concern themselves with unions? For example, in television situation comedies, how many families are working class? Lindblom has presented an appropriate summary of the dominance of business values:

The bias in policy making is of course not limited to interest-group participation. Elected and appointed proximate policy makers are overwhelmingly from the more favored classes; in the federal government 60 percent of them come from business and professional families. They will therefore seek out and listen to interest-group leaders with whose desires they are already sympathetic. To be sure, officials do not see themselves as representing the interests of some classes against others; rather it is that they see the general interest in the light of their own group affiliations, a phenomenon conspicuous in small-town politics in which, in any easy relation between business and public officials, both see the public interest as equivalent to what they agree on. Every man is, of course, a product of early and continuing indoctrinations reflecting family and group socioeconomic status. What is more, the prestige of middle-class attitudes and political preferences is so overwhelming in some countries, the United States included, that many of the disadvantaged themselves subscribe to them, thus endorsing and perpetuating the very bias in policy making against which they might be expected to protest.[13]

Organizational activity, viewed in terms of the *preferences communicated*, is equally conservative. Those who participate in organizational activity are, for example, more economically conservative than those who do not. Further, their activity has an impact upon leader response only if leaders have been sensitized by a high rate of voting. Voting, in itself, has *no impact* upon leader behavior. However, in areas where voting participation is high, organizational groups have their greatest impact—a decidedly conservative one. Thus, voters become the unwitting cannon fodder for the active minority.[14]

Lobbying

Lobbying is defined as any communication directed at a legislator with the hope of influencing his decision. The lobbyist plays a very functional role in the legislative process. He provides an important communication link between non-governmental elites and their legislators; communications flow both ways as a legislator learns about the interest of non-governmental elites, and these elites are influenced to support the legislator. The lobbyist presents demands on the legislative system from organized interests, participates in negotiations leading to resolution of conflicts, and helps to facilitate elite support for public policy through his involvement in these decisions.

The Federal Regulation of Lobbying Act of 1946 requires the registration of names and spending reports of anyone who "solicits, collects or receives money or any other thing of value to be used principally to aid in . . . the passage and defeat of any legislation by the Congress of the United States." However, enforcement of this law is quite lax, and many of the larger lobby groups—for example, the National Association of Manufacturers, the National Bankers Association, the Americans for Constitutional Action—have never registered as lobbyists. Only about 300 groups register as lobbyists each year, and only about $4 million per year is reported as having been spent for lobbying activities. But these figures grossly underestimate the extent of lobbying activity in Congress. The law only requires reports on money spent on direct lobbying before Congress, not money spent for public relations or for campaign contributions.

Further, many hundreds of lobbyists do not register on the pretext that they are not really lobbyists, but lawyers, researchers, or educational people. However, more restrictive legislation on lobbying might violate the First Amendment freedom to "petition the government for a redress of grievances."

Political scientists examining the political activity of a group's elite tend to infer the values of the group's followers from the group's lobbying actions, when in fact lobbyists and other organization leaders have much the same function in relation to members as do societal elites to masses in general. They make opinions more often than they follow them.

Whatever the nature of the goals of the group, an organization is dominated by its active minority. An organization is composed of formal leaders, active followers, and passive followers, the latter group consisting of the majority of members. A "realistic" theory would have leaders (including lobbyists) representing "virtually"—by means of shared values—the aspirations of their followers. Actually, leaders accommodate only those factions represented by active members, whose values are not necessarily reflective of the values of most members. Since in most cases the followers are not especially interested in political activities, lack of accurate representation is not crucial to their continued membership. Only when the leaders go beyond the limits of acceptable behavior, and thus become highly visible, will they encounter much opposition

The discrepancy between leaders' and followers' beliefs is greater than leaders perceive it to be. Interest group leaders pride themselves on their ability to sense intuitively the feelings of followers. However, like all elites, they are inclined to attribute to followers ideologies which the followers do not possess.

For example, the fact that labor union leaders support civil rights legislation does not mean that union members support it. Civil rights are not likely to receive much support among the membership of unions. However, in spite of the absence of a clear chain of communication between leaders and followers, leaders can still exert lobbying pressure based on the number of their followers. Legislators may operate upon the *assumption* that these numbers are convertible into a deliverable vote. In Oregon, for example, the Oregon Education Association is regarded as powerful by legislators primarily because it has a large membership. The inference is that these members can be turned out to vote in a block; actually, few of the members can correctly identify the position of the organization, and fewer still are likely to follow the advice of group leaders. Therefore, power is not necessarily a function of *actual* resources but rather of *perceived* resources.

However, the surest way to dissipate such a resource is to allow it to be put to the test. An inexperienced lobbyist might threaten to defeat a legislator at the polls, but most skilled lobbyists never mention electoral defeat, because they know that the threat is an empty one. Threats are ineffective in influencing behavior, in any case; fear-arousing communications produce negative reactions. If directly threatened, a legislator may take an adamant position to prove that he is independent. Independence is a highly valued trait in American political lore, and legislators are reluctant to contradict their image of themselves. Unless the threat is capable of being enforced immediately, it is usually ineffective.[15] However, if the threat is only implied, and thus no one has seen evidence that the threat is ineffective, it retains its influence.

The general lack of a one-to-one relationship between the policy statements of the lobbyist and the voting preferences of the members of the organization is most conspicuous when the lobbyist advocates positions unrelated to the immediate self-interest of the members. For example, Edelman notes:

The officers of the AFL-CIO, in lobbying for a civil rights bill and liberal tariff policies, get some immediate status benefit from posing as statesmen influential in the general affairs of state. The rank-and-file members, who do not share in this benefit, are likely to find the objectives of such legislation remote from their experience and sometimes find that they clash with perceptions of immediate interests: economic or status rivalry with Negroes or employment in an industry losing its market to foreign goods. Congressmen who ignore the official labor position on civil rights or foreign trade can accordingly be fairly confident that the votes and the lofty rhetoric will often be found in different places.[16]

The political resources of the lobbyists are not immediately convertible into power. The legislator, however, possesses a resource that is highly valued by the lobbyist: his vote. Therefore, the lobbyist seeks to create goods desired by the legislator so that the legislator's resource will be used to the benefit of the lobbyist's organization. The key resource that a lobbyist may develop is *information*. Information may be technical, dealing with the details of legislation; or it may be political, concerning the impact of legislation upon the attitudes and behavior of a public. The degree to which a lobbyist can use information as a resource depends upon the existence to competing sources of information. In state legislatures, the informational role of the lobbyist is more important because legislators do not have personal or committee staffs. National legislators, on the other hand, are difficult for lobbyists to see, because their other sources of information are usually adequate for their tasks. Thus, recent estimates of the effects of lobbying in Congress indicate that the efforts of lobbyists have been highly exaggerated by popular commentators.[17]

Also, lobbyists can occasionally be more effective in state politics because of the absence of professionalism among state legislators. State legislators are comparative amateurs. The turnover in state legislatures is very high; in any given session, a substantial proportion of the legislators are "freshmen." This inexperience makes it difficult for them to acquire an "in group" identification with their colleagues. The institutional life of the state legislature is consequently more permeable by outside forces.

Successful lobbying has little to do with "pressure." In fact, successful lobbying is *negatively* related to the application of pressure techniques. Groups that are perceived by legislators to be the most pressure-oriented are least likely to achieve satisfactory results. The smaller, persistent groups that concern themselves with tangible rewards have no resources for the application of pressure; yet they are successful, especially at the administrative level, because their personnel gradually identify with the day-to-day problems of a particular industry. This identification results in the desire to protect the group from non-industry attackers. Agencies originally designed by legislation (in victories won by larger groups) to regulate an industry in the "public interest" frequently are converted to agencies defending the industry against its competition. The members of the agency come to share the values of the regulated industry. This type of interest group's success, while less visible than symbolic victories, is more meaningful in terms of the allocation of tangible resources.

The Oil Industry and the Energy Crisis: A Case Study

The activities of the oil industry in the energy crisis of 1973–74 present an almost classic example of how a well-organized lobbying group with a near monopoly on critical information can influence government policy making and acquire a beachhead for its interest within the institutional framework of government. The oil industry has always enjoyed special benefits from government in the way of tax benefits and easy access to both elected and appointed officials. However, environmental and international setbacks caused profits of the major companies to dip in the early seventies. The industry responded with massive contributions to the 1972 re-election campaign of Richard Nixon. On January 1, 1974, Representative Les Aspin (D-Wisc.) released a 58-page report on oil industry contributions to the President's 1972 re-election, showing that 413 company officers and principal stockholders contributed a total of almost $5 million to the campaign.

When the oil-producing Arab nations of the Middle East announced in the fall of 1973 an embargo on oil exports to the United States, there was a great deal of publicity about possible shortages of petroleum products. The oil industry had been predicting the current shortage increasingly since the spring of 1970, and given the fact that it was the only source of industry-wide statistics, few people disputed the industry's story. Although the Arab nations accounted for only a fraction of the oil supply used by the nation, and although later evidence seemed to dispute the effectiveness of the embargo in actually reducing supplies of crude oil, the industry urged the government to institute a rationing system for oil products and offered its assistance.

At the same time the Arabs announced the embargo, they also raised the price of their oil fourfold. This led to an enormous jump in oil company profits as the crude oil price increases were used to justify increased retail prices. Again, given the complex nature of the multinational oil companies and the lack of independent cost data, few people were in a position to dispute the industry argument that higher prices and record profits were unavoidable in a time of shortage of oil products to consumers.

The oil industry waged an intensive publicity campaign in the newspapers and on television defending its increased profits and urging the government to institute a rationing system to allocate scarce oil supplies. The industry claimed high profits were necessary to provide an incentive for individual companies to develop new sources of energy. The *Oil and Gas Journal*, a trade publication reflecting the views of the American Petroleum Institute (API), the industry lobbying organization, editorialized that the "profit gains such as those being shown this year must become commonplace. . . . oil companies can make higher profits palatable to the public and government, only as they translate them into investments that will produce more fuel." The *Journal* urged the government to call upon the industry for "assistance" in instituting a rationing system and said that Department of Interior officials "confirm they are looking into the legal aspects of enlisting industry executives on a large scale in a formal operational capacity (to install mandatory allocation of oil) as well as in an advisory role."[18] Industry confirmation of the push for formal, widespread participation of oilmen came from Frank N. Ikard, president of the API. Ikard, an ex-congressman from Texas who served on the tax-writing House Ways and Means Committee, noted that petroleum supply and distribution operations are tremendously complex: "In view of this the government should promptly recruit knowledgeable experts from the private sector in the day-to-day implementation of its program.

"Damn lines are worse than ever."

Szep, reprinted by permission

Simply creating an industry advisory group won't do the job. Oil executives must be able to talk with one another and with top government officials to act quickly to minimize disruption of essential public services and economic activity."[19]

The following week the National Petroleum Council (NPC), an industry organization made up of oil company executives, with quasi-official advisory capacity to the Department of Interior, and responsible for developing statistics used to project U.S. energy needs and resources, said that "mandatory rationing of all petroleum fuels—gasoline, distillates and heavy fuels—should be undertaken in the U.S. on a national scale immediately." The NPC argued that the nation must establish priorities and determine where cuts in demand should be made. "The general public would undoubtedly prefer some discomforts and inconveniences to idle plants and high unemployment," concluded the NPC.[20] In an editorial entitled, "Rationing is the Answer only if Experts Operate It," the *Oil and Gas Journal* developed the point:

[Rationing involves] a complex producing, processing, and distribution system demanding immediate and accurate decisions by knowledgeable experts. An intricate intelligence system must be maintained to spot critical areas and antici- pate needs. Constant product exchanges and transportation shifts must be ef- fected to keep the system in balance. Unless the administration enlists the ser- vices of hundreds of experienced oil-operating people, fuel rationing will only compound the shortages into chaos. There just are not enough career government people knowledgeable in operations of the energy system to man the 12 regional and 50 state offices administering the program. There's no time to train them. The only sensible approach is to call in those already trained. Legislation is needed to give emergency antitrust and conflict of interest clearances to free the pool of talent in the petroleum industry for public service. Congress and the Nixon administration should clear these obstacles quickly.[21]

What benefits did the industry hope to gain in return for assuming responsibility for allocating the nation's energy supplies? Another *Oil and Gas Journal* editorial answered the question by stating that "new supplies and not rationing are the ultimate energy solution," and outlined a program for the future:

What is involved are assurances to private industry of free price and reasonable environmental regulations that will not outpace technological capability to com- ply. . . . Operators must know they can market their coal, oil, or gas over a time frame and at a price that will justify the investment of large sums on a new supply venture. . . . It's too easy for price regulators to pull the rug from under prices.
   Coal operators also need market assurances—for instance, that relaxed regula- tions on sulphur will continue until stock-gas equipment will permit compliance with cleaner, stricter standards.
   Other decisions on the environment likewise are overdue: New drilling offshore. Low rating of nuclear-power plants. Ban on strip-mining. In short, nuclear energy and coal eventually must share with petroleum the burden of supplying the nation's needs. And the need to increase supply must not be obscured by the hue and cry over rationing, allocation, shifting refinery yields, Sunday closings, car pools, 50-m.p.h. speed limits, cool houses in winter, or turning off display lights all over the country. The country doesn't have to settle for this kind of future life style. It still has the possibility for energy growth if it adroitly manages its resources.[22]

The editorial went on to applaud a Department of Interior plan to call up 250 "executive reservists" from the industry, saying this "will bring oilmen and gasmen into the government in a major way."

   On November 8, 1973, representatives of 20 major oil companies met with State Department officials at the Interior Department and agreed to establish a task force in New York City for pooling information about the location and destination of crude oil in the world. The meeting was held under the auspices of Duke Ligon, an ex-executive from Continental Oil Company, now serving as director of the Office of Oil and Gas at the Interior Department. The companies represented were members of the Emergency Petroleum Supply Committee, an industry group which meets with government representatives present. Industry sources argued that what was needed to help alleviate the fuel shortages was a policy that would enable oil companies to work together within the United States on pipeline construction, the building of deepwater ports, and exchanges of fuels in different parts of the country. Such cartelization of the industry would require such sweeping waivers of the antitrust laws as had not been given for domestic operations since World War II, but industry sources reported that government officials at State and Interior were "completely receptive" to the idea.

Not all government officials were so sympathetic to the industry, however. Senator Thomas J. McIntyre (D-N.H.) asked the Federal Trade Commission (FTC) to stop the six-month-old "massive advertising campaign" designed to convince the American people that the oil industry is "relatively blameless" for the current shortages. McIntyre said, "We are being told that the shortages are the result of misguided government policies and the uncontrolled consumer appetite for petroleum products. The companies have even suggested the environmental controls have been a major contributing factor to our present crisis." He went on to say:

This mass media assault is not only disgusting but blatantly false and deceptive. The firms fail to tell consumers that it was the industry which urged that the quota system be adopted to limit imports into this country and that the government granted the industry a number of incentives such as oil depletion allowance, intangible drilling cost tax deductions, foreign investment credits, and others which the industry said would protect this country's domestic oil supply. The energy crisis will require a tremendous sacrifice by each American and it is a tragedy that a number of major oil companies have attempted to turn this energy crisis into a vehicle to improve their tarnished public image, destroy competition, implement enormous price increases, and radically alter national public policy.[23]

The Office of Petroleum Allocation was established in the Interior Department in late November 1973, with retired Vice Admiral Eli T. Reich as its head. Reich immediately announced that he planned to draw in 225 oil industry persons within six months to run the program. At the same time, Secretary of Interior Rogers C. B. Morton revealed that 250 oil executives would be recruited by the government to run the various fuel allocation programs. An Interior Department spokesman said "there is no antitrust or conflict of interest involved" in bringing oilmen into government positions. However, President Nixon informally asked the Senate to exempt the oil companies from antitrust laws and other conflict of interest regulations, but he was turned down.

In early December President Nixon established the Federal Energy Administration to coordinate national energy policy, with William H. Simon as head. Simon's appointment was seen as a "plus" by the oil industry. The *Oil and Gas Journal* noted that "incentives to develop domestic resources, and access to them, will have a most articulate and able advocate in . . . Simon."[24] White House energy advisor John Love again asked Congress to grant exemptions from the antitrust laws to oil and other energy companies because "they will be forced to cooperate and plan for mutual action" to implement the proposed emergency energy act.

At the same time Senator Lee Metcalf (D-Mont.) charged that oil companies and a few banks dominate federal energy policy through an "interlocked apparatus" that virtually excludes other concerned segments. Metcalf supported his charge of an "interlocked apparatus" with detailed examples: —The White House had recently partially activated the Emergency Petroleum and Gas Administration Executive Reserve, which in event of national emergency is to direct the petroleum industry in the government's behalf. In key positions were twenty-four officials from ARCO, twelve from Sun Oil, eleven from Northern National Gas, and ten from Gulf. The Emergency Petroleum Supply Committee, an advisory committee that is required to include members from all segments of the oil industry, was completely dominated by the major companies. —Other government advisory committees had fifty-four representatives from Standard Oil of Indiana and Socol, forty-six from Exxon, thirty-three from Mobil, twenty from Texaco, twenty from Gulf, seventeen from Citgo and twenty-one from Phillips.[25]

A Senate committee investigating the causes of fuel shortages focused on the Office of Emergency Preparedness, whose function it was to regulate oil imports. The committee reported that "the agency's director, retired Army General George A. Lincoln relied for guidance upon executives of major oil companies that stood to benefit from tight restrictions on imports."[26] The investigating committee concluded that the OEP provided "a classic case of a bureaucracy setting a course of action not in response to the nation's needs but to secure its own comfort."

Although the Emergency Energy Act was voted down in December, and Congress failed to waive antitrust and conflict of interest provisions to allow formal appointment of oil executives to government agencies dealing with energy, the *Oil and Gas Journal* announced that "Simon Finds Roundabout Means of Using Oilmen's Expertise." The "roundabout means" was the establishment by Simon of "citizen advisory committees" to provide "expert counsel and information." Simon said that "a prime objective in establishing the committees would be to ensure that the great diversity of interests and talents in our society are considered in the decision-making process and fully utilized." The committees were made up of over 100 oil executives who would act as advisors to Simon in Washington and on six regional committees throughout the country.[27]

An investigation by Representative Benjamin S. Rosenthal (D-N.Y.) showed that 58 ex-oilmen held key FEO jobs within three months of its formation. The 58 employees included an assistant administrator, two deputy assistant administrators, two acting division directors, two fuel distribution specialists, three economists, two office directors, 16 industrial specialists, three case resolution officers, and assorted technical experts and advisors. The list also showed 14 former oil-company people holding jobs in the FEO's key Office of Policy, Planning and Regulation, which acts on pricing matters, draws up regulations, and considers general policy questions.

The FEO defended its position by denying that it had a "deliberate policy of hiring professionals from the oil industry . . . although where such people are available and can be utilized to assist us, we have not declined to employ them." The FEO said its policy was "to employ those persons most qualified to assist in moving in an expeditious and knowledgeable manner to deal with the current national energy emergency." Congressman Rosenthal called the policy an "incestuous game of musical chairs that is played so frequently by industry and government."[28] Whatever the ultimate resolution of the energy crisis, it seems clear that the oil industry is in a firm position to strongly influence, if not control, the development and implementation of future energy legislation.

Poverty Programs and Interest Groups

Another good example of the success of interest groups in the administrative process occurs, ironically, with the passage of the Economic Opportunity Act in 1964. This act, the pride of the war on poverty, provided clear symbolic satisfaction to the "have-nots." The Job Corps, VISTA, and the Office of Economic Opportunity had a firm legislative mandate to uplift the poverty-stricken.

It is in the administration of the act, however, that the real allocation processes can be discovered. The rhetoric surrounding the Community

Action Program takes direct aim on the local power structures; it indicates a desire to shake up the establishment:

The local organization applying for a Community Action Program must satisfy only one basic criterion: It must be broadly representative of the interests of the community. It may be a public agency. . . . Or it may be a private non-profit agency which has the support of the relevant elements of the community. . . .[29]

The law and the rhetoric were intended to delegate decision-making authority to interest groups, in accordance with the pluralist belief that such groups are "broadly representative." As these groups stepped forward, or were newly created, in response to the availability of large sums of money, they became officially recognized by the governmental bureaucracy. Once recognized, they used their official recognition as a resource to prevent the emergence of still newer groups. The political conflict within the war on poverty consists largely of a struggle for control of the administration, with the result that a new establishment is created—those groups with the greatest stake in the program: ". . . the organizations newly organized had such narrow constituencies that their demands were usually narrow . . . rather than calls for broad reform which would improve education for all those in their class or ethnic group."[30]

Thus the war on poverty, as administered, satisfied the restricted needs of specialized groups, not the needs of the poor. Those portions of the population not specifically organized around immediate, tangible goals are excluded. Who, for example, benefits when group demands result in the appointment of a black principal of a ghetto school?

The creation of a new, privileged set of interest groups has been the only appreciable impact of the war on poverty. Small groups of elites, blessed with official recognition, have gained the authority to spend federal money. Leaders of such groups, appropriately coöpted, become protective of the new *status quo*. Their struggle is largely over control of resources. They do battle with previously established welfare groups, and the poor are forgotten. The argument is not, "how can we eliminate poverty?" but rather, "which set of elites shall rule?"[31]

Studies of participation by "the poor" in various poverty programs are consistent in their findings that the more affluent segments of the lower strata are more likely to be incorporated into administrative positions. Through prior involvement in welfare activities, these people are more organizationally adept. Program officials, anxious to produce visible evidence of program integrity, facilitate the participation of the more skilled "nearly poor." Hence, those with knowledge of opportunities, learned from exposure to other service agencies, are recruited. Thus,

Similar types of affiliation patterns have been found to exist among the poor as for the total range of socioeconomic groups: the participants are more likely to come from the relatively affluent segments of the population. One consequence is that these programs are not reaching those persons with the greatest needs.[32]

Thus, the groups most effective as mediators between their members and government are small, cohesive groups that represent finite but well-articulated interests. These elite groups are best able to concentrate their resources and activities where they can attain tangible rewards for their members. Governmental administrators tend to be the targets for groups of this type. Large groups are characterized by broad, hazily defined goals, and their activities tend to be directed at legislators rather than at administrators. What rewards such groups receive tend to be symbolic.

The Unequal Distribution of Resources

We have argued that much of the energy of pressure groups is dissipated by the receipt of symbolic rewards. Such rewards create the *illusion* of pluralist competition and equal access to political resources. In fact, political resources are *not* equally available to all groups seeking to influence public policy. Conspicuously absent from the successful group process are those organizations seeking to articulate the demands of various powerless strata in society: "protest" groups. By the very nature of their demands and their constituency, such groups are doomed to a short life and political failure.

As an illustration of such a failure, consider the example of the Newark Community Union Project.[33] Organized in 1964 by members of the Students for a Democratic Society and some residents of Newark's South Ward, the NCUP was meant to mobilize ghetto residents into a social protest movement. However, rather than seek the broad and symbolic rewards typical of such movements, NCUP organizers concentrated on specific, tangible problems within the ghetto. During the period from 1964 to 1968, three issues were focused upon.

The first issue was housing. Ghetto residents were paying exorbitant rents for inadequate housing. After months of presenting the problem to the attention of various local agencies had brought no success, a rent strike was begun. In response the tenants were evicted and, in some cases, arrested, and the strike ended. The strikers learned the hard way that laws dealing with rent collection and eviction are swiftly enforced, while those dealing with violations of building codes were unenforceable. In short, the rent strike was a failure.

The next NCUP effort concerned the apparently trivial matter of a traffic light at a dangerous intersection. The issue was, however, especially salient to residents of the ghetto because of deaths and injuries to children from speeding cars. In this case, after rallies, petitions, and letter writing campaigns, the mayor granted an audience and agreed to install the light. Thus a "victory" had apparently been achieved. However, nothing happened. After more protests, demonstrations, and delays, the matter was finally referred to the State Bureau of Motor Vehicles, which declared that traffic lights could be installed only after a survey of traffic conditions—a survey which was never made. Soon after, residents of a white middle-class community were able to get a traffic light installed 28 days after they submitted a petition containing 50 signatures. The light in the ghetto was never installed.

The next effort by NCUP was an attempt to challenge the dominant Democratic leadership electorally. In 1965, the United Freedom Ticket, a coalition of various minority groups, asked NCUP to support an insurgent black Democrat in his fight to challenge the regular Democratic nominee to the state legislature. Against the organization and influence of the regular Democratic organization, defeat was inevitable. Less than half the blacks (as compared to two thirds of the whites) voted, and the United Freedom Ticket candidate drew less than 5 percent of the vote.

Thus in every attempt to win even a minor victory the protest group was defeated. Not only did NCUP lose every issue it contested, but the organization was subject to harrassment (wire-taps, arrests on trumped-up charges, evictions, etc.) by city officials. After about three years NCUP ceased to exist.

The lessons are clear. Although pluralist interest-group theory argues that effective organizations and use of political resources gives everybody an equal opportunity to win, this opportunity is in fact restricted to established, relatively conservative interests. In Newark, there may have been a plurality of interests, but these interests coalesced to defend themselves against an assault from an organization viewed as a threat. Clearly, then, organization is no guarantee of even the opportunity to contest issues legitimately. If a protest group is to survive, it must produce results. Since established elites can effectively deny even the most trivial victory, the protest group is doomed. It cannot compete, and thus is not a participant in the "normal" interest group process. In order to convert potential power into actual power, an organization must have some political resources with which to begin the process. But protest groups have none. They have no money; their constituency—although numerically impressive—is apathetic, and their values are a direct challenge to the established structure of authority. Withholding rent payments, temporary disruption of traffic, and unsuccessful electoral challenges are regarded by the established elites as minor threats to be nipped in the bud, rather than as bargaining resources. Parenti points out the closed nature of the interest group system:

Those who are most needful of substantial reallocations are by that very fact usually farthest removed from the resources necessary to command such reallocations and least able to make effective use of whatever limited resources they possess.[34]

How Well Do Groups Integrate the Individual?

There remains the question of the meaning of group membership for the individual and for the society. Belonging to an organization has beneficial consequences for the individual, and through him for the society, *if we assume that stability is a desirable societal attribute.* Although membership in voluntary groups is highly related to social status (which, as we know, contributes to feelings of efficacy), membership in a group contributes to an individual's efficacy no matter what his social status. In measuring "subjective competence" (feelings of personal power toward government), Almond and Verba found that members of political organizations believed themselves to be more competent than members of nonpolitical organizations, who in turn felt more competent than people who did not belong to an organization.[35] These consequences of group membership on the attitude of the individual are not necessarily related to an objective measurement of the ability of the organization to mediate for the individual. Indeed, most people do not regard organized group activity as the most efficient method of influencing governmental decisions. Thus, integrative functions, to the extent they are performed at all, are performed by voluntary associations because they provide the *opportunity* for influence, not necessarily because they provide evidence of influence.

Members of organizations, whatever the nature of the organization, are more active and interested in political affairs, and they are more committed to, and satisfied with, "the system." For instance, members of organizations are more in accord than are non-members with community preferences. Community influences are mediated through organizations, contributing to a general commitment on the part of members to the concept of the community. For instance, community preferences can be defined in terms of partisan division of the vote. The votes of members of two or more associations are more closely correlated with community preferences than the votes of members of one organization, and the votes of members of one organization are more clearly related to community preferences than the votes of non-members. Group members in Democratic communities are more likely to vote Democratic than non-members.[36] Coleman has speculated that the reason for the relationship between high turnout and defeat of local referenda (e.g., school bonds and fluoridation) is that a high turnout indicates that people unattached to the community (through voluntary associations) are stimulated to vote negatively. In "normal" elections only a small core of community identifiers vote, thus insuring the success of the referenda.[37] In the high turnout election the participation of unaffiliated individuals is much greater, while the participation of members of associations remains constant.

As was mentioned at the beginning of the chapter, many political scientists believe that groups have a stabilizing influence on the individual because overlapping memberships create conflicting demands, and thus modify the effects of each single group on the individual. But membership in voluntary associations is stabilizing in itself, not because of overlapping membership. Few people belong to more than one organization. Even among those who do, memberships are likely to be cumulative rather than conflicting. People associate with reinforcing groups; most political discussion takes place among partisans rather than among adversaries. If a member encounters conflict in a group, a natural response is to reduce his activity. If activity is reduced, the leadership of the organization acquires more discretion rather than less.

Further, due to the ability of people to compartmentalize conflicting values, and also because of the desire to avoid dissonance, people can have loyalty to two sets of values (and to the organizations that reflect these values), even though they are in conflict. As we noted earlier, beliefs do not have to be constraining. Presumably, a Catholic member of a labor union dominated by Communists would have a difficult conflict to resolve, provided there was a strong commitment to both ideologies. A study of just such a conflict reached the following conclusions: "Perhaps the most important finding in this study of cross pressures is the small number of individuals who evidenced awareness of conflicting influences."[38]

The Conservative Influence of Organizations

Organizations perform a conservative, stabilizing function for the society. Formal associations do not cause social change. Of course, the goals of associations vary, some being more radical than others. But in general, organizations that survive, even if they began as radical, become moderate as organizational perpetuation and maintenance of bureaucracy displace the original goals:

Phillip Selznick's theory of bureaucracy states that the running of an organization creates problems not related to original goals. These goals of internal relevance assume an increasing proportion of time and may gradually be substituted for externally directed goals. The day-to-day behavior of the permanent staff and active participants (a minority of the membership) becomes centered around proximate goals of primarily internal importance, modifying or "displacing" the stated goals of the organization.[39]

Messinger has described this development as a shift from the implementation of the values of the organization to maintaining the structure as such, even if this means the loss of the organization's central mission.[40] Organizations thus come to be dominated by those who have the greatest stake in the existing social system. This is not to suggest that organizations seek no change, but that the extent of change they seek is minimal. If they achieve even a portion of what they wish to achieve, then they have established a stake in the ongoing system and have a rational basis for moderate politics. Social stability is apparently a product of the organizational system, not necessarily because of overlapping affiliations, but because of the inevitable nature of organizations. Associations that begin with a radical ideology must modify their views to attract the sustained membership necessary for organizational health. Organized labor, for example, is not as radical a force as it once was, even though business executives treat it as such.

Pressure for substantial social change (as distinguished from incremental or moderate change) comes from forces outside the associational structure. Even leaders of "radical conservative" groups (for example, the Daughters of the American Revolution and the American Legion) display more commitment to the system than does the general population. Most liberals are accustomed to thinking of the American Legion as an instrument of the radical right, without concern for civil rights and freedom of speech. Yet studies show that the leaders of the American Legion are more committed to democratic rules than are unaffiliated citizens.[41] Since all organizations develop bureaucracies that resist change, groups serve to stabilize the social system, irrespective of the official ideology of the organizations.

Since groups serve society by cementing their members to the established social system, those who seek an alteration in this system find organizations an unsatisfactory mechanism. It is true that some groups are created with radical change in mind, but the process of bureaucratization and the evolution of the position of the membership from "have-nots" to "haves" gradually reduces the commitment of any organization to substantial change. Impoverished people and blacks have gained little from groups because the group structure is dominated by people with a favored position in society. Violent protest is the most effective method of entry into the political process for segments of society effectively barred from other forms of participation. Ironically, if deprived peoples succeed in organizing and achieving a more equitable distribution of rewards, violence will probably decline, to be replaced by organizational activity. In time, the new organizations (for example, the "new left" groups) will develop their own commitment to the *status quo,* thus making likely the development of more radical groups.

As agents of integration, then, groups function quite effectively. Not only do group members tend to feel efficacious, but they are also more active and interested in political affairs, are more satisfied with the political system, and identify more readily with the community. Because they contribute to the social integration of their members, organized interest groups have a conservative, stabilizing influence on society.

Summary

Pluralism asserts that organized interest groups provide an effective means of participation in the political system for the individual. It contends that the individual can make his voice heard through membership in the organized groups that reflect his views on public affairs. Pluralists further contend that competition among organized interests provides a balance of power to protect the interests of the individual. Interest groups divide power among themselves and hence protect the individual from rule by a single oppressive elite.

Earlier we pointed out that pluralism diverges from classical democratic theory. Even if the plural elite model accurately portrays the reality of American politics, it does not guarantee the implementation of democratic values. Our analysis of interest groups produced the following propositions:

1. Interest-group membership is drawn disproportionately from middle- and upper-class segments of the population. The pressure-group system is not representative of the entire community.

2. Leadership of interest groups is recruited from the middle- and upper-class population.

3. Business organizations predominate among organized interest groups.

4. Organizations tend to become conservative as they acquire a stake in the existing social order. Therefore, pressures for substantial social change must generally come from forces outside the structure of organized interest groups.

5. Generally mass membership groups achieve only symbolic success and smaller, more cohesive groups are able to achieve more tangible results.

6. There is a great deal of inequality among organized interest groups. Business and producer groups with narrow membership but cohesive organization are able

to achieve their tangible goals at the expense of broad, unorganized groups seeking less tangible goals.

7. Organized interest groups are governed by small elites whose values do not necessarily reflect the values of most members.

8. Business groups and associations are the most highly organized and active lobbyists in Washington and in the state capitals.

References

[1]Gabriel A. Almond and Sidney Verba, *The Civic Culture: Political Attitudes and Democracy in Five Nations* (Boston: Little, Brown and Co., 1965), p. 245.

[2]David B. Truman, *The Governmental Process* (New York: Alfred A. Knopf, 1951).

[3]Arnold Rose, *The Power Structure* (New York: Oxford University Press, 1967), p. 6.

[4]Almond and Verba, *The Civic Culture*, p. 249.

[5]E. E. Schattschneider, *The Semisovereign People: A Realist's View of Democracy in America* (New York: Holt, Rinehart and Winston, 1960), p. 35.

[6]Sidney Verba and Norman H. Nie, *Participation in America* (New York: Harper and Row, 1972), p. 208.

[7]Roberto Michels, *Political Parties: A Sociological Study of the Oligarchical Tendencies of Modern Democracy* (New York: Dover, 1959; originally published in English in 1915), esp. p. 248.

[8]Harmon Zeigler, "Interest Groups in the States," in Herbert Jacob and Kenneth N. Vines, eds., *Politics in the American States* (Boston: Little, Brown and Co., 1965), p. 109.

[9]Schattschneider, pp. 31–34.

[10]Murray Edelman, *The Symbolic Uses of Politics* (Urbana: University of Illinois Press, 1964), pp. 24–26.

[11]Joseph R. Gusfield, *Symbolic Crusade: Status Politics and the American Temperance Movement* (Urbana: University of Illinois Press, 1963), p. 173.

[12]Andrew Hacker and Joel D. Aberbach, "Businessmen in Politics," *Law and Contemporary Problems*, 27 (Spring

[13]Charles E. Lindblom, *The Policy-Making Process* (Englewood Cliffs, N.J.: Prentice-Hall, 1968), p. 68.

[14]Verba and Nie, *Participation in America*, pp. 322–330.

[15]Harmon Zeigler and Michael A. Baer, *Lobbying: Interaction and Influence in American State Legislatures* (Belmont, Calif.: Wadsworth Publishing Co., 1969), pp. 120–121.

[16]Edelman, *The Symbolic Uses of Politics*, p. 124.

[17]See, for example, Lester W. Milbrath, *The Washington Lobbyists* (Chicago: Rand McNally, 1963).

[18]*The Oil and Gas Journal* (November 12, 1973), p. 85.

[19]*The Oil and Gas Journal* (November 12, 1973), p. 101.

[20]*The Oil and Gas Journal* (November 12, 1973), p. 33.

[21]*The Oil and Gas Journal* (November 19, 1973), p. 17.

[22]*The Oil and Gas Journal* (November 19, 1973), p. 11.

[23]The *Washington Post*, November 23, 1973, p. 10.

[24]*The Oil and Gas Journal* (December 10, 1973), p. 30.

[25]The *Washington Post*, December 6, 1973, p. A-11.

[26]The *Washington Post*, December 14, 1973, p. 1.

[27]*The Oil and Gas Journal*, (December 24, 1973), p. 15.

[28]The *Washington Post*, March 6, 1974, p. 12.

[29]U.S. House of Representatives, *To Mobilize the Human and Financial Resources of the Nation to Combat Poverty in the United States*, 88th Congress, 2nd sess., 1964, H.R. 10440, pp. 17–18. Cited in Theodore J. Lowi, *The End of Liberalism* (New York: W. W. Norton & Co., 1969), p. 236.

[30]Paul E. Peterson, *City Politics and Community Action* (doctoral dissertation, University of Chicago, 1967), pp. 14–15. Cited in Lowi, *op. cit.*, p. 246.

[31]For an excellent elaboration of this idea, see Lowi, *op. cit.*, ch. 8.

[32]Russell L. Curtis, Jr. and Louis A. Zurcher, Jr., "Voluntary Associations and the Social Integration of the Poor," *Social Problems*, 18 (Winter 1971), 353.

[33]This discussion is taken from Michael Parenti, "Power and Pluralism: A View from the Bottom," *Journal of Politics*, 32 (August 1970), 501–530.

[34]Parenti, p. 530.

[35]Almond and Verba, *The Civic Culture* p. 253.

[36]Robert D. Putnam, "Political Attitudes and the Local Community," *American Political Science Review*, 60 (September 1966), 646–648.

[37]James S. Coleman, *Community Conflict* (New York: Free Press, 1957), p. 19.

[38]Martin Kriesberg, "Cross-Pressures and Attitudes: A Study of the Influence of Conflicting Propaganda on Opinions Regarding American-Soviet Relations," *Public Opinion Quarterly*, 13 (Spring 1949), 8.

[39]Harmon Zeigler, *Interest Groups in American Society* (Englewood Cliffs, N.J.: Prentice-Hall, 1964), p. 81.

[40]Sheldon L. Messinger, "Organizational Transformation: A Case Study of a Declining Social Movement," *American Sociological Review*, 20 (February 1955), 10.

[41]Samuel A. Stouffer, *Communism, Conformity, and Civil Liberties* (New York: John Wiley, 1966), p. 31.

Selected Additional Readings

Edelman, Murray. *The Symbolic Uses of Politics.* Chicago: University of Illinois Press (Illini Books edition), 1967. (See Chapter 5, page 188.)

Engler, Robert. *The Politics of Oil.* Chicago: The University of Chicago Press (Phoenix Books edition), 1961. Although somewhat dated, this book provides important historical background concerning the power of the American oil industry and its relationships to government—both at home and abroad. Particularly useful to the argument made in this chapter of the *Irony* are the sections on the oil lobby, the use of public relations, and the entry of oil corporation officials into appointive government positions.

Key, V. O., Jr. *Politics, Parties and Pressure Groups.* New York: Thomas Y. Crowell Co., 1967. (See Chapter 7, page 252.)

Olson, Mancur, Jr. *The Logic of Collective Action: Public Goods and the Theory of Groups.* New York: Schocken Books, 1968. This work is well written, dealing with the rational basis for interest-group activity. Individuals are the units of analysis, and Olson constructs a model of individual motivation for collective behavior based upon the assumption of rationality.

Schattschneider, E. E. *The Semisovereign People: A Realistic View of Democracy In America.* New York: Holt, Rinehart and Winston, 1960. (See Chapter 5, page 189.)

Scoble, Harry M. *Ideology and Electoral Action: A Comparative Case Study of the National Committee for an Effective Congress*. San Francisco: Chandler, 1967. A single interest group, the National Committee for an Effective Congress, is subjected to intensive study in this book. Scoble describes its history, its ideology, its organization, and its activities. Additionally, he relates his observations to interest group theory and compares the NCEC to other types of interest groups.

Verba, Sidney and Norman H. Nie. *Participation in America: Political Democracy and Social Equality*. New York: Harper and Row, 1972. In this text Verba and Nie present an exhaustive treatment of citizen participation in American politics. After establishing an impressive theoretical framework within which to view participation, the authors undertake an extensive empirical investigation of the socioeconomic, racial, and organizational correlates of participation. They conclude with a section on the impact of participation on citizen policy preferences and leader responsiveness.

Zeigler, Harmon and Peak, Wayne. *Interest Groups in American Society*, 2nd ed. Englewood Cliffs, N.J.: Prentice-Hall, 1972. This comprehensive study of the composition and roles of interest groups in the political system of the United States discusses the development of interest group theory, the relationship of such theory to broader aspects of democratic political thought, and empirical data concerning group phenomena.

CHAPTER 9

THE PRESIDENCY IN CRISIS

If the majority does not rule, who does? Decision making by governmental elites is a process of bargaining, accommodation, and compromise among the dominant interests in American society. Governmental elites act essentially as go-betweens, mediating, seeking policies that are mutually beneficial to the major interests—industrial, financial, labor, farm, military, bureaucratic, and so on. Governmental elites in America do not command; they seek consensus.

Accommodation and compromise, as the prevailing style of American politics, are made possible by the consensus existing among elite groups in the nation—a consensus that includes fundamental agreement among the elites on the worth of the system itself. Compromise is possible because elites do not perceive their interests as irreconcilable. If elite differences in America were fundamental, it would be difficult to find acceptable accommodations, bargains, or compromises.

Bargaining among elites does not have to be explicit; direct communication is not always necessary when elites already understand the interests of other elites. Of course, explicit contracts, by formalizing agreements among elites, minimize the chance of misunderstanding. In international politics, these contracts appear in the form of treaties; in domestic politics, they appear in the form of wage contracts, government defense contracts, and so on. (Probably the most famous example of an explicit agreement or contract among the elites is the Constitution of the United States itself.) But most bargaining assumes the form of implicit or tacit understandings, in which elites agree to render support for each other in exchange for "good will" and expectations of future support. "You scratch my back and I'll scratch yours" is the traditional style of policy making in America.

It is ironic that Richard Nixon's crisis in the presidency stemmed largely from his misunderstanding of the accommodationist style of American politics. Nixon believed that his election by an overwhelming majority of the nation's voters entitled him to govern the nation. But in reality his election only gave him the opportunity to engage in consultation, accommodation, and cooperation with other elites. Nixon's personal style—his shyness, introspection, and reclusiveness—contributed further to his isolation from the establishment. He surrounded himself with loyal but colorless, younger, uninfluential men, who eventually led to his undoing. Established elites felt shut out of presidential decision making; their frustration turned to suspicion and eventually to hostility. Nixon's painful experience demonstrates conclusively that the president is merely one individual in a larger elite membership. The president does not stand *above* America's elites, but rather *among* them. Election to the nation's highest office—even by an overwhelming majority—does not entitle anyone to ignore established elites.

Separation of Powers—Ambition to Counteract Ambition

The potential power of government officials worried the Founding Fathers. They were not so much concerned with the possibility of a *minority* seizing control of the national government as with the possibility that the *majority* of people might gain access to the legitimate use of force and threaten the established men of principle and property. There was a real fear that, even under the republican and federal structure of the American government, a majority might still be able to "outnumber and oppress the rest." The Founding Fathers, therefore, sought to place additional obstacles in the way of "an unjust and interested majority."

To provide some "precautions" against mass movements that might threaten the rights of property, the Founding Fathers devised two different but related arrangements—separation of powers and checks and balances. These arrangements had two goals: first, to make it more difficult for the masses to capture control of the entire government; and second, to prevent governmental elites from abusing their power and threatening the interests of non-governmental elites.

The idea of a *separation of powers* —that is, the dividing of power among the three branches of national government—was derived from the writings of an early French political scientist, Baron Montesquieu, whose two volumes on *The Spirit of the Laws* appeared about 1748. Montesquieu wrote:

In every government there are three sources of power: the legislative, the executive and the judiciary power. . . . When the legislative and executive powers are united in the same person, or in the same body of magistrates, there can be no liberty. . . . Again, there is not liberty if the judiciary be not separated from the legislative and executive.[1]

Montesquieu's doctrine was widely accepted by American elites in 1787. In *The Federalist* No. 47, James Madison echoed Montesquieu:

No political truth is certainly of greater intrinsic value or is stamped with the authority of more enlightened patrons of liberty, than that the accumulation of all powers, legislative, executive, and judiciary in the same hands, whether of one, a few, or many, and whether hereditary, self-appointed, or elective, may justly be pronounced the definition of tyranny.[2]

The separation of powers concept is expressed in the opening sentence of the first three articles of the Constitution, which establishes separate legislative, executive, and judicial branches of government. To further separate these powers, each of the major decision-making bodies in the national government is chosen by a different constituency—the House by voters in the several legislative districts, the Senate by the state legislatures and later by the voters of whole states, the president by "electors" chosen by the voters in whole states, and the judiciary by the president with the consent of the Senate. A sharp differentiation is also made in the terms of office of each of these decision-making bodies, so that a complete renewal of government by popular majority at one stroke is impossible. The House is chosen for two years, and the Senate for six; but the entire Senate is not chosen in one election, for one third of the senators go out every two years. The president is chosen every four years, and the judges of the Supreme Court hold office for life. Thus the people are restrained from bringing about immediate changes in government policy.

The idea of *checks and balances* supplemented the notion of separating power. "Ambition must be made to counteract ambition."[3] Not only did the Founding Fathers want separate branches of government to be responsive to different constituencies, they also wanted to give each branch of the national government some opportunity to control the operations of the others. The separate branches of the American government are not independent but, rather, interdependent. There is really a sharing of power among the branches of the national government, not a separating of power; for each branch participates in the activities of every other branch.

Thus, an elaborate system of overlapping powers and responsibilities was established. The president shares the legislative powers through his veto and through his responsibility to make recommendations to Congress about legislation he believes to be necessary and expedient. He can also convene special sessions of Congress. But the appointing power of the president is shared by the Senate, as is his treaty-making power; and Congress can override effective presidential vetoes. The president must execute the laws; but in order to do so he must rely upon executive departments, and these must be created by Congress. Moreover, the executive branch cannot spend money that has not been appropriated by Congress. The president appoints judges of the Supreme Court, but only with the consent of the Senate. And the Supreme Court can determine when the president has acted outside the Constitution or the laws of Congress and can even invalidate laws of Congress which are contrary to the Constitution. Finally, Congress possesses the ultimate check on the president and the Supreme Court through its powers of impeachment and removal from office.

Those who criticize the United States government for its slow, unwieldy processes should realize that this characteristic was deliberately built into the government by its founders. These cumbersome arrangements—the checks and balances and the fragmentation of authority that make it difficult for government to realize its potential power over private interests (business, industry, banks, and labor)—were designed by the Founding Fathers to protect the private interests from governmental interference and to shield the government from an unjust and self-seeking majority. If the system handcuffs government and makes it easy for established groups to oppose change, then the system is working as the Founding Fathers intended.

The Founding Fathers planned well. The system of intermingled powers and conflicting loyalties that they established is still alive today. Of course, some things have changed: senators are now directly elected by the voters, and the president is more directly responsible to the voters than was originally envisioned. But the basic arrangement of checks and balances endures. Presidents, senators, representatives, and judges are chosen by different constituencies; their terms of offices vary, and their responsibilities and loyalties differ. This system makes majority rule impossible.

Sources of Presidential Power

The president's real power does not depend upon his formal authority, but upon his abilities at persuasion. The president does not command American elites, but he stands in a central position in the elite structure. The responsibility for the initiation of public policy falls principally upon the president and his staff and executive departments. He has a strong incentive to fulfill this responsibility; for in the eyes of a large segment of the American public, the president is responsible for everything that happens in the nation during his term of office, regardless of whether he has the authority or the capacity to do anything about it. At the very least, there is a general public expectation that every president, even a president committed to a "caretaker" role, will put forth some sort of policy program.

Through the power of policy initiation alone, the president's impact on the nation is considerable. The president sets the agenda for public decision making. The president's programs are presented to Congress in various presidential messages and in his budget, and the president thereby largely determines what the business of Congress will be in any session. Few major undertakings ever get off the ground without presidential initiation; the president frames the issues, determines their context, and decides their timing.

The powers of the presidency and the importance of this office in the American political system vary with political circumstances and with the personalities of the men who occupy the office. In debates about the real extent of executive power, the contrasting views of Presidents William Howard Taft and Theodore Roosevelt are often quoted as examples of the different approaches individuals take to the presidency. Taft once said:

The true view of the executive function is, as I conceive it, that the president can exercise no power which cannot be fairly and reasonably traced to some specific grant of power or justly implied and included within such express grant as proper and necessary to its exercise. Such specific grants must be either in the federal constitution or in the pursuance thereof. There is no undefined residuum of power which can be exercised which seems to him to be in the public interest.[4]

The alternative view was held by Theodore Roosevelt:

I decline to adopt the view that what was imperatively necessary for the nation could not be done by the president unless he could find some specific authorization to do it. My belief was that it was not only his right but his duty to do anything that the needs of the nation demanded, unless such action was forbidden by the Constitution or by the laws. Under this interpretation of executive *power I did and caused to be done many things not previously done by the president and the heads of departments. I did not usurp the power, but I did greatly broaden the use of executive power.*[5]

On the whole, evaluations of a presidential performance are likely to weigh favorably the more activist approach to the office. Taft, Herbert Hoover, and Dwight Eisenhower, who took more restricted views of the presidency, are usually downgraded in comparison with Woodrow Wilson, Theodore and Franklin Roosevelt, and Harry Truman, who were much more active presidents.

It is sometimes argued that the presidency has grown more powerful in the twentieth century, but few presidents have been more powerful than Abraham Lincoln, as Wilfred Binkley comments:

Unquestionably, the highwater mark of the exercise of the executive power in the United States is found in the administration of Abraham Lincoln. No President before or since has pushed about the degrees of executive power so far into the legislative sphere . . . Under the war power he proclaimed the slaves of those in rebellion emancipated. He devised and put into execution his peculiar plan of reconstruction. With disregard of law he increased the army and navy beyond the limits set by statute. The privilege of the writ of habeas corpus was suspended wholesale and martial law declared. Public money in the sum of millions was deliberately spent without Congressional appropriation. Nor was any of this done innocently. Lincoln understood his constitution. He knew, in many cases, just how he was transgressing, and his infractions were consequently deliberate. It is all the more astonishing that this audacity was the work of a minority president performed in the presence of a bitter congressional opposition even in his own party.[6]

Yet, on the whole, presidents of the twentieth century have exercised greater power and initiative than those of the nineteenth century. This increase in power has occurred, first of all, because of America's greater involvement in world affairs and the resulting *increase in the importance of military and foreign policy.* The Constitution gives the president unmistakable and far-reaching powers in foreign and military affairs: the president is given the power to send and receive ambassadors and to make treaties (with the advice and consent of the Senate), and is made commander-in-chief of the armed forces. In effect, these powers give him almost exclusive authority over foreign and military policy in the nation.

A second factor contributing to the power of the president in the twentieth century has been *the growth of the executive branch* which he heads. The federal bureaucracy has grown into a giant elite structure, and the president's constitutional powers as chief executive place him at the top of this structure. The Constitution gives the president broad, albeit vague, powers to "take care that the laws be faithfully executed" and to "require the opinion in writing of the principal officer of each of the executive departments upon any subject relating to the duties of their respective offices." This clause gives the president general executive authority over the 2.5 million civilian employees of the federal bureaucracy. Moreover, the president has the right to appoint (and the right to remove) the principal officers of the executive branch of government. The Senate must consent to appointments, but not removals. A major addition to the president's constitutional authority over the executive branch came in the Budget and Accounting Act of 1921, in which Congress vested in the president the control of the initiation and execution of the federal budget. Budgetary control is a major weapon in the hands of the president, for it can mean the life or death of an administrative agency. While it is true that Congress must appropriate all monies spent by executive departments, nonetheless, the president has responsibility for formulating the budget. Congress may cut a presidential budget request and even appropriate more than the president asks for a particular agency or program, but by far the greatest portion of the president's budget is accepted by Congress.

The third reason for the importance of the presidency in the twentieth century can be traced to technological improvements in the mass media and *the strengthening of the role of the president as party leader and molder of mass opinion.* Television brings the president directly in contact with the masses, and the masses have an attachment to the president which is unlike their attachment to any other public official or symbol of government. Fred I. Greenstein has classified the "psychological functions of the presidency"[7]: First, the president "simplifies perception of government and politics" by serving as "the main cognitive 'handle' for providing busy citizens with some sense of what their government is doing." Second, the president provides "an outlet for emotional expression" through public interest in his and his family's private and public life. Third, the president is a "symbol of unity" and of nationhood (as the national shock and grief over the death of a president clearly reveals). Fourth, the president provides the masses with a "vicarious means of taking political action," in the sense that he can act decisively and effectively while they cannot do so. Finally, the president is a "symbol of social stability," in that he provides the masses with a feeling of security and guidance. Thus, for the masses, the president is the most visible elite member.

The president has many sources of formal power (see Table 9-1); he is chief administrator, chief diplomat, commander-in-chief, chief of state, party leader, and voice of the people. But despite the great powers

Table 9-1 / Formal Presidential Powers

Chief administrator
  Implement policy—"Take care that laws be faithfully executed."
  Supervise executive branch of government.
  Appoint and remove policy officials.
  Prepare executive budget.

Chief legislator
  Initiate policy—"Give to the Congress information of the State of the Union and recommend
    to their consideration such measures as he shall judge necessary and expedient."
  Veto legislation passed by Congress.
  Convene special sessions of Congress "On extraordinary occasions."

Party leader
  Control national party organization.
  Control federal patronage.
  Influence (not control) state and local parties through prestige.

Chief diplomat
  Make treaties ("with the advice and consent of Senate").
  Make executive agreements.
  Power of diplomatic recognition—"to send and receive ambassadors."
  Represent the nation as chief of state.

Commander-in-chief
  Command U.S. Armed Forces—"the President shall be Commander-in-chief of the army and
    the navy."
  Appoint military officials.
  Initiate war.
  Broad war powers.

of the office, no president can monopolize policy making. The president functions within an established elite system, and he can only exercise power within the framework of the elite system. The choices available to the president are limited to those alternatives for which he can mobilize elite support. He cannot act outside existing elite consensus, outside of the "rules of the game." The president must be sensitive to the interests of major elites—business, agriculture, military, education, bureaucratic, and so on.

Of course, on some issues the president may have greater opportunity for mobility and a larger number of alternatives for which he can find elite support. But on many questions of domestic and foreign policy, the president is hedged in by other governmental elites—Congress, the Supreme Court, and party leaders—and by the demands of influential business, financial, agricultural, and military elites. The Congress can clearly frustrate the president when it chooses to do so, particularly on budgetary questions. Similarly, the Supreme Court may restrict presidential actions. For example, in 1952, within three months after President Truman ordered the government to seize the steel industry to end a strike during the Korean War, the Supreme Court held his action unconstitutional, and the steel mills were returned at once to the owners.

President Truman also encountered strong opposition from governmental, military, and private elites when he dismissed General Douglas MacArthur from his command in Korea for failure to carry out presidential orders. This action led to cries of impeachment in the Congress, owing to the great following that the distinguished general had in Washington and the country. Many presidents have been forced to discard or modify policies because of negative responses from industry, farmers, doctors, union leaders, and so on.

Issues in Presidential Power

For decades, the intelligentsia in America praised the presidency and scorned the Congress. Textbooks taught students that the hope of the nation rested with a powerful president; the Congress was viewed as unprogressive, dilatory, even reactionary. Strong presidents—Lincoln, Roosevelt, Truman—were eulogized; weak presidents—Coolidge, Hoover, Eisenhower—were ridiculed. Leading establishment scholars, e.g. Harvard political scientist Richard Neustadt, taught that presidents should conduct themselves in ways which would maximize their power.[8] Americans were led to believe that the president, as the only official elected by *all* of the people, would use his power to "do good."

But then came two successive presidents—Johnson and Nixon —who were distrusted by most of the nation's intellectuals. The result has been an abrupt reversal of establishment views regarding the presidency. The Vietnam War and Watergate convinced liberal intellectuals that the presidency was too powerful and that the Congress must be prepared to check the actions of unruly presidents. Today most commentators, journalists, intellectuals, and, of course, senators and congressmen, argue the importance of curtailing the president's war-making powers, overseeing the activities of the White House, and protecting the nation from the abuses of presidential power.

From time to time in America's political history, both liberals and conservatives have jumped from one side of the argument about presidential power to the other, depending on the current political situation. The lesson to be learned is that arguments over presidential power can never be removed from their political context.

The War-Making Controversy The American colonists who declared their independence from Britain in 1776 were deeply suspicious of standing armies, and of a king who would send British troops to the colonies. This distrust carried over after independence, contributing to a determination among the Founding Fathers to subject military affairs to civilian control. The Second Continental Congress had general oversight over the conduct of the military during the Revolutionary War. It commissioned George Washington to be Commander-in-Chief but instructed him "punctually to observe and follow such orders and directions . . . from this or a future Congress." But George Washington himself chaired the Constitutional Convention of 1787, and he recognized the need for a strong chief executive who could respond quickly to threats to the nation. Moreover, he was aware of the weaknesses of civilian militia, and he favored the establishment of a national army and navy.

The Constitutional Convention of 1787 *divided* the war power between Congress and the president. Article I Section 8 says: "The Congress shall have the power to . . . provide for the common defense . . . to declare war . . . to raise and support armies . . . to provide and maintain a navy . . . to make rules for the government and regulation of the land and naval forces. . . ." Article II Section 2 says: "The President shall be Commander-in-Chief of the army and navy of the United States. . . ." In defending the newly written Constitution, the *Federalist* papers construed the president's war powers narrowly, implying that the war-making power of the president was little more than the power to defend against imminent invasion when Congress was not in session. But historically the president has exercised much more than strictly defensive war-making powers. Since 1789 U.S. forces participated in military actions overseas on more than 150 occasions, but Congress has declared war only five times: the War of 1812, the Mexican War, the Spanish-American War, World War I, and World War II. Supreme Court Justice William H. Rehnquist wrote before he was elevated to the Court, "It has been recognized from the earliest days of the Republic, by the President, by Congress and by the Supreme Court, that the United States may lawfully engage in armed hostilities with a foreign power without Congressional declaration of war. Our history is replete with instances of 'undeclared wars' from the war with France in 1789-1800 to the Vietnamese War."[9] The Supreme Court has generally refused to take jurisdiction in cases involving the war powers of the president and Congress.

Thus, while Congress retains the formal power to "declare war," in modern times wars are seldom "declared." Instead, they are begun by direct military actions, and the president as Commander-in-Chief of the armed forces determines what military actions will be undertaken by the United States. Over the years Congress generally acceded to the supremacy of the president in military affairs. Not until the Vietnam War has there been serious congressional debate over who shall have the power to commit the nation to war. In the past, Congress tended to accept the fact that under modern conditions of war only the president has the information-gathering facilities, the speed, and the secrecy for reaching quick military decisions during periods of crisis.

The war in Vietnam was not an unprecedented use of the president's war-making powers. John Adams fought a war against the French without a congressional declaration; Thomas Jefferson fought the Barbary Pirates; every president in the nineteenth century fought the Indians; Abraham Lincoln carried presidential war-making powers beyond anything attempted by any president before or since; Woodrow Wilson sent troops to Mexico and a dozen Latin American nations; Franklin D. Roosevelt sent U.S. destroyers to protect British convoys in the North Atlantic before Pearl Harbor; and Harry Truman committed American forces to a major war in Korea. So when President Johnson initiated bombing attacks on North Vietnam in 1965 and eventually committed more than one half million men to the battle, he was not really assuming any powers that had not been assumed by presidents before him. Perhaps his greatest mistake was his failure to achieve either a military or diplomatic solution to the war.

The Johnson Administration maintained that the president had ample authority to undertake U.S. armed intervention in Vietnam. It rested this authority first on the president's power as Commander-in-Chief of the armed forces. The Johnson Administration also claimed that the Southeast Asian Treaty Organization (SEATO), which had been approved by the Senate, recognized the right of the South Vietnamese government to appeal to any signatory of that pact for protection against communist aggression. The administration was careful to point out that every step of the U.S. commitment in South Vietnam had been taken only after a formal request for help from the Saigon government. The Johnson Administration also claimed congressional authorization for its intervention from the Gulf of Tonkin Resolution, approved by Congress in 1964. This joint resolution of both houses of Congress was passed after the United States reported that two American destroyers had been attacked by North Vietnamese PT boats. It declared congressional support for the president's "determination to take all necessary measures" to repel attacks on U.S. forces to prevent further aggression. It said that the United States was prepared "as the President determines" to use force if necessary to assist the nations of Southeast Asia to repel aggression.

In the early days of the Vietnam War there was strong support for the war effort among the liberal leadership of the nation, and no one really questioned the president's power to commit the nation to war. However, by 1969 most of the liberal leadership in Congress who had supported the war in its early stages now rushed to assume the image of doves. Indeed, senators argued over who had been the first to change his mind about the war. Moreover, now there was a *Republican* president and a *Democratic* Congress, and congressional attacks on presidential policy became much more partisan. Thus, as opposition to the Vietnam War grew in public opinion, and with different parties in control of the presidency and Congress, the members of Congress now sought to reassert the role of Congress in making decisions leading to war.

Congress began by repealing the Tonkin Gulf Resolution in 1970. President Nixon did not oppose the repeal of the Tonkin Gulf Resolution, maintaining that it had not been relied upon for authority to conduct the war anyhow. The President did not consult with Congress when he sent U.S. troops into Cambodia in 1970. The President contended that as commander-in-chief he had the sole authority to conduct the war as he saw fit and to protect American troops in Vietnam. A series of attempts was made in Congress to curtail the president's war-making powers by cutting off money for U.S. military activity in Southeast Asia. It was generally recognized that Congress did not have the authority to end the Vietnam War by congressional declaration. However, Congress could set a date after which it would not permit any government funds to be spent in the support of U.S. troops in Southeast Asia. Nonetheless, despite attempts by antiwar congressmen to get their colleagues to cut off funds for the war, no such action was taken by the Congress until after President Nixon announced a peace agreement in 1973. Congress then cut off funds for continued bombing in Cambodia. But it is important to note that Congress has never voted to cut off funds to support armies in the field.

In 1973, the Congress passed a War Powers Act that was designed to restrict presidential war-making powers. The President vetoed the bill, but the Watergate affair appeared to undermine the President's support in this struggle with Congress, and Congress overrode the President's veto. The act provides an interesting example of the continuing struggle over checks and balances in the American government. It provides that:

I. In the absence of a declaration of war by Congress, armed forces could be committed to hostilities or to "situations where imminent involvement in hostilities is clearly indicated by the circumstances" only:
   1. To repel an armed attack on the United States or to forestall the "direct and imminent threat of such an attack."
   2. To repel an armed attack against U.S. armed forces outside the United States or to forestall the threat of such attack.
   3. To protect and evacuate U.S. citizens and nationals in another country if their lives were threatened.

4. Pursuant to specific statutory authorization by Congress, not to be inferred from any existing or future law or treaty unless specific authorization was provided.

II. Required the president to promptly report to Congress the commitment of forces for such purposes.

III. Limited to 60 days the length of involvement of U.S. forces unless Congress by specific legislation authorized their continued use.

IV. Authorized Congress to end a presidential commitment by a concurrent resolution—an action which does not require the president's signature.

Senator Jacob K. Javits (R-N.Y.) defended the act: "It would not 'deprive the President of authority essential to the security of our country.' It would permit him to follow his own judgment in responding to emergencies, but would subject unauthorized action to a time limit of 60 days. The important thing is that at some stage . . . (a presidential decision) ceases to be repelling or retaliating against an attack and becomes a basic commitment to war. . . . That requires the concurrence of Congress."[10] And so did Senator Herman E. Talmadge (D-Ga.): "The single most important decision . . . a nation can make is the decision to go to war. . . . In the recent past, the President, acting alone, has determined whether we followed a course of war or peace. The decision is too great for one man to make. . . ."[11]

But President Nixon argued that the War Powers Act is "clearly unconstitutional" because it attempts to "automatically terminate after 60 days . . . the President's constitutional powers as Commander-in-Chief of the Armed Services." "No overt Congressional action would be required to cut off these powers—they would disappear automatically unless Congress extended them." Moreover, Nixon argued that to end American involvement by a congressional resolution would be to deny the president his constitutional role in approving legislation. Not only is the act unconstitutional, warned the President, but it also "seriously undermines this nation's ability to act decisively and convincingly in times of international crisis."[12]

The combination of executive failures in Vietnam and executive abuses in Watergate has encouraged Congress to reassert its powers relative to the executive branch. The War Powers Act may be more symbolic than instrumental in times of real crisis: the Congress has supported the president in the initial stages of every U.S. overseas military involvement, including Vietnam. Hence it is unlikely that a real constitutional confrontation will ever come about between the president and Congress over its implementation. However, the War Powers Act reminds the president once again that he is a member of a larger elite group. Even his command of America's military depends on broad elite consensus.

The Impoundment Controversy The Constitution grants to the Congress the power to appropriate money for public purposes: "No money shall be drawn from the Treasury, but in consequence of appropriations made by law." There is no doubt that the president cannot spend money which has not been appropriated by Congress. But can the president decline to spend money which has been appropriated? Over the years, many presidents have impounded funds appropriated by Congress—that is, refused to spend them. Recently, impoundment has involved billions of dollars and has become a major irritant in presidential-congressional relations.

Historically, the practice of impoundment arose when presidents confronted changing conditions obviating the necessity of expenditures already approved by Congress, or when presidents succeeded in accomplishing the purposes of a program with less expenditure of funds than originally envisioned. Generally, Congress welcomed the return of the money to the Treasury.

In recent years, however, presidents have impounded funds because they disagreed with the objectives of the appropriations, or because they placed a low priority on the programs and a high priority on cutting government spending. In some cases, appropriations were impounded by a president after a presidential veto of the appropriation measure had been overridden by Congress. Indeed, in some cases, Congress has specifically directed the president to spend monies for designated purposes, incorporating anti-impoundment language into law.

Conflict over impoundment, of course, was exacerbated with a liberal Democratic Congress and a more conservative Republican president. The impoundment controversy antedated the Watergate affair, but certainly the Watergate scandal contributed to an awakening interest in Congress in curtailing Nixon's powers.

Presidents have argued that the "executive power" includes the power to control expenditures of executive agencies. Moreover, Congress often gives the president conflicting instructions. For example, the Full Employment Act of 1946 and the Economic Stabilization Act direct the president to avoid inflating government spending, and Congress maintains an overall debt limit on the U.S. Treasury. Presidents have argued that these objectives can take priority over congressional appropriations and entitle him to make spending cuts where he thinks necessary to maintain a balanced budget and avoid inflation. Finally, presidents have historically withheld funds from programs which were not working properly, arguing that many manpower, health, and welfare programs had outlived their usefulness.

In contrast, congressional spokesmen have contended that the president is constitutionally required to "faithfully execute" the laws of Congress, including appropriation measures. The president cannot frustrate the laws of Congress by refusing to spend money for programs established by Congress, simply because the president does not agree with the purposes of the programs. To date, lower federal courts have generally upheld the Congress on this point, particularly where the law specifically mandates the president to spend money for the purposes of an act. But the Supreme Court has not yet produced a definitive decision in the matter, and presidential impoundment continues.

The Executive Privilege Controversy   Executive privilege is an assertion of the right of the president to withhold information, documents, or testimony from either the Congress or the courts if, in the opinion of the president, it is necessary to do so in the interest of national security or the proper functioning of the Executive. The notion of "executive privilege" is derived from the constitutional separation of legislative, executive, and judicial branches of government: the presidency is a popularly elected and constitutionally independent office; neither the Congress nor the courts can compel presidential action or interfere with the functioning of the Executive. The claim of executive privilege is made not only relative to information affecting national security and international diplomacy; it has been claimed on *all* communications between presidents and their own advisors and cabinet members. This is to insure that advisors can be completely candid in their conversations with the president. The legislative branch enjoys a specific constitutional protection of privilege: Article I Section 6 provides that "for any Speech or Debate in either House, they shall not be questioned in any other Place." Presidents have asserted the same privilege, but there is no specific language in the Constitution granting it.

Executive privilege was first invoked against Congress by President George Washington in 1796, when he refused a request by the House of Representatives for documents relating to the controversial Jay Treaty with Great Britain. According to Washington, "a just regard to the Constitution and to the duty of my office . . . forbids a compliance with your request." A Library of Congress study reports that between 1961 and 1972, President Kennedy invoked executive privilege thirteen times, President Johnson twice, and President Nixon nine times.[13] However, Congress has never sanctioned the notion of executive privilege, and it has always been a sensitive topic in presidential-congressional relations. Congressional critics of executive privilege argue that it can be used to frustrate congressional oversight of executive actions, and to cover up fraud and corruption in office.

Executive privilege was first invoked against the courts by President Thomas Jefferson in 1807. Supreme Court Chief Justice John Marshall, then presiding over the trial of former Vice President Aaron Burr for treason, issued a subpoena to President Thomas Jefferson to appear at the trial and bring certain documents from his files bearing on the case. Marshall argued: "That the President of the United States may be subpoenaed, and examined as a witness, and required to produce any paper in his possession, is not controverted." The president, Marshall argued, was subject to law as any other person; the English principle that the King could do no wrong did not apply to the president. But Jefferson saw things differently. He sent the documents to the trial in Richmond, but declined to appear in person. He argued that the Constitution placed higher obligations on him than answering court subpoenas, which would "withdraw him entirely from his constitutional duties" and "leave the nation without an executive branch." More importantly, if the president were obliged to honor court orders, then the doctrine of separation of powers would be destroyed.

The second president ever to be served a court subpoena was Richard Nixon. He was served subpoenas in the Watergate affair from both the Senate Watergate Committee and from former Special Prosecutor Archibald Cox. Nixon invoked executive privilege against both the Congress and the Special Prosecutor:

I must decline to obey the command of that subpoena. In doing so I follow the example of a long line of my predecessors as President of the United States who have consistently adhered to the position that the President is not subject to compulsory process from the courts.

The independence of the three branches of our government is at the very heart of our constitutional system. It would be wholly inadmissible for the President to compel some particular action by the courts. It is equally inadmissible for the courts to seek to compel some particular action from the President. [14]

The issue finally reached the Supreme Court in *United States* v. *Richard M. Nixon*, when the second Watergate Special Prosecutor, Leon Jaworski, subpoenaed the President for tapes of presidential conversations with his aides in the White House. A unanimous Supreme Court recognized the legitimacy of executive privilege, but held that such privilege did not extend to criminal cases, where the public interest in a fair trial outweighed the public interest in presidential confidentiality. Chief Justice Warren Burger cited the landmark case of *Marbury* v. *Madison* in holding that the president is not above the rule of law nor

Executive privilege

Szep, reprinted by permission.

insulated from orders of the judicial branch. The Court said that executive privilege was not absolute, but limited to "military, diplomatic, or sensitive national security secrets" and other areas "essential to the effective discharge of the President's powers." Even in criminal cases, the court said that judges must carefully weigh the competing claims of the president, the prosecution, and the defendants; and that judges must screen presidential material themselves to make sure that only relevant criminal evidence is given out.

It is clear that the Supreme Court was trying to assert judicial supremacy over the Executive, but at the same time to prevent constant harassment of the president from 400 federal court judges seeking presidential material. But it is possible that the case will be cited by many prosecutors and defendants in future cases in attempts to gain access to presidential files, documents, and conversations. President

Nixon agreed to abide by the Supreme Court's decision in this case. Since he was facing imminent impeachment, he was too weak to offer further resistance. But the question of executive privilege is likely to be raised again in the future.

The Resignation of Richard Nixon

The president must govern the nation within the boundaries of elite consensus. Mass opinion can be manipulated, but elite opinion is a powerful restraint on executive action. Voters may elect the president, but elites determine what he does in office.

The forced resignation of President Nixon is one of the most dramatic illustrations of the president's dependence upon elite support in the nation's history. A president who was re-elected by an overwhelming majority of the nation's voters found himself obliged to resign his office less than two years after his landslide victory. It is our contention that Nixon's threatened impeachment and subsequent resignation was more than a product of specific misdeeds or improprieties in office. Instead, Nixon's demise was a result of 1) his general isolation from established elites, 2) his failure to adopt an accommodationist style of politics, and 3) his frequent disregard of traditional "rules of the game."

Impeachment as a Political Process   The Constitution defines an impeachable offense as "treason, bribery, or other high crimes and misdemeanors." But impeachment is not really a *legal* process—it is a political process. And Nixon's offenses were political, perhaps more than criminal.*

---

*The only precedent for a presidential impeachment—the impeachment and trial of Andrew Johnson in 1868—was also political in character. There was no evidence of President Johnson's personal involvement in a crime for which he could be indicted and found guilty in a court of law. Johnson was a Southern Democrat, a U.S. Senator from a seceding state (Tennessee) who had remained loyal to the Union. Lincoln chose him as Vice President in 1864 as a gesture of national unity. When Johnson acceded to the presidency after Lincoln's assassination, he resisted attempts by "radical" Republicans in Congress to restructure Southern society by force. When Johnson dismissed some federal officials who opposed his conciliatory policies, Congress passed a Tenure of Office Act over Johnson's veto, forbidding executive removals without Senate consent. Johnson contended that the act was an unconstitutional infringement of his powers as Chief Executive. (Years later the Supreme Court agreed, holding that the power of removal is an executive power, and specifically declaring that the Tenure of Office Act had been unconstitutional.) When Johnson dismissed his "radical" Republican Secretary of War, Edwin M. Stanton, Congress was enraged. The House impeached Johnson on a party line vote, charging that Johnson had violated the Tenure of Office Act. The Civil War had left a legacy of bitterness against Johnson as a Southerner and a Democrat. But following a month-long trial in the Senate, the result was 35 guilty, 19 not guilty—one vote short of the necessary two-thirds vote for removal. Seven Republicans joined the 12 Democrats in supporting the President. John F. Kennedy, in his book *Profiles in Courage*, praised the strength and courage of those senators who resisted popular emotions and prevented the President's removal. See Michael Les Benedict, *The Impeachment and Trial of Andrew Johnson* (New York: W. W. Norton, 1973).

Alexander Hamilton, in *The Federalist* No. 65, expressed his awareness of the impossibility of a nonpolitical impeachment proceeding:

A well-constituted court for the trial of impeachments is an object not more to be desired than difficult to be obtained in a government wholly elective. The subjects of its jurisdiction are those offenses which proceed from the misconduct of public men . . . from the abuse of violation of some public trust . . . which may with peculiar propriety to be denominated POLITICAL. . . . The prosecution of them . . . will seldom fail to agitate the passions of the whole community, and to divide it into parties more or less friendly or inimical to the accused. In many cases it will connect itself with the pre-existing factions, and will enlist all their animosities, partialities, influence and interest on one side or the other; and in such cases there will always be the greatest danger that decision will be regulated more by the comparative strength of the parties than by the real demonstrations of innocence or guilt.[15]

Congressman Robert Drinan, of the House Judiciary Committee which recommended impeachment, is a Jesuit priest and flamboyant spokesman for liberal causes. He explained it even more directly: "The first illusion we have to break is that you have to prove a criminal offense to impeach the President. This is a political offense."[16] Nixon's former Attorney General Richard Kliendienst put it succinctly, if somewhat cynically: "To impeach the President, you don't need facts, you don't need evidence—all you need is votes."[17]

The House Judiciary Committee voted in early August 1974 to recommend to the full House of Representatives "the impeachment and trial and removal from office" of President Richard M. Nixon. The Committee charged that the President:

. . . using the powers of his high office, engaged personally and through his close subordinates and agents, in a course of conduct or plan designed to delay, impede, and obstruct the investigation of such unlawful entry; to cover up, conceal, and protect those responsible; and to conceal the existence and scope of other unlawful activities.[18]

Democrats on the committee were united against the President, but Republicans were split, with a majority supporting him. Shortly after the formal vote, however, newly subpoenaed court tapes tended to support the charge that Nixon himself, although he had no knowledge of the original break-in at Watergate, did in fact order the FBI to restrict its investigation of this offense and implied to investigators that the break-in was a CIA operation, which it was not.[19] Following this revelation, pro-Nixon Republicans on the committee announced that they had changed their minds and would vote to impeach when the vote was taken by the full House of Representatives. Senator Hugh Scott, Senate

Republican leader, Representative John Rhodes, House Republican Leader, and Senator Barry Goldwater, former GOP presidential candidate, met with the President to inform him he could expect to be impeached by the full House, and removed from office by a two-thirds vote of the Senate. In a dramatic nationwide television speech on August 8, 1974, Richard Nixon announced his resignation—the first president in the history of the nation to resign this high office:

From the discussions I have had with congressional and other leaders, I have concluded that because of the Watergate matter I might not have the support of the Congress that I would consider necessary to back the very difficult decisions and carry out the duties of this office in the way the interests of the nation will require.

I have never been a quitter. To leave office before my term is completed is abhorrent to every instinct in my body.

As President I must put the interests of America first. America needs a full-time president and a full-time Congress, particularly at this time with problems we face at home and abroad.

To continue to fight through the months ahead for my personal vindication would almost totally absorb the time and attention of both the President and the Congress in a period when our entire focus should be on the great issues of peace abroad and prosperity without inflation at home.

Therefore, I shall resign the presidency effective at noon tomorrow. [20]

The formal charges against the president were serious, but they were not the real cause of his ouster. Nixon's demise was not a result of the fact that the Democratic national headquarters was wiretapped and burglarized; that the president's top White House staff and the president himself attempted to cover up the Watergate affair with illegal payments to defendants and promises of executive clemency; that the president withheld taped conversations and documents bearing on the Watergate investigation from prosecutors, courts, and Congress; that ITT (International Telephone and Telegraph) made a large campaign contribution and settled a government antitrust suit out of court; that the milk industry made a large campaign contribution and received an increase in milk price supports; that the president took advantage of legal loopholes in his own income tax returns and used government funds to make improvements on his own homes.

Nor was Nixon's resignation a result of mass demands for his removal. He was re-elected with a landslide 62 percent of the vote five months *after* the initial Watergate arrests. He achieved an all-time high approval rating in the public opinion polls *after* initial reports of a cover-up. Even after two years of Watergate scandal dominating the news from Washington, public opinion remained divided on whether or not he should be impeached.

Isolation from Established Elites   Nixon's ouster was, first of all, a result of his isolation from established elites and the suspicion, distrust, and hostility generated by his isolation. Nixon was never fully accepted by established Eastern elites. Despite his apprenticeship in a top Wall Street law firm, he was always regarded as opportunistic, uncultured, and middle class by the Eastern corporate and financial leaders he served, by influential segments of news media, and by intellectuals in prestigious universities and foundations. Nixon was upwardly mobile, competitive, self-conscious, boorish; he stood in marked contrast to the wealthy, cool, self-assured, aristocratic John F. Kennedy. Nixon fought his way up from rooms over his father's grocery store, through the local, unprestigious Whittier College (California), to Duke Law School (North Carolina), by self-sacrifice and hard work, long hours studying, and pleasures and luxuries postponed. In 1952, when the dominant Eastern Republicans nominated Eisenhower over the Ohio Senator Robert Taft, they chose Richard Nixon as Eisenhower's running mate in a gesture to the losing Western and Midwestern interests. Even so, shortly thereafter, they nearly dumped him from the ticket when it became known that his early career was financed by a "slush fund" set up by wealthy Californians. Nixon resorted to a "dirty trick": he appealed for mass support in his famous nationally televised "Checkers" speech. His appeal was effective, and it drowned the Republican headquarters in a sea of letters and telegrams from sympathetic viewers. The Eastern leadership kept Nixon on the ticket, but they never forgot this resort to demagoguery.

Nixon always stood closer to the new-rich Southern and Western elites than to the Eastern establishment. Nixon was a self-made man in the political world who shared with self-made men of the business world an aggressive instinct, a sense of competition, and a belief in traditional, individualistic values. Yet Nixon tried to straddle both factions in America's elite structure. He served humbly as vice president under Eisenhower; he courted the favors of Nelson Rockefeller; he went to work on Wall Street; and he frequently voiced support of liberal and moderate programs and policies. Indeed, his vacillation between factions led to cynical references to the "New Nixon," the "New New Nixon," and "Tricky Dick." But his personal friends were Sun Belt Cowboys such as Charles "Bebe" Rebozo (who started his career as a gas station attendant, opened a successful tire recapping business, expanded into Florida real estate, and later established the Key Biscayne Bank), and Robert Abplanalp (inventor of the spray valve used on aerosol cans and co-owner of Nixon's Key Biscayne Florida and San Clemente California properties). And Nixon's admiration of Texan John Connally was undisguised.

When Nixon came to the presidency, he found a giant Washington bureaucracy, overwhelmingly liberal in its politics, and more responsive to the news media, influential interest groups, and key senators and congressmen than to the Chief Executive. This is how it has always been in Washington. But Nixon sought to gather up the reins of power over the bureaucracy by adding to the size and powers of his own White House staff. He attempted to centralize decision making in the White House—his national security advisor Henry Kissinger became more powerful than the Secretary of State or Secretary of Defense; his domestic affairs advisor John Ehrlichman became more powerful than the secretaries who headed the domestic departments, and his Chief of Staff H. R. Haldeman became more powerful than anyone else, determining what information the President received and implementing presidential orders. Not only did this style of administration win the President the lasting enmity of the Washington bureaucracy, but it also contributed to his isolation from other elites. Unlike Roosevelt and Kennedy, who deliberately encouraged multiple and often competitive channels of information, Nixon became a prisoner of a single information system.

Nixon's long-standing hostility toward the press, a hostility that was more than reciprocated, contributed immeasurably to his isolation. But it was Nixon himself who, in reaction to a hostile press, cut himself off from the dialogue with influential publics.

In the 1972 presidential campaign, Nixon divorced himself from his party and operated through his own Committee to Re-Elect the President, rather than the Republican National Committee. He abandoned GOP governors and congressmen and concentrated on amassing the largest possible majority for himself. He gained his landslide majority, but at the price of alienating elite support even within his own party.

James David Barber writes:

The President himself took action after action . . . moving suddenly, on his own, either without consulting key officials or against their fervent advice . . . Nixon was repeatedly leaving his top administrative officials and Congressional party leaders in the dark—unable to consent or oppose because they did not know.

Progressively, Nixon isolated himself not only from legislative and executive powers that be, but from his own aides, setting his assistant H. R. Haldeman to the task of keeping the horde at a distance.[21]

Failure at Accommodation Nixon's personality made it difficult for him to engage in the friendly, hand-shaking, back-slapping politics that his predecessor Lyndon Johnson had developed into a fine art. As a consequence Nixon never really fit comfortably into the accommodationist style of elite interaction. Nixon did not really enjoy politics. He was by nature a "loner." His major decisions were not made in White House gatherings of top officials and advisors, but alone in the presidential retreat at Camp David or at his San Clemente or Key Biscayne homes far from the hubbub of Washington.

Nixon also cut himself off from other elites—congressmen and senators could not reach the President, phone calls were shifted to aides, and key influentials outside of the government were seldom if ever consulted. Only the "Germans" at the White House—Haldeman, Ehrlichman, Ziegler, and Kissinger—had direct access to the president. They stood as a "Berlin Wall" isolating the President from other elites—because the President wanted it that way. The influential news media (eg. CBS News, the *Washington Post*, and the *New York Times*), who Nixon

"Ask not what your king can do for you, but what you can do for my country."

Szep, reprinted by permission.

(correctly) perceived as his enemies, were aggressively shut out; Nixon held fewer press conferences than any president since Herbert Hoover.

Nixon complained that his critics blew up a petty incident—the Watergate break-in—out of all proportion to its importance. And indeed the burglary of a party headquarters was trivial compared to ending the Vietnam War, or the trip to China, or the Middle-Eastern crisis. But Watergate's importance grew as the President escalated his defense, challenged the powers of other elites, asserted his own authority, and offended the Congress, the courts, and the press. Liberal writer Arthur Schlesinger, Jr. condemns Nixon in highly partisan terms, but acknowledges that: "Despite Senator McGovern's efforts to rouse the conscience of the electorate, most Americans regarded 'the Watergate caper' with indifference if not with complacency till well into 1973, and they began to react only after the issue had changed from the original depredation to the subsequent obstruction of justice. . . . The expansion and abuse of Presidential power constituted the underlying issue, the issue that, as we have seen, Watergate raised to the surface, dramatized and made politically accessible."[22]

It was the President's style to confront crisis directly, to avoid surrender, to test his own strength of character against adversity. His gut instinct in a crisis was to "fight like hell" rather than to bargain, accommodate, and compromise. Nixon viewed "politics" as a burden to be borne, rather than an art to enjoy. James David Barber believes that such political figures eventually became rigid:

Such a President will, eventually, freeze around some adamant stand—as did Wilson in the League of Nations fight, Hoover in refusing relief to Americans during the Depression, and Johnson in the Vietnam escalation. Increasingly, as his stance rigidifies, he will see compromise as surrender, justify his cause as sacred, plunge into intense and lonely effort, and concentrate his enmity on specific enemies he thinks are conspiring against him.[23]

As the Watergate affair broadened and intensified, Nixon increasingly viewed it as a test of his strength and character. He perceived a conspiracy of liberal opponents in Congress and the news media to reverse the 1972 election outcome. He became rigid in his stance on executive privilege, withholding tapes and documents. He came to believe he was defending the presidency itself.

Violating Rules of the Game We have already suggested that the Watergate bugging and burglary of Democratic national headquarters, and the actions of the White House Plumbers unit, violated established "rules of the game." (See Chapter 1.) Elites and masses in America have generally condoned repressive acts against communists, subversives, and "radicals." But when these tactics are turned against established political opposition—Democrats, liberals, and assorted presidential critics—then elite consensus is clearly violated.

Yet despite all of the revelations by the media—the Watergate cover-up, the activities of the Plumbers, the ITT case, the dairy industry case, the President's tax returns and home improvements—Nixon would not have been forced to resign if he had publicly repented and cooperated with Congress, the news media, and representatives of the Eastern establishment in cleansing his administration.

The direct stimulus to Nixon's impeachment was his firing of Attorney General Elliot Richardson and Special Prosecutor Archibald Cox in October 1973. The story of Richardson and Cox illustrates very clearly the necessity of the President's accommodating established elites. As the Watergate scandal broadened in early 1973, and evidence of a cover-up was exposed, the President's top two White House advisors—Chief of Staff H. R. Haldeman and Domestic Advisor John Ehrlichman—were dismissed. Attorney General Richard G. Kliendienst resigned because, he said, he would be uncomfortable in prosecuting so many close associates. At this point, the President and key elites in Congress appeared to reach an understanding. The President would appoint an Eastern establishment representative, Elliot Richardson, as Attorney General, who would appoint a Harvard professor, Archibald Cox, as Special Prosecutor, and Cox would have complete independence in conducting his investigations of Watergate. This pledge was made to the Senate during confirmation hearings on Richardson's appointment as Attorney General.

But when Cox was installed in office, he recruited a highly partisan staff of liberal attorneys, and expanded his own investigative activities well beyond the Watergate break-in and cover-up. Later, Nixon began to suspect a conspiracy to destroy him. When Nixon appeared to reach an agreement with the Senate Watergate Committee's Chairman and Vice-Chairman, Senators Sam Ervin (D) and Howard Baker (R), to allow Senator Stennis to listen to certain taped conversations in lieu of turning over the tapes to the courts, Cox demurred and insisted on hearing the tapes himself. Cox cited the original promise to give him full independence in pursuing his investigation. Attorney General Richardson backed up his former Harvard Law School professor. Nixon acted abruptly in the "Saturday Night Massacre" to dismiss both Cox and Richardson.

In firing Cox and Richardson, President Nixon made his most serious error. He not only broke a solemn pledge made to the Congress, but more importantly he cut his last ties with the Eastern establishment. (Former Harvard Professor and Rockefeller Foundation scholar Henry Kissinger would remain as Secretary of State to conduct crucial foreign affairs, but the President was now stripped of establishment support in his efforts to avoid impeachment.) Richardson and Cox represented a good-faith effort on the part of the Eastern establishment to correct the errors of the Nixon Administration. In rejecting these efforts, the President further isolated himself from established elites.

Yet no one in the news media, the Congress, the Democratic Party, or the intellectual community could seriously consider impeaching Richard Nixon as long as Vice President Spiro Agnew was next in line of succession. Agnew was even more isolated from established elites than Nixon; indeed, Agnew publicly attacked the "effete intellectual snobs" of the Eastern establishment and openly criticized the news media—"a tiny enclosed fraternity of privileged men." So removing Agnew was a prerequisite to any serious impeachment movement.

Agnew was extremely vulnerable to attack; the task of removing him was relatively easy. Agnew had served his political apprenticeship as Baltimore County Manager before moving on to the governorship of Maryland and the vice presidency. It was widely known that Baltimore was one of the nation's most corrupt city and county governments. Indeed, for years Washington cocktail parties had been spiced by stories of scandal implicating the Vice President. So all that was required was a thorough investigation—one which revealed that Agnew received cash payments from Maryland contractors as county manager and governor, and, more importantly, continued to receive such payments as vice president.* Agnew resigned after his indictment, pleaded no contest to the charge of income tax fraud (failure to report the payments as income for tax purposes), was convicted and given a suspended sentence. Nixon was now open to direct frontal attack.

Nixon's final line of defense was legal and technical—a feeble plea to abide by the constitutional definition of impeachment, "high crimes and misdemeanors." But the President was really forced to resign because of political acts—his isolation from establishment elites, his failures in accommodationist politics, and his misunderstanding of the rules of elite interaction. As Barber explains:

---

*There are few senators, congressmen, or governors who have not accepted contributions from highway and building contractors. This industry is a major source of political campaign financing. However, most politicians place the money received in separate campaign finance accounts and use this money for campaign purposes rather than personal living expenses. If the money is used for personal living expenses, it becomes taxable income under federal tax laws, and it is more likely to be regarded as a "bribe" than a "campaign contribution."

If this country is to avoid more presidential crises, we need to elect Presidents who enjoy the politics of persuasion—the process of evoking consent, rather than commanding or coercing it. Further, our chief executives should be people committed to working within the balance of institutional roles we have inherited from the Constitutional Tradition.[24]

The Irony of Richard Nixon It is ironic that Richard Nixon saw himself as a tribune of the people—"the great silent majority"—pitting himself against a liberal establishment that was not popularly elected and did not reflect grass-roots sentiments. Nixon believed he understood "Middle America," and he probably did, since he was Middle American himself. But in the end, established elites were able to turn Middle America against him. In six months in 1973, Nixon suffered the steepest plunge in public opinion approval ratings ever recorded. Public opinion is unstable, changeable, and susceptible to manipulation by the mass media.

Richard Nixon failed to understand that without elite support, even landslide victories at the polls are meaningless. Popular majorities elect a president, but they do not permit him to govern. A president can govern only with the support of the nation's elite—a costly lesson Nixon learned in his "final crisis."[25]

Undoubtedly pluralist writers will present Nixon's forced resignation as an illustration of the working of American pluralism—executive wrongdoing that was corrected by the operation of our system of checks and balances, competitive parties, and a free press. Such an interpretation fits the prevailing ideology of multiple competitive centers of power, checking each other and protecting against the abuse of power.

But complacency about the survival of democratic values is unwarranted. The White House "horrors" are typical of the behavior of elites when they feel threatened by crisis situations. Nixon was an "outsider" to the liberal establishment. He rejected many opportunities to accommodate with his liberal opposition. Would Watergate-type abuses have been uncovered in a liberal administration? Would Watergate abuses have been uncovered except for the chance occurrence of the capture of the original Watergate burglars? Will future periods of mass unrest be treated any differently by elites because of Watergate?

The president is the only national official elected by all of the people, but recent events have greatly weakened the presidency. Over the years the major thrust for reform in the nation has been led by strong presidents—from Jefferson and Jackson and Lincoln, to Wilson, Roosevelt, and Truman—not the Congress. Weakening the presidency—making the president's very tenure in office a function of his popularity with the press, his temporary standing in opinion polls, and his resulting support in the Congress—can weaken the thrust for reform and the opportunity for change. A presidential democracy has the capacity to react more quickly and decisively to national and international events than a parliamentary democracy. And the forced resignation brings us closer to parliamentary democracy than this nation has ever been in the twentieth century.

Gerald Ford: A New Search for Consensus

President Gerald R. Ford is the first president of the United States wholly selected by the Congress, with no popular vote of the people (or even presidential electors) involved in his rise to the vice presidency or the presidency. It would be ironic if the first president ever to acquire that office without any popular vote turned out to be an effective and successful chief executive.

Ford's early performance in office suggests that he understands fully the compromising and accommodationist style of American politics. Ford is open and accessible to both the news media and Congress. He seldom acts without extensive consultation with Congress. Despite Ford's conservative voting record as a Republican congressman, he seeks to accommodate liberals as well as conservatives, Democrats as well as Republicans; he consults with blacks, labor, women, and other minorities who seldom saw the inside of the White House during the Nixon years. Ford's selection of former New York Governor and liberal Republican Nelson Rockefeller as vice president clearly indicated the new president's desire to make peace with the "Eastern establishment" within his own party and to assure the nation that his administration would reflect a broad elite consensus.

While many critics attacked President Ford's pardon of ex-President Nixon as placing Nixon above the law and subverting the judicial process, it was clear that Ford was searching for a way to end divisiveness and polarization in America:

I deeply believe in equal justice for all Americans whatever their station or former station. But . . . the facts as I see them are that a former President of the United States, instead of enjoying equal treatment with other citizens accused of violating the law, would be cruelly and excessively penalized. . . . During this long period of delay and potential litigation, ugly passions would again be aroused, and our people would again be polarized in their opinion, . . . my conscience says that it is my duty, not merely to proclaim domestic tranquility, but to use every means I have to ensure it.*

---

*Text of President's Gerald Ford's pardon of former President Richard Nixon, September 8, 1974.

Thus, Ford acted, even at the expense of his own popularity, in a way which he hoped would restore national consensus.

Other Executive Elites

The presidency is not one man, but more than five thousand permanent employees in the executive office of the president (see Figure 9-1), which is composed of the White House Office, the Bureau of the Budget, the Council of Economic Advisers, the National Security Council, the National Aeronautics and Space Council, the Office of Emergency Planning, and the Office of Science and Technology. In addition, there is the presidential Cabinet, consisting of heads of twelve major executive departments. Finally, there are more than forty independent agencies that function outside of the regular departmental organization of the executive branch, including the Interstate Commerce Commission, the Federal Reserve Board, the Federal Trade Commission, the Federal Power Commission, the Federal Communications Commission, the Securities and Exchange Commission, the National Labor Relations Board, the Civil Aeronautics Board, and the Atomic Energy Commission.

The White House Staff   Closest to the president is a group of aides and assistants who work with him in the White House Office. These aides and assistants perform whatever duties the president assigns them, and the president organizes the White House Office as he sees fit. There is usually a Chief of Staff, a press secretary, an appointment secretary, and one or more special assistants for liaison with Congress. Some of the president's assistants have ad hoc assignments, while others have a particular speciality. Theodore Sorensen, Special Assistant to President Kennedy, defined the role of the White House staff as the auxiliary eyes and ears of the president, with responsibilities as broad as those of the president.[26]

Increasingly White House staff men have come to exercise great power in the name of the president. They frequently direct affairs in the name of the president ("The president has asked me to tell you. . . ." "The president wants you to. . . ." etc.), but the president may have little direct oversight of their activities. Even more serious is the fact that staff men come into power with little preparation or experience for elite membership. Often their training consists of nothing more than serving as "advance men" in presidential election campaigns—scheduling presidential appearances, handling campaign advertising, and fetching coffee and doughnuts. Staff men are valued not for their independent contributions to policy but rather for their personal loyalty to the president.

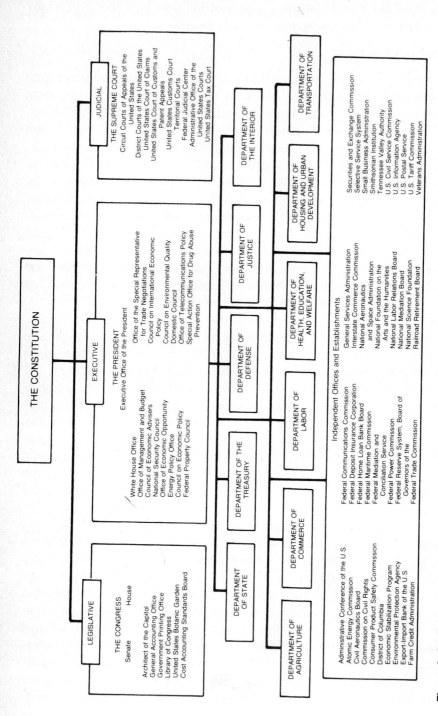

Figure 9–1. The governmental organization of the United States. (From *U.S. Government Manual*, 1973–74.)

When President Johnson praised his staff, for example, it was in terms like these:

[Domestic advisor Jack Valenti] is about the best fellow with me. He gets up with me every morning. He stays with me until I go to bed at night, around midnight, and he is the only one who can really take it. The rest of these fellows are sissies.[27]

Frequently, in recent presidential administrations, these men have embarrassed the president: Truman's personal secretary went to jail for fixing a tax case; Eisenhower's "Assistant to the President," Sherman Adams, retired in disgrace for accepting expensive gifts; Johnson's White House advisor, Walter Jenkins, was convicted of a homosexual assault; and Nixon's original White House staff were nearly all indicted in the Watergate scandal.

Executive Agencies   The Office of Management and Budget (OMB) is the largest agency in the executive office of the president. The function of OMB is to prepare the budget of the United States for the president to submit to Congress. No money may be spent by the federal government without appropriations by Congress, and all requests for congressional appropriations must be cleared through OMB. This gives OMB great power over the executive branch of government. Since all agencies request more money than they can receive, the primary responsibility for reducing budget requests rests with the bureau. The bureau reviews, reduces, and approves estimates submitted by departments and agencies (subject, of course, to their appeal to the president), and it also continuously scrutinizes the organization and operations of executive agencies in order to recommend changes that would promote efficiency and economy. Like members of the White House staff, the top officials of OMB are solely responsible to the president, and they are supposed to reflect the president's goals and priorities in their decision making.

The Council of Economic Advisers, created by the Employment Act of 1946, is composed of three professional economists of high standing, appointed by the president with the consent of the Senate. The functions of the council are to analyze trends in the economy and to recommend to the president the fiscal and monetary policies necessary to avoid both depression and inflation. In addition, the council prepares the Economic Report which the Employment Act of 1946 requires the president to submit to Congress each year. The Economic Report, together with the annual budget message to Congress, give the president the opportunity to assess broadly the major policies of his administration.

The National Security Council resembles a cabinet; it is composed of the president as chairman, the vice president, the Secretary of State, the Secretary of Defense, and the director of the Office of Emergency Planning (a minor unit in the executive office). The chairman of the Joint Chiefs of Staff and the director of the Central Intelligence Agency are advisors to the Security Council. The staff of the council is headed by a special assistant to the president for national security affairs. The purposes of the National Security Council are to advise the president on security policy and to coordinate foreign, military, and domestic policies. However, presidents do not rely exclusively on the National Security Council for direction in major foreign and military decisions.

Cabinet officers in the United States are powerful because they sit at the heads of giant administrative organizations. The Secretary of State, the Secretary of Defense, the Secretary of the Treasury, the Attorney General, and, to a lesser extent, the other departmental secretaries are all men of power and prestige in America. But the Cabinet, as a council, rarely makes policy.[28] Seldom does a strong president hold a Cabinet meeting to decide important policy questions. More frequently, he knows what he wants and is inclined to hold Cabinet meetings to help him sell his views. John F. Kennedy preferred to meet with individual Cabinet members on particular policy issues rather than to hold formal or regular Cabinet meetings, which he believed were "unnecessary and involve a waste of time."

There are forty independent executive agencies that function outside of the departmental organization. Some are small and obscure, while others are large and powerful. The independent regulatory commissions are usually headed by boards or commissions of five to eleven members appointed by the president but free from direct responsibility to him. Members are appointed for fixed overlapping terms and are not easily removed from office. The first important regulatory agency was the Interstate Commerce Commission, created in 1887; it was followed by the Federal Reserve Board (1913), the Federal Trade Commission (1915), the Federal Power Commission (1920), the Federal Communications Commission (1934), the Securities and Exchange Commission (1934), the National Labor Relations Board (1935), the Civil Aeronautics Board (1938), and the Atomic Energy Commission (1946). All of these regulatory commissions engage in policy making, regulation, and quasi-judicial activities, mostly in the economic sphere. These commissions exercise tremendous power in the fields of transportation (railroads, buses, trucks, pipelines, the merchant marine, and airlines), of communications (telephone, telegraph, radio, and television), of power and natural resources (electricity, water and flood control, and natural gas), of unfair trade practices in industry and commerce, of unfair labor practices in labor-management relations, and of banking practices, credit policies, issuance of securities, and trading in national stock markets.

The regulatory commissions generally represent the industry they are supposed to regulate, rather than "the people." One reason is that commission members are usually selected from the industry that they are supposed to regulate. As Marver Bernstein points out, "Expertness plays into the hands of regulated interest."[29] The commissions usually regard the industries they are supposed to regulate as clients who need to be promoted and protected. While the commissions may act against wayward members of an industry, they seldom do anything that is not clearly acceptable to industry leaders. This point is well illustrated in the operation of the Federal Reserve System. The Federal Reserve Board (FRB) is composed of seven men appointed by the president with the consent of the Senate for staggered terms of fourteen years; a chairman is designated by the president from among its members. The Federal Reserve Board is essentially the governing board of the nation's banking system. However, Federal Reserve Board members are generally bankers themselves, and financial support for the Federal Reserve System comes from payments made by banks that are members of the system (while only half of the nation's banks are members of the Federal Reserve System, this half possesses over 85 percent of all deposits). The policies of the FRB toward the supply of money and credit in the nation, which profoundly affect the state of the economy, generally reflect the views of bankers in economic matters. Neither the president nor Congress has direct control over the activities of the FRB.

Summary

Governmental elites in America do not command; they seek consensus. Governmental decision making involves bargaining, accommodation, and compromise among governmental and non-governmental elites. Our examination of the crisis of the presidency provides clear evidence of the consensual nature of elite interaction, and the heavy price a president must pay if he fails to pursue accommodationist politics.

1. The "separation of powers" system was designed to make it difficult for masses to capture control of the entire government, and to prevent governmental elites from abusing their power and threatening the interests of private elites. Not only did the Founding Fathers want separate branches of government to be responsive to different interests, they also wanted to give each branch of the national government some opportunity to control and check the activities of the

others. In other words, the system was designed to insure bargaining and compromise.

2. The president is the first among equals of America's elites. His real power depends not on his formal authority but on his abilities of persuasion. Moreover, the president must still function within the established elite system. The choices available to him are limited to alternatives for which he can mobilize elite support. Despite the president's access to mass opinion, he can be effectively checked by other public and private elites.

3. Traditionally, presidential decisions were usually made in consultation with key elite members inside and outside of government. These decisions reflect elite consensus, and, moreover, are incremental—they involve marginal shifts in public policy rather than radical changes in national purposes or objectives.

4. In the twentieth century, presidential power has increased as a result of the increased importance of military and foreign policy in national life—areas in which the president has greatest constitutional powers. The growth of the executive branch of government, and the increased visibility of the president in the mass media, also contribute to the growth of presidential power.

5. Controversies over presidential power can never be removed from their political context. Recently Congress has sought to curtail presidential powers over war-making, impoundment of appropriated funds, and "executive privilege."

6. The movement to impeach President Nixon was a dramatic illustration of the president's dependence upon elite support. A president must govern within the boundaries of elite consensus or face removal from office. The president can be removed not only for "high crimes and misdemeanors," but also for *political* offenses—violating elite consensus.

7. The forced resignation of Nixon was a product not only of specific crimes or improprieties in office, but also of his isolation from established elites, his failure to adopt an accommodationist style of politics, and his disregard of traditional rules of the game.

8. Popular majorities may select the president, but they do not permit him to govern. A president with an overwhelming electoral majority in November can find himself fighting to hold onto his elected office the next year. A president can only govern with the support of the nation's elite.

References

[1]Baron de Montesquieu, *The Spirit of the Laws.*

[2]James Madison, Alexander Hamilton, and John Jay, *The Federalist* No. 47 (New York: Modern Library, 1937).

[3]Madison, Hamilton, and Jay, *The Federalist* No. 51.

[4]William Howard Taft, *Our Chief Magistrate and His Powers* (New York: Columbia University Press, 1938), p. 138. Reprinted in John P. Roche and L. W. Levy (eds.), *The Presidency* (New York: Harcourt, Brace & World, 1964), p. 23.

[5]From Arthur B. Tourtellot, *Presidents on the Presidency* (Garden City, N.Y.: Doubleday & Co., 1964), pp. 55–56.

[6]Wilfred E. Binkley, *President and Congress* (New York: Alfred A. Knopf, 1947), p. 127.

[7]Fred I. Greenstein, "The Psychological Functions of the Presidency for Citizens," in Elmer E. Cornwell (ed.), *The American Presidency: Vital Center* (Chicago: Scott, Foresman and Co., 1966), pp. 30–36.

[8]Richard Neustadt, *Presidential Power* (New York: Wiley, 1960).

[9]Quoted in *Congressional Quarterly*, "The Power of the Pentagon" (Washington: Congressional Quarterly, Inc., 1972), p. 42.

[10]*Ibid.*, p. 43.

[11]*Ibid.*

[12]*Ibid.*

[13]*Congressional Quarterly* (February 10, 1973), p. 295.

[14]*Congressional Quarterly* (July 28, 1973), p. 2032.

[15]Madison, Hamilton, and Jay, *The Federalist* No. 65.

[16]*Congressional Quarterly* (January 26, 1974) p. 159.

[17]*Congressional Quarterly* (January 26, 1974) p. 127.

[18]House Judiciary Committee, Bill of Impeachment Against Richard M. Nixon, reprinted in *Newsweek*, August 5, 1974.

[19]Transcript of subpoenaed conversations between President Richard M. Nixon and H. R. Haldeman on June 23, 1972 (six days after the break-in), reprinted in *Time*, August 19, 1974.

[20]National television address of President Richard M. Nixon, August 8, 1974.

[21]James David Barber, *The Presidential Character* (New Jersey: Prentice-Hall, Inc., 1972), pp. 423–424.

[22]Arthur Schlesinger, Jr., *The Imperial Presidency* (Boston: Houghton Mifflin, 1973), p. 265.

[23]James David Barber, "Tone-Deaf in the Oval Office," *Saturday Review* (January 12, 1974), p. 14.

[24]*Ibid.*, p. 11.

[25]For further information on Richard M. Nixon's career, see his partial autobiography, *Six Crises* (Garden City, N.Y.: Doubleday, 1962).

[26]See Theodore C. Sorensen, *Decision Making in the White House* (New York: Columbia University Press, 1963).

[27]Quoted in James David Barber, *The Presidential Character* (Englewood Cliffs: Prentice-Hall, Inc., 1972), p. 81.

[28]See Richard F. Fenno, Jr., *The President's Cabinet* (Cambridge, Mass.: Harvard University Press, 1959).

[29]Marver H. Bernstein, *Regulating Business by Independent Commissions* (Princeton, N.J.: Princeton University Press, 1965), p. 118.

Selected Additional Readings

Barber, James David. *The Presidential Character: Predicting Performance in the White House.* Englewood Cliffs, N.J.: Prentice-Hall (paperback edition), 1973. This extremely readable book seeks to classify presidents along two continua—an "active-passive" baseline, according to the amount of energy and enthusiasm displayed in the exercise of presidential duties, and a "positive-negative" baseline, dealing with the degree of happiness or "fun" each president displayed in manipulating presidential power. Using these two baselines, Barber classifies the modern presidents into four types—active-positive (F.D.R., Truman, Kennedy), active-negative (Wilson, Hoover, Johnson), passive-positive (Taft, Harding), and passive-negative (Coolidge, Eisenhower). President Nixon is analyzed while in office to demonstrate the predicitive capacity of these concepts.

Lindblom, Charles E. *The Intelligence of Democracy.* New York: Free Press, 1965. Lindblom analyzes the democratic decision-making process and prescribes the "best" way of making decisions. He discusses in depth the implications of incremental decision making.

Gold, Gerald, ed. *The White House Transcripts.* New York: Bantam Books Inc., 1974. This is one of several publications which reproduce in its entirety the "Submission of Recorded Presidential Conversations to the Committee on the Judiciary of the House of Representatives by President Richard Nixon." Later versions of the recordings (including the House Judiciary Committee's version) contain some important variations from the material reported in this version.

Halberstam, David. *The Best and the Brightest.* New York: Random House, 1972. (See Chapter 4, page   .)

Neustadt, Richard. *Presidential Power.* New York: John Wiley, 1960. Neustadt focuses on the attributes of the individuals who occupy the office of the president rather than the attributes of the office itself. Instead of a discussion of the roles and formal powers attached to the presidential office, this book focuses on the ability of the president to use his personality, persuasive abilities, professional reputation, public prestige, etc., to increase his power and influence.

Rossiter, Clinton. *The American Presidency,* 2nd ed. New York: New American Library of World Literature (Mentor Books edition), 1964. This classic traditional work on the roles and powers of the president was originally published in 1956. It discusses the several roles of the president (Chief of State, Chief Executive, Commander in Chief, Chief Diplomat, Chief Legislator, Chief of Party, Chief Manager of Prosperity, etc.). In addition, Rossiter discusses the several limitations of the president's powers, the historical and modern presidency and the "hiring, firing, retiring, and expiring of presidents."

Schlesinger, Arthur, Jr. *A Thousand Days.* New York: Houghton Mifflin, 1965, and *The Imperial Presidency.* Boston: Houghton-Mifflin, 1973. *A Thousand Days* is an entertaining and instructive chronicle of the Kennedy Administration, devoted mostly to historical accounts of executive decision making, primarily in the area of foreign policy. In the *Imperial Presidency,* Schlesinger, Jr. describes the changes in the modern Presidency under Richard Nixon which he believes have resulted in an alarming concentration of power in just one man—Nixon. The argument runs directly counter to an earlier liberal point of view which held that the presidency—especially the presidency in the hands of Democrats—was not sufficiently powerful to push public-regarding public policy through a conservative, obstructionist Congress.

Wildavsky, Aaron. *The Politics of the Budgetary Process.* Boston: Little, Brown, 1964. An excellent book describing with considerable clarity the process of federal budgetmaking. He concludes "budgeting turns out to be an incremental process, proceeding from a historical base, guided by accepted notions of fair shares, in which decisions are fragmented, made in sequence by specialized bodies, and coordinated through multiple feedback mechanisms." (p. 62) The importance of this book is that it demonstrates the politics of policy formation and the extreme difficulties to be encountered in attempting radical change.

CHAPTER 10:

CONGRESS: THE LEGISLATIVE ELITE

Congress was established to represent the "people" in policy making. But how does Congress "represent" the people, and who are "the people" that Congress represents? It is our contention that because of the way congressmen are elected, Congress tends to represent local elites in America and thereby injects a strong parochial influence into national decision making. Congressmen are part of local elite structures; they retain their local businesses, club memberships, and religious affiliations. Also, congressmen are recruited by local elites rather than national elites. They are not responsible to national political leaders but rather to leaders within their home constituency. Thus, congressmen represent many small segments of the nation, rather than the nation as a whole.

The Social Backgrounds of Congress: The Class Bias

The "representational bias" of Congress begins with recruitment. Senators and representatives are seldom recruited from the masses, but have their origins in the well-educated, prestigiously employed, successful, and affluent upper and upper-middle classes. The occupations of the fathers of congressmen are a reasonably accurate indicator of the class origins of congressmen; and with few exceptions, congressmen are the sons of professional men, business owners and managers, or successful farmers and land owners.[1] Only a small minority are the sons of wage earners or salaried workers. When this fact is compared with the occupational characteristics of the labor force in 1900, which is about the period when many of our present congressmen were born, the overrepresentation of upper-class families is clear. In 1900, wage earners and salaried workers formed the overwhelming majority of the population.

The occupational characteristics of congressmen themselves also show that they are generally of higher social standing than their constituents; professional and business occupations dominate the halls of Congress. One reason for this is, of course, that candidates for Congress are more likely to be successful if their occupations are socially "respectable" and provide opportunities for extensive public contacts. The lawyer, insurance man, farm implement dealer, and real estate man establish in their business the wide circle of friends necessary for political success. Another more subtle reason is that candidates and elected congressmen must come from occupational groups with flexible work responsibilities. The lawyer, landowner, or business owner can adjust his work to the campaign and then the legislative schedule, but the office manager cannot.

The overrepresentation of lawyers as an occupational group in Congress and other public offices is particularly marked, since lawyers constitute no more than two tenths of 1 percent of the labor force.[2] Lawyers have always played a prominent role in the American political system. Twenty-five of the 52 signers of the Declaration of Independence and 31 of the 55 members of the Continental Congress were lawyers. The legal profession has also provided 70 percent of the presidents, vice presidents, and Cabinet officers of the United States; 50 percent of the United States senators from 1947 to 1957; and 56 percent of the members of the House of Representatives from 1949 to 1951. In 1973, 63 percent of the senators and 48 percent of the representatives were lawyers. Lawyers are in a reasonably high-prestige occupation, but so are physicians, businessmen, and scientists. Why then do lawyers, rather than members of these other high-prestige groups, dominate Congress?

It is sometimes argued that the lawyer brings a special kind of skill to Congress. The lawyer's occupation is the representation of clients; therefore, he makes no great change in occupation when he moves from representing clients in private practice to representing constituents in Congress. Also, the lawyer is trained to deal with public policy as it is reflected in the statute books, so he may be reasonably familiar with public policy before entering Congress. But professional skills alone cannot explain the dominance of lawyers in public office. One answer is evident in the fact that of all the high-prestige occupations, only lawyers can really afford to neglect their careers for political activities. The physician, the corporate businessman, and the scientist find the neglect of their vocation for political activity very costly. But political activity can be a positive advantage to the occupational advancement of a lawyer—free public advertising and opportunities to make contacts with potential clients are two important benefits. Another answer is the fact that lawyers naturally have a monopoly on public offices in the law and the court system, and the offices of judge or prosecuting attorney often provide lawyers with steppingstones to higher public office, including Congress.

To sum up, information on the occupational background of congressmen indicates that more than high social status is necessary for election to Congress. It is also helpful to have experience in interpersonal relations and public contacts, easy access to politics, and a great deal of free time to devote to political activity.[3]

Congressmen are among the most educated occupational groups in the United States. They are much better educated than the populations they represent. Of course, their education reflects their occupational background and their middle- and upper-class origins.

White Anglo-Saxon Protestants (WASPs) are substantially overrepresented in Congress. About two thirds of the House, and three fourths of the Senate, are Protestant. The main minority groups—blacks, Catholics, Jews, and foreign-born—have fewer seats in Congress than their proportion of the population would warrant. Religious denominations of high social status, such as Episcopalians and Presbyterians, are regularly overrepresented in Congress. About one third of the United States senators and representatives are affiliated with the Congregational, Presbyterian, Episcopalian, or Unitarian churches. Although the representation of Catholics and Jews has been increasing in recent years, evidence indicates that these minorities can only win representation in Congress in districts in which they constitute a majority or near majority. Nearly all Catholic and Jewish congressmen are elected from Northern and industrial states, notably from major cities; Mississippi, Georgia, and South Carolina send congressional delegations composed largely of Baptists and Methodists; whereas New York City sends delegations almost solidly Catholic and Jewish. Apparently congressmen must be of the religious and ethnic backgrounds dominant in their districts.

If blacks were to have representation in Congress equal to their proportion of the population, there would be 43 blacks in the House of Representatives and ten in the Senate. However, until 1966, when Republican Edward Brooke of Massachusetts was elected, no black was ever popularly elected to the Senate; and in the Ninety-third Congress (1971–1973), there were 12 blacks in the House of Representatives. Their districts were chiefly the black ghetto areas of these large cities—Chicago, New York, Philadelphia, Los Angeles, Cleveland, and Baltimore. All were Democrats.

Elite-Mass Interaction: Legislators and the Folks Back Home

Larger Constituencies Give Legislators More Freedom A congressman must concern himself with the interests of local elites; he is not as free as the president or the executive elites to direct himself to national problems or concerns. Moreover, a congressman represents a more homogeneous constituency than the president; a congressman's constituency is usually well defined—rural or urban, mining or manufacturing or agricultural, defense-oriented or cotton-producing or citrus-growing. A president, on the other hand, must please a much wider and more heterogeneous constituency. No single interest need dominate his judgment; he is freer to seek bargains, accommodations, and compromises among separate elites. He is freer to be concerned about the general welfare, and he can take a more cosmopolitan view of national affairs. Similarly, senators, who represent larger constituencies than representatives, are somewhat less parochial and are freer to be concerned about the general public welfare. Lewis A. Froman presents evidence that senators support "liberal" measures more often than do representatives, and he suggests that this difference in political behavior may result from the narrower constituencies of representatives and the localism of their political orientation.[4]

The inference here is not that larger constituencies are more liberal, but rather that they are more heterogeneous. There is more of an opportunity to pick and choose from among the various demands. The comparative liberalism of the Senate appears to be remarkably stable. A study of all employment, housing, health care, education, and welfare measures from 1955 through 1970 reveals the Senate to be consistently more inclined toward spending for such legislation.[5] What does such a phenomenon tell us about the representation of constituents by legislators? Is the Senate or the House of Representatives "right," that is, more reflective of the opinions of its constituents?

Take, for example, a variety of the most politically "hot" topics discussed widely in the media during the 1970s. A CBS poll revealed that, as expected, the Senate was more "liberal" than the House, but that *both*

Table 10-1 / Comparison of Public and Congressional Opinion on Key Policy Issues, 1970

	Public	U.S. House Members	U.S. Senators
1. Vietnam: Percent say "speed up our withdrawal"	27	30	45
2. Defense: Percent say "place less emphasis" on military weapons programs	30	37	45
3. Guaranteed Income: Percent approve at least "$1600 for a family of four or more"	48	65	76
4. Civil Rights: Percent say government should go farther to improve blacks' conditions	53	58	76
5. Supreme Court: Percent deny it gives "too much consideration to rights of people suspected of crimes"	29	36	56

Source: Robert S. Erickson and Norman Luttbeg, *American Public Opinion* (New York: John Wiley, 1973), p. 257.

representative bodies were more "liberal" than the mass public. (See Table 10–1.) Such a finding comes as no surprise to those who have followed our argument. We argue that elites (in this case, representatives) are typically more committed to the principles of democratic government than are masses. Here we find the elites also more sympathetic to the acceptance of new ideas. Note, however, that the congruence between the members of the House of Representatives and the public is greater than the congruence between the Senate and the public.

Obviously, such findings provide no more than a clue to the nature of the representative process. The table says nothing about the sharing of policy preferences between particular sets of constituents and their representatives. If we turn to such a match-up, we begin to see that the process of representation is considerably more complex than simply speaking for "the people."

It is not rare to find two senators from the same state voting in opposition to each other on a variety of issues. On one of the key issues of 1972, the withdrawal from Indochina amendment to the military aid authorization bill, twenty-six states were represented by senators who voted in opposition to each other. There are a considerable number of states habitually represented by senators whose philosophy and voting behavior are rarely congruent. The Americans for Democratic Action, a liberal group, and the Americans for Constitutional Action, a conservative organization, provide "grades" by regularly assessing the performance of representatives, which illuminate the point. (See Table 10–2.)

Table 10-2 / Selected Senators' Performance Assessed by ADA and ACA

	(1972) ADA Rating	(1972) ACA Rating
Arkansas		
McClellan (D)	10	69
Fulbright (D)	50	22
Idaho		
Church (D)	70	17
McClure (R)	0	94
*Iowa		
Hughes (D)	97	10
Miller (R)	13	82
Michigan		
Hart (D)	95	5
Giffin (R)	15	74
New Hampshire		
McIntyre (D)	35	33
Cotton (R)	0	76
New York		
Buckley (Cons)	10	45
Javitz (R)	80	15
North Dakota		
Burdick (D)	75	14
Young (R)	5	82
Utah		
Moss (D)	70	15
Bennett (R)	5	90

*1971

Source: Compiled from Michael Barone, Grant Ujifusa, and Douglas Matthews, *The Almanac of American Politics* (Boston: Gambit, 1974).

Unless we assume that voters in such states prefer that their representation be, in effect, neutralized, we need to look closer at the communication between the leaders and the led.*

Elites: The Relevant Constituents   What can we make of this apparent confusion? Let us answer with another, more basic question: Who *are* the

---

*A particularly intriguing case is South Dakota, represented for years by Karl Mundt, a staunch conservative, and by George McGovern, temporary leader of the "New Politics." McGovern, long an opponent of the War in Vietnam, became a stand-in for Robert Kennedy in 1968 after the assassination. Re-elected in 1968, his voting record became steadily more liberal. His ADA rating jumped from 43 in 1968 to 84 in 1970. Mundt, in contrast, stood even more firmly in support of the war than Richard Nixon, and compiled a voting record rated by the ADA as between 0 and 6. In 1972, this liberal-conservative balance was shattered. McGovern's voting record reverted to its pre-New Politics moderation with an ADA rating of 45. Mundt's replacement, James Abourezk (D.), compiled a substantially more liberal voting record (63). Thus, McGovern became the *conservative* half of the equation!

constituents of a congressman? The relevant political constituency of a congressman is not the general population of the district; it is the elite (or elites) of the district.

We should think of a constituency *not* as an aggregate body of people, but as a relatively small group of political activists. Such activists are those with the time, interest, and skill to communicate about political events. Consequently, they are of a disproportionately high social status, as high (or higher) than their representatives. For the great mass of the people, Congress is simply an institution with very low salience. A study commissioned by the Senate Subcommittee on Intergovernmental Relations discovered some grim facts about the public's awareness of Congress.

Only 59 percent of a national sample of Americans could identify *one* senator from their state, and barely half were aware of his party affiliation. With regard to the *second* senator, only a paltry 39 percent even knew his name! Members of the House of Representatives, those allegedly closer to their constituents, fared even worse. Only 46 percent could identify their representative, and only 41 percent were aware of his political affiliation. Further, impressive minorities were ignorant of even the most rudimentary institutional arrangements. For example, 20 percent were under the impression that Congress included the Supreme Court![6] Such confusion leads to an inability to assess performance, even in the most general terms. We know, for instance, that a person's party identification colors his perception of governmental performance. Thus, Democrats should be expected to rate Democratic-controlled Congresses more favorably. However, individual party identification operates in such a way as to inflate estimation of congressional performance when the White House, rather than Congress, is controlled by the party of individual preference. The "government," rather than its components, is being assessed.

It is important to realize that the poll was taken in the midst of the Watergate investigation, a time when attention was probably at its sharpest focus! Even the most tumultuous events apparently fail to stimulate the mass of the population to acquire the most elementary knowledge about Congress. One cannot expect the "man on the street" to write a congressman whose name he does not know.

An excellent example is provided by the debate upon, and ultimate defeat of, the funding for the Supersonic Transport in 1970 and 1971. Heavily lobbied against by environmental groups, vigorously supported by the President, viewed as necessary for economic survival by a depressed aircraft industry, extensively covered by the media, the target of a Senate filibuster of two weeks, the SST became a symbol of the struggle of environmentalists against unchecked industrial expansion. In this particularly bitter fight, Common Cause made one of its first appearances. Common Cause, the latest in a series of "citizen lobbies," led the fight against a strong coalition of business and labor groups, guided by the administration. Here, then, are "the people"* defeating the "establishment." Soon after Congress voted to terminate funds to the SST, a poll of selected congressional districts revealed more than two thirds of the respondents were uncertain of their representative's position. Among those claiming to know, about half were wrong. As Erikson and Luttbeg explain: "Thus, the voters were almost totally unaware of how their Congressman voted on an issue that had commanded a major share of newspaper headlines for a period of months."[7]

Such lack of policy-oriented information means that even when a congressman is known, such knowledge is likely to be based upon vague impressions rather than specific policy positions taken, or for that matter, even a more general knowledge of the main thrust of a congressman's position. Hence, Miller and Stokes found that, among those who offered a reason for candidate choice, only 7 percent indicated that their choice had any "discernible issue content." By this general definition of issue content (for example, the congressman is "for the working man"), only a tiny fraction of the population can qualify as an attentive public. If more stringent standards are imposed, such as detailed information about policy stands, only a "chemical trace" of the population qualify as attentive.

But surely legislators are not totally free of input from their districts. *Somebody* communicates, on some issues. After all, we read of floods of letters demanding the impeachment of President Nixon. Approximately 15 percent of the population has *ever* written a letter to their congressman, and 3 percent of the population accounts for over two thirds of congressional mail. During periods of turmoil the flow of letters becomes more urgent. Thus about one third of the public claims to have written in regard to the Watergate scandal. Even if we disallow the normal tendency to inflate, and assume the figure to be accurate, one can hardly regard one third of the population as indicative of a veritable flood. Yet it is generally assumed that the Watergate scandal involved widespread popular response. Certainly, Watergate stimulated an unusually high public communication, but only by comparison with "normal" times. However, even in situations approaching a state of siege, the flow of communication is unrepresentative. As Miller and Stokes put it:

The communication most Congressmen have with their districts inevitably puts them in touch with organized groups and individuals who are relatively well

---

*Common Cause, like all organizations, is disproportionately representative of the middle to upper social classes.

informed about politics . . . as a result, his sample of contacts with a constituency . . . is heavily biased.[8]

The relevant constituents of a congressman, then, are the active, interested, and resourceful elites of his home district. Usually these are the key economic elites of his district. In an agricultural district, they are the leaders of the American Farm Bureau Federation and the major agricultural producers—cotton producers, wheat growers, dairymen, tobacco growers, peanut producers, or others. In the Southwest, a congressman's key constituents may be oil producers or cattlemen; in the mountain states, the copper, lead, and silver mining interests; in upper New England, the lumber, granite, and fishing interests; in central Pennsylvania and West Virginia, the coal interests and leaders of the United Mine Workers. In more heterogeneous urban constituencies, there may be a variety of influential constituents—bankers and financial leaders, real estate owners and developers, owners and managers of large industrial and commercial enterprises, top labor leaders, and the owners and editors of newspapers and radio and television facilities. In certain big city districts with strong, disciplined party organizations, the key constituents of a congressman may be the city's political and governmental elites—the city or county party chairmen or the mayor. And, of course, anyone who makes major financial contributions to a congressman's campaign is always considered an important constituent, for many congressmen are hard put to find enough money to finance the increasingly expensive costs of campaigning.

Sending the Message to Legislators

The messages which are transmitted from the elite of the constituency to its representative tend, in most cases, to be in *agreement* with the representative's known policy preferences. Representatives, like most people, tend to associate with people with whom they agree. Contacts with the constituency will then be maintained largely through those who knew him before he was elected, and who continue the association. Two thirds of the representative's information about constituency preferences are gained through such personal contact, with another 25 percent obtained by mail. Thus, representatives, in effect, hear what they want to hear. Perhaps this example of selective perception helps explain why one so frequently hears conflicting reports of public opinion. Barry Goldwater, for example, was allegedly perplexed about his presidential aspirations in 1964. On the one hand, his mail offered a source of considerable encouragement. On the other hand, poll data suggested that his chances were slim. In an ingenious examination of the Goldwater campaign, the Survey Research Center of the University of Michigan found an explanation. Among the tiny minority of active communicators, Goldwater held a clear lead over Johnson. Further, in Goldwater's "public," those with whom he communicated, his position against the growth of bureaucracy in federal government is supported by a 3 to 1 ratio. However, the vast majority of less active constituents did not show this concern, nor did they support the Goldwater candidacy.[9] Small wonder that Goldwater was perplexed! Similarly, during the height of the Vietnam War, congressional mail (originating from less than 3 percent of the population), was nearly twice as hawkish as was the population.

Constituency communications, then, are sources of encouragement. Consider the ebb and flow of communication surrounding the investigation of Watergate. At various junctures, most usually when President Nixon has made a public statement, we learn that his mail is quite favorable. Simultaneously, Senator Ervin's committee indicated *its* mail was equally favorable. As V. O. Key notes: "Those who write letters to the White House tend to write in support or approbation rather than in criticism. . . . The tendency to write letters of approval doubtless gives Presidents, Senators, Congressmen, and other officials a distorted notion of the nature of public response to their actions and positions."[10] Two legislators from the same constituency, who take opposing points of view on a particular issue, are therefore probably speaking the truth when they claim (as they usually do) that an overwhelming majority of their mail supports the position they have taken.

As we have seen, communication of legislators with local *elites* is relatively intense. Given the fact that elite opinions are not those of the masses, a general lack of congruence between what the masses want and what the legislator actually does is hardly surprising. On particularly salient issues, those issues which minimize the distortion in communication, the congruence between legislative performance and constituency demand can be relatively high. On civil rights issues, for instance, congressional voting and constituency opinion is highly correlated. On most other issues, however, the correlation between constituency attitude and legislative behavior are low. That is to say, if the constituents knew what their representative was doing, they would not be particularly happy (or unhappy, since Congress is of such low salience). Except for the few major issues—such as civil rights—the "average" constituent would say of his representative's behavior: "I don't like it; I don't dislike it; I just don't think about it very much."

The English political philosopher Edmund Burke's classic question about representation—Should the legislator be guided by his party, his constituents, or his own conscience?—is thus somewhat artificial, but by no means irrelevant. Granted that constituents form the weakest link in the chain (the congressional party and one's personal judgment are much more immediate), there is the intriguing question of what legislators believe about their constituency and about their appropriate representative roles.

In viewing their task, representatives indicate a dominant concern with the role of "tribune." Such a role orientation is defined by Roger Davidson as the "discover, reflector, or advocate of popular needs and wants."[11] Clearly, the dominance of the role suggests a desire to "represent," that is, do what "the people" want. As one congressman expressed it: "Represent the people . . . that's the first duty . . . do exactly what the name 'Representative' implies." Such a response is typical of elites, whose idealistic images of government belie their power.

However, having said that elites are not cynical, keep in mind that tribunes have to "discover" opinion. Perceiving oneself as a spokesman for the people is hardly a limiting concept. Virtually every tyrant from Caligula to Hitler has perceived himself as representing the "true will" of the people. In seeking the people's will, legislators fall prey to a typical occupational disease of elites: exaggeration of mass awareness of their activities. In most cases, their perception of constituency opinion is in error, but their vote is significantly correlated with their *perception* of constituency opinion. In other words, representatives think they are reflecting opinion; indeed, they *want* to represent opinion. They err in perception rather than intent.

Legislators believe people know what they are up to. They believe their individual actions have such an impact upon the electorate that a "wrong" vote could cost them dearly. This false attribution of attention is one of the many "sub-ironies" of democracy. If legislators really believed what political scientists tell them, perhaps they would behave quite differently! Their mistaken image of their own self-importance is the strongest link to mass opinion, even if they err in their perceptions of such opinion.

One should also remember that representation involves a great deal more than voting. There is also the well-developed process of securing economic benefits for the constituency. Defense industries and military bases are especially important constituents in a large number of congressional districts, because of the very visible economic benefits that derive from them for the district. Fewer than 75 of the 435 members of the House of Representatives do *not* have a major defense plant or a military installation in their district. The opening, expansion, cut-back, or closing of military bases is of vital interest to the congressman whose district is concerned, as is the awarding of prime military contracts.

Congressmen work very hard to secure military bases or contracts for their district. An often-cited example of the congressional quest for military-industrial constituents is the state of Georgia, which is represented by the chairman of the Senate Armed Services Committee, Richard B. Russell, and until his retirement in 1965, by the chairman of the House Armed Services Committee, Carl M. Vinson. A general once remarked regarding military installations in Georgia, "One more base would sink the state." Georgia, hardly an industrial state, ranked tenth in prime military contracts. When the first C5-A cargo plane was completed, President Johnson warmly complimented the Georgia delegation for landing the contract for their state: "I would have you good folks of Georgia know that there are a lot of Marietta, Georgias scattered throughout the fifty states . . . all of them would like to have the pride that comes from this production . . . but all of them don't have the Georgia delegation."[12]

Such efforts on the behalf of local elites probably produce more insurance for longevity than a "good" voting record. In any case, since congressmen are products of the social system in their constituency, they share its dominant goals and values. They have deep roots in the social system of their constituency—many organizational memberships, many overlapping leadership positions, lifetime residency, close ties with social and economic elites, shared religious affiliations, and so on. A congressman is so much "of" his constituency that he needs little direct prompting or supervision from local elites, and conflicts seldom occur between his own views and the dominant views in his constituency.

While we cannot say with assurance what the representative process *is,* we certainly know what it is *not.* It is not the representation of the will of "the people." At best, representation is intra-elite communication.

The Re-election of Incumbents

There are, of course, elections. The ultimate reprisal for a congressman who fails to keep his ear to the ground is to be sent packing. Congressmen, of course, subscribe to the popular theory of representative government, summarized by Charles O. Jones: "[Election time] is the period of accounting: either the representative is instructed further, or he is defeated for malrepresentation, or he is warned, or he is encouraged."[13]

Actually, we know that very little of this accounting takes place. In brief, incumbents rarely lose. Indeed, if we accept the standard theory of election, Americans are ecstatic over the performance of Congress. Roughly 81 percent of the senators who seek re-election win; and a whopping 93 percent of House members who seek re-election win also.

A glance at Table 10–3 will bring us back to our earlier point from another perspective. Popular support for Congress is diminishing; criticism is increasing. But are the rascals to be thrown out? Clearly not. Not only are incumbents routinely returned to their seats; the postwar trend is toward even greater safety for incumbents. Notice the continuation of the trend in 1974, the year of an alleged revulsion against incumbents as a consequence of a general negative reaction to politics.

Table 10-3 / Popular Support for Congress and Re-election of Incumbents

	% of Public Expressing Positive Rating of Congress	% Sen. Incumbents Re-elected.	% House Incumbents Re-elected.
1948		65%	
1950		80	
1952		74	
1954		85	95%
1956		86	96
1958		65	91
1960		96	94
1962		90	96
1964		93	88
1965	64%		
1966	49	96	90
1967	38		
1968	46	83	96
1969	34		
1970	34	88	95
1971	26		
1972	24	84	93
1974	29	92	90

Such a finding should not be surprising. We know that the electorate has a marked inability to identify their representatives in Congress. We can imagine how many voters can identify his opponent. Name familiarity—in the absence of any knowledge of issues—can be a powerful advantage. The average voter, if he is aware of the incumbent, is likely to perceive him favorably and vote for him.

Additionally, incumbents are likely to have developed a more effective political organization and a stable network of communication with local elites. The assiduous incumbent can use his franking privilege for mailing newsletters, polls, and other information; he can appear at various public events, call news conferences, address organizational meetings, and, in general, make himself as visible as possible with a minimum of expense.

By developing such ties with local elites, and because the "smart money" will back a winner, incumbents have more to spend, thus maximizing exposure. Incumbents are generally able to raise almost twice as much as challengers. Regardless of party, Senate incumbents in 1972 spent an average of $480,000 to get re-elected, while their challengers spent, on the average, $244,000. In the House, the cost is less, but the discrepancy equal. Incumbents spent roughly $50,000, their challengers, $30,000.

The growing influence of incumbency upon electoral success calls our attention again to the discussion of the constituency–legislator linkage. The cue for voters is incumbency (name familiarity), rather than issue position or even party affiliation (as the role of incumbency grows, the role of party identification is weakened). Clearly, then, Congress is an institution which can generally operate free of mass reprisals: "We have neither a Democratic nor a Republican party. Rather, we have an incumbency party which operates a monopoly."[14]

Congress and the President: An Unstable Balance of Power

What is the difference between the role of Congress and the role of other elites? Policy proposals are initiated outside Congress; Congress's role is to respond to proposals from the president, executive and military elites, and interested non-governmental elites. Congress does not merely ratify or "rubber stamp" decisions, it plays an independent role in the policy-making process. But this role is essentially a deliberative one, in which Congress accepts, modifies, or rejects the policies initiated by others. For example, the national budget, perhaps the single most important policy document, is written by executive and military elites and modified by the president before it is submitted to Congress. Congress may make further modifications, but it does not formulate the budget. Of course, Congress is a critical obstacle through which appropriations and revenue measures must pass. But sophisticated lawmakers are aware that they function as arbiters rather than initiators of public policy. As Robert Dahl explains:

The Congress no longer expects to originate measures but to pass, veto, or modify laws proposed by the Chief Executive. It is the President, not the Congress, who determines the content and substance of the legislation with which Congress deals. The President is now the motor of the system; the Congress applies the brakes. The President gives what forward movement there is in the system; his is the force of thrust and innovation. The Congress is the force of inertia–a force, it should be said, that means not only restraint, but stability in politics.[15]

The relationship between Congress and other policy-making elites is not necessarily stable. Whether Congress operates merely to ratify the decisions of others, or to assert its voice independently depends upon a variety of factors: the aggressiveness and skill of the president, the strength of congressional leadership, and so on. Nevertheless, except in cases of unusually passive presidents (such as Eisenhower), Congress—however tenacious it appears in rejecting policy—rarely *initiates* policy.

From a constitutional point of view, of course, the potential for power in Congress is very great. Article I empowers Congress to levy taxes, borrow and spend money, regulate interstate and foreign commerce, coin money, declare war, maintain armies and navies, and a number of other important functions, including the passing of all laws "necessary and proper" to carry out these powers.

The Historical Perspective   The pendulum swings back and forth between congressional and executive power, but the general trend since Roosevelt has been in the direction of the president. Powerful executives such as Lincoln and Roosevelt overrode Congress, almost by sheer force and determination; weaker ones, such as McKinley and Harding, found themselves helpless.* A key event in the struggle for power between Congress and the president was the depression of the 1930s and the creation of massive federal programs under the auspices of the New Deal. In response to economic crisis, Congress, with its cumbersome decision-making process, simply gave up. Roosevelt's first act was to close all banks by executive order, explaining that he intended to use executive power to wage war against depression just as he would do in the event of foreign invasion. In the early days of the New Deal, senators and congressmen voted for bills they had never even read; the average debate for major legislation was three hours!

Granted that these were exceptional events, it is nevertheless true that Roosevelt's "revolution" remained intact. While Congress recovered more of an active role in domestic affairs (confined, however, to the modification of executive-sponsored legislation), its role in foreign affairs has been diminished to the point of acquiescence, if that. Under the pressure of cold-war ideology, the president frequently assumed that information should be withheld; that "national security" made it imperative that congressional participation be minimized. Huge military appropriations bills routinely passed both houses with only a single day of debate, and usually without amendment. Thus, the decision to commit troops to Korea was

---

*The case of McKinley is especially interesting with the Vietnam War so close at hand. The sinking of the *Maine* in 1899 (precipitating the Spanish-American War) was as suspicious as the attack upon U.S. vessels in the Gulf of Tonkin. In both cases, however, the attack served to minimize rational discourse. In the case of McKinley, Congress forced the reluctant President to war. In the case of Vietnam, President Johnson's escalation was undertaken with only cursory attention to Congress.

made with only the most cursory communication; the decision to escalate in Vietnam was technically approved, with two days' debate, and two dissenting votes.

However, the disappointments of the Vietnam War led to congressional resurgence. This resurgence was evident in the 1970 repeal of the Gulf of Tonkin resolution. It became more apparent when Congress amended a foreign aid bill to prohibit the use of ground forces in Southeast Asia, and ultimately imposed upon President Nixon a deadline for all military activity in Vietnam. The culmination of the process of renewed congressional vigor was the passage of legislation—over presidential veto—limiting presidential power to commit troops to combat without congressional approval (Ironically, the President was given two months of unchecked war power before congressional approval was required.)

Nixon Breaks the Rules and is Penalized   The forces leading to more balanced distribution of influence was thus at hand before Watergate. President Nixon's centralization of executive authority in the White House staff challenged the established network between Congress and the various executive departments such as the Department of Health, Education and Welfare, Department of Agriculture, and Department of Commerce. Through the years, executive departments—and their bureaus— had developed an elaborate network of relationships with congressional committees and interest groups. This "subsystem" was challenged by a vast expansion of the White House staff. Nixon employed far more personal assistants than had any of his predecessors. Kennedy and Johnson averaged about 20, but in 1972 Nixon had 48. The total on the White House payroll rose from 266 in 1954 to 600 in 1971. Additionally, the Executive Office staff (as distinguished from the personal staff) grew from 1175 in 1954 to 1664 under Kennedy to 5394 during Nixon's presidency. In Nixon's first term, the operating cost of the Executive Office doubled from $31 million to $71 million.

The consequences, as Arthur Schlesinger, Jr. points out, was a radical reduction in the influence of the "normal" channels of communication:

What all this signified, and what was far more crucial than the increase in numbers and budget, was the centralization of White House substantive operations. By Nixon's time, White House aides were no longer channels of communication. They were powerful figures in themselves, making decisions in their own right, more powerful than members of the Cabinet —Kissinger more powerful than the Secretary of State [William Rogers] or Defense [Melvin Laird]. Haldeman and

Ehrlichman more powerful than the forgotten men who headed the domestic departments. But they were not, like members of the Cabinet, subject to confirmation by the Senate or (pre-Watergate) to interrogation by committees of the Congress.[16]

The result of the reduction of the influence of experienced bureaucrats, and the inflation of the influence of inexperienced amateurs, was a rapid deterioration of the bargaining and compromise which usually characterize legislative-executive relations.

The expansion of executive influence, a consequence of the demands of cold-war diplomacy, was never seriously challenged with regard to foreign policy until Nixon. In domestic matters, the president has had a much more difficult time. As Aaron Wildavsky has observed:

From the end of the 1930's to the present (what may roughly be called the modern era), presidents have often been frustrated in their domestic programs. . . . In the realm of foreign policy there has not been a single major issue on which presidents, when they were serious and determined, have failed.[17]

Nixon's foreign policy setbacks were thus extraordinary. However, such defeats were at least a partial consequence of his destruction of normal communication channels, and his unusually vigorous effort to reduce the role of Congress in *domestic* policy.

To say that the president initiates domestic policy is not to say that Congress is a rubber stamp; typically no more than half of the legislative program of a president is approved. Thus, Presidents Eisenhower, Kennedy, and Johnson requested about 4,500 separate pieces of legislation from the period 1953–1968. A slight majority were not granted.

Lyndon Johnson: How It Should Be Done   Under such circumstances, the executive office normally engages in an intensive process of bargaining, lobbying, consultation, and using external pressure on Congress. Particularly useful is the device of recruiting congressional assistance in the drafting of legislation. The relationship between Lyndon Johnson and Wilbur Mills (D-Ark.), chairman of the House Ways and Means Committee, is illustrative of these techniques. The issue was a tax increase, or more precisely a surcharge, as a device to slow the rate of inflation.

President Johnson's economic advisors were firm in their recommendations of a surcharge, as distinguished from a tax increase; organized business and labor clearly would not go along with an increase, nor would the majority of members of the House Ways and Means Committee, which has the responsibility of initiating revenue-producing legislation.

If not an increase, what? Johnson personally consulted Mills, who checked with key representatives. Johnson recalls that "With Chairman Mills, we worked on the draft of the tax message as if we were working up a bill in Executive session or in conference. . . ."[18] Mills, however, insisted on substantial cuts in government spending to accompany the surcharge. Johnson viewed such cuts as threatening to his social programs, but agreed to some reductions. These compromises, while satisfying Mills, opened the door to a more vigorous assault on the "Great Society" programs. Each proposed cut resulted in the demand for even greater reductions in expenditures. The suggested reductions eventually reached $6 billion; Johnson was hoping for $4 billion. Both sides seemed unable to modify their expectations, but finally Mills won. The Senate-House Conference Report recommended a reduction of $6 billion. Now, although Johnson was under increasing pressure (from the AFL-CIO, Urban Coalition, and other loyalists of the Great Society programs) to hold out to the bitter end, Johnson did not. He indicated that, even though the additional $2 billion reduction would endanger his domestic programs, he would trade this cost against the benefit of a surcharge, and thus the bill became a law.

Several crucial components of Johnson's mixed success deserve enunciation. First, he carefully involved Mills and other key congressmen at every phase of the negotiation. As Johnson remarked, "We made many mistakes, but failure to inform and brief the Congress was not one of them." (Johnson's willingness to share information apparently did not extend to foreign policy; e.g., the Gulf of Tonkin Resolution). Second, the Cabinet—especially the Departments of the Treasury and Commerce— were heavily involved. Through them, other normal subsystem participants were recruited. The American Bankers' Association and National Association of Manufacturers, two particularly active lobbying organizations, cooperated with appropriate cabinet officials. While business organizations were not difficult to bring into line, organized labor, sensing a major impact on the Great Society programs, was more difficult. Labor lobbyists were, in Johnson's words, "stalking the Hill," urging defeat of the legislation. Johnson held a meeting with AFL-CIO president, George Meany, and later recalled, "We talked the problem out. Several days later the labor lobbyists quietly lowered their voices."[19]

Nixon the Radical Revolutionary Such are the ways of bargaining among elites. The key participants—the president, two cabinet officials, leaders of articulate interest groups, and the chairman of a key House Committee—all knew and respected each other. Although tempers occasionally flared, the end result was really never in doubt. When the surcharge was approved, the elite participants disbanded their coalitions, only to form new ones on other issues, as they had done in the past.

With Nixon's election, the subsystem was subverted. As we have seen, the Cabinet was reduced to impotence, with major decision-making authority centering in the Executive Office. Thus, one group of the "normal" elite was replaced. The replacements were *not* known, and were widely mistrusted. The "old boy" network was shattered.

The uncomfortable feeling generated in the Congress by the disruption of communication patterns was exacerbated by Nixon's use of a variety of devices to strengthen his hand vis à vis Congress. The two most conspicuous devices were impoundment of funds authorized by Congress and executive privilege. Neither technique was unique to the Nixon presidency, but he carried them well beyond the established practice. Nixon impounded far more money than any previous president, and he did so—as it seemed to Congress—for the purpose of frustrating congressional will. Normally, impoundment was used for routine financial management, but Nixon's approach was to seek the alteration of *policy*. Programs which he viewed with disapproval were subject to impoundment, to the extent that $15 billion (roughly 20 percent of controllable funds) went unspent in 1973.

Such an interpretation of the Constitution was viewed by influential senators, notably Sam Ervin (D-N.C.) as a serious breach of the constitutional provision for separation of powers between the executive and legislative branches, all the more so since Nixon's communication network excluded established legislative elites.

Equally unusual was Nixon's use of the doctrine of executive privilege to avoid releasing information to Congress. Made famous by Nixon's use of executive privilege to resist inquiry into the Watergate affair, it actually was used far more extensively on other legislative matters. Nixon claimed an immunity from Congress and inquiry that extended to his many White House aides. Nixon prohibited Haldeman, Ehrlichman, and Kissinger from providing congressional testimony. Indeed, prior to his becoming Secretary of State (even though he was Nixon's most influential foreign policy decision maker), Henry Kissinger had never testified before Congress. William Rogers, Secretary of State, *had* testified. However, he apparently knew so little about the content of foreign policy (unless he was withholding information) that he assured the Senate Foreign Relations Committee, one week before the Cambodia invasion of 1970, that no increased military activity was anticipated in Southeast Asia.

Under pressure from the Watergate investigation, Nixon extended the claim of executive privilege to include all documents received by the president—and any members of his staff, past or present, in connection with official duties. Thus, Nixon argued, in effect, that Congress had no right to any information at all.

Such behavior was, in the literal sense, revolutionary. Although Nixon's electoral mandate was interpreted (publicly) as a demand for the return to the simpler virtues of the American past (individualism, restoration of authority to the states, etc.), his approach to Congress demonstrated that his disregard for established patterns of interaction was consistent with a revolutionary concept of the traditional distribution of influence. Kevin Phillips, a Nixon advisor, articulated the philosophy of Nixon's revolution:

> The "separation of powers" concept . . . may in fact be obsolete: an eighteenth century theory turned late twentieth century malfunction that is beginning to cause dangerous trouble. . . . "separation of powers" must be rated as one of the best dignified mistakes of the eighteenth century. . . . Congress's separate power is an obstacle to modern policymaking. . . . To marshal executive-branch power on behalf of his "New American Revolution," President Nixon is necessarily trying to end-run not only Congress, but the bureaucratic structure built up under the Democrats from 1933 to 1966.[20]

Congress—as we shall see—is an institution characterized by a fragmented power structure. Committee chairmen have traditionally maintained rarely challenged authority over the fate of legislation. Given such a structure of influence, it was impossible for either house to respond to Nixon's challenge in any manner other than a normal glacial, sporadic pattern. No single person, even leaders of the majority party, could organize a cohesive counter-attack. Nevertheless, a response gradually developed.

First of all, Nixon began his first term under a rather unusual handicap. Not since the presidency of Zachary Taylor in 1849 had a president entered office faced with opposition majorities in both the Senate and House. Nevertheless, he won on 74 percent of the 119 roll-call votes which represented a test of support for his views. Although facing potentially hostile majorities, Nixon found his own party difficult to control. His major defeat of the year was the rejection of Clement Haynsworth as a Supreme Court Justice. On this vote, the Senate Republican leadership voted against the President. An ominous key to the future was provided by Senator Charles Mathias (R-Md.), who angrily condemned the White House staff as "Prussians." Nevertheless, there was no precipitous decline in congressional support. The next year, in fact, Nixon won major victories with tough crime legislation and further deployment of the Anti-Ballistic Missile System.

It was in 1971 that the tide began to turn against the President. It is hardly coincidental that 1971 was the year Nixon began his plan to restructure government in earnest. While he was still winning at about the same rate, much of his legislation was simply never put to a vote; and major defeats, such as the refusal of Congress to fund the Supersonic Transport, provided growing evidence of Nixon's increased loss of control.

Nixon's problems with Congress were exacerbated by the 1972 election. Although he won a landslide victory, his campaign was conducted completely aloof from the campaigns of congressional Republicans, the Republican National Committee, or any normal Republican campaign operation. Not only did he ignore the established communication network in congressional relations, he insisted on a campaign which excluded the participation of Republican elites. While regarding the victory as a personal mandate, he had done nothing to increase his party's strength in Congress. Indeed, the party lineup in 1973 was the same as when Nixon began his first term. He began the year optimistically, continuing his efforts to achieve revolution. However, Watergate made most other problems minor. In the first seven months of 1973, Nixon's victory record had declined to 43 percent—the first time since 1953 that a president had managed a losing record.

The deterioration was massive, cutting across party and regional identification. As Table 10–4 indicates, the Southerners and Republicans were least likely to rebel; even here, however, the erosion of support was apparent. Nixon's special appeal to the South (the nomination of Southern-

Table 10-4 / Presidential Support, 1972–1973

	East		Midwest		South		West	
	1972	1973	1972	1973	1972	1973	1972	1973
Senate								
Democratic	36%	29%	40%	28%	60%	39%	29%	25%
Republican	63	47	66	55	73	62	64	59
House								
Democratic	48	28	44	28	48	44	45	30
Republican	70	58	63	60	58	67	63	64

Source: Compiled from *Congressional Quarterly Almanac*, vols. 27–28 (Washington, D.C.: Congressional Quarterly Service, 1973–1974).

ers to the Supreme Court, resistance to integration, etc.) did not prevent the Southern Democrats in the Senate from abandoning him. Indeed, the most visible desertion occurred among this group. Such staunch Nixon supporters as Eastland (D-Miss.), Long, (D-La.), and Ervin (D-N.C.), showed marked disinclination to go along. At no time in modern history has a president's legislative program been in such a shambles. The lesson is clear: Intra-elite bargaining and compromise are an established style Nixon did not play by elite rules, and he suffered a terrible cost.

Whether Congress is institutionally capable of regaining the initiative from a crippled president is very much in doubt. Congress, as we have seen, is accustomed to *responding* (even negatively) to presidential initiative. It is not accustomed to the development of a separate legislative program. The clearest response to the weakened presidency was the successful attempt, in 1974, to provide congressional direction (by means of centralization of budgeting authority) to the development of the federal budget, formerly the exclusive domain of the president. Whether Congress can implement the new plan is uncertain.

The Elaborate Procedures of Legislative Elites

The rules and procedures of Congress are elaborate but important to the functioning of legislative elites. A great deal of legislative debate concerns rules and procedures; and many policy questions turn on the question of proper procedure. Legislative procedures and rules make the legislative process fair and orderly; without established customs, rules, and procedures, it would be impossible for 435 men to arrive at collective decisions about the thousands of items submitted to them during a congressional session. Yet the same rules also delay or obstruct proposed changes in the *status quo;* they strengthen Congress's conservative role in policy making. Congressional procedures offer many opportunities to defeat legislation and many obstacles to the passage of legislation. Of course, it is not surprising that an elite that functions as an arbiter of public policy should operate under rules and procedures that maximize deliberation and grant advantages to those who oppose change.

Congress follows a fairly standard pattern in the formal process of making laws. Table 10–5 describes briefly some of the more important procedural steps in bill passage. Bills are generally drafted in the president's office, in executive departments, or in the offices of interested elites, but they must be formally introduced into Congress by members of the House or Senate. A bill may be introduced in either the House or the

Table 10-5 / How a Bill Becomes a Law

1. *Introduction.* Most bills can be introduced in either house. (In this table, the bill is first introduced in the Senate.) It is given a number and referred to the proper committee.
2. *Hearings.* The committee may hold public hearings on the bill.
3. *Committee action.* The full committee meets in executive (closed) session. It may kill the bill, approve it with or without amendments, or draft a new bill.
4. *Calendar.* If the committee recommends the bill for passage, it is listed on the calendar.
5. *Debate, amendment, vote.* The bill goes to the floor for debate. Amendments may be added. The bill is voted on.
6. *Introduction to the second house.* If the bill passes, it goes to the House of Representatives, where it is referred to the proper committee.
7. *Hearings.* Hearings may be held again.
8. *Committee action.* The committee rejects the bill, prepares a new one, or accepts the bill with or without amendments.
9. *Rules Committee consideration.* If the committee recommends the bill, it is listed on the calendar and sent to the Rules Committee. The Rules Committee can block a bill or clear it for debate before the entire House.
10. *Debate, amendment, vote.* The bill goes before the entire body, is debated and voted upon.
11. *Conference Committee.* If the bill as passed by the second house contains major changes, either house may request a conference committee. The conferees — five persons from each house, representing both parties — meet and try to reconcile their differences.
12. *Vote on conference report.* When they reach an agreement, they report back to their respective houses. Their report is accepted or rejected.
13. *Submission to the president.* If the report is accepted by both houses, the bill is signed by the speaker of the House and the president of the Senate and is sent to the president of the United States.
14. *Presidential action.* The president may sign or veto the bill within ten days. If he does not sign and Congress is still in session, the bill automatically becomes a law. If Congress adjourns before the ten days have elapsed, it does not become a law. (This is called the "pocket veto.") If the president returns the bill with a veto message, it may still become a law if passed by a two-thirds majority in each house.

Senate, except that bills for raising revenue are required by the Constitution to begin in the House. Upon introduction, a bill is referred to one of the standing committees of the House or the Senate, which may: (1) recommend it for adoption with only minor changes; (2) virtually rewrite the bill into a new policy proposal; (3) ignore the bill and prevent its passage through inaction; (4) kill it by majority vote. The full House or Senate *may* overrule the decision of its committees, but this is a rare occurrence. Most members of Congress are reluctant to upset the prerogatives of the committees and the desires of recognized leaders. Therefore, committees virtually have the power of life or death over every legislative measure.

The Importance of Congressional Committees Committee work is essential to the legislative process; Congress as a body could never hope to review all the measures put before it. As early as 1885, Woodrow Wilson described the American political process as "government by the standing committees of Congress." But in the process of reducing legislative work to manageable proportions, the committees exercise considerable influence over the outcome of legislation. A minority of the legislators, sometimes a single committee chairman, can delay and obstruct the legislative process.

In the Senate, the most prestigious committees are Foreign Relations, Appropriations, and Finance. In the House, the most powerful committees are the Rules Committee, Appropriations, and Ways and Means. (The 20 standing committees of the House and the 15 of the Senate are listed in Table 10–6 and 10–7.) To expedite business, most standing committees create subcommittees to handle particular matters falling within their jurisdiction. This practice further concentrates power over particular subject matter in the hands of a small number of congressmen. A great deal of power lies in the hands of subcommittee members, especially the chairmen; interested elites cultivate the favor of powerful subcommittee chairmen as well as committee chairmen.

In examining legislation, a committee or subcommittee generally holds public hearings on bills deemed worthy by the chairman or, in some cases, by the majority of the committee. Influenced by the legal profession, from which a majority of congressmen are drawn, the committees tend to look upon public hearings as trials in which contestants present their side of the argument to the committee members, the judges. Presumably, during this trial the skillful judges will sift facts on which to base their decisions. In practice, however, committees use public hearings primarily to influence public opinion, influence executive action, or, occasionally, to discover the position of major elite groups on the measure under consideration. Major decisions are made in executive session in secret.

The membership of the standing committees on agriculture, labor, interior, insular affairs, and judiciary generally reflects the interest of particular elite groups in the nation. Farm interests are represented on the agricultural committees; land, water, and natural resource interests are represented on interior and insular affairs; congressmen with labor ties and urban industrial constituencies gravitate toward the labor committee; and lawyers dominate the judicial committees of both houses.

In view of the power of congressional committees, the assignment of congressmen to committees is one of the most significant activities of Congress. In the House of Representatives, the Republicans assign their members to committees through a Committee on Committees that consists of one representative from each state sending a Republican to Congress. Each representative votes with the strength of his state delegation. But the real business of this committee is conducted by a subcommittee appointed by the Republican party leader. The subcommittee fills committee

Table 10-6 / The Standing Committees of the Senate

Committee	Name	State	First Elected	% Vote in Last Election	Age	ADA* Rating	Busing**	Cambodia*** Bombing
Foreign Relations	Fulbright	Ark.	1944	59	69	50	AGN	AGN
Appropriations	McClellan	Ark.	1942	61	76	10	AGN	AGN
Finance	Long	La.	1948	U	56	15	FOR	FOR
Agriculture	Talmadge	Ga.	1956	78	61	10	AGN	AGN
Armed Services	Stennis	Miss.	1947	88	73	0	AGN	ABS
Judiciary	Eastland	Miss.	1942	58	70	5	AGN	FOR
Commerce	Magnuson	Wash.	1944	65	69	60	FOR	AGN
Banking	Sparkman	Ala.	1946	62	75	0	ABS	FOR
Rules	Cannon	Nev.	1958	58	62	25	AGN	ABS
Interior	Jackson	Wash.	1952	82	62	40	ABS	FOR
Post Office	McGee	Wyo.	1958	56	59	35	FOR	ABS
Public Works	Randolph	W. Va.	1958	66	72	40	AGN	AGN
Government Operations	Ervin	N.C.	1954	61	76	10	AGN	ABS
D.C.	Eagleton	Mo.	1968	51	45	70	FOR	AGN
Labor	Williams	N.J.	1958	55	55	85	FOR	AGN
Aeronautics and Space	Moss	Utah	1958	56	63	70	FOR	AGN
Veterans Affairs	Hartke	Ind.	1958	50	55	65	ABS	AGN

Source: Compiled from Barone, *et al., The Almanac of American Politics.*

* The rating by the Liberal Americans For Democratic Action. Scores represent percentage of votes in agreement with ADA positions in 1972 and 1973.

** Use of federal funds to force districts to transport students to different schools to achieve racial balance.

***Prohibition of funds for use in Cambodia or Laos (a yes vote is against bombing. Those who so voted are listed here as "against").

Table 10-7 / The Standing Committees of the House

Committee	Name	State	First Elected	% Vote in Last Election	Age	ADA* Rating	Busing*	Cambodia* Bombing
Rules	Madden	Ind.	1942	57	82	81	FOR	AGN
Appropriations	Mahon	Tex.	1934	U	74	6	AGN	FOR
Ways and Means	Mills	Ark.	1938	U	65	19	AGN	AGN
Armed Services	Herbert	La.	1940	U	73	0	AGN	FOR
Bank and Commerce	Patman	Tex.	1929	U	81	13	AGN	FOR
Agriculture	Poage	Tex.	1936	U	75	6	AGN	FOR
Education and Labor	Perkins	Ky.	1948	62	62	38	FOR	AGN
Government Operations	Holifield	Cal.	1942	67	71	50	FOR	AGN
Public Works	Blatnik	Minn.	1947	76	63	50	FOR	AGN
Judiciary	Rodino	N.J.	1948	80	65	88	FOR	AGN
Interstate and Foreign Commerce	Staggers	W. Va.	1949	70	67	31	AGN	FOR
Foreign Affairs	Morgan	Pa.	1944	61	68	69	FOR	AGN
Interior and Insular	Haley	Fla.	1952	58	75	0	AGN	FOR
Science and Aeronautics	Teague	Tex.	1946	72	64	6	AGN	ABS
Post Office and Civil Service	Dulski	N.Y.	1958	72	59	50	AGN	AGN
Veterans Affairs	Dorn	S.C.	1950	75	58	19	FOR	FOR
Merchant Marine and Fisheries	Sullivan	Mo.	1952	69	–	38	AGN	AGN
D.C.	Diggs	Mich.	1954	86	52	88	FOR	AGN
Internal Security	Ichord	Mo.	1960	62	48	19	AGN	FOR
House Administration	Hays	Ohio	1948	70	63	38	AGN	FOR

Source: Compiled from Barone, *et al., The Almanac of American Politics.*

*See Table 10-6.

vacancies with freshman congressmen and members who are requesting transfer from other committees. The Committee on Committees considers the career backgrounds of congressmen, their seniority, and their reputation for "soundness," which usually means adherence to conservative policy positions. Often, the chairman of a standing committee tells the Committee on Committees whom he prefers to have on his committee. Democrats in the House are assigned by a Committee on Committees composed exclusively of Democrats on the prestigious Ways and Means Committee. In the Senate, Republican committee positions are filled by a Committee on Committees, and Democratic committee positions are selected by a steering committee appointed by the Democratic floor leader. Usually, only senators with seniority are eligible for major committee positions in the Senate, such as Foreign Relations, Armed Services, and Appropriations.

Committee chairmen are very powerful. They usually determine which bills will be considered by the committee, whether or not public hearings will be held, and what the agenda of the committee will be. The chairman of the committee is officially consulted on all questions relating to his committee; this procedure gives him status with the executive branch and with interested non-governmental elites. Only occasionally is the chairman's decision about a committee matter overruled by a majority within the committee.

The Seniority System   The practice of awarding chairmanships according to seniority is another guarantee of conservatism in the legislative process. The member of the majority party having the longest continuous service on the committee becomes chairman; the member of the minority party with the longest continuous service on the committee is the ranking minority member. Therefore chairmen are not chosen by their own committees, by their own party, or by the House and Senate as a whole. They are chosen by the voters of non-competitive congressional districts, for the congressmen from these districts are likely to stay in office the longest. Thus, the major decisions in Congress are made by men from areas where party competition and voter participation is low; in the past, these areas have been Southern and rural constituencies and big city machine constituencies. In both chambers, the seniority system works against the competitive urban and suburban districts. In 1971, both parties modified seniority to allow review and ratification by the party caucus. In practice, neither party caucus has challenged the seniority tradition, with the conspicuous exception of the Senate Budget Committee, established in 1974 to provide central budgetary control.

As can be seen in Tables 10–6 and 10–7, the seniority system has a "redistributive" effect. In both the Senate and House, Southerners hold approximately half of the committee chairmanships. The committees are ranked in an order of descending prestige. This ranking indicates more firmly the effects of seniority; the top Senate chairmanships are held by Southerners. In the House, with the important exception of the Rules Committee, one has to drop down to eighth most prestigious committee to find a chink in the Southern armor.

Seniority lends a rather conservative cast to the congressional leadership (remember, however, that Congress is more liberal than its constituents). Consider, for example, the Senate committee leadership: Fulbright (D-Ark.), McClellan (D-Ark.), Long (D-La.), Talmadge (D-Ga.), Stennis (D-Miss.), and Eastland (D-Miss.). Except for Fulbright, these senators are distinguished by their conservative voting records. Three (Eastland, Stennis, and Talmadge), are consistent supporters of the "conservative coalition" (see Table 10–11, p. 362). When the Democrats are able to organize Congress, conservative interests are overrepresented. When Republicans are able to organize Congress, this is not the case, since the South does not elect as many Republicans as do other regions of the country.

Conspicuous by their absence in key committee assignments are legislators from the most populous states in the country—New York, California, and Illinois. Also notably absent are senators whose public visibility far exceeds their influence: Goldwater, Kennedy, Humphrey, McGovern, and Muskie. In the world of the Senate, their power is considerably less than that of, say, Senator Eastland of Mississippi, whose influence over the appointment of Supreme Court justices is legend. Eastland came to the Senate in 1942, when Edward Kennedy was ten years old.

As their influence *within* Congress grows, so does the tendency of high-seniority legislators to identify with Congress as an institution, to the decline of possible constituency influences. Two factors are at work here. On the one hand, legislators get to know each other well (a legislator can see a colleague, but not a constituent, on a regular basis). On the other hand, older legislators probably have learned from experience that the expected vigorous constituency response to a perceived "unpopular" vote simply does not materialize. Having learned the low visibility of his behavior, the experienced congressman may develop a more realistic view of the electorate: ". . . after several terms, I don't give a damn any more. I'm pretty safe now and I don't have to worry about reaction in the district."[21] Also, legislators learn about their constituency; their colleagues learn about them. They develop expertise, specializing in certain kinds of legislation, and are viewed as credible sources of information. As one congressman phrases it: "That's the beauty of the seniority system—there are informed, experienced people on each Committee you can consult."[22] Indeed, when congressmen really need advice, in the majority of cases, they will turn to someone of higher seniority.

Initial committee assignment is, of course, not strictly made according to seniority. Once a committee assignment is made, the legislator can remain, building up seniority. First, though, each party must make its selection. In the Senate, as we stated earlier, the Democratic Steering Committee and Republican Committee on Committees have this task. In the House, Democratic committee assignments are controlled by that party's members of the Ways and Means Committee, while the Republicans use a Committee on Committees. Common to all these units is the fact that the process is handled by small groups of senior members.

The first consideration is whether or not an assignment will improve the probability of the legislator's re-election. Since control of Congress depends upon re-election, efforts are made to place party members where they can do the most good. Thus, as we noted, the major interests in a constituency are represented on the appropriate committee.

Matching the interests of back-home elites with committee assignments is only part of the assignment process. Perhaps more crucial, especially with regard to assignments to prestigious committees, is demonstrated "responsibility." One demonstrates responsibility in a very well-defined manner:

[The responsible legislator] understands the pressure on the members with whom he cannot always agree and avoids pushing an issue to the point where his opponents suffer political embarrassment. On specific issues, no matter how firm his convictions and no matter how great the pressures upon him, he demonstrates a willingness to compromise. He is a moderate, not so much in the sense of his voting record and personal ideology, but rather in the sense of a moderate approach; he is not to be found on the uncompromising extremes of the political spectrum. . . . A responsible legislator is . . . one who does not believe that the Congress is the proper place to initiate drastic and rapid changes in the direction of public policy. On the contrary, he is more inclined to be a gradualist, and to see public policy as a sort of synthesis of opposing viewpoints. . . . Even in an instance in which party leaders feel compelled to appoint a member of a dissident wing of the party in order to gain greater cooperation, they will tend to select the member who most closely conforms to the norms of responsibility. (Masters, House Committee Assignments)[23]

Screening out potential dissidents occasionally produces some bizarre assignments. Thus Herman Badillo and Shirley Chisholm from New York were initially assigned to the House Agriculture Committee, causing

Badillo to remark that "There isn't any crop in my district except mari-juana." Subsequently, both were able to convince the leadership to change their assignments. However, Bella Abzug of New York, an un-relenting critic of the War in Vietnam, was unable to gain an assignment to the Armed Services Committee, and now toils on Government Opera-tions and Public Works.

The system has its critics and its defenders. Those most active in seeking a modification in seniority are: (1) those with low seniority; (2) those without formal leadership positions, (3) those from urban districts, and (4) those with a more liberal voting record.[24] Typical is Michael T. Harrington (D-Mass.), thirty-seven years old, elected in 1969, who rates a strong 94 from the ADA. He laments: "Bills are not passed because the nation wants or needs them—they are passed because senior chairmen have agreed to let them through. Until that system is dumped, much campaign discussion dissolves into rhetoric."

Supporters of seniority (those whose characteristics contrast with those reformers on the four points listed above) talk more in terms of the rewards of experience, the development of expertise, and the nurturing of stability in relationships. The maintenance of the "subsystem" is greatly enhanced by seniority: the established network of relationships between interest groups, executive agencies, and committees would flounder in its absence.

The most central consequence of seniority is to reduce conflict. By automatically resolving the issue of committee assignments, party dis-putes are avoided in most cases. The benefits of avoiding possibly ir-reparable party disputes are gained at the cost of an incremental, gradual decision-making process.

Legislative Procedure In the House of Representatives, after a standing committee reports a bill that it has considered favorably, a special rule or order must be issued by the Rules Committee before the bill can be considered by the membership of the House. This means that in the House of Representatives bills must be approved by the Rules Committee as well as the standing committee. (The only exceptions are bills reported by the House Appropriations and the Ways and Means Committees; their bills may be considered at any time as "privileged motions.") The Rules Committee can kill a bill by shelving it indefinitely. It can insist that the bill be amended as the price of permitting it on the floor and can even substitute a new bill for the one framed by another committee. The Rules Committee determines the extent of the debate that will be permitted on the floor of the House on any bill and the number and kind of amendments that may be offered from the floor. The only formal limits on Rules Committee authority are the "discharge petition" (which is rarely used and hardly ever successful) and "calendar Wednesday," a cumbersome procedure that permits standing committees to call up bills that have been blocked by the Rules Committee. The Rules Committee, clearly the most powerful single committee in Congress, is dominated by senior members elected from non-competitive districts.

In the Senate, control of floor debate rests with the majority leader. But the majority leader does not have the power to limit debate; once a senator has the floor, he may talk as long as he pleases, and he may yield the floor to whomever he chooses. If enough senators wish to talk a bill to death in a filibuster, they may do so. This device permits a small minority to tie up the business of the Senate and prevent it from voting on a bill. Under Rule 22 of the Senate, debate can be limited only by cloture. When 16 members sign a petition for a cloture, cloture must be voted upon, and a two-thirds vote of the senators present ends the filibuster. But cloture has been successful only six times in the history of the Senate. It has been a major weapon in civil rights legislation; the Civil Rights Act of 1964 passed the Senate through a cloture petition. But generally senators agree to protect each other's right of unlimited debate. Like the Rules Committee in the House, the filibuster is a means by which a small elite can defend itself against majority preferences.

Of the 10,000 bills introduced into Congress every year only about 1,000, or one in ten, becomes law. After a bill has been approved by the standing committee in the Senate or by the standing committee and the Rules Committee in the House, it is reported to the floor for a vote. Usually the most crucial votes come on the amendments to the bill that are offered to the floor (however, amendments may be prevented in the House by the Rules Committee). Once major amendments have either been defeated or incorporated into the bill, the bill usually picks up broad support, and the vote on final passage is usually a lopsided one in favor of the bill.

One of the most conservative features of American government is its bicameralism; the complicated path that a bill follows in one house must be repeated in the other. A bill must pass both branches of Congress in identical form before it can be sent to the president for his signature. However, the Senate often amends a House bill, and the House usually amends Senate bills. This means that even after a bill has passed both houses, it must be resubmitted to the originating house to see if it will concur with the changes made by the other. If either house declines to accept changes in the bill, specific differences must be ironed out by an ad hoc joint committee, called a conference committee. Disagreements between the houses are so frequent that from one third to one half of all public bills, including virtually all important ones, must be referred to conference committees after passage by both houses.

Members of conference committees are appointed by the presiding officers of each house, but are usually drawn from the two standing committees that handled the bill in each house. Since the final bill produced by the conference committee is generally accepted by both houses, conference committees have tremendous power in determining the final form of legislation. Reports of conference committees must be accepted or rejected as a whole; they cannot be further amended. Conference committees are held in secret and are unrecorded; they hold no hearings and listen to no outside testimony. The bill that emerges from their deliberations may not represent the view of either house and may contain items never considered by either house. Conference committees have sometimes been characterized as a "third house" of Congress, whose members are not elected by the people, keep no record of their work, and perform entirely in secret—and there can be no debate about their product.

Elites within Elites—The Congressional Establishment

There is a power hierarchy among federal governmental elites. This power hierarchy is supported by protocol, by the distribution of formal constitutional powers, by the powers associated with party office, by the committee and seniority systems of Congress, and by the "informal folkways" of Washington. According to the protocol of Washington society, the highest social rank is held by the president, followed by former presidents and their widows, the vice president, the Speaker of the House, members of the Supreme Court, foreign ambassadors and ministers, the Cabinet, United States senators, governors of states, former vice presidents, and finally congressmen.

The Constitution grants greater formal powers to senators than to representatives. There are only 100 senators; therefore, each senator is more visible than a representative in the social and political life of Washington, as well as in his home state. Also, senators have a special authority in foreign affairs not accorded to representatives, for the Senate must advise and consent by a two-thirds vote to all treaties entered into by the United States. The threat of Senate repudiation of a treaty makes it desirable for the president to solicit Senate views on foreign affairs; generally the Secretary of State works closely with the Foreign Relations

Committee of the Senate. Influential senators undertake personal missions abroad and serve on delegations to international bodies. Another constitutional power afforded senators is to advise and consent on executive appointments, including Supreme Court members, Cabinet members, federal judges, ambassadors, and other high executive officials. Even though the Senate generally approves the presidential nominations, the added potential for power contributes to the difference between the influence of senators and of House members. Finally, senators are elected for a six-year term and from a broader and more heterogeneous constituency. Thus, they have a longer guaranteed tenure in Washington, more prestige, and greater freedom from minor shifts in opinion among non-governmental elites in their home states.

Senators can also acquire additional power through their political roles; they often wield great power in state parties and can usually control federal patronage dispensed in their state. The power of the Senate to confirm nominations has given rise to the important political custom of "senatorial courtesy." Senatorial courtesy gives individual senators who are of the same party as the president a virtual veto power over major appointments—federal judges, postmasters, customs collectors, and so on—in their state. When presidential nominations are received in the Senate, they are referred to the senator or senators from the state involved. If the senator declares the nominee "personally obnoxious" to him, the Senate usually respects this declaration and rejects the appointment. Thus, before the president submits a nomination to the Senate, he usually makes sure that the nominee will be acceptable to his party's senator or senators from the state involved.

Party leadership roles in the House and the Senate are major sources of power in Washington. (See Tables 10–8 and 10–9 for a list of Senate and House leaders for the 93rd Congress.) The Speaker of the House of Representatives, who is elected by the majority party of the House, exercises more power over public policy than any other member of the House or Senate. Before 1910 the Speaker appointed all standing committees and their chairmen, possessed unlimited discretion to recognize members on the floor, and served as chairman of the Rules Committee. But in 1910, a group of progressives, led by George Norris, severely curtailed the authority of the Speaker. Today he shares power over the appointment of committees with the Committee on Committees; committee chairmen are selected by seniority, not by the Speaker; and the Speaker no longer serves as chairman of the Rules Committee. However, the Speaker retains considerable authority. He refers bills to committees, appoints all conference committees, rules on all matters of House procedure, recognizes

Table 10-8 / Senate Party Leadership

	Senator	State	Yr. First Elected	% of Last Election	Age	ADA* Rating	Busing* Vote	Cambodia* Bombing Vote
President Pro Tempore	Eastland	Miss.	1942	58%	70	5	Agn	For
Majority Leader	Mansfield	Mont.	1952	61	71	80	For	Agn
Majority Whip	Byrd	W. Va.	1958	78	56	35	Agn	Agn
Dem. Conf. Secretary	Moss	Utah	1958	56	63	70	For	Agn
Minority Leader	Scott	Penn.	1958	52	74	35	For	For
Rep. Pol. Com Chmn.	Tower	Texas	1961	54	49	0	Agn	For
Rep. Conf. Chmn.	Cotton	N.H.	1954	59	74	0	Agn	Abs
Rep. Conf. Secretary	Bennett	Utah	1950	54	76	5	Agn	Abs

Source: Compiled from Barone et al., *The Almanac of American Politics.*

Table 10-9 / House Party Leadership

	Representative	State	Yr. First Elected	% of Last Election	Age	ADA* Rating	Busing* Vote	Cambodia* Bombing
Speaker	Albert	Okla.	1946	93%	66	Speaker votes only to break tie		
Majority Leader	O'Neil	Mass.	1952	99	62	69	For	Agn
Majority Whip	McFall	Cal.	1956	63	56	44	For	For
Minority Leader	Rhodes	Ariz.	1952	57	58	6	Agn	For
Minority Whip	Anderson	Illinois	1960	72	52	44	For	Agn

Source: Compiled from Barone et al., *The Almanac of American Politics.*
*See Table 10-6

those who wish to speak, and generally directs the business of the floor. More importantly, he is the principal figure in House policy formulation, leadership, and responsibility; although he shares these tasks with standing committee chairmen, he is generally "first among equals" in his relationship with them.

Next to the Speaker, the most influential party leaders in the House are the majority and minority floor leaders and the party whips. These party leaders are chosen by their respective party caucuses, which are held at the beginning of each congressional session. The party caucus, composed of all the party's members in the House, usually does little more than elect these officers; it makes no major policy decisions. The floor leaders and whips have little formal authority; their role is to influence legislation through persuasion. Party floor leaders are supposed to combine parliamentary skill with persuasion, good personal relationships with party members, and close ties with the president and administration. They cannot deny party renomination to congressmen who are disloyal to the party, but they can control committee assignments and many small favors in Washington so a maverick congressman will have a difficult time becoming an effective legislator. The whips, or assistant floor leaders, keep members informed about legislative business, see that members are present for important floor votes, and communicate party strategy and position on particular issues. They also serve as the eyes and ears of the leadership, counting noses before important votes are taken. Party whips should know how many votes a particular measure has, and they should be able to get the votes to the floor when the roll is called.

The vice president of the United States, who serves as president of the Senate, has less control over Senate affairs than the Speaker of the House has over House affairs. The vice president votes only in case of a tie, and he must recognize senators in the order in which they rise. The majority party in the Senate also elects from its membership a president pro tempore who presides in the absence of the vice president.

The key power figures in the Senate are the majority and minority leaders. The majority leader usually has great personal influence within the Senate and is a powerful figure in national affairs. The majority leader, when he is of the same party as the president, is in charge of getting the president's legislative program through the Senate. He has somewhat less formal authority than the Speaker of the House, but he has the right to be the first senator to be heard on the floor; and, with the minority floor leader, he determines the Senate's agenda. He can greatly influence committee assignments for members of his own party. But on the whole, his influence rests upon his powers of persuasion. It is widely recognized that the most effective majority leader in recent times was Lyndon Johnson, Senate majority leader from 1953 to 1960.

The committee system and the seniority rule also create powerful congressional figures, the chairmen of the most powerful standing committees—particularly the Senate Foreign Relations, Appropriations, and Finance Committees, and the House Rules, Appropriations, and Ways and Means Committees. Chairmen of the standing committees acquire their power because the members of each house respect the authority of their committees. The standing committee system is self-sustaining, because each committee and committee chairman tends to regard an attack upon the authority of one committee or committee chairman as a threat to all. If one committee or committee chairman can be bypassed on a particular measure, other committees and committee chairmen can be bypassed on other measures. Hence, committee chairmen and ranking committee members tend to stand by each other and support each other's authority over legislation assigned to their respective committees. Committee chairmen or ranking committee members are also respected because of their seniority and experience in the legislative process. Committee chairmen are often experts in parliamentary process as well as in the substantive area covered by their committees. Finally, and perhaps most importantly, committee chairmen and ranking committee members acquire power through their relationships with executive and private elites who are involved in the policy area within the jurisdiction of the committee. "Policy clusters"—alliances of leaders from executive agencies, congressional committees, and private business and industry—tend to emerge in Washington. Committee chairmen, owing to their control over legislation in Congress, are key members of these policy clusters. One policy cluster might include the chairmen of the House and Senate committees on agriculture, the Secretary of Agriculture and other key officials of the Department of Agriculture, and the leaders of the American Farm Bureau Federation. Another vital policy cluster would include the chairmen of the House and Senate Armed Services Committees; the Secretary and Under-Secretaries of Defense; key military leaders, including the Joint Chiefs of Staff; and the leadership of defense industries such as Lockheed and General Dynamics. These alliances of congressional, executive, and private elites determine most public policy within their area of concern.

Power also accrues to key senators and congressmen by virtue of custom and informal folkways. Professor David B. Truman writes that Congress "has its standards and conventions, its largely unwritten system of obligations and privileges. . . . The neophyte must conform, at least in some measure, if he hopes to make effective use of his position."[25] A new member of Congress should expect to "go along" with the customs of Congress if he wishes to "get along." These informal folkways appear more important in the Senate, where there are fewer formal controls over members than in the House. Donald Matthews has described some of the folkways of the Senate as: respect for the seniority system; good behavior in floor debate; humility in freshmen senators; a willingness to perform cheerfully many thankless tasks, such as presiding over floor debate; deference to senior members; making speeches only on subjects on which you are expert or which concern your committee assignment or your state; doing favors for other senators; keeping your word when you make an agreement; remaining friendly toward your colleagues, whether you are in political agreement with them or not; and speaking well of the Senate as an institution.[26]

Ralph K. Huitt describes the Senate type as:

. . . a prudent man, who serves a long apprenticeship before trying to assert himself, and talks infrequently even then. He is courteous to a fault in his relations with his colleagues, not allowing political disagreements to affect his personal feelings. He is always ready to help another Senator when he can, and he expects to be repaid in kind. More than anything else he is a Senate man, proud of the institution and ready to defend its traditions and prerequisites against all outsiders. He is a legislative workhorse who specializes in one or two policy areas. . . . He is a man of accommodation who knows that "You have to go along to get along;" he is a conservative, institutional man, slow to change what he has mastered at the expense of so much time and patience.[27]

This image of the insider brings to mind the opposite role: the outsider, a senator whose eyes and mind are upon other political opportunities. Such men (often willingly) find themselves assigned to glamorous but relatively powerless committees. Hence the absence of the "household word" senators—McGovern, Muskie, Goldwater, Kennedy —from the inside club. Edward Kennedy is a particularly apt example, since he once successfully challenged the insular traditions of the Senate. Of Kennedy it was written:

On his own the amiable Teddy might someday have become at best a fringe member of the club, but he is associated with Robert F., who like John F., is the archetype of the national kind of politician that the club regards with suspicion. It's believed correctly that the Kennedy family has always looked on the Senate as a means to an end, but not an end in itself.[28]

Yet, shortly after this was written, Kennedy defeated Russell Long (D-La.), for the position of Majority Whip. However, Kennedy did not make good in his new role. He was soon replaced by a true Senate man, Robert Byrd (D-W.Va.).

Senators and prominent reporters have described the Senate "establishment" as the "inner club" where power in the Senate and in Washington is concentrated. The establishment is composed primarily of conservative senators from both parties who have acquired great seniority and control key committee chairmanships. The establishment consists of those senators who have learned the folkways of the Senate over a long period of time and who now appear to be running the Senate. In 1963, United States Senator Joseph S. Clark of Pennsylvania attacked the Senate "establishment" as "the antithesis of democracy."[29] He charged that it was composed of political conservatives from the Democratic South and the Republican Midwest who had acquired seniority and who controlled appointment to committees and other important posts. William S. White also talks of the "inner club" in the Senate, composed of men who "express consciously or unconsciously the deepest instincts and prejudices of 'the Senate type.'" For White, a Senate type is one who displays "tolerance toward fellows, intolerance toward any who would in any real way change the Senate," and commitment toward the Senate as "a career in itself, a life in itself, and an end in itself."[30]

In summary, it seems clear that there are elites within elites. There are elites within the House, the Senate, and the executive branch who exercise disproportionate control over government and who are not representative even of the majority of governmental elites. Power within the House and Senate appears to flow downward from senior party leaders and influential committee chairmen, whose dominance in congressional affairs is seldom challenged by the rank-and-file congressmen. Senator Clark writes: "The trouble with Congress today is that it exercises negative and unjust powers to which the governed, the people of the United States, have never consented. . . . The heart of the trouble is that power is exercised by minority, not majority, rule."[31]

Conflict and Consensus: Party Voting in Congress

Studies of roll-call voting in Congress show that political parties play a minor to major role in legislative conflict, depending upon the issue.[32] Party votes, those roll-call votes in which a majority of voting Democrats oppose a majority of voting Republicans, occur on less than *half* of all the roll-call votes taken in Congress. Roll-call voting follows party lines more often than it follows sectional, urban-rural, or any other divisions that have been studied. How much cohesion exists within the

Table 10-10 / Party Voting in Congress

	Party Votes as Percentage of Total Votes	Party Support* Democrats	Party Support* Republicans
1955–1960			
Senate	41%	69%	70%
House	48	70	69
1961–1964			
Senate	44	65	66
House	49	71	72
1965			
Senate	42	63	68
House	52	70	71
1966			
Senate	50	57	63
House	41	62	68
1967			
Senate	35	61	60
House	36	67	74
1968			
Senate	32	51	60
House	35	59	64
1969			
Senate	36	62	63
House	31	61	62
1970			
Senate	35	58	56
House	27	55	60
1971			
Senate	42	64	63
House	38	61	67
1972			
Senate	36	57	64
House	27	58	61

*Party support: Average percentage of times a congressman voted with his party majority in disagreement with the other party's majority.

Source: Compiled from *Congressional Quarterly Almanac*, Vols. XI–XXVII (Washington, D.C.: Congressional Quarterly Service, 1955-1972).

parties? Table 10–10 shows the number of party votes that have been taken in Congress in recent years and the average support Democratic and Republican congressmen have given to their parties. Democrats and Republicans appear equally cohesive, with members of both parties voting with their party majority more than two thirds of the time. Party voting appears more frequent in the House than in the Senate.

Bipartisan votes, those roll calls in which divisions are not along party lines, occur most frequently in the areas of foreign policy and defense matters. Bipartisan agreement also appears on appropriation bills and roll calls where there is little dispute. Recently bipartisan voting has settled issues of federal aid to education, highway beautification, water pollution, voting rights, presidential continuity, and increases in federal employees' pay and veterans' benefits.

Conflict between parties occurs most frequently over issues involving social welfare programs, housing and urban development, economic opportunity, medical care, anti-poverty programs, health and welfare, and the regulation of business and labor. Party conflict is particularly apparent in the budget, the most important policy document of the national government. The budget is identified as the product of the president and carries the label of his party. On some issues, such as civil rights and appropriations, voting will follow party lines during roll calls on preliminary motions, amendments, and other preliminary matters, but swing to a bipartisan vote on passage of the final legislation. This means that the parties have disagreed on certain aspects of the bill, but compromised on its final passage.

Many of the issues that cause conflict between the Democratic and Republican parties are related to the conflict of government and private initiative. In general, Democrats have favored: lower tariffs; federal subsidies for agriculture; federal action to assist labor and low-income groups through social security, relief, housing, and wage-hour regulation; and generally a larger role for the federal government in launching new projects to remedy domestic problems. Republicans, on the other hand, have favored higher tariffs, free competition in agriculture, less government involvement in labor and welfare matters, and reliance on private action.

Further, each party supports the president to a different degree. The president generally receives greater support from his own party than from the opposition party in Congress. President Johnson received the support of 64 percent of all Senate Democrats and 74 percent of the House Democrats on the 274 roll calls in 1965 presenting clear-cut tests for support for his views. In contrast, the Republicans in both houses supported President Johnson on less than half of these presidential support votes. Democrats rarely opposed the President's program, while Republicans frequently did. However, Republicans were much more critical of the President's domestic programs than of his foreign policy programs.

Party lines are hazy when it comes to issues involving veterans, civil service, public works, and states' rights; and differences between the parties on foreign policy are practically non-existent. Before World War II, Democrats tended to support United States international involvement, while the Republicans were heavily committed to neutrality and "isolationism." Now, only the question of foreign aid divides the parties significantly in foreign affairs; Democrats generally give greater support to foreign aid than Republicans.

To some extent, party influences act as a check to the decentralization inherent in the committee system. Yet one should bear in mind that party votes do not occur on *most* of the issues voted upon in a given session. The probability of a legislator voting in accordance with the party leadership is only slightly better than chance. It seems that the feeling of party identification is more significant than actual party voting.

The Conservative Coalition

Although party voting appears more important than regional alignments, one regional voting block can be identified on a significant number of issues in Congress. As David Truman explains, "the evidence is clear that there [is] a solid and sharply identifiable die-hard element among the Southern Democrats, whose opposition extend[s] well beyond the issues of intense regional loyalty to almost a whole range of questions growing out of the strains and stresses to which the American society has been subjected in the mid-twentieth century." On the civil rights votes, this block of Southern Democrats votes in opposition to a majority of both Northern Democrats and Republicans.

More significant, however, is the "conservative coalition" of Southern Democrats and Republicans who oppose the Northern Democrats. In recent years this coalition has occurred on about 20 percent of all congressional roll calls (see Table 10–11). The coalition votes together on such issues as aid to depressed areas, minimum wage laws, federal aid to education, public housing, urban renewal, medical care for the aged, taxation, and other domestic welfare questions. Not all Southern Democrats or Republicans vote with the coalition; a roll-call coalition is defined as any roll call in which a majority of voting Southern Democrats and a majority of voting Republicans oppose a majority of Northern Democrats. The coalition generally has less concern for the public than the president or the Northern Democrats do, and it has resisted the expansion of federal power and the increase of federal spending programs.

The coalition was highly successful during the Eisenhower Administration and, to some extent, during the Kennedy years. But when Johnson won an overwhelming victory in the presidential election of 1964, he carried into office enough Northern Democratic congressmen to help him break the back of the conservative coalition in the 1965 session of Congress. The coalition lost almost two thirds of the coalition roll calls

Table 10-11 / The Conservative Coalition in Congress, 1958-1972

	Percentage of Coalition Roll Calls to Total	Percentage of Coalition Victories on Coalition Roll Calls
1958		
Senate	19%	86%
House	15	64
1959		
Senate	13	65
House	13	91
1960		
Senate	22	67
House	20	35
1961		
Senate	32	48
House	20	74
1962		
Senate	15	71
House	13	44
1963		
Senate	19	44
House	13	67
1964		
Senate	17	47
House	11	67
1965		
Senate	24	39
House	24	25
1966		
Senate	30	51
House	19	32
1967		
Senate	18	54
House	22	73
1968		
Senate	25	80
House	23	63
1969		
Senate	18	67
House	39	71
1970		
Senate	26	64
House	20	70
1971		
Senate	28	86
House	31	79
1972		
Senate	25	63
House	29	79

Source: Compiled from the *Congressional Quarterly Almanac*, Vols. XVIII–XXIX (Washington, D.C.: Congressional Quarterly Service, 1962-1972).

in 1965. However, the Republican victories in the mid-term congressional elections of 1966 strengthened the coalition. Even though the coalition emerged on only 20 percent of the roll-call votes in recent years, it is important to keep in mind that, when the coalition appears, it wins more often than not. It is an extremely potent force, especially when it finds itself in agreement with the president, as has been the case since 1968. While Nixon has been losing influence with Congress, when the coalition supports him, his chances improve.

Summary

This analysis of Congress produces several propositions which enable us to refine elite theory, and apply it to a specific institution:

1. Congress tends to represent locally organized elites, who inject a strong parochial influence in national decision making. Congressmen are responsible to national interests that have a strong base of support in their home constituencies.

2. A congressman's relevant political constituency is not the general population of his district, but its local elite. Less than half the general population of a congressman's district knows his name; fewer still have any idea of how he voted on any major issue. Only a tiny fraction ever express their views on a public issue to their congressman.

3. With the possible exception of civil rights questions, most congressmen are free from the influence of popular preferences in their legislative voting. However, a congressman's voting record generally reflects the socioeconomic makeup of his home district. Congressmen are products of the social system in their constituency; they share its dominant goals and values.

4. Congress seldom initiates changes in public policy. Instead it responds to policy proposals initiated by the president, executive and military elites, and interested non-governmental elites. The congressional role in national decision making is usually a deliberative one, in which Congress responds to policies initiated by others.

5. Congressional committees are important to communication between governmental and non-governmental elites. "Policy clusters," consisting of alliances of leaders from executive agencies, congressional committees, and private business and industry, tend to develop in Washington. Committee chairmen are key members of these policy clusters, because of their control over legislation in Congress.

6. The elaborate rules and procedures of Congress delay and obstruct proposed changes in the *status quo*. The rules and procedures of Congress strengthen its conservative role in policy making. It is a difficult process for a bill to become a law; congressional procedures offer many opportunities to defeat the legislation and many obstacles to the passage of legislation.

7. An elite system within Congress places effective control over legislation in the hands of a relatively few members. Most of these congressional "establishment" members are conservative congressmen from both parties who have acquired great seniority and therefore control key committee chairmanships.

8. Most bills that are not killed before the floor vote are passed unanimously. The greatest portion of the national budget is passed without debate. What con-

flict exists in Congress tends to follow party lines more often than any other factional division. Conflict centers on the implementation of domestic and foreign policy; seldom is there any conflict over the major directions of policy.

References

[1]See Donald Matthews, *Social Background of Political Decision Makers* (New York: Doubleday & Co., 1954).

[2]Heinz Eulau and John D. Sprague, *Lawyers in Politics* (Indianapolis, Ind.: Bobbs-Merrill Co., 1964).

[3]See Joseph A. Schlesinger, *Ambition and Politics* (Chicago: Rand McNally, 1966).

[4]Lewis A. Froman, *Congressmen and Their Constituencies* (Chicago: Rand McNally, 1963).

[5]Sam Kernell, "Is the Senate More Liberal Than the House?" *Journal of Politics*, 35 (May 1973), pp. 332–336.

[6]Committee on Government Operations, Subcommittee on Intergovernmental Relations, *Confidence and Concern: Citizens View American Government* (Washington, D.C.: Government Printing Office, 1973), pp. 72–77.

[7]Robert S. Erikson and Norman Luttbeg, *American Public Opinion* (New York: John Wiley, 1973), p. 281.

[8]Warren Miller and Donald Stokes, "Constituency Influence in Congress," *American Political Science Review*, 57 (March 1963), p. 55.

[9]Philip E. Converse, A. R. Clausen, and Warren E. Miller, "Electoral Myth and Reality: The 1964 Election," *American Political Science Review*, 54 (June 1965), pp. 321–336.

[10]V. O. Key, Jr., *Public Opinion and American Democracy* (New York: Alfred A. Knopf, 1961), p. 418.

[11]Roger H. Davidson, *The Role of the Congressman* (New York: Pegasus, 1969), p. 79.

[12]See *Congressional Quarterly*, Special Report, "The Military Industrial Complex," May 24, 1968.

[13]Charles O. Jones, "The Role of the Campaign in Congressional Politics," in M. Kent Jennings and Harmon Zeigler, eds., *The Electoral Process* (Englewood Cliffs, N.J.: Prentice-Hall, 1966), p. 21.

[14]Fred Westheimer, quoted in *Congressional Quarterly* (December 1, 1973), p. 3130.

[15]Robert Dahl, *Pluralist Democracy in the United States* (Chicago: Rand McNally, 1967), p. 136.

[16]Arthur Schlesinger, Jr., *The Imperial Presidency* (Boston: Houghton Mifflin Co., 1973), pp. 221–222.

[17]Aaron Wildavsky, "The Two Presidencies," *Transaction* (December 1966), p. 7.

[18]Lyndon B. Johnson, "Congress and the Presidency," in Theodore Lowi and Randall B. Ripley, eds., *Legislative Politics, U.S.A.*, 3rd ed. (Boston: Little-Brown, 1973), p. 243.

[19]*Ibid.*, p. 252.

[20]Kevin Phillip, "Our Obsolete System," *Newsweek*, April 23, 1973, p. 13.

[21]John W. Kingdon, *Congressmen's Voting Decisions* (New York: Harper and Row, 1973), p. 62.

[22]*Ibid.*, p. 88.

[23]Nicholas A. Masters, "Committee Assignments in the House of Representatives," *American Political Science Review*, 56 (June 1961), p. 352.

[24]Roger H. Davidson, David M. Kovenock, and Michael K. O'Leary, *Congress in Crisis: Politics and Congressional Reform* (Belmont, Calif.: Wadsworth Publishing Co., 1966), pp. 67–91.

[25]David B. Truman, *The Governmental Process* (New York: Alfred A. Knopf, 1955), p. 344.

[26]Donald R. Matthews, "The Folkways of the United States Senate: Conformity to Group Norms and Legislative Effectiveness," *American Political Science Review*, 53 (December 1959), pp. 1064–1089.

[27]William S. White, *The Citadel: The Story of the U.S. Senate* (New York: Harper & Row, 1956), Chapter VII.

[28]Cited in Nelson Polsby, "Goodbye to the InnerClub," in Lowi and Ripley, *Legislative Politics, U.S.A.*, p. 132.

[29]Joseph S. Clark, *The Senate Establishment* (New York: Hill & Wang, 1963).

[30]White, *The Citadel*, p. 84.

[31]Joseph S. Clark, *Congress: The Sapless Branch* (New York: Harper & Row, 1964), pp. 22–23.

[32]See Malcolm E. Jewell and Samuel C. Patterson, *The Legislative Process in the United States* (New York: Random House, 1966); William J. Keefe and Morris Ogul, *The American Legislative Process* (Englewood Cliffs, N.J.: Prentice-Hall, 1964).

Selected Additional Readings

Clark, et al., Joseph S. *The Senate Establishment.* New York: Hill and Wang, 1963. Clark's book contains speeches made on the Senate floor that deal with power relationships in the Senate, especially the disproportionate power of the conservative coalition.

Davidson, Roger H. *The Role of the Congressman.* New York: Pegasus, 1969. Davidson's focus is upon the legislator's image of his job.

Huitt, Ralph K. and Robert L. Peabody. *Congress: Two Decades of Analysis.* New York: Harper and Row, 1969. Seven authoritative essays—Ralph K. Huitt's major contributions on the United States Senate and the executive-legislative process and Robert L. Peabody's critical review of scholarship and trends in legislative research during the last two decades—are collected in this volume.

Kingdon, John W. *Congressmen's Voting Decisions.* New York: Harper and Row, 1973. This book is the result of an intensive issue-by-issue examination of how decisions were reached by individual members of the U. S. House of Representatives in 1969. Focusing on one issue at a time, Kingdon employs interviews with selected congressmen to determine how they reached their decision concerning their vote on the issue. The result is a highly informative and readable text reflecting the complex relationships between the actors—the individual congressman, his constituents, fellow congressmen, party leaders in and out of Congress, interest group lobbyists, the executive branch, his staff, and the media—and the decision-making process—structural influences, information problems, and decision norms.

White, William S. *The Citadel: The Story of the U.S. Senate.* New York: Harper and Row, Co., 1956. Though White's attitude toward the Senate is reverential when compared to Clark's critical view, *The Citadel* contains much information in an easy, enjoyable, if somewhat dated book.

CHAPTER 11

COURTS: ELITES IN BLACK ROBES

The Supreme Court of the United States, and the federal court system, is the most elitist institution in American government. Nine men—none of whom are elected and all of whom serve for life—possess ultimate authority over all of the other institutions of American government. These men have the power to void the acts of popularly elected presidents, Congresses, governors, state legislators, school boards, and city councils. There is no appeal from their decisions about what is the "supreme law of the land," except perhaps to undertake the difficult task of amending the Constitution itself.

Many of the nation's most important domestic policy decisions have been made by the Supreme Court rather than the president or Congress. It was the Supreme Court which took the lead in eliminating segregation from public life, insuring separation of church and state, defining rights of criminal defendants and the powers of law enforcement officials, insuring voters equality in representation, defining the limits of free speech and free press, and declaring abortion to be a fundamental right of women. Courts, then, are deeply involved in policymaking—on such diverse issues as school segregation, busing, public school prayers, federal aid to church-supported schools, capital punishment, police brutality, crime and law enforcement, malapportionment, pornography, censorship, and abortion. Indeed, sooner or later in American politics, most important policy questions are decided by judges—men who are not elected to office and cannot be removed for anything other than "treason, bribery, or high crimes and misdemeanors." As de Tocqueville observed as early as 1835: "Scarcely any political question arises in the United States that is not resolved, sooner or later, into a judicial question."[1]

Judicial Review as an Elitist Principle

The undemocratic character of judicial power in America has long been recognized. The Founding Fathers viewed the federal courts as the final bulwark against mass threats to principle and property. In *The Federalist* No. 78, Hamilton wrote:

By a limited Constitution I understand one which contains certain specified exceptions to the legislative authority; such, for instance, as that it shall pass no bills of attainder, no ex post facto laws, and the like. Limitations of this kind can be preserved in practice no other way than through the medium of courts of justice, whose duty it is to declare all acts contrary to the manifest tenor of the Constitution void. Without this, all the reservations of particular rights or privileges would amount to nothing.[2]

In *Marbury v. Madison*, the historic decision establishing the power of judicial review, John Marshall argued persuasively that: 1) The Constitution is "the supreme law of the land," and the laws of the United States and of the States must be made in pursuit thereof; 2) Article III of the Constitution gives to the Supreme Court the judicial power, which includes the power to interpret the meaning of laws, and, in case of conflict between laws, decide which law shall prevail; 3) the courts are sworn to uphold the Constitution, therefore, they must declare void a law that conflicts with the Constitution.

Since 1803, the federal courts have struck down more than eighty laws of Congress and uncounted state laws that they believed conflicted with the Constitution. Judicial review and the power to interpret the meaning and decide the application of law are the major sources of power for judges.

The decision of the Founding Fathers to grant federal courts the power of judicial review of *state* decision is easy to understand. After all, it is stated in Article VI that the Constitution and the laws and treaties of the national government are the supreme law of the land, "anything in the Constitution or laws of any state to the contrary notwithstanding." Federal court power over state decisions is probably essential in maintaining national unity, for fifty different state interpretations of the meaning of the United States Constitution or of the laws and treaties of Congress would create unimaginable confusion. Thus, the power of federal judicial review over state constitutions, laws, and court decisions is seldom questioned.

However, at the national level, why should the views of an appointed court about the meaning of the Constitution prevail over the views of an elected Congress and an elected president? Congressmen and presidents are sworn to uphold the Constitution, and it can reasonably be assumed that they do not pass laws that they believe to be unconstitutional. Since laws must be approved by majorities of those voting in both houses and must have the president's formal approval, why should the Founding Fathers have allowed the decisions of these bodies to be set aside by the federal courts?

The answer appears to be that the Founding Fathers distrusted both popular majorities and elected officials who might be influenced by popular majorities. They believed that government should be limited so that it could not attack principle and property, whether to do so was the will of the majority or not. So the courts were deliberately insulated against popular majorities; to insure their independence, judges were not to be elected, but appointed for life terms. Originally, it was expected that they would be appointed by a president who was not even directly elected himself and confirmed by a Senate that was not directly elected. Only in this way, the writers of the Constitution believed, would they be sufficiently protected from the masses to permit them to judge courageously and responsibly.

The Making of a Judge

The social backgrounds of judges reflect close ties with the upper social strata of society. John R. Schmidhauser reports that over 90 percent of the Supreme Court Justices serving on the Court between 1789 and 1962 were from socially prominent, politically influential, upper-class families.[3] Over two thirds of the Supreme Court justices ever serving on the Court attended prestigious or Ivy League law schools (Harvard, Yale, Columbia, Pennsylvania, N.Y.U., Michigan, Virginia, etc.). No blacks served on the Supreme Court until the appointment of Associate Justice Thurgood Marshall in 1967. Henry Abraham depicts the typical Supreme Court justice: "White, generally Protestant . . .; fifty to fifty-five years of age at the time of his appointment; Anglo-Saxon ethnic stock . . .; high social status; reared in an urban environment; member of a civic-minded, politically active, economically comfortable family; legal training; some

The Role of the Courts in the American System: Views of the Founders

Marshall in support of judicial review:

> It is emphatically the province and duty of the judicial depart-
> ment to say what the law is. Those who apply the law to par-
> ticular cases, must of necessity expound and interpret that
> rule. If two laws conflict with each other, the courts must de-
> cide on the operation of each.
>
> So if a law be in opposition to the constitution; if both the
> law and the constitution apply to a particular case, so that the
> court must decide that case conformably to the law, disregard-
> ing the constitution; or conformably to the constitution, disre-
> garding the law; the court must determine which of these con-
> flicting rules governs each case. This is of the very essence of
> judicial duty.
>
> If, then, the courts are to regard the constitution, and the
> constitution is superior to any ordinary act of the legislature,
> the constitution, and not such ordinary act, must govern the
> case to which they both apply. . .

Chief Justice John Marshall in *Marbury v. Madison* (1803).

Gibson in opposition to judicial review:

> The Constitution and the right of the legislature to pass the Act,
> may be in collision. But is that a legitimate subject for judicial
> determination? If it be, the judiciary must be a peculiar organ,
> to revise the proceedings of the legislature, and to correct its
> mistakes. And in what part of the Constitution are we to look
> for this proud pre-eminence? Viewing the matter in the oppo-
> site direction, what would be thought of an Act of Assembly in
> which it should be declared that the Supreme Court had, in a
> particular case, put a wrong construction of the Constitution of
> the United States, and that the judgment should therefore be
> reversed? It would doubtless be thought a usurpation of judi-
> cial power. But it is by no means clear, that to declare a law
> void which has been enacted according to the forms prescribed
> in the Constitution, is not a usurpation of legislative power.
> . . . It is the business of the judiciary to interpret the laws, not
> scan the authority of the lawgiver; and without the latter, it

cannot take cognizance of a collision between a law and the Constitution. . .

Chief Justice Gibson of the Pennsylvania Supreme Court, in *Eakin v. Raub* (1825).

Hamilton in defense of life terms for judges:

> The standard of good behavior for the continuance in office of the judicial magistracy is certainly one of the most valuable of the modern improvements in the practice of government. In a monarchy it is an excellent barrier to the despotism of the prince; in a republic it is a no less excellent barrier to the encroachments and oppressions of the representative body. And it is the best expedient which can be devised in any government to secure a steady, upright, and impartial administration of the laws. . . . If then, the courts of justice are to be considered as the bulwarks of a limited Constitution against legislative encroachments, this consideration will afford a strong argument for the permanent tenure of judicial offices, since nothing will contribute so much as this to that independent spirit in the judges which must be essential to the faithful performance of so arduous a duty.
>
> Alexander Hamilton, *The Federalist*, Number 78.

Hamilton on behalf of an elitist judiciary:

> Hence it is that there can be but few men in the society who will have sufficient skill in the laws to qualify them for the station of judges. And making the proper deductions for the ordinary depravity of human nature, the number must be still smaller of those who unite the requisite integrity with the requisite knowledge. These considerations apprise us that the government can have no great option between fit characters; and that a temporary duration in office which would naturally discourage such characters from quitting a lucrative line of practice to accept a seat on the bench would have a tendency to throw the administration of justice into hands less able and less qualified to conduct it with utility and dignity.
>
> Alexander Hamilton, *The Federalist*, Number 78.

type of public office; generally well educated."[4] Of course, social background does not necessarily determine judicial philosophy. But as Schmidhauser observes: "If . . . the Supreme Court is the keeper of the American conscience, it is essentially the conscience of the American upper-middle class, sharpened by the imperative of individual social responsibility and political activism, and conditioned by the conservative impact of legal training and professional legal attitudes and associations."[5]

All federal judges are appointed by the president and confirmed by the Senate. The recruitment process which brings the names of potential appointees to the president's desk is highly political. Herbert Jacob reports that 80 percent of federal judges have held political office some time in their career prior to appointment.[6] (See Table 11-1.) Less than one

Table 11-1 / The Supreme Court

Justices	Position Held at Time at Appointment
Chief Justice:	
Warren Burger	Judge, U.S. Court of Appeals
Associate Justices:	
William O. Douglas	Member, Securities and Exchange Commission
Thurgood Marshall	U.S. Solicitor General
William J. Brennan, Jr.	Justice, Supreme Court of New Jersey
Potter Stewart	U.S. Deputy Attorney General
Byron R. White	U.S. Deputy Attorney General
Harry A. Blackmun	Judge, U.S. Court of Appeals
Lewis F. Powell, Jr.	Private practice
William H. Rehnquist	Assistant Attorney General

third of the nation's Supreme Court justices have had prior experience as judges. Few Supreme Court justices are promoted through the federal court system; political support and friendship with the president is a more promising avenue toward high judicial appointment. Generally, agreement with the political philosophy of the president is a necessary criteria for consideration. Of course, once appointed, a Supreme Court justice can pursue a policy course at variance with the president, and many have done so. The Attorney General's office assists the president in screening candidates for all federal judgeships; after the choice is narrowed, the president usually requests the American Bar Association to comment on the qualifications of the proposed nominees.

The president's formal nomination of a federal judge must be confirmed by a majority vote of the U.S. Senate. Until recently the Senate Judiciary Committee, which holds hearings and recommends confirmation to the full Senate, has accepted nominations of the president with a minimum of dissent. (The Senate has failed to approve only 28 of the 130

Supreme Court nominations ever sent to it.) The prevailing ethos was that a popularly elected President deserved the opportunity to appoint his own judges; that the opposition party in Congress would have its own opportunity to appoint judges when it captured the presidency; and that partisan bickering over judicial appointments should be avoided. But in recent years presidential-congressional cooperation on Supreme Court nominations has broken down on several occasions. In 1968 President Lyndon Johnson nominated his own lawyer, prominent Washington attorney Abe Fortas, to the Chief Justiceship of the Supreme Court. Fortas was already serving as an Associate Justice owing to an earlier Johnson appointment. A coalition of liberal (anti-Johnson) Democrats and Republicans in Congress complained of "cronyism," and information concerning Fortas' financial affairs was used to discredit his nomination and force his resignation from the Court.

Later, when President Nixon nominated two Southern federal judges to the Supreme Court—Clement F. Haynsworth and G. Harold Carswell—similar tactics were employed in Congress to halt these presidential nominations. President Nixon charged that the Senate, by withholding confirmation of his Southern conservative nominees, was infringing upon his "constitutional responsibility"; Nixon had actually campaigned for office pledging to alter the liberal stance of the Warren Court, and he believed he had a constitutional mandate to do so. Eventually, the Senate confirmed the president's nomination of other conservatives —Burger, Blackmun, Powell, and Rehnquist.

Presidents usually nominate judges who share their own political philosophy. Actually, this might be considered a democratizing influence on the Court, assuming that the people elect a president because of their agreement with *his* political philosophy. But Supreme Court justices frequently become independent once they reach the Court. Former Chief Justice Earl Warren, as Republican governor of California, had swung critical delegate votes to Eisenhower in the 1952 Republican Convention. When he was rewarded with the Chief Justiceship by a grateful president, there was little in Warren's background to suggest that he would lead the most liberal era in the Court's history. Later Eisenhower would complain that the Warren appointment was "the biggest damn mistake I ever made."[7]

The Special Style of Judicial Policy Making

The power of the courts to shape American life is cloaked in an *appearance of objectivity.* Because judges are appointed for life and legally accountable to none, they maintain the fiction that they are *not* engaged in policy making but merely "applying" the law to specific cases. To admit otherwise would spotlight the conflict between judicial power and the democratic myth of policy making by elected representatives.

Former Supreme Court Justice Owen J. Roberts once defended the myth of judicial objectivity:

It is sometimes said that the court assumes a power to overrule or control the action of the people's representatives. This is a misconception. The Constitution is the supreme law of the land ordained and established by the people. All legislation must conform to the principles it lays down. When an act of Congress is appropriately challenged in the courts as not conforming to the constitutional mandate, the judicial branch has only one duty—to lay the article of the Constitution which is involved beside the statute which is challenged and to decide whether the latter squares with the former. All the court does, or can do, is to announce its considered judgement upon the question. The only power it has, if such it may be called, is the power of judgement. [8]

Carl Brent Swisher admits of some judicial policy making but still clings to the notion of judicial objectivity: "The court determines the facts involved in particular controversies brought before it, relates the facts to the relevant law, settles the controversies in terms of the law, and more or less incidentally makes new law through the process of decision." [9]

This mechanistic theory of judicial objectivity is acknowledged as a myth by many of the nation's better judicial thinkers. For example, former Justice Felix Frankfurter once observed:

The meaning of "due process" and the content of terms like "liberty" are not revealed by the Constitution. It is the Justices who make the meaning. They read into the neutral language of the Constitution their own economic and social views . . . Let us face the fact that five Justices of the Supreme Court are the molders of policy rather than the impersonal vehicles of revealed truth. [10]

The Courts also maintain the *fiction of non-partisanship*. Judges must not appear to permit political considerations to affect their decisions. *After* they are appointed to the federal bench, they are expected to have fewer direct ties to political organizations than congressmen. They must not appear to base their decisions on partisan considerations, or party platforms, or to bargain in the fashion of legislators. Perhaps as a result of their non-partisan appearance, courts enjoy a measure of prestige that other government institutions lack. Court decisions become more acceptable to the public if the public believes that the courts dispense unbiased justice.

Courts function under *special rules of access*. For example, courts seldom initiate policies or programs themselves in the fashion of Con-

"*I'm happy to say that my final judgment of a case is almost always consistent with my prejudgment of the case.*"

Drawing by Dana Fradon; © 1973 *The New Yorker Magazine, Inc.*

gress or the executive branch. Instead, courts wait until a case involving a policy question is brought before them. The Constitution gives jurisdiction to federal courts only in "cases and controversies." Courts do not issue policy pronouncements, rules, or order on their own initiative. For example, courts do not declare a law of Congress or an action of the president unconstitutional immediately upon its passage or occurrence. Nor do the federal courts render advisory opinions prior to congressional or executive action. Instead, the courts assume a passive role and wait until a case comes before them which directly challenges a law of Congress or action of the president.

To gain access to the federal courts, we must present a *case* in which the federal courts have *jurisdiction*. A case must involve two disputing parties, one of which must have incurred some real damages as a result of the action or inaction of the other. The *federal* courts will accept jurisdiction based on: 1) *the nature of the parties*—a case in which the United States government is a party; or a controversy between two or more states, or between a state and a citizen or another state, or between citizens of different states; or a case involving a foreign nation or citizen; or 2) *the nature of the controversy* —a case which arises under the Constitution (a "constitutional question") or under the laws and treaties of the United States. Congress has further limited the jurisdiction of federal courts in cases between citizens of different states by requiring that the dispute must involve over $10,000. All other cases must be heard in state courts.

Judicial policy making occurs in a *legalistic style*. Facts and arguments are presented to the courts in formal testimony, cross examination, legal briefs, and oral arguments; all of these presentments are highly ritualized. Legal skills are generally required to make these presentments in a fashion that meet the technical specifications of the courts. Decorum in court proceedings is highly valued in order to convey a sense of dignity; seldom do legislative or executive offices function with the same degree of decorum.

These distinctive features of judicial policy making—the appearance of objectivity, the fiction of non-partisanship, special rules of access, limited jurisdiction, and legalistic style—all contribute to the power of the courts. These features help to legitimize court decisions, to win essential support for them, and thus contribute to influence of judges in the political system.

The Structure of the Federal Court System

The federal court system consists of three levels of courts with general jurisdiction, together with various special courts (a Court of Claims, a Customs Court, a Patent Court, and the Court of Military Appeals). Only the Supreme Court is established by the Constitution itself, although the number of Supreme Court justices—traditionally nine—is determined by Congress. Article III authorized Congress to establish "such inferior courts" as it deems appropriate. Congress has designed a hierarchical court system consisting of nearly one hundred *U.S. federal district courts* and eleven *U.S. circuit courts of appeals*, in addition to the *Supreme Court of the United States*. (See Figure 11-1.)

Federal district courts are the trial courts of the federal system. Each state has at least one district court, but larger states have more. (New York, for example, has four.) There are over three hundred federal district judges, appointed for life by the president and confirmed by the Senate. The president also appoints a U.S. marshal for each district court to carry out orders of the court and maintain order in the courtroom. Federal

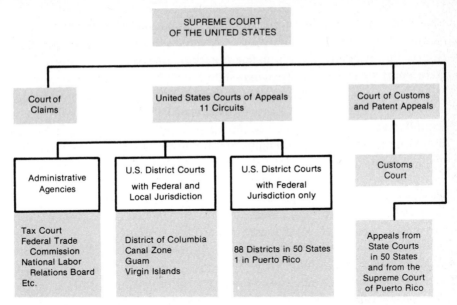

Figure 11-1. The United States court system. (From *The United States Courts: Their Jurisdiction, and Work*, Committee on the Judiciary, House of Representatives, Washington, D.C.: U.S. Government Printing Office, 1969, p. 3.)

district courts hear criminal cases prosecuted by the U.S. Department of Justice, as well as civil cases. As trial courts, the district courts make use of both grand juries (juries composed to hear evidence and, if warranted, to indict a defendant by bringing formal criminal charges against him) and petit, or regular juries (juries which determine guilt or innocence). District courts may hear as many as 300,000 cases in a year.

Circuit courts of appeals are appellate courts. They do not hold trials or accept new evidence but consider only the record of the trial courts and oral or written arguments (briefs) submitted by attorneys. Federal law provides that every individual has a right to appeal his case, so courts of appeals have little discretion in hearing appeals. There are nearly one hundred circuit court judges, appointed for life by the president and confirmed by the Senate. Normally three judges serve together on a panel to hear appeals. Over 90 percent of the cases decided by circuit courts of appeals are ended at this level. Further appeal to the Supreme Court is not automatic, but must be granted by the Supreme Court itself. Hence, for most cases, the decision of the circuit court of appeals is final.

The Supreme Court of the United States is the final interpreter of all matters involving the U.S. Constitution and federal laws and treaties, whether the case began in a federal district court or in a state court. The

Supreme Court has original jurisdiction in some cases (authority to serve as a trial court), but this jursidiction is seldom used. Appellate jurisdiction is the Supreme Court's major function. Appeals may come from a state court of last resort (usually state supreme courts) or from lower federal courts. The Supreme Court determines for itself whether to accept an appeal and consider a case. It may do so if there is "a substantial federal question" presented in the case, or if there are "special and important reasons." Appeal can be granted by any four justices. However, most cases submitted to the Supreme Court, on "writs of appeal" and "writs of certiorari," are denied; and the Court need not give any reason for denying appeal or certiorari.

In the early days of the Republic, the size of the U.S. Supreme Court fluctuated, but since 1869 its membership has remained at nine—a chief justice and eight associate justices. The supreme court is in session each year from October through June, hearing oral arguments, accepting written briefs, conferring among themselves, and rendering opinions.

Majority opinions of the Supreme Court are usually written by a single justice who summarizes majority sentiment. Concurring opinions are written by justices who vote with the majority but who feel the majority opinion does not fully explain their own reasons. A dissenting opinion is written by a justice who is in the minority; such opinions have no impact on the outcome of the case. Written opinions are printed, distributed to the press, and published in *U.S. Reports* and other legal reporting services.

Activism Versus Self-Restraint in Judicial Policy Making

Great legalists have argued the merits of activism versus self-restraint in judicial decision making for more than a century.[11] One view argues for self-restraint in judicial policy making: since justices are *not* popularly elected, the Supreme Court should move cautiously and avoid direct confrontation with legislative and executive authority. Justice Felix Frankfurter wrote:

The only check upon our own exercise of power is our own sense of self-restraint. For the removal of unwise laws from the statute books appeal lies, not to the courts, but to the ballot and to the processes of democratic government.[12]

But Frankfurter was arguing a minority position on the Court. The dominant philosophy of the Warren Court was one of judicial activism. As Harvard Law Professor Archibald Cox, dismissed Watergate Special Prosecutor, posed the question: "Should the Court play an active creative role in shaping our destiny, equally with the executive and legislative branches? Or should it be characterized by self-restraint, deferring to the legislative branch whenever there is room for policy judgement and leaving new departures to the initiative of others?"[13]

Clearly the Warren Court believed it should shape constitutional meaning to fit its own estimate of the needs of contemporary society. In defense of a broad and flexible construction of the Constitution, it can be argued that if the fundamental law of the land does not change over time to fit a changing society dozens of new constitutional amendments would be required each generation. The strength of the American Constitution lies in its flexibility—its relevance to contemporary society.

Nonetheless, the notion of self-restraint is reflected in a number of self-imposed maxims of interpretive philosophy—maxims which are generally, but not always, followed by the Supreme Court:

1. The Court will not pass upon the constitutionality of legislation in a non-adversary proceeding but only in a real case.

2. The Court will not anticipate a question on constitutional law in advance of the necessity of deciding it. The Court does not decide hypothetical cases.

3. The Court will not formulate a rule of constitutional law broader than is required by the precise facts to which it is to be applied.

4. The Court will not pass upon a constitutional question, if there is also present some other ground upon which the case may be disposed of.

5. The Court will not pass upon the validity of a law if the complainant fails to show that he has been injured by the law, or if the complainant has availed himself of the benefits of the law.

6. When there is doubt about the constitutionality of a law, the Court will try to interpret the meaning of a law so as to give it a constitutional meaning and avoid the necessity of declaring it unconstitutional.

7. All remedies available in lower federal courts or state courts must have been exhausted before the Supreme Court accepts review.

8. The constitutional issue must be crucial to the case, and it must be substantial rather than trivial, before the Court will invalidate a law.

9. Occasionally, the Court defers to Congress and the president and classifies an issue as a "political question," and refuses to decide it. The Court has stayed out of foreign and military policy areas.

10. If a law is held unconstitutional, the Court will confine the holding only to the particular section of the law that is unconstitutional, thus not affecting the rest of the statute.[14]

Courts are also limited by the principle of *stare decisis*, which means that the issue has already been decided in earlier cases. Reliance upon precedent is a fundamental notion in law. Indeed, the underlying *common law* of England and the United States is composed simply of past decisions. Students of the law learn what the law is through the case-study method—the study of previous decisions. Reliance on precedent gives stability to the law: if every decision is new law, then no one would know what the law would be from day to day. But the Supreme Court frequently discards precedent. Justice William O. Douglas, who seldom feels restrained by legal precedent, justified disregard of precedent as follows:

the decisions of yesterday or of the last century are only the starting points . . . a judge looking at a constitutional decision may have compulsions to revere the past history and accept what was once written. But he remembers above all else that it is the Constitution which he swore to support and defend, not the gloss which his predecessors may have put on it. So he comes to formulate his own laws, rejecting some earlier ones as false and embracing others. He cannot do otherwise unless he lets men long dead and unaware of the problems of the age in which he lives do his thinking for him.[15]

Distinguished jurists have long urged the Supreme Court to exercise self-restraint. A law may be unwise, unjust, unfair, or even stupid, and yet still be constitutional. One cannot equate the wisdom of a law with its constitutionality; and the Court should decide only the constitutionality and not the wisdom of a law. Justice Oliver Wendell Holmes once lectured his colleague, 61-year-old Justice Stone:

Young man, about 75 years ago I learned that I was not God. And so, when the people . . . want to do something I can't find anything in the Constitution expressly forbidding them to do, I say, whether I like it or not, "Goddamn it, let 'em do it."[16]

But the actual role of the Supreme Court in America's power struggles suggests that the Court is indeed prepared to equate wisdom with constitutionality. Broad phrases in the Fifth and Fourteenth Amendments establishing constitutional standards of "due process of law" and "equal protection of the laws" are frequently cited in attacks on laws believed to be unfair or unjust. Most Americans have come to believe that unwise laws must be unconstitutional, and that the courts have become the final arbiter of fairness and justice.

The Supreme Court in Elitist Perspective

The Supreme Court is best understood as an elitist institution, rather than as a conservative or liberal institution in American government. During the 1930s, the Supreme Court was a bastion of conservatism; it attacked the economic programs of the New Deal and clung to the earlier elite philosophy of rugged individualism. Yet the Warren Court was criticized as too liberal in its orientations toward equality of the law, church-state relations, and individual rights before the law. The apparent paradox can be understood if we view the Court as an exponent of the dominant elite philosophy, rather than as a constant liberal or conservative element in national politics. When the dominant elite philosophy was rugged individualism, the Court reflected this fact, just as it reflects a liberal philosophy today. Of course, owing to the insulation of the Court even from other elites, through life terms and independence from the executive and legislative branches, there is a time lag between changes in elite philosophy and the Court decisions reflecting these changes.

Before the Civil War, the Supreme Court was spokesman first for the Federalists under John Marshall and later for Southern planters and slaveholders under Roger Taney. Marshall, who served as Chief Justice for 34 years, helped to elevate the Supreme Court to a position of importance in American government corresponding to that of Congress and the president. Rulings by his court helped establish the authority of the national government over the states and protect the rights of property. Taney, Marshall's successor, retreated from Marshall's nationalism and defended property rights in land and slaves. In *Dred Scott* v. *Sanford*, Taney declared that slavery was constitutionally protected and invalidated the Missouri Compromise by declaring that Congress did not have the power to exclude slavery from any of the territories.

Following the emergence of industrial capitalism in the second half of the nineteenth century, the Supreme Court became the spokesman for the prevailing elite philosophy of social Darwinism. The Court struck down the federal income tax; it prevented prosecutions of corporations under the Sherman Antitrust Act, while applying this act against labor unions; and it struck down child labor laws and laws limiting the work week. The Court gave such a restrictive interpretation of the interstate commerce clause that it prevented federal regulation of the economy. It interpreted the "due process" clause of the Fifth and Fourteenth Amendments and the contract clause of Article II, Section 10, in such a way as to protect business enterprise from almost any form of government regulation. Justice Oliver Wendell Holmes lamented, "the Fourteenth Amendment does not enact Mr. Herbert Spencer's *Social Statics*. . . . A constitution is not intended to embody a particular economic theory whether of paternalism . . . or of laissez faire."[17] But Holmes was writing a minority opinion. The majority impulse of the Court was to read social Darwinism into the Constitution itself and to give it constitutional protection.

The Supreme Court's greatest crisis occurred when it failed to respond swiftly to changes in elite philosophy. When Franklin D. Roosevelt became president in 1933, the Supreme Court was committed to the philosophy of rugged individualism. In a four-year period, 1933–1937, the Court made the most active use of the power of judicial review over congressional legislation in its history, in a vain attempt to curtail the economic recovery programs of the New Deal. It invalidated the National Industrial Recovery Administration, nullified the Railroad Retirement Act, invalidated the National Farm Mortgage Act, and threw out the Agricultural Adjustment Act. Having denied the federal government the power to regulate manufacturing, petroleum, mining, agriculture, and labor conditions, the Court reaffirmed the notion that the states could not regulate hours and wages. By 1936, it appeared certain that the Court would declare the Social Security Act and the National Labor Relations Act unconstitutional.

The failure of the Court to adapt itself quickly to the new liberalism of the national elite led to its greatest crisis. Roosevelt proposed to "pack" the Court by expanding its size and adding new liberal members. But the nation's leadership itself was divided over such a drastic remedy; the Court had served the interests of the established order so well over its history that Congress was reluctant to accept Roosevelt's plan. Moreover, at a critical point in the debate, the Court changed its attitude, with Chief Justice Hughes and Justice Roberts making timely changes in their position. In *National Labor Relations Board v. Jones & Laughlin Steel Corporation*, the Court expanded the definition of interstate commerce to remove constitutional barriers to government regulation of the economy.[18] The power of the federal government to establish a social security system was upheld in a series of decisions that struck down the "due process" objections to social and economic legislation. And the contract clause was reinterpreted to permit Congress and the states to regulate wages, hours, and conditions of work.

A liberal concern for the underprivileged in America was reflected in the development of civil rights law by the Supreme Court under the leadership of Chief Justice Earl Warren. The Court firmly insisted that no person in America should be denied equal protection of the law. It defended the right of blacks to vote, to attend integrated schools, and to receive equal justice in the courts; it upheld the power of Congress to protect blacks from discrimination in public accommodations, employment, voting, and housing. It ruled that discrimination against any group of voters by state legislatures in the apportioning of election districts was unconstitutional. It protected religious minorities (and the nonreligious) from laws establishing official prayers and religious ceremonies in public schools. The Court also protected defendants in criminal cases from self-incrimination through ignorance of their rights, through the subtlety of law enforcement officials in extracting confessions, or through lack of legal counsel.

It is interesting, however, that the Court was noticeably less concerned with civil liberty when the cold-war ideology of liberal establishment was involved. In *Dennis* v. *United States* the Court permitted the prosecution of communists for merely "advocating" the overthrow of the government[19] and in *Communist Party, U.S.A.* v. *Subversive Activities Control Board*, it upheld the right of government to require the registration of "subversive" organizations.[20] It permitted congressional committees to interrogate citizens about their political views and upheld loyalty oaths and loyalty-security programs. But by the late 1960s, after a decline of cold-war ideology among the nation's elite, the Court began to protect "communists" and "subversives" from some of the harsher provisions of federal law.

Popular predictions that the Burger Court, with four Nixon appointees including Chief Justice Warren Burger, would reverse the liberal decisions of the Warren Court are based on a misunderstanding of the elitist character of the Court. Supreme Court efforts to end racial segregation under law, insure equality in representation, and maintain separation of church and state are fundamental commitments of the national elite. Hence, there is little likelihood of a rollback of the landmark decisions of the Warren Court in these areas. The Burger Court extended the doctrine of *Brown* v. *Topeka* to uphold Court-ordered busing of children to end racial imbalance in public schools with a history of segregation under law (Southern school districts).[21] However, the Court refused to extend the busing requirement to force independent suburban school districts to bus students into central cities to achieve racial balance in predominantly black city schools. The Burger Court also struck down state payments to church schools for nonreligious instruction.[22] Only in the area of rights of criminal defendants has the Burger Court altered the direction of Warren Court holdings; even here, the Burger Court has not reversed any earlier holdings but merely failed to extend them further.

Perhaps the most sweeping declaration of individual liberty in the Supreme Court's history was the recent assertion of the constitutional right of women to have abortions in the first six months of pregnancy. The ultimate impact on society of this decision—on population growth, the environment, and the role of women in society—may be as far-reaching as any decision ever rendered by the Court. Certainly this decision clearly indicates that the Supreme Court continues to be a powerful institution capable of affecting the lives of virtually all Americans.

Recognizing the elitist character of the U.S. Supreme Court, Professor John P. Roche once described the Court as:

. . . a Platonic graft on the democratic process—a group of wise men insulated from the people have the task of injecting truth serum into the body politic, of acting as an institutional chaperone to insure that the sovereign populace and its elected representatives do not act unwisely.[23]

Summary

Many of the nation's most important policies are determined by the Supreme Court of the United States. Indeed, most political questions sooner or later end up in the courts. Yet any fair examination of the court system in America will reveal the elitist character of judicial decision making.

1. The Supreme Court is established as the most elitist branch of the national government. Nine men—none of whom are elected and all of whom serve for life—can void the acts of popularly elected presidents, Congresses, governors, legislatures, school boards, and city councils.

2. The principle of judicial review of congressional acts grew out of the Founding Fathers' distrust of popularly elected officials who could be influenced by popular majorities. Judicial review enables the courts to protect constitutional principles against attacks by elected bodies.

3. The social backgrounds of judges reflect close ties to upper-class segments of society. Presidents may attempt to influence court decisions in their selection of judges, but life terms make judges independent of presidential or congressional influence once they are appointed.

4. Judicial decision making takes on an appearance of objectivity, maintains the fiction of non-partisanship, employs special rules of access, and reflects a legalistic style. These features help to legitimize the decisions of men who have no electoral mandate.

5. Since judges are not popularly elected, some scholars and jurists have urged self-restraint in judicial policy making. This means the Court should decide only the constitutionality of a law, not its wisdom; the Court should not substitute its own judgment for the judgment of elected representatives. But over the years judicial activism has strengthened the power of judges. Broad phrases in the Constitution such as "due process of law" and "equal protection of the law" have been used to strike down laws which the Court believed to be unfair or unjust.

6. Over its history the Supreme Court has not been consistently liberal or conservative, but rather reflective of dominant elite philosophy. The greatest crisis in the Court's history occurred in the 1930s when dominant elites accepted New Deal "liberalism," but the Court continued to reflect the "rugged individualism" of an earlier era. Contrary to popular beliefs, the Burger Court has not reversed any of the landmark decisions of the Warren Court. Instead,

it has continued to reflect prevailing liberal establishment concerns for civil rights, equality in representation, and separation of church and state. The Burger Court's assertion of the constitutional right to have abortions may be one of the most important decisions in the Court's history.

References

[1]Alexis de Tocqueville, *Democracy in America* (New York, Mentor Books, 1956), p. 73.

[2]James Madison, Alexander Hamilton, John Jay, *The Federalist* No. 78 (New York: The Modern Library, 1937), p. 505.

[3]John R. Schmidhauser, *The Supreme Court* (New York: Holt, Rinehart and Winston, 1960), p. 59.

[4]Henry Abraham, *The Judicial Process* (New York: Oxford University Press, 1962), p. 58.

[5]Schmidhauser, *The Supreme Court*, p. 59.

[6]Herbert Jacob, *Justice in America* (Boston: Little, Brown, 1965), p. 95.

[7]Joseph W. Bishop, "The Warren Court is Not Likely To Be Overruled," *New York Times Magazine*, September 7, 1969, p. 31.

[8]*U.S. v. Butler*, 297.

[9]Carl Brent Swisher, "The Supreme Court and the Moment of Truth," *American Political Science Review*, 54 (December 1960), p. 879.

[10]Felix Frankfurter, "The Supreme Court and the Public," *Forum*, 83 (June 1930) pp. 332–334.

[11]Frank Jerone, *Law and the Modern Mind* (New York: Coward-McCann, 1930); Benjamin N. Cardozo, *The Nature of the Judicial Process* (New Haven: Yale University Press, 1921); Roscoe Pond, *Justice According to Law* (New Haven: Yale University Press, 1951).

[12]*West Virginia State Board of Education* v. *Barnette*, 319 U.S. 624 (1943).

[13]Archibald Cox, *The Warren Court* (Cambridge: Harvard University Press, 1968), p. 2.

[14]See Henry Abraham, *The Judicial Process* (New York: Oxford University Press, 1962), pp. 310–326.

[15]Justice William O. Douglas "Stare Decisis," *The Record*, New York City Bar Association, April 1947.

[16]As quoted by Charles P. Curtis, *Lions Under the Throne* (Boston: Houghton-Mifflin, 1947), p. 281; also cited by Abraham, p. 325.

[17]*Lochner v. New York*, 198 U.S. 45 (1905).

[18]*National Labor Relations Board* v. *Jones and Laughlin Steel Corp.*, 301 U.S. 1 (1937).

[19]*Dennis v. U.S.*, 341 U.S. 494 (1951).

[20]*Communist Party, U.S.A.* v. *Subversive Activities Control Board*, 367 U.S. 1 (1961).

[21]*Swann v. Charlotte-Mecklenburg Board of Education*, 39 L.W. 4437 (1971).

[22]*Lemon v. Kurtzman*, 403 U.S. 602 (1971).

[23]John P. Roche, *Courts and Rights*, 2nd ed. (New York: Random House, 1966), pp. 121–122.

Selected Additional Readings

Abraham, Henry J. *The Judicial Process*. New York: Oxford University Press, 1968. This book is one of the most comprehensive introductions to the basics of the judicial process. It provides both a sound theoretical introduction to the nature, sources, and types of law and a thorough "nuts and bolts" knowledge of the staffing, organization, and technical processes involved in the judicial process. There are four extensive bibliographies dealing with American Constitutional law, biographies and autobiographies of and by justices of the United States Supreme Court, comparative constitutional law, and civil liberties.

Jacob, Herbert. *Justice in America*. 2nd ed. Boston: Little, Brown, 1972. Jacob addresses this text to the question of how well American courts administer civil and criminal justice. He views the courts as political, policy-making institutions and examines their participants, procedures, and restraints. Special attention is given to "out-of-court settlements, plea-bargaining, and political justice and injustice."

Schmidhauser, John S. *The Supreme Court*. New York: Holt, Rinehart, and Winston, 1960. Although somewhat dated, *The Supreme Court* is still one of the best historical treatments of the development of the Court as an institution. It examines changes in the organization, procedures, and personnel of the Court over time.

Schubert, Glendon. *Judicial Policy-Making*. Glenview, Ill.: Scott, Foresman, 1965. This book by judicial behavioralist Glendon Schubert views the judicial process as an integral part of the political system. After first examining the relationship of the courts to other structural elements in the political system, Schubert focuses upon the judicial process itself as a policy-making system. He offers a "systemic model of judicial policy-making" and discusses it in terms of its "policy inputs, conversion, and outputs." Also included in the book is an evaluation of several approaches to the study of judicial policy making, including the "traditional, conventional, and behavioral."

CHAPTER 12

AMERICAN FEDERALISM:

ELITES IN STATES AND COMMUNITIES

There are more than 90 thousand state and local governments in America
—states, counties, cities, towns, boroughs, villages, special districts,
school districts, and public authorities. Legally, states are the important
units of government in America; they are endowed with all governmental powers not vested specifically in the national government or
reserved to the people by the U.S. Constitution. All other governmental
jurisdictions are subdivisions of states; states may create, alter, or abolish
these other units of government by amending state laws or constitutions.
Over time, the number of local governments in America has been decreasing, mostly because of the consolidation of small school districts. Even so,
the multiplicity of governments in America is still impressive.[1]

Decentralization—decision making by sub-elites—reduces strain
on the national political system and on national elites by keeping many
issues out of the national arena. Conflict between sub-elites is resolved by
allowing each to pursue its own policies within the separate states and
communities and not battling over a single national policy to be applied
uniformly throughout the land. For example, sub-elites who wish to raise

taxes and spend more money for public schools can do so in their own states and communities, and sub-elites who wish to reduce taxes and eliminate educational "frills" can also do so within their own states and communities. As Robert Dahl explains:

Their local governments permit Americans to take or to keep many questions out of the great arena of national politics, and therefore out of a strictly either-or kind of conflict; they make it possible for Americans to deal with many problems in different ways, ways presumably more in harmony with local tastes and values than any national solution could possibly be. To this extent, presence of a vast network of local government with a good deal of autonomy has probably reduced by a considerable margin the severity of conflict that a wholly national system would run into. By denationalizing many conflicts, local governments can reduce the strain on national political institutions. Importance of denationalizing conflicts can hardly be overestimated, particularly in a large country like the United States where there is a great diversity in resources and local problems.[2]

The masses play an even smaller role in state and local politics than they do in national politics. The news media emphasize national politics rather than state or community politics. Very few citizens know who their *state* senator or *state* representative is, or who their councilmen or county commissioners are. We can expect 55 to 60 percent of the nation's eligible voters to cast ballots in presidential elections, but turnout in state gubernatorial elections in non-presidential years is generally less than 50 percent. Municipal elections often attract fewer than 20 or 30 percent of the eligible voters.

Federalism: The Division of Power Between Nation and States

The Constitution divides power between two separate authorities, the nation and the states, each of which can directly enforce their own laws on individuals through their own courts. In a disputed area, only the Constitution can determine whose authority is legitimate. American federalism differs from a "unitary" political system in that the central government has no legal authority to determine, alter, or abolish the power of the states. At the same time, American federalism differs from a confederation of states, in which the national government is dependent upon its states for power. The American system shares authority and power constitutionally and practically. National and state power are sometimes considered as the opposite ends of a seesaw—if national powers are increased, then state power must decline. But, although national power has expanded over the years, so has the power of states and communities. States and communities perform more services, employ more people, spend more money, and have a greater impact on the lives of their citizens than they have ever had in the past.

The Constitution, in the Tenth Amendment, "reserves" to the states the power to protect and advance the public health, safety, welfare, or morals. This means that the national government may enact no laws dealing directly with housing, streets, zoning, schools, health, police protection, crime, and so on. However, the national government may *tax* or *borrow* or *spend money* to contribute to the general welfare. Thus, Congress cannot outlaw billboards on highways, because billboard regulation is not among the enumerated powers of Congress in the Constitution. But the national government, through its power to tax and spend, can provide financial grants-in-aid to the states to build highways, and then pass a law threatening to withdraw financial aid if the states do not outlaw billboards themselves. Thus, the federal government can indirectly enforce its decisions in such areas as highways and billboard regulation, even though these fields are "reserved" to the states.

The federal government is expanding its power in states and communities by the use of grants-in-aid. During the Great Depression of the 1930s the national government used its taxing and spending powers in a wide variety of areas formerly reserved to states and communities. Grant-in-aid programs to states and communities were initiated for public assistance, unemployment compensation, employment services, child welfare, public housing, urban renewal, highway construction, and vocational education and rehabilitation. The inadequacy of state and local revenue systems contributed significantly to the increase of national power in states and communities. Federal grants-in-aid to state and local governments have expanded rapidly in recent years (see Table 12-1) not only in terms of dollar amounts, but also in terms of the percentage of the total

Table 12-1 / Federal Grants to States and Communities, 1932–1975

Year	Total Federal Grants (in millions of dollars)	Federal Grants as Percent of State-Local Revenue
1932	232	2.9%
1938	800	7.2
1942	858	6.5
1950	2,486	9.7
1955	3,131	8.3
1960	7,040	13.5
1965	10,904	14.6
1970	23,954	18.3
1975	51,732	22.4

Source: Special Analysis Budget of the United States Government 1975.

revenue of states and communities that comes from the federal government.

Whenever the national government contributes financially to state or local programs, the state or local officials are left with less discretion than they would have otherwise. Federal grants-in-aid are invariably accompanied by congressional standards or "guidelines" that must be adhered to if states and communities are to receive their federal money. Often Congress delegates to federal agencies the power to establish the conditions attached to grants. Federal standards are designed to insure compliance with national minimum standards, but they are bound to annoy state and local leaders. Sometimes protests from state and local leaders are loud enough to induce Congress to yield to the views of sub-elites.

State or communities can reject federal grants-in-aid if they do not wish to meet federal standards, and some have done so. But it is difficult to resist the pressure to accept federal money. They are "bribed" by the temptation of much-needed federal money; and they are "black-mailed" by the thought that other states and communities will get the federal money if they do not, although the money was contributed in part by federal taxation of their own citizens.

In short, through the power to tax and spend for the general welfare and through the conditions attached to federal grants-in-aid, the national government can exercise important powers in areas originally "reserved" to the states. Of course, federal grants-in-aid have enabled many states and communities to provide necessary and desirable services that they could not have afforded without federal aid, and federal guidelines have often improved standards of administration, personnel policies, and fiscal practices in states and communities. Further, federal guidelines have helped to insure that states and communities will not engage in racial discrimination in federally aided programs. However, many commentators are genuinely apprehensive that states and communities have surrendered many of their powers to the national government in return for federal money. They argue that the role of states and communities in the American federal system has been weakened considerably by federal grant-in-aid programs and the conditions which are attached to them, because the centralization of power in Washington and the increased role of the national government in state and community affairs limits the individuality of state and local elites.

Elite Structures in the States

Elite structures vary among the fifty states, but observers generally agree that economic elites are the most influential. The authors of The Legisla-

tive System interviewed state legislators in four states, asking them which interests were perceived as most powerful.[3] In all four states, business interests were named the "most powerful groups" more often than any other interests; educational and labor interests, although important, were ranked below business interests in perceived influence. Agricultural interests, government interests (associations of city, county, and township governments, and government employee associations), ethnic interests, and religious, charitable, and civic interests were given only minor mention by state legislators.

It is difficult to measure the relative strength of economic interests in all fifty states. The strength of any interest group is a function of many factors, including resources, organization, leadership, prestige, "cohesion" (unity), and "access" (contacts) to decision makers. Some years ago, the American Political Science Association questioned social scientists in the several states, asking them to judge whether interest groups in their state were strong, moderately strong, or weak.[4] Their judgments are open to challenge, but they are probably the best testimony of interest-group strength in the states. This classification of the states in terms of the strength of their interest groups does not focus exclusively upon economic interests; but it is reasonable to assume that the judgments of these observers were heavily influenced by economic factors.

Table 12–2 shows the relationship between the perceived strength of interest groups in the states, the level of inter-party competition, the degree of party cohesion, and the socioeconomic environments in the states. States with stronger interest groups are more likely to be (1) one-party states, rather than competitive two-party states; (2) states in which parties in the legislatures show little cohesion and unity; (3) states which are poor, rural, and agricultural. Wealthy, urban, industrial states may have more interest groups, but it is difficult for a single interest to dominate the political scene. In contrast, the poorer, rural, agricultural states with relatively backward economies may have fewer interest groups, but the interest groups are stronger and may exercise considerable power over public policy.[5] These findings lend some empirical support to James Madison's belief that "the smaller the society, the fewer the number of interests, and the greater the likelihood that a single interest will dominate."[6] Madison believed that the larger the political society, the less likely a single elite was to dominate its politics.

Let us divide the state elite systems into types to facilitate the identification of elite patterns in state politics. First, in the *single unified elite* system, usually found in a state with a non-diversified economy and weak, non-competitive parties, a cohesive group of economic interests dominates state politics. A good example of this type of elite system is

Table 12-2 / The Strength of Pressure Groups in Varying Political and Economic Situations

Social Conditions	Types of Pressure System*		
	Strong (24 states)†	Moderate (14 states)‡	Weak (7 states)§
Party competition			
One-party	33.3%	0.0%	0.0%
Modified one-party	37.5%	42.8%	0.0%
Two-party	29.1%	57.1%	100.0%
Cohesion of parties in legislature			
Weak cohesion	75.0%	14.2%	0.0%
Moderate cohesion	12.5%	35.7%	14.2%
Strong cohesion	12.5%	50.0%	85.7%
Socioeconomic variables			
Urban	58.6%	65.1%	73.3%
Per capita income	$1,900.	$2,335.	$2,450.
Industrialization index	88.8	92.8	94.0

*Alaska, Hawaii, Idaho, New Hampshire, and North Dakota are not classified or included.

†Alabama, Arizona, Arkansas, California, Florida, Georgia, Iowa, Kentucky, Louisiana, Maine, Michigan, Minnesota, Mississippi, Montana, Nebraska, New Mexico, North Carolina, Oklahoma, Oregon, South Carolina, Tennessee, Texas, Washington, Wisconsin.

‡Delaware, Illinois, Kansas, Maryland, Massachusetts, Nevada, New York, Ohio, Pennsylvania, South Dakota, Utah, Vermont, Virginia, West Virginia.

§Colorado, Connecticut, Indiana, Missouri, New Jersey, Rhode Island, Wyoming.

Source: Harmon Zeigler, "Interest Groups in the States," in Herbert Jacob and Kenneth Vines (eds.), *Politics in the American States* (Boston: Little, Brown and Co., 1965), p. 116.

Maine, of which Duane Lockard writes: "In few American states are the reins of government more openly, more completely in the hands of a few leaders of economic interest groups than in Maine."[7] Specifically, power, timber, and manufacturing—"the big three"—have combined into a cohesive economic elite, due to their key position in the economy of the state. Over three fourths of the state is woodland, and most of this land is owned by a handful of timber companies and paper manufacturers. The timber interests, combined with power companies and textile and shoe manufacturers, control Maine politics to protect their own economic well being. The predominant authority of the big three is rarely challenged with a significant degree of organization or sustained effort.

The deep South states also display the cultural homogeneity and unified elites characteristic of non-diversified or agricultural economies. In addition, Southern elites have traditionally benefited from the general consensus among the white masses that the black must be kept "in his place, and that any efforts by national elites to rearrange racial patterns must be met by a unified white community."[8] Competition among Southern elites is considered particularly dangerous, since a split might contribute to black political influence. Occasionally, "populist" candidates have arisen from the masses to temporarily challenge the dominance of the planting, landowning, and financial elites in Southern states. But once in power, the demagogues have seldom implemented populist programs; more frequently they have become instruments of the established elites whom they castigated in campaign oratory.

A second type of elite structure we shall label *a dominant elite among lesser elites*. This structure is also found in states with a non-diversified economy, although the states may display a reasonably competitive party system, with moderate party cohesion in the legislature. The distinctive feature of the dominant elite among lesser elites structure is the prevailing influence of a single company or industry. A classic example of this elite structure is Montana, where the Anaconda Company has exercised unparalleled influence for almost a century. In a state in which the extraction of minerals is the major non-agricultural source of personal income, Anaconda is the largest employer. In Montana politics, Anaconda is known simply as "the company." The immensity of the Anaconda empire is described by Thomas Paine:

Its strength rests not only in its wealth and resources but also in its elaborate network of relationships with key citizens, banks, legal firms and business organizations throughout the state. Rare is that unit of local government—county, city, or school district—that does not have among its official family an associate, in some capacity, of the Anaconda Company.[9]

However, some leaders, such as Burton K. Wheeler, have built a political career out of opposition to the company, and the company has been forced to accept defeat on certain occasions when faced with a strong combination of lesser elites. In 1959, Anaconda sold its chain of newspapers in the state and assumed a somewhat less visible role in electoral politics. In recent years, Anaconda has remained as quiet as possible, confining itself to legislation directly affecting its economic interests.

The position of Anaconda in Montana is roughly parallel to the position of single dominant economic interests in other states, such as oil in Texas, or DuPont in Delaware. Doubtless the reputation of these interests for absolute control of a state far exceeds their actual exercise of control over public policy; there are many issues in Delaware, for instance, in which the DuPont Corporation and the DuPont family do not become actively involved. Yet it is unlikely that the state of Delaware would ever enact legislation adversely affecting the DuPont Corporation. Likewise, the reputation for oil control of Texas politics is exaggerated. The chairman of the Texas Democratic Executive Committee once said:

"It may not be a wholesome thing to say, but the oil industry today is in complete control of state politics and state government."[10] This is an overstatement that one frequently hears in political circles; many issues in state politics are of little concern to the oil interests. However, it is unlikely that Texas politicians will ever oppose the oil depletion allowance in the federal tax structure, for this is a matter of direct and vital concern to the oil producers.

A *bipolar elite* structure is most likely to be found in an industrial, urban, competitive state with strong and cohesive political parties. Michigan is the prototype of this form of elite structure. While Michigan's economy is industrial rather than agricultural, it is non-diversified and heavily dependent upon the automotive industry; the automobile manufacturers are the largest single employer. But automobile manufacturers do not dominate Michigan politics, because organized labor has emerged as an effective counter-elite to the automobile manufacturers. Joseph La Palombara concludes that "no major issues of policy (taxation, social legislation, labor legislation, etc.) are likely to be decided in Michigan without the intervention, within their respective parties and before agencies of government, of automotive labor and automotive management."[11] Labor and management elites in Michigan each have "their own" political party, and polarization in the elite system is accompanied by strong competition between well-organized, cohesive, and disciplined Democratic (labor) and Republican (management) party organizations.

A *plural elite* structure is typical of a state with a highly diversified economy. California may have the most diversified economy of any state in the nation, with thriving agricultural interests, timber and mining resources, and manufacturing enterprises that run the gamut from cement to motion pictures. The railroads, the brewers, the race tracks, the motion pictures, the citrus growers, the airplane manufacturers, the insurance companies, the utilities, the defense contractors, and a host of other economic interests co-exist in this state. No one economic interest or combination of interests dominates California politics. Instead, a variety of elites govern within specific issue areas; each elite concentrates its attention on matters directly affecting its own economic interest. Occasionally, the economic interests of elites may clash, but on the whole co-existence, rather than competition, characterizes the relationships among elites. Political parties are somewhat less cohesive and disciplined in the plural elite system. Economic elites, hesitating to become too closely identified with a single party, even make financial contributions to opposing candidates to insure that their interests will be protected regardless of which party or candidate wins office.

Single Elites in American Communities

One of the earliest studies of community elites was the classic study of Middletown, conducted by Robert and Helen Lynd in the middle 1920s, and again in the mid-1930s.[12] In Muncie, Indiana, the Lynds found a monolithic power structure dominated by the owners of the town's largest industry, the "X" family. Community power was firmly in the hands of the business class, which controlled the economic life in the city, particularly through its ability to control the extension of credit. The city was run by a "small top group" of "wealthy local manufacturers, bankers, the local head managers of . . . national corporations with units in Middletown, and . . . one or two outstanding lawyers." Democratic procedures and governmental institutions were window dressing for business control. The Lynds described the typical city official as a "man of meager caliber" and as a "man whom the inner business control group ignores economically and socially and uses politically." Perhaps the most famous passage from the Lynds' study was a comment by a Middletown man made in 1935:

If I'm out of work, I go to the X plant; if I need money I go to the X bank, and if they don't like me I don't get it; my children go to the X college; when I get sick I go to the X hospital; I buy a building lot or house in the X subdivision; my wife goes downtown to buy X milk; I drink X beer, vote for X political parties, and get help from X charities; my boy goes to the X YMCA and my girl to their YWCA; I listen to the word of God in a X subsidized church; if I'm a Mason, I go to the X Masonic temple; I read the news from the X morning paper; and, if I'm rich enough, I travel via the X airport.[13]

W. Lloyd Warner, who studied Morris, Illinois, in the 1940s, describes a power structure somewhat similar to that encountered by the Lynds in Muncie. About one third of all of the city's workers had jobs in "The Mill," which Warner says dominated the town:

The economic and social force of the mill affects every part of the life of the community. Everyone recognizes its power. Politicians, hat in hand, wait upon Mr. Waddell, manager of The Mill, to find out what he thinks on such important questions as "Shall the tax rate be increased to improve the education our young people are getting?"—"Should the city support various civic and world enterprises?"—"Should new industries enter the town and possibly compete with The Mill for the town's available labor supply?" They want to know what Mr. Waddell thinks. Mr. Waddell usually lets them know.[14]

Hollingshead studied the same town (sociologists seem to prefer to disguise the names of towns they are studying: Warner called the town Jonesville; Hollingshead called it Elmtown), and his findings substantially confirmed Warner's.[15] And in sociologist Floyd Hunter's influential study of Atlanta, Georgia,[16] community policy is described as originating in a group composed primarily of business, financial, religious, and education leaders rather than from the people of the community.

According to Hunter, admission to the circle of influentials in Atlanta is based primarily on one's position in the business and financial community. Hunter explains that the top power structure concerns itself only with major policy decisions and that the leadership of certain substructures—economic, governmental, religious, educational, professional, civic, and cultural—then take their cues and communicate and implement the policies decided at the top level.

[The substructures] are subordinate . . . to the interests of the policy makers who operate in the economic sphere of community life in the regional city. The institutions of the family, church, state, education, and the like draw sustenance from economic institutional sources and are thereby subordinate to this particular institution more than any other. . . . Within the policy-forming groups the economic interests are dominant [p. 94].

The top power holders seldom operate openly. "Most of the top personnel in the power group are rarely seen in the meetings attended by the associational understructure personnel in Regional City [Atlanta] [p. 90]." Hunter describes the process of community action as follows:

If a project of major proportions were before the community for consideration—let us say a project aimed at building a new municipal auditorium—a policy committee would be formed. . . . Such a policy committee would more than likely grow out of a series of informal meetings, and it might be related to a project that has been on the discussion agenda of many associations for months or even years. But the time has arrived for action. Money must be raised through private subscription or taxation, a site selected, and contracts let. The time for a policy committee is propitious. The selection of the policy committee will fall largely to the men of power in the community. They will likely be businessmen in one or more of the large business establishments. Mutual choices will be agreed upon for committee membership. In the early stages of policy formulation there will be a few men who make basic decisions. . . . Top ranking organizational and institutional personnel will then be selected by the original members to augment their numbers; i.e., the committee will be expanded. Civic associations and the formalized institutions will next be drawn into certain phases of planning and initiation of the projects on a community-wide basis. The newspapers will finally carry stories, the ministers will preach sermons, the associations will hear speeches regarding plans. This rather simply is the process, familiar to many, that goes on in getting any community project underway [pp. 92–93].

Note that in Hunter's description of community decision making, decisions tend to flow *down* from top policy makers (composed primarily of business and financial leaders) to the civic, professional, and cultural association leaders, the religious and educational leaders, and the government officials who implement the program. The masses of people have little direct or indirect participation in the whole process. Policy does not go up from associational groupings or from the people themselves.

The top group of the power hierarchy has been isolated and defined as comprised of policy makers. These men are drawn largely from the businessmen's class in Regional City. They form cliques or crowds, as the term is more often used in the community, which formulate policy. Committees for the formulation of policy are commonplace; and on community-wide issues, policy is channeled by a "fluid committee structure" down to institutional, associational groupings through a lower-level bureaucracy which executes policy [p. 113].

According to Hunter, elected public officials are clearly part of the lower-level institutional substructure that *executes* policy, rather than formulating it. Finally, Hunter found that this whole power structure is held together by "common interests, mutual obligations, money, habit, delegated responsibilities, and in some cases by coercion and force [p. 113]."

Hunter's findings in Atlanta reinforce the elite model, and they are discomforting to those who wish to see America governed in a truly democratic fashion. Hunter's research challenges the notion of popular participation in decision making, or grassroots democracy; it raises doubts as to whether cherished democratic values are being realized in American community life.[17]

Plural Elites in American Communities

Pluralist models of community power stress the fragmentation of authority, the influence of elected public officials, the importance of organized group activity, and the roles of public opinion and elections in determining public policy. Who, then, rules in the pluralist community? "Different small groups of interested and active citizens [rule] in different issue areas with some overlap, if any, by public officials, and occasional intervention by a larger number of people at the polls."[18] Citizens' influence is felt not only through organized group activity, but also through elites anticipating the reactions of citizens and endeavoring to satisfy their demands. Leadership in community affairs is exercised not only by elected public officials, but also by interested individuals and groups who confine their participation to one or two issue areas. The pluralist model regards interest and activity, rather than economic resources, as the key to elite membership. Competition, fluidity, access, and equality characterize community politics.

In his significant study of power in New Haven, political scientist

Robert A. Dahl admits that community decisions are made by "tiny minorities," who are not representative of the community as a whole in terms of social class.[19] However, Dahl challenges the notion that the elite system in American community life is pyramidal and cohesive and unresponsive to popular demands. Dahl studied major decisions in urban redevelopment and public education in New Haven, as well as the nominations for mayor in both political parties. In contrast to Hunter's highly monolithic and centralized power structure in Atlanta, Dahl found a polycentric and dispersed system of elites in New Haven. Influence was exercised from time to time by many elites, each exercising some power over some issues but not over others. When the issue was urban renewal, one set of leaders was influential; in public education, a different group was involved.

Business and financial elites, who in Hunter's study dominate Atlanta, are only one of many influential elites in New Haven. According to Dahl:

> The economic notables, far from being a ruling group, are simply one of many groups out of which individuals sporadically emerge to influence the politics and acts of city officials. Almost anything one might say about the influence of the economic notables could be said with equal justice about a half dozen other groups in the New Haven community [p. 72].

Yet at the same time, Dahl finds that the total number of people who are involved in all community decisions in New Haven are still only a tiny minority of the community. For example, Dahl writes:

> It is not too much to say that urban redevelopment has been the direct product of a small handful of leaders [p. 115].
> The bulk of the voters had virtually no direct influence on the process of nomination [p. 106].
> The number of citizens who participated directly in important decisions bearing on the public schools is small [p. 151].

Moreover, Dahl notes that persons exercising leadership for each issue are of higher social status than the rest of the community, and that these middle- and upper-class elite members possess more of the skills and qualities required of leaders in a democratic system.

Obviously, Dahl's New Haven parallels the pluralist model. However, it is very important to observe that New Haven is not a democracy in the sense that we defined democracy earlier. Not all of the citizens of New Haven participated in the decisions that affected their lives, and not all of the citizens had an equal opportunity to influence public policy.

Aaron Wildavsky's study of Oberlin, Ohio, revealed, if anything, an even more pluralistic structure of decision making than Dahl found in New Haven. Oberlin was a reaffirmation of small-town democracy, where "the roads to influence . . . are more than one; elites and non-elites can travel them, and the toll can be paid with energy and initiative as well as wealth."[20]

Wildavsky studied eleven community decisions in Oberlin, including such diverse issues and events as the determination of municipal water rates, the passage of the fair housing ordinance, the division of United Appeal Funds, and a municipal election. He found "that the number of citizens and outside participants who exercise leadership in most cases is an infinitesimal part of the community."[21] but that no person or group exerted leadership on all issue areas. To the extent that overlap among leaders in issue areas existed, the overlap involved public officials —the city manager, the mayor, and city councilmen—who owed their positions directly or indirectly to "expressions of the democratic process through a free ballot with universal suffrage." Leaders often competed among themselves and did not appear united by any common interest. Persons exercising leadership were of somewhat higher social status than the rest of the community, but it was not status or wealth that distinguished leaders from non-leaders; it was their degree of interest and activity in public affairs.

Edward Banfield's excellent description of decision making in Chicago also fails to reveal a single "ruling elite," although the structure of influence is centralized. Banfield finds that Mayor Daley's political organization, rather than a business or financial elite, is the center of Chicago's influence structure. According to Banfield:

Civic controversies in Chicago are not generated by the efforts of politicians to win votes, by differences about ideology or group interest, or by the behind-the-scenes efforts of a power elite. They arise, instead, out of the maintenance and enhancement needs of large formal organizations. The heads of an organization see some advantage to be gained by changing the situation. They propose changes. Other large organizations are threatened. They oppose, and a civic controversy takes place.[22]

It is not usually business organizations that propose changes in Chicago; "in most of the cases described here the effective organizations are public ones, and their chief executives are career civil servants." Though business and financial leaders played an important role in Chicago politics, they did not constitute a single elite.

After studying seven major decisions in Chicago, Banfield concluded that political heads such as Mayor Daley, public agencies, and civic associations employed top business leaders to lend prestige and legitimacy to policy proposals. The "top leaders" of Chicago—the Fields, McCormacks, Ryersons, Swifts, and Armours—and the large corporations—Inland Steel, Sears Roebuck, Field's Department Store, and the Chicago Title and Trust Company—were criticized less for interfering in public affairs than for "failing to assume their civic responsibilities." Few top leaders participated directly in the decisions studied by Banfield. Banfield admits that this fact is not proof that the top business leadership did not influence decisions behind the scenes; and he acknowledges the widespread belief in the existence of a ruling elite in Chicago. He quotes the head of a black civic association as saying: "There are a dozen men in this town who could go into City Hall and order an end to racial violence just like you or I could go into a grocery store and order a loaf of bread. All they would have to do is say what they wanted and they would get it."[23] Banfield states that top business leaders in Chicago have great "potential for power"—"Indeed, if influence is defined as the *ability* to modify behavior in accordance with one's intentions, there can be little doubt that there exist 'top leaders' with aggregate influence sufficient to run the city"[24]—but he maintains that these top leaders do not, in fact, run the city. Business leaders, divided by fundamental conflicts of interest and opinion, do not have sufficient unity of purpose in community politics to decide controversial questions. They have no effective communication system that would enable them to act in concord; and they lack the organization to carry out their plans, even if they could agree on what should be done.

Sub-Elites: A Comparative View

Differing descriptions of the structures of power in American communities may be a product of the differences among social scientists in theory and methods of research. It is likely, however, that community power structures in the United States range from monolithic elites to very dispersed pluralistic elites. Unfortunately, we do not yet know enough about community power structures across the nation to estimate the frequency of different structures.

The key to understanding community power is relating the types of power structure to local social, economic, and political conditions. For example, we may find that large communities with a great deal of social and economic diversity, a competitive party system, and a variety of well-organized, competing interest groups have pluralist elite systems.

On the other hand, small communities with a homogeneous population, a single dominant industry, non-partisan elections, and few competing organizations may be governed by a single cohesive elite.

One of the most important comparative studies of community power was made by Agger, Goldrich, and Swanson, an intensive study of "power and impotence" in four American communities during a fifteen-year period.[25] These scholars identified four types of power structure, based upon the degree of citizen participation and influence and the degree of competition and conflict among political leaders (Table 12–3).

Table 12-3 / Types of Power Structures

Political Leadership	Distributions of Political Power among Citizens	
	Broad	Narrow
Convergent	Consensual mass	Consensual elite
Divergent	Competitive mass	Competitive elite

Source: Robert Agger, Daniel Goldrich, and Bert Swanson, *The Rulers and the Ruled*, abridged edition (North Scituate, Mass.: Duxbury Press, 1972), p. 38.

If many citizens shared political influence and two or more leadership groups competed with each other, the community was said to have a "competitive mass" power structure. If many citizens shared political influence, but little disagreement or conflict occurred among leaders, the community's power structure was termed "consensual mass." If few citizens shared political influence and leaders rarely disagreed among themselves, the power structure was said to be "consensual elite." If few citizens shared political influence but leaders divided into competing groups, the community was said to have a "competitive elite" structure.

The "consensual elite" structure most closely resembles the monolithic or single elite model described earlier, because citizen influence is limited and leaders share a single ideology. The "competitive mass" structure most closely resembles our pluralist model, inasmuch as many citizens share power and competition occurs among leadership groups. The "ideal" community is probably the "consensual mass" type, in which influence is widely shared among the citizens and little conflict occurs among leaders. The municipal reform movement envisions such a community, in which democracy prevails and "reasonable men" agree to govern in "the public interest."

The authors also proposed a typology of community "regimes" based upon the recognized "rules of the game" in community politics and the degree to which people believe that citizens can be politically effec-

Table 12-4 / Types of Regimes

Sense of Political Effectiveness	Probability of Illegitimate Sanctions Being Used	
	Low	High
High	Developed democracy	Guided democracy
Low	Undeveloped democracy	Oligarchy

Source: Robert Agger, Daniel Goldrich, and Bert Swanson, *The Rulers and the Ruled,* abridged edition (North Scituate, Mass.: Duxbury Press, 1972), p. 44.

tive (Table 12–4). When the "rules of the game" are followed by political leaders, the regime is labeled a "developed democracy" if citizens believe they can influence policy, and an "undeveloped democracy" if they believe they cannot. If leaders frequently resort to illegitimate means— including loss of employment, discrimination, or severe social ostracism—to curtail political participation or free expression, the regime is labeled either a "guided democracy," if public confidence remains high, or an "oligarchy," if people no longer feel they can affect policy.

The Rulers and the Ruled study produced many interesting findings about community power. The "competitive mass" type of power structure (pluralist) is related to a "developed democracy" regime. A sense of political effectiveness among citizens and adherence to the rules of games by leaders is essential for the development of broad citizen participation in community affairs and the emergence of competitive leadership groups. A lack of political confidence among residents and a widespread belief that political activity is useless often result in a monopoly of political leadership and a "consensual elite" (monolithic) power structure.

If leadership changes from competitive to consensual, the distribution of power changes from mass to elite. In other words, with the disappearance of competition among leadership factions, citizen participation declines, fewer issues are submitted to popular referenda, and the power distribution becomes more elitist. Conversely, when the distribution of power changes from elite to mass—that is, when an increasing number of people begin to "crack" the power structure—political competition is likely to increase.

A "competitive mass" (pluralist) type of power structure will be more stable through time if the competing leadership groups represent high and low socioeconomic classes than if the competitors represent the same socioeconomic class. Pluralism depends in part upon socioeconomic cleavages in the community being represented by separate leadership groups. When competitive leaders represent the same socioeconomic class, competition can easily disappear over time, and the power structure can become "consensual" rather than "competitive."

Agger, Goldrich, and Swanson also find that "developed democracy" regimes and "competitive mass" power structures are less likely to occur in communities in which the major industries are home-owned. Economic leaders of home-owned industries tend to be members of a single group of political leaders that discourage competition. The prominence of these people influences some groups in their communities to refrain from political activity because they fear illegitimate political sanctions, even though the actual use of these sanctions is relatively infrequent. Interestingly, Agger, Goldrich, and Swanson found no relationship between community size or growth rate and either the type of regime or the nature of the power structure in the four communities they studied.

Summary

The existence of political sub-elites within the larger American political system permits some decentralization of decision making. Decentralization, or decision making by sub-elites, reduces potential strain on the consensus of national elites. Each sub-elite is allowed to set its own policies in its own state and community, without battling over a single national policy to be applied uniformly throughout the land. Let us summarize the propositions that emerge from our consideration of American federalism and our comparative analysis of elites in states and communities.

1. Debate over state versus national power reflects the power of various interests at the state and national level. Currently, the liberal public-regarding elites dominant at the national level generally assert the supremacy of the national government. In contrast parochial, conservative, rural interests dominant in some states and communities, but with less power at the national level, provide the backbone of support for "states rights."

2. Although national elites now exercise considerable power in states and communities, particularly through federal "grant-in-aid" programs, this growth of national power has not necessarily reduced the power of state and local governments. State and local government activities are not declining, but growing and expanding.

3. Economic elites in states and communities are generally ranked as the "most powerful groups" by legislators.

4. States with the most cohesive elite system are likely to be one-party states, not competitive two-party states; states in which political parties show little cohesion and unity; and states that are poor, rural, and agricultural. Wealthy, urban, industrial states have more elite groups, but it is difficult for a single elite to dominate the political scene.

5. Scholars have described American communities in terms reflecting both single elite and plural elite models. Yet even the plural elite studies conclude that "the key political, economic, and social decisions" are made by "tiny minorities." They also find that these "tiny minorities" are recruited from the upper- and middle-class community. Few citizens participate in community decisions that affect their lives.

6. There is conflicting evidence about the extent of competition among community elites, the extent of elite concentration, the fluidity of elites, the ease of access to elite membership, the persistence of elite structures over time, the relative power of economic elites, and the degree of mass influence. Some scholars have reported a polycentric structure of power with different elite groups active in different issue areas and a great deal of competition, bargaining, and sharing of power among elites.

7. Elite structures in communities are related to the community's size, economic function, and social composition. Small communities with a homogeneous population, a single dominant industry, a weak party structure, and few competing organizations are more likely to be governed by a single cohesive elite. Larger communities with social and economic diversity, a competitive party system, and well-organized competing interest groups are more likely to have plural elite systems.

8. Monolithic power structures are associated with a lack of political confidence among residents and with a widespread belief that political activity is useless. A plural elite system is associated with a sense of political effectiveness among citizens and with adherence to the rules of the game by leaders.

References

[1] For a comprehensive survey of government and politics in American states and communities, see Thomas R. Dye, *Politics in States and Communities* (Englewood Cliffs, N.J.: Prentice-Hall, 1969).

[2] Robert Dahl, *Pluralist Democracy in the United States* (Chicago: Rand McNally, 1967), p. 181.

[3] John Wahlke, et al., *The Legislative System* (New York: John Wiley, 1964).

[4] See Belle Zeller, *American State Legislatures* (New York: Thomas Y. Crowell Co., 1954), pp. 190–191.

[5] Harmon Zeigler, "Interest Groups in the States," in Herbert Jacob and Kenneth A. Vines (eds.), *Politics in the American States* (Boston: Little, Brown and Co., 1965), p. 114.

[6] James Madison, Alexander Hamilton, John Jay, *The Federalist* No. 10 (New York: Modern Library, 1937).

[7] Duane Lockard, *New England State Politics* (Princeton, N.J.: Princeton University Press, 1959), p. 79.

[8] See V. O. Key, Jr., *Southern Politics* (New York: Alfred A. Knopf, 1948).

[9] Thomas Paine, "Under the Copper Dome: Politics in Montana," in Frank H. Jonas (ed.), *Western Politics* (Salt Lake City: University of Utah Press, 1961), pp. 197–198.

[10] Robert Engler, *The Politics of Oil* (New York: Macmillan Co., 1961), p. 354.

[11] Joseph La Palombara, *Guide to Michigan Politics* (East Lansing: Michigan University, Bureau of Social and Political Research, 1960), p. 104.

[12]Robert S. and Helen M. Lynd, *Middletown* (New York: Harcourt, Brace & World, 1929); and *Middletown in Transition* (New York: Harcourt, Brace & World, 1937).

[13]Lynd and Lynd, *Middletown in Transition*, p. 74.

[14]W. Lloyd Warner, *Democracy in Jonesville* (New York: Harper & Row, 1949), p. 10.

[15]August B. Hollingshead, *Elmtown's Youth* (New York: John Wiley, 1949).

[16]Floyd Hunter, *Community Power Structure* (Chapel Hill: University of North Carolina Press, 1953).

[17]For a more pluralist view of Atlanta's power structure, see Kent Jennings, *Community Influentials* (New York: Free Press, 1964).

[18]Aaron Wildavsky, *Leadership in a Small Town* (Totowa, N.J.: Bedminister Press, 1964), p. 8.

[19]Robert Dahl, *Who Governs?* (New Haven, Conn.: Yale University Press, 1961).

[20]Wildavsky, p. 214.

[21]Wildavsky, p. 265.

[22]Edward Banfield, *Political Influence* (New York: Free Press, 1961), p. 263.

[23]Banfield, p. 289.

[24]Banfield, p. 290.

[25]Robert Agger, Daniel Goldrich, and Bert Swanson, *The Rulers and the Ruled*, abridged edition (North Scituate, Mass.: Duxbury Press, 1972).

Selected Additional Readings

Agger, Robert, Daniel Goldrich, and Bert Swanson. *The Rulers and the Ruled.* North Scituate, Mass.: Duxbury Press, 1972. This book presents an in-depth study of "power and impotence" in four American communities over a fifteen-year period.

Dahl, Robert A. *Who Governs?* New Haven: Yale University Press, 1961. This is perhaps the most important pluralist community power study. Using a "decisional approach," Dahl finds the existence of a number of elites making decisions in different issue areas.

Hunter, Floyd. *The Power Structure.* Chapel Hill: University of North Carolina Press, 1953. Although classical elitism has its origins in European sociological theory, much of the current American controversy over elitism has been the result of community power research. Hunter's *The Power Structure* was one of the first community power studies reporting elitist results. His use of the "reputational method" in this study of Atlanta set the scene for a heated debate with the pluralists Dahl and Polsby.

Ricci, David M. *Community Power and Democratic Theory: The Logic of Political Analysis.* New York: Random House, 1971. (See Chapter 1, page 29.)

Walton, John. "Substance and Artifact: The Current Status of Research on Community Power Structures." *American Journal of Sociology,* 72 (1966), 430–438. Walton makes an extensive survey of community power literature and finds that the use of the reputational method tends to yield elitist results, while use of the decisional method tends to yield pluralist results.

CHAPTER 13

PROTEST MOVEMENTS:

CHALLENGE TO DOMINANT ELITES

The place of blacks and other economically deprived groups in American society has been a central domestic issue of American politics since the first black slaves were brought to the United States in 1619. The American nation as a whole, with its developing (if ambiguous) democratic tradition, has felt strong sentiments against slavery, segregation, and discrimination. But white America has also harbored an ambivalence toward blacks—a recognition of the evils of inequality but a reluctance to take steps to eliminate it. Gunnar Myrdal, writing in 1944, captured the essence of the American racial dilemma:

The "American dilemma" . . . is the ever-raging conflict between, on the one hand, the valuations preserved on the general plane which we shall call the "American creed," where the American thinks, talks, and acts under the influence of high national and Christian precepts, and, on the other hand, the valuation on specific planes of individual and group living, where personal and local interests; economic, and social, and sexual jealousies; considerations of community prestige and conformity; group prejudices against particular persons or types of people; all sorts of miscellaneous wants, impulses, and habits dominate his outlook. [1]

Myrdal's formulation of the American dilemma has much in common with the more general attitudes of the American masses toward democracy: commitment to abstract ideals, but substantially less commitment to the behavior that follows from these ideals. As it was pointed out earlier, elites need pay little attention to mass opinion in making most policy decisions; for the most part, the masses are ignorant of and apathetic about policy issues. But the attitudes of white masses toward blacks are important for two reasons: (1) Civil rights is so visible an issue that elite behavior is more circumscribed by mass opinion than is normally the case; and (2) since blacks constitute only a small portion of the total population, they are largely dependent upon the benevolence of the white majority.

The struggle of blacks for full citizenship can be viewed as a dialogue—sometimes violent, sometimes peaceful—between the demands

Dist. Publishers-Hall Syndicate

© Jules Feiffer

of black counter-elites and the response of dominant white elites. Although the dialogue receives its most complete articulation in the behavior of elites, its base is in the attitudinal structure of the masses. Each group of elites interprets (and consequently distorts) the aspirations of the masses whom they pretend to represent. And each group interprets and distorts the aspirations of the opposing group as well.

That there should be such a struggle at all in the United States is a demonstration of the extent to which racial feelings take precedence over moral and constitutional requirements. The language of the Fourteenth Amendment leaves little doubt that the original purpose of this amendment was to achieve full citizenship and equality for American blacks.

All persons born or naturalized in the United States, and subject to the jurisdiction thereof, are citizens of the United States and of the state wherein they reside. No state shall make or enforce any law which shall abridge the privileges or

immunities of citizens of the United States; nor shall any state deprive any person of life, liberty, or property without due process of law; nor deny to any person within its jurisdiction the equal protection of the law.

However, 100 years after the ratification of this amendment, the National Advisory Commission on Civil Disorders wrote: "Our nation is moving toward two societies, one black, one white—separate and unequal."[2] The commission strongly implicated whites in the failure of blacks to share equally in the affluence of American society.

What white Americans have never fully understood—but what the Negro can never forget—is that white society is deeply implicated in the ghetto. White institutions created it, white institutions maintain it, and white society condones it.[3]

The commission thus assumed that whites must solve the problem that they created. This assumption is a radical reversal of the American consensus that each *individual* can achieve anything he wishes in this open society. The generally negative reaction of governmental elites and of the masses to the report of the Commission on Civil Disorders indicates how radical is the idea that environmental rather than individual circumstances are the reason for ghetto life and violence.

In recent years, the civil rights movement has undergone a substantial shift in goals and in techniques. Beginning with efforts to remove legal discrimination, principally in the South, the civil rights movement has lately turned its attention toward economic inequalities in the North. As Bayard Rustin observes: "The very decade which has witnessed the decline of legal Jim Crow has also seen the rise of *de facto* segregation in our most fundamental socioeconomic institutions."[4] Americans can understand legal discrimination; and the majority—even a strong minority in the South—agree that such discrimination is inconsistent with the norms of a democratic society. However, the idea that society as a whole has a responsibility to reduce economic inequalities is alien to the myths and symbols that cement white society together.

The Historical Background of Black Subjugation

The period of slavery is of more than historical interest; we are still feeling the impact of the brutality of this period. The scars of the rigidly enforced obedience system and the matriarchal family structure characteristic of slavery are still present today. Elkins has compared Southern slavery to Nazi concentration camps in its effects upon personality.[5] Both institutions were closed and highly authoritarian; both produced, for the most part, total obedience to the authority figure. In concentration camps, for example, guards were frequently viewed as father figures. Correspondingly, among slaves, the master often represented a father figure. Slavery, by rewarding obedience and compliance, negatively sanctioned individual effort and achievement. Even today, Southern blacks are, in comparison to those of Northern origin, passive and non-militant. The relative acquiescence of those blacks whose backgrounds are closest to slavery is a remnant of the dependent position of the slave upon his master.

Another factor with consequences that blacks are still struggling to overcome is the "deculturation" of the slaves. That is, blacks from many different cultures were thrown together, and there was no common cultural buffer to make it possible for them to resist the psychological effects of the economic and social conditions of slavery. The condition of slavery became their dominant institution—an institution that molded the personality of the blacks. For example, slaves, in order to survive within the system, developed child-rearing practices that emphasized obedience rather than achievement; and the descendants of these slaves still show the effects of this training.

McClelland, who has developed devices to measure need for achievement, found that lower-class blacks who are the group least removed from the effects of slavery, have the lowest need for achievement of any minority group. McClelland found, on the other hand, that middle-class blacks are uniformly higher in the need for achievement than are middle-class whites. This illustrates, first, that it is not being black that reduces the need for achievement and, second, that achieving members of the minority groups need to be more motivated than achieving members of majority groups. Since most blacks are lower class, however, they are unable to break out of the pathology of the ghetto. Ghetto norms reinforce the traditions of the past.[6]

Slavery also hindered the development of a strong family life. Since many slave-owners separated families on the auction block, the slave household developed a matri-focal pattern. After slavery was abolished, poverty in the ghetto strengthened the mother-centered tradition. Even now, about one fourth of the non-white families, compared to only 9 percent of the white families, have female heads.[7]

In 1865, the Thirteenth Amendment abolished slavery everywhere in the United States. The Fourteenth Amendment, which was passed in 1867 by a Republican Congress that intended to reconstruct Southern society after the Civil War, made "equal protection of the laws" a command for every state to obey. The Fifteenth Amendment, passed in 1869, provided that the right to vote could not be abridged by either federal or state governments "on account of race, color, or previous condition of servitude." In addition, Congress passed a series of civil rights statutes in the 1860s and 1870s guaranteeing the new black freedman protection in the exercise of his constitutional rights. The Civil Rights Act of 1875 specifically outlawed segregation by owners of public accommodation facilities. Between 1865 and the early 1880s, the success of the civil rights movement was reflected in widespread black voting throughout the South, the presence of many blacks in federal and state offices, and the almost equal treatment afforded blacks in theaters, restaurants, hotels, and public transportation.

But by 1877, support for reconstruction policies began to crumble. In what has been described as the Compromise of 1877, the national government agreed to end military occupation of the South, give up its efforts to rearrange Southern society, and lend tacit approval to white supremacy in that region. In return, the Southern states pledged their support for the Union, accepted national supremacy, and agreed to permit the Republican candidate, Hayes, to assume the presidency, although the Democratic candidate, Tilden, had received a majority of the popular vote in the disputed election of 1876. The Supreme Court adhered to the terms of this compromise. In the famous Civil Rights Cases of 1883, the Supreme Court declared unconstitutional those federal civil rights laws preventing discrimination by private individuals. By denying Congress the power to protect blacks from discrimination, the Court paved the way for the imposition of segregation as the prevailing social system of the South. In the 1880s and 1890s, segregation was imposed in public accommodations, housing, education, employment, and almost every other sector of private and public life. By 1895 most Southern states had passed laws requiring segregation of the races in education and in public accommodations.

In 1896, in the famous case of *Plessy* v. *Ferguson*,[8] the Supreme Court upheld state laws requiring segregation of the races. Even though segregation laws involved state action, the Court held that segregating the races did not violate the equal protection clause of the Fourteenth Amendment so long as the persons in each of the separated races were treated equally. Schools and other public facilities that were "separate but equal" won constitutional approval.

The violence that occurred during this period was almost entirely one-sided and consisted of attacks by whites upon blacks. Grimshaw refers to this type of racial violence as "Southern style."[9] The pattern of race relations at the turn of the century was clearly one of violent repression, the exclusion of blacks from jobs and labor unions, and rigid segregation. Blacks had lost most of what they had gained during Reconstruction.

Twentieth-Century Responses

The First Civil Rights Organizations As a result of the repressive pattern of the late nineteenth century, the first black organizations emerged. The National Association for the Advancement of Colored People (NAACP) and the National Urban League were formed in 1909 and 1910, respectively. Both of these organizations reacted against Booker T. Washington's acceptance of the inferior status of blacks, and both worked closely with white liberals. These organizations, depending as they did upon the goodwill of whites, chose a strategy of seeking black equality through court action and other legal means. They were (and still are) moderates, dominated by middle-class blacks and upper-class whites. They accepted the premise that meaningful change can be obtained within the framework of the American legal system. They were (and are) conservative in the sense that their techniques require commitment to the institutional *status quo*. They specifically disavowed any attempt to change or overthrow the basic political and economic structure of the society, for the changes they sought were limited to the inclusion of blacks in the existing society. In other words, they took literally the ideology and premises of the American democratic system.

When the concentration of blacks in Northern cities increased the potential for mass action, a new style of violence began to emerge. A series of grievances, such as discrimination in housing and transportation, is expressed by the black community. As grievances build and expression becomes more aggressive, a precipitating incident occurs; and blacks respond by attacking whites or their property. The Northern style riot differs substantially from the Southern style violence; blacks no longer remain passive victims but become active participants. The "Northern style" riot made its first appearance in Springfield, Illinois, in 1908.

Perhaps the first important black counter-elite was Marcus Garvey. Since the NAACP was an avowedly elitist organization both in membership and appeal, the Universal Negro Improvement Association was organized by Garvey, a West Indian, to articulate the feelings of a latent black nationalism. Garvey's programs for a separate black nation in Africa held considerable appeal for improverished blacks, especially as white bigotry, in the form of the Ku Klux Klan, spread north in the wake of black economic advance. Garvey's appeal was essentially similar to that of the Black Muslims of the 1950s and 1960s and the more radical black nationalists of the late 1960s. Like the Muslims, Garvey urged his followers to practice personal frugality and establish a high level of morality. Like the nationalists, he sought to teach blacks that "black" is a color of which one could be proud rather than ashamed. At one time, Garvey had a following estimated at three million, but his movement collapsed in the middle 1920s. However, the response from the black masses was very important, for Garvey's appeal rested on the assertion that blacks would never achieve what the NAACP insisted that they could achieve—an equal share in the American economic system. As Myrdal observes, the Garvey movement "tells of the dissatisfaction so deep that it mounts to hopelessness of ever enjoying a full life in America."[10]

The period following the Korean War, marked by enormous legal and symbolic victories, was crucial in the development of the relationship between blacks and whites. The long labors of the NAACP paid off in the historic *Brown* v. *Board of Education of Topeka*[11] decision in which the Court reversed the *Plessy* v. *Ferguson* doctrine of "separate but equal." This decision symbolized the beginning of a new era of high expectations among blacks. While elected elites had remained silent on civil rights and, in fact, exhibited substantial hostility, an appointed elite, the Supreme Court, declared that blacks and whites were equal in the eyes of the law.

However, the hostility of *elected* elites continued throughout the 1950s. With World War II over, the Fair Employment Practices Commission—symbolic though it was—was destroyed, and no civil rights legislation could pass through the gauntlet of Congress. In 1948, for example, attempts to re-establish the Fair Employment Practices Commission, to outlaw poll taxes, to eliminate segregation in public transportation, and to pass a federal anti-lynching law were all unsuccessful. The Dixiecrat Revolt of 1948, led by Strom Thurmond, was in direct response to the increasing commitment of the Democratic party to civil rights and indicated the strength of the "conservative coalition" in the Senate and House. This coalition of Southern Democrats and Northern Republicans was able to block civil rights legislation regularly, and it held firm through the 1950s.

Brown v. *Board of Education of Topeka* marked the beginning, not the end, of the political battle over segregation. Segregation would not be abolished merely because the Supreme Court had declared it unconstitutional. Unless the political power of the white majority in the South were successfully challenged by another political elite with equal resources, the pattern of segregation would remain unchanged. Segregation was widespread and deeply ingrained. Seventeen states required segregation, and the Congress of the United States required segregation in Washington, D.C. Four other states (Arizona, Kansas, New Mexico, and Wyoming) authorized segregation at local option.

The Supreme Court, in not ordering immediate desegregation, snatched the tangible portion of the victory away from blacks. The Court placed primary responsibility for enforcing this decision upon local officials and school boards, thus in effect returning power to the white sub-elites in the South. As a result, during the 1950s the white South developed a wide variety of schemes to resist integration. Ten years after *Brown v. Board of Education of Topeka*, only about 2 percent of the blacks in the South had actually been integrated; the other 98 percent remained in segregated schools. In short, the decision meant nothing to the overwhelming majority of blacks, whose frustrations were intensified by the discrepancy between the declarations of the Supreme Court and the behavior of the local officals. Legally they were victorious, but politically they were impotent, since the South stubbornly refused to abide by the decision of the Court.

The continuation of this symbolic victory and tangible defeat reoriented the civil rights movement away from the removal of legal restrictions and toward the removal of *de facto* segregation and unequal socioeconomic institutions.

That this phase of the civil rights movement is strongly elitist should be carefully noted. The bargaining and exchanges took place largely between the NAACP and the Supreme Court, both of which were insulated from both white and black masses. The elite orientation of the NAACP, as previously noted, meant that its leadership accepted the prevailing values of white elites. Its attraction was to the "talented tenth"—the minority of upper-class, educated blacks. Its strategy was the "rules of the game"—litigation, not protest. White elites, especially those most removed from mass sanction, found NAACP values quite compatible with their own. The educated blacks of the NAACP sought only the removal of legal barriers in order to provide equality of opportunity. Being educated, they regarded education as the key to success. NAACP leadership, being economically successful on the whole, gained a relatively higher degree of acceptance by white elites. Thus, they were culturally at the periphery of the black community. The success of the NAACP depended largely upon the maintenance of "good connections" with white elites, and the organizational leadership did not intend to risk its favored position by identifying with those sections of the black community unacceptable to the white elites.

Creative Disorder and Hostile Outbursts   The first stage in the reorientation of the civil rights movement toward creative disorder began in

1955, immediately after the *Brown* v. *Board of Education of Topeka* decision. Certainly the symbolic importance of this decision cannot be overestimated; and despite the fact that tangible benefits were minimal, the decision undoubtedly stimulated the escalation of black expectations and demands. Additional elite sanctions, such as President Eisenhower's sending troops to Little Rock, Arkansas, in support of the 1954 decision (in spite of the fact that he disapproved of the Court's decision), gave further support to the rising expectations of blacks. Now the executive branch, in addition to the judiciary, had committed itself to the legal equality of blacks. Kenneth Clark assesses the importance of official sanction as follows:

> . . . This [civil rights] movement would probably not have existed at all were it not for the 1954 Supreme Court school desegregation decision which provided a tremendous boost to the morale of Negroes by its clear affirmation that color is irrelevant to the rights of American citizens. Until this time the Southern Negro generally had accommodated to the separation of the black from the white society.[12]

Dramatic support for Clark's hypothesis can be found in the 1955 refusal of a black to ride in the back of a bus in Montgomery, Alabama. Her act resulted in the Montgomery boycott and the first significant evidence of a shift away from the legalism of the NAACP. Ironically, the shift of the civil rights movement away from the NAACP occurred at least partially because of the legal successes of the older organization.

The Montgomery bus boycott illustrated the general relationship between elites and masses. The work of the NAACP was conducted exclusively by black elites. Their work stimulated mass behavior, which in turn required mass-oriented leadership. The need for mass-oriented leadership was filled initially by Martin Luther King, who was catapulted into prominence by the bus boycott. The Southern Christian Leadership Conference (SCLC) emerged in 1957 as the first Southern-originated civil rights group. Although substantially more militant than the older black organizations, it was nevertheless explicitly nonviolent. Mass demonstrations were to be used to challenge the legality of both legal and *de facto* segregation and to prick the consciences of white elites.

The tactics of the SCLC were expanded upon by the Student Nonviolent Coordinating Committee (SNCC), which was created from the next phase of direct action, the sit-in demonstrations and freedom rides of the 1960s. In February 1960, at Greensboro, North Carolina, the first sit-ins were conducted by North Carolina Agricultural and Technical College students. These sit-ins were followed by others, and SNCC was organized in order to coordinate this new student protest. SNCC, unlike the SCLC, encouraged blacks to feel proud of being black. The Congress on Racial Equality, which had been created in the 1940s, emerged from limbo to lead the freedom rides, which challenged the Jim Crow laws of transportation facilities. Many thousands of students participated in these extremely dangerous freedom rides.

The vigor with which the freedom rides and sit-ins were pursued indicated that the civil rights movement was committed to direct action. However, even this new phase of the civil rights movement was not a mass movement; the participants were still relatively privileged in comparison to the black masses. The most frequent participants in the confrontations of the early 1960s were urban students, who were substantially less prejudiced and bitter against whites than were later leaders. These students had a very tolerant and optimistic attitude toward the white community. The freedom riders were not despair-driven anarchists but optimistic young people. The relatively privileged youths were disappointed in the unwillingness of the white society to recognize their merit. According to Matthews and Prothro:

This resulted in a sense of relative deprivation when they compared their chances with those of middle-class whites and the values professed by the white community. Thus the active protestors felt deprived by "white" or general American standards of judgment at the same time they felt relatively advantaged by Negro standards. [13]

This phase of the black civil rights movement can thus best be explained by the relative-deprivation hypothesis advanced by Crane Brinton. He argues that revolutions are most likely to be led not by those at the bottom of the status pyramid, but by those who are more privileged than the masses they lead. [14]

In 1963, in Birmingham, Alabama, prolonged demonstrations were conducted on the broadest front yet conceived by civil rights leaders. Demands to end discrimination in public accommodations, employment, and housing were presented to the white elite of Birmingham. Under the leadership of Martin Luther King, these demonstrations were committed to nonviolence. Probably because of the broad nature of the demands, participation in these demonstrations reached the grass roots of the black community for the first time. All strata of the black community were involved.

Birmingham was, as we have mentioned, the beginning of a new militancy on the part of all classes of blacks. But it was also the signal for an escalation of violence on the part of whites. In Mississippi, Medgar Evers was shot; in Alabama, a white postman, participating in the civil rights march, was ambushed and killed. Violence was sanctioned by

Southern elites, as was their custom. No one was punished for the murder of Medgar Evers, and Alabama Governor George Wallace stood at the door of the University of Alabama to prevent a black from entering. In Birmingham, a bomb killed four black girls who were attending Sunday school; and this was the twenty-first bombing and the twenty-first time that the bombers were never apprehended. These incidents gave evidence of the increasing tension between the races.

The Civil Rights Act of 1964 The Birmingham demonstrations were another landmark in the civil rights movements. As a partial consequence of the repressive behavior of Southern elites toward these peaceful demonstrations, the Kennedy Administration was moved to propose significant civil rights legislation. The Birmingham demonstration of 1963 began what was to become the Civil Rights Act of 1964 and the first significant entry of Congress into the civil rights field.

The Civil Rights Act of 1964 passed both houses of Congress by more than a two-thirds favorable vote; it won the overwhelming support of both Republican and Democratic congressmen. It ranks with the Emancipation Proclamation, the Fourteenth Amendment, and *Brown v. Board of Education of Topeka* as one of the most important steps toward full equality for blacks in America. The act provides:

I. That it is unlawful to apply unequal standards in voter registration procedures or to deny registration for irrelevant errors or omissions on records or applications.

II. That it is unlawful to discriminate or segregate persons on the grounds of race, color, religion, or national origin in any place of public accommodation, including hotels, motels, restaurants, movies, theatres, sports areas, entertainment houses, and other places which offer to serve the public. This prohibition extends to all establishments whose operations affect interstate commerce or whose discriminatory practices are supported by state action.

III. That the Attorney General shall undertake civil action on behalf of any person denied equal access to a public accommodation to obtain a federal district court order to secure compliance with the act. If the owner or manager of a public accommodation continues to discriminate, he shall be in contempt of court and subject to preemptory fines and imprisonment without trial by jury. [This mode of enforcement gave establishments a chance to mend their ways without punishment, and it also avoided the possibility that Southern juries would refuse to convict persons for violations of the act.]

IV. That the Attorney General shall undertake civil actions on behalf of persons attempting orderly desegregation of public schools.

V. That the Commission on Civil Rights, first established in the Civil Rights Act of 1957, shall be empowered to investigate deprivations of the right to vote, to study and collect information regarding discrimination in America, and to make reports to the president and Congress.

VI. That each federal department and agency shall take action to end discrimination in all programs or activities receiving federal financial assistance in any form. This action shall include termination of financial assistance.

VII. That it shall be unlawful for any employer or labor union with 25 or more persons after 1965 to discriminate against any individual in any fashion in employment, because of his race, color, religion, sex, or national origin, and that an Equal Employment Opportunity Commission shall be established to enforce this provision by investigation, conference, conciliation, persuasion, and, if need be, civil action in federal court.

The Civil Rights Act of 1964, while largely symbolic, did result in some tangible gains for Southern blacks. The withdrawal of federal grant-in-aid money as a sanction was a remarkable innovation in federal enforcement of civil rights. When the United States Office of Education began to apply pressure in the South, progress was impressive in comparison with the previous ten years. The lessons of this astonishing increase are quite clear: in order to convert symbolic into tangible victories, a tangible sanction must be utilized. However, the Civil Rights Act of 1964 contained an amendment that forbade government agencies to issue any orders achieving racial balance in areas that did not have legally segregated schools in the past. Thus, the United States Office of Education could not issue desegregation guidelines outside the South, and the act, therefore, had no effect on the plight of blacks in the ghettos.

Nevertheless, the 1964 Civil Rights Act was a symbolic victory nearly equal to that of the 1954 *Brown v. Board of Education of Topeka* decision. One hundred years after the end of the Civil War, the three branches of the federal government had declared themselves to be in sympathy with black Americans.

In this phase of the civil rights movement, the dominance of the NAACP was broken, and more militant action was undertaken. Black elites, even those who successfully challenged NAACP hegemony, were still largely of middle-class origin. By appealing to the conscience of white elites they were able to extend symbolic victories to the legislative process. Though resulting in minimal tangible reallocations, such victories contributed to a loss of control by black elites of the black masses. The masses, activated by symbolic victories, began to rebel against black elites. This rebellion took place in the ghetto.

Life in the Ghetto

The ghettos were initially created when blacks migrated into, and whites out of, slum areas. This migration has gradually been declining, but the ghettos are well established. Only about one half of the American black population lives in the South; the other half lives in the central cities of the North. Fully 98 percent of the black population increase in recent years has taken place in the central cities, while 77 percent of the white population increase has occurred in the suburbs.[15] Thus, the central cities are becoming black and the suburbs white.

All major American cities are characterized by a high degree of residential segregation. In 1960, the segregation index for the 707 largest cities was 86.2, meaning that 86 percent of all blacks lived in essentially all-black areas in the cities. In the larger cities outside of the South, those containing over two thirds of the black population, segregation indexes are unusually high. For example, the segregation index of Chicago was 92.6; that of New York, 79.3; that of Los Angeles, 81.8; that of Detroit, 84.5; and that of Philadelphia, 87.1. These figures have remained quite stable and in many cases have actually increased since 1960. Consequently, Taeuber and Taeuber conclude:

In the urban United States there is a very high degree of segregation of the residences of whites and Negroes. This is true for cities in all regions of the country and for all types of cities—large and small; industrial and commercial, metropolitan and suburban. It is true whether there are hundreds of thousands of Negro residents or only a few thousand. Residential segregation prevails regardless of the relative economic status of the white and Negro residents. It occurs regardless of the character of local law and policies and regardless of the extent of other forms of segregation or discrimination.[16]

The physically crowded conditions in ghettos are pathological and conducive to violent collective behavior. Some of the more overt manifestations of the pathology of ghetto life can be observed in the remarkably high crime rate. Table 13–1 indicates the remarkable persistence of criminal activity within the ghetto. Crimes against persons are extremely high, and the presence of police seems to make little difference. Police departments apparently tolerate substantially more violence among blacks, even though they assign more patrolmen to ghetto areas.

Table 13-1 / Incidence of Crime and Patrolmen Assignments per 100,000 Residents in Four Chicago Police Districts, 1965

Economic Makeup of Districts	Crimes against Persons	Crimes against Property	Patrolmen Assignments
High income white	80	1,038	93
Low-middle income white	440	1,750	133
Mixed high-low income white	338	2,080	115
Low income Negro	1,618	2,508	243

Source: Report of the National Advisory Commission on Civil Disorders (Washington, D.C., 1968), p. 267.

Lawlessness in the ghetto is seemingly sanctioned by both whites and blacks and has become a way of life. For example, until the riots, there were no "law and order" protests against crime and violence in the ghetto. So long as the victims of black violence were blacks, the white society remained complacent. Similarly, although the probability of being a victim of a violent crime is 78 percent higher for non-whites than it is for whites, it is the whites who now express concern about the maintenance of "law and order."

The poverty of the ghetto undoubtedly contributes to the high incidence of crime. While there has been substantial improvement in the economic position of blacks in recent years, this improvement is not bringing the ghetto population appreciably closer to the white standard of living. It is customary to compare the relation of white to non-white income to ascertain the extent of the progress; and it is true that black income, as a proportion of white income, has been increasing. However, the dollar difference between the white and the black median family incomes has actually been increasing. In 1952, the difference in per capita income between the two races was $1,415; in 1966, it was $2,908; in 1972, it was $4,685. Thus, although blacks have made absolute economic gains, they are increasingly falling behind whites. Further, the unemployment rate among blacks remains twice as high as for whites (10 percent versus 5 percent), a ratio virtually identical to that in 1964. Education is supposed to be the key to success, but a significant discrepancy exists in the lifetime earnings of whites and blacks at identical educational levels. Moreover, the discrepancy between black and white incomes increases as education increases. That is, the more education a black achieves, the less is the dollar value of the education to him (see Table 13–2). Given two equally motivated people—one white and one black—it is worth substantially more to the white to get as much education as he can. Since the income gap widens as education increases, a non-white college graduate earns less in a lifetime than a white with only an eighth-grade education.

Table 13-2 / Median Income for all Males (25 years old and over) by Race and Education, 1969

Years of Schooling	Black Male	White Male	Ratio
Elementary — less than 8	$3,000	$ 3,600	.82
8	4,300	5,500	.79
High School 1–3	5,200	7,300	.71
4	6,100	8,600	.71
College 1–3	7,100	9,600	.74
4 or more	8,600	12,400	.69

Source: *Current Population Reports,* Series P-60, No. 75, Table 47, p. 105.

Inequality *among* blacks is much greater than *among* whites. The black social class structure resembles a pyramid. Most of the black population is at the bottom of the pyramid, with only a few blacks at the top.[17] The white social class structure, on the other hand, is diamond-shaped; there are a few whites at both the top and the bottom, and most whites are in the middle. This is proved economically. The inequality of income distribution is greater among blacks than among whites and is not improving.

This persisting inequality of income among blacks is evidence of the politics of tokenism. A few blacks attain middle-class economic status, but in so doing they lose contact with the ghetto. These blacks who are at the top of the pyramid, are looked upon by whites as examples of what can be accomplished in an egalitarian society. Actually, the relationship of these few middle-class blacks to the black masses is so remote as to make them useful primarily as symbolic rewards for white liberal elites. They are certainly not useful as practical or even symbolic leaders for the ghetto blacks. This, however, may be changing as more middle-class blacks appear and feel isolated from *both* the white middle class *and* the lower-class blacks. Under these conditions, middle-class blacks would be able to develop their own identity.

White and Black Mass Perceptions of Black Urban Violence

A polarization of attitudes between the black and white masses, resulting in differing perceptions of the same events, is developing. Consider the different perceptions of black violence. Since whites believe that blacks are treated equally with whites, they feel that the riots are caused by agitators, communists, and hoodlums. In Detroit, for example, 70 percent of the whites believed the riots were completely irresponsible, unjustifiable, and the work of criminals. In contrast, 71 percent of the blacks believed that the riots were the result of wide-spread mistreatment and social injustice.[18] Clearly, blacks do not see riots as random or individual behavior, but instead as a spontaneous protest against unfair economic deprivation. Remove these conditions, they argue, and you will remove the cause of the riots. The essential difference between the attitudes of blacks and whites, therefore, is that to whites the riots have little social meaning but to blacks they are of great social significance.

Strangely, although whites do not attach any social significance to the riots, they view them as planned rather than spontaneous. The conspiracy theory of riots dominates the attitudes of whites. Whites also believe that only a tiny minority of the black population riots or is in sympathy with violence, though they simultaneously exhibit some tendency to believe that blacks are more violent by nature than whites. But among black explanations for the riots, phrases like "want to be treated like a human being" occur time and time again. These phrases are rarely heard as whites explain riots. When asked, for example, "What do you think is the most important thing the city government can do to keep a disturbance from occurring?" about half the whites, but only one tenth of the blacks, say "more police control."[19]

The polarity of black and white attitudes is well illustrated in the reaction of both groups to the explosive symbol "Black Power." Whites, responding negatively, see "Black Power" as synonymous with "black rule," but the majority of blacks see the symbol as meaning "black pride" and a fair share of the economic rewards of American society. Such symbols operate to create cohesion among blacks, irrespective of socioeconomic status.

Ironically, income inequalities between middle-class and lower-class blacks operate to strip the black population of many potential leaders. For example, efforts in Northern cities to speed up residential integration at the middle-class level skim off those blacks whose life styles are middle class and co-opt them into the white society in limited numbers. Those who remain behind—the overwhelming majority of blacks—cannot accept the leadership of those who leave the ghetto; for upwardly mobile blacks often try to outdo middle-class whites in conformity and achievement. It is noteworthy that demands for integration are made largely from the upwardly mobile segments of the black population who want to get out of the ghetto and are frequently critical of lower-class blacks. The fact that some black property has been attacked in recent riots attests to the hostility which exists among blacks. As Kenneth Clark observes: "The ghetto develops a sinister power to perpetuate its own pathology, to demand conformity to its norms; it ridicules, drives out, or isolates those who seek to resist these norms or even transform them."[20]

The psychology of the ghetto, argues Clark, produces cynicism, suspicion, and fear of the outside world. The ghetto psychology consequently prevents the development of potentially effective leaders, thus contributing to the cycle of pathology. The pathology of the ghetto also manifests itself in the attitudes and life patterns of blacks. Basically, ghetto life encourages both severe alienation and extreme mental illness. Self-identity problems of blacks are especially acute. Since about one fourth of the families in the ghetto have female heads, black boys are deprived of the benefits of socialization into manhood by a male model. Consequently, their problems of sexual identification are intense. Matriarchal traditions, begun by slavery and enhanced by poverty, also lower the self-esteem of black males. Lowered self-esteem, as we have seen, reduces achievement motivations; and reduced achievement motivations often result in economic failure and, occasionally, individual violence, in order to compensate for the loss of self-esteem.

Discrimination is also substantially harder on males than females. The black male was most humiliated by segregation; keeping the black "in his place" usually meant keeping the *male* in his place.

The popularity of Africana among blacks may be linked to problems of self-esteem. However, the popularity of African music, styles of dress, and hair styles should not be confused with a genuine desire for separatism or a return to Africa. No more than one fourth of the black population is genuinely separatist; and separatism is no more than an extreme desire to develop a more favorable self-image. There is a substantial yearning by American blacks for some sort of cultural identity.

Among the black masses, there is the persistent belief that whites are not in sympathy with them. Only one third see whites as well intentioned, while two thirds see them as either hostile or indifferent.[21] The white masses feel that this suspicion is unjustified, since they are willing to express a verbal commitment to civil rights. But most whites, denying the existence of discrimination, avoid any responsibility for the conditions in the ghetto. Only one fifth of the whites, compared to two fifths of the blacks, believe that blacks are discriminated against in employment. Denying the existence of discrimination makes it possible for whites to blame black problems on blacks themselves, specifically upon their lack of ambition and industriousness.[22] Since we have seen that ghetto life does lower aspiration levels, there is some surface truth to these white beliefs. Actually, however, lower aspiration levels and lower actual achievement are environmentally induced; they are not inherent characteristics of blacks. As we noted earlier, middle-class blacks have higher achievement levels than middle-class whites.

Police in the Ghetto

To many ghetto dwellers, the police are the symbol of white oppression. "Police brutality" has become a theme with enormous emotional impact among blacks. James Baldwin's description of the attitude of ghetto dwellers toward police cannot be improved upon. He notes that:

. . . *their very presence is an insult, and it would be, even if they spent their entire day feeding gumdrops to children. They represent the force of the white world, and that world's real intentions are, simply, for that world's profit and ease, to keep the black man corralled here in his place. The badge, the gun and the holster, and the swinging club make vivid what will happen should this revolution become overt. . . . He moves through Harlem, therefore, like an occupying soldier in a bitterly hostile country; which is precisely what, and where, he is, and is the reason they walk in twos and threes.*[23]

Since the policeman's role in the ghetto is that of a symbol of white authority and repression, even the most exemplary behavior on his part would risk offense to the ghetto dwellers. And, of course, the behavior of many policemen is far from exemplary. The white masses strongly reject the idea that police behavior in the ghettos has been brutal or even discriminatory; only a small proportion of whites accept without reservation the possibility that blacks might be subject to rough treatment and disrespect by police. Seventy-two percent of the whites believe that blacks are treated the same as whites.[24] Of course, dissatisfaction with the police among the black masses runs very deep; Table 13–3 shows the extent of this hostility.

Table 13-3 / Black and White Mass Perceptions of the Police: Percentage Agreeing with Various Statements

	Black	White
The police do not come quickly when called.	51%	27%
The police do not show respect and use insulting language.	38	16
The police frisk and search without good reason.	36	11
The police are too rough when arresting.	35	10

Source: Supplementary Studies for The National Advisory Commission on Civil Disorders (Washington, D.C., July 1968), p. 44.

Given this state of high tension between police and ghetto residents, it is almost invariable that a police action is the precipitating event immediately preceding a riot. A routine arrest made in an atmosphere of increasing tensions and black exasperation by previous perceptions of police hostility is usually the trigger for large-scale rioting. Blacks feel by a two-to-one margin that police brutality is a major cause of disorder, an idea that is rejected by whites by an eight-to-one margin.

Studies of police attitudes have uncovered a substantial reservoir of anti-black bias. For instance, Albert Reiss reported the following information to the Kerner Commission:

In predominantly Negro precincts, over three fourths of the policemen expressed prejudice or highly prejudiced attitudes towards Negroes. . . . What do I mean by extreme prejudice? I mean that they describe Negroes in terms that are not people terms. They describe them in terms of the animal kingdom. . . .[25]

Peter Rossi also studied the police in the cities that suffered violence. He finds that policemen feel that blacks are pushing too hard. Seventy-nine percent of the police do not believe that blacks are treated worse than the whites; and, like most whites, the policemen cannot see the need for any further push toward equality. They exhibit fairly strong anti-black attitudes; for example, 49 percent do not approve of the idea of whites and blacks socializing, and 56 percent are disturbed at blacks moving into white neighborhoods.[26] In an accurate estimate of black opinion, the police believe that only a small minority of blacks regard them as their friends, whereas a substantial majority the whites do so. However, policemen cannot understand why blacks resent them. Still, it is interesting that the police view themselves in much the same terms as blacks view them as to their status in the ghetto: The policemen feel alone in a strange and hostile land.

Table 13–4 compares the attitudes of police and educators about the causes of riots. We can see that the police perceive riots as acts of criminal irresponsibility, whereas educators view the riots as produced by economic and social grievances. Police are more inclined to think that blacks are basically violent and that they have been misled by militants and criminals. Educators are more inclined to think that riots are caused not by the basic violence of blacks but by the unwillingness of whites to listen to their complaints.

The goal of the police is generally not to reduce the long-term problems of the ghetto but to effect short-term control of riots. They wish to suppress riot activity vigorously, and they are angered by the leniency they perceive in judges and courts.* Police in the ghetto also have strong negative attitudes toward black civil rights groups and toward federal poverty agencies. They perceive the civil rights groups as contributors to violence and the poverty agencies as misguided social reform institutions that do not understand the legitimacy of force.

The attitudes of the police are understandable in view of the recruitment and socialization processes through which they pass. Police are recruited from the social classes most likely to have anti-black biases—the lower-middle and working classes. Moreover, very few police

---

*Because their occupation is a hazardous one that tends to develop strong in-group ties, the police also view lack of public support as a major problem. However, they need not worry about lack of support among the white community; 54 percent of the whites favor Mayor Daley's order to shoot looters on sight, and an even higher proportion favor a national holiday to honor the police (Gallup Opinion Index, Report No. 37, July 1968, p. 17). Clearly, the police are emerging as heretofore unappreciated heroes in the eyes of whites.

Table 13–4 / Views of Policemen and Educators about Blacks: Percentage Agreeing with Various Statements

	Police	Educators
Negroes are basically violent.	28%	8%
Riots are caused by police brutality.	9	33
Riots are caused by nationalists and militants.	77	46
Criminal elements are involved in riots.	69	33
Unheard Negro complaints are involved in riots.	31	70

Source: Supplemental Studies for the National Advisory Commission on Civic Disorders (Washington, D.C., July 1968), p. 96.

have had college training. Since we know that education is positively correlated with tolerance, we would expect that the police, being disproportionately representative of the uneducated classes, would be as typically intolerant as the average lower-class white.

In addition to the initial anti-black bias, occupational socialization probably strengthens the attitudes of policemen. The element of danger in policemen's jobs makes them naturally suspicious. Also, since policemen are engaged in enforcing rules, they become overly concerned with authority, and are politically and emotionally conservative. Jerome Skolnick observes: "It was clear that a Goldwater type of conservatism was the dominant political and emotional persuasion of police. I encountered only three policemen (out of 50) who claimed to be politically 'liberal,' at the same time asserting that they were decidedly exceptional."[27]

Add to these police attitudes the fact that the crime rate in ghettos is unusually high, and we have the makings of another vicious circle. One officer describes the operation of this circle:

The police have to associate with lower-class people, slobs, drunks, criminals, riff-raff of the worst sort. Most of these . . . are Negroes. The police officers see these people through middle-class or lower-middle-class eyeballs. But even if he saw them through highly sophisticated eyeballs he can't go into the street and take this night after night. When some Negro criminal says to you a few times, "Take off that badge you white mother fucker and I'll shove it up your ass," well it's bound to affect you after a while. Pretty soon you decide they're all just niggers and they'll never be anything but niggers. It would take not just an average man to resist this feeling, it would take an extraordinary man to resist it, and there are very few ways by which the police department can attract extraordinary men to join it.[28]

The Desegregation Issue

Another agent of white society in the ghetto is the schools. *De facto* school segregation in Northern ghettos—that is, segregated housing patterns coupled with neighborhood schools—has continued unabated, even as token integration has been achieved in the South. Approximately three quarters of all black pupils in Northern cities attend *de facto* segregated schools—that is, schools in which 90 percent or more of their classmates are black. Whereas in the South there has been some progress toward integration, in the North process of segregation is actually increasing.[29] This increase in *de facto* segregation in the North has occurred because the Negro population in the central cities has grown and because school officials have taken little action to achieve racial balance.

Although the majority of both races prefer integration, at least at the level of verbal commitment, white parents oppose many of the measures that would make integrated education possible. White parents have successfully fought busing of students in most Northern cities. What whites have in mind, when they say that it is permissible for blacks and whites to attend the same schools, is a balance in which most of the children are white. For example, although a majority of whites approve the idea of integration, two thirds of them would not want to send their child to a school where more than half are black. One third of the whites object to sending their children to schools in which approximately half the pupils are black.[30]

Partially because of such unshakeable opposition, it was not until the years 1968–71 in a series of major decisions on school integration that the Supreme Court finally began to give form to desegregation legally required by the Brown decision of 1954. In 1969 the Court discarded the "all deliberate speed" formula and ruled that no further postponement could be constitutionally permitted *(Alexander v. Holmes, 1969)*. Then, in 1971, in the *Swann v. Charlotte-Mecklenburg* case, the Court finally faced the full implications of the earlier Brown decision.

The school board of Charlotte, North Carolina argued that their segregated school system was the innocent byproduct of a racially neutral neighborhood school policy. Given that neighborhoods reflect economic status and income differentials between blacks and whites, it was only "natural" that some schools would be overwhelmingly white and others overwhelmingly black.

The Court, however, refused to accept this defense and ruled that school authorities must do whatever necessary including busing children to different schools outside their neighborhood, to achieve integration. If there had once been official school segregation, the Court reasoned authorities had a positive obligation to produce integration immediately. It soon became apparent that this decision would have as great an impact in the North as it would in the South. Almost every state in the country with more than a token non-white population had at one time or another requirements or practices which resulted in some form of school segregation. As Table 13–5 shows, there was actually a higher degree of segregation in many *Northern* states than Southern states.

Table 13-5 / Racial Isolation in Northern and Southern States, 1970

State	% Black	% Segregated
U.S. Average	14.9	38.2
North Carolina	29.4	12.2
Arkansas	24.7	15.5
South Carolina	40.9	17.2
Virginia	24.1	20.9
Connecticut	9.0	21.3
Massachusetts	4.5	2.7
Florida	23.1	21.9
Mississippi	50.8	29.9
Georgia	33.2	30.8
New Jersey	15.4	36.3
Louisiana	40.4	37.1
Wisconsin	4.2	37.7
Alabama	34.3	38.9
Texas	15.3	41.9
Ohio	12.1	42.8
Pennsylvania	11.8	44.3
Maryland	24.2	45.7
California	9.2	46.7
Michigan	13.4	49.8
Tennessee	21.2	50.1
Illinois	18.2	71.2

Source: Department of Health, Education and Welfare, July 18, 1971.

The civil rights movement began with the goal of achieving equal opportunity by repealing acts of official discrimination. However, it soon became apparent that integration and equality of opportunity would require fundamental changes in a predominantly white society. This federally inspired "social engineering" came into increasing conflict with traditional local prerogatives, particularly in the neighborhood school system where local elites predominate. White resistance stiffened, and from 1966 on, local protests spurred increasing congressional attacks on school desegregation requirements.

Richard Nixon made his opposition to busing a central issue in his 1968 campaign for election, saying, "I oppose any action by the Office of Education which goes beyond a mandate of Congress. A case in point is the busing of students to achieve racial balance in schools." He also opposed "withdrawing federal funds to force a local school board to balance its schools racially, by busing children all over the city." Since the withholding of federal funds is the prime method by which the government can enforce compliance with the law, Nixon's election in 1968 largely removed the executive from the arena of enforcing desegregation. The role of the Justice Department also changed significantly. In contrast to its previous vigorous prosecution of noncompliance, it now pleaded with the Supreme Court for a delay in desegregation. The federal courts were left to bear the burden of desegregation without the active assistance of the executive branch and with increasing criticism from the legislative branch.

Decisions requiring extensive busing were handed down in Texas, Virginia, Tennessee, Florida, Mississippi, Georgia, and elsewhere. Soon federal judges handed down decisions requiring substantial transportation of children in a number of Northern cities as well. When lower-court decisions in Richmond and Detroit suggested the assignment of pupils across city-suburban lines on a city-wide basis, suburban resentment was immediate and intense. Millions of white people all over the country who had been unaffected by the Southern cases suddenly felt threatened. Polls showed that 82 percent of the public opposed mandatory busing, whereas only 18 percent supported it. Blacks themselves were evenly divided on the question.[31]

In 1971 the House of Representatives adopted a series of amendments designed to restrict the power of the courts and executive agencies to require urban desegregation by busing. President Nixon again made clear his opposition to busing in his 1972 campaign for re-election. By the end of 1972 the House passed a measure drastically curtailing the power of federal courts to order busing even within a single school district. In effect, the bill would have repealed the Supreme Court decision in the *Swann* case. Indicative of the widespread support for the anti-busing measure was the fact that a number of Northern congressmen who had once been fervent civil rights supporters supported the bill. A majority of the Senate was ready to vote for the bill, and it was defeated only when civil rights supporters killed the measure by use of a filibuster.

In December 1973, the House again voted 221 to 192 to ban the busing of students farther than the school nearest their homes. In an amendment denounced by black members of the House, Rep. John D. Dingell, a liberal Democrat from Michigan, proposed to "save more than 78 million gallons of fuel a year" by not busing school children farther than physically necessary and thus aid in coping with the energy crisis.

Political opposition to busing children for the purpose of achieving racial balance in the school comes mainly from parents who fear their children will be transported into the violent crime-ridden culture of the ghetto. They fear that their children will be exposed to what black children have long had to cope with—rape, robbery, extortion, mugging, dope addiction—which have made ghetto schools blackboard jungles where surviving is more important than learning. Many white parents moved to the suburbs at great cost to themselves to obtain a better education for their children, and they do not appreciate the prospect of federal judges ordering their children back to ghetto schools. Generally, white parents are less fearful of black pupils being transported to white schools (as long as blacks remain a minority) than they are of white pupils being transported to predominantly black schools. Thus, limited one-way busing over relatively short distances is politically feasible. But the specter of large-scale two-way busing, transporting white children ten to thirty miles from the suburbs to the ghetto, is another matter.

The widespread fear of busing between suburbs and central cities seemed to be at the heart of the Supreme Court's 5 to 4 ruling, on July 25, 1973, striking down Detroit's plan to integrate the school system by merging it with white neighboring districts. With all of Nixon's appointees to the Court voting together in the majority, the Court effectively halted busing across school district lines. Consequently, the continued segregation of northern cities was guaranteed. Since the suburbs are white and the central cities are black, the decision was a major victory for the white middle and upper classes. However, those whites, mostly the lower classes, still living within the central city (e.g., those unable to afford the exodus to the suburbs), still faced the probability of busing. Hence, a major disturbance in September 1974 occurred in Boston when intra-city busing began. The Supreme Court decision—coupled with continuing protest by those whites remaining in the central city—solidified the division of metropolitan areas into black central cities and white suburbs.

President Nixon has recommended that Congress legislate a "moratorium" on court-ordered busing until after the Supreme Court has considered the issue again and come to a clear and binding decision. Some congressional critics of court-ordered busing have proposed a constitutional amendment prohibiting federal courts from ordering racial balancing in public schools. Public opinion polls consistently show heavy public opposition to busing. But supporters of busing argue that black children have a constitutional right to equal educational opportunity and that busing is a necessary tool in achieving this constitutional right. The supporters are a very small minority, and the probability of busing is at best remote.

In spite of the psychological advantages accruing to black children from genuinely integrated schools, and in spite of the increases in educational achievement that occur, there is also strong resistance among educational elites to racial balancing in classrooms. An example of such resistance is the behavior of superintendents. Crain found that superintendents of large school districts generally professed to be "color blind." In general, they oppose the classification of schools as "segregated" or "integrated." However, by refusing to consider racial balance a problem for schools, they impede the process of integration. The official ideology of some members of the educational establishment—"keeping politics out of the schools"—means avoiding social and political issues and minimizing public criticism. It also means, as Crain observes, that ". . . the interaction between civil rights leaders and school superintendents has the preconditions for conflict. They literally do not speak the same language."[32]

Riot, Revolution, or Repression?

Rising Expectations and Revolt   We have classified urban violence as a phase in a social movement. Why did it occur in the 1960s, and what is the next phase? The crime statistics in Table 13–6 indicate that mass racial violence increased steadily up to 1968, when it declined significantly. At the same time, individual crimes of violence and crimes against persons increased rapidly. What meaning can be made of these seemingly contradictory trends? Much of the decline in civil disturbances undoubtedly reflects the winding down of the Vietnam War, but we might also infer from the above data that the nature of political protest is undergoing a dramatic change in this country. Since the essentially peaceful days of "non-violent civil disobedience" characteristic of the late fifties and early sixties, political protest has grown steadily more violent in America. It has also moved underground as the established elites learned to cope more efficiently and effectively with openly organized militant groups and mass demonstration tactics of protest. Therein lies a possible explanation of the meaning behind the decline in mass protest and the increase in violent crime against person and property. A theoretical reason suggested for the increase in racial violence in the past 20 years is that blacks have hopes of bettering their condition. Totally subservient people seldom revolt. When things are looking up, but not far enough up, violence is likely to erupt. It is not those who have accepted poverty as a way of life but those who are rising in the social order who become the most intense advocates of change.

Table 13-6 / Trends in Crime Statistics

| | | **Crime Rates** | | | | |
		Total	Murders	Rape	Robbery	Assault
Crime Rate Per 100,000	1960	160	5	10	60	85
	1965	198	5	12	71	110
	1967	251	6	14	102	129
	1968	295	7	16	131	142
	1969	325	7	18	147	152
	1970	361	8	19	171	163
	1971	393	9	20	187	177
	1972	398	9	22	180	187
1960–1970 % Increase		126%	60%	90%	186%	92%

| | **Civil Disturbances & Related Deaths** | | | |
Period	Total	Major[1]	Other[2]	Deaths
1967, June–Oct.	52	12	40	87
1968, all year	80	26	54	83
1969, all year	57	8	49	19
1970, all year	76	18	58	33
1971, all year	39	10	29	10
1972, all year	21	2	19	9
1973, Jan.–March	4	1	3	2

[1]*Major* = characterized by: 1) vandalism 2) arson 3) looting or gunfire 4) outside police used 5) more than 300 involved (excluding police) 6) 12 hours or longer duration.

[2]*Other* = Any of 1 to 4 above; duration at least three hours and more than 150 involved (excluding police).

Source: Statistical Abstract of the U.S., 1973

James C. Davies has pointed to the disparity between *expectations* and *actual* reward, rather than the absolute level of reward deprivation, as the key factor in revolutionary movements.[33] As noted earlier in the chapter, while the economic well-being of blacks has increased over the past 20 years, it is still much less than that of whites and, more significantly, it is growing at a much lesser rate. The *differences* between the economic well-being of whites and blacks is actually *increasing* in a time when black expectations are not decreasing. It is Davies's theory that masses do not revolt until they *perceive* the possibility of actually bettering their lot in life, while at the same time *perceiving* that their attempts to do so are being thwarted. Persons with a long-standing history of deprivation, or those who are severely repressed, are not likely to perceive any real hope of alleviating their distressed condition. Only when forces not of their own making cause them to hope—justifiably or not—that conditions can become better will they perceive that change is possible and seek further gains. Thus, expectations tend to rise as perceptions of material or social well-being rise.

Davies postulates that as long as the gulf between their expectations and their perception of actual conditions does not grow too immense, the deprived and repressed minorities will not engage in revolutionary activity. However, if their perception of want satisfaction does not keep pace with their rising expectations, the underprivileged will eventually revolt, for there is a critical point at which the gulf becomes intolerable.

Black violence in America lends itself to analysis through the use of Davies's model. Two factors have contributed to the rise in black expectations in the past two decades: (1) the Southern black emigration to the Northern cities, with the concomitant anticipation of economic betterment; and (2) the symbolic rewards flowing from federal desegregation policies. Although these factors conspired to raise the expectations of blacks, they failed to make good their promises. Moreover, the white backlash, particularly as manifested in the stiffening resistance against the use of busing to achieve school integration, tended to dull symbolic gratification as well as impede the progress of further reform.

That black expectations were on the ascendance as long ago as 1954 is attested to by the fact that, in that year, 64 percent of them, compared to only 53 percent of the whites, thought that life would be getting better for them.[34] By 1972, however, only 47 percent of non-whites expressed satisfaction with the future, compared to 59 percent of the whites.[35] The riots and mass violence in the 1960s indicate that black expectations have not been sufficiently realized.

The extent to which diffuse and vaguely defined violence becomes organized and carefully channeled violence depends in the long run upon white elite reaction. Separatism and support for violence among blacks is not confined to a few radicals. Most blacks—even most rioters—favor racial harmony, but nationalism attracts a substantial minority. More blacks participated in riots than many whites realize; it is likely that between 10 percent and 30 percent have actually participated in various hostile outbursts. Further, fully 60 percent of those who have participated would be willing to do so again; and 54 percent of all blacks who did not and would not riot are sympathetic with the rioters. Clearly, the rioters are not outcasts in the eyes of other blacks. They are not outside agitators but indigenous members of the black community.[36]

The data also indicate that elite reaction to rioting as a tactic in rebellion was quick and effective. Police forces throughout the country were provided with larger budgets, trained in riot-control techniques, and equipped with various new weapons such as tear gas and helicopters. Within two years of the initiation of a counter-intelligence campaign by the FBI, the number of civil disturbances in the country peaked and began to decline. At the same time, violent crime continued to increase. The number of police officers killed by felons, for example, has grown steadily since 1963 (Table 13–7).

Table 13-7 / Police Officers Killed: 1963 to 1971

	1963	1964	1965	1966	1967	1968	1969	1970	1971
Total Killed	88	88	83	99	123	123	125	146	178
By Felons	55	57	53	57	76	64	86	100	126
In Accidents	33	31	30	42	47	59	39	46	52

Source: U.S. Federal Bureau of Investigation, *Uniform Crime Reports for the United States,* annual.

Terrorism and Repression A careful distinction between "terror" and "terrorism" should be drawn. "Terror" is intimidation by the powerful, and "terrorism" is attempted control by intimidation by the powerless, helpless, and would-be powerful. Terror is used as a means of social control by all police states, and terrorism has been familiar to Europeans since at least the days of the *fin de siècle* anarchist movement in the late nineteenth century. In the twentieth century, terrorism that is well organized and planned with definite, long-term aims was used successfully by the Algerians in their fight for independence from France in the 1950s. Since then it has become a tactic of almost every guerrilla movement in the world, with particular refinements added by the Viet Cong, the Palestinian Black September group, the Irish Revolutionary Army (IRA), and the Tupamaro guerrillas of Uruguay.

In the past six years, American intelligence experts have chronicled 432 major acts of international terrorism, including 235 bombings, 93 hijackings, and at least 57 kidnapings. At least 196 people died and another 300 were injured as a result of these operations, and ransom payments and property damage have run into millions of dollars. However, it has only been in recent years that calculated political terror has become a domestic affair. Although the Ku Klux Klan and the Weathermen can perhaps be cited as basically terrorist organizations, most observers feel that the murder of black Oakland school superintendent Marcus Foster and the kidnaping of heiress Patricia Hearst by an organization calling itself the Symbionese Liberation Army (SLA) were the first acts in the United States of political terror of the kind so common internationally. The Symbionese Liberation Army is believed to have had its origins in a multi-racial discussion group program conducted between outsiders and inmates in California's Soledad Prison and depicts itself as revolutionary shock troops dedicated to fighting members of the "high ruling class and big business."

The SLA movement appears to be an outgrowth of black and student protest politics of the 1960s. Both manifestations of political protest have declined, but they have left a residue of extremely frustrated young people who see no chance to achieve their goals peacefully through conventional political channels or of persuading a large number of ordinary people to accept their vision for a new kind of society.

Terrorism enables such numerically insignificant people (the SLA is thought to number only about 25) to call attention to themselves and their goals by deeds that are more direct and more threatening than anything this country has experienced—a more explicit and more directed version of the mass political protest of the 1960s. Although many of the goals of the terrorists appear so idealistic and far-reaching as to be unrealistic without a total change in basic social institutions, tactics such as political assassination and kidnaping work to make law-enforcement officials and authority in general look impotent. If terrorists, who operate in super-secret, hard-to-infiltrate small groups, succeed in disabling authority, it makes authority invalid and encourages the feeling that nobody can do anything to stop their terrorism.

In a modern complex society with advanced public communications systems, a small group of ideologically motivated individuals can have a political impact far out of proportion to its size. The SLA succeeded in gaining national attention for its ideas and has involved thousands of people in meeting its ransom demands. In addition to wreaking havoc vastly disproportionate to its numbers, terrorist groups can inspire fear in society and generate other extra-legal groups. As the study of urban riots has shown, violence is infectious and spreads quickly.

Documents released by Attorney General William B. Saxbe on March 7, 1974, showed that the FBI has carried on an extensive secret counter-intelligence campaign against radical political groups on both the left and the right since October 12, 1961, when the Bureau began secret disruptive tactics against the Socialist Workers Party. On September 2, 1964, the campaign expanded to include the Ku Klux Klan and on August 25, 1967, expanded again to include "militant black nationalist hate groups." The purpose of the campaign was to destroy organizations the FBI considered violence-prone and to topple their leaders from whatever power and influence they had amassed in the black and white communities. In describing the goals of the black militant campaign, the FBI said it intended to:

—"Prevent the coalitions of militant black nationalist groups" because it feared "the beginning of a true black revolution."

—"Prevent the rise of a 'messiah' who could unify and electrify the militant black nationalist movement." The documents listed several potential "messiahs," but those names were censored out.

—"Prevent violence on the part of black nationalist groups. . . . Through counter intelligence, it should be possible to pinpoint potential troublemakers and neutralize them before they exercise their potential for violence."

—"Discredit militants in the eyes of responsible blacks, white liberals and black radicals."

The documents argued that the primary targets of the counter-intelligence "should be the most violent and radical groups and their leaders," and instructed field agents to report counter-intelligence activities regularly, to obtain FBI headquarters approval for each operation, and to make sure "that there is no possibility of embarrassment to the Bureau." The operations were officially terminated by a previously released memo dated April 28, 1971.

In April 1974, the liberal Democratic mayor of San Francisco instituted a "stop and search" program whereby police could interrogate black men fitting a vaguely defined "profile" of a murder suspect. Thus, terrorism brings on repression by the elites, which, in turn, can lead to increased terroristic acts and increased repression in an escalating cycle. Urban violence, then, is a black counter-elite movement directed against—and condemned by—both white and black established elites. As is the case when established elites lose control of any social movement, the mode of action is violent and unstable. Nobody is really in charge.

The Women's Movement and the Problem of Group Consciousness

After more than two decades of highly visible protest, both peaceful and violent, the plight of blacks and other non-white minorities is well known. While black activity constituted the major portion of the civil rights movement in the early 1960s, toward the end of the decade, Chicanos and Indians became restive. In neither case, however, was the organizational intensity of the blacks matched. The Chicano movement is virtually totally absorbed by Cesar Chavez's union organization efforts (see p. 260). Locked in a life-and-death struggle for survival, the union has severely limited the range of its activities. The Indian movement suffers from a different disadvantage. Problems of survival, of necessity, make mass movements difficult, and Indians suffer a standard of living far worse than that of blacks. The plight of Indians attracted considerable attention during the late 1960s, and a militant mood began to develop among some Indians, notably Vine Deloria, leader of the National Congress of American Indians. Sporadic violent outbursts (e.g., the seizure of Alcatraz and the occupation of Wounded Knee, South Dakota) did not, however, mobilize a movement comparable in scope to the black movement. In terms of organizational activity, the women's movement emerges as the logical successor to the civil rights protests of the 1960s.

However, only within recent years have an increasing number of women come to view themselves as a distinct group facing economic and social discrimination similar to that suffered by blacks. It is not so much that the economic condition of women has worsened (which it has), but that some active women have moved away from the traditional stereotypes and role patterns defined for them by the dominant culture and are seeking new sources of identity.

Protest movements have a spill-over effect. As the traditional civil rights movement declined, organizationally, its message of discrimination was received—and acted upon—by women. However, as we shall see, women's movements have experienced different problems than other protests, due primarily to a problem of identification. Are women a "group"? That is, are their attitudes, behaviors, and problems unique to women *as* women? With blacks such a question is absurd; with women it is less so. Women, whether oppressed or not, are *not* a minority. Thus, other groups' identities (Republican, Episcopalian, etc.) have minimized attitudinal differences between men and women. Examine any array of poll data comparing differences between blacks and whites; then compare differences in attitude between men and women. In virtually every case (with the notable exception of attitudes toward issues dealing exclusively with sex, such as nudity in plays and movies), men and women have similar attitudes.

A good illustration of this similarity can be found in attitudes toward what has come to be known as "the quality of life." Consider Table 13–8, which measures degree of satisfaction with a variety of conditions. In every case, women appear about as satisfied as men—hardly the conditions for radical protest. Further, there is some evidence that the

Table 13-8 / Percent Expressing Satisfaction with Living Conditions

	Male	Female	Black	White
Standard of living	71%	71%	48%	74%
The work you do	80	78	55	82
Your family income	62	60	38	64
The future facing you & your family	54	51	37	55
Your children's education	62	60	49	63
Your housing situation	73	74	52	77

Source: Gallup Political Index, December 1973.

general level of satisfaction among women is *increasing*. Take, for an example, job satisfaction. Seventy-eight percent of the women are currently satisfied with their work. In 1949, 66 percent of women indicated satisfaction. In contrast, the percentage of blacks expressing satisfaction has not changed.

After an exhaustive survey of possible differences in attitude between men and women, Erikson and Luttbeg conclude: "Differences in the political attitudes of men and women are so slight as to deserve only brief mention. . . . In political attitudes and voting, men and women are seldom different."[37] Even on the question of liberalized abortion laws—defined by women activists as a key to the women's liberation movement—men and women have virtually identical attitudes (two thirds of both groups are in favor of liberalization of abortion). Ironically, women are somewhat less likely than men to favor liberalized divorce laws.

Not surprisingly, the activity of women's organizations are directed toward "consciousness raising," that is, creating uniquely female attitudes, or a "group consciousness" similar to that of blacks.

The raw material for such a group consciousness is there; tangible evidence of economic discrimination against women is unequivocal. As Table 13–9 shows, the median income of women is about one-half that of

Table 13-9 / Median Income of Males and Females, 1950–1971

	Males	Females	Ratio
1950	2831	1559	.55
1955	3797	1926	.51
1960	4822	2348	.49
1965	5907	2771	.47
1968	7080	3380	.48
1969	7659	3598	.47
1970	8036	3844	.48
1971	8371	4019	.48

Source: Compiled from U.S. Department of Commerce, Bureau of the Census, *The American Almanac* (New York: Grosset and Dunlap, 1974), p. 334.

males, and the income gap is widening. To some extent, economic discrimination against women is a consequence of the fact that women find entry into highly remunerative occupations difficult and are forced to settle for more drudgery and less money. Some occupations (for example, nursing, secretarial work) are almost exclusively female; others (especially the more highly paid professions) are male dominated. However, even within occupational and educational categories, there is evidence of economic discrimination. Thus, the income of the average professional woman is 60 percent of that of the average professional man; the income of the average woman college graduate is 63 percent of that of the average male college graduate. Further, women are less likely to go to college and are less likely to finish if they start. Even though more women are now entering college, the graduating class of the "average" university will contain about twice as many men as women.

Under such circumstances, creating a group consciousness should not be difficult. However, the women's movement is only now developing out of the ashes of the black protests of the 1960s. Women's liberation formally began with the founding of the National Organization for Women in 1966. NOW's membership is expanding rapidly, as is that of the National Women's Political Caucus, dedicated to the recruitment and election of women to political office.

Some tangible results of the women's movement are apparent, especially with regard to equal employment. Under a 1967 executive order, federal funds can be terminated to federal contractors which discriminate in the hiring or promotion of women. The most effective use of this lever has been among colleges and universities, many of which stand to lose substantial federal grants.

Such successes, however, apply only to the elite of women, the minority who have been able to earn advanced degrees. Still nascent is a sense of identity for the masses of women, especially working-class women. Thus, a recent poll revealed that 42 percent of women favored "efforts to strengthen and change women's status in society," while 43 percent were opposed. Further, two thirds believed that women get "as good a break as men." An equally strong percentage of men denied discrimination. Yet, while denying discrimination, the majority of women believe that their opportunity to become the executive of a company is not as great as that of an equally educated man.[38] Inferentially, one can see that there is a strong feeling among women that there *should* be discrimination at higher levels of employment.

The ambivalence of women toward work is well illustrated by the issue of child care centers. Whereas substantial majorities of both men and women support federally funded day care centers, 71 percent of the women also believe that "taking care of a home and raising children is more rewarding for a woman than having a job."

The organizational heart of the women's movement is the small group meeting. Groups form, meet for a while, and disband, leaving the long-range development of goals and strategy in the hands of the active minority. Communication between the active minority and passive majority is sporadic, and the aspirations of the active minority are poorly understood. There is substantial hostility on the part of the masses to the efforts of the activists to generate change in sex roles. Protest activity is particularly poorly received, as is protest activity by other economically disadvantaged groups. About half of the women interviewed in 1971, for instance, agreed that "leaders of women's organizations are trying to change women into men."

Further, from 75 to 95 percent of women vote like their husbands. While this does not necessarily mean women vote in accordance with the wishes of their husbands (indeed, the opposite may just as easily be true), the development of an independent political voice is certainly hampered. Thus, in 1972, in spite of the conspicuous identification of women activists with the McGovern candidacy, the proportion of women voting for McGovern was virtually identical with the proportion of men voting for McGovern (38 v. 37 percent). Further, the turnout among women was slightly lower than the turnout among men.

The basic problem of the women's movement is the heterogeneity of women. As analytical and organizing concepts, race, education, and social class are substantially more important. Heterogeneity is especially apparent among married women, who are more inclined to identify with the status of their husband. For instance, only one woman in six would be more likely to vote for a woman candidate for president; but among single women the ratio increased to one in three. Perhaps, then, the key to the future of the women's movement (that is, the development of group identification) depends less upon the activities of the active minority of women than upon the evolution of social and economic trends (increased divorce rate, lower birth rate), which operate independently of organizational efforts. However, the passage of the Equal Rights Amendment, still far from certain, might interact with social and economic trends to escalate the process of group identification, and the similarities in behavior and attitude which would follow such identification.

The amendment, in generating intense controversy, may serve as a catalyst for the women's movement, in the same way that Brown v. Board of Education generated a decade of black protest. The amendment may provide a crucial factor, heretofore lacking, in the women's movement; opposition. Until now, the women's movement has not aroused a "backlash" comparable to, say, busing. However, the Equal Rights Amendment has been rejected by twelve states, and is eight shy of the required 38. The vitality of the women's movement, ironically, may be strengthened as opposition increases. There must be an enemy.

Summary

How do American elites cope with mass activism? Generally, established elites can depend upon mass apathy. But occasionally mass activism replaces apathy, and this activism is extremist, unstable, and unpredictable. America has experienced a long history of mass movements led by a wide variety of counter-elites from Shay's Rebellion of the eighteenth century to recent black militancy. But the place of blacks in American society has been the central domestic issue of American politics. We chose to examine the movement for black equality within the context of elite theory to observe political activism among subservient people and the reaction of dominant elites to this activism. In many ways, the recent political activism among blacks is typical of mass movements—it is unstable and unpredictable; it expresses resentment toward the established order; it is made up of people who seldom participate in democratic politics and do not always understand the "rules of the game"; it is highly flammable and can produce violence; it has produced a variety of counter-elites; and it has threatened the established order. However, we must be cautious in developing generalizations about mass movements based upon black experience in America. For blacks must contend not only with white *elites*, but also with white *masses*. Contrary to the general assumption of elite theory, the white masses *do* have opinions about civil rights and race relations, and elite behavior is more circumscribed by mass opinion than is normally the case. Hence, the relationship between white elites and black masses is complicated by the role of the white masses. Yet elitism offers many insights into the nature of the black struggle in America and the way in which this nation has responded to black demands.

1. Prevailing myths and symbols of the American nation are drawn from democratic theory; these include a recognition of the rights of minorities, a commitment to the value of individual dignity, and a commitment to the value of equal opportunity for all people. Although committed to these abstract ideals, white elites have consistently failed over the course of American history to implement these ideals in public policy.

2. Centuries of slavery and segregation have left black masses poorly educated, unskilled, poorly housed, poverty-stricken, frequently unemployed, segregated, and subject to a variety of social pathologies. White elites generally expect individual blacks to solve these problems individually. Black counter-elites charge that white elites created these problems and are obliged to resolve these problems with black masses as a group.

3. White elites are willing to accept individual blacks on a near-equal basis only if these blacks accept the prevailing consensus and exhibit white middle-class values. White elites are less willing to accept black masses who have not assimilated prevailing middle-class values.

4. Public-regarding liberal elites are prepared to eliminate legal barriers to provide equality of opportunity under the law for individual blacks, but they are not prepared to take massive action to eliminate absolute inequalities ("leveling"), which would bring black masses up to average white standards of living.

5. Historically white elites have been willing to sacrifice the interests of blacks to avoid cleavage among themselves that would impair national consensus and unity. The propensity to sacrifice black interests for white unity was evidenced in the years before the Civil War, in the Compromise of 1877, throughout the long period of segregation, and in the moderate, go-slow approach of recent civil rights legislation.

6. The first governmental institution to act and achieve equality of opportunity for blacks in America in the twentieth century was the Supreme Court. This institution was structurally the farthest removed from the influence of white masses, and was the first to apply liberal public-regarding policies to the blacks. Elected elites who are more accessible to white masses were slower to act on black rights than appointed elites.

7. Elected white elites did not respond to black requests until faced with a prolonged campaign of nonviolent civil disobedience, public demonstrations, and creative disorder and crises. Generally elites have responded by making the most minimal changes in the system consistent with maintaining stability. Often these changes are only symbolic. No revolutionary changes have been contemplated by elites even when they are faced with massive civil disorder.

8. The elimination of legal discrimination and the guarantee of equality of opportunity has been achieved largely through the efforts of black middle-class groups who share a dominant elite consensus and who appeal to the conscience of white elites to extend that consensus to include blacks.

9. The successes of black elites in achieving symbolic goals has helped to activate black masses. Once activated, these masses have turned to goals that went beyond accepted elite consensus—for example, demands for *absolute* equality have replaced demands for equality of opportunity. New mass-oriented black counter-elites have emerged to contend with established middle-class black elites. Middle-class black elites have relatively little influence with masses in the ghettos. Mass counter-elites have less respect for the "rules of the game" than either white elites or established middle-class black leaders.

10. Liberal public-regarding white elites have wanted to extend equality of opportunity to individual blacks, but other goals had higher priority—notably the war in Vietnam, the cold war in Europe, and the maintenance of a large defense establishment. Consequently, many of the appeals from established middle-class black leaders are set aside, and the demands of black masses ignored.

11. Mass urban violence in the ghettos has confounded both white elites and the established black leadership. Black leaders reprimanded black masses, and the cleavage between black leaders and black masses became apparent. Mass-oriented black counter-elites have developed new slogans and tactics to exploit mass activism and violence.

12. Urban violence is a form of political activity on the part of black masses in the ghetto. The rioters (counter-elites) are representative of the black masses in

socioeconomic composition, but they express greater racial hostility and a higher level of political information and awareness than the masses.

13. Protest movements have a spill-over effect; they run from group to group in a ripple-like fashion. Groups only recently engaged in protest activity, such as women, have not developed the group consciousness of more severely repressed groups.

References

[1] Gunnar Myrdal, *An American Dilemma*, Vol. I (New York: McGraw-Hill Book Co., 1964), p. lxxi.

[2] *Report of the National Advisory Commission on Civil Disorders* (Washington, D.C., 1968), p. 1.

[3] *Report of the National Advisory Commission on Civil Disorders*, p. 2.

[4] Bayard Rustin, "From Protest to Coalition Politics," in Marvin E. Gettleman and David Mermelstein (eds.), *The Great Society Reader* (New York: Vintage Books, 1967), p. 265. A short discussion of *de facto* segregation appears later in this chapter.

[5] Stanley M. Elkins, *Slavery: A Problem in American Institutional and Intellectual Life* (New York: Universal Library, 1963).

[6] David C. McClelland, *The Achieving Society* (Princeton, N.J.: D. Van Nostrand Co., 1961), pp. 376–377.

[7] U.S. Department of Commerce, Bureau of the Census, *Current Population Reports*, P-20, No. 125, 116, 106, 100, 88, 83, 75, 67, 53, 44, 33, and 26.

[8] *Plessy v. Ferguson*, 163 U.S. 537 (1896).

[9] Allen D. Grimshaw, "Lawlessness and Violence in America and Their Special Manifestations in Changing Negro-White Relationships," *Journal of Negro History*, 44, 1 (January 1959), 67.

[10] Myrdal, *An American Dilemma*, Vol. II, p. 749.

[11] *Brown v. Board of Education of Topeka*, 347 U.S. 483 (1954).

[12] Kenneth B. Clark, "The Civil Rights Movement: Momentum and Organization," in Talcott Parsons and Kenneth B. Clark (eds.), *The Negro American* (Boston: Beacon Press, 1966), p. 610.

[13] Donald R. Matthews and James W. Prothro, *Negroes and the New Southern Politics* (New York: Harcourt, Brace & World, 1966), p. 424.

[14] Crane Brinton, *The Anatomy of Revolution* (New York: Vintage Books, 1965), pp. 100–105.

[15] Report of the National Advisory Commission on Civil Disorders, p. 390.

[16] Karl E. Taeuber and Alma F. Taeuber, *Negroes in Cities* (Chicago: Aldine Publishing Co., 1965), pp. 35–36.

[17] St. Clair Drake, "The Social and Economic Status of the Negro in the United States," in Parsons and Clark, *The Negro American*, p. 17.

[18] Alberback and Walker, "The Meanings of Black Power," p. 17.

[19] "The Uses of Violence," in *Supplementary Studies for the National Advisory Commission on Civil Disorders*, p. 48.

[20] Kenneth B. Clark, *Dark Ghetto: Dilemmas of Social Power* (New York: Harper & Row, 1965), p. 62.

[21]William Brink and Louis Harris, *The Negro Revolution in America* (New York: Simon and Schuster, 1964), p. 126; see also "Racial Views of Racial Issues," in *Supplementary Studies for the National Advisory Commission on Civil Disorders* (Washington, D.C., July 1968), p. 25.

[22]Brink and Harris, pp. 138–153; see also "White Beliefs about Negroes," in *Supplementary Studies for the National Advisory Commission on Civil Disorders*, July 1968.

[23]James Baldwin, *Nobody Knows My Name* (New York: Dell, 1961), p. 62.

[24]"White Beliefs about Negroes," in *Supplementary Studies for the National Advisory Commission on Civil Disorders*, p. 30.

[25]*Report of the National Advisory Commission on Civil Disorders*, p. 306.

[26]*Gallup Opinion Index*, Report No. 25 (July 1967), p. 19.

[27]J. H. Skolnick, *Justice without Trial* (New York: John Wiley, 1967), p. 61.

[28]James Q. Wilson, *Varieties of Police Behavior* (Cambridge, Mass.: Harvard University Press, 1968), p. 43.

[29]"Racial Isolation in the Public Schools," *A Report of the United States Commission on Civil Rights*, 1967, pp. 3–7.

[30]See Paul B. Sheatsley, "White Attitudes toward the Negro," in Parsons and Clark, *The Negro American*, pp. 303–324.

[31]*Gallup Political Index*, July 1972.

[32]Robert L. Crain, *The Politics of School Desegregation* (Chicago: Aldine Publishing Co., 1968), p. 123.

[33]James C. Davies, "Toward a Theory of Revolution," *American Sociological Review*, 27 (February 1962), p. 6.

[34]Thomas F. Pettigrew, "Social Evolution Theory: Consequences and Applications," *Nebraska Symposium on Motivation*, 1967, p. 295.

[35]*Gallup Political Index*, November 1972.

[36]Supplementary Studies for the National Advisory Commission on Civil Disorders, p. 55.

[37]Robert S. Erikson and Norman R. Luttbeg, *American Public Opinion: Its Origins, Content, and Import* (New York: John Wiley, 1973), p. 205.

[38]*Gallup Political Index*, September 1970.

Selected Additional Readings

Banfield, Edward C. *The Unheavenly City Revisited: A Revision of the Unheavenly City*. Boston: Little, Brown, 1974. This book is an analysis, from a somewhat unusual viewpoint, of the problems of the people of urban America and of the cities in which they live. Banfield argues that the "poor" in America are not as unfortunate as they might first appear to be. It is only relative to the affluence of middle- and upper-class Americans that the poor seem deprived. In an absolute sense, however, they are not generally "poor," especially as compared to the poor of Europe or Asia. This book is frequently cited in our discussion of civil rights and the problems of the poor.

Clark, Kenneth B. *Dark Ghetto: Dilemmas of Social Power*. New York: Harper and Row (Harper Torchbook edition), 1967. *Dark Ghetto* is a particularly incisive analysis of the life of American blacks in urban ghetto areas and of the pathologies this life produces.

Matthews, Donald R. and James W. Prothro. *Negroes and the New Southern*

Politics. New York: Harcourt, Brace and World, 1966. This is one of the pioneering works on the changing political role of the Southern black. It considerably updates some of Myrdal's earlier comments on Southern politics.

Myrdal, Gunnar. *An American Dilemma,* Vol. I: *The Negro in a White Nation.* Vol. II: *The Negro Social Structure.* New York: McGraw-Hill, 1964. Originally published in 1944, this remains one of the most comprehensive studies dealing with the situation of blacks in America. It draws broadly from many disciplines.

Report of the National Advisory Commission on Civil Disorders. New York: Bantam Books, 1968. Popularly called "The Kerner Report," this volume is the most comprehensive study of major urban riots in the United States available today. It presents a detailed discussion of the factors underlying past riots and offers recommendations for avoiding such confrontations in the future.

Pomper, Gerald. *Elections in America: Control and Influence in Democratic Politics.* New York: Dodd, Mead, and Co., 1968. Chapter 9 contains a discussion of the development of the civil rights movement in America. The emphasis is on the changing status of blacks in American society and on the impact such change has had on American voting patterns.

Theodore, Athena, ed. *The Professional Woman.* Cambridge: Schenkman Publishing Co., 1971. A collection of essays and articles dealing with the social, economic, political, cultural, and moral problems faced by women in their professional lives.

CHAPTER 14

WHITHER DEMOCRACY?

SOME CONCLUSIONS

The Alienation of the Masses

As the nation approaches its two hundredth anniversary, confidence in its government has hardly ever been lower. Americans distrust the men and institutions which decide the course of public policy. An unpopular war in Vietnam, the Watergate affair, the continued antipathy between mass media and two successive presidential administrations, the resignation of a President, and his subsequent pardon have gradually eroded whatever confidence Americans had in their governing elites.

The alienation of Americans toward government goes beyond dissatisfaction or opposition to particular politicians or parties. A national survey conducted by pollster Louis Harris in 1973 revealed that a *majority* of Americans give alienated replies to general questions about American society. Sociologists and political scientists have used these questions as barometers of alienation and powerlessness for many years, and the trend is clear. Table 14–1 reveals that in 1973, 76 percent of the people agreed with the statement, "The rich get richer and the poor get poorer," compared to only 45 percent in 1966. The number of people who agree that "what you think doesn't count much anymore" rose from 37 to 61 percent in the same period. And the idea that "people running

447

Table 14-1 / Trends in Mass Alienation and Powerlessness

Agreement with Statement	1973 %	1966 %
The rich get richer and the poor get poorer.	76	45
What you think doesn't count much anymore.	61	37
People running the country don't really care what happens to you.	55	26
		Undecided omitted.

Source: U.S. Senate, Committee on Intergovernmental Relations, *Confidence and Concern: Citizens View American Government* (Washington: Government Printing Office, 1973), p. 30.

the country don't really care what happens to you" is agreed to by 55 percent of the people, compared to 26 percent in 1966.

Few people believe that government improves their lives. The federal government is the worst culprit—a plurality of Americans believe that it makes their lives *worse*. State and local governments fare better—most Americans believe they do no great harm. (See Table 14–2.)

Table 14-2 / Mass Feelings Toward Government

	How Has Government Changed Your Life?		
	Improved it	Made it Worse	No Change
Federal Government	23%	37%	34%
State Government	27	14	52
Local Government	28	11	54
			Undecided omitted

Source: U.S. Senate, Committee on Government Operations, Subcommittee on Intergovernmental Relations, *Confidence and Concern: Citizens View American Government* (Washington: Government Printing Office, 1973), p. 42-43.

Perhaps even more disturbing is the widespread feeling that the quality of life in America is declining. Nearly half (46 percent) of the American public believe that the quality of their life has *declined* in the last decade; 15 percent believe it has stayed the same; and 35 percent believe it has improved. (See Table 14–3.) Interestingly, *elites* think the

Table 14-3 / Elite and Mass Attitudes on the Quality of Life

	Has the Quality of Life Improved Since 1963?		
	Improved	Become Worse	Stayed Same
Total Public	35	46	15
Selected Leaders	61	20	16

Source: U.S. Senate, Committee on Government Operations, Subcommittee on Intergovernmental Relations, *Confidence and Concern: Citizens View American Government* (Washington: Government Printing Office, 1973), p. 231.

quality of life is improving—61 percent of a national leadership sample believed life had improved over the decade, and only 20 percent believed it had grown worse. Thus, elites and masses are clearly differentiated in their respective notions of whether things are getting better or worse in this nation.

Mass distrust of a democratic government is an invitation to tyranny. When asked what they thought were the nation's biggest problems, Americans listed inflation, lack of integrity in government, crime, welfare, federal spending, taxes, pollution, and overpopulation well ahead of racial justice, health care, or housing. This suggests that there is no widespread mass demand for traditional liberal reforms. More ominous, perhaps, is the willingness of fully 67 percent of the American people to agree with the statement: "It's about time we had a strong federal government to get this country moving again." Some may interpret this reply as a demand for greater integrity, honesty, etc.; but a more realistic interpretation is that the nation would welcome a strong leader—perhaps even an authoritarian figure. Democracy is at its weakest when the citizenry loses confidence in its governing elites.

The Inevitability of Elites

The elitism we have ascribed to American society is not a unique corruption of democratic ideas attributable to capitalism, war, "Watergate," the "military-industrial complex," or any other events or people in this nation. Elitism is a necessary characteristic of *all* societies. There is no "solution" to elitism, for it is not *the* problem in a democracy. There have been many mass movements, both "left" and "right" in their political ideology, which have *promised* to bring power to the people. Indeed, the world has witnessed many "successful" mass movements which have overthrown social and political systems, often at great cost to human life, promising to empower the masses. But invariably they have created *new* elite systems which are at least as "evil," and certainly no more democratic, than the older systems which they replaced. Revolutions come and go—but the masses remain powerless. The question, then, is not how to combat elitism or empower the masses or achieve revolution, but rather how to *build* an orderly, humane, and just society.

Let us summarize some of the reasons why mass democracy is not really feasible. First of all, in a large society the influence of a single individual on societal decisions, even assuming political equality, is so tiny as to render participation in mass democracy fruitless. As the society grows larger, the individual shrinks—in influence, power, liberty, and the capacity for shaping the decisions which affect his life. As Rousseau observed: "Thus, the subject remaining always one, the rela-

.on of the sovereign increases in proportion to the number of citizens. From which it follows that the more the state grows, the more liberty diminishes." The chance that a particular individual in a society of 200 million people can affect the outcome of an election, a referendum, or other societal decision is infinitesimal. An individual who has only one two-hundred-millionth of a say in the outcome of issues cannot be personally effective. This would be true even under conditions of perfect equality.

Inequalities among men are inevitable, and these inequalities produce differences in political power. Men are not born with the same abilities, nor can they acquire them by education. Modern democrats who recognize that inequality in *wealth* is a serious obstacle to political equality propose to eliminate such inequality by taking from the rich and giving to the poor, to achieve a "leveling" which they believe is essential to democracy. But despite their mass appeal, these schemes consistently run astray—in part because of the ingenuity of the men who have acquired wealth in defeating them. But *even if* inequalities of *wealth* were eliminated, differences among men in intelligence, organizational skills, leadership abilities, knowledge and information, drive and ambition, and interest and activity would remain. Such inequalities are sufficient to assure oligarchy, even if wealth were uniform. Moreover, de Tocqueville's warning about equality deserves consideration:

I believe that it is easier to establish an absolute and despotic government among a people in which the conditions of society are equal than among any other; and I think that if such a government were once established among such a people, it not only would oppress men, but would eventually strip each of them of several of the highest qualities of humanity.[1]

Moreover, it is impossible for a mass to govern. The mass must delegate governing responsibilities to representatives, and by so doing they create a governing minority who will be distinguished from the masses in behavior, role, and status. This is true no matter what system of accountability is established. Delegation of authority creates a governing elite. Yet delegation is essential, if for no other reason than that people are unwilling to spend all of their time in decision-making activity—attending meetings, acquiring information, debating, and so on. Organization inevitably means oligarchy. Mosca demonstrated that even European socialist parties espousing democracy were in fact oligarchies:

When his work is finished, the proletarian can think only of rest, and of getting to bed in good time. His place is taken at meetings by the bourgeois, by those

who come to sell newspapers and picture postcards, by clerks, by young intellec-
tuals who have not yet got a position in their own circle, people who are glad to
hear themselves spoken of as authentic proletarians and to be glorified as the
class of the future.[2]

The authoritarianism of "revolutionary" parties today confirms Mosca's earlier observations. Participatory democracy is a romantic fiction.

The Futility of Protest

Many students who read this book lose their innocence. "How can I, an 18-year-old freshman from Central Oregon, ever attempt to wage battle against the all-powerful elite?" "*The Irony of Democracy* certainly does not make me eager to take advantage of the opportunity to register to vote. I almost feel it is futile." Obviously, there is frustration, a sense of helplessness, and anger over our claim (in Chapter 1) that "the future of American democracy depends upon the wisdom, responsibility, and resourcefulness of the nation's elite."

"Revolutionary" movements are led by elites, and even the much-heralded "counter-culture" is dominated by a few intellectuals. The only way to avoid elite rule is to decentralize decision making to the point of absurdity. (Even the New England town meeting drew sparse attendance.) A particularly relevant example of the inevitability of elite rule is community control over schools and other governmental functions, now so much in demand. The phrase itself is illusory, because there is really no *community* as such, but rather an articulate group of community leaders who wish to contest for power with an established elite (in most cases the central administration of schools). Paul Goodman's definition of decentralization, while not incorrect in its assumptions, misses the point: "Decentralizing is increasing the number of decision-making units and the number of the initiators of public policy; increasing the awareness of individuals of the whole function in which they are involved; and establishing as much face to face association with decision makers as possible. *People are directly engaged in the function.*"[3] Goodman's point is correct, up to a point, for (obviously) increasing the number of decision-making centers increases opportunities to influence decisions. But do not assume that the word "people" means "masses," for it does not. Further, do not assume that the content of decisions would be altered appreciably by a shift in the locus. A social system which has institutionalized the consensus values we have described in this book is not likely to be appreciably changed by tinkering with political institutions.

At this point in the development of our society, institutional reforms (e.g., making political parties "more democratic," abolishing the seniority system in Congress, etc.) are futile. Political institutions are not agencies of change but rather reflections of the dominant values of society. Changing the shape of an institution without changing its underlying value structure accomplishes nothing.

One short-term method of change is protest. But protests are *prima facie* evidence of little political power. (The protests of the 1960s and early 1970s, beginning with the civil rights demonstrations and culminating in student uprisings, have in every case been undertaken because of the realization that "normal" channels of political influence were not accessible.) Consequently, as stated clearly in the text, one cannot expect that long-term social change can develop out of protest activity.

Protest, even peaceful protest, is not viewed with favor by either elites or masses. In spite of overwhelming evidence on this point, student protesters persist in the belief that their actions will "awaken the public." Indeed, these actions will awaken the public, and its elite representatives will respond, but the response will be grim and repressive. That the backlash to protest, especially student protest, is inevitable must be understood if our argument against the possibility of radical change through protest is to be understood. As Wilson and Lipsky have argued, the protesters' basic problem is that they have no resources to exchange for political benefits, and their protests reduce even further the opportunities for coalitions with groups who have actual or potential resources.[4] It is consequently of little political significance that blacks and students form an alliance, for both groups suffer from the same problem: no exchangeable resources. Take, for example, protests about the Vietnam war. According to the Survey Research Center, adult "doves" were quite antagonistic toward Vietnam War protesters: A clear majority were negative, and almost one fourth declared themselves extremely hostile. Thus the natural target for a coalition—that part of the adult population opposed to the war—was alienated.[5]

Whether or not student protesters consciously sought coalition with those who shared their values, their tactics achieved the opposite effect. That any alternative tactic of protest could succeed in building coalitions is doubtful. But clearly the fierce hostility of the mass suggests that it is in no mood to tolerate dissent, even when peaceful. It may be helpful to potential protesters to know that, in spite of media coverage sympathetic to the youthful protesters, adults (even doves) approve of what has been labeled a police riot at the 1968 Democratic Convention in Chicago. The adult population also thought that the four slain Kent State students *got what they deserved*. That part of the electorate which was *not* alienated by students (and which agreed with their goals) came to less than 3 percent.[6]

Student protest leaders practice selective perception with consummate skill. If there were to be "power to the people," then the student protesters would find themselves in a far worse situation than those who were so brutally attacked at the Chicago convention. A genuine "people's revolution" in America would begin with a reign of terror in which first radical students and then blacks would be threatened with brutal extermination. Of course, this is precisely the point of *The Irony of Democracy*, and why radical political movements accomplish only repressive political responses. As Slater puts it: "If the matter is left to a collision of generational change it seems to me inevitable that a radical right revolution will occur as a last ditch effort to stave off change."[7]

A further point to be made about the "youth revolt" is that it is not anything of the sort. The vanguard of the new generation is exactly that—an elite, or "an elite-to-be." The evidence is clear that, at least politically, there is no youth culture. For instance, outside the South, Wallace captured a disproportionately high vote among those under 30. While expressing in extreme form the values of traditional America, Wallace attracted large numbers of younger voters. So let the college radical avoid deceiving himself:

Although privileged young college students, angry at Vietnam, saw themselves as sallying forth to do battle against a corrupted and cynical older generation, a more head-on confrontation at the polls, if a less apparent one, was with their own agemates who had gone from high school to the factory instead of college, and who were appalled by the collapse of patriotism and respect for the law that they saw around them.[8]

Charles Reich asserts that there is an emerging culture that is noncompetitive, more "humane," and less materialistic and confining (he calls it Consciousness III), which will spread through the entire population by the force of its own appeal and without the need for broad-gauged, concerted proselytizing.[9] He finds the new-left activism of the 1960s a failure but offers another alternative: "when self is recovered the power of the corporate state will be ended as miraculously as a kiss breaks a witch's evil enchantment."[10] But students should not take such statements seriously. If those who reject the old culture simply conduct their personal lives in a manner somewhat different from the traditional style (even to the point of living in communes), then, unless one seriously expects most adults to reverse their values, social change will be left to participants in the "old culture." Further, Consciousness III is hardly as idyllic as it is portrayed to be by Reich. Although it includes some genuinely humane values, it also includes hard narcotics, terrorism, violence (presumably Charles Manson and Patricia Hearst are liberated persons) but more often only superficial changes in life style. For example, Reich attaches considerable importance to clothes and rock music. We cannot find much evidence that such symbols of change are very meaningful. That someone wears his hair long, likes rock music, and smokes grass are not usually good indicators of his political values. So the spread of Consciousness III beyond the campuses of our colleges and universities is superficial, and it contains no viable political expression.

The Dilemma of American Politics

The dilemma of American politics today is not really much different from that faced by the Founding Fathers in 1787—how to protect individuals in a democratic system where majorities rule from the excesses and injustices of both *majorities* and *minorities*. James Madison warned that protection against *majority* oppression "is the real object to which our inquiries are directed." But the question is not only how to restrain the masses, but also how to control elites. The threat to democratic values arises not only from unrestrained majorities, but also ruling minorities.

The masses are anti-democratic and therefore cannot be relied upon to govern democratically. Despite a superficial commitment to the symbols of democracy, the people are not attached to the ideals of individual liberty, toleration of diversity, freedoms of expression and dissent, or equality of opportunity. On the contrary, these are more likely to be the values of elites. Masses are authoritarian, intolerant, anti-intellectual, nativistic, alienated, hateful, and violent. Mass politics is extremist, unstable, and unpredictable. The masses are not committed to democratic "rules of the game;" when they are politically activated, they frequently go outside these rules to engage in violence. Moreover, mass politics frequently reflects the alienation and hostility of the masses by concentrating upon scapegoats. The scapegoats can be any minority who are somehow differentiated from the majority of the masses—Jews, blacks, Catholics, immigrants, students, intellectuals, etc.

The masses are fatally vulnerable to tyranny. Extremist movements —reflecting authoritarianism, alienation, hostility, and prejudice— are more likely to be based in masses than elites. Hannah Arendt writes: "A whole literature on mass behavior and mass psychology demonstrated and popularized the wisdom, so familiar to the ancients, of the affinity between democracy and dictatorship, between mob rule and tyranny."[11] The masses, feeling in themselves the power of the majority, cannot be trusted to restrain themselves in dealing with dissenting minorities. Tolerance of diversity is a quality acquired only through years of socialization. The authoritarianism of the masses is unavoidable, given their authoritarian childhood experiences and family relationships, their limited education and restricted cultural opportunities, their monotonous job experiences, and their orientation toward immediate gratification. Efforts to re-educate or resocialize the masses are futile. Two hundred years ago Jefferson proposed universal free public education as a prescription for mass ignorance, incompetence, and alienation. Today the masses in America average twelve years of free public education, but, if anything, they appear less capable of governing in a wise and humane fashion than the masses of Jefferson's time.

Yet we have also learned that democracy is not always safe in the hands of elites—even democratically elected elites. Throughout this nation's history elites themselves have posed threats to democracy—from the Alien and Sedition Acts, to Woodrow Wilson's "Red Scare," to Roosevelt's incarceration of thousands of Japanese Americans, to Truman's "loyalty" programs, to the present Watergate "horrors." Restrictions on mass political activity—the forcible break-up of revolutionary parties, restrictions on the public appearances of demagogues, the suppression of literature expressing hatred or advocating revolution or violence, the equipping and training of additional security forces, the jailing of violence-prone radicals and their co-conspirators, and so on—are continuing threats to a democratic society.

Elite repression—the abandonment of democratic values by the nation's established leadership—is a characteristic response to mass protest activity. While it may be comforting to argue that Watergate was unique and unprecedented, or that it was a product of a conservative ideology, neither statement is true. All elites are capable of repressive measures when they feel threatened by mass unrest.

Of course, repression in a free society is a contradiction. We cannot logically curtail liberty—even the liberty of a demagogue—in order to preserve a free society. James Madison considered and rejected repression as a means of controlling mass movements, and pointed out the inconsistency of repression in a free society:

Liberty is to faction [mass movements] what air is to fire, an element without which it instantly expires. But it could not be less folly to abolish liberty, which is essential to political life, because it nourishes faction, than it would be to wish the annihilation of air, which is essential to animal life, because it imparts to fire its destructive agency. [12]

In short, repression is not really a serious instrument for an elite committed to the values of individual dignity, personal freedom, and tolerance of diversity.

If this dilemma—the protection of individual liberties against the assaults of majority and elite excess—is troublesome today, there is every indication that it may become even more serious in the future.

In the winter of 1973–74, as Americans shivered in the dawn waiting for a few gallons of gasoline, suddenly the warnings of ecologists became alarmingly real. Similarly, as inflation cut deeply into the earning power of the average wage-earner, the predictions of economists became tangible and terrifying. Americans perceived not only an abstract decline in the quality of life, but a tangible deterioration. Nineteen seventy-three may prove to be a year which—in retrospect—divided one age (the age of affluence) from another (the age of scarcity).

The political processes of the first age may prove to be luxuries which cannot be afforded in the second. In an age of affluence, democracies—albeit the symbolic variety described in these pages—could be tolerated because there had been considerable slack in the system. The economic problems of industrial societies—how to achieve an appropriate distribution of existing and future wealth—was one that could be debated and subjected to interelite negotiation. The problem was one of *distribution*. The stakes of the dispute were serious, but not too serious. Thus, "wars on poverty" come and go, the distribution of wealth remains stable, but protest is confined and isolated, as was the case with the riots of the 1960s.

In an age of scarcity, hardship is much more widespread, as the problem shifts from distribution of abundant resources to *conservation* of scarce resources. Chillingly symptomatic of the protest of the new age was the truckers' strike of 1974, in response to scarce and expensive fuel. Truckers—previous beneficiaries of the age of affluence or "middle Americans"—became so outraged that they engaged briefly in the techniques of protest previously confined to the ghetto. Two truckers were killed, and dozens were injured by gunshot, rocks, and bottles. National Guardsmen were called out in eight states.

There are several significant aspects to the truckers' strike. First, as previously mentioned, it was led by frustrated *middle* Americans. Second, the source of the truckers' frustration was *not* the policy of the United States or any political subdivision. Rather, the scarcity of fuel—and the attendant rise in price—were caused by a complicated *international* reallocation of resources. In the 1960s, the national government at least had the authority to provide symbolic satisfaction to rioters. In the 1970s, the nation-state may no longer be the effective decision maker.

In an age of scarcity, problems which materially affect an individual's quality of life may be so linked with international systems that national decisions are futile. Examples come readily to mind. Consider, for instance, the "population explosion." World population is approximately 3.6 billion. However, one third of the population lives in areas—such as the United States—where population stability is being achieved. For such areas, population will become stable at about 50 percent larger than it is now. For the remainder of the world, the balance of population and available resources is approaching a grim solution: mass starvation. Assuming, therefore, that the "developed" nations effectively stabilize population, will they not in any case be victims of the scarcity which ensues as the world's resources are exhausted?

Similarly, pollution is a global problem, as is inflation. In these cases there is little that a nation-state, acting individually, can do. Additionally, there is the problem of the technology, or competence, required to understand, much less influence, the problems which accompany the age of scarcity. We know that masses have little knowledge of contemporary politics; what can we expect them to understand about international re-allocation of scarce resources? Indeed, we now know that even recent American presidents, especially Nixon, found themselves incapable of understanding the complexities of the international monetary system.

Size and complexity, then, reduce the notion of participation by masses—and in some cases, elected elites—to an unrealistic dream. Moreover, the continued inability of national governments to provide relief can lead to widespread civil unrest, of which the truckers' strike is indicative. Necessarily, governments' attention would shift from resource allocation to controlling civil unrest. In times of anxiety, the pressures toward authoritarianism are intense, as we learned from Watergate.

However, even assuming no widespread social unrest, there are other reasons why "democracy" may be unsuitable to an age of scarcity. An end to democracy, accompanied by a drastic restriction of individual liberty, may be the only course available. As Heilbroner predicts: " . . . the passage through the gantlet ahead may be possible only under governments capable of rallying obedience far more effectively than would be possible in a democratic setting. If the issue for mankind is survival, such governments may be unavoidable, even necessary."[13]

If the present political game is survival, rather than the division of abundant resources, the power of *technological elites* over elected elites may relegate government "by the people" (even when "the people" are the elite) to antiquity. The greater the technological power we bring to bear in the struggle against scarcity, the more the political power of existing elites must be sacrificed to the technological elite. In a world where only the most careful planning can prevent rapid deterioration of the quality of life, social control, drastic restrictions in individual freedom, and rule by "experts" are inevitable. Bargaining among competing elites, much less mass participation, could not be tolerated.

References

[1]Alexis de Tocqueville, *Democracy in America*, Vol. 2 (New York: Vintage Books, 1955), p. 336.

[2]Gaetano Mosca, *The Ruling Class* (New York: McGraw-Hill, 1939), p. 332.

[3]Paul Goodman, "Notes on Decentralization," in Irving Howe (ed.), *The Radical Papers* (Garden City, N.Y.: Doubleday, 1966), p. 190 (emphasis added).

[4]James Q. Wilson, "The Strategy of Protest: Problems of Negro Civic Action," *Journal of Conflict Resolution*, 3 (September 1961), pp. 291–303; Michael Lipsky, "Protest as a Political Resource," *American Political Science Review*, 68 (December 1968), 1144–1158.

[5]Philip E. Converse, et. al., "Continuity and Change in American Politics: Parties and Issues in the 1968 Election," *American Political Science Review*, 69 (December 1969), 1087.

[6]*Ibid.*, p. 1088.

[7]Philip E. Slater, *The Pursuit of Loneliness* (Boston: Beacon Press, 1970), p. 126.

[8]Converse, *et al., op. cit.*, p. 1104.

[9]Charles A. Reich, *The Greening of America* (New York: Random House, 1970).

[10]*Ibid.*, p. 295. For an alternate, more realistic appraisal, see Joe Olexa, *Search for Utopia* (doctoral dissertation, University of Oregon, 1971).

[11]Hannah Arendt, *The Origins of Totalitarianism* (New York: Harcourt Brace Jovanovich, 1951), pp. 309–310.

[12]James Madison, Alexander Hamilton, and John Jay, *The Federalist*, No. 10.

[13]Robert L. Heilbroner, *An Inquiry into the Human Prospect* (New York: W. W. Norton & Co. Inc., 1974), p. 110.

THE CONSTITUTION OF

THE UNITED STATES OF AMERICA

We the People of the United States, in Order to form a more perfect Union, establish Justice, insure domestic Tranquility, provide for the common defense, promote the general Welfare, and secure the Blessings of Liberty to ourselves and our Posterity, do ordain and establish this Constitution for the United States of America.

Article I

Section 1. All legislative Powers herein granted shall be vested in a Congress of the United States, which shall consist of a Senate and House of Representatives.

Section 2. The House of Representatives shall be composed of Members chosen every second Year by the People of the several States, and the Electors in each State shall have the Qualifications requisite for Electors of the most numerous Branch of the State Legislature.

No Person shall be a Representative who shall not have attained to the age of twenty five Years, and been seven Years a Citizen of the United States, and who shall not, when elected, be an Inhabitant of that State in which he shall be chosen.

Representatives and direct Taxes shall be apportioned among the several States which may be included within this Union, according to their respective Numbers, *which shall be determined by adding to the whole Number of free Persons, including those bound to Service for a Term of Years, and excluding Indians not taxed, three fifths of all other persons.*[1] The actual Enumeration shall be made within three Years after the first Meeting of the Congress of the United States, and within every subsequent Term of ten Years, in such Manner as they shall by Law direct. The Number of

[1]Superseded by the 14th Amendment. Throughout, italics are used to indicate passages altered by subsequent amendments.

Representatives shall not exceed one for every thirty Thousand, but each State shall have at Least one Representative; and until such enumeration shall be made, the State of New Hampshire shall be entitled to chuse three, Massachusetts eight, Rhode-Island and Providence Plantations one, Connecticut five, New-York six, New Jersey four, Pennsylvania eight, Delaware one, Maryland six, Virginia ten, North Carolina five, South Carolina five, and Georgia three.

When vacancies happen in the Representation from any State, the Executive Authority thereof shall issue Writs of Election to fill such Vacancies.

The House of Representatives shall chuse their Speaker and other Officers; and shall have the sole Power of Impeachment.

Section 3. The Senate of the United States shall be composed of two Senators from each State, chosen by the *Legislature thereof,*[2] for six Years; and each Senator shall have one Vote.

Immediately after they shall be assembled in Consequence of the first Election, they shall be divided as equally as may be into three Classes. The Seats of the Senators of the first Class shall be vacated at the Expiration of the second Year, of the second Class at the Expiration of the fourth Year, and of the third Class at the Expiration of the sixth Year, so that one third may be chosen every second Year; *and if Vacancies happen by Resignation, or otherwise, during the Recess of the Legislature of any State, the Executive thereof may make temporary Appointments until the next Meeting of the Legislature, which shall then fill such Vacancies.*[3]

No Person shall be a Senator who shall not have attained to the Age of thirty Years, and been nine Years a Citizen of the United States, and who shall not, when elected, be an Inhabitant of the State for which he shall be chosen.

The Vice President of the United States shall be President of the Senate, but shall have no Vote, unless they be equally divided.

[2] See 17th Amendment.
[3] See 17th Amendment.

The Senate shall chuse their other Officers, and also a President pro tempore, in the Absence of the Vice President, or when he shall exercise the Office of President of the United States.

The Senate shall have the sole Power to try all Impeachments. When sitting for that Purpose, they shall be on Oath or Affirmation. When the President of the United States is tried, the Chief Justice shall preside: And no Person shall be convicted without the Concurrence of two thirds of the Members present.

Judgment in Cases of Impeachment shall not extend further than to removal from Office, and disqualification to hold and enjoy any Office of Honor, Trust or Profit under the United States: but the Party convicted shall nevertheless be liable and subject to Indictment, Trial, Judgment and Punishment, according to Law.

Section 4. The Times, Places and Manner of holding Elections for Senators and Representatives, shall be prescribed in each State by the Legislature thereof; but the Congress may at any time by Law make or alter such Regulations, except as to the Places of chusing Senators.

The Congress shall assemble at least once in every Year, and such Meeting shall be on the first Monday in December, unless they shall by Law appoint a different Day.[4]

Section 5. Each House shall be the Judge of the Elections, Returns and Qualifications of its own Members, and a Majority of each shall constitute a Quorum to do Business; but a smaller Number may adjourn from day to day, and may be authorized to compel the Attendance of absent Members, in such Manner, and under such Penalties as each House may provide.

Each House may determine the Rules of its Proceedings, punish its Members for disorderly Behaviour, and, with the Concurrence of two thirds, expel a Member.

Each House shall keep a Journal of its Proceedings, and from time to time publish the same, excepting such Parts as may in their Judgment require Secrecy; and the Yeas and Nays of the Members of either House on any question shall, at the Desire of one fifth of those Present, be entered on

[4] See 20th Amendment.

the Journal.

Neither House, during the Session of Congress, shall, without the Consent of the other, adjourn for more than three days, nor to any other Place than that in which the two Houses shall be sitting.

Section 6. The Senators and Representatives shall receive a Compensation for their Services, to be ascertained by Law, and paid out of the Treasury of the United States. They shall in all Cases, except Treason, Felony and Breach of the Peace, be privileged from Arrest during their Attendance at the Session of their respective Houses, and in going to and returning from the same; and for any Speech or Debate in eiher House, they shall not be questioned in any other Place.

No Senator or Representative shall, during the Time for which he was elected, be appointed to any civil Office under the Authority of the United States, which shall have been created, or the Emoluments whereof shall have been encreased during such time; and no Person holding any Office under the United States, shall be a Member of either House during his Continuance in Office.

Section 7. All Bills for raising Revenue shall originate in the House of Representatives; but the Senate may propose or concur with Amendments as on other Bills.

Every Bill which shall have passed the House of Representatives and the Senate, shall, before it become a Law, be presented to the President of the United States; If he approve he shall sign it, but if not he shall return it, with his Objections to that House in which it shall have originated, who shall enter the Objections at large on their Journal, and proceed to reconsider it. If after such Reconsideration two thirds of that House shall agree to pass the Bill, it shall be sent, together with the Objections, to the other House, by which it shall likewise be reconsidered, and if approved by two thirds of that House, it shall become a Law. But in all such Cases the Votes of both Houses shall be determined by Yeas and Nays, and the Names of the Persons voting for and against the Bill shall be entered on the Journal of each House respectively. If any Bill shall not be returned by the President within ten Days (Sundays excepted) after it shall have been presented to him, the Same shall be a Law, in like Manner as if he had signed it, unless the Congress by their Adjournment prevent its Return, in which Case it shall not be a Law.

Every Order, Resolution, or Vote to which the Concurrence of the Senate and House of Representatives may be necessary (except on a question of Adjournment) shall be presented to the President of the United States; and before the Same shall take Effect, shall be approved by him, or being disapproved by him, shall be repassed by two thirds of the Senate and House of Representatives, according to the Rules and Limitations prescribed in the Case of a Bill.

Section 8. The Congress shall have Power To lay and collect Taxes, Duties, Imposts and Excises, to pay the Debts and provide for the common Defence and general Welfare of the United States; but all Duties, Imposts and Excises shall be uniform throughout the United States;

To borrow Money on the credit of the United States;

To regulate Commerce with foreign Nations, and among the several States, and with the Indian Tribes;

To establish an uniform Rule of Naturalization, and uniform Laws on the subject of Bankruptcies throughout the United States;

To coin Money, regulate the Value thereof, and of foreign Coin, and fix the Standard of Weights and Measures;

To provide for the Punishment of counterfeiting the Securities and current Coin of the United States;

To establish Post Offices and post Roads;

To promote the Progress of Science and useful Arts, by securing for limited Times to Authors and Inventors the exclusive Right to their respective Writings and Discoveries;

To constitute Tribunals inferior to the Supreme Court;

To define and punish Piracies and Felonies committed on the high Seas, and Offences against the Law of Nations;

To declare War, grant Letters of Marque and Reprisal, and make Rules concerning Captures on Land and Water;

To raise and support Armies, but no Appropriation of Money to that Use shall be for a longer Term than two Years;

To provide and maintain a Navy;

To make Rules for the Government and Regulation of the land and naval Forces;

To provide for calling forth the Militia to execute the Laws of the Union, suppress Insurrections and repel Invasions;

To provide for organizing, arming, and disciplining, the Militia, and for governing such Part of them as may be employed in the Service of the United States, reserving to the States respectively, the Appointment of the Officers, and the Authority of training the Militia according to the discipline prescribed by Congress;

To exercise exclusive Legislation in all Cases whatsoever, over such District (not exceeding ten Miles square) as may, by Cession of particular States, and the Acceptance of Congress, become the Seat of the Government of the United States, and to exercise like Authority over all Places purchased by the Consent of the Legislature of the State in which the Same shall be, for the Erection of Forts, Magazines, Arsenals, dock-Yards, and other needful Buildings;—And

To make all Laws which shall be necessary and proper for carrying into Execution the foregoing Powers, and all other Powers vested by this Constitution in the Government of the United States, or in any Department or Officer thereof.

Section 9. The Migration or Importation of such Persons as any of the States now existing shall think proper to admit, shall not be prohibited by the Congress prior to the Year one thousand eight hundred and eight, but a Tax or duty may be imposed on such Importation, not exceeding ten dollars for each Person.

The Privilege of the Writ of Habeas Corpus shall not be suspended, unless when in Cases of Rebellion or Invasion the public Safety may require it.

No Bill of Attainder or ex post facto Law shall be passed.

No Capitation, or other direct, Tax shall be laid, unless in Proportion to the Census or Enumeration herein before directed to be taken.

No Tax or Duty shall be laid on Articles exported from any State.

No Preference shall be given by any Regulation of Commerce or Revenue to the Ports of one State over those of another: nor shall Vessels bound to, or from, one State, be obliged to enter, clear, or pay Duties in another.

No Money shall be drawn from the Treasury, but in Consequence of Appropriations made by Law; and a regular Statement and Account of the Receipts and Expenditures of all public Money shall be published from time to time.

No Title of Nobility shall be granted by the United States: And no Person holding any Office of Profit or Trust under them, shall, without the Consent of the Congress, accept of any present, Emolument, Office, or Title, of any kind whatever, from any King, Prince, or foreign State.

Section 10. No State shall enter into any Treaty, Alliance, or Confederation; grant Letters of Marque and Reprisal; coin Money; emit Bills of Credit; make any Thing but gold and silver Coin a Tender in Payment of Debts; pass any Bill of Attainder, ex post facto Law, or Law impairing the Obligation of Contracts, or grant any Title of Nobility.

No State shall, without the Consent of the Congress, lay any Imposts or Duties on Imports or Exports, except what may be absolutely necessary for executing its inspection Laws: and the net Produce of all Duties and Imposts, laid by any State on Imports or Exports, shall be for the Use of the Treasury of the United States; and all such Laws shall be subject to the Revision and Controul of the Congress.

No State shall, without the Consent of Congress, lay any Duty of Tonnage, keep Troops, or Ships of War in time of Peace, enter into any Agreement or Compact with another State, or with a foreign Power, or engage in War, unless actually invaded, or in such imminent Danger as will not admit of delay.

Article II

Section 1. The executive Power shall be vested in a President of the United States of America. He shall hold his Office during the Term of four Years, and, together with the Vice President, chosen for the same Term, be elected, as follows:

Each State shall appoint, in such Manner as the Legislature thereof may direct, a Number of Electors, equal to the whole Number of Senators and Representatives to which the State may be entitled in the Congress: but no Senator or Representative, or Person holding an Office of Trust or Profit under the United States, shall be appointed an Elector.

The Electors shall meet in their respective States, and vote by Ballot for two Persons, of whom one at least shall not be an Inhabitant of the same State with themselves. And they shall make a List of all the Persons voted for, and of the Number of Votes for each; which List they shall sign and certify, and transmit sealed to the Seat of the Government of the United States, directed to the President of the Senate. The President of the Senate shall, in the Presence of the Senate and House of Representatives, open all the Certificates, and the Votes shall then be counted. The Person having the greatest Number of Votes shall be the President, if such Number be a Majority of the whole Number of Electors appointed; and if there be more than one who have such Majority, and have an equal Number of Votes, then the House of Representatives shall immediately chuse by Ballot one of them for President; and if no Person have a Majority, then from the five highest on the List the said House shall in like Manner chuse the President. But in chusing the President, the Votes shall be taken by States, the Representation from each State having one Vote: A quorum for this Purpose shall consist of a Member or Members from two thirds of the States, and a Majority of all the States shall be necessary to a Choice. In every Case, after the Choice of the President, the Person having the greatest Number of Votes of the Electors shall be the Vice President. But if there should remain two or more who have equal Votes, the Senate shall chuse from them by Ballot the Vice President.[5]

The Congress may determine the Time of chusing the Electors, and the Day on which they shall give their Votes; which Day shall be the same throughout the United States.

No Person except a natural born Citizen, or a Citizen of the United States, at the time of the Adoption of this Constitution, shall be eligible to the Office of President; neither shall any Person be eligible to that Office who shall not have attained to the Age of thirty five Years, and been fourteen Years a Resident within the United States.

In Case of the Removal of the President from Office, or of his Death, Resignation, or Inability to discharge the Powers and Duties of the said Office, the Same shall devolve on the Vice President, and the Congress may by Law provide for the Case of Removal, Death, Resignation or Inability, both of the President and Vice President, declaring what Officer shall then act as President, and such Officer shall act accordingly, until the Disability be removed, or a President shall be elected.[6]

The President shall, at stated Times, receive for his Services, a Compensation which shall neither be encreased nor diminished during the Period for which he shall have been elected, and he shall not receive within that Period any other Emolument from the United States, or any of them.

Before he enter on the Execution of his Office, he shall take the following Oath or Affirmation:—"I do solemnly swear (or affirm) that I will faithfully execute the Office of President of the United States, and will to the best of my Ability, preserve, protect and defend the Constitution of the United States."

Section 2.　The President shall be Commander in Chief of the Army and Navy of the United States, and of the Militia of the several States, when called into the actual Service of the United States; he may require the Opinion, in writing, of the principal Officer in each of the executive Departments, upon any Subject relating to the Duties of their respective Offices, and he shall have Power to grant Reprieves and Pardons for Offences against the United States, except in Cases of Impeachment.

He shall have Power, by and with the Advice and Consent of the Senate, to make Treaties, provided two thirds of the Senators present concur; and he shall nominate, and by and with the Advice and Consent of the Senate, shall appoint Ambassadors, other public Ministers and Consuls, Judges of the supreme Court, and all other Officers of the United States, whose Appointments are not herein otherwise provided for, and which shall be established

---

[5] Superseded by the 12th Amendment.

[6] See 25th Amendment.

by Law: but the Congress may by Law vest the Appointment of such inferior officers, as they think proper, in the President alone, in the Courts of Law, or in the Heads of Departments.

The President shall have Power to fill up all Vacancies that may happen during the Recess of the Senate, by granting Commissions which shall expire at the End of their next Session.

Section 3. He shall from time to time give to the Congress Information of the State of the Union, and recommend to their Consideration such Measures as he shall judge necessary and expedient; he may, on extraordinary Occasions, convene both Houses, or either of them, and in Case of Disagreement between them, with Respect to the Time of Adjournment, he may adjourn them to such Time as he shall think proper; he shall receive Ambassadors and other public Ministers; he shall take Care that the Laws be faithfully executed, and shall Commission all the Officers of the United States.

Section 4. The President, Vice President, and all civil Officers of the United States, shall be removed from Office on Impeachment for, and Conviction of, Treason, Bribery, or other high Crimes and Misdemeanors.

Article III

Section 1. The judicial Power of the United States, shall be vested in one supreme Court and in such inferior Courts as the Congress may from time to time ordain and establish. The Judges, both of the supreme and inferior Courts, shall hold their Offices during good Behaviour, and shall, at stated Times, receive for their Services, a Compensation, which shall not be diminished during their Continuance in Office.

Section 2. The judicial Power shall extend to all Cases, in Law and Equity, arising under this Constitution, the Laws of the United States, and Treaties made, or which shall be made, under their Authority;—to all Cases affecting Ambassadors, other public Ministers and Consuls;—to all Cases of admiralty and maritime Jurisdiction;—to Controversies to which the United States shall be a Party—to Controversies between two or more States;—*between a State and Citizens of another State*[7];—between Citizens of different States;—between Citizens of the same State claiming Lands under Grants of different States, *and between a State or the Citizens thereof, and foreign States, Citizens, or Subjects.*[8]

In all Cases affecting Ambassadors, other public Ministers and Consuls, and those in which a State shall be Party, the supreme Court shall have original Jurisdiction. In all the other Cases before mentioned, the supreme Court shall have appellate Jurisdiction, both as to Law and Fact, with such Exceptions, and under such Regulations as the Congress shall make.

The Trial of all Crimes, except in Cases of Impeachment, shall be by Jury; and such Trial shall be held in the State where the said Crimes shall have been committed; but when not committed within any State, the Trial shall be at such Place or Places as the Congress may by Law have directed.

Section 3. Treason against the United States, shall consist only in levying War against them, or in adhering to their Enemies, giving them Aid and Comfort. No Person shall be convicted of Treason unless on the Testimony of two Witnesses to the same overt Act, or on Confession in open Court.

The Congress shall have Power to declare the Punishment of Treason, but no Attainder of Treason shall work Corruption of Blood, or Forfeiture except during the Life of the Person attainted.

Article IV

Section 1. Full Faith and Credit shall be given in each State to the public Acts, Records, and judicial Proceedings of every other State. And the Congress may by general Laws prescribe the Manner in which such Acts, Records, and Proceedings shall be proved, and the Effect thereof.

Section 2. The Citizens of each State shall be entitled to all Privileges and Immunities of Citizens in the several States.

A Person charged in any State with Treason, Felony, or other Crime, who shall flee from Justice, and be found in another State, shall on Demand of the executive Authority of the State from which he fled, be deliv-

[7] See 11th Amendment.
[8] See 11th Amendment.

ered up, to be removed to the State having Jurisdiction of the Crime.

No Person held to Service or Labour in one State, under the Laws thereof, escaping into another, shall, in Consequence of any Law or Regulation therein, be discharged from such Service or Labour, but shall be delivered up on Claim of the Party to whom such Service or Labour may be due.[9]

Section 3.   New States may be admitted by the Congress into this Union; but no new State shall be formed or erected within the Jurisdiction of any other State; nor any State be formed by the Junction of two or more States, or Parts of States, without the Consent of the Legislatures of the States concerned as well as of the Congress.

The Congress shall have Power to dispose of and make all needful Rules and Regulations respecting the Territory or other Property belonging to the United States; and nothing in this Constitution shall be so construed as to Prejudice any claims of the United States, or of any particular State.

Section 4.   The United States shall guarantee to every State in this Union a Republican Form of Government, and shall protect each of them against Invasion; and on Application of the Legislature, or of the Executive (when the Legislature cannot be convened) against domestic Violence.

Article V

The Congress, whenever two thirds of both Houses shall deem it necessary, shall propose Amendments to this Constitution, or, on the Application of the Legislatures of two thirds of the several States, shall call a Convention for proposing Amendments, which, in either Case, shall be valid to all Intents and Purposes, as Part of this Constitution, when ratified by the Legislatures of three fourths of the several States, or by Conventions in three fourths thereof, as the one or the other Mode of Ratification may be proposed by the Congress; Provided that no Amendment which may be made prior to the Year One thousand eight hundred and eight shall in any Manner affect the first and fourth Clauses in the Ninth Section of the first Article; and that no State, without its Consent, shall be deprived of its equal Suffrage in the Senate.

[9]See 13th Amendment.

Article VI

All Debts contracted and Engagements entered into, before the Adoption of this Constitution, shall be as valid against the United States under this Constitution, as under the Confederation.

This Constitution, and the Laws of the United States which shall be made in Pursuance thereof; and all Treaties made, or which shall be made, under the Authority of the United States, shall be the supreme Law of the Land; and the Judges in every State shall be bound thereby, any Thing in the Constitution or Laws of any State to the Contrary notwithstanding.

The Senators and Representatives before mentioned, and the Members of the several State Legislatures, and all executive and judicial Officers, both of the United States and of the several States, shall be bound by Oath or Affirmation, to support this Constitution; but no religious Test shall ever be required as a Qualification to any Office or public Trust under the United States.

Article VII

The Ratification of the Conventions of nine States, shall be sufficient for the Establishment of this Constitution between the States so ratifying the Same.

Done in Convention by the Unanimous Consent of the States present the Seventeenth Day of September in the Year of our Lord one thousand seven hundred and eighty seven and of the Independence of the United States of America the Twelfth.In witness whereof We have hereunto subscribed our Names.

ARTICLES IN ADDITION TO, AND AMENDMENT OF, THE CONSTITUTION OF THE UNITED STATES OF AMERICA, PROPOSED BY CONGRESS, AND RATIFIED BY THE SEVERAL STATES, PURSUANT TO THE FIFTH ARTICLE OF THE ORIGINAL CONSTITUTION:

Amendment I

(Ratification of the first ten amendments was completed December 15, 1791.)

Congress shall make no law respecting an establishment of religion, or prohibiting the free exercise thereof; or abridging the freedom of speech, or of the press; or the right of the people peaceably to assemble, and to petition the Government for a redress of grievances.

Amendment II

A well regulated Militia, being necessary to the security of a free State, the right of the people to keep and bear Arms, shall not be infringed.

Amendment III

No Soldier shall, in time of peace be quartered in any house, without the consent of the Owner, nor in time of war, but in a manner to be prescribed by law.

Amendment IV

The right of the people to be secure in their persons, houses, papers, and effects, against unreasonable searches and seizures, shall not be violated, and no Warrants shall issue, but upon probable cause, supported by Oath or affirmation, and particularly describing the place to be searched, and the persons or things to be seized.

Amendment V

No person shall be held to answer for a capital, or otherwise infamous crime, unless on a presentment or indictment of a Grand Jury, except in cases arising in the land or naval forces, or in the Militia, when in actual service in time of War or public danger; nor shall any person be subject for the same offence to be twice put in jeopardy of life or limb; nor shall be compelled in any criminal case to be a witness against himself, nor be deprived of life, liberty, or property, without due process of law; nor shall private property be taken for public use, without just compensation.

Amendment VI

In all criminal prosecutions, the accused shall enjoy the right to a speedy and public trial, by an impartial jury of the State and district wherein the crime shall have been committed, which district shall have been previously ascertained by law, and to be informed of the nature and cause of the accusation; to be confronted with the witness against him; to have compulsory process for obtaining witnesses in his favor,

and to have the Assistance of Counsel for his defence.

Amendment VII

In Suits at common law, where the value in controversy shall exceed twenty dollars, the right of trial by jury shall be preserved, and no fact tried by a jury, shall be otherwise reexamined in any Court of the United States, than according to the rules of the common law.

Amendment VIII

Excessive bail shall not be required, nor excessive fines imposed, nor cruel and unusual punishments inflicted.

Amendment IX

The enumeration in the Constitution, of certain rights, shall not be construed to deny or disparage others retained by the people.

Amendment X

The powers not delegated to the United States by the Constitution, nor prohibited by it to the States, are reserved to the States respectively, or to the people.

...................................Amendment XI (1798)

The Judicial power of the United States shall not be construed to extend to any suit in law or equity, commenced or prosecuted against one of the United States by Citizens of another State, or by Citizens or Subjects of any Foreign States.

...................................Amendment XII (1804)

The Electors shall meet in their respective states and vote by ballot for President and Vice-President, one of whom, at least, shall not be an inhabitant of the same state with themselves; they shall name in their ballots the person voted for as President, and in distinct ballots the person voted for as Vice-President, and they shall make distinct lists of all persons voted for as President, and of all persons voted for as Vice-President, and of the number of votes for each, which lists they shall sign and certify, and transmit sealed to the seat of the government of the United States, directed to the President of the Senate;—The President of the Senate shall, in the presence of Senate and House of Representatives, open all the certificates and the votes shall then be counted;—The person having the greatest number of votes for President, shall be the President, if such number be a majority of the whole number of Electors appointed; and if no person have such majority, then from the persons having the highest numbers not exceeding three on the list of those voted for as President, the House of Representatives shall choose immediately, by ballot, the President. But in choosing the President, the votes shall be taken by states, the representation from each state having one vote; a quorum for this purpose shall consist of a member or members from two-thirds of the states, and a majority of all the states shall be necessary to a choice. And if the House of Representatives shall not choose a President whenever the right of choice shall devolve upon them, *before the fourth day of March next following*.[10] then the Vice-President shall act as President, as in the case of the death or other constitutional disability of the President.—The person having the greatest number of votes as Vice-President shall be the Vice-President, if such number be a majority of the whole number of Electors appointed, and if no person have a majority, then from the two highest numbers on the list, the Senate shall choose the Vice-President; a quorum for the purpose shall consist of two-thirds of the whole number of Senators, and a majority of the whole number shall be necessary to a choice. But no person constitutionally ineligible to the office of President shall be eligible to that of Vice-President of the United States.

.............................**Amendment XIII** (1865)

Section 1. Neither slavery nor involuntary servitude, except as a punishment for crime whereof the party shall have been duly convicted, shall exist within the United States, or any place subject to their jurisdiction.

Section 2. Congress shall have the power to enforce this article by appropriate legislation.

.............................**Amendment XIV** (1868)

Section 1. All persons born or natural-

[10] Altered by the 20th Amendment.

ized in the United States, and subject to the jurisdiction thereof, are citizens of the United States and of the State wherein they reside. No State shall make or enforce any law which shall abridge the privileges or immunities of citizens of the United States; nor shall any State deprive any person of life, liberty, or property, without due process of law; nor deny to any person within its jurisdiction the equal protection of the laws.

Section 2. Representatives shall be apportioned among the several States according to their respective numbers, counting the whole number of persons in each State, excluding Indians not taxed. But when the right to vote at any election for the choice of electors for President and Vice President of the United States, Representatives in Congress, the Executive and Judicial officers of a State, or the members of the Legislature thereof, is denied to any of the male inhabitants of such State, being twenty-one years of age, and citizens of the United States, or in any way abridged, except for participation in rebellion, or other crime, the basis of representation therein shall be reduced in the proportion which the number of such male citizens shall bear to the whole number of male citizens twenty-one years of age in such State.

Section 3. No person shall be a Senator or Representative in Congress, or elector of President and Vice President, or hold any office, civil or military, under the United States, or under any State, who, having previously taken an oath, as a member of Congress, or as an officer of the United States, or as a member of any State legislature, or as an executive or judicial officer of any State, to support the Constitution of the United States, shall have engaged in insurrection or rebellion against the same, or given aid or comfort to the enemies thereof. But Congress may by a vote of two-thirds of each House, remove such disability.

Section 4. The validity of the public debt of the United States, authorized by law, including debts incurred for payment of pensions and bounties for services in suppressing insurrection or rebellion, shall not be questioned. But neither the United States nor any State shall assume or pay any debt or obligation incurred in aid of insurrection or rebellion against the

United States, or any claim for the loss or emancipation of any slave; but all such debts, obligations, and claims shall be held illegal and void.

Section 5. The Congress shall have power to enforce, by appropriate legislation, the provisions of this article.

...............................**Amendment XV** (1870)

Section 1. The right of citizens of the United States to vote shall not be denied or abridged by the United States or by any State on account of race, color, or previous condition of servitude.

Section 2. The Congress shall have power to enforce this article by appropriate legislation.

...............................**Amendment XVI** (1913)

The Congress shall have power to lay and collect taxes on incomes, from whatever source derived, without apportionment among the several States, and without regard to any census or enumeration.

...............................**Amendment XVII** (1913)

The Senate of the United States shall be composed of two Senators from each State, elected by the people thereof, for six years; and each Senator shall have one vote. The electors in each State shall have the qualifications requisite for electors of the most numerous branch of the State legislatures.

When vacancies happen in the representation of any State in the Senate, the executive authority of such State shall issue writs of election to fill such vacancies: *Provided,* That the legislature of any State may empower the executive thereof to make temporary appointments until the people fill the vacancies by election as the legislature may direct.

This amendment shall not be so construed as to affect the election or term of any Senator chosen before it becomes valid as part of the Constitution.

...............................**Amendment XVIII** (1919)

Section 1. *After one year from the ratification of this article the manufacture, sale, or transportation of intoxicating liquors within, the importation thereof into, or the exportation thereof from the United States and all territory subject to the jurisdiction thereof for beverage purposes is hereby prohibited.*

Section 2. *The Congress and the several States shall have concurrent power to enforce this article by appropriate legislation.*

Section 3. *This article shall be inoperative unless it shall have been ratified as an amendment to the Constitution by the legislatures of the several States, as provided in the Constitution, within seven years from the date of the submission hereof to the States by the Congress.*[11]

...............................**Amendment XIX** (1920)

The right of citizens of the United States to vote shall not be denied or abridged by the United States or by any State on account of sex.

Congress shall have power to enforce this article by appropriate legislation.

...............................**Amendment XX** (1933)

Section 1. The terms of the President and Vice President shall end at noon on the 20th day of January, and the terms of Senators and Representatives at noon on the 3rd day of January, of the years in which such terms would have ended if this article had not been ratified; and the terms of their successors shall then begin.

Section 2. The Congress shall assemble at least once in every year, and such meeting shall begin at noon on the 3rd day of January, unless they shall by law appoint a different day.

Section 3. If, at the time fixed for the beginning of the term of the President, the President elect shall have died, the Vice President elect shall become President. If a President shall not have been chosen before the time fixed for the beginning of his term, or if the President elect shall have failed to qualify, then the Vice President elect shall act as President until a President shall have qualified; and the Congress may by law provide for the case wherein neither a President elect nor a Vice President elect shall have qualified, declaring who shall then act as President, or the manner in which one who is to act shall be selected, and such person shall act accordingly until a President or Vice President shall have qualified.

Section 4. The Congress may by law

---

[11] Repealed by the 21st Amendment.

provide for the case of the death of any of the persons from whom the House of Representatives may choose a President whenever the right of choice shall have devolved upon them, and for the case of the death of any of the persons from whom the Senate may choose a Vice President whenever the right of choice shall have devolved upon them.

Section 5. Sections 1 and 2 shall take effect on the 15th day of October following the ratification of this article.

Section 6. This article shall be inoperative unless it shall have been ratified as an amendment to the Constitution by the legislatures of three-fourths of the several States within seven years from the date of its submission.

............................**Amendment XXI** (1933)

Section 1. The eighteenth article of amendment to the Constitution of the United States is hereby repealed.

Section 2. The transportation or importation into any State, Territory, or possession of the United States for delivery or use therein of intoxicating liquors, in violation of the laws thereof, is hereby prohibited.

Section 3. This article shall be inoperative unless it shall have been ratified as an amendment to the Constitution by conventions in the several States, as provided in the Constitution, within seven years from the date of the submission hereof to the States by the Congress.

............................**Amendment XXII** (1951)

Section 1. No person shall be elected to the office of the President more than twice, and no person who has held the office of President, or acted as President for more than two years of a term to which some other person was elected President shall be elected to the office of President more than once. But this Article shall not apply to any person holding the office of President when this Article was proposed by the Congress, and shall not prevent any person who may be holding the office of President, or acting as President, during the term within which this Article becomes operative from holding the office of President or acting as President during the remainder of such term.

Section 2. This article shall be inopera-

tive unless it shall have been ratified as an amendment to the Constitution by the legislatures of three-fourths of the several States within seven years from the date of its submission to the States by the Congress.

............................**Amendment XXIII** (1961)

Section 1. The District constituting the seat of Government of the United States shall appoint in such manner as the Congress may direct:

A number of electors of President and Vice President equal to the whole number of Senators and Representatives in Congress to which the District would be entitled if it were a State, but in no event more than the least populous State; they shall be in addition to those appointed by the States, but they shall be considered, for the purposes of the election of President and Vice President, to be electors appointed by a State; and they shall meet in the District and perform such duties as provided by the twelfth article of amendment.

Section 2. The Congress shall have power to enforce this article by appropriate legislation.

............................**Amendment XXIV** (1964)

Section 1. The right of citizens of the United States to vote in any primary or other election for President or Vice President, for electors for President or Vice President, or for Senator or Representative in Congress, shall not be denied or abridged by the United States or any state by reason of failure to pay any poll tax or other tax.

Section 2. The Congress shall have the power to enforce this article by appropriate legislation.

............................**Amendment XXV** (1967)

Section 1. In case of the removal of the President from office or of his death or resignation, the Vice President shall become President.

Section 2. Whenever there is a vacancy in the office of the Vice President, the President shall nominate a Vice President who shall take office upon confirmation by a majority vote of both Houses of Congress.

Section 3. Whenever the President transmits to the President pro tempore of the Senate and the Speaker of the House of

Representatives his written declaration that he is unable to discharge the powers and duties of his office, and until he transmits to them a written declaration to the contrary, such powers and duties shall be discharged by the Vice President as Acting President.

Section 4. Whenever the Vice President and a majority of either the principal officers of the executive departments or of such other body as Congress may by law provide, transmit to the President pro tempore of the Senate and the Speaker of the House of Representatives their written declaration that the President is unable to discharge the powers and duties of his office, the Vice President shall immediately assume the powers and duties of the office as Acting President.

Thereafter, when the President transmits to the President pro tempore of the Senate and the Speaker of the House of Representatives his written declaration that no inability exists, he shall resume the powers and duties of his office unless the Vice President and a majority of either the principal officers of the executive departments or of such other body as Congress may by law provide, transmit within four days to the President pro tempore of the Senate and the Speaker of the House of Representatives their written declaration that the President is unable to discharge the powers and duties of his office. Thereupon Congress shall decide the issue, assembling within forty-eight hours for that purpose if not in session. If the Congress, within twenty-one days after receipt of the latter written declaration, or, if Congress is not in session, within twenty-one days after Congress is required to assemble, determines by two-thirds vote of both Houses that the President is unable to discharge the powers and duties of his office, the Vice President shall continue to discharge the same as Acting President; otherwise, the President shall resume the powers and duties of his office.

..............................Amendment XXVI (1971)

Section 1. The right of citizens of the United States, who are 18 years of age or older, to vote shall not be denied or abridged by the United States or any state on account of age.

Section 2. The Congress shall have the power to enforce this article by appropriate legislation.

INDEX